TROADES

Euripides

Troades

Edited with Introduction and Commentary
by
DAVID KOVACS

OXFORD
UNIVERSITY PRESS

OXFORD
UNIVERSITY PRESS

Great Clarendon Street, Oxford, OX2 6DP,
United Kingdom

Oxford University Press is a department of the University of Oxford. It furthers the University's objective of excellence in research, scholarship, and education by publishing worldwide. Oxford is a registered trade mark of Oxford University Press in the UK and in certain other countries

First Edition published in 2018

Impression: 1

Published in the United States of America by Oxford University Press
198 Madison Avenue, New York, NY 10016, United States of America

British Library Cataloguing in Publication Data
Data available

Library of Congress Control Number: 2017963195

ISBN 978-0-19-929615-6

Printed and bound by
CPI Group (UK) Ltd, Croydon, CR0 4YY

Preface

In 1988 Euripides' *Trojan Women* was put on by the University of Virginia Department of Drama. This was accompanied by a symposium on the play at which members of the Department of Classics gave papers. The play was effectively performed, and the papers were good. There was also a lunch for those participating in the event. I remember sitting next to the young woman who played Andromache and asking her how she was enjoying the role. 'Oh', she said, 'it's a lovely part, and I have enjoyed it very much. Still, I can't help but feel a bit envious of some of the other actresses. Cassandra waves those flaming torches, Hecuba has the business with Astyanax on Hector's shield, and Helen wears that stunning red dress, whereas I don't have anything to distract the audience from what I'm saying.'

It is the purpose of a commentary on a Greek tragedy to encourage its readers to listen closely to what the characters are saying. At the level of the individual line or sentence, commentators explain grammar that is in any way difficult; point out matters of tragic style or metre or the style or metre of the particular tragic poet; see whether a passage gives the sense the context seems to require and whether it is written in the expected style, and if not, whether conjectural alteration of the text commends itself. At the level of the speech or scene or lyrical piece, they try to grasp the whole to which its parts contribute, and to note important issues in any dispute to try to determine what attitudes the audience are being invited to take toward the parties to it. At the level of the whole work, they try to see what sort of place the world of the play is (e.g. what the gods contribute to the action and whether any misfortune human agents meet with is presented as personally deserved), and wherein lies whatever unity the work possesses.

As regards the interpretation of the whole play, the present volume argues that certain views about Euripides that have dominated scholarship from the early nineteenth century until recently and continue to have advocates have made it difficult to take in its characters' words and what they might imply. One such view, first put forward in 1839, is that the play is Euripides' response to the Athenian destruction of Melos. Another is the notion, derived from (some parts of) the biographical tradition rather than from the plays themselves, that Euripides was a disbeliever in the gods and that therefore (a big 'therefore' this) he cannot be inviting his audience to enter into the spirit of tragic drama as practised by his predecessors and contemporaries, a form of drama that always involves the gods. The two *Tendenzen* are for this play related: those who think that Euripides is chastising the Athenians will be unreceptive to the notion that in the last analysis it was the gods who destroyed Troy since that would imply the same about Melos. My introduction and commentary are an effort to hear what is in the text.

At the other end of the scale from the interpretation of the whole are the many points of detail where the text must be either explained or emended or corruptions cordoned off by means of obeli. Our earliest complete text of *Troades* is from the late thirteenth century AD, some seventeen centuries after Euripides first wrote the play down for his actors to perform, and the damage the text has sustained during those centuries of hand copying has not been slight. The work of restoration has been facilitated by centuries of scholarship that has paid close attention to the regularities of tragic style. This has resulted in worthwhile emendations to the text of our play, based on these regularities, made by a whole succession of scholars from the sixteenth to the twenty-first centuries.

The basic strategy of the commentary in textual matters is to demonstrate, in fuller detail than any previous commentary on the play, how it exemplifies Euripides' characteristic means of expression. (Differences from the practice of the other tragedians are also noted.) There are lengthy sections of the play where only slight alteration is necessary to produce sense that the context leads us to expect and style that is paralleled elsewhere in the tragic corpus. This serves to make more plausible the heuristic assumption that Euripides is a polished and careful author and thereby increases the likelihood that, where the manuscripts give us a clumsy or slipshod one, they are wrong.

Diggle's 1981 OCT marked a considerable advance in establishing the text of *Troades*, restoring sense by paying attention to tragic idiom, metre, and a variety of other matters, knowledge of which can help an editor produce a text in which readers can feel greater confidence. I have continued his work, and my text differs from his in some one hundred places (some of these are already in my Loeb edition).[1] A few have important

[1] Some of my readers may wish to know what I consider to be my most important interventions, both sceptical and conservative, in the text. In my notes to 28–44, 95–7, 114, 153, 156, 184–9, 274, 276, 289–91, 310, 477–8, 508, 547–50, 589–90, 591–3, 702–5, 718, 737, 879, 916–18, 998–1001, 1018, 1095, 1223, and 1320–1 I discuss places where I print or propose a conjecture and Diggle gives the paradosis (sometimes obelized). I delete lines or words at 22, 38, 424–6, 637, and 1295–6. I argue that there is good reason to reconsider the assignment of speakers in 577–600. On the conservative side I defend what is transmitted in my notes on 71, 445, 555–7, 604–5, 831–2, 975–6, 1059, 1242–4 (ὑμνήθημεν),

consequences for the interpretation of the play. Some, however, are more purely technical, and, following the practice of Barrett's *Hippolytos*, I have set off by means of an em-dash discussions of less moment so those so inclined may skip over them and pursue the main argument.

Another emphasis of the commentary is visible stage action. Contrary to what the actress I quote above said, what the audience can see in a Greek tragedy is no distraction from what the actors say: stage action—the torches, Hector's shield, and the rest—reinforces verbal meaning, and so I have paid close attention to the clues in the text that allow us to reconstruct the physical performance.[2] The visible actions implied by the text are set out in paragraphs headed *Staging*.

This book was begun a long time ago. Its progress toward completion was set back in 2009, when a health crisis intervened. Since then I have been the recipient of visiting fellowships that gave me access to first-rate libraries: I spent a year as Visiting Research Fellow at Jesus College, Oxford, in 2010–11; I was a Tytus Fellow at the University of Cincinnati in the summer of 2013; and I spent Michaelmas Term of 2016 as Visiting Fellow Commoner at Trinity College, Cambridge. I am extremely grateful to these bodies for the encouragement they provided to my work.

Hilary O'Shea of Oxford University Press welcomed my proposal for a commentary on *Troades* and helped me establish a template for the whole. Charlotte Loveridge, who succeeded her, and Georgina Leighton, her assistant, have been prompt in answering queries. To my copy editor, Timothy Beck, I here express my gratitude for his heroic efforts in bringing my unruly manuscript into good order.

I must also acknowledge kind permission, in two regards, given by Jeffrey Henderson, editor of the Loeb Classical Library, and Harvard University Press. My translations in the commentary occasionally repeat phrases or sentences found in my Loeb translation of the play, and I am grateful to Professor Henderson and Harvard University Press for allowing this reuse. I also gratefully acknowledge their permission to use the electronic form of my Loeb text as the basis for my present one: I have introduced

and 1269–70. In the following are places I rescue a text from incomprehensibility by marking or proposing a lacuna: see my notes on 380, 435–9, 440–1, 561, 570, 860–2, 1206, 1212, and 1251–2. (These perhaps deserve to stand on the conservative side of the ledger since they save every letter of what is transmitted.) I have used obeli where Diggle does not at 310, 316/17, 595, 640, 674, 717, 721, 1087, 1172, 1188, and 1252. There is a significant alteration of punctuation at 511–12.

[2] Considerations of how the *eisodoi* are used help to prove what the text already suggests (see 707n), that the Greek who enters in the second episode is not Talthybius but a different herald.

many alterations in the Greek, but it was a great convenience that I had the Loeb document to alter and did not need to retype the entire text.

Over the years I have had the good fortune to be able to discuss (either in person or by email) textual problems and other matters relevant to this play with Martin Cropp, Roger Dawe, James Diggle, Stephen Kelly, Nicholas Lane, and Ruth Scodel. Three people read the entire manuscript when it was finished. Justina Gregory agreed to read it as a favour to me and made the kind of judicious comments I had hoped to receive from her. Oxford University Press secured the services of two highly regarded experts on Greek tragedy, James Diggle and Patrick Finglass. I am grateful for their many valuable suggestions on both substance and style. I have used the initials JD and PJF to signal suggestions made to me by them, either in their reports to the Press or in other communications. Suggestions on the text sent to me or made in person by Nicholas Lane are signalled with his initials.

Lastly, I have been fortunate over the years to be able to have many long discussions of Euripidean textual problems with the late Sir Charles Willink. He had an extraordinary feel for tragic lyric, and I learned a great deal from discussions with him. He also gave me a draft of his *Cantica euripidea*, a work he never published. Suggestions marked 'Willink unpub.' are to be found in this manuscript. As a mark of my personal affection for him I dedicate the present volume to his memory.

D.K.
University of Virginia

Contents

Abbreviations

The following are works cited by author name or initial alone and works cited by abbreviated title. I cite the fragments of Greek tragedy from B. Snell et al., *Tragicorum graecorum fragmenta* (Göttingen 1971–2007), the fragments of Greek epic from M. L. West, *Greek epic fragments* (Cambridge, Mass. 2003), and the fragments of early philosophy from D. W. Graham, *The texts of early Greek philosophy* (Cambridge 2010). For fragments of Stesichorus F. indicates the fragments as edited by Finglass in M. Davies and P. J. Finglass, *Stesichorus: the poems* (Cambridge 2015).

Adesp. Trag.	R. Kannicht and B. Snell (eds), *Tragicorum graecorum fragmenta*, vol. 2, *Fragmenta Adespota* (Göttingen 1980, rev. edn 2007).
Allen–Italie	J. T. Allen and G. Italie, *A concordance to Euripides* (Berkeley 1954; rpt Groningen 1970).
Barlow	S. Barlow (ed.), *Euripides: Trojan Women* (Warminster 1986).
Beekes	R. Beekes, *Etymological dictionary of Greek*, 2 vols (Leiden, Boston 2010).
Biehl	W. Biehl (ed.), *Euripides: Troades* (Heidelberg 1989).
Breitenbach	W. Breitenbach, *Untersuchungen zur Sprache der euripideischen Lyrik* (Stuttgart 1934; rpt Hildesheim 1967).
Bruhn	E. Bruhn, *Anhang*, in F. W. Schneidewin and A. Nauck, *Sophokles*, vol. 8 (Berlin 1899).
Burges	G. Burges (ed.), *Euripidis Troades* (Cambridge 1807).
Collard–Cropp	C. Collard and M. Cropp (eds), *Euripides: fragments*, vols 1 and 2 (Cambridge, Mass. 2008).
DK	H. Diels and W. Kranz, *Die Fragmente der Vorsokratiker, Griechisch und Deutsch*, 5th edn (Berlin 1934–7).
Diggle	J. Diggle (ed.), *Euripidis tragoediae*, vol. ii (Oxford 1981).
Diggle, *Studies*	J. Diggle, *Studies on the text of Euripides: Supplices, Electra, Heracles, Troades, Iphigenia in Tauris, Ion* (Oxford 1981).
DNP	*Der neue Pauly: Enzyklopädie der Antike* (Stuttgart 1996–2003).

Ellendt	F. Ellendt, *Lexicon Sophocleum* (Berlin 1872; rpt Hildesheim 1965).
Eur. Alt.	D. Kovacs, *Euripidea Altera* (Leiden, New York 1996).
Eur. Tert.	D. Kovacs, *Euripidea Tertia* (Leiden, Boston 2003).
GEF	M. L. West (ed.), *Greek epic fragments* (Cambridge, Mass. 2003).
GP	J. D. Denniston, *The Greek particles*, 2nd edn with corrections (Oxford 1959).
Italie	G. Italie, *Index Aeschyleus* (Leiden 1964).
Jackson	J. Jackson, *Marginalia scaenica* (Oxford 1955).
Jocelyn	H. D. Jocelyn (ed.), *The tragedies of Ennius* (Cambridge 1967). (Abbreviated as J. following fragment numbers.)
KA	R. Kassell and C. Austin (eds), *Poetae Comici Graeci* (Berlin and New York, 1983–).
Kannicht	R. Kannicht (ed.), *Tragicorum graecorum fragmenta*, vol. 5, *Euripides* (Göttingen 2004). (Abbreviated as K. following fragment and testimonium numbers.)
KB	R. Kühner and F. Blass, *Ausführliche Grammatik der griechischen Sprache: Erster Teil: Elementar- und Formenlehre*, 2 vols, 3rd edn (Hannover, Leipzig 1890; rpt Hannover 1966).
KG	R. Kühner and B. Gerth, *Ausführliche Grammatik der griechischen Sprache: Zweiter Teil: Satzlehre*, 2 vols, 3rd edn (Hannover, Leipzig 1898; rpt Hannover 1966).
Kiefner	G. Kiefner, *Die Versparung: Untersuchungen zu einer Stilfigur der dichterischen Rhetorik am Beispiel der griechischen Tragödie, unter Berücksichtigung des σχῆμα ἀπὸ κοινοῦ*, Klassischphilologische Studien, Heft 25 (Wiesbaden 1964).
Lee	K. H. Lee (ed.), *Euripides: Troades* (Basingstoke 1976).
LIMC	H. C. Ackerman and J.-R. Gisler, *Lexicon Iconographicum Mythologiae Classicae* (Zürich 1981–2009).
LHS	M. Leumann, J. B. Hoffman, and A. Szantyr, *Lateinische Grammatik* (Munich 1965–77).
Loeb	D. Kovacs (ed., trans.), *Euripides: Trojan Women, Iphigenia among the Taurians, Ion* (Cambridge, Mass. 1999).
LSJ	H. G. Liddell and R. Scott, *A Greek–English Lexicon*, revised by H. S. Jones with a revised supplement (Oxford 1996).

Manuwald	G. Manuwald (ed.), *Tragicorum Romanorum fragmenta vol. ii: Ennius* (Göttingen 2012). (Abbreviated as M. following fragment numbers.)
Moorhouse	A. C. Moorhouse, *The syntax of Sophocles*, *Mnemosyne* Supplement 75 (Leiden 1975).
MT	W. W. Goodwin, *Syntax of the moods and tenses of the Greek verb* (London 1875; rpt Bristol 1965).
Murray	G. Murray (ed.), *Euripidis tragoediae*, vol. ii (Oxford 1913).
Musgrave	S. Musgrave (ed.), *Euripidis quae extant omnia*, vol. 2 (1778).
Parmentier	L. Parmentier and H. Grégoire (eds), *Euripide*, vol. 4 (Paris 1925).
Scodel	R. Scodel, *The Trojan trilogy of Euripides*, *Hypomnemata* 60 (Göttingen 1980).
SD	E. Schwyzer, *Griechische Grammatik: auf der Grundlage von Karl Brugmanns griechischer Grammatik*, 4 vols, 2nd vol. completed by A. Debrunner (Munich 1934–71).
Seidler	A. Seidler (ed.), *Euripidis tragoediae*, vol. 1, *Troades* (Leipzig 1812).
SFP i and ii	*Euripides: Selected Fragmentary Plays*: i, ed. C. Collard, M. J. Cropp, and K. H. Lee (Warminster 1995); ii, ed. C. Collard, M. J. Cropp, and J. Gibert (Warminster 2004).
Smyth	H. W. Smyth, *Greek Grammar* (Cambridge, Mass. 1956).
Wackernagel	D. R. Langslow (ed. and tr.), *Jacob Wackernagel: lectures on syntax* (Oxford 2009). This is a translation of J. Wackernagel, *Vorlesungen über Syntax*. 2nd edn (Basel 1950–7) with the addition of further unpublished material.
West	M. L. West, *Greek metre* (Oxford 1982).
Wilamowitz	U. von Wilamowitz-Moellendorff, *Griechische Tragödien Uebersetzt*, iii (Berlin 1906).

Commentaries, whether on Euripides, other tragic texts, or other Greek or Latin works, are given in the form 'Barrett on *Hipp.* 794', 'West on *Od.* 1.109–12', or 'Austin on *Aen.* 2.325–6' apart from cases where the reference is to an introduction or an appendix. Ancient works are generally abbreviated as in LSJ and the *Oxford Latin Dictionary*, but note *Herc.* for *Heracles* and *Hcld.* for *Heraclidae*.

Introduction

Many readers, from antiquity to the present, have found *Troades* a deeply moving experience. To take an example from antiquity, Plutarch tells us (*Pelopidas* 29.4–6) that Alexander, the fourth-century tyrant of Pherae, was so stirred by the play that he left the performance early so that his fellow citizens would not see him weep for the troubles of Hecuba when he had no tears for the Pheraeans he killed. But because of its episodic structure the play has frequently been regarded as poorly made. Lattimore's 1958 introduction concludes by saying 'In candor one can hardly call *The Trojan Women* a good piece of work, but it seems nevertheless to be a great tragedy.' Enthusiasm for it is often the result of the belief that it is Euripides' response to the Athenians' conquest of the neutral island of Melos, a belief which this Introduction will call into question. The belief that the play is, in effect, a political allegory about Athens' foreign policy has had the result that parts of the play that do not support such a view have been ignored. It is the aim of this commentary to interpret the entire play and to recover the perspective from which the whole makes sense.

1. THE DATE OF THE PLAY AND RELATED PROBLEMS

1.1. Year and festival

Three ancient notices give us information about the date of the play. The first, Aelian, *VH* 2.8, gives us the Olympiad in which it was produced, tells us that it won second prize, and also provides us with the names of the other three plays produced with it:

κατὰ τὴν πρώτην καὶ ἐνενηκοςτὴν ὀλυμπιάδα, καθ' ἣν ἐνίκα Ἐξαίνετος ὁ Ἀκραγαντῖνος ςτάδιον, ἀντηγωνίςαντο ἀλλήλοις Ξενοκλῆς καὶ Εὐριπίδης.

καὶ πρῶτός γε ἦν Ξενοκλῆς, ὅςτις ποτὲ οὗτός ἐςτιν, Οἰδίποδι καὶ Λυκάονι καὶ Βάκχαις καὶ Ἀθάμαντι ςατυρικῶι. τούτου δεύτερος Εὐριπίδης ἦν Ἀλεξάνδρωι καὶ Παλαμήδει καὶ Τρωιάςι καὶ Cιςύφωι ςατυρικῶι. γελοῖον δέ (οὐ γάρ;) Ξενοκλέα μὲν νικᾶν, Εὐριπίδην δὲ ἡττᾶςθαι, καὶ ταῦτα τοιούτοις δράμαςι. τῶν δύο τοίνυν τὸ ἕτερον· ἢ ἀνόητοι ἦςαν οἱ τῆς ψήφου κύριοι καὶ ἀμαθεῖς καὶ πόρρω κρίςεως ὀρθῆς, ἢ ἐδεκάςθηςαν. ἄτοπον δὲ ἑκάτερον καὶ Ἀθηναίων ἥκιςτα ἄξιον.[1]

The other two notices, scholia on Aristophanes' *Wasps* 1326 and *Birds* 842, give the exact year, 416/5, and we may specify March or April since tetralogies, so far as our evidence goes, were presented only at the City Dionysia. The date of the play raises questions of the relation of *Troades* to contemporary political events, especially the destruction of Melos, which preceded the play by three months or so, and the Sicilian Expedition, which may have left shortly after the Dionysia and was under discussion in the winter months preceding the play. Scholarship, ancient, medieval, and modern, went on until well into the nineteenth century without thinking that anything had to be said on the play's connection with these events. Then quite suddenly the consensus view was that these connections had been proved beyond a doubt. In recent decades a much more hesitant and sceptical approach to the question has gained ground. I compare below the case in favour of the connection with Melos and the case against. A further section discusses the play in relation to Sicily.

1.2. Contemporary events: Melos

In the Athenian-calendar year of 416/5 the Athenians attacked and conquered the neutral island of Melos, which had refused to become a tributary member of the Athenian empire. After starvation had reduced the Melians to dire straits and some of the islanders had betrayed the city, they surrendered. The Athenians killed all the adult males and enslaved the women and children. Later that same year Euripides produced *Troades*, a play in which a city has been conquered, its men killed, and its women made slaves. Is the play to be understood as alluding to current events?

[1] 'In the 91st Olympiad [416/5–413/2], when the stade-race was won by Exaenetus of Acragas, Xenocles and Euripides competed against each other. The first prize was won by Xenocles, whoever *that* is, with *Oedipus*, *Lycaon*, *Bacchae*, and the satyr-play *Athamas*. Euripides was second with *Alexandros*, *Palamedes*, *Trojan Women*, and the satyr play *Sisyphus*. For Xenocles to win and Euripides to lose is a laughable result, surely, especially since the latter was presenting plays like these. One or the other therefore must be the case: either those whose votes decided the contest were thoughtless and ignorant and lacking in good judgement, or they were bribed. Either conclusion is strange and unworthy of the Athenians.'

1.2.1. Troades *and Melos: the chronological argument for a connection*

For some hundred and fifty years (1839–1987) the majority of scholars have said 'yes', pronouncing it self-evident that *Troades* reflects the fate of Melos. Thus Schöll 1839: 75–6 writes:

> If Euripides now [i.e. after the fall of Melos] filled a tragedy with the bitterest depictions of disgrace felt and bewailed by women robbed of country, husbands, and children and reduced to slavery . . . , was he not displaying to the Athenians their own callousness and showing in its ugliest colours the taste for conquest that they were still gratifying in the Sicilian venture?[2]

Norwood 1920: 245 is forthright in making the play an allegory: 'No spectator could doubt that "Troy" is Melos, "the Greeks" Athens.' The view that the play has Melos in view was the standard one until 1987 and has still found numerous supporters in the three decades since then.[3]

The implication of this argument is that the audience were intended to feel outrage at the sufferings of the Trojan women and then shame that they themselves had done something similar at Melos. But the audience is unlikely to have reacted with outrage since this emotion is not evoked by what is expected or normal. The enslavement of the Trojan women is what is expected from several points of view. (1) In the *Iliad* Hector (6.448–65), Priam (22.59–71), and Andromache (24.728–32) describe the fall of Troy they are certain is coming, a fall entailing the enslavement of its women. That women are enslaved when a city is captured is the epic norm.[4] Lyric

[2] Wenn nun Euripides eine Tragödie füllte mit den bittersten Schilderungen der Schmach, wie solche des Vaterlands, der Gatten und Kinder beraubte, zur Sklaverei entwürdigte Weiber fühlen und klagen, . . . hieß dies nicht den Athenern ihre eigene Härte vorhalten, und die Eroberungslust, welcher sie in der Unternehmung gegen Sizilien noch nachhingen, ihnen von der häßlichsten Seite zeigen?

[3] Virtually all the arguments for a connection with Melos were made between 1839 and 1923. The following are later scholars who accept the contemporary reference (Melos or earlier massacres) without adding anything either new or plausible (some curiosities or qualifications are noted in parenthesis): Delebecque 1951: 245–6 and 254–7 (parallels in wording between *Troades* and the Melian Dialogue are noted: perhaps Euripides took part?), Vellacott 1954: 14–15, Lattimore 1958: 122–4, Goossens 1962: 520–7, Conacher 1967: 136, Lesky 1972: 391, Engl. trans. 290 (the Melos connection, though unprovable, should be accepted as fact because it was previously accepted), Biehl 1973: 135, Kuch 1973: 113 (the enslavements in *Andromache*, *Hecuba*, and *Troades* should not be correlated with particular fifth-century incidents but reflect the general temper of the times), Lee: ix–x and xiv (there is a reference, but Melos is not the play's central theme), Barlow: 26–7 (Melos 'might have influenced Euripides'), Croally 1994: 232–4, Kuch 1998, Clay 2005: 7, Burian 2009: 4–7, Griffith and Most 2012: 77–9.

[4] See *Il.* 9.591–4, *Od.* 8.523–30, 9.39–42.

tells the same tale. Stesichorus' *Iliupersis*, as we can gather from the *Tabula Iliaca Capitolina* (see Davies–Finglass on fr. 105), dealt with the fate of all the Trojan women in Euripides' play. Contemporary visual arts attest the theme as well: enslaved Trojan women were depicted by Polygnotus in a large painting in the Cnidian Lesche at Delphi (Paus. 10.25–7), and there was a similar picture in the Stoa Poikile in Athens (Paus. 1.15.2). Tragedy assumes enslavement in consequence of war, as shown by the Chorus's words at *Septem* 108–10 and 321–68 and Creon's at *Antigone* 199–202. (2) Prose sources state the principle that a conqueror had the right to treat the vanquished as he liked: see Heraclit. fr. 59 Graham, Hdt. 9.122, Xen. *Cyr.* 7.5.73, *Mem.* 4.2.15 (Socrates!), *Dissoi Logoi* 3.5 Graham, and Arist. *Pol.* 1.6, 1255a6–7. Kiechle 1958: 132–8 and Kuch 1973: 107–9 note that in the archaic period the more humane practice of *anastasis* (forced migration) tended to replace massacre and enslavement, particularly where a city surrendered before being forcibly captured, but the older practice was not a dead letter.[5] It certainly remained in force when Greeks dealt with non-Greek cities.[6] Thus, even an audience inclined to evaluate what they saw in contemporary terms would find nothing here that obviously called for outrage. (3) Persons or groups recently enslaved in consequence of war figure in eleven of the thirty-one tragedies that survive from the fifth century.[7] This theme, to be sure, is more in evidence in *Troades* than in most plays, but it is roughly as prominent in *Hecuba*,[8] where scholars have not seen an extradramatic reference. It must have been prominent in Sophocles' *Aichmalotides*, as well as in his *Aias Locros* and *Lakainai*. Euripides' audience in 415, accustomed to seeing this motif in tragedy, would have no reason to think that the poet was alluding to the recent past. The choice of enslaved women as the play's subject is insufficient to prove a link with Melos.[9]

[5] See the instances discussed in Kuch 1973: 118n34.

[6] See Kuch 1973: 119n35.

[7] These are, in addition *to Troades*, *Agamemnon* (Cassandra), *Choephoroi* (chorus), *Ajax* (Tecmessa), *Trachiniae* (Iole and other captives from Oechalia), *Andromache* (Andromache), *Hecuba* (Hecuba, chorus, Polyxena), *Electra* (Clytaemestra's Trojan slaves), *Iphigenia Taurica* (Iphigenia and the chorus), *Helen* (chorus), and *Orestes* (the Phrygian). Choruses of captive women figured in Aeschylus' *Threissai* and Sophocles' *Aichmalotides*.

[8] Slavery is lamented by Polydorus (55–8), the Chorus (100–3, 444–83), Hecuba (157–8, 232–7, 415, 614–15, 798, 809–11, 822–3), and Polyxena (349–66, 420, 551–2)—and noted by Odysseus (135), Talthybius (494–6), and Polymestor (1095–6, 1120, 1252–3); and loss of homeland by Hecuba (619–23) and the Chorus (905–42). Cassandra's concubinage also comes in for mention (824–7).

[9] A curiosity is Murray 1965 (1946): 65, who says that Euripides treats 'the proudest conquest wrought by Greek arms in legend' in a way that reveals 'not glory at all but shame and blindness and a world swallowed up in night'. This implies that the treatment

1.2.2. Arguments for a connection: anti-war sentiment in Troades?

But there are two passages that have been constantly cited in the literature to show that the *Tendenz* of *Troades* is quasi-pacifist, that it demonstrates the folly of all wars except those fought in defence of one's homeland. These passages need to be examined in detail to see whether the conclusions drawn from them are justified.

1. Murray 1965 (1946): 66 quotes Poseidon's words at *Tro.* 95–7. Like many others he thinks that Poseidon calls anyone who sacks cities a fool *tout court*, and he says that the coming fate of the sackers of Troy must have made the sackers of Melos uneasy. The anti-war interpretation is also in Steiger 1900: 364–6, who calls Poseidon's lines an exhortation to peace (*Friedensmahnung*), and by Goossens 1962: 524–6, who says that Poseidon condemns wars such as those against Troy or Melos. But Poseidon and Athena have had a conversation of almost fifty lines before Poseidon speaks these three verses. That conversation makes it plain that what was foolish about the Greeks' behaviour was not that they sacked Troy but that they failed to punish Ajax for dragging Cassandra from Athena's temple. The whole prologue makes it clear that in sacking Troy the Greeks were doing precisely what Athena wanted them to do, for she is named four times (10, 24, 46–7, 72) as Troy's destroyer. The standard interpretation makes Poseidon's three lines a complete non sequitur in relation to what precedes: 'The Greeks are about to perish because of their failure to punish Ajax's impiety against Athena, who helped them sack Troy; therefore it is foolish to sack cities.' If Euripides had wanted Poseidon to drive home the point—and it would certainly need driving home for an Athenian audience in the fifth century[10]—that a war of conquest is inevitably lethal for the

of the Trojan legend in Homer was a sunny exercise in Greek self-congratulation and showed no empathy with the sorrows of the defeated, this being Euripides' novel importation. Murray's uncritical belief that Euripides was a pioneer of the human spirit has led him to trivialize his epic predecessor.

[10] Green 1999: 98 points out that fifth-century Greece 'consisted of mutually antagonistic and competitive states that regarded warfare as a natural and inevitable way of life, peace simply as a continuation of war by different means. There could hardly be a more radical contrast than that with our own post-nuclear age, which regards war by definition as the greatest conceivable disaster, to be avoided at all costs, and its instigators as criminals or moral imbeciles.' Scodel 2012: xxiii says 'War, for Greeks, seemed often to be an inescapable evil, and they could not imagine that it would ever vanish.' See also Carter 2007: 134–5. These widely accepted generalities should be borne in mind by interpreters of Euripidean tragedy.

conqueror, he could easily have set it in a context that would reinforce this idea rather than rendering it unintelligible.[11] Since tragic poets were not bound to reproduce the story line of earlier poets, he need not have made Ajax's impiety the reason for Athena's change of heart and could have had her anger arise from some circumstance that is the natural outcome of sacking a city, for example the burning of her shrine. Alternatively, Poseidon or Athena could have said something to imply that sackers of cities are prone to commit impieties such as that of Ajax. But they do not do so, and if Poseidon's statement that sacking cities is foolish is to seem a reasonable conclusion from what has gone before, this point will have to be made.[12] At 95–7n below I argue that the change of a single letter integrates the lines into their context.[13] What they mean is that it is a foolish man who, after destroying his enemies, himself meets with a destruction he could easily have avoided. Neither Athena nor Poseidon, it should be noted, is remotely plausible as an opponent of war per se.

2. The other passage is *Tro.* 400–2, from the first *rhesis* of Cassandra:

> *φεύγειν μὲν οὖν χρὴ πόλεμον ὅϲτιϲ εὖ φρονεῖ·*
> *εἰ δ' ἐϲ τόδ' ἔλθοι, ϲτέφανοϲ οὐκ αἰϲχρὸϲ πόλει*
> *καλῶϲ ὀλέϲθαι, μὴ καλῶϲ δὲ δυϲκλεέϲ.*

For Steiger 1900: 367–70 Cassandra is the mouthpiece of the poet, who is urging the Athenians not to sail against Sicily. Parmentier 17 takes the lines as Euripides' statement that only wars of defence are ever justified and concludes that the poet is reproving the Athenians for their unprovoked attack on Melos: Cassandra is denouncing all wars of choice. Is it plausible to read such a general admonition out of these lines? There are reasons to demur.

Ever since the Persian invasion of 480/79 Athens had been pursuing an aggressive policy toward both the Persians and the other cities of Greece. She had consolidated the Delian League under her own control and used its resources to fight wars not only in Asia Minor but also in Greece and as far away as Egypt, a stance that alarmed the more conservative states of the Peloponnese. There were, to be sure, Athenian leaders such as Cimon

[11] It could be urged that Poseidon deprecates the sacking of cities because the sackers lose the self-control necessary to avoid violating sanctuaries. But Poseidon offers no hint of such reasoning.

[12] Furthermore, Euripides could easily have substituted other figures for Poseidon and Athena, figures neither of whom was involved in destroying Troy and who might have uttered the warning against sacking cities out of a sense of disinterested justice.

[13] An additional reason for thinking that all is not well is that the transmitted text cannot be convincingly punctuated: different editors mark a pause either after *πόλειϲ* or *τύμβουϲ θ'* or *κεκμηκότων* or *δούϲ*, without being able to give a convincing reason for their choice.

and Thucydides, the son of Melesias, who wanted their city to be less confrontational, but interludes of comparative quietism were only brief interruptions of a stance—taken by Themistocles, Pericles, and others—of what we might call foreign-policy dynamism, a determination to 'pay any price, bear any burden, meet any hardship' in pursuit of Athenian greatness.[14] This energetic policy is articulated in all three of the speeches Thucydides puts in the mouth of Pericles,[15] and Athens' critics describe it in similar terms.[16] It must have had wide support at Athens. Aethra speaks along these lines at *Supplices* 314–25, where she reproves her son Theseus for not taking on the possibly risky war against Thebes (a war of choice, not a war to defend Athens) and tells him that a policy of frequent risk-taking means greatness, whereas quietism means obscurity. Theseus echoes these same sentiments at 339–45 and 571–7. It is hard to believe that Euripides himself had no sympathy whatever for this point of view or that he expected his audience to reject it.[17] Now, we are asked to believe, Euripides, through the mouth of Cassandra, is telling his countrymen that only defensive wars are legitimate.

Surely, though, if he had wanted to persuade the Athenians to alter their policy so radically, he would not have made such an earnest point by inserting it as an *obiter dictum* into a rhetorical θέcιc παράδοξoc ('The Trojans, who lost the war, were really the victors'). That seems an ineffective way to argue a case that needed skilled advocacy. To regard this passage as Euripides' personal message to the Athenians is to assume that the poet chose offhand and ineffectual means to warn his countrymen against a policy of aggression when better means were available.

The quasi-pacifist interpretation also misrepresents what Cassandra says. In the first part of her speech she contrasts the Greeks and the Trojans in regard to the advantages they have foregone or enjoyed. She says that

[14] I borrow a phrase from John F. Kennedy's Inaugural Address to show how Athenian πολυπραγμοcύνη might have looked to those who supported it.

[15] See Thuc. 1.141.3 (the Spartans, unlike the Athenians, do not wage wars abroad), 2.36.2 (toil by the previous generation has resulted in empire), 2.39.2 (we wage war on land and sea at many places at once), 2.41.4 (we have forced every land and sea to be a highway for our daring), 2.63.2–3 (if we adopt quietism as a policy, it will be the ruin of Athens). There is further evidence of prices paid, burdens born, and hardships met in the list of the casualties sustained by the Erechtheid tribe (it was more usual for all ten tribes to list their war dead on a single stele) during the campaigning season of 460 or 459: see Meiggs and Lewis 1969: 73–6. The prescript names Cyprus, Egypt, Phoenicia, Halieis, Aegina, and Megara as battle locations and says that all these men died in the same year. It is hard not to read such an inscription as a boast: here is what our tribe sacrificed for the good of Athens.

[16] The Corinthians at Thuc. 1.70.8–9 (the Athenians give no rest to themselves or others).

[17] Similar sentiments also at *Hcld.* 329–32 and e.g. fr. 745.

the costs to the Greeks of getting Helen back—the sacrifice of Iphigenia and the death of so many Greeks abroad—were not justified: even those not killed were deprived of their loved ones for ten years. The Trojans, by contrast, suffered none of these disabilities; thus far the prudential argument for the thesis that the Trojans are the winners. The second part, however, moves from the subject of comforts lost or enjoyed to that of glory: Hector would not have won fame if his country had not been attacked. Military renown is regarded as a good thing in itself, and Hector would have been the poorer had he missed it. The lines about Paris (398–9) stray even farther from the moral argument for avoiding war, for they claim that had he not married Helen (a marriage disastrous to his country), he would have forfeited renown. Fame—the fame of killing enemy soldiers and even the dubious fame of marriage-by-theft with Helen—is a consolation for death and the measure of a successful life. Therefore when Cassandra says 'So, while anyone with sense should avoid war, if it comes to war, to die nobly is an adornment for one's city, just as an ignoble death is a disgrace', the point she is making is that while war clearly has its drawbacks (this is a subsidiary and concessive point, as the μέν shows), Trojan participation in *this* war (a war of choice, be it noted, since Helen could have been given back) has brought glory not achievable by other means. It is only when these three lines are taken from their context and their grammatical form ignored that they give quasi-pacifist sense. Thus neither the temporal juxtaposition of enslaved Trojan women with enslaved Melian women nor the two particular passages constantly appealed to have the probative value the Melian thesis requires.

1.3. *Troades* and Melos: evidence against a connection

1.3.1. Chronology

Chronology, as we have seen, has been invoked as proving the connection between *Troades* and Melos, though it does not do so. In fact chronology, when examined closely, shows that the play could *not* have been conceived and written under the impact of Melos. In 1987 A. M. van Erp Taalman Kip demonstrated on the basis of Thucydides that Melos fell mid-December at the earliest and that Euripides needed to have his plays ready well before that date.[18] The poet may have needed to write his tetralogy

[18] She acknowledges (p. 414) that the chronological problem was first noticed by Scodel: 139. But consciousness of it seems to have induced Schöll 1839: 69–70 and Planck 1840: 7–10 to date the trilogy to December of 415 at the Rural Dionysia, perhaps in Piraeus. This, however, contradicts the dating of the *Wasps* scholiast, who would have put *Wasps* eight (not seven) years earlier than the trilogy if it had occurred in the

in time to show it to the eponymous archon shortly after he assumed office around 1 July. He certainly needed to have a complete text in order to begin what must have been weeks of rehearsals (the Chorus were amateurs, and there were four plays to prepare). The idea that Euripides began even one of the four plays as late as December for a performance at the Dionysia in March to April is intuitively unappealing. There was simply not enough time between the fall of Melos and the Dionysia of 415 for Euripides to have conceived, written, and rehearsed a play alluding to it.[19]

1.3.2. Some attempts to answer the chronological objection

To answer this objection, some have alleged that Euripides must have made last-minute alterations in light of recent history in the course of rehearsals. Kuch 1998: 153 claims 'That the Melian catastrophe had an effect on the nascent production and also on the text of a drama that had as its theme precisely such a disaster is obvious (*liegt nahe*). We may presume revisions in the verbal and dramaturgical structure that made the play more pointed (*eine verschärfende Nacharbeit läßt sich... vermuten*)'. But since neither he nor Croally 1994: 232 gives examples of anything that looks like such a revision, this is assertion ('obvious', 'we may presume') in place of argument. It would have been easy, for example, for Euripides to have inserted into Poseidon's prologue some lines such as 'the Trojan men who were captured have all been put to the sword' or to have given some similar announcement to Talthybius in the first episode.

Kuch 1998: 153 also suggests that the play as originally written by Euripides 'was a poetic reflection of the new, harsh tenor of the times' as exemplified in events in Mytilene, Plataea, Hysiae, and Scione. This is a second line of defence for the view that the play is a comment on the Peloponnesian War, especially Athens' behaviour in it: it needn't be a reaction to Melos per se since recent history presented a series of such measures against defeated populations.[20] Yet since this way of conducting war had been in evidence since Mytilene and Plataea, the 'emotional shock' Kuch (p. 147) says Melos administered (and which had always figured in arguments for an extra-dramatic reference) loses much of its plausibility.

archon year 415/4. Furthermore, a festival in which most of the audience came from one deme does not seem a likely choice for a major first performance. There is also no evidence that tetralogies were put on anywhere but at the City Dionysia.

[19] Hornblower 2008: 219 comes to this same chronological conclusion.

[20] Mastronarde 2010: 77n27 also thinks *Troades* is an anti-war play inspired by events that antedate Melos.

Croally 1994: 232n170 has a last line of defence: 'Most important, though, is the fact that the writing of the play is not really the issue: it was a matter for the audience to decide in March whether they saw the play as a response (as *their* response) to Melos' (emphasis in the original). But surely what Euripides wrote into his play *is* an important issue. If the poet did not write Melos into *Troades* but the audience read Melos out of it, there was a failure of communication. Furthermore, we have, on the one hand, direct access to the text of the play, which Croally concedes may not have been written with Melos in mind. On the other we have no direct access to the mind of the first audience, and Croally's claim that they understood the play as a reference to recent events is unsupported. We have no evidence that the Athenians, either with or without Euripides' help, were conscience-stricken about what they had done at Melos, and there is some evidence (see § 1.3.7 below) that they felt complacent about it.

We may provisionally conclude that the evidence in favour of the Melos allusion is weak and that the chronological argument, previously regarded as strong evidence in its favour, is strong evidence against it.

1.3.3. Complimentary references to Athens

Euripides makes the Chorus express a longing to be sent to Athens and not to Sparta (208–13). This does not sound as if the poet is rebuking Athens for the way it is conducting its war with Sparta.[21] The Chorus's rejection of Sparta is given a motivation within the play in their hatred of Helen and Menelaus. They give no explanation of their preference for Athens. The *prima facie* explanation is that the play is not anti-Athenian and that Euripides is doing what he regularly does, describing Athens in favourable terms. Anyone familiar with Euripides knows that he makes frequent complimentary references to his city (nor are these confined to plays earlier than *Troades*). Some passages contain assertions of Athenian valour (*Hcld.* 191–4, 303–6, *Supp.* 188–92), justice (*Supp.* 377–80), blessedness (*Med.* 824–50, *Herc.* 1405), freedom (*Hcld.* 198, 957–8, *Supp.* 403–8, 518–21), or antiquity (*Hcld.* 69, *Ion* 589–90). At other times the compliment takes the form of an honorific epithet: 'famous' at *Hcld.* 38, *Hipp.* 423, 760, 1094, 1459, *Ion* 8, 30, 590, 1030; 'blessed' at *Alc.* 452, *IT* 1088; 'holy' at *El.* 1319, *Ion* 184; 'god-built' at *Hipp.* 974, *IT* 1449; 'shining' at *Alc.* 452, *IT* 1130; 'great and fair-choired' at *Hcld.* 358–9. Athens is sometimes honorifically designated as the city of one or another of its legendary heroes such as Erechtheus or Cecrops (*Med.* 1384, *Supp.* 658, *El.* 1289) or as

[21] The point is also made by Knox 1985: 334.

'the city of Pallas' (*Med.* 771, *Hipp.* 30, *Supp.* 377, *Herc.* 323, *IT* 960, 1014, *Ion* 12, 235). In still other places details of Athenian cult or legend are mentioned with what to most has seemed evident affection: see *IT* 945–6, 958–60, 1450–61, and *Ion* throughout. Someone not defending a thesis would say that when the Chorus in *Troades* refer to Athens as 'the famous and blessed land of Theseus', this is likely to have a similar laudatory intent. Kuch, defending the 'Troy equals Melos' thesis, says (1998: 150n23) that the Chorus's praise of Athens glorifies the 'mythical ideal' of long ago, which 'has nothing in common . . . with contemporary Athens', but the distinction between past and present Athens is not in the text, and the audience are given no encouragement to make it. Athens, it should be noted, gets laudatory mention at the beginning of the second stasimon (803) as well.

1.3.4. Heralds, Menelaus, Neoptolemus

If the Greeks, as stand-ins for the Athenians, are the villains of the piece, one would expect them to behave more villainously than they do in our play. Euripides knew well how to portray heralds who are the emissaries of tyrannical power: see those in *Heraclidae* and *Supplices*. The heralds[22] in our play exhibit neither cruelty nor the jack-in-office insolence of men whose person is sacred and who therefore may act as odiously as they like,[23] and they show a degree of sympathy with the Trojan women that is hard to understand if their masters are meant to be portrayed as villainous. To be sure, the herald who comes to fetch Astyanax gives testimony against his masters when he finds the news he is reporting almost too bad to tell (713–17) and wishes that a more hard-hearted man than himself had his job to carry out (786–9). But the decision to kill Hector's son is no novelty designed to evoke outrage but firmly fixed in the poetic tradition. In any case the heralds themselves are portrayed as humane. Nor are they alone in showing decency. Menelaus treats Hecuba not with cruelty or contempt but with humanity. Neoptolemus is another case: we do not see him, but though he is in haste to leave Troy to deal with his grandfather Peleus' expulsion by Acastus, he accedes to Andromache's request that her son be buried, that Hector's shield be his coffin, and that the boy be brought to Hecuba to be adorned for burial (1133–44). Such characterizations, while puzzling for those who take the Melian line, are unsurprising for readers or spectators who see the play as a tragedy rather than an

[22] I argue that *Troades* has more than one: see below § 2.3 and 707n.

[23] At 424–6 Cassandra accuses Talthybius of being such a hateful herald, but there is no justification for the outburst. See note *ad loc.*

indictment in the form of a historical allegory: in a story where Greek and Trojan will both be brought low by the agency of the gods (see § 1.3.5 below) there is no reason to make one side wholly sympathetic and the other wholly unsympathetic. But a poet bent on rebuking his countrymen for cruelty would have been well advised, one would suppose, to proceed differently.

1.3.5. The gods in the play

A poet intending to present the Melians allegorically as the victims of the Athenians will studiously avoid suggesting that the gods destroyed Melos, yet in our play it is repeatedly said that the gods destroyed Troy: see 10, 23–4, 46–7, 59, 72, 561, 597, 612–13, 775–7, 857–8, 867, 1060–70, 1203–6, and 1240–5. By contrast, outbursts against Greek cruelty or aggression are rare (562–7, 628, 764–5, 1188–91)[24] and are outnumbered by execrations of Helen (131–7, 498–9, 766–73, 780–1, 881–2, 987–97, 1004–9, 1100–17), who of course has no counterpart in the destruction of Melos (or in that of the other cities Athens attacked and subdued). Those who see the play as an allegory about Athenian aggression avoid saying anything about this theme. Yet it is clearly in the text, and interpreters deserve censure if they leave out part of the play they are claiming to interpret.

1.3.6. Did Euripides' contemporaries think of him as critical of Athens?

It would seem from our evidence that throughout much of his career Euripides received a chorus every time he had plays to perform, possibly as often as every other year.[25] If he had been perceived by the Athenians as critical of their policies, as the anti-Athenian view of the play implies, it does not seem likely that he would have been allowed to compete so frequently.[26] Yet the productivity of the last decade of his life suggests that he continued to enjoy the support of the archon. The Romantic model of the artist as someone willing to rebuke his own country exercises a strong appeal today, but if this model had any anticipations in the ancient world, it is hard to find them.[27] In any case, nothing said in antiquity about

[24] Lines 366–82 and 1158–65 are about Greek stupidity.

[25] See Stevens 1956: 91–2.

[26] The point is made by Carter 2007: 133, who, however, seems to leave open the possibility—unprovable, in his view—that Euripides was criticizing the Athenians.

[27] Aristophanes looks like an instance, but it is unclear how seriously his jibes at Athenian policy were meant to be taken. One of the meanings of the verb κωμῳδεῖν is 'lampoon, ridicule', and we may fairly conclude from this that obloquy was part of the

Euripides suggests that he was such a person.[28] The silence of Aristophanes on this subject is particularly noteworthy.

No ancient source suggests that there is any connection between *Troades* and contemporary events. (Contrast, e.g., the scholiast on *Andromache* 445, who sees in Menelaus' treachery a reference to Spartan treaty violation.) In particular, Aelian, who in nearby chapters discusses fifth-century Athenian foreign-policy decisions in an informed way, can think of no reason for Euripides' defeat in 415 except the incompetence or venality of the judges. Yet if the play had been perceived by the audience as a criticism of Athenian policy, an explanation of the defeat would lie ready to hand: some of the judges would certainly have taken offence.

1.3.7. The supposed 'message' of Troades *and Athenian views on war*

The presupposition of the Melian interpretation of *Troades* is that Euripides wants the Athenians to see how wrongly they have acted at Melos (or at Scione, if Melos is chronologically impossible). But, as Green 1999 points out, the Athenians in the Peloponnesian War seem to have thought about their treatment of other *poleis* in prudential, not moral, terms. When they debated the fate of Mytilene, the decision not to massacre the men and enslave the women and children was made, according to Thucydides, on grounds of τὸ ξυμφέρον: which policy, mildness or severity, would serve Athenian interests better?[29] It was only after the loss of the fleet at Aegospotami, when the Athenians feared (Xen. *Hell.* 2.2.3) that they might be treated as they had treated Scione, Melos, and other *poleis*, that anyone, so far as we know, cast doubt on the wisdom of Athenian policy. Likewise, the only hesitation anyone is reported to have felt about the Sicilian adventure is that it might fail and cause damage to Athens: even Socrates is reported by Plutarch, *Nicias* 13.6 to have thought that the expedition was a mistake *because it would result in harm to Athens.* A further indication of this frame of mind is that a little more than a year after Melos (414) Aristophanes in *Birds* 185–6 has Peisetairos say that he and Euelpides will starve out the gods 'with a Melian hunger'. This is

comic poet's job. Comic poets are a special case. There is no evidence that Euripides availed himself of an essentially comic licence. See next note.

[28] All the ancient testimonia to Euripides' life are collected in Kannicht's *TrGF* 5.1. The majority are translated in Kovacs 1994b: 1–141.

[29] Compare the debate in Diod. Sic. 13.20–3 on the fate of the Athenian prisoners in Sicily (cited by Green 1999: 98). Diodorus' account, probably based on Philistus, is likewise centred on τὸ ξυμφέρον. This suggests that the terms of the Mytilenaean debate have not suffered a Thucydidean distortion.

clearly meant to get a laugh, and it suggests that the Athenians, including Aristophanes, suffered no qualms of conscience about Melos. Dealing harshly with enemies, whether by starvation or massacre and enslavement, was simply one available option, to be considered on its practical merits.[30] Did Euripides think he could persuade the Athenians to repent of their aggressive ways just by representing the misery of Trojan captives? That does not seem likely nor that he would have simply spat into the wind, alienating his fellow citizens by an attempt that showed little promise of success.

1.3.8. Further arguments against the allegorical interpretation

There are important differences between the fates of the two cities. (a) Troy is burnt to the ground so that it will never be inhabited again, and the Greeks have no intention of seizing the land for their own use. Melos, by contrast, is not burnt but taken over by Athenian cleruchs.[31] (b) In *Troades* virtually no mention is made of the killing of captured Trojan soldiers (there is only the single phrase *καράτομος ἐρημία* 564), whereas the historical record emphasizes this point in connection with the Peloponnesian treatment of Plataea and Hysiae and the Athenian treatment of Mytilene, Scione, and Melos. (c) Melos was delivered into enemy hands by treachery from within, Troy by a clever ruse. (d) Arguably the most emotionally searing moments in the play are the taking away of Astyanax to be killed and the adorning of his dead body by Hecuba. This killing was forecast in Andromache's speech in *Iliad* 24 and narrated in the *Iliupersis*. Euripides has therefore produced his most intense pathos from an incident derived from an epic story that corresponds to nothing in recent history. Vellacott 1975: 166 says 'the killing of Astyanax is used to give particular point to the indictment of Athens'. But in fact it makes it clear that the poet is *not* indicting Athens.[32] Our sources tell us that the Athenians killed adult males but mention no one else.[33]

For further arguments against the Melian interpretation see § 4.7 below.

[30] Recall the boast of Pericles (Thuc. 2.41.4) that Athens has everywhere left *μνημεῖα κακῶν τε κἀγαθῶν ἀίδια*, 'undying memorials of harms inflicted and benefits conferred'. See Rusten *ad loc.*, who cites Adam on Pl., *Rep.* 331E, Dover 1974: 180–4, and Page on *Med.* 809–10. Further on the ethic of helping friends and harming enemies in Blundell 1989.

[31] Also, as Carter 2007: 133 points out, Troy was a formidable enemy that took ten years to capture, while Melos fell in a matter of months.

[32] The sacrifice of Polyxena, not part of the main action but mentioned three times, likewise has no counterpart in the Melos affair.

[33] See also Sidwell 2001: 34–5 for other dissimilarities.

Before 1987 the Melian interpretation was the consensus view,[34] though there were dissenters.[35] The number of disbelievers or agnostics on this question has increased of late,[36] though some remain committed to the notion of Euripides the outsider, who criticizes his countrymen for their own good.

1.4. Contemporary events: the Sicilian expedition

It has also been suggested that *Troades* alludes to possible Athenian designs of conquest in Sicily.[37] Sicily is mentioned by the Chorus, along with Athens, Thessaly, and Thurii on the instep of Italy, as a comparatively desirable place in which to endure servitude. Is this a warning against the Sicilian Expedition? Parmentier 14 raises the difficulty that the request to help Egesta that occasioned the expedition was made around the time the play was performed or only a short time before. Euripides could not have known as he was writing his play that his countrymen would have to decide whether to make this intervention. Nor would he have known what their decision would be.[38] Still, since Thucydides tells us (3.86) that the Athenians had conceived the idea of conquering the island as far back as 426, the idea that Euripides was warning his countrymen of a decision they might be tempted to take is not a chronological impossibility.

But the reference to the island in the *parodos* does not suggest that the poet is warning his audience against conquest. (1) Sicily keeps company on this list with places that enjoyed friendly relations with Athens. Several cities of Thessaly were her allies, and in the period immediately preceding the production of *Troades* they had served as a counterweight to neighbouring Macedonia, which under Perdiccas had attempted to thwart the designs of Athens on several occasions: see below 214–17n. Connections between Thurii and Athens were close: though it was not formally an Athenian colony, its population was preponderantly Athenian. Sicily

[34] For a list of scholars who see a contemporary reference in the play see above, n. 3.

[35] Macurdy 1905: 93–5, Pertusi 1952: 253, Steidle 1968: 55, Lloyd-Jones 1983: 146, Erbse 1984: 72, and Lefkowitz 1986: 54–5.

[36] Gregory 1991: 179n2, Kovacs 1997, Roisman 1997, Green 1999, Sidwell 2001, and Hornblower 2008: 219. Scodel 2012: xxiii–xxiv says it is 'not really an antiwar play' and 'does not endorse pacifism', a view also expressed by Lloyd 1994: 54–5. Rutherford 1998: 179 appears to be agnostic, and Carter 2007: 133 is explicitly so.

[37] See Steiger 1900: esp. 364–70 and 397n35, Wilamowitz 287–91 (Wilamowitz's admirers may be surprised to see pages from his hand as vague and dithyrambic as these), Delebecque 1951: 24–54, Pohlenz 1954: 371–2, and Burian 2009: 4.

[38] Some scholars have got round this difficulty by claiming that Euripides had prophetic powers and knew that the expedition would be voted and would prove catastrophic: see Wilamowitz 288–9, Delebecque 1951: 246, Pohlenz 1954: 372, Vellacott 1954: 15, Lee x, Clay 2005: 7–8. I know of no evidence to substantiate such a claim.

resembles these in that it too had several cities with close ties, some of long-standing, to Athens: Egesta, Leontini, Camarina, Naxos, and Catane were all either formally allied by treaty or had showed their good will to Athens in the recent past.[39] (2) Neither Thessaly nor Thurii belong to a list of states Athens was likely to try to overrun by force, which makes against the idea that Euripides is hinting at possible conquest. (3) The terms in which all three places are discussed are similarly laudatory: Thessaly is fertile, Sicily has had brilliant success in the pan-Hellenic games, and Thurii's river enriches a land of heroes. Had Euripides been intent on dissuading the Athenians from conquest, he would surely have had to mention their military prowess and their love of liberty.[40] A mention of Sicily in this company and in these terms looks like a compliment to Athens' allies of the present day. It does not look at all like a warning against Athenian overreach, and it would never have been taken as such if scholars had not convinced themselves that Euripides *must of course* have been against this war.[41] Scholars who care about evidence or its lack will have to admit that the evidence for the well-beloved figure of Euripides the anti-war gadfly, the conscience of Athens, is not extant but must be manufactured. On Euripides' ostensible attitude toward Athens, as revealed by comments in the plays, see § 1.3.3 above.

2. STAGING

2.1. The evidence

We possess virtually no ancient stage directions for Greek tragedy or comedy: tragic and comic poets wrote down only the words their actors

[39] An alliance between Egesta and Athens is the subject of an inscription, *IG* I³ 11 dating from the 450s. A treaty with Leontini of unknown date was renewed in 433/2 (see Meiggs and Lewis 1969: 175–6). In the war of 427/6 between Syracuse and Leontini, Camarina was allied with Leontini and hence with the Athenians who took her side (Thuc. 3.86.2). Nicias (Thuc. 6.20.3) mentions Naxos and Catane as likely to stand by Athens.

[40] This last point is made well by Perrotta 1925: 289: 'Whoever speaks of [Sicily and Italy's] "prosperity", though not necessarily a supporter of a colonial venture, is not its determined adversary either.' (Note that the phrase εὔανδρον γᾶν in 229, which might have been a warning against conquest, is used of Thurii, not Sicily.)

[41] Several scholars in the nineteenth and twentieth centuries—including two who are convinced he was a pacifist—are prepared to admit that Euripides might well have been caught up in the general enthusiasm for the Sicilian expedition: see Decharme 1895: 204–5, Nestle 1901: 316, Grégoire 1933: 93–7, Goossens 1962: 530–4, and Green 1970: 101–2. And for all we know to the contrary, he *could* have been a supporter. Those whose stomachs are not strong enough for a Euripides who cheers on wars of conquest may have Euripides the giver of innocent compliments. As far as I can see, Euripides the stern warner against imperial ventures is not available.

and chorus were to speak or sing since they directed and produced the plays themselves and could tell the cast in person what visible actions they were to perform, what props they were to use, when to make their entrances and exits, and which point of entry to use. Because of this lack of explicit written evidence, scholarship on tragedy for a long time tended to ignore the visual component of the genre and to treat the scripts as works for reading only. In this they were encouraged by Aristotle, who in the *Poetics* (1453b1–15) seems to regard *opsis*, the visual dimension, as of merely subsidiary importance.

But a number of scholars—Hourmouziades 1965, Steidle 1968, and especially Taplin 1977 and 1978—have made serious efforts to recover the basic stage directions associated with ancient productions and also to evaluate the contribution of these visual cues to a play's meaning.[42] The first aim is helped by the fact that much of what the audience saw is 'doubled' in the text by explicit comments from the characters, e.g. someone announces the entrance of characters or their mode of entrance (on a wagon, for instance) or notes that they are weeping or kneeling in supplication. These 'embedded' stage directions are a reliable basis for reconstructing the stage action. Theoretically there could also be other actions unmentioned in the text, but as we have no access to these, it seems best not to invent 'dumb show' out of whole cloth. Since so many actions are doubled in words, it has seemed reasonable to make the assumption (in principle unprovable) that whenever there is significant action on the tragic stage, it is mentioned or alluded to in the words of the characters.[43] Further study has allowed us to see what effect is produced by, e.g. the act of grasping someone's knees in supplication or the entrance of a character late in the play by an *eisodos* that has been unused since the play's beginning. There is a 'grammar' of dramatic action that conveys its meaning much as does the grammar of the Greek language.[44] One of the aims of the present edition is to make progress in recovering the visual component of *Troades* and in understanding the contribution this makes to the play as a whole and to the trilogy to which it belongs.

[42] Further contributions in Halleran 1984, Seale 1982, Rehm 1992, Wiles 1997 and 2000, and Rehm 2002.

[43] Only one counter-example is known to me: when the Queen first enters at *Persae* 159 the words of the text do not specify her mode of entrance, and only at her second entrance (see 607–9) do we learn that she had previously come in a wheeled conveyance. Taplin 1977: 75–9 gives a plausible explanation for the omission: in earlier Aeschylean tragedy, before the *skēnē* was invented, the normal mode of entry was by wheeled vehicle, and only departures from this (like the Queen's second entrance) are marked in the text.

[44] See Fraenkel (p. 305) on *Ag.* 613f.

2.2. The acting area

The acting area available to Euripides in the Theatre of Dionysus at Athens was dominated at the back by a wooden building called the *skēnē*. This usually represents the outer façade of a palace, and behind it is usually to be imagined a courtyard and, beyond that, the house itself. (In *Troades* the *skēnē* represents a more humble abode, a military hut belonging to Agamemnon, housing those of the Greek captive women who have not yet been assigned to masters.[45]) The *skēnē* has a large central door of two inward-opening[46] panels. This door is flanked by two smaller doors, which are often used in comedy to represent separate houses but in tragedy are mostly ignored.[47] The roof of the *skēnē*, reached by a ladder or stairs behind or within the *skēnē*, can be used for the appearance of gods or can represent an upper storey occupied by mortals (Antigone and the Paidagogos in the prologue of *Phoenissae* and Orestes, Pylades, and Hermione in the *exodos* of *Orestes*), and in one case, Euripides' *Supplices*, it represents a high cliff from which Evadne leaps to her death. Between the *skēnē* and the audience is the *orchēstra* (place for dancing), where the Chorus sing and dance their entrance song (*parodos*) and the other musical pieces (the choral odes or *stasima* and the lyric interchanges with the actors or *amoibaia*) that punctuate the drama. This space is circular in the well-preserved theatre at Epidaurus. The *orchēstra* at the Theatre of Dionysus in Athens in the second half of the fifth century may have been circular, but some polygonal figure such as a trapezoid is also possible.[48] At the edge of the *orchēstra*, right in front of the *skēnē*, there was probably a shallow stage of no more than a metre or two in depth (the normal place for actors to perform) and communicating with the *orchēstra* by steps at one or more places.

2.3. Assigning the *eisodoi*

For entrances and exits the three principal routes are the door of the *skēnē* and two ramps or gangways, leading into the *orchēstra* from the audience's right and left. By convention, one of these *eisodoi* was used for entrances

[45] In our play there are two places only, 139 and 177, where this is called the hut of Agamemnon. See 177n.

[46] For the evidence see Hourmouziades 1965: 16.

[47] Hourmouziades 1965: 24–5 raises the possibility that the two semi-choruses in *Troades* might have entered by the two side doors but admits that the text provides no conclusive proof that they did so.

[48] In favour of a polygonal *orchēstra* see Gebhard 1974 and Isler 2002: 261 (who quotes no evidence). In favour of a circular shape see Scullion 1994: 38–41 and the second chapter of Wiles 1997. *Adhuc sub iudice lis est.*

from or exits to locations abroad (the foreign *eisodos*) and the other was for destinations in the same city (the local *eisodos*). These are used in a schematically consistent way, so that if a character leaves by an *eisodos*, his subsequent return will be by the same *eisodos*.

How were the *eisodoi* used in our play? One of them leads to the Greek agora, the place where the army assembles to take its decisions. For ease of visualization let us arbitrarily say that this is on the right from the audience's point of view.[49] Down the same *eisodos* lies the tomb of Achilles at which Polyxena is sacrificed, plausibly imagined as near the assembly place. (Cf. 626–7 where Andromache, who has just come from the agora, mentions seeing the tomb and adorning Polyxena's body on her way.) This right-hand entrance ramp constitutes, for this play, the local *eisodos*. The other, the left, *eisodos* leads, I will argue, to the ships of Agamemnon, Menelaus, and Neoptolemus. It is the foreign *eisodos*. A third destination is the city of Troy, imagined as visible in the distance to those on stage. I discuss its assignment to an *eisodos* in § 2.4.

The scheme of Greek agora to the right and ships to the left is the one that, in my judgement, makes the best sense of the movements implied in the text. Talthybius at the beginning of the first episode enters by the *eisodos* from the Greek assembly with the news of the assignment of Cassandra to Agamemnon. In theory Agamemnon's ship could lie in the quarter from which he has come, and he could have retraced his steps, bringing Cassandra back with him. But in the next scene this option is much less plausible, for when Andromache appears, en route to the ship of Neoptolemus, there are two reasons why she should exit by means of the other *eisodos*. First, since she is on her way to Neoptolemus' ship, it makes little sense for her to come to the tent where the unassigned captives are being kept and then turn and retrace her steps. Second, she is being transported along with booty from Troy on a wagon, and for this conveyance to execute a U-turn in the *orchēstra* would be awkward. Menelaus likewise appears from the direction of the Greek assembly since he reports the Greek decision to give him a free hand in punishing his errant wife. Theoretically he could have returned in the same direction, but clarity and simplicity are served by putting all the ships down the same *eisodos*, the one marked since the first episode as leading to foreign parts. If Menelaus and Helen exit left, as well as Cassandra and Andromache, the play

[49] According to Pollux, *Onomasticon* 4.126–7, however, the right *eisodos* represents by convention the entrance from the country or harbour and the left *eisodos* the entrance from the city. Pollux (second century AD) may be describing later convention: some representations of Greek tragedy on fifth- and fourth-century vases show arrivals from abroad entering from the left. I assign the two *eisodoi* with full knowledge that the choice is arbitrary.

consists, visually, of a series of movements from right to left: Cassandra, Andromache, Astyanax, and Helen all leave toward the sea, as do Hecuba and the Chorus at the end.

There is only one indication in the text that is hard to square with the above schema. It seems a generally accepted principle that the two *eisodoi* should represent schematically two separate directions, and I noted above that when a character exits by an *eisodos*, his later reappearance will be by the same *eisodos*. Yet in our text Talthybius, who has on this scheme exited to the left at 461 with Cassandra, reappears from the Greek assembly (i.e. from the right) at 706. But the same text that poses a problem for this schema contains a feature that is problematic on any showing, and both problems have the same solution. The speaker indications in the manuscripts call this entering character 'Talthybius', and it is clear (707–8, 710–11, 786–9) that he is a herald. But Hecuba, who has conversed at length with Talthybius in the preceding episode, is unable to recognize this herald (*τίν'* 707). The arriving character is a new servant of the Greek army (as *τίν' αὖ* strongly suggests), and we should recall that the *Iliad* knows of three Greek heralds (Talthybius, Eurybates, and Hodios).[50] The new arrival is a different herald, as suggested already by the scholiast *ad loc*. See also 707n.[51]

2.4. Which *eisodos* leads to Troy?

The last piece of the puzzle is the location of Troy. There are good reasons to put it on the left. When the herald returns (1123) with the body of Astyanax, who has been hurled from the battlements, he mentions (1126–31) that he has seen Neoptolemus set sail with Andromache. Troy would thus seem to lie down the same *eisodos* as Neoptolemus' ship, which we have already seen good reason to put on the left. What the herald brings with him tells the same tale, for he brings both the body of Astyanax (1134), recovered from below the walls of Troy, and the shield of Hector (1136–7), last seen departing for Neoptolemus' ship. Lying in this same direction is

[50] Yoon 2012: 25n63, commenting on a lecture I gave in Oxford that discussed, among other things, the identity of the herald of the second episode, admits that 707 is hard to explain on the hypothesis that he is Talthybius but suggests that Hecuba's eyesight may be failing. There is, however, no indication of this in the play. She does not address the objection that this herald comes from the Greek assembly, whereas Talthybius had left by the other *eisodos*.

[51] If the 'Talthybius' of our mss. is actually two separate characters, we can explain why describing his characteristics has proved so difficult for scholars: see Sullivan 2007: 472, who cites the incompatible views of Lee, Webster 1967, Conacher 1967, Gilmartin 1970, and Dyson and Lee 2000.

the River Scamander.[52] A further indication that the same *eisodos* leads to both Troy and the ships is 1275–6, where Hecuba, aware that she will soon be departing for the ships, tells herself to hurry so that she may say farewell to the city. There is no indication that she is moving in a different direction from that proposed by the Herald.[53]

The disadvantage of the left *eisodos* for Troy is that judged in realistic spatial terms, this assignment involves having the Trojan women move from Troy on the left to the Greek agora on the right, then from the agora to the hut of Agamemnon, and then back to the ships on the left. But the first two legs of this journey (only the first leg as regards Andromache) are ἔξω τοῦ δράματος, having occurred before the play begins. What the audience actually see is a virtually uniform right-to-left movement. Further, the only entrance by the left *eisodos* is that at 1123. The significance of this single entry from the left is discussed below.

The only other inconvenience to this view is that the herald who enters at 1260 from the right, was, if Talthybius, last seen exiting left at 461. He is not the anonymous herald who exited at 1155, who almost certainly departed leftward to dig Astyanax's grave: see the *Staging* note before 1156–1206. Hence he cannot be the herald who enters at 1260, for that man enters from the right: it would make no sense for him to come *from* the direction of Troy in order to shout orders *to* Greek soldiers in Troy. If he is Talthybius (and some connections are observable), it was eight hundred lines earlier that he had last been seen exiting left, and the discrepancy might pass unnoticed, unlike the blatant mistake Carcinus made in this regard (see Arist. *Poet.* 1455a26–8). There is also the possibility of calling him *ΚΗΡΥΞ Β*.

What, then, is the visual contribution of these exits and entrances to the meaning of the play? The three episodes and the *exodos* all end with leftward exits by Cassandra, Andromache, Astyanax, Helen, and Hecuba with Chorus, so this visually unifies them in spite of their disparate character. Of these four acts, three begin with an entrance from the right (Talthybius, Herald, Menelaus). The fourth, in which a herald enters bearing the body of Astyanax and the shield of Hector, is the only one from the left. When an *eisodos* is used for an entrance for the first time late in a play

[52] Wilamowitz 356 claims on the basis of 1151 that the river must have been represented on the painted scenery. But then one would have expected a deictic at 29. For the deictic at 1151 see commentary *ad loc.*

[53] The schema outlined here lines up almost exactly with the map of the Trojan battlefield printed by Strauss Clay 2011: 104. To achieve perfect congruence it would be necessary only to move the agora to the centre of the Greek camp. To someone looking from the left side of the diagram the agora would be to the right and both Troy and the sea would be to the left.

or has been used only once near the beginning (as happens with the foreign *eisodos* in *OT*), rarity of use serves to highlight that entrance. What is highlighted here may be the final destruction of Troy's future, symbolized by the death of Hector's son.

2.5. Entrances and exits in *Troades*

The entrances and exits of Poseidon and Athena in the *prologos* (1, 48, 86, 97) were probably made above ground level, as argued in the commentary. The actor who played Poseidon will have entered by climbing the stairs or ladder behind the *skēnē* and appearing on the rooftop and will have exited the same way. Athena might have done the same, but Poseidon's command ἀλλ' ἕρπ' Ὄλυμπον (92) suggests the possibility that she arrived and departed by means of the *mēchanē*, the stage crane used for aerial entrances.

Subsequent entrances and exits, together with evidence from the text, may be summarized as follows:

153: first semi-chorus enters from the *skēnē*. They are followed by the second semi-chorus in 176.

230: Talthybius with servants enters by the right *eisodos* (see 238, 240, 264, 274, 277).

308: Cassandra enters from the *skēnē*.

461: Talthybius and Cassandra exit by the left *eisodos*, toward Agamemnon's ship (see 455–7).

568: Andromache and Astyanax enter from the right on a wagon (entrance from the agora is implied by Andromache's assignment to Neoptolemus: see 657–8).

709: an unnamed Herald with attendants enters from the right (see 710–11).

789: Andromache departs by the left *eisodos* on the wagon; the Herald exits in the same direction, his attendants carrying or escorting Astyanax (786).

860: Menelaus with attendants enters by the right *eisodos* (in 873–5 he says he has obtained permission from the army to treat Helen as he likes).

880: Menelaus' attendants exit into the *skēnē*. They re-enter with Helen at 895.

1059: Menelaus with attendants and Helen exits by the left *eisodos*.

1118: the Herald enters by the left *eisodos* with attendants carrying the body of Astyanax and the shield of Hector (1136).

1155: the Herald exits by the left *eisodos*, leaving two attendants behind (see 1246).

1200: two attendants of Hecuba enter the *skēnē* and emerge at 1207 carrying adornments for Astyanax.

1250: the Herald's attendants exit left with Astyanax's body on the shield.

1260: a herald (perhaps Talthybius, last seen exiting left at 461) enters from the right and shouts toward the left *eisodos* the order to set Troy on fire. He is accompanied by soldiers from Odysseus, who are to escort Hecuba to her master's ship (see 1271–2).

1331: the Herald and Hecuba, escorted by Odysseus' men, exit by the left *eisodos*, followed by the Chorus in 1332.

2.6. Actors and roles

Euripides had three actors at his disposal. One of them played Hecuba, who is onstage from the beginning to the end. The other two divided the other roles. A possible scheme is as follows:

Actor I: Hecuba.

Actor II: Poseidon, Talthybius, Andromache, Menelaus, Herald of *Exodos* (Talthybius or another).

Actor III: Athena, Cassandra, Herald of second episode, Helen.

Non-speaking roles: attendants of Hecuba, attendants of Talthybius, attendants of the Herald of the second episode, attendants of Menelaus, attendants of Herald of the *Exodos*.

2.7. Props and costume

What other matters must the producer attend to? One thing he need not worry about is any representation of the city of Troy: this is imagined as offstage, visible to the actors (1256–9) but invisible to the audience and near enough that Talthybius' shouted orders to fire the city (1260–4) can be heard. The items actually needed are these:

1. two torches for Cassandra to brandish (298–350);
2. a wagon, laden with Trojan spoils including Hector's armour, on which Andromache and Astyanax make their entrance (568);
3. a shield, carried in at 568 on the wagon and reappearing at 1123 with the Herald (see 1136–7);
4. adornments of clothing and jewellery to deck the body of Astyanax (1207) and a garland with which Hecuba decorates the shield of Hector (1223).

Details of costume include the provision of appropriate masks to designate characters who are male or female, old or young, free or slave, plus the following:

1. Poseidon and Athena will have been clothed in a fashion suitable for divinities, with the former additionally carrying a trident and the latter being equipped with helmet, spear, aegis, and shield.
2. Hecuba, we may suppose, was costumed in royal dress now smudged with dirt; the same may be true of Andromache; Hecuba's hair is cropped in mourning (see 141–2).
3. The chorus members, unlike the servants in *Andromache* or the Chorus of *Hecuba*, are not Hecuba's slaves but free matrons and maidens of Troy and will have been costumed accordingly.
4. Talthybius and the Anonymous Herald I have argued for at § 2.3 and at 707n below will have carried the herald's staff and worn perhaps other recognizable marks of their office.
5. Cassandra was marked as Apollo's prophetess both by a garland of laurel about her head and by something worn on her body, plausibly to be identified with the ἀγρηνόν mentioned by Pollux, a reticulated garment falling from shoulder to thigh (see 256–8n and 329n).
6. Helen, we know, was not dressed in rags nor was her hair cropped in grief like Hecuba's (1025–6), but we have no indication whether she was spectacularly attired or not. (Had she dressed particularly well, we might have expected Hecuba to note this fact and not merely the negative fact that her clothing was not ragged or her hair cut short.) Her mask will have given some conventional indication of her remarkable beauty.

3. TRILOGY

3.1. A connected trilogy

The Aelian passage quoted above (§ 1.1) gives us, in addition to the Olympiad in which *Troades* was produced, the names of its companion plays. The three tragedies are all set in either the city of Troy or the Greek camp before it, and the first play dramatizes an important antecedent to the Trojan War, the second an incident in the Greek camp during its course, and the third the war's aftermath. The question thus arises whether these three plays constitute a connected trilogy or *Inhaltstrilogie*, i.e. a series of plays that make an artistic whole, each in principle incomplete without the others.[54] It was characteristic of Aeschylus to enter three closely connected tragedies and a related satyr play at the City Dionysia,[55] and he may well be the inventor of the connected trilogy. Such a grouping, a *Lycurgeia*, is also attributed to Aeschylus' competitor Polyphrasmon (*TrGF* 7 T 3). Though the *Inhaltstrilogie* was not characteristic, as far as we can tell, of later practice,[56] Aeschylus' nephew Philocles wrote a *Pandionis* (*TrGF* 24 T 6c). Meletus, the prosecutor of Socrates (or possibly his father) produced an *Oedipodeia* (*TrGF* I DID C 24) in a year not far from the end of the century (see Scodel 17n14). A fourth-century inscription says that a *Telepheia* by 'Sophocles' was produced for a deme festival (*TrGF* I DID B 5.8). This might have been the grandson of the great Sophocles, but it could also have been a reperformance of three plays on the Telephus theme attested for the fifth-century Sophocles, as argued by Finglass 2015a: 214 and n41.

The plays of 415, however, are much less closely connected than those of the *Oresteia*, where *Choephori* picks up (with the lapse of a few years) from the end of *Agamemnon*, and *Eumenides* carries on almost seamlessly from *Choephori*. *Troades*, by contrast, does not join up with *Palamedes*, which in its turn is considerably later than *Alexandros*.[57] So why should we assume, as most scholars since Schöll 1839 have done, that Euripides intended the tragedies of 415 as an artistic whole and—just as important—that the first audience would have recognized them as such? Why

[54] I speak here of connected trilogies, not tetralogies, since the satyr play, though drawn from the same cycle of myth, often stands outside the temporal sequence of the first three plays: Aeschylus' satyric *Proteus* of 458, for example, dramatizes an event earlier in the story than the trilogy that preceded it. Euripides' *Sisyphus* is set earlier in time than its companion tragedies and is furthermore only tangentially connected to the Trojan story. (Sansone 2015 argues that the satyr play was in fact performed first, but if it was, it is odd that it is always mentioned last.)

[55] In fact, however, as is pointed out by Yoon 2016: 258–62, we have secure attestations for Aeschylus of only four productions of mythologically connected plays, the *Oresteia*, the Theban plays, the *Lycurgeia*, and the Egyptian plays. Gantz 1979 and 1980 and *TrGF* 3: 111–19 give plausible connected offerings of Aeschylus, but they are conjectural only. The tetralogy should not be assumed to be his default setting.

[56] A sentence in the *Suda* Sophocles entry (T 2.5–6 Radt) seems to claim that Sophocles was the first to write unconnected plays; that is not literally true, as Aeschylus' offerings of 472 make clear. The text here is uncertain, and Yoon 2016: 262–3 points out that the emendation *τετραλογίαν* for transmitted *cτρατολογεῖcθαι* lacks transmissional probability. If it should happen, nevertheless, to be correct, I would supplement as follows: *ἦρξεν τοῦ δράμα<τι> πρὸc δρᾶμα ἀγωνίζεcθαι ἀλλὰ μὴ <τετραλογίαι πρὸc> τετραλογίαν*.

[57] The looseness of the connections is pointed out by Planck 1840 and Mayerhoefer 1908: 61–3, both of whom argue against an *Inhaltstrilogie*.

should we not regard them as three separate and unconnected plays presented at the same festival, their common derivation from the same cycle of myth being extrinsic and accidental? Scodel 11–19 discusses this question, giving full weight to the evidence against connectedness but arguing persuasively for it. I will not summarize her argument here since it should be read by anyone who cares about this question, but merely add a few further considerations that corroborate the idea of a connected trilogy.

1. As far as our evidence goes, it was normal practice for three unconnected tragedies to be drawn from geographically distinct cycles of myth, e.g. Aeschylus in 472, Sophocles or Mesatus in the year of Aeschylus' Danaid trilogy, and Euripides in 438, 431, and 412, as well as in his posthumous production. It is true that of Xenocles' plays of 415 *Oedipus* and *Bacchae* are drawn from Theban legend (if we assume that the second dealt with the death of Pentheus), but *Lycaon* is not. To judge from the record, therefore, poets did not produce three tragedies drawn from the same mythic cycle if they were not meant to form a trilogic offering. As for audience perception, the announcement of the titles of the three plays would have alerted them that they were about to see such a trilogy: Aeschylus' plays were put on after his death, perhaps not at the Dionysia, as the tradition in antiquity claimed,[58] but often enough to remind the audience of the nature of most of his offerings.[59] An Athenian audience, viewing three plays drawn from the same cycle, would surely have regarded them as connected.
2. Not only are our three plays drawn from the Trojan cycle, but they also stand in the same order as in the mythical narrative. Since order of presentation was chosen by the poet, this further advertises the unity of the three tragedies. (By contrast, of Xenocles' two Theban plays of 415 the first, *Oedipus*, occurs several generations later than the third, which belongs to the lifetime of Cadmus, the city's founder.)

To be sure, Euripides' plays of 415, taken as an *Inhaltstrilogie*, are the only instance of such a grouping in his work,[60] but as Scodel (18) points

[58] Biles 2006–7 gives the grounds for scepticism on this point. Lamari 2015 seems less sceptical.

[59] In addition to Aeschylean plays revived in other venues, the pseudo-Aeschylean Prometheus trilogy—possibly the work of Aeschylus' son Euphorion and possibly produced as the work of Aeschylus—may have been produced in 431 or earlier: see West 1990: 67–72.

[60] The mention together of *Oenomaus* and *Chrysippus* in the fragmentary hypothesis (hypothesis (g) in Diggle's OCT) to *Phoenissae* does not prove that the three plays

out, Euripidean tragedy shows many signs of influence by Aeschylus, and it would not be surprising if he reverted, on one occasion or more, to the larger form used by his great predecessor. It would be irrational to assert that three plays drawn from the same cycle of myth and presented in the same order as the mythical narrative were unconnected merely because connected trilogies were rare in the second half of the fifth century.[61] As Scodel (19) says, 'Though the public may have been relatively indifferent to the trilogy as a form, it is hard to believe that they could have seen the *Alexander* and *Troades* on the same day and made no connection. The older members of the audience had been brought up on Aeschylus.' We should make the heuristic hypothesis of unity and see whether what is known about the two lost tragedies coheres in any way with *Troades*. Here is a summary of what is known or conjectured with strong probablity about them.

3.2. *Alexandros*

We are fortunate in having a number of sources—a papyrus *hypothesis*, several substantial papyrus fragments, a number of quotations by ancient authors, fragments of a translation or adaptation of the play by the Latin dramatist Ennius, and representations of the story on ancient works of art—to help us reconstruct this play.[62] In spite of our good fortune a number of problems remain, as we will see. The play's action reports or dramatizes

were produced together, and there are good reasons for thinking they were not: see Mastronarde on *Phoenissae*, pp. 11–14 and 36–8.

[61] Koniaris 1973 tries to prove that the plays of 415 do not form a connected whole, but his arguments are weak. He claims, for example, that Alexandros in the first play, though the bearer of a curse, was wholly admirable but was portrayed in *Troades* as culpable. But it seems impossible to prove from the fragments that he was portrayed as admirable, and his defects are made clear in his decision in judging the goddesses to prefer his own sexual satisfaction to his country's success in war. Koniaris correctly infers that in *Alexandros* divine power (which he calls predestination) was about to produce Troy's ruin but claims on the basis of 34–5 and 373 that in *Troades* Helen's free decision is the principal cause. But the lines in question do not prove this (see the discussions *ad locc.*), and his argument also ignores the numerous places in *Troades* where the gods are blamed for Troy's fall (see above § 1.3.5). Scodel (15) says justly that the article is 'poorly argued and simplistic in its assumptions'.

[62] The fragments may be consulted in Kannicht, in *SFP* ii, and in Collard–Cropp. Numbers preceded by F and T refer respectively to the fragments and testimonia on the play to be found in Kannicht's edition, whose numeration is followed in the other two editions mentioned. Fragments of Ennius' *Alexander* (plus some lines likely to come from there) are cited by both Manuwald's and Jocelyn's fragment numbers. I have replaced Jocelyn's Roman numerals with Arabic ones and added the lines of his continuous numeration where appropriate. Additionally P. Oxy. 5183 is a further tragic fragment, possibly from *Alexandros*: see Henry 2014. In view of the uncertainties about

the surprising rescue of Alexandros, son of Priam and Hecuba, from death (1) at the time of his birth, (2) on the occasion of his arraignment by his fellow shepherds, and (3) when Deiphobus and Hecuba conspired to kill him because of his success in the athletic games in which he had been allowed to compete. Since the audience have been aware since the beginning of the play that Alexandros will prove to be the downfall of Troy, they know that his rescue, though perceived as a happy event by the Trojans, in fact seals their destruction.

3.2.1. Prologue

A papyrus *hypothesis* of *Alexandros*[63] gives us the play's first line (or rather its last seven syllables) and most of its basic storyline, both the antecedent events mentioned in the prologue and actions within it, whether enacted or reported.[64] By contrast, about many details of the management of the plot—the speaker of the prologue, the identity of the Chorus, the nature of the attempt to kill Alexandros, whether Cassandra appeared twice, and so forth—evidence is lacking.

The beginning of the summary (lines 4 through 14) gives the action that precedes the opening of the play: Hecuba's dream that she gave birth to a firebrand that was to destroy Troy; the decision to expose the child she was carrying; his being raised among shepherds by the man entrusted with the exposure; the institution of lavish games in his memory; and his showing himself, as he grew up, to have qualities superior to his servile circumstances. All this will have been narrated in the prologue, whose first line (F 41a) is:

× – ⏑ – ×] *καὶ τὸ κλεινὸν* [*Ἴ*]*λιον.*

Ennius, as we have noted, translated or adapted Euripides' play. In his *Alexander* fr. 18 J., fr. adesp. 76 M., we have a description of the dream, in which Hecuba gives birth to a firebrand that consumes the city. The prologue probably contained the comment on the march of time (F 42).[65] At

attribution and interpretation I have not attempted to bring it to bear on my reconstruction.

[63] On the nature of these prefaces see the beginning of the Commentary, devoted to the *hypothesis* to *Troades*.

[64] The *hypothesis* was first published in Coles 1974: 1–22. Diggle 1998a: 80–1 and Kannicht 174–6 re-edited the papyrus and noted subsequent suggestions. There is a re-edition with thorough discussion in Meccariello 2014: 119–30.

[65] It might also have included the explanation, given in *Alexander* fr. 16 M., 20 J. (= F 42d), for Paris' second name, 'Alexandros': 'warder-off of men', given to him to recognize his protection of the herds from marauders. The *hypothesis* (lines 6–7) says

Kovacs 2015 I give reasons for thinking that the prologue was spoken by a divinity, e.g. Athena or Hermes. It could well have contained the couplet announcing that Zeus has decided to bring ruin on both Trojans and Greeks (F 1082, Euripidean but no play title given):

> Ζεὺϲ γὰρ κακὸν μὲν Τρωϲί, πῆμα δ' Ἑλλάδι
> θέλων γενέϲθαι ταῦτ' ἐβούλευϲεν πατήρ.

This forecast of the Διὸϲ βουλή fits well in a speech by Athena or Hermes, as does the phrase Ζεὺϲ ... πατήρ.[66]

3.2.2. *First episode*

We next learn (and here we have the beginning of the play's action) that since Paris behaved insolently toward the other herdsmen (slaves like himself), they brought him for punishment to Priam, who did not chastise him but allowed him to compete in the games. This will have formed the main part of the first episode and will have been acted, not reported: we know that the other shepherds formed a secondary chorus (T v). But the *hypothesis* abbreviates since the trial of Paris did not immediately follow the prologue. We are told (T v) that the main chorus was already in place when the chorus of shepherds entered. We know something about what the main chorus did before the secondary chorus arrived: there is among the papyrus fragments of the play a passage in which the Chorus Leader urges Hecuba to stop grieving for the son she exposed so many years ago.[67] This scene of consolation fits most economically before the arrival of Alexandros with his accusers: the prologue mentioned the lamentation of Hecuba for her lost son, and it is a natural sequence that the report of this grief be followed by its dramatization.[68] Probably the *hypothesis* gives us what was the main content of the first episode, omitting those parts of it that precede the entrance of Alexandros.

That the Chorus were women is suggested by their attitude of sympathy with Hecuba's loss.[69] We may suppose that their entrance was motivated

that his foster-father raised him, Ἀλέξανδρ[ον Π]άριν προϲαγορεύϲαϲ. The Greek is ambiguous, but it might mean that the foster-father called by the name of Paris (presumably from the πήρα in which he was exposed) the boy the world later knew as Alexandros.

[66] These lines are assigned to *Alexandros* as fr. 45 by Snell 1937. In ταῦτ' ἐβούλευϲεν the pronoun, to judge from what the quoter Strabo says, refers to Paris' abduction of Helen. This is consistent with the situation here, where neither the journey to Sparta nor the Trojan War have yet happened.

[67] F 46, with which FF 43–5 also cohere.

[68] See e.g. *Med.* 20–3 followed by 96–165.

[69] On the other hand their emphasis on the philosophical control of emotions (F 43: cf. F 45 and F 46.5) may point in the other direction. The secondary chorus and the

either by the news that their queen was distressed (compare *Hippolytus*, *Andromache*) or by the sounds of her lamentation (cf. *Medea*, *Heraclidae*, *Troades*, *Helen*, and *Prometheus Vinctus*). So the action of the play seems to have begun with the entrance of the Chorus, who had a dialogue with Hecuba about the loss of her son. Preceding the *parodos* there might have been a monody by Hecuba.

3.2.3. *The entrance of Cassandra*

At the end of F 46, we have what looks like an entrance announcement: the Chorus leader says that she sees someone approaching (δέδορκα is certain):

× – δέ]δορκα παῖδα κ[
× – ⏑]ν ἀδύτων ω[

The verb δέδορκα is often used in entrance announcements (see *Med.* 1118, *Andr.* 545, *El.* 339, and *Tro.* 707), and the first two syllables of 11 were probably καὶ μὴν or καὶ δή. The entrant most probably had a name beginning with kappa. The mention of ἀδύτων, 'shrine', in the genitive (indicating place from which) and the initial kappa strongly suggest that the entrant is Cassandra. Wilamowitz's supplement, καὶ μὴν δέ]δορκα παῖδα Κ[αccάνδραν cέθεν, gives good sense and style.

The *hypothesis* (lines 25–8) has her entering later in the play and prophesying about Alexandros just before the recognition is brought about by his foster-father. Kannicht suggests that in the first episode she is just passing through (*hoc quidem loco fabulae quasi praeteriens tantum modo in scaenam inducitur*), but since this is both without parallel and arguably pointless, we are entitled to conclude that Cassandra entered here to be a participant in the scene. As we will see, there are indications in this very entrance announcement (her haste or distressed demeanour) that Cassandra will deliver a prophecy *in this scene*, which can only have been about Alexandros. I can see no reason why Euripides would have brought her on twice to do the same thing.[70] It is simpler to assume that this is her scene and that the *hypothesis* has misrepresented the timing of her appearance. Hamilton 1976: 67–8 gives numerous examples where the *hypotheseis*

main chorus are of different sexes in *Hippolytus*, Euripides' *Supplices*, and *Antiope*. In *Phaethon* both the main and the secondary chorus are female. In Aeschylus' *Supplices* the secondary chorus might be either male or female. We cannot exclude on formal grounds a main chorus that is male.

[70] Occam's razor may be invoked in the form *uaticinia uesana non sunt multiplicanda praeter necessitatem*.

to extant plays distort the order of events. A close parallel is the *hypothesis* to *Troades*, which puts Agamemnon's taking of Cassandra as his mistress (first episode) after Menelaus' taking away of Helen (third episode). In these *hypotheseis* smoothness and parallelism trump accuracy, and two women have been mentioned together because, we may suppose, each has been taken away by an Atreid. This parallels the dislocation I suggest in the *hypothesis* to *Alexandros*: its author has paired by means of *μέν* and *δέ* the warning of Cassandra that the young man must be destroyed with the attempt on his life by Deiphobus and Hecuba.[71]

The very end of F 46 (lines 11–12) raises several questions that might as well be dealt with here.

> *καὶ μὴν δέ]δορκα παῖδα Κ[αϲϲάνδραν ϲέθεν*
> *ϲτείχουϲαν] ἀδύτων ω[.* 12

12 *ϲτείχουϲαν* Diggle | *ὧ[δε Φοιβείων πάροϲ* Wilamowitz

In 12 Diggle's *ϲτείχουϲαν* accords with Euripides' practice in such announcements. By contrast there are two problems with Wilamowitz's supplement for the end of the line. First, Cassandra is not coming to the temple of Phoebus but surely has left it for the *skēnē*, which must represent the Trojan royal palace. The *skēnē* is where the herdsmen bring Paris to be judged by Priam, and it is presumably from it that Hecuba has emerged to have her dialogue with the Chorus. Cassandra must enter by the local *eisodos*, at whose end is to be imagined the temple of Apollo. For Wilamowitz's *πάροϲ* we could read Webster's *ἄπο* (Webster 1967: 167).

A second problem is *ὧδε*, which all editors of these fragments known to me mention, with no objection raised and no alternative named. In Wilamowitz's reconstruction it must mean 'hither'. This is common in Sophocles, but there is no certain instance in Euripides.[72] We must reject *ὧ[δε* in this sense. Two alternatives suggest themselves. (1) If we read *ὧδε*, it expresses degree, not direction, e.g. *ϲτείχουϲαν] ἀδύτων ὧδε λαιψηρῶϲ ἄπο* (or *ϲυννεφῆ πάρα*), i.e. the Chorus point out either the speed of Cassandra's entrance or the gloominess of her demeanour. (2) Euripides wrote some other word beginning with omega. Such words (especially ones giving us the trochee we require) are rare. The only plausible candidate

[71] If we regard lines 25–8 of the *hypothesis* as narrated out of order, we can take *παραγενηθέντα* to refer to Alexandros' *first* appearance on stage, a meaning it most often bears: see Kovacs 1984: 50–1.

[72] *Ion* 208 is corrupt, and it is not certain that *ὧδε* means 'hither'; the word was restored by Meineke at F 74, but transmitted *ὅδε* is printed by Kannicht. *ὧδε* occurs some seventy times in Euripides, and the fact that there is no certain instance of the word in a directional sense is a significant pointer to Euripidean usage.

is ὠκύϲ, which suggests ϲεμνῶν ἀπ']αδύτων ὠ[κὺν αἴρουϲαν πόδα, pointing to the swiftness of her entrance.[73] Cassandra, then, enters either in haste (cf. her running entrance at *Tro.* 306–7) or in evident distress (e.g. ὧδε ϲυννεφῆ), presumably because Apollo has told her something disturbing she feels she must report.

The remains of Ennius' *Alexander* give Cassandra sung lines (*fr. incert.* 151.12–15 M., *Alexander* 17.43–6 J.) as well as spoken dialogue (*fr. incert.* 151.3–11 and 16–18 M., *Alexander* 17.34–42 and 47–9 J.). Euripides' normal practice is to portray an extraordinary state of mind by the use of monody, which is then followed by spoken verse.[74] After her entrance Cassandra probably sang an excited prophecy, unintelligible to Hecuba and the Chorus, about the role of a young shepherd in causing the expedition of the Greeks against Troy. This was followed by a *rhesis* or a stichomythic interchange in which Cassandra told Hecuba what she learned from the god about the dangerous person who would shortly arrive in Troy. Some excited spoken lines will have been uttered after she has caught sight of Alexandros entering with his accusers. These will have identified him not as the son of Hecuba but as Troy's destroyer.[75] She will have returned by the *eisodos* shortly before the chorus of shepherds entered with Paris, uttering the prophecy that the man who had already judged the goddesses would bring a spirit of ruin, a Fury or Erinys, to Troy (*fr. incert.* 151.16–18 M., *Alexander* 17.47–9 J.).[76] The entrance song of the chorus of shepherds and any ensuing dialogue with Hecuba will have given the actor who played Cassandra time to put on the costume and mask of Priam. Hecuba will have remained on stage and taken part in the trial scene.

3.2.4. *Some questions about Cassandra*

The Cassandra scene must have told the audience what, in this play, Cassandra's relation was to Apollo, her 'back story'. Aeschylus' Cassandra

[73] Or κινοῦϲαν] ἀδύτων ὠ[κὺν ἐκ Φοίβου (or ἐκ ϲεμνῶν) πόδα.

[74] On this sequence see Dale on *Alc.* 280ff. In *Alexandros* the order monody–dialogue is confirmed by Cicero, *De div.* 2.112 (citing *fr. incert.* 151.16 M., *Alexander* 17.47–9 J.) as 'a bit later than (*paulo post*)' the lyric utterance of 43.

[75] Neither at this point nor later in the play, where the *hypothesis* appears to put her prophecy, is it necessary to suppose that she actually said that the young man was Hecuba's long-lost son rather than merely a danger to the city. It would arguably diminish the force of the *peripeteia* if someone on stage identified Paris as the exposed child before his foster-father did. Cf. *OT*, where Oedipus is first identified by Teiresias as the killer of Laius and only later shown to be his son.

[76] On the idea of a human being as an *Erinys*, see 457n. I see no justification for Jocelyn's claim (p. 218) that 'Ennius' emphasis is on the wickedness of Helen herself'. For *Furiae* as agents of divine destruction see the *Thesaurus Linguae Latinae* 6.1.1613–14.

tells the Chorus that she cheated Apollo of her promised favours and that, since he could not take back the prophetic gift, he caused her to be disbelieved (*Ag.* 1202–13). She also explains that the god is now bringing her to Argos to be killed by Clytaemestra (*Ag.* 1136–9 and 1275–8). But Euripides, if we may judge from what is said in *Troades*, presents her story rather differently. Cassandra retains her virginity not by cheating Apollo but because he granted it to her as a gift (*Tro.* 41–4, 253–4). There is no trace of enmity between the god and his prophetess but only of friendly relations (*Tro.* 329–30, 451–4). Furthermore, Cassandra seems to prophesy not primarily on the basis of second sight like her namesake in Aeschylus but because Apollo himself tells her the future (*Tro.* 356–7, 428–30).[77] It is reasonable to believe that in *Alexandros* Cassandra explained the history of her relations with Apollo. This need not have involved straight exposition but could have been conveyed by comments made in passing.

If she and the god are still on friendly terms, we face the question why she is disbelieved, since this motif belongs to a version where Apollo is taking his revenge on her. Here we must confess ignorance. She is disbelieved on one level, of course, because she is regarded as mad (see *Tro.* 348–50, 406–10, 417), a belief her wild behaviour will have caused. In Aeschylus it is Apollo who causes Cassandra to be disbelieved, and perhaps in Aeschylus her raving manner is part of her punishment by Apollo. By contrast we do not know how long Euripides' Cassandra has acted like a madwoman. It may have been a recent phenomenon, perhaps designed to discredit her particular prophecies about Paris, which must be disbelieved if the city is to fall.[78] As it happens, there is a passage of Ennius—no play title given but with Cassandra attested as its subject—that suggests that her wild behaviour is a recent phenomenon (*fr. incert.* 151.1–2 M., *Alexander* fr. 17.32–3 J.):

> sed quid oculis rabere visa est derepente ardentibus?
> ubi illa paul<ul>o ante sapiens virginali' modestia?

But why does she[79] suddenly appear to be raving, with eyes aflame? Where is that wise maidenly modesty she had a short time before?

[77] But *frr. incert.* 16–18 M., *Alexander* 17.47–9 J., may be Cassandra describing a vision only she can see.

[78] F 62g (ἄκραντα γάρ μ' ἔθηκε θεcπίζειν θεόc, κτλ.), quoted by Plut. *Mor.* 821B, represents Cassandra as *always* disbelieved before the event. But Plutarch names neither play nor poet. Sophocles wrote an *Alexandros*, as did Nicomachus of Alexandria. *Pace* Collard 2004: 86 we cannot conclude from the fact that Cic. *Att.* 8.11.3 speaks of Cassandra as a prophet *cui nemo credidit* before quoting from Ennius' *Alexander* that Ennius' and Euripides' plays had these lines. Cicero may be speaking of the general story of Cassandra, not the one dramatized by Ennius or Euripides.

[79] Timpanaro 1996: 19 recommends Lambinus' correction to the second person *visa es*. This is likely to be correct for Ennius, who probably had no chorus, but the 3rd-person form would fit better in the mouth of the *coryphaeus*.

The speaker of these lines knows a Cassandra who acts with maidenly propriety. It is tempting to translate it into Greek trimeters and put it with the entrance announcement[80] we have in F 46, e.g.

καὶ μὴν δέ]δορκα παῖδα Κ[ασσάνδραν σέθεν
σεμνῶν ἀπ'] ἀδύτων ὠ[κὺν αἴρουσαν πόδα. 12
<τί δ' ὄμμ' ἔχουσα πυρσὸν ἐξέστη φρενῶν,
καὶ ποῦ 'στιν αἰδὼς παρθένειος ἡ πάρος;>

Euripides' Cassandra may well have said something to answer this question.[81] Ennius *fr. incert.* 151.3–9 M., *Alexander* 17.34–40 J., gives her lines that explain (if we read *namque* in 36) that she has been sent by Apollo, who by his prophecies has driven her mad against her will: she apologizes for the disgrace this causes her mother. One cannot prove from this passage that in Ennius Cassandra's madness is a recent development, but the Ennius quotation is compatible with this suggestion. We know that Euripides took pains with details like these and that, when he introduced mythical novelties, he adjusted other elements of his plays to be compatible with them. Although we cannot say in this particular instance what caused the Trojans to disbelieve Cassandra, there are ways to explain it that do not involve Apollo's enmity, and we are entitled to suppose that Euripides adopted one of them.

3.2.5. *The trial of Alexandros*

The remainder of the first episode will have been taken up by the trial of Alexandros before Priam. Our only guide, apart from a few book fragments that could come from this *agon*, is the *hypothesis*, which raises on this point as many questions as it answers (I cite the text from Diggle 1998a: 80).

οἱ δ' ἄλλοι νομεῖς διὰ τ̣ὴν ὑπ̣ερήφανον συμβίωσιν δ̣ήσαντες ἐπ̣[ὶ] Πρίαμον ἀνήγαγον αὐτόν̣· ἀ̣π̣ο̣λο̣γηθεὶς [δ]ὲ ἐπ̣ὶ τοῦ δυνάστο̣υ̣ . . . . .[.] . . . . . .[.(.)] ρ̣ειτο κ̣α̣ὶ τοὺς διαβάλ̣λοντ̣α̣ς ε . . . . [.]υς ἔλαβε καὶ τῶν ἐπ' αὐτῶ̣ι̣ τελ[ο]υ̣μέ̣νων ἀγώνων εἰάθη μετασχεῖ̣ν̣.

[80] On the tendency of Ennius to replace iambic trimeters with longer metres such as the septenarius see Jocelyn on frr. 84, 105, 107, 108, and 109.

[81] It is at least possible that F 62e represents part of Cassandra's explanation, e.g.

μῆτερ, τὸ θεῖον ἀβλαβ]ὴς ἤκουσ' ἔπος
Φοίβου δέ μ' αὐτὸ ῥῆμα β]ακχεύει φρένα[ς.

'I was sound of mind, mother, when I heard the god's word, but the very utterance of Phoebus caused my mind to rave.' (For transitive *βακχεύω* see LSJ s.v. II, all examples from Euripides. For the 'construction of part and whole', see *Tro.* 408.)

The other herdsmen because of his haughty behaviour bound him and brought him before Priam. <Having defended himself> in the presence of the king he [verb unknown] and convicted [?] his <several?> accusers [post διαβάλλοντας suppl. ἑκ̣ά̣ϲ̣τ̣[ο]υϲ Coles] and was allowed to take part in the contests performed in his honour.

One of the most surprising things is the statement that Priam, after acquitting Paris on the charge of arrogance, gave him permission to enter the games. Is this in addition to the acquittal or did Paris himself ask permission to compete? What aspect of Paris' behaviour was his principal offence? He might have been arrogant in other ways[82] but also have offended his fellow shepherds by saying that he, though a slave, deserved to compete in the games. This would explain Priam's permission, which otherwise seems gratuitous. According to Hyginus, *Fabulae* 91, Paris demanded to compete because a favourite bull of his had been taken away to be a prize in the games. Did this bull figure in Euripides? The possibility cannot be excluded. Such a motive need only have been mentioned in passing. More prominence, however, might have been given to something that would not have been a motive but an emboldenment: Paris might well have felt that someone who had judged three goddesses in a beauty contest—and had been offered royal power and success in war as well as the hand of the world's most beautiful woman—was no ordinary person. There is also the likelihood (see F 42d) that he had demonstrated unusual physical prowess in repelling robbers who tried to steal the herds.

The trial—to judge from the number of fragments assigned to the speeches of prosecution and defence that comprised it—was staged rather than reported.[83] With Priam as judge and Paris as defendant, who was the prosecutor? Some earlier scholars gave this role to Deiphobus, but it is hard to see what reason he could have at this point to intervene in a quarrel between slaves. The *hypothesis* is inexplicit, but since it was the shepherds who initiated this action, it seems reasonable that the accuser should be one of them, perhaps the *coryphaeus* of the secondary chorus.[84] We are accustomed to speeches of two to four lines from the mouth of a *coryphaeus*, but *Herc.* 252–74 is an example of something more

[82] Arist., *Rhet.* 2.24, 1401b20–3, mentions a speech of defence (author not named) put in the mouth of Paris, who claims that being aloof and herding by himself on Ida was the act of a μεγαλόψυχος. Does this reflect Alexandros' defence in our play against a charge of ὑπερηφανία?

[83] In Kovacs 1984 I argued that the trial of Paris was reported and that the book fragments commonly assigned to it come from an *agon* later in the play in which Hecuba accuses Paris before Priam. I now retract this suggestion.

[84] In 1984: 50 I dismissed the idea without any discussion. But the *hypothesis* later provides evidence for it, τοὺϲ διαβάλλονταϲ ε . . . [.]υϲ, discussed below.

lengthy. There are not many secondary choruses in extant tragedy, but note that one of Hippolytus' huntsmen, who may have been the *coryphaeus* of the secondary chorus, has a dialogue with him.

Still, there seems to be a lot of material in the accusation fragments, perhaps too much to assign to a *coryphaeus*. The suggestion of Cropp 2004: 39 that Hecuba speaks against Paris is both possible and attractive.[85] It is possible since Hecuba is likely to have been onstage when the shepherds arrived and to have remained there. It is also dramatically attractive to have an initial encounter between mother and son before the part of the play where their relationship is revealed: a hostile encounter between an unrecognized mother and child figures in *Ion* and *Cresphontes*. A motive for her intervention also lies ready to hand: if the *coryphaeus* briefly set out the charges against Paris, which might have included his claiming the right to participate in the games, Hecuba, who had persuaded Priam to found the games in honour of her lost son, might well have felt that to allow a slave to participate would diminish the honour. A short speech of accusation may have been made by the *coryphaeus* and answered briefly by Paris. Then Hecuba may have spoken at greater length and been answered in her turn. This has the merit of explaining the otherwise puzzling τοὺϲ διαβάλλονταϲ ϵ . . . [.]υϲ ἔλαβϵ: Paris will have answered both his accusers.[86]

The staging, then, may have proceeded as follows. Paris was led by the herdsmen, his hands bound behind him, to a place in front of the *skēnē*. This secondary chorus will have sung an entrance song, which would give the actor playing Cassandra time to change into the mask and costume of Priam. Priam could have been sent for or have entered by chance at the moment when he was needed, as at *Alcestis* 507–8 and *Antigone* 385–6. The *coryphaeus* will have made a short speech of complaint against Paris, whose reply might have incorporated F 57, which accuses the other herdsmen of being slaves not in name alone but also in actuality.[87] The charge against them makes sense if they regard anything but slavish behaviour as

[85] It is impossible, of course, if Priam and Hecuba were played by the same actor, as maintained by Scodel 40–1. But since the presence (postulated by her and others) of Deiphobus in the *agon* is not only unproven but positively unlikely, the actors could be assigned, without splitting roles, as follows: actor 1: Hecuba (present onstage virtually throughout the whole play); actor 2: Cassandra, Priam, Deiphobus, the Herdsman; actor 3: the προλογίζων, Paris, Messenger, Hector.

[86] If τοὺϲ διαβάλλονταϲ ἑ̣κάϲ̣τ[ο]υϲ (the reading in Kannicht) is correct, ἑκάϲτουϲ may have been used loosely for ἑκατέρουϲ because the first speech of accusation was made in the name of more than one person.

[87] Kannicht thinks the fragment is a disparagement of Priam's sons, but he gives no reason why a charge of servility should be levelled against them. He also cites Matthiae, who thinks they are Deiphobus' description of the herdsmen. But even supposing

evidence of pride. Hecuba will then have made a lengthier accusation. To this speech I would assign F 48:

> σοφὸς μὲν οὖν εἶ, Πρίαμ', ὅμως δέ σοι λέγω·
> δούλου φρονοῦντος μᾶλλον ἢ φρονεῖν χρεὼν
> οὐκ ἔστιν ἄχθος μεῖζον οὐδὲ δώμασι
> κτῆσις κακίων οὐδ' ἀνωφελεστέρα.

Though you are wise, Priam, I nevertheless tell you this: there is no greater trouble and no worse or more harmful possession for a house than a slave who has more intelligence than he ought to have.

There is good reason to assign these lines to her and not to the *coryphaeus*: in Euripides when persons of servile status address their royal betters, they almost never call them by their names.[88] Hecuba, then, is likely to be the speaker. It must be noted that when she says that such a slave is a bad possession, she implies he must be got rid of. Hecuba is hostile to this slave because he is either too proud or too clever.[89] She may be asking that he be killed. If so, there is piquant irony in the fact that Hecuba, who recently lamented the death of the child her husband once exposed, is now trying, unwittingly, to kill him.[90]

Deiphobus to have a part in this scene, he would have no reason to disparage Paris' accusers.

[88] I have already established (1984: 52n10) that Deiphobus could not be the speaker of this fragment, but a shepherd may also be almost certainly excluded. In the extant plays of Euripides slaves (I do not include recently enslaved persons such as Andromache or the Chorus in *Hecuba* in this category) addressing royal persons use ἄναξ (7× in Euripides, 1× in *Rh.*), δέσποτα (2×), and δέσποινα (15×); when there is a pronounced difference in age we find παῖ (17×), τέκνον (21× plus 1× with parents' name in genitive), θύγατερ (7× plus 1× with mother's name in genitive), πρέσβυ (2×), and γεραιέ or γεραιά (2×); some further vocatives are γύναι (2×), ὦ τᾶν (1×), and ὦ τάλαινα (1×). If against these examples (some ninety) we set five counter-examples of a royal person's name in the vocative (*Med.* 1122, *Hipp.* 1157, *Hel.* 597, *Pho.* 88, and *Ba.* 434) and six examples, all from *Iphigenia Aulidensis* (and all from portions of the play regarded with deep suspicion by Diggle), of name plus ἄναξ (*IA* 3, 13, 30, 133, 414, and 436), we can conclude that the leader of the secondary chorus is unlikely to be the one who addressed the king of Troy as Πρίαμε. The same conclusion is suggested by the fragment's confident paraenetic tone. Hecuba is a far more reasonable choice.

[89] See the discussion of the text of this fragment below. It is more plausible to apply ἀνωφελεστέρα, which must mean 'more harmful' (see Barrett on *Hipp.* 634–7), to a clever slave than to a proud one. When Hippolytus at *Hippolytus* 640–4 says he does not want a clever wife in his house since they get up to mischief, he is making a similar point.

[90] If Hecuba does indeed ask for the death penalty (the alternative proposal would be to sell him, but this seems a bit tame), there is a potential new setting for one of the fragments often put later in the play. In Kovacs 1984: 59 I pointed out how awkward it would be to fit F 62i (οἴμοι, θανοῦμαι διὰ τὸ χρήσιμον φρενῶν κτλ.) into a scenario in which Paris is the victim of a surprise attack. A possible location for it, different from

The issues raised in our putative two speeches of accusation and the two in reply can be guessed only in the most general terms: the fragments likely to belong to this debate are so general that it is sometimes difficult to see which side of the debate a fragment is arguing. The herdsmen's general accusation of arrogant behaviour may have been substantiated in various ways (see above), but if he intended to enter the games that fact would have been part of the evidence against him. As noted above, F 57 would be an effective beginning to Paris' reply. He perhaps went on to cite the goddesses' confidence in his judgement as an indication that his view of himself did not exceed his merits. He might have mentioned his defence of the herds.[91] He may also have mentioned some indication of his conspicuous intelligence since this appears to figure in Hecuba's speech of accusation.[92]

Priam, we know, decided in Paris' favour. We probably have his verdict in F 60, which leaves to the judgement of time to determine whether Paris is noble (χρηcτόν) or base (κακόν). A choral ode will have covered the time needed for the games to take place. Possibly from this stasimon are the lyric FF 61b and 61c, which discuss noble birth. In the first of these the Chorus say that εὐγένεια as commonly understood is an arbitrary convention: *real* nobility consists in the possession of qualities such as wisdom and intelligence, and these are the gifts of a god and not the product of being born into a wealthy house. The second appears to be attempting a

the one I proposed then, is at the start of Paris' reply to Hecuba: Paris remarks how unfair it is that his very excellences are the reason he is (apparently) about to die. This could be followed by F 56 (ἄναξ, διαβολαί, κτλ.), in which he begins his defence by protesting against the power of slander and the ability of eloquence to distort the truth. But F 62i could have come from Paris' (presumed) refuge at an altar if he feared he might be dragged away or otherwise forced to leave: see below, n. 101, and text thereto.

[91] I suggest the possibility that three fragments, sometimes assigned to Paris' accuser, might have been spoken by Paris. (1) In F 49 ('slaves are all belly and have no thought for the future') we might have the words of someone defending himself against a slave's accusations and disparaging the class of slaves as a whole for their lack of intelligence and foresight. This would fit Paris since he is a man under attack for possessing those qualities. (2) F 50 in Paris' mouth might be intended to discredit the shepherds' accusation: Paris could be claiming that he has incurred the hatred of his fellow slaves by acting in his masters' interest, and that it is this hatred, rather than facts or justice, that explains the charges. (3) Paris does not think of himself as one of the κακοί, and in the course of the Judgement he has chosen to marry above his putative station, so F 59 (ἐκ τῶν ὁμοίων κτλ.) could be a comment distinguishing himself from his servile attackers.

[92] If the fragment is correctly transmitted in Stobaeus (an inscription on a herm in Copenhagen has μεῖζον instead of μᾶλλον in line 2), part of the charge against Paris was that he was too intelligent for his station: φρονοῦντοc μᾶλλον is the comparative of φρονοῦντοc *simpliciter*, and would here mean 'more intelligent'.

similar 'persuasive definition' of εὐγένεια, claiming that only the morally good deserve to be called εὐγενεῖϲ. Both these fragments reverse the expectations embodied in epinician, where the noble birth of the *laudandus* is emphasized.[93] Like Homer in the *Odyssey*, Euripides elsewhere disparages the high-born and arrogant by contrasting them with loyal and decent folk of lowly station: see e.g. *El.* 380–5 with Kovacs 1998: 144–5. Here, however, the Chorus draw their 'enlightened' conclusions from a false premise since Paris is in fact a prince. He is proof that the nobly born have a φύϲιϲ that will come out in spite of lowly nurture, for it is his royal ancestry that causes him to stand out from the environment in which he was raised. For better or for worse (it will be the latter for his city), he is the scion of Troy's kings.

3.2.6. The second episode

This episode, of which we have a long stretch of partial lines, will have consisted of a messenger scene, announcing the result of the games, followed by a scene in which Deiphobus enters with Hector and, against the advice of his brother, plots to kill Paris.[94] After the first stasimon someone expresses eagerness for news of the games (fr. 15 M., 19.62–3 J.). Since the Chorus seem in F 61d to be the ones conversing with the messenger, which they would not be doing if Hecuba were on stage, she probably came out subsequent to the Messenger's stichomythic summary of his main points. (Kannicht compares *IT* 1284–1303 and 1304–1419.) Hecuba will have been the recipient, along with the Chorus, of the detailed account of the games, including the young man's victory. It is in this speech that I would put F 54 on the inability of noble birth or wealth to foster hard work, a reflection on the defeat of the noble sons of Priam by someone thought to be of lowly origins.[95]

3.2.7. The plot against Paris' life

In the remainder of the episode a plot against Paris' life is set in motion.[96] In F 62a Deiphobus, incensed at being defeated by a slave, is urged by

[93] See Cropp 2004: 76–8 and Carey 2012: 32–3.

[94] There may have been a formal *agon*, as suggested by Karamanou 2011.

[95] The imperfect with ἄρα indicates that the speaker has just learned the truth of his maxim that wealth and luxury do not train men up into manly excellence. The only proof of this in the play is Paris' success in the games. The comment therefore must be subsequent to that success.

[96] Hecuba, presumably, remains on stage, and then Hector and Deiphobus enter, which means that the actor who plays the Messenger must re-enter in the costume and

Hector not to take the defeat too much to heart, but he is obdurate. One may reasonably assume that Hector exits at some point: since he tried to counteract Deiphobus' resentment of Paris' victory over him, his presence in the scene in which Paris' death is plotted would be a hindrance. According to the *hypothesis* Deiphobus demanded that Hecuba should kill the young man. It is hard to glean much that is useful from FF 62b, col. ii and 62c, but in F 62d.25 Hecuba says that Paris must die by a hand whose owner is masked by a lacuna.[97] Later in the same fragment (62d.29) occur the words 'hither, so that he may fall into a trap'. Perhaps when the *hypothesis* speaks of Hecuba 'killing' Paris, it means 'luring him to a place where he may be killed'. If Hecuba lured him into the palace[98] to be killed, a messenger must have been sent to him. The time for the delivery of the message and the arrival of Paris may have been covered by a choral ode or *amoibaion*, parts of which might be visible in F 62d.43–50.

3.2.8. *The attack on Paris*

Cropp suggests that at F 62d.51–3 we may have the first words of Paris after his new entrance. It is possible that the 'victory song' mentioned in 53 may represent the fictitious grounds for inviting him to the palace. We are now in the third episode,[99] and perhaps the attempted murder takes up the remainder of it. Since it is unlikely that the attack on him took place before the eyes of the audience, he was probably lured into the palace by

mask of either Hector or Deiphobus. There must have been either a conversation between Hecuba and the Chorus Leader to 'cover' the Messenger's exit and his change of costume before his re-entry as one of the sons of Priam; or there could have been a choral ode. It is true that F 62a.2–3 announces the arrival of the two sons of Hecuba, and entrances after a stasimon are usually not announced. But there are exceptions to this rule (see 230–4n), so the choral ode cannot be ruled out. The stasimon described above, containing persuasive definitions of εὐγένεια, could easily have followed the messenger scene, reacting to its apparent demonstration that noble birth in its commonly accepted sense is meaningless.

[97] Even if the correct supplement is τῆι]δε (Crönert) the passages cited by di Giuseppe 2012: 148–9 show that this does not necessarily imply that Hecuba herself means to wield the sword.

[98] Scodel 35 says that after a stasimon Hecuba may have returned with a weapon and retainers, which suggests that the attack on Paris took place in front of the audience. This, however, would be without parallel. For the luring of someone into the house to be murdered see *Hec.* 1011–22, *El.* 1124–33, *Herc.* 701–25, *Or.* 1321–52, and *Antiope* F 223.28–45.

[99] Karamanou 2017: 19 suggests that Paris does not enter until the second episode, in which case the third would contain the messenger speech and the plotting scene, and we would already be in the fourth episode or the *exodos* when Paris makes his second entrance. She could be right. The same result would obtain if a choral ode separated the departure of the messenger from the arrival of Hector and Deiphobus.

Hecuba so that Deiphobus could attack him with a weapon. He will have made his exit from the palace at a run and taken up the posture of a suppliant at the altar in the *orchēstra*.[100]

3.2.9. The ending

We know that Hecuba's attempt on his life was foiled, that his recognition as the son of Priam and Hecuba was effected by the herdsman who raised him as his son, and that he was received back into his family of origin. It seems dramatically plausible, as well as attested on Etruscan works of art, for Paris' life to be saved by his escape to an altar and for his recognition to be accomplished while he was a suppliant there. An obvious question is whether Hecuba—and she must be the one on the scene rather than Deiphobus—intended to respect the altar or whether she set in motion some action to force Paris to abandon it. Here we have to make our best guess how favourably Euripides intended his audience to view Hecuba in this play. On the sympathetic side she has kept alive the memory of the son she was forced to expose twenty years earlier. But against this we must set her falling in with the scheme of Deiphobus to kill Paris for no other reason than that his success at the games had made the princes of Troy look bad. (Contrast Creusa, who decides to kill Ion in the belief that Xuthus is attempting to smuggle his bastard son onto the throne of Athens.) Hecuba is also acting against the known wishes of her husband in helping to kill a young man Priam had tried and found not guilty. That she may have intended to remove him from the altar by force or trickery cannot be excluded.[101] If her commitment to the basic principles of piety is somewhat shaky, that would merely align her with other members of the Trojan royal house such as Laomedon, twice guilty of offences against

[100] The iconographic evidence for Paris at the altar is discussed by Cropp 2004: 45–6 and Karamanou 2013. According to Hyginus 91 Paris took refuge at the altar of Zeus Herkeios. The identity of the altar, however, is problematical, as pointed out by Karamanou 2017: 28–31: the altar to this god stood in the courtyard, i.e. behind the façade of the stage building, and could have been shown only by means of the *mēchanē*.

[101] At Kovacs 1984: 59–60 I argued against assigning F 62i (*οἴμοι, θανοῦμαι διὰ τὸ χρήσιμον φρενῶν, κτλ.*) to a putative scene in which Paris was a suppliant at an altar on the grounds that altars are regularly respected in tragedy. But tragedy in fact shows examples where persons of determined impiety either directly violate sanctuary by dragging suppliants away (*Heraclidae*), build fires at the altar to force them to abandon their position (threatened in *Heracles*), or trick them from their refuge by false promises (*Andromache*). We cannot therefore eliminate the possibility that Hecuba has indicated that she intends to remove Paris by force and that Paris' words belong here, showing his realization that his death is inevitable. Another possible location for the fragment is suggested in n. 90 above.

Zeus Horkios (see below 799–818n), and her son Alexandros, who will soon sail to Sparta and commit a grave offence against Zeus Xenios.

The *hypothesis* tells us that his foster-father came along and—since Paris' life was in danger—was forced to reveal that the young man was the son Priam and Hecuba had exposed. This leaves unanswered an important question: was the herdsman's nick-of-time arrival due to chance, or was he sent for by someone, either Paris or Priam?[102] The chance arrival of the foster-father (which would not have been a mere coincidence but an instance of divine guidance of affairs, for which there is a parallel in the unexpected appearance of Aegeus in *Medea*)[103] is attractive in some ways and probably could have been managed comfortably even if the shepherd did not appear earlier in the play as, for example, the speaker of the prologue. Initial dialogue might have proceeded as follows:

Χο. καὶ μὴν γέροντα τόνδ' ἄγροικον εἰcορῶ
cτείχοντα δεῦρο· μῶν τι καινὸν ἐξερεῖ;
Αλ. ὦ χαῖρε, πάτερ· ἐγὼ δὲ θαυμάζω c' ὁρῶν·
τίc γάρ cε χρεία πρὸc πόλιν τήνδ' ἤγαγεν;
ἢ τἄμ' ἀκούcαc ἦλθεc ἀρκέcων κακά;
ΠΟΙΜΗΝ
ὦ χαῖρε, τέκνον· ὃ δέ μ' ἐρωτήcαc ἔχειc,
ὑπῆλθέ μ' ἵμερόc τιc—ἀγνοῶ πόθεν—
ὄχλουc τε Τρώων εἰcιδεῖν καὶ δώματα.
cὺ δ', ὦ τέκνον μοι, τίνοc ἕκατι cυμφορᾶc
ἱκέτηc καθίζειc βωμὸν Ἑρκείου Διόc;

The Shepherd's admission that his appearance in Troy was due to an impulse he could not quite explain would perhaps convey the point that it was no mere accident.[104] But it is also possible that either Paris sent a request to him for help or that Priam, suspecting that all was not as it seemed, summoned his servant in order to question him.

Presumably, in the rejoicing that ensued (the *hypothesis* breaks off with a hint of a glad reunion between Hecuba and her son), the reasons that led to his exposure in the first place were forgotten. Since Alexandros has almost certainly already judged the goddesses and accepted the bribe of Helen from Aphrodite,[105] he may have announced his intention to sail to

[102] The latter is suggested tentatively by Scodel 34.

[103] See Kovacs 1993, where it is shown that the coming along of Aegeus precisely when Medea needs a place of refuge is to be seen not as a meaningless coincidence but as divinely ordained.

[104] On the 'I know not how' theme as an indicator of divine causation see Kovacs 2002: 209 and also Mastronarde on *Pho.* 33, 49, and 413.

[105] Wilamowitz 260n1 points out that the *Cypria* apparently knows nothing of Hecuba's dream and Paris' subsequent exposure and gives a plausible reason why there

Sparta. In any case the play will have ended, in spite of the happy scene of reunion, on a note of foreboding.[106] There can have been no *deus ex machina* to prophesy what lies in store for Troy: this would make the reintegration of Paris into the household a psychological impossibility.

3.2.10. *The gods and the destruction of Troy*

The story type to which the Alexandros myth belongs is that of the 'curse child', that is, a child predicted to be the cause of ruin to his family or his city. His parents are warned by an oracle, a dream, a portent, or other supernatural means, and an attempt is made to avert the prophecy by killing the child, but he survives and goes on to produce the prophesied ruin. In most instances it is clear that (a) the warning was never intended as a genuine means of escape; (b) the child's survival is the result of providential direction of circumstances, not accident; and (c) the ruin in question is not caused by some impersonally determined destiny but by the hostility of some particular god or of the gods collectively. It seems likely that Zeus or the gods intend Troy's destruction, that Paris is their instrument, and that this is why he survives three attempts to kill him.

That the gods as destroyers of Troy are in the background of *Troades* is evident from the numerous passages that mention them in this capacity: see 10, 23–4, 46–7, 59, 72, 561, 597, 612–13, 775–7, 857–8, 867, 1060–70, 1203–6, and 1240–5. Helen's importance in that play is derived from her part in this scheme. Though Hecuba tries to argue that Aphrodite had nothing to do with Helen's departure from Sparta, she is clearly wrong: see

was no exposure then and why one was later invented: when the epics were written, it was regarded as perfectly natural for the son of a king to herd livestock on a mountainside. When custom changed, poets who told the story were led to invent the exposure, with Paris raised as a shepherd, and his later reintegration into the royal house (the earliest extant mention of Hecuba's dream is Pi., *Pae.* 8 fr. 52iA). In our play, therefore, the exposure implies that Paris is not going to herd animals on Ida—or judge the goddesses there—once he is recognized as a Trojan prince. Note also Cassandra's *iudicauit* in Ennius' translation (*fr. incert.* 151.16 M., *Alexander* 17(d).48 J.). Those who think that *iudicauit* could refer to the future cite *compleuit* in *fr. incert.* 151.15 M., *Alexander* 17.46 J., but not only is there a variant *complebit*, but the immediately preceding *adueniet* helps make the future reference of the perfect, if it is genuine, plain.

[106] In 1984: 64 I tried to capture, with some *exempli gratia* play-ending anapaestic dimeters, how the mood of rejoicing at the recovery of a long-lost son could be combined with a sense of doom palpable to the audience: I had the Chorus describe Paris as φάοϲ ἥδιϲτον and say that he shone on the Trojans in the manner of a gleaming fire (νῦν δ᾽ εὐδαίμων πυρὸϲ αἰθομένου τοῖϲ Τρωϲὶ δίκην ϲέλαϲ εὐφεγγὲϲ λάμπει φανερῶϲ), a benign and eulogistic version of the image of him as a destructive torch. No one would venture to say that Euripides *must* have ended his play in this fashion, but he almost always uses anapaests for the final utterance, and lines like these would do the needful.

e.g. 973–4n. Her attempt to locate the responsibility for the Trojan War on the shoulders of the individual Helen alone is a failure since Zeus' daughter was playing the part designed for her by her father. No matter how *Alexandros* is reconstructed, it is apparent that in this play Paris' survival was no accident (cf. *Tro.* 597). The gods saved his life to allow him to be the means of Troy's destruction, a destruction caused by his stealing of Helen. As I argue in my introductory note to the third episode, any assessment of Helen's trial that fails to take this into account is going to be badly mistaken. Hecuba may be the Queen of Sorrows in *Troades*, but that does not mean her views are correct.

3.3. *Palamedes*

The play had as its subject the judicial murder of Palamedes engineered by Odysseus.[107] One motive was that when Odysseus pretended to be mad in order to avoid service in the Trojan War, Palamedes saw through the pretense and unmasked it. Another was jealousy: Palamedes' inventions, such as that of letters and numbers, put Odysseus' cleverness in the shade.

In the *Cypria* (F 27 West) Odysseus simply murdered Palamedes by drowning him. In the tragic poets, however, the revenge took the form of a false accusation of treason. According to mythographical sources (Apollod. *epit.* 3.8, Hyg. *fab.* 105, Serv. on *Aen.* 2.81, Σ *Or.* 432), which reflect the myth as handled in tragedy, Odysseus buried gold under Palamedes' hut and arranged for a forged letter from Priam to be found. The letter specified a sum of gold the Trojans were paying Palamedes to betray the Greek cause. The letter and the exact agreement between the sum named in the letter and the money planted under the hut convinced the Greeks that Palamedes was guilty, and he was stoned to death. His brother Oeax wrote the story of this judicial murder on the blades of several oars and threw them into the Aegean. They reached Greece, where Nauplius, the father of Oeax and Palamedes, avenged his son's death by setting false beacons on the coast of Euboea to lure the Greek ships onto the rocks.

Different mythographers describe the action differently, and attempts have been made to identify a single tragic poet as the source for each account, but this is rendered difficult by the contamination of one storyline with details from another. In the scholion to *Orestes* 432, often thought to represent the plot of Euripides' play, the conspirators force a Trojan captive to write the letter 'in Phrygian characters' and then kill him. The

[107] A summary of the various versions of the Palamedes story is given by Davies–Finglass on Stesich. fr. 175.

Trojan prisoner figures also in the quite different account of Apollodorus. But in Euripides' play, as we know from F 578, Palamedes is credited with having invented writing for the Greeks (the more usual version made Cadmus the inventor of the alphabet), and it is arguably an important theme of Euripides' play that the hero was undone by his own invention, not by a different form of writing. The Trojan prisoner also figures as a bearer of the letter (though not as its writer) in Hyginus. It seems more likely that in Euripides Odysseus wrote out the letter himself.

The plot described in the last paragraph but one probably gives the substance of Euripides' play. There must have been a staged trial, an *agon*, in which Odysseus spoke for the prosecution, and one of his points is given in F 580, which argues that everyone is susceptible to money. The only part of Palamedes' defence we have is F 578, in which he argues that he has done great service to humanity by his inventions, such as that of writing, which permits communication over distance, allows an heir to check the amount bequeathed to him, and prevents men from quarreling over an agreement whose terms may be misremembered or misrepresented by one of the parties to it. We do not know what he said to rebut the charge of treason.

Likewise the play's fragments and testimonia do not give us enough information to reconstruct what happened in its other episodes. They also leave at least two important questions unanswered. The first is whether Odysseus acted alone in securing the death of Palamedes. In some retellings of the story he not only has the help of Diomedes as a second prosecutor but wins over to his side Agamemnon, the judge in the case, who merely pretends to be impartial. The latter possibility has a parallel in *Hecuba*, where Agamemnon feigns impartiality in Polymestor's case but has secretly promised not to punish Hecuba for blinding him and murdering his sons. If others besides Odysseus were in on the plot to convict Palamedes, the guilt on the Greek side extends beyond Odysseus himself. We learn in *Troades* that the impiety of the lesser Ajax was shared by his comrades when they failed to punish it. It seems unlikely, however, that the Greek army as a whole can have been culpable in the Palamedes affair.

A second question is raised when we consider who spoke the prologue. Since in order to understand the plot the audience must know that the evidence against Palamedes has been planted, and since the planting is unlikely to have been carried out during the course of the play, these things must have been revealed to the audience by someone who knew the facts. Some have suggested Odysseus as προλογίζων, but it seems contrary to Euripidean practice that someone so unsavoury should deliver the prologue: can we imagine e.g. Menelaus as the προλογίζων of *Andromache* or Lycus of *Heracles*? Conceivably a servant of Odysseus who was aware of what was going on without sharing in the plot might have told the audience what he knew, but equally it might have been a god. Poseidon is the father of Palamedes' father Nauplius (see *IA* 198) and hence would be a strong candidate. We know from a fragment of a *hypothesis* to the play that Nauplius appeared in Troy after the execution of Palamedes and threatened to punish Agamemnon for his son's death.[108] If Poseidon spoke the prologue, he could well have foretold that the oars on which the story of Palamedes' death was written would reach Nauplius not by chance but by his own dispensation and that the Greeks would be punished for killing him. (The divine causation could also have been conveyed in the *exodos*.) The Chorus may well have consisted of soldiers under Palamedes' command.

3.4. Some connecting features

Our knowledge of *Alexandros* is incomplete and of *Palamedes* quite exiguous. Nevertheless, the elements of plot and theme thrown up by the fragments show suggestive similarities with *Troades*.[109]

3.4.1. Things common to all three plays

1. There are trial scenes in all three plays. In *Alexandros* the title figure is accused of ὑπερηφανία but is acquitted: there is some doubt, in view of the sequel, about the justice of the verdict. In *Palamedes* the inventive hero is accused of treason, tried, and unjustly convicted. In *Troades* Helen is arraigned on the grounds that it was of her own free will that she left Sparta, no appeal to the goddess Aphrodite allowed, and she is convicted (unjustly, as I argue in the introduction to the third episode).

2. In all three plays people mistake their blessing for their bane or vice versa or are warned against doing so. In the first play Hecuba and Priam are overjoyed to recover their lost son and forget the prophecy that he would prove the ruin of his city. A second irony is Paris' complaint (F 62i) that his very excellences are proving to be the cause of his death,[110] though of course he escapes being killed in the end. In the second play Odysseus

[108] See Luppe 2011 and Meccariello 2014: 332–3.

[109] Attempts to see thematic connections among the three plays include Schöll 1839, Murray 1965 (1946): 68–70, Parmentier 3–9, Murray 1932, Snell 1937: 65–8, Murray 1946, Webster 1966, Webster 1967: 177–81, Scodel 1980: especially 64–121, and Kovacs 1997.

[110] Similar are Andromache's complaint (657–60) that her wifely excellence reached the ears of the Greeks with the result that Neoptolemus chose her as his prize; and her complaint (742–3, if genuine, and 744) that the excellence of Hector doomed his son.

contrives that the Greeks shall regard their most effective benefactor as a traitor. A second irony is that part of the evidence against Palamedes is the forged letter from Priam that his own invention of letters and numbers made possible. In the second episode of the third play Cassandra sees beneath the circumstances of her coming enslavement to Agamemnon the consoling news that she will be the cause of his death at the hands of his wife. Hecuba is unable to understand this, and she likewise fails to take in the good news that she herself will never be Odysseus' slave but will die near the Hellespont and be buried in a place that will keep her name alive. She likewise does not understand Andromache's contention (636–42) that death is the only amelioration of her own circumstances she can hope for. In the third episode she presses for the death of Helen, whom she blames for the fall of her city: in fact, she is merely the instrument of her father Zeus's intention to destroy both Greeks and Trojans and is not a primary agent at all. Hecuba's forensic triumph over Helen gives her joy, but her intended revenge will never be achieved. From a more distant past comes the picture in the first stasimon of the Trojans welcoming the wooden horse as an offering to their patron goddess, an offering that would prove their ruin.[111]

3.4.2. Connections between Alexandros *and* Troades

1. The image, from Hecuba's dream in *Alexandros*, of Paris as a fatal torch or firebrand recurs at *Troades* 922. More impressively, the metaphor is made visible in the *exodos* of *Troades*, whose final section dramatizes the actual firing of the city.

2. The role of the gods in the destruction of Troy was clearly part of what Cassandra prophesied in *Alexandros*. A fragment of Ennius' Latin translation of the play calls Helen *Furiarum una* (*fr. incert.* 151.16–18 M., *Alexander* 17.47–9 J.), and there can be little doubt that in calling Helen an Ἐρινύς Cassandra was expressing a theological point, that Helen was the instrument, as the literal Erinyes are, of Zeus-caused destruction. This is the same theology that Aeschylus expresses at *Agamemnon* 744–9. A similar theological point is made when Cassandra at *Troades* 457 calls herself an Erinys because she will cause Agamemnon's death.

[111] Murray (1932 and 1946) treats this mistaking of blessing for bane and vice versa in the Trojan trilogy. He regards this theme as a Euripidean novelty and gives it the name *paracharaxis*, 'restamping the coinage', a concept he takes from Diogenes the Cynic (too late, of course, to influence Euripides). But the split between appearance and reality is a basic tragic theme, and there is no need to invoke Cynic philosophers when Aeschylus and Sophocles are available.

3. In the first play Cassandra's prophecies about Paris and the future of Troy were certainly discounted. In the third play Hecuba (168–72, 348–50), the Chorus (341–2, 406–7), and Talthybius (408, 415, 417) all regard her as mad, and Hecuba (490–7) discounts her daughter's prophecy that she will never endure slavery (427–30).

4. At *Troades* 597 Andromache attributes the survival of Paris to 'the malice of the gods'. Although in the present state of our knowledge we cannot substantiate the claim that it was divine malignity that caused Paris in *Alexandros* to survive, it is eminently plausible that it did: at three points (his exposure, the trial before Priam, and the attack engineered by Deiphobus) his life was in danger, and yet he lived to make his fatal voyage to Sparta.

5. Cassandra's prophecy of Hecuba's metamorphosis into a hound and her burial at Cynossema was alluded to in *Alexandros* (F 62h) and recurs at *Troades* 428–30.

3.4.3. Connections between Palamedes *and* Troades

The most prominent connection is that *Palamedes* shows the Greeks laying the foundation for their own destruction by their treatment of Nauplius, whose anger at his son's judicial murder they apparently ignore. He is the one who will set false beacons on the coast of Euboea, a fact glancingly alluded to in *Troades*: see 90n.

Odysseus is only an offstage character in *Troades* (721–4), but the warmth of Hecuba's denunciation of him when he is named as her master (277–92) and the length of Cassandra's gloating description (426–43) of the troubles awaiting him on his homeward journey and at home may owe something to his unsavoury role in *Palamedes*.

3.5 *Sisyphus*

It is impossible to integrate Euripides' satyr play into the discussion of the tetralogy since little is known of either its plot or its themes. To be sure, there is a highly interesting fragment about the gods (*TrGF* I 43 Critias F 19) attributed in some sources to Euripides (the name of the play is not specified, but the speaker is Sisyphus) that puts forth a theory of the origin of religion. The introduction of law, the fragment claims, rescued man from a primitive, beastly state characterized by violence. But since people disobeyed the law when no one was watching, a clever man invented the all-seeing gods to persuade them that everything they did, said, or thought was known by them and would, if criminal, be punished. This fragment clearly argues for atheism.[112] It would be interesting to trace the connections between it and the various passages in *Troades* where Hecuba, Andromache, or the Chorus arraign the gods for their malice, ingratitude, stupidity, or indifference (see 597–600, 820–59n, 1060–80n, 1204–6n, 1240–2, 1280–1, and the introductory note to the *exodos*, especially the fourth and sixth paragraphs) or propound new-fangled accounts of them (see 884–8n, 969–86, and the last paragraph of the introductory note to the third episode).

But it is difficult to believe that the fragment is by Euripides given the external evidence. The principal quoter, Sextus Empiricus, attributes it to Critias, one of the Thirty Tyrants. Other sources, beginning with the doxographer Aëtius, ascribe it to Euripides. We are told by an ancient life of Euripides that three plays of his, *Pirithous*, *Rhadamanthys*, and *Tennes*, were regarded as spurious, and one of these, *Pirithous*, is described at Athenaeus 11.496A as the work of *either* Critias *or* Euripides. Clearly some scholars in Alexandria concluded that *Pirithous* and the play containing Sisyphus' atheistic argument, though widely regarded as being by Euripides, were not his work.[113] These scholars did not merely deny the play to Euripides but assigned it to Critias. This cannot be simply conjecture on their part since Critias was not an obvious guess for the author of a dramatic fragment (only one other play is ascribed to him), and no other testimony connects him with atheist views.[114] The Alexandrians must have taken his name from the didascalic record. Euripides' *Sisyphus* of 415 was surely named there, as well as, under a different year, a play by Critias

[112] This is disputed by Pechstein 1998: 307–10, who thinks the passage does not deny the traditional gods (*θεοί*) but only a remarkable *δαίμων* with powers like those attributed to the gods by Socrates, e.g. the power to read men's thoughts. But (1) *δαίμων* and *θεός* are commonly synonymous in poetry, and nothing in the fragment distinguishes between the two; and (2) the fragment explicitly says (16) that the clever man *τὸ θεῖον εἰσηγήσατο*, which implicitly equates *δαίμων* and *θεός*. O'Sullivan 2012 attempts to shift the emphasis of the argument from the falsity to the usefulness of belief in the gods and sees the fragment as atheistic but not hostile to religion. Whitmarsh 2014, who stresses connections between theological and poetic fictions, calls it 'a powerful cocktail of religious heterodoxy' (111). For a possible context for the fragment see n. 120 below.

[113] Wilamowitz 1875: 161–72 and 1927: 446–7 (see also a personal communication of Wilamowitz published in Bremer and Calder 1994: 211–16) argued that the three tragedies judged spurious in antiquity and the satyr play *Sisyphus* were a tetralogy by Critias misattributed to Euripides. We need not assign all four plays to a single *didascalia* in order to feel the force of his argument that the Sisyphus fragment is unlikely to be Euripidean. For the history of scholarship on this question see Collard–Cropp 2.629–35.

[114] The attempt by Dihle 1977 to show that Critias' name got attached to the fragment by a mistake in transmission cannot be regarded as anything but a long-shot guess. This conjecture in any case does not explain why *Pirithous* is assigned to Critias.

of the same name. The Alexandrians may have possessed both plays and assigned one to each poet. The plays may both have continued to circulate with Euripides' name on them even after the Alexandrians had sorted them out. If we ask ourselves whether it is more likely that a fragment written by Critias should be misattributed to Euripides or vice versa, the answer is obvious.[115] It is hard to know how much weight, if any, to attribute to certain metrical features that are hard to parallel in Euripides (the evidence of enjambment is dismissed by Collard–Cropp 2.634n4), but at least one scholar has noted that its language does not have a Euripidean feel.[116] In recent decades several attempts have been made to reclaim the fragment for Euripides,[117] but the case must be regarded as weak. To discuss the fragment in connection with the plays of 415 BC, with which it probably has nothing to do, would be rash.

I have suggested that not only Critias' play but also Euripides' *Sisyphus* survived long enough to be included in the Alexandrian library. In favour of the survival of the Euripides play only negative evidence is available: we are not told, as we are about Euripides' *Theristai* of 431, that it did not reach Alexandria. But Aelian *Varia Historia* 2.8 believed he had read the four plays of 415, which he admired. That both plays reached Alexandria is assumed by Snell in *TrGF* 1—he prints the atheistic fragment as the work of Critias and explicitly says (p. 170) that other fragments of a *Sisyphus*, along with a *hypothesis*, belong to Euripides' play. Kannicht's revision of *TrGF* 1 says nothing to contradict Snell on this point. It is confusing, therefore, that in *TrGF* 5 Kannicht prints a lacunose *hypothesis*[118] and two fragments of a *Sisyphus* among the fragments of Euripides and yet states his view (p. 659; see also Kannicht 1996: 27) that Euripides' play

[115] Pechstein 1998: 191 says there is as little reason to trust the ancient ascription of *Sisyphus* to Critias as that of *Rhesus* to Euripides, but this ignores the *utrum in alterum* argument.

[116] Scodel 125 says that it 'does not really sound like the work of Euripides'.

[117] Dihle 1977 was the first substantive attack (he had precedessors in Kuiper 1907 and Page 1950: 120–3) against the Wilamowitz hypothesis. Scodel 122–37 and Pechstein 1998: 185–92 attempt to vindicate the fragment for Euripides. The latter prints it under the heading 'Unsichere Fragmente' because only the identity of the speaker, not the play title, is attested, and we know that Sisyphus was a character in Euripides' satyric *Autolycus*. Collard 1995 argues for Euripides as the author of *Pirithous* but says (188) that the case for assigning the atheistic fragment to Critias is 'very much stronger' than for assigning *Pirithous* to him.

[118] In fact there are two badly preserved *hypotheseis* of plays beginning with sigma (P. Oxy. 2455, frr. 5 and 7) that could be summaries of Euripides' *Sisyphus*. It is likely that one of them is such. This is an indication (not, alas, a proof) that the Alexandrians possessed Euripides' play. (Meccariello 2014: 369–75 combines frr. 5 and 7 with fr. 6 as summarizing *Sciron*, leaving nothing for *Sisyphus*. But she admits that frr. 5 and 7 cannot be part of the same *hypothesis* and is forced to regard them as alternatives.)

did not survive to Alexandria.[119] It remains to speculate what Euripides' and Critias' plays may have been about.

F 673 K of Euripides' *Sisyphus* has someone rejoicing that Heracles has arrived and that some foul person (*μιαρόν*) has been killed. We do not know who this person is, and it is only a presumption that it was Heracles who destroyed him. What Heracles is doing in a Sisyphus play is far from clear. The only known connection between them is tenuous, that when Heracles had brought the horses of Diomedes to Eurystheus, Sisyphus stole them from Eurystheus. But since Sisyphus in no version steals the horses from Heracles, the episode of the horses is unlikely to furnish the play's plot. Pechstein 1998: 216–17 suggests that Euripides' *Sisyphus* may have taken place in the Underworld, where Heracles must go to carry out one of his labours and where Sisyphus endures punishment. This could be right, and it would be further proof that the atheist fragment does not belong to this play since in the Underworld there would be no audience to whom an argument that the gods do not exist might be addressed.[120] In fact we know nothing about the plot of either play. Euripides' play might have concerned the siring of Odysseus (thus Bethe 1927: 374), the story, alluded to repeatedly in tragedy, that Sisyphus managed to trick his way into the bed of Anticleia and is thus the father of Odysseus (whose devious ways are thereby given a genetic explanation). This would provide a connection of sorts with *Palamedes* and also with the uncomplimentary references to Odysseus in *Troades*, but we have no way to confirm or disconfirm this guess. For all we know, both plays may have dramatized this same tale.

4. TOWARD AN INTERPRETATION OF *TROADES*: THEMES AND UNITY

Unlike, e.g., Sophocles' *Oedipus Tyrannus* or Euripides' *Hippolytus*, or even the plays of Euripides with double plots, such as *Andromache* or *Heracles*, *Troades* is almost completely episodic: it lacks the kind of unity

[119] It would appear that he came to his view subsequent to his revision of Snell and printed the fragments and *hypothesis* in *TrGF* 5 because he did not wish them to be completely omitted.

[120] As evidence that the fragment is not really atheistic Pechstein 1998: 309–10 notes that Sisyphus, who has been dealing with the gods throughout his entire life, is not the man to maintain that they do not exist. But Sisyphus could be saying what he knows to be false (he was a great liar) if he were trying to convince someone that they do not exist in order to persuade him or her to do something unlawful. In the Underworld such an argument would obviously not work, but perhaps the audience for Sisyphus' argument was Anticleia.

that allows one to see actions earlier in the play leading to the dénouement at the end. To be sure, the scene where Astyanax is sent to his death must precede the scene where his corpse is adorned for burial, but the Cassandra episode and the Helen episode have no consequences later in the play, and as far as plot is concerned the Cassandra, Andromache, and Helen episodes could have been presented in any order. The biggest questions interpretation has to answer are (1) why Euripides chose to make a play consisting of discrete episodes; (2) what explains their order; and (3) what is the unity to which they contribute.

1. The first is the hardest to answer since we cannot know what other options presented themselves to Euripides' mind for his third play. The trilogy could easily have ended with a fateful action on the Greek side, an *Ajax*, in which the son of Oïleus, having forcibly removed Cassandra from the altar of Athena, persuades the Greeks not to punish him, with fateful consequences for all concerned. (The action would have nicely paralleled that of *Alexandros*, where the son of Priam likewise escapes death and thereby seals the fate of Troy.) We can, however, see in general that in choosing to write a play in which three members of the Trojan royal house appear, together with a chorus of Trojan women, he has decided to end his trilogy with an emphasis not on the fate of the Greeks but on that of the Trojans. The Ajax theme, of course, is dealt with in the prologue.

2. As for the order of the episodes, their sequence observes a rule of increasing pathos (a rule to which the Helen episode is an exception whose purpose we can see). First comes the comparatively cheerful episode where Cassandra, instead of lamenting the loss of her Apollo-granted virginity and her coming death, anticipates taking revenge upon the Greeks in the person of Agamemnon. The Andromache episode starts on a note of pathos, which deepens further as the episode continues: it begins with Hector's widow lamenting her concubinage to the son of her husband's slayer and the ruin of her happiness; it ends with the taking away of Astyanax. The Helen episode, placed just before the *exodos*, arrests the march toward pathos by its intellectual argumentation, thereby serving as a foil to set off the final portion of the play portraying the complete destruction of Troy. There Hecuba laments the death of her grandson as she prepares him for burial and she and the Chorus wail amid the scene of Troy's final conflagration.

3. The unity to which these episodes contribute, it will be argued below, is a meditation on the ways of the gods, sometimes inscrutable, sometimes perfectly intelligible, and the fragility of human happiness.

4.1. Prologue and *parodos*

Poseidon's monologue presents the destruction of Troy as the result of the action of two spiteful divinities, Athena and Hera. He offers nothing beyond their spite to explain Troy's fall, to which he seems resigned. (In *Alexandros* both Cassandra and the prologue speaker, likely to be a divinity such as Hermes, will have made it clear why Zeus intends harm to both Greeks and Trojans, so such an explanation is not needed here.) When Athena enters with the news that the Greeks have offended her by their failure to punish the lesser Ajax, the audience can have no difficulty in understanding that in failing to uphold the goddess's *timē* the Greeks have angered her and that this will be have serious consequences. When the two divinities have departed, Hecuba's aria laments the misfortunes of Troy, which she cannot understand. She has harsh words for Helen, seeing her as the cause of the ruin of Priam, herself, and Troy. The audience will have remembered that Cassandra in *Alexandros* had cast Helen in the role of an Erinys, a spirit of destruction sent by Zeus.

The *parodos*, consisting of an *amoibaion* of the Chorus with Hecuba and two purely choral stanzas, dilates on the misery that is theirs: the only amelioration of their lot would be slavery in some comparatively benign place such as Athens, Thessaly, Sicily, or Thurii.

4.2. The Cassandra episode and the first stasimon

To call Cassandra's entrance surprising is to understate the matter: it administers a shock as great as any in tragedy. Early in the episode Talthybius tells Hecuba that her daughter is to be the slave concubine of Agamemnon, and Hecuba reacts with horror at the sacrilege involved in violating her Apollo-dedicated virginity. Yet when Cassandra is brought forth from the *skēnē*, she is carrying torches as if in a bridal procession and singing her wedding hymn, and she exhorts her mother to rejoice in her good fortune. Cassandra, as we have already noted, had a role in *Alexandros*, where she revealed her brother's judgement of the three goddesses and predicted that Helen would come as an Erinys and ruin Troy if Paris were allowed to live. Where everyone else saw good fortune in the recovery of the long-lost Alexandros, she had predicted that ruin would come from it. Now, with that ruin accomplished, she administers a *post eventum* solace, consoling her mother and the Chorus with the thought that their Greek foes will not be unscathed. In the divine dispensation of events the future is revealed to be as surprising as it is inevitable. Cassandra contributes a sense of the latter as she describes Agamemnon's death, which she alone knows is coming. That she, his slave, should be the instrument of his destruction is a Euripidean paradox. In the first play she described Helen as an Erinys, bringing divinely wrought ruin on Troy. Now she herself is the Erinys (457), and it is her job to visit destruction on the Greeks in the person of Agamemnon. She also reports Apollo's prophecy that Hecuba will die and be buried in the Troad and that the man who claims the queen as his slave will suffer terrible woes both on his journey and when he reaches home. The world is not governed by blind chance. Though the gods may act from motives obscure to mortal eyes, it is they who determine human life. What they bring is often unpredictable by human reasoning.

Though the Chorus have shown no understanding of Cassandra's divine perspective, their choral ode touches on a related paradox, a theme central to the play and to the whole trilogy, the propensity of mortals to welcome as blessing what is in fact their bane, as the Trojans welcomed the horse. The stasimon is thus symmetrical with the episode, which emphasizes that what looks like a bane (sexual slavery) may contain an element of unexpected blessing (the triumph over one's enemies).

4.3. The Andromache episode and the second stasimon

This episode administers the play's second-biggest shock, the sudden arrival of a herald to take Astyanax away to his death. The original audience were naturally familiar from the allusion in the *Iliad* and from the epic cycle and Stesichorus (see 706–89n) with the story that he was hurled from Troy's battlements, but it seems likely that Euripides is deliberately encouraging them to forget that this event is coming. (See the introductory note to the second episode.) They can then enter into Hecuba's hopes for the child's future (702–5) and experience to the full the *peripeteia* of his actual fate. In the scene that precedes the herald's entrance, Andromache informs Hecuba of the sacrifice of Polyxena, whose fate she compares favourably with her own: Polyxena is dead and beyond the reach of woe, while she herself must live life as the chosen spoil of the son of her husband's slayer. There is an irony about this that is characteristic of the trilogy (see § 3.4.1) since it was, as she points out, her very virtues that led Neoptolemus to choose her. (Astyanax too is destroyed by his very excellences: see 744 with note and a similar comment in *Alexandros* F 62i.) She is left with a choice of disloyalty to the memory of Hector or incurring the hatred of her new master. To these predictions of misery Hecuba replies by holding out hope (632–3, 697–705). But as is usual in a tragedy about downfall, hopes for a happy future are uttered only to be refuted by events. Hecuba is wrong about the future. By contrast Andromache is wrong about the past when she says (766–73) that Helen can be no daughter of Zeus. But the alternative paternities she proposes for Helen are not far from the mark: she was brought into the world as an Alastor (spirit of ruin), and her siring had in view death and slaughter.

The effect of the second stasimon on an audience that has just lived through the emotionally searing departure of Astyanax is likely to have been one of relief: the narrative of Telamon's attack on Troy, highly ornamented and romantic, has the effect of distancing the listener from the miseries at hand. The second stanzaic pair recalls an earlier day in Troy when the gods took a favourite (Ganymede) and a husband (Tithonus) from their midst. It expresses elegiac sadness that the gods no longer feel love for the city and now look on its destruction without sadness or compunction. It is characteristic of both Hecuba and the Chorus in this play that they tax the gods with indifference to Troy's suffering and forgetfulness of their once close ties to her. But as a reference in the next episode (865–8) makes clear, the Trojans have paid the penalty for Alexandros' offence against Zeus Xenios. The Chorus themselves give evidence against their complaint that the gods are unjust when they allude (809) to Laomedon's perjured promise to Heracles.

4.4. The Helen episode and the third stasimon

In a play depicting the fall of Troy principally as the result of Greek aggression it is hard to see what place there could be for a debate on Helen's responsibility. Even if Helen is as blameworthy as one could wish, her elopement with Paris would be without effect unless the Greeks were determined to wade through blood to get her back and unless the Trojans were determined to keep her at the risk of losing their city. To devote an entire episode to the question of her guilt would be a distraction from the issue at hand. Concentration on the role of the daughter of Zeus in the fall of Troy makes sense only from a theological perspective.

The third episode is the most explicitly theological in the play since the workings of the gods in the world are the subject of its central debate between Helen and Hecuba. Detailed arguments on the interpretation of this debate—who is the winner, who is the loser, and why, dramaturgically speaking, Euripides has written it this way—will be found in the introduction to the episode, as well as in the notes on 884–8, 914–65, and 969–1032. In brief I argue that Helen, frivolous though she may be, is correct in her explanation of the Judgement of Paris and its consequences and does not deserve the sentence of death passed against her, a sentence which, as the audience know, will not in any case be carried out. By contrast, Hecuba, as shown by her prayer to Zeus and her speech of accusation, follows a rationalist line with regard to the gods that is out of keeping with the world as it is actually represented in both play and trilogy. Why Hecuba, on whom so much of the audience's sympathy is focused throughout, should be made to argue (in the play's terms) mistakenly is a real question, and several explanations are available. (See the introduction to the episode in the commentary.) But although Menelaus is convinced by her argument, the idea that we are actually meant to regard her as correct in her judgement can be ruled out: the Judgement of Paris is a fact, and the consequences of it are the hatred of Hera and Athena for Troy. That these issues are raised here at all is a further indication, if any is needed, of the importance of the gods to both play and trilogy.

The third stasimon reproaches Zeus, in effect, with stupidity: the Trojans made all manner of offerings to him, offerings which presumably delighted him, and yet in allowing Troy to fall he has lost them all (*σοι* in 1071 is dative of disadvantage). The pathos of the Chorus's situation is not obliterated, and they go on to mention the death of their husbands and the enslavement of themselves and their children, who may be separated from their mothers. They express the wish (under the circumstances it can be no prayer) that Zeus's lightning may descend on Menelaus' ship and kill Helen. (Lightning, as we know from the prologue, will descend, but Menelaus' ship will not be sunk.) But in calling her the daughter of Zeus (1109) they provide good reason for thinking that this will never happen.

4.5. The *exodos*

The last portion of the play is in two parts that treat two themes, the burial of Astyanax and the firing of the city. The first, mostly spoken, part conveys vividly the sense of all that has been lost in the hurling of Astyanax from the walls of Troy: he was cut off before he reached his prime, yet he was the true son of his father, whom he so closely resembled. (The latter suggests that the Greek decision to kill him, though hard-hearted, was prudent: he would have been a formidable warrior and could well have refounded Troy, as Hecuba herself suggested to Andromache that he might.) In the second part, which begins in dialogue and ends in strophic lyric, the burning of the city is the culmination of Hecuba's dream, with which *Alexandros* began: Paris the torch-child has done his work.

4.6. *Troades* and archaic Greek thought: poetry and theology

One of the best attested themes of fifth-century Attic tragedy is the mutability of the human condition not only because of the limitations of human knowledge but also because of the propensity of the gods to overthrow human prosperity. This, of course, is a theme tragedy inherits from earlier poetry. It is pervasive in Herodotus as well, and even Thucydides, whose pages are inhospitable to the divine dimension, will occasionally touch on it, e.g. Pericles' remark (2.64.3) that all things are naturally prone to diminish. According to Aristotle (*Poetics* 1453a22–30) a tragedy that ends in misery for the character or characters with whom we have come to sympathize is doing what a tragedy ought to do, and he says that a *peripeteia*, a swift change of fortune, is characteristic of the best tragedies.[121]

Troades begins with the Trojan women in misery and ends with their being only slightly more miserable (Astyanax is dead, Troy is in flames, and Hecuba and the Chorus are being marched into a life of servitude, but at the play's start their city was already destroyed and their husbands dead). Nevertheless, the trilogy as a whole shows an earlier starting point when Troy and its people had no notion of the troubles that lay in store for them. A similar *metabolē* awaits the Greeks, who are portrayed as sovereign in *Palamedes* but are doomed to destruction at sea because of decisions taken shortly before *Troades* opens. In the only one of the three tragedies whose text we can read in its entirety, statements about the mutability of human fortunes and the propensity of the gods to destroy human happiness are made early and often. Much of the evidence takes the form of explicit statements by gods and by Cassandra, one of their accredited spokespersons. Statements by Hecuba, the Chorus, or Andromache reinforce these themes both when they express similar sentiments and when they pointedly deny what the audience know to be true. I laid out this evidence in Kovacs 1997. There is further elaboration in the commentary: for the role of the gods in Troy's fall see on 10, 41–4, 72, 597–600, 766–71, 799–818, 820–59, 866, 973–4, 1060–80, and the introduction to the *exodos*; for the gods as destroyers of the Greeks see on 95–7 and 457; for the role of the gods in the world see the introduction to the third episode and the notes on 884–8 and 987–90; for generalities about the instability of human fortunes see on 509–10, 1203–4, and 1204–6. There are similar emphases in the excellent discussion of the play's unity in Heath 1987a: 108–11.

[121] There are only two mentions of the gods in the *Poetics*, and Aristotle recommends that each action follow as the necessary or probable result of what has gone before and that the divine (which he calls *τὸ ἄλογον*), if admitted at all, be kept *ἔξω τοῦ δράματος*. This does not describe the tragedies we have but is a distortion produced by his apologetic stance vis-à-vis Plato's *Republic*.

4.7. Two views of the play compared

Burian 2009: 6n9 writes, 'It should be said that this decoupling of Melos from *Trojan Women* has been welcomed as a way to defang the play politically', and he cites as an example of such defanging my 1997 reading of play and trilogy that emphasizes the instability of fortune and the fallibility of human understanding. Now if *Troades* had left Euripides' pen equipped with fangs, extracting them would, of course, disfigure his design, but we have only the unsupported word of Burian and other allegorical interpreters that the play was ever intended to bite the Athenians. No ancient source says or suggests that Euripides used this play—or any of his plays—to criticize or call into question the policies of Athens, and some passages imply the reverse: for Aelian the second-place verdict was surprising, which it would not be if it was meant as a devastating critique. Furthermore, if we were looking, even in the undiscriminating manner of Nestle 1901—who was unconcerned that many of the fragments have for us no dramatic home and cannot therefore be properly evaluated—for *prima facie* evidence in the plays and fragments that Euripides ever held up his own city to criticism, there is little to reward the search. What we find instead are harsh words against Sparta (*Andr*. 445–52) and trenchant criticisms of undemocratic regimes together with the praise of democracy and *isonomia* (*Supp*. 429–41), which Euripides' fellow citizens would have had every right to take as an encomium of themselves. In § 1.3.3 above I cite a large number of passages that praise Athens, including two from *Troades*. From passages that praise peace or deprecate war (fr. 369, *Supp*. 481–93) it would be unwise to conclude an opposition to Athenian policy. There are passages, cited in § 1.2.2 above, where sympathetic characters seem to be speaking in favour of a policy of dynamism not unlike the one pursued by Pericles and his successors. In short, there is no *prima facie* evidence for the proposition that Euripides disapproved of Athens' use of force in the world and quite a bit of *prima facie* evidence against it.

By contrast, if one wished to demonstrate that one of Euripides' most persistent tragic themes is the radical uncertainty of the human condition, its exposure to vicissitude in either direction, the deceptiveness of both hope and despair, one could have examples by the cartload. Sudden change for the worse is constantly portrayed (e.g. *Hippolytus*, *Andromache*, *Supplices*, *Heracles*, *Phoenissae*, *Orestes*, *Bacchae*) and constantly commented on (e.g. *Herc*. 508–12). The *peripeteia* toward happiness is also much in evidence (e.g. *Alcestis*, *Iphigenia Taurica*, *Ion*, *Helen*) and the object of pointed remark (e.g. *Andr.* 1284–8). I have shown that these themes run like an unmistakable red thread through *Troades* and are in evidence in the fragments of one of its two companion tragedies. The whole divine dimension of the action makes against interpretations that see the play as a reaction to Athenian foreign policy, and those who follow this interpretation tend to ignore this material. When I am alleged to have 'defanged' *Troades* by showing that it does not berate the Athenians in a manner evident nowhere else in Euripides, it seems fair to reply that it is the political interpretation, not the theological one, that is an act of mutilation. Large parts of the tragedy that we have, being incapable of integration into the anti-Athenian scheme, stand as witness against a view of the play that, for all the credit it enjoyed between 1839 and 1987, should be looked on as a temporary and regrettable aberration.

5. MANUSCRIPTS AND PAPYRI; EDITORIAL PRINCIPLES

Ancient sources give the number of Euripides' plays as ninety-two, including some whose authorship was disputed. Of these we have eighteen (seventeen tragedies and one satyr play) plus *Rhesus*, one of the disputed plays.[122] We have only seven plays of Sophocles and only six of Aeschylus. Just why the plays of Euripides we can read survived and the varying means of their survival makes a complicated story, which will be presented here in outline.[123]

The Library of Alexandria set about collecting all of Greek literature, and this included the tragic poets. Though some of Euripides' plays did not survive to Alexandria, some seventy-eight did and received the attention of scholars there. In the course of the last centuries of antiquity attention was increasingly fixed on ten plays (*Alcestis*, *Medea*, *Hippolytus*, *Andromache*, *Hecuba*, *Troades*, *Phoenissae*, *Orestes*, *Bacchae*, and *Rhesus*), with the result that the rest were little copied. These ten plays, which were annotated in antiquity (the comment survives in abbreviated form in our scholia), are called the Selection. In the mediaeval period there was a further reduction of scope, and large numbers of copies were made of three of the ten, *Hecuba*, *Orestes*, and *Phoenissae*, the so-called Byzantine triad, with consequent neglect of the others.

[122] For a convincing reconciliation of the various numbers (plays written, performances at the Dionysia, plays that survived to Alexandria) in the biographical tradition, see Kannicht 1996.

[123] Other treatments of the transmission of Euripides' text are Turyn 1957, Barrett on *Hipp.*, pp. 45–90, Zuntz 1965, Kannicht on *Hel.*, pp. 1.78–129, Biehl 39–42, Kovacs 2005, Parker on *Alc.*, pp. lvii–lxvii, Mastronarde 2017, and Finglass forthcoming.

But by lucky chance an ancient manuscript survived to the fourteenth century containing nine further plays beginning with the letters epsilon, eta, iota, and kappa, part of a complete works of Euripides arranged in alphabetical order.[124] A copy of this into the new minuscule hand was made under the direction of Demetrius Triclinius. This book, which also contains the 'select' plays except for *Troades*, now resides in the Laurentian Library in Florence and is referred to as the Laurentianus (L). Triclinius made several sets of changes to it based in part on his understanding of metre. L and the Palatinus (P), a copy made of L before the last set of changes, are our sole witnesses to these nine plays.

In terms of their transmission there are essentially three groups of plays, the 'alphabetic' plays transmitted in L and P, the non-triadic 'select' plays, of which the numbers vary from sixteen manuscripts for *Hippolytus* and two for *Bacchae*, and the triad, of which there are scores of copies. *Troades* belongs to the non-triadic selection.

What the reader needs to know about the mediaeval manuscripts of *Troades* is set out in succinct Latin in the preface to Diggle's second OCT volume, pp. vi–viii. I summarize this information here before making some further remarks.

The text descends to us in two families. (See the stemma in Diggle's edition, p. vii.) On one side is the Vaticanus (V) and its apographs Neap. and Va (the latter are only occasionally cited). On the other side is the Palatine manuscript (P) and the first 610 lines of the Harley manuscript (Q): both are copied from the same source, one independent of V. (The remainder of the play in Q, designated q by Diggle, was copied from an apograph of V.) Both families provide access to readings that deserve to be considered genuine.

The three principal manuscripts vary in date, V belonging to the thirteenth century, P to the fourteenth, and Q to the early sixteenth.[125] This has led, at various points in the history of editing the play, to a prejudice in favour of the readings of V over P and Q. But readings of an older manuscript are not necessarily better than those of a younger one since the truth can be lost in one branch of the tradition and preserved in another even though its representatives happen to be later. Each case, each set of variants, must be assessed on its own merits.

There is one anomaly that should be mentioned: *Troades* is transmitted in P but is missing from L, the only play (apart from a portion of *Bacchae*) of which this is true. For the 'alphabetical' plays (and *Rhesus*) the text of P

[124] A tenth play, *Bacchae*, though one of the Selection, survives only in L and P.

[125] Wilson 1966: 337 identifies the hand as that of Gian Francesco Burana, born in 1474 and redates it from *c.*1475 to *c.*1500.

is copied from L. In the triad there is no particular affinity between the two manuscripts.[126] For the non-triadic select plays, though it is not clear what the relationship is, it seems to be a close one: they represent a distinct branch of the tradition.[127] Though L lacks *Troades*, P's text is probably derived from an L-like source, possibly the exemplar of L.[128]

Troades has not benefitted much from papyrus or inscription finds. P. Oxy. 4564 has parts of 340–6. It confirms λυγράν in 344 against the variants in P and Q. It assigns 341–2 to Talthybius, an assignment reported in the scholia but not found in any manuscript. (The assignment to the *coryphaeus* is overwhelmingly more probable, and Carrara 2009: 424 suggests that this may be the remnant of a post-classical version in which the Chorus is left out or reduced.) Schubart and Wilamowitz 1907: xvii no. 6 is an inscribed wooden tablet containing 876–9. It appears to be a text dictated to pupils in a school. Each trimeter occupies two lines with the division at the caesura. Its two textual novelties are mere errors.

What general principles should editors follow in editing this text? They must be aware that it has been subjected to corruptions of several different kinds. As noted above, the truth may be found in either branch of the tradition, so variants must be assessed on their merits where rational assessment is possible. In addition to corruption we must not neglect the possibility of interpolation even though interpolation, whether by actors or by others, does not seem to have affected this play deeply. A third source of corruption is accidental omission. When a passage fails to make sense even though all of its words seem germane to the subject under discussion (and hence none of them is easily challengeable), this may be an indication that something has been omitted. In choosing where to mark a lacuna the editor must be guided by the possibility in some cases or the impossibility in others of providing a plausible *exempli gratia* supplement. It is a point in favour of such a diagnosis if marking a lacuna can restore sense while leaving all the transmitted words unaltered.

[126] See Diggle 1991: 111.

[127] Vitelli 1890: 287–300, followed by Barrett 73, Zuntz 35–8, and Diggle 1983: 340 [= 1994: 251] argues that in the non-triadic select plays (apart from *Rhesus*) P is a copy of a copy of L. Zuntz 1965: 264–5 suggests that its ultimate archetype may be different from that of the other manuscripts of the non-triadic selection and may be the result of the recopying into the minuscule script of a different uncial manuscript. One piece of evidence for this is the uncial error *ΛΙ* for *Ν* at *Tro.* 122.

[128] P was corrected by a second hand, p, in the sixteenth century, but there is no reason to think its readings pass on genuine tradition: of the seventeen p readings in this play cited by Diggle only its readings at 483, 736, 931, and 935 *might* be thought too good to be his conjectures.

6. RECEPTION OF *TROADES* AND EURIPIDES

Recent scholarship has devoted considerable attention to documenting the ways in which Euripides' plays were 'received', i.e. what poets, playwrights, or artists in other media have made out of his works. Twentieth-century productions and adaptations of *Troades* are discussed in Goff 2009: 78–135. Other treatments of reception in this sense are Hall 2004, Gildenhard and Revermann 2010, G. Kovacs 2014, Lauriola 2015, Gamel 2016, and van Zyl Smit 2016. A fairly recent production is noticed at <http://www.theguardian.com/world/2016/apr/20/ queens-of-syria-refugees-trojan-women-adaptation-uk-tour>. For the history of reception by those who are not artists but scholars, critics, historians, philosophers, or theologians see Funke 1965/6, Kuch 1978, Heath 1987b, and Michelini 1988.

Sigla

MANUSCRIPTS

V	Vaticanus gr. 909 (end of thirteenth century)
V^{ac}	V before it was corrected
V^{pc}	V after correction, whether by the original scribe or another
P	Palatinus gr. 287 (beginning of fourteenth century)
P^{ac}	P before correction
P^{pc}	P after correction, whether by the original scribe or another
p	the Italian corrector of P (end of fifteenth century)
Q	Harleianus 5734, lines 1–610 (*c.*1500)

Neap.	Neapolitanus 165 (fourteenth century, apograph of V)
Va	Palatinus gr. 98 (fourteenth century, apograph of V)
Haun.	Hauniensis 417 (fifteenth century, apograph of Va)
q	Harleianus 5743, lines 611–1332 (fifteenth to sixteenth century, apograph of Va)

GNOMOLOGIA

gB	Vaticanus Barberini gr. 4 (*c.*1300)
gE	Escorialensis gr. X.1.13 (beginning of fourteenth century)

PAPYRI

P. Oxy. 2455 fr. 13 col. xii, part of a *hypothesis*, second century CE
P. Oxy. 4564 contains parts of lines 340–6, end of third to fourth century CE
P. Oxy. 1176, fr. 37, col. III.21–2 (Satyrus' *Life of Euripides*), lacunose quotation of line 886, second century CE

INSCRIBED TABLET

Schubart and Wilamowitz 1907: 98, a wooden tablet containing parts of lines 876–9, first century CE

Σ a reading attested by the scholiast
Σ^{l} the lemma cited by the scholiast
Σ^{i} a reading inferrable from the scholiast's paraphrase
~ indicates that a quoter does not have the reading or conjecture just cited
[] words judged to be spurious
<> words supplied *exempli gratia* to fill a postulated scribal omission
†† words judged to be corrupt for which there is no certain or plausible emendation
⁎ a letter that can no longer be read because it was erased or obliterated

ΥΠΟΘΕϹΙϹ ΤΡΩΙΑΔΩΝ

Μετὰ τὴν Ἰλίου πόρθηϲιν ἔδοξεν Ἀθηνᾶι τε καὶ Ποϲειδῶνι τὸ τῶν Ἀχαιῶν ϲτράτευμα διαφθεῖραι, τοῦ μὲν εὐνοοῦντοϲ τῆι πόλει διὰ τὴν κτίϲιν, τῆϲ δὲ μιϲηϲάϲηϲ τοὺϲ Ἕλληναϲ διὰ τὴν Αἴαντοϲ εἰϲ Καϲϲάνδραν ὕβριν. οἱ δὲ Ἕλληνεϲ κληρωϲάμενοι περὶ τῶν αἰχμαλωτίδων γυναικῶν τὰϲ ἐν ἀξιώμαϲιν ἔδωκαν Ἀγαμέμνονι μὲν Καϲϲάνδραν, Ἀνδρομάχην δὲ Νεοπτολέμωι, Πολυξένην δὲ Ἀχιλλεῖ. ταύτην μὲν οὖν ἐπὶ τῆϲ τοῦ Ἀχιλλέωϲ ταφῆϲ ἔϲφαξαν, Ἀϲτυάνακτα δὲ ἀπὸ τῶν τειχῶν ἔρριψαν. Ἑλένην δὲ ὡϲ ἀποκτενῶν Μενέλαοϲ ἤγαγεν, Ἀγαμέμνων δὲ τὴν χρηϲμωιδὸν ἐνυμφαγώγηϲεν. Ἑκάβη δὲ τῆϲ μὲν Ἑλένηϲ κατηγορήϲαϲα, τοὺϲ ἀναιρεθένταϲ δὲ κατοδυραμένη τε καὶ κηδεύϲαϲα, πρὸϲ τὰϲ Ὀδυϲϲέωϲ ἤχθη ϲκηνάϲ, τούτωι λατρεύειν δοθεῖϲα.

τὰ τοῦ δράματοϲ πρόϲωπα· Ποϲειδῶν, Ἀθηνᾶ, Ἑκάβη, χορὸϲ ἐξ αἰχμαλωτίδων Τρωιάδων, Ταλθύβιοϲ, Καϲϲάνδρα, Ἀνδρομάχη, Μενέλαοϲ, Ἑλένη.

argumentum habent VPQ, linearum 1–6 frustula P. Oxy. 2455 fr. 13 col. xii 1 *πόρθηϲιν* PQ: *-θωϲιν* V: [*Π*] | *ἔδοξεν* hoc loco non habuit *Π* 2 *διαφθεῖραι* V: *-φεῖραι* P: *-φθαρῆναι* Q 3 *καϲϲάνδραν* Q: *καϲά-* VP: uide Fraenkel ad A. *Ag.* 1035 4 *κληρωϲάμενοι…γυναικῶν* VQ: *ἐκληρώϲαντο τὰϲ αἰχμαλωτίδαϲ τῶν γυναικῶν* P: *κληρωϲαμεν]οι̣ τω̣[ν] αιχμαλ[* *Π* | *τὰϲ* V: *τὰϲ γὰρ* PQ: *τοιϲ* *Π*, sicut coniecerat Seidler | post *Αγαμεμνο]νι* explicit *Π* 5 *καϲϲάνδραν* Q: *καϲά-* VP | *ἀνδρομάχη* V | *δὲ* PQ: *μὲν* V 6 *ἀχιλλεῖ* VQ: *τῷ ἀχ-* P | *οὖν* om. Q | *ἀχιλλέωϲ* V: *εἰρημένου* P: *προειρ-* Q 7 *ἀποκτενῶν* uoluit Aldina: *-κτείνων* VPQ 9 *τὸν ἀναιρεθέντα* Diggle | *δὲ* PQ: *μὲν* V | *κατοδυραμένη* V: *-ομένη* PQ | *τε καὶ* PQ: *καὶ* V | *καὶ* <*τὸν Ἀϲτυάνακτα*> Kirchhoff 10 *κηδεύϲαϲα* V: *θρηνήϲαϲα* P: *θρηνήϲαϲα καὶ κηδεύϲαϲα* Q | *τούτω(ι)* PQ: *-ων* V 11 *ἑκάβη* post *χορὸϲ…τρωιάδων* V | *ἐξ* om. P: cf. ind. pers. Ionis et Phoen. 11–12 *αἰχμαλωτίδων* PQ *-ώτων* V 12 *καϲϲάνδρα* Q: *καϲά-* VP

The Characters

Poseidon
Athena
Hecuba
Talthybius, a Greek herald
Cassandra
Andromache
Herald (see 707n)
Menelaus
Helen
Chorus of captive Trojan women

Non-speaking roles: Astyanax, servants belonging to Hecuba, Talthybius, the Herald, and Odysseus

Scene: before the military hut of Agamemnon in the Greek camp before Troy

ΕΥΡΙΠΙΔΟΥ ΤΡΩΙΑΔΕϹ

ΠΟϹΕΙΔΩΝ

Ἥκω λιπὼν Αἰγαῖον ἁλμυρὸν βάθοϲ
πόντου Ποϲειδῶν, ἔνθα Νηρῄδων χοροὶ
κάλλιϲτον ἴχνοϲ ἐξελίϲϲουϲιν ποδόϲ.
ἐξ οὗ γὰρ ἀμφὶ τήνδε Τρωϊκὴν χθόνα
Φοῖβόϲ τε κἀγὼ λαΐνουϲ πύργουϲ πέριξ
ὀρθοῖϲιν ἔθεμεν κανόϲιν, οὔποτ' ἐκ φρενῶν
εὔνοι' ἀπέϲτη τῶν ἐμῶν Φρυγῶν πόλει·
ἣ νῦν καπνοῦται καὶ πρὸϲ Ἀργείου δορὸϲ
ὄλωλε πορθηθεῖϲ'· ὁ γὰρ Παρνάϲϲιοϲ
Φωκεὺϲ Ἐπειὸϲ μηχαναῖϲι Παλλάδοϲ
ἐγκύμον' ἵππον τευχέων ϲυναρμόϲαϲ
πύργων ἔπεμψεν ἐντὸϲ ὀλέθριον βάροϲ.
[ὅθεν πρὸϲ ἀνδρῶν ὑϲτέρων κεκλήϲεται
δούρειοϲ ἵπποϲ, κρυπτὸν ἀμπίϲχων δόρυ.]
ἔρημα δ' ἄλϲη καὶ θεῶν ἀνάκτορα
φόνωι καταρρεῖ· πρὸϲ δὲ κρηπίδων βάθροιϲ
πέπτωκε Πρίαμοϲ Ζηνὸϲ ἑρκείου θανών.
   πολλοῖϲ δὲ κωκυτοῖϲιν αἰχμαλωτίδων
βοᾶι Ϲκάμανδροϲ δεϲπόταιϲ κληρουμένων.
καὶ τὰϲ μὲν Ἀρκάϲ, τὰϲ δὲ Θεϲϲαλὸϲ λεὼϲ

1 *αἴγαιον* V | *ἁλμυρὸν* Q: *ἀλ-* VP: *ἁλμυροῦ* Burges 2 *νηρῄδων* V: *-ηίδων* PQ | *χοροὶ* V et Aristid. 44.9: *-ὸϲ* PQ 3 *ποδί* Aristid. 6 *ὀρθοῖϲ* V 9 *παρνάϲϲιοϲ* VΣ: *-νάϲιοϲ* PQ 11 *ἵππων* P | *ξυναρμόϲαϲ* P 12 *βρέταϲ* V, fort. recte 13–14 del. Burges 13 *κληθήϲεται* PQ 14 *ἀμπίϲχων* V: *ἀμφί-* PQ: *ἀμπιϲχὼν* L. Dindorf 15 *ἀγάλματα* Σ^γρ 17 *ἑρκείου* Musgrave: *-κίου* VPQΣ (*ἑ-* VΣ et fort. Q) 18–27 post 44 transposui: 23–7 post 44 trai. G. Wagner 29 *δεϲπόταιϲ* Lane: *-αϲ* VPQ

εἴληχ' Ἀθηναίων τε Θηςεῖδαι πρόμοι.
ὅςαι δ' ἄκληροι Τρωιάδων, ὑπὸ ςτέγαις
ταῖςδ' εἰςί, τοῖς πρώτοιςιν ἐξῃρημέναι
ςτρατοῦ, ςὺν αὐταῖς δ' ἡ Λάκαινα Τυνδαρὶς
Ἑλένη, νομιςθεῖς' αἰχμάλωτος ἐνδίκως.
τὴν δ' ἀθλίαν τήνδ' εἴ τις εἰςορᾶν θέλει,
πάρεςτιν, Ἑκάβην κειμένην πυλῶν πάρος
[δάκρυα χέουςαν πολλὰ καὶ πολλῶν ὕπερ]·
ἧι παῖς μὲν ἀμφὶ μνῆμ' Ἀχιλλείου τάφου
οἰκτρὰ τέθνηκε τλημόνως Πολυξένη·
φροῦδος δὲ Πρίαμος καὶ τέκν'· ἣν δὲ παρθένον
μεθῆκ' Ἀπόλλων δρομάδα Καςςάνδραν ἄναξ,
τὸ τοῦ θεοῦ τε παραλιπὼν τό τ' εὐςεβὲς
γαμεῖ βιαίως ςκότιον Ἀγαμέμνων λέχος.
πολὺς δὲ χρυςὸς Φρύγιά τε ςκυλεύματα
πρὸς ναῦς Ἀχαιῶν πέμπεται· μένουςι δὲ
πρύμνηθεν οὖρον, ὡς δεκαςπόρωι χρόνωι
ἀλόχους τε καὶ τέκν' εἰςίδωςιν ἄςμενοι
[οἳ τήνδ' ἐπεςτράτευςαν Ἕλληνες πόλιν].
ἐγὼ δέ (νικῶμαι γὰρ Ἀργείας θεοῦ
Ἥρας Ἀθάνας θ', αἳ ςυνεξεῖλον Φρύγας)
λείπω τὸ κλεινὸν Ἴλιον βωμούς τ' ἐμούς·
ἐρημία γὰρ πόλιν ὅταν λάβηι κακή,
νοςεῖ τὰ τῶν θεῶν οὐδὲ τιμᾶςθαι θέλει.
ἀλλ', ὦ ποτ' εὐτυχοῦςα, χαῖρέ μοι, πόλις
ξεςτόν τε πύργωμ'· εἴ ςε μὴ διώλεςεν
Παλλὰς Διὸς παῖς, ἦςθ' ἂν ἐν βάθροις ἔτι.

ΑΘΗΝΑ

ἔξεςτι τὸν γένει μὲν ἄγχιςτον πατρὸς
μέγαν τε δαίμον' ἐν θεοῖς τε τίμιον,
λύςαςαν ἔχθραν τὴν πάρος, προςεννέπειν;

Πο. *ἔξεςτιν· αἱ γὰρ ςυγγενεῖς ὁμιλίαι,*

31 *τε* VΣ^{l}: *δὲ* PQ 32 *Τρωιάδων*] *παρθένων* $\Sigma^{\gamma\rho}$ 34 *δ' ἡ* V: *ἡ* PQ 37 *ἑκάβην κειμένην* V: *-η -μένη* PQ 38 del. Prinz | *δάκρυα χέουςαν* V: *δακρυχέουςα* PQ 39 *ἀχιλλείου* P^{pc}(*-ίου* P^{ac}) Q: *-ιλείου* V 40 *οἰκτρὰ* PQ$\Sigma^{\gamma\rho}$: *λάθρα* V | *τλῆμον ὡς* P 41 *παρθένον*] *πάροιθεν* P 42 *καςςάνδραν* pQ: *καςά-* VP 22 u. del. Hartung | *ἐπεςτράτευςαν* P(*ἐπ' ἐςτρ-*)Q: *ἐςτρ-* V 23 *θεᾶς* V 24 *ἥρας τ' ἀθήνας τ' αἳ* (*αἳ* V^{pc})V 47 *πολλὰς* P | *παῖς*] *ςε* Q 48 *τῶν* Q | *γένει*] *ἐν γένει* V 49 *μέγαν δὲ* Elmsley

ἄναcc᾽ Ἀθάνα, φίλτρον οὐ cμικρὸν φρενῶν.
Αθ. ἐπῄνεc᾽ ὀργὰc ἠπίουc· φέρω δὲ coὶ
κοινοὺc ἐμαυτῆι τ᾽ ἐc μέcον λόγουc, ἄναξ.
Πο. μῶν ἐκ θεῶν του καινὸν ἀγγελεῖc ἔποc,
ἢ Ζηνὸc ἢ καὶ δαιμόνων τινὸc πάρα;
Αθ. οὔκ, ἀλλὰ Τροίαc οὕνεκ᾽, ἔνθα βαίνομεν,
πρὸc cὴν ἀφῖγμαι δύναμιν, ὡc κοινὴν λάβω.
Πο. οὔ πού νιν, ἔχθραν τὴν πρὶν ἐκβαλοῦcα, νῦν
ἐc οἶκτον ἦλθεc πυρὶ κατηιθαλωμένην;
Αθ. ἐκεῖcε πρῶτ᾽ ἄνελθε· κοινώcηι λόγουc
καὶ cυμπονήcειc ἃν ἐγὼ πρᾶξαι θέλω;
Πο. μάλιcτ᾽· ἀτὰρ δὴ καὶ τὸ cὸν θέλω μαθεῖν·
πότερον Ἀχαιῶν ἦλθεc οὕνεκ᾽ ἢ Φρυγῶν;
Αθ. τοὺc μὲν πρὶν ἐχθροὺc Τρῶαc εὐφρᾶναι θέλω,
cτρατῶι δ᾽ Ἀχαιῶν νόcτον ἐμβαλεῖν πικρόν.
Πο. τί δ᾽ ὧδε πηδᾶιc ἄλλοτ᾽ εἰc ἄλλουc τρόπουc
μιcεῖc τε λίαν καὶ φιλεῖc ὃν ἂν τύχηιc;
Αθ. οὐκ οἶcθ᾽ ὑβριcθεῖcάν με καὶ ναοὺc ἐμούc;
Πο. οἶδ᾽· ἡνίκ᾽ Αἴαc εἷλκε Καccάνδραν βίαι.
Αθ. κοὐδέν γ᾽ Ἀχαιῶν ἔπαθεν οὐδ᾽ ἤκουc᾽ ὕπο.
Πο. καὶ μὴν ἔπερcάν γ᾽ Ἴλιον τῶι cῶι cθένει.
Αθ. τοιγάρ cφε cὺν coὶ βούλομαι δρᾶcαι κακῶc.
Πο. ἕτοιμ᾽ ἃ βούληι τἀπ᾽ ἐμοῦ. δράcειc δὲ τί;
Αθ. δύcνοcτον αὐτοῖc νόcτον ἐμβαλεῖν θέλω.
Πο. ἐν γῆι μενόντων ἢ καθ᾽ ἁλμυρὰν ἅλα;
Αθ. ὅταν πρὸc οἴκουc ναυcτολῶc᾽ ἀπ᾽ Ἰλίου.
καὶ Ζεὺc μὲν ὄμβρον καὶ χάλαζαν ἄcπετον
πέμψει δνοφώδη τ᾽ αἰθέροc φυcήματα·
ἐμοὶ δὲ δώcειν φηcὶ πῦρ κεραύνιον,
βάλλειν Ἀχαιοὺc ναῦc τε πιμπράναι πυρί.

52 *μικρὸν* P 53 *δὲ coὶ* Seidler: *δέ coι* VPQ 55 *κοινὸν* PQ | *ἀγγέλλειc* PQ 57 *ἔνθ᾽ ἐβαίνομεν* P 58 *πρὸc ἣν* Q 59 *οὔ* Wecklein: *ἦ* VPQ | *νιν* V: *νυν* P: *νῦν* Q | *νῦν*] *νιν* V^{ac} 60 *οἶκον* P^{ac} | *κατηιθαλωμένην* Elmsley: -*ηc* VPQ 62 *cυμπονήcειc* PQ: *cυνθελήcειc* V 64 *οὕνεκ᾽ ἦλθεc* PQ 65 *θέλων* Q^{ac} 68 *λείαν* Q | *τύχηc* V: -*η(ι)* PQ(-*ῆι* Q) et gE et Cyrill. c. Iul. 175 B (PG 76.767 Migne) 70 *εἷλε* V et Cyrill. | *καccάνδραν* Q: *καcά-* PV 71 *κοὐδέν γ᾽* PQ et Cyrill.: *κοὐδὲν* V: *κοὐ δείν᾽* Nauck 72 *ἔπερcάν γ᾽* Victorius: -*cάν τ᾽* VQ: *ἔπερcατ᾽* P 75 *δύcτηνον* V 76 *μένουcιν* PQ | *ἁλμυρὰν* Q: *ἀλ-* VP 78 *χάλαζα* P 79 *πέμψειν* Porson | *δνοφώδη* Dindorf: *γνο-* VPQ et *Σ* Lycoph. 382 | *ἐθέροc φηcήματα* P^{ac} ut uid.

cὺ δ' αὖ, τὸ cόν, παράcχεc Αἰγαῖον πόρον
τρικυμίαιc βρέμοντα καὶ δίναιc ἁλόc,
πλῆcον δὲ νεκρῶν κοῖλον Εὐβοίαc μυχόν,
ὡc ἂν τὸ λοιπὸν τἄμ' ἀνάκτορ' εὐcεβεῖν
εἰδῶc' Ἀχαιοὶ θεούc τε τοὺc ἄλλουc cέβειν.

Πο. *ἔcται τάδ'· ἡ χάριc γὰρ οὐ μακρῶν λόγων*
δεῖται· ταράξω πέλαγοc Αἰγαίαc ἁλόc.
ἀκταὶ δὲ Μυκόνου Δήλιοί τε χοιράδεc
Cκῦρόc τε Λῆμνόc θ' αἱ Καφήρειοί τ' ἄκραι
πολλῶν θανόντων cώμαθ' ἕξουcιν νεκρῶν.
ἀλλ' ἕρπ' Ὄλυμπον καὶ κεραυνίουc βολὰc
λαβοῦcα πατρὸc ἐκ χερῶν καραδόκει,
ὅταν cτράτευμ' Ἀργεῖον ἐξιῆι κάλωc.
μῶροc δὲ θνητῶν ὅcτιc ἐκπορθεῖ πόλειc,
ναοὺc δὲ τύμβουc θ', ἱερὰ τῶν κεκμηκότων,
ἐρημίαι δοὺc αὐτὸc ὤλεθ' ὕcτερον.

ΕΚΑΒΗ

ἄνα, δύcδαιμον· πεδόθεν κεφαλήν,
ἐπάειρε δέρην· οὐκέτι Τροία
τάδε, καὶ βαcιλῆc ἐcμεν Τροίαc.
μεταβαλλομένου δαίμονοc ἀνέχου.
πλεῖ κατὰ πορθμόν, πλεῖ κατὰ δαίμονα,
μηδὲ προcίcτη πρῶιραν βιότου
πρὸc κῦμα πλέουcα τύχαιcιν.
αἰαῖ αἰαῖ.
τί γὰρ οὐ πάρα μοι μελέαι cτενάχειν,
ἧι πατρὶc ἔρρει καὶ τέκνα καὶ πόcιc;
ὦ πολὺc ὄγκοc cυcτελλόμενοc
προγόνων, ὡc οὐδὲν ἄρ' ἦcθα.
τί με χρὴ cιγᾶν, τί δὲ μὴ cιγᾶν;
τί δὲ θρηνῆcαι;

82 *παράcχεc* P: *-έcχεc* Q: *πάραcχε* V | *αἴγαιον* V 84 *νεκρὸν* Q 86 *cέβειν*] *τίειν* Herwerden 89 *μυκίνου* VΣ^1 93 *χερὸc* P^{ac} ut uid. 94 *Ἀργεῖον* Canter: *-είων* VPQ | *κάλοc* P^{ac} 95 *γε* gB | *ἐκπέρcαc* Reiske | *πόλιc* Q 96 *ναοὺc δὲ* Blomfield: *ναούc τε* VPQ | post *πόλειc* grauius dist. Kirchhoff 1852, post *τύμβουc θ'* *Σ*, post *κεκμηκότων* Page, post *δούc* West 97 *δούc* <*cφ'*> Page ap. Diggle | <*κ*>*αὐτὸc* Holzhausen, praeeunte West 99 *δέρην* <*τ'*> Musgrave 101 *ἀνέχου* VPQ: *ἄνcχου* Nauck 111 del. Tyrrell

δύϲτηνοϲ ἐγὼ τῆϲ βαρυδαίμονοϲ
ἄρθρων κλίϲεωϲ, ὡϲ διάκειμαι,
νῶτ' ἐν ϲτερροῖϲι ταθεῖϲα.
οἴμοι κεφαλῆϲ, οἴμοι κροτάφων
πλευρῶν θ', ὥϲ μοι πόθοϲ εἱλίξαι
καὶ διαδοῦναι νῶτον ἄκανθάν τ'
εἰϲ ἀμφοτέρουϲ τοίχουϲ μελέων,
ἐπιοῦϲ' αἰεὶ δακρύων ἐλέγουϲ.
μοῦϲα δὲ χαὔτη τοῖϲ δυϲτήνοιϲ
ἄταϲ κελαδεῖν ἀχορεύτουϲ.

πρῷραι ναῶν, ὠκείαιϲ
Ἴλιον ἱερὰν αἳ κώπαιϲ
†δι' ἅλα πορφυροειδέα καὶ
λιμέναϲ Ἑλλάδοϲ† εὐόρμουϲ,
αὐλῶν <ϲὺν> παιᾶνι ϲτυγνῶι
ϲυρίγγων τ' εὐφθόγγων φωνᾶι
βαίνουϲαι, πλεκτάϲ, Αἰγύπτου
παίδευμ', ἐξηρτάϲαϲθ', <αἰαῖ,>
αἰαῖ, Τροίαϲ ἐν κόλποιϲ,
τὰν Μενελάου μεταϲιϲόμεναι
ϲτυγνὰν ἄλοχον, Κάϲτορι λώβαν
τῶι τ' Εὐρώται δύϲκλειαν·
ἃ ϲφάζει μὲν
τὸν πεντήκοντ' ἀροτῆρα τέκνων
†Πρίαμον, ἐμέ τε μελέαν Ἑκάβαν†
ἐϲ τάνδ' ἐξώκειλ' ἄταν.
οἴμοι, θάκουϲ οἵουϲ θάϲϲω
ϲκηναῖϲ ἐφέδρουϲ Ἀγαμεμνονίαιϲ.
δούλα δ' ἄγομαι

114 νῶτ' ἐν ϲτερροῖϲι ταθεῖϲα Hartung: ν- ἐν ϲτερροῖϲ λέκτροιϲι ταθεῖϲα fere VPQ (ϲτεροῖϲ V, ϲτέρνοιϲ PQ, ϲτερροῖϲ Haun. teste Kirchhoff): ϲτερροῖϲ λέκτροιϲι ταθεῖϲα, ceteris deletis Seidler 119 ἐπιοῦϲ' Musgrave: ἐπὶ τοὺϲ VPQ: ἐπαειδούϲηι Scheidweiler 122 λιαῶν P | ὠκείαιϲ Tyrrell: ὠκεῖαι VPQ 124 δι' ἅλ' <Αἰγαίαν> Willink 125 λιμέναϲ θ' Seidler et Hermann, deleto in 124 καὶ 126 <ϲὺν> Page 127 φωνᾶ(ι) PQ: -αῖϲ V 128 πλεκτάϲ Musgrave: πλεκτὰν VP: λεκτὰν Q 129 παίδευμ' Tyrrell: παιδείαν VPQ | ἐξηρτάϲαϲθ' Kovacs: -τήϲαϲθ' VPQ | <αἰαῖ> Page 136 ἐμὲ δ' αὖ μελέαν ceteris deletis Lenting 138 θάκουϲ' Q | οὓϲ PQ 139 ἐφέδρουϲ Bothe: -οϲ VPQ | Ἀγαμεμνονίαιϲ Valckenaer: -είαιϲ VPQ 140 δοῦλ' ἄγομαι V

γραῦc ἐξ οἴκων πενθήρη
κρᾶτ᾽ ἐκπορθηθεῖc᾽ οἰκτρῶc.
ἀλλ᾽ ὦ τῶν χαλκεγχέων Τρώων
ἄλοχοι μέλεαι
καὶ κοῦραι, δύc<νυμφοι> νύμφαι,
τύφεται Ἴλιον, †αἰάζομεν†.
μάτηρ δ᾽ ὡcεὶ πτανοῖc κλαγγὰν
ὄρνιc, ἐξάρξω ᾽γὼ μολπάν,
οὐ τὰν αὐτὰν οἵαν ποτὲ δὴ
cκήπτρωι Πριάμου διερειδομένου
ποδὸc ἀρχεχόρου πλαγαῖc Φρυγίουc
εὐκόμποιc ἐξῆρχον θεούc.

ΗΜΙΧΟΡΙΟΝ Α´

Ἑκάβα, τί θροεῖc; τί δὲ θωΰccειc; str. 1
ποῖ λόγοc ἥκει; διὰ γὰρ μελάθρων
ἄιον οἴκτουc οὓc οἰκτίζηι.
διὰ δὲ cτέρνων τάρβοc ἀίccει
Τρωιάcιν, αἳ τῶνδ᾽ οἴκων εἴcω
δουλείαν αἰάζουcιν.

Εκ. *ὦ τέκν᾽, Ἀχαιῶν πρὸc ναῦc ἤδη*
κινεῖται κωπήρηc χείρ.

Ημ. *οἳ ᾽γώ, τί θέλουc᾽, ἦ πού μ᾽ ἤδη*
ναυcθλώcουcιν πατρίαc ἐκ γᾶc;

141 *πενθήρη* PQΣ^{i}: *-ρει* V | ante *πενθήρη* (*-ει*) uocabula *κουρᾶ(ι) ξυρήκει* (Alc. 427) quae habent VPQΣ del. Murray (*ξυρήκει* iam del. Bothe) 142 *ἐκπορθηcεῖc᾽* P 143 *χαλκεχέων* V 145 *κοῦραι* Aldina: *κόραι* VPQ | *δύc<νυμφοι> νύμφαι* Kovacs: *δύcνυμφαι* VPQ 146 *αἰάζομεν* VPQΣ^{i}: *-ζωμεν* Aldina: metrum sanaret *αἰάζω μέν*, ante quae fort. indicanda est lacuna, e.g. *<αἰαῖ· πρὸc ναῦc ἤδη χωρεῖ cτρατὸc Ἑλλάνων·> αἰάζω μέν, κτλ.* ut intelligi possint 159–60 147 *ὡcεὶ* VQΣ^{i}: *ὡcεί τιc* P | *πτανοῖc* V^{pc}QΣ^{i}: *παν-* V: *πτην-* P 148 *ὄρνιc* Dindorf: *ὄρνιcιν ὅπωc* VPQ | *μολμὰν* V^{ac} 150 *διερειδομένου* Herwerden: *-μένα* VP(*δ᾽ ἐρ-* P) QΣ 151 *παιδὸc* V | *ἀρχαιχόρου* P | *πλαγαῖc* Seidler: *πλαγγ-* V: *πληγ-* PQ | *Φρυγίουc* Wilamowitz: *-αιc* VPQ et Σ ut uid. 153 *ΗΜΙΧΟΡΙΟΝ Α´* Musgrave: *Χο.* VPQ | *Ἑκάβα* Kovacs: *-η* VPQ 154–5 *ποῖ λόγοc ἥκει* et *ἄιον οἴκ* om. P et spatiis uacuis relictis primitus Q (suppl. q) 156 *τάρβοc* Wecklein (noluit Seidler): *φόβοc* VPQ 159 *Ἀχαιῶν* Schroeder: *Ἀργείων* VPQ 160 *κοπήρηc* V^{ac} 161 *Ημ.* Musgrave: *Χο.* VQ: om. P | *οἳ ᾽γώ* Kirchhoff: *οἳ ἐγὼ μελέα* V: *οἳ ᾽γὼ* (*οἳ ᾽ἐγὼ* Q) *τλάμων* (*-ον* P^{ac}) PQ | *μ᾽ ἤδη* V: *με δὴ* Q: *γε δὴ* P 162 *ναυcθλώcουcι* V^{ac}: *-ώcc-* V^{pc}P: *ναύc᾽ ἀθλώcουcι* Q | *πατρίαc* Burges: *-ώ(ι)αc* VPQ | *ἐπὶ* P

Εκ. οὐκ οἶδ', εἰκάζω δ' ἄταν.
Ημ. ἰὼ ἰώ.
μέλεαι, μόχθων ἐπακουcόμεναι,
Τρῳάδεc, ἔξω κομίcαcθ' οἴκων·
cτέλλουc' Ἀργεῖοι νόcτον.
Εκ. ἒ ἔ.
μή νύν μοι τὰν
ἐκβακχεύουcαν Καccάνδραν,
αἰcχύναν Ἀργείοιcιν,
πέμψητ' ἔξω,
μαινάδ', ἐπ' ἄλγεcι δ' ἀλγυνθῶ.
ἰὼ ἰώ.
Τροία Τροία δύcταν', ἔρρειc,
δύcτανοι δ' οἵ c' ἐκλείποντεc
καὶ ζῶντεc καὶ δμαθέντεc.

ΗΜΙΧΟΡΙΟΝ Β'

οἴμοι. τρομερὰ cκηνὰc ἔλιπον ant. 1
τάcδ' Ἀγαμέμνονοc ἐπακουcομένα,
βαcίλεια, cέθεν· μή με κτείνειν
δόξ' Ἀργείων κεῖται μελέαν;
ἢ κατὰ πρύμναc ἤδη ναῦται
cτέλλονται κινεῖν κώπαc;
Εκ. ὦ τέκνον, ὀρθρεύουcαν ψυχὰν
ἐκπληχθεῖc' ἦλθον φρίκαι.
Ημ. ἤδη τιc ἔβα Δαναῶν κῆρυξ;
τῶι πρόcκειμαι δούλα τλάμων;

163 *Εκ.* Musgrave: om. VPQ   164 *Ημ.* VQ: *Χο.* P | μόχθον V | ἐπακούcομαι Q   166 ἔξω κομίcαcθ' Aldina: ἔξω κομίζεcθ' VPQ: ἐξορμίζεcθ' Headlam   167 πέλλουc' V   168 ἒ ἔ Q: ἓ ἕ VP: αἰαῖ Dindorf   169 καccάνδραν PQ: καcά- V   171, 170 hoc ordine Murray   171 αἰcχύνην PQ | <ἔν γ'> Ἀργείοιc uel Ἰδαίαιcιν Kovacs   170 πέμψετ' PQ   172 ἄλγει V ('nihilo deterius' Diggle)   173 ἰὼ ἰώ V: ἰὼ PQ: del. Seidler: uide ad 193–4   174 δύcτανόν P | c' ἐκλείποντεc Burges: c' ἐκλιπόντεc VQ: cε λιπ- P   176 *ΗΜΙΧΟΡΙΟΝ Β'* Musgrave cum *Σ*: *Χο.* VPQ   182 ὀρθρεύουcαν Aldina: ὀρθρεύου cὰν VPQΣ^{li} 183 Hecubae contin. Aldina: choro trib. VPQ   184 *Ημ.* Seidler: om VPQ   185 τλᾶμον P

Εκ. ἐγγύς που κεῖcαι κλήρου.
Ημ. ἰὼ ἰώ.
τίς μ’ Ἀργείων ἢ Φθιωτᾶν
ἢ νηcαίας ἄξει χώρας
δύcτανον πόρcω Τροίας;
Εκ. φεῦ φεῦ.
τῶι δ’ ἁ τλάμων
ποῦ πᾶι γαίας δουλεύcω γραῦς,
ὡς κηφήν, ἁ δειλαία,
νεκροῦ μορφά,
νεκύων ἀμενηνὸν ἄγαλμα,
αἰαῖ αἰαῖ,
τὰν παρὰ προθύροις φυλακὰν κατέχους’
ἢ παίδων θρέπτειρ’, ἃ Τροίας
ἀρχαγοὺς εἶχον τιμάς;

Χο. αἰαῖ αἰαῖ. ποίοις δ’ οἴκτοις str. 2
τάνδ’ ἂν λύμαν ἐξαιάζοις;
οὐκ Ἰδαίοις ἱcτοῖς κερκίδα
δινεύους’ ἐξαλλάξω·
νέατον τοκέων δώματα λεύccω,
νέατον· μόχθους <δ’> ἕξω κρείccους,
ἢ λέκτροις πλαθεῖς’ Ἑλλάνων

186 Hec. notam om. Q 187 *Ημ.* Musgrave: *Χο.* VP: om. Q | ante *τίς* Hec. notam habet P | *μ’* VΣ^{1}: *με* PQ | *φθιωτᾶν* Q: *-ὰν* P: *-ῶν* V 188 *νηcαίας…χώρας* Wecklein: *-αν…-αν* VPQ | *ἄξει* Brodaeus: *μ’ ἄξει* V: *ἥξει* PQ 189 *πόρcω* Dindorf: *πρόcω* VΣ: *πόρρω* PQ$\Sigma^{\gamma\rho}$ 190 *Εκ.* Bothe: *Χο.* P: om. VQ | ante *τῶι* Hec. notam habet P 191 *πᾶ* V: *παῖ* PQ 192 *κηφὴν ἁ* Q: *cκηφὴν ἁ* P: *κηφήνα* V 193–5 sic mutilos exhibent PQ: *νεκύων ἀμενηνὰ* (*ἀμενη* Q)/*παρὰ προθύροις*/*ἢ* (*c’ ἢ* Q) *παίδων θρέπτηρας* (*θρέπτειν* Q) 193 *ἄγαλμα, / αἰαῖ αἰαῖ* post Hermann (*ἒ ἔ* uel *αἰαῖ* semel) Diggle: *ἄγαλμ’ ἢ* VΣ^{1} (desunt PQ): *ἄγαλμα* (del. *ἢ*) Lachmann | *δειλαία…ἄγαλμα* habent gB et gE 194 *παρὰ* PQ: *παρά τε* VΣ^{1} 195 *θρέπτειρ’* Va: *θέπτειρ’* V: de PQ uide supra 197 *Χο.* PΣ: *Εκ.* VQ 198 *τάνδ’ ἂν* Wilamowitz: *τὰν cὰν* VPQ | *ἐξαιάζοις* Wilamowitz: *-αιάζεις* V: *-ετάζεις* PQ 199 *Χο.* VQ: *Εκ.* P | *ἱcτοῖς* Aldina: *-οῖcι* V PQΣ^{1} 200 *ἐξαλάξω* V201 *Εκ.* praescr. V | *νέατον* Seidler: *-οι* V (*νεάτοι*) PQΣ^{1} | *τοκέων δώματα* Parmentier (*τοκέων* iam Wilamowitz): *τεκέων cώματα* VPQ: *τοκέων cήματα* Wilamowitz | *λεύcω* V 202 *νέατον* Seidler: *-τοι* VPQ | <δ’> Seidler 203 *πλαcθεῖς’* V

(ἔρροι νὺξ αὕτα καὶ δαίμων)
ἢ Πειρήνας ὑδρευομένα
πρόσπολος οἰκτρὰ ϲεμνῶν ὑδάτων.
τὰν κλεινὰν εἴθ' ἔλθοιμεν
Θηϲέωϲ εὐδαίμονα χώραν.
μὴ γὰρ δὴ δίναν γ' Εὐρώτα
τάν <τ’> ἐχθίϲταν θεράπναν Ἑλέναϲ,
ἔνθ' ἀντάϲω Μενέλαι δούλα,
τῶι τᾶϲ Τροίαϲ πορθηταῖ.

τὰν Πηνειοῦ ϲεμνὰν χώραν, ant. 2
κρηπῖδ' Οὐλύμπου καλλίϲταν,
ὄλβωι βρίθειν φάμαν ἤκουϲ'
εὐθαλεῖ τ' εὐκαρπείαι·
τάδε δεύτερά μοι μετὰ τὰν ἱερὰν
Θηϲέωϲ ζαθέαν ἐλθεῖν χώραν.
καὶ τὰν Αἰτναίαν Ἡφαίϲτου
Φοινίκαϲ ἀντήρη χώραν,
Ϲικελῶν ὀρέων ματέρ', ἀκούω
καρύϲϲεϲθαι ϲτεφάνοιϲ ἀρετᾶϲ,
τάν τ' ἀγχιϲτεύουϲαν γᾶν
†Ἰονίωι ναύται πόντωι†,
ἃν ὑγραίνει καλλιϲτεύων
ὁ ξανθὰν χαίταν πυρϲαίνων
Κρᾶθιϲ ζαθέαιϲ παγαῖϲι τρέφων
εὔανδρόν τ' ὀλβίζων γᾶν.

204 αὕτα Seidler: αὐτὰ VPQ 205 ἢ PΣ: ἣ Q: ἦ V | ὑδρευομένα Heiland: -ϲομένα V (-α cum ι subscr.) PQ 206 οἰκτρὰ om. VQ | ὑδάτων Hermann: ὑδάτων ἔϲομαι VPQ | πρόπολοϲ ϲεμνῶν ὑδάτων ἔϲομαι Dindorf 207 Χο. praescr. P | ἔλθοιμι e Σ 210 enucleauit et defendit Meridor 210 Εκ. praescr. P | δὴ δίναν VΣ^{l}: ἐν δίνα(ι) PQ 211 <τ’> Musgrave | θεράπναν Q (Θεράπναν Σ^{i}): -άπαν V: -άπεναν P^{ac} (-άπαιναν P^{pc}) 212 ἀντάϲωμαι Q 213 τῆϲV 215 κριπίδ'V 216 ὄλβονPQ 217 εὐκαρπείαι Burges: -πία(ι) VPQ 218 τάδε VQΣ^{li}: τὰ P 219 ἐλθεῖν om. PQ 223 καρύϲϲεϲθαι Dindorf: καρύϲϲεϲθε V: κηρύϲϲεϲθαι PQΣ | τ' ἀρετάϲ PQ 225 ἰωνίω P | ναύται (ι adscr.) PQ: -τα V | fort. ἄιον αὖ θάλλειν πάντωϲ 226 ὑγραίνει V et Σ Lycoph. 1021: ὑδρ- PQ 227 πυρϲαίνων V et Σ Lycoph.: πυρϲεύων V^{sl}Q (nisi -ϲαύων Q): πυρδεύων P 228 κρᾶθιϲ Va: κράθ- VΣ: κράνθ- P: κρᾶνθ- Q | παγαῖϲι Seidler: πηγ- VPQ

—καὶ μὴν Δαναῶν ὅδ' ἀπὸ cτρατιᾶc
κῆρυξ, νεοχμῶν μύθων ταμίαc,
cτείχει ταχύπουν ἴχνοc ἐξανύτων.
τί φέρει; τί λέγει; δοῦλαι γὰρ δὴ
Δωρίδοc ἐcμὲν χθονὸc ἤδη.

ΤΑΛΘΥΒΙΟC

Ἑκάβη—πυκνὰc γὰρ οἶcθά μ' ἐc Τροίαν ὁδοὺc
ἐλθόντα κήρυκ' ἐξ Ἀχαιικοῦ cτρατοῦ—
ἐγνωcμένοc δὴ καὶ πάροιθέ coι, γύναι,
Ταλθύβιοc ἥκω καινὸν ἀγγελῶν λόγον.
Εκ. †τόδε τόδε φίλαι γυναῖκεc ὃ† φόβοc ἦν πάλαι.
Τα. ἤδη κεκλήρωcθ', εἰ τόδ' ἦν ὑμῖν φόβοc.
Εκ. αἰαῖ, τίνα πόλιν Φθιάδοc εἶπαc ἢ
Καδμείαc χθονόc;
Τα. κατ' ἄνδρ' ἑκάcτη κοὐχ ὁμοῦ λελόγχατε.
Εκ. τίν' ἄρα τίc ἔλαχε; τίνα πότμοc εὐτυχὴc
Ἰλιάδων μένει;
Τα. οἶδ'· ἀλλ' ἕκαcτα πυνθάνου, μὴ πάνθ' ὁμοῦ.
Εκ. τοὐμὸν <μὲν> τίc ἆρ'
ἔλαχε τέκοc, ἔνεπε, τλάμονα Καccάνδραν;
Τα. ἐξαίρετόν νιν ἔλαβεν Ἀγαμέμνων ἄναξ.
Εκ. ἦ τᾶι Λακεδαιμονίαι νύμφαι
δούλαν; ὤμοι μοι.
Τα. οὔκ, ἀλλὰ λέκτρων cκότια νυμφευτήρια.
Εκ. ἦ τὰν τοῦ Φοίβου παρθένον, ᾇι γέραc ὁ
χρυcοκόμαc ἔδωκ' ἄλεκτρον ζόαν;

230 *Χο.* praescr. VPQ 231 νεογμῶν PQ 232–4 cτείχει ταχύπουν ἴχνοc et τί φέρει; τί λέγει; et Δωρίδοc ἐcμὲν spatiis uacuis relictis om. P et primitus Q (suppl. q): cτείχει ... λέγει habet gE 232 ἐξανύτων praemonente Porson Burges: -νύων VPQ et gE 235 οἶcθ' εἰc τ- Q 236 ἀχαιικοῦ Q: ἀχαικ- VP 237 ἐγνωcμένωc V | δὴ Mistchenko: δὲ VPQ | πάροιθεν V | u. del. Dobree 238 ταλθίβιοc V | κοινὸν PQ | ἀγγελῶν Q: -έλων $\mathrm{VP^{ac}}$: -έλλων $\mathrm{P^{pc}}$ 239 τόδε alterum del. Matthiae | γυναῖκεc V: τρω(ι)άδεc PQ | τόδε, φίλαι γυναῖκεc, τόδε Τρωϊάδεc Diggle 240 κεκλήρωcθ' εἰc V 241 τίνα πόλιν Willink: τίνα (τίν' V) ἢ Θεccαλίαc πόλιν VPQ | Φθιάδοc Hartung: ἢ Φθιάδοc VPQ | εἶπαc ἢ καὶ V 244 *Εκ.* PQ: *Χο.* V | ἔλαχον PQ 245 μένει Hermann: -νεῖ VPQ 247 τοὐμὸν <μὲν> post Nauck (τοὐμὸν <δὴ>) Willink | ἆρ' Kirchhoff: ἄρ' PQ: om. V 248 τέκνον Q | ἔνεπε Seidler: ἔνν- VPQ | καccάνδραν PQ: καcά- V 249 ἔλαχεν Q 250 ἦ $\mathrm{V^{pc}Q^{pc}}$: ἢ $\mathrm{V^{ac}P\Sigma^{l}}$: de $\mathrm{Q^{ac}}$ incertum | νύμφη P 251 ὤμοι μοι Hermann: ἰώ μοι (μοί V) VPQ 253 ἢ $\mathrm{V^{ac}}$ 254 ζόαν Dindorf (noluit Seidler): ζωάν VPQ

Τα. ἔρωϲ ἐτόξευϲ’ αὐτὸν ἐνθέου κόρηϲ.
Εκ. ῥῖπτε, τέκνον, ζαθέουϲ κλά-
δαϲ καὶ ἀπὸ χροὸϲ ἐνδυ-
τῶν ϲτεφέων ἱεροὺϲ ϲτολμούϲ.
Τα. οὐ γὰρ μέγ’ αὐτῆι βαϲιλικῶν λέκτρων τυχεῖν;
Εκ. τί δ’ ὃ νεοχμὸν ἀπ’ ἐμέθεν ἐλάβετε τέκοϲ;
ποῦ μοι <νῦν κυρεῖ>;
Τα. Πολυξένην ἔλεξαϲ ἢ τίν’ ἱϲτορεῖϲ;
Εκ. ταύταν· τῶι πάλοϲ ἔζευξεν;
Τα. τύμβωι τέτακται προϲπολεῖν Ἀχιλλέωϲ.
Εκ. οἴμοι ἐγώ· τάφωι πρόϲπολον ἐτεκόμαν.
ἀτὰρ τίϲ ὅδ’ ἢ νόμοϲ ἢ τί
θέϲμιον, ὦ φίλοϲ, Ἑλλάνων;
Τα. εὐδαιμόνιζε παῖδα ϲήν· ἔχει καλῶϲ.
Εκ. τί τόδ’ ἔλακεϲ;
ἆρά μοι ἀέλιον λεύϲϲει;
Τα. ἔχει πότμοϲ νιν, ὥϲτ’ ἀπηλλάχθαι πόνων.
Εκ. τί δ’ ἁ τοῦ χαλκεομήϲτοροϲ Ἕκτοροϲ δάμαρ,
Ἀνδρομάχα τάλαινα; τίν’ ἔχει τύχαν;
Τα. κοίτην ϲφ’ Ἀχιλλέωϲ ἔλαβε παῖϲ ἐξαίρετον.
Εκ. ἐγὼ δὲ τῶι πρόϲπολοϲ ἁ τριτοβάμο-
νοϲ χερὶ δευομένα βάκτρου,
γεραιὸν κάρα;
Τα. Ἰθάκηϲ Ὀδυϲϲεὺϲ ἔλαχ’ ἄναξ δούλην ϲ’ ἔχειν.
Εκ. ἒ ἔ·
ἄραϲϲε κρᾶτα κούριμον, ἕλκ’ ὀνύχεϲϲι
δίπτυχον παρειάν.

255 fort. ἔρωϲ <γ’> | ἐνθέτου Q | κόρηϲ PQ et gB et gE: κούρηϲ V 256 κλάδαϲ Stanley: κληίδαϲ PQ: κλειίδαϲ V 259 αὐτῆ P: -ὴ V: -ὴν Q 260 δ’ ὃ Tyrwhitt: δὲ τὸ VP: δὲ τὸν Q 261 <νῦν κυρεῖ> Diggle 263 ταύτην V 264 ἀχιλέωϲ V 265 οἴμοι VQ: ὤμοι P 266 ἢ prins V: ἦν PQ | τί om. P 268 ἔχειν V^{pc} 270 λεύϲει P^{ac} ut uid. 271 πόνων V et gB: κακῶν PQ 272 ἁ Dindorf: ἡ VPQ | χαλκεομήϲτοροϲ Burges: -μήτοροϲ V: -μίτοροϲ PQ: cf. Hesych. χαλκεομήϲτοροϲ· ἰϲχυόφρονοϲ (Kirchhoff: χαλκεομίϲτωρ· ἰϲχυροφόροϲ cod.) | δάμαρ del. Bothe 273 Ἀνδρομάχα Seidler: -χη VPQ 274 κοίτην ϲφ’ (κοίτην iam Burges) Kovacs: καὶ τήνδ’ VPQ 275 τριτοβάμονοϲ PQ et gB: τριβάμ- VΣ 276 γεραιὸν κάρα Wecklein: γεραιῶ(ι) κάρα(ι) VPQ et gB 278 ϲ’ erasum in P 278 ἒ ἔ VQ: ἔ ἔ P et gB 279 ἄραϲϲα P 280 ὀνύχεϲϲι Aldina: -εϲι VPQ

ἰώ μοί μοι.
μυcαρῶι δολίωι λέλογ-
χα φωτὶ δουλεύειν,
πολεμίωι δίκαc, παρανόμωι δάκει,
ὃc πάντα τἀκεῖθεν ἐνθάδ' <ἀνcτρέφει,
τὰ δ'> ἀντίπαλ' αὖθιc ἐκεῖcε
διπτύχωι γλώccαι,
φίλα τὰ πρότερ' ἄφιλα τιθέμενοc πάλιν.
γοᾶcθέ <μ'>, ὦ Τρωιάδεc·
†βέβακα δύcποτμοc,†
οἴχομαι ἁ τάλαινα, δυcτυχεcτάτωι
προcέπεcον κλήρωι.

Χο. τὸ μὲν cὸν οἶcθα, πότνια· τὰc δ' ἐμὰc τύχαc
τίc ἆρ' Ἀχαιῶν ἢ τίc Ἑλλήνων ἔχει;

Τα. ἴτ', ἐκκομίζειν δεῦρο Καccάνδραν χρεὼν
ὅcον τάχιcτα, δμῶεc, ὡc cτρατηλάτηι
ἐc χεῖρα δούc νιν εἶτα τὰc εἰληγμέναc
καὶ τοῖcιν ἄλλοιc αἰχμαλωτίδων ἄγω.
ἔα· τί πεύκηc ἔνδον αἴθεται cέλαc;
πιμπρᾶcιν—ἢ τί δρῶcι—Τρωιάδεc μυχούc,
ὡc ἐξάγεcθαι τῆcδε μέλλουcαι χθονὸc
πρὸc Ἄργοc, αὑτῶν τ' ἐκπυροῦcι cώματα
θανεῖν θέλουcαι; κάρτα τοι τοὐλεύθερον
ἐν τοῖc τοιούτοιc δυcλόφωc φέρει κακά.
ἄνοιγ' ἄνοιγε, μὴ τὸ ταῖcδε πρόcφορον
ἐχθρὸν δ' Ἀχαιοῖc εἰc ἔμ' αἰτίαν βάληι.

Εκ. οὐκ ἔcτιν, οὐ πιμπρᾶcιν, ἀλλὰ παῖc ἐμὴ
μαινὰc θοάζει δεῦρο Καccάνδρα δρόμωι.

ΚΑϹϹΑΝΔΡΑ

ἄνεχε, πάρεχε, φῶc φέρε· cέβω φλέγω— str.
ἰδοὺ ἰδού—

282 λέλογχα VQ: λέγ- P: λέλοχα gE 285 ὃc] ἓ ἕ gB | τἀκεῖθεν V et gB: τἀκεῖc' PQΣ: κεῖθεν Σ^{i} 285–6 <ἀνcτρέφει, τὰ δ'> post Wilamowitz (<cτρέφει, τὰ δ'>) Diggle 288 φίλα…ἄφιλα Seidler: ἄφιλα…φίλα VPQ et gB | πάλιν praeeunte Seidler Wilamowitz: πάντων VPQ 289 γοᾶcθέ <μ'> Hartung | Τρωιάδεc Hartung: τρ- με VPQ 291 τάλαινα V et gE: τάλαινα ἃ PQ | προcέπεcα PQ (προcπ- Q) et gE 293 ἆρ' Aldina: ἄρ' VPQ 296 χεῖραc VQ | δούc νιν PQ: δῶμεν V | εἰληγμέναc Heath: εἰλεγ- VPQ (ἠλ- Q) Σ^{l}: utrumque Σ^{i} 297 αἰχμαλωτίδαc λέγω PQ 298 αἴθεται PQ: ἵcταται V 300 μέλλουcαι PQΣ: -cι V 301 αὑτῶν QΣ^{i} αὐ- VPΣ^{l} 308 φέρε Bothe ex Σ (uide etiam Σ Ar. Au. 1720): φέρω VPQ et Σ Ar. Vesp. 1326 309 ἰδοὺ ἰδού quae post ἄναξ 310 habent VPQ huc trai. Hermann

λαμπάϲι †τόδ'† ἱερόν. ὦ Ὑμέναι' ἄναξ,
μακάριοϲ ὁ γαμέταϲ·
μακαρία δ' ἐγὼ βαϲιλικοῖϲ λέκτροιϲ
κατ' Ἄργοϲ ἁ γαμουμένα.
Ὑμὴν ὦ Ὑμέναι' ἄναξ·
ἐπεὶ ϲύ, μᾶτερ, †ἐπὶ δάκρυϲι καὶ†
γόοιϲι τὸν θανόντα πατέρα †πατρίδα τε†
φίλαν καταϲτένουϲ' ἔχειϲ,
ἐγὼ δ' ἐπὶ γάμοιϲ ἐμοῖϲ
ἀναφλέγω πυρὸϲ φῶϲ
ἐϲ αὐγάν, ἐϲ αἴγλαν,
διδοῦϲ', ὦ Ὑμέναιε, ϲοί,
διδοῦϲ', ὦ Ἑκάτα, φάοϲ,
παρθένων ἐπὶ λέκτροιϲ
ἇι νόμοϲ ἔχει.

πάλλε πόδ' αἰθέριον <*ἄναγ'*> *ἄναγε χορόν—* ant.
εὐὰν εὐοῖ—
ὡϲ ἐπὶ πατρὸϲ ἐμοῦ μακαριωτάταιϲ
τύχαιϲ· ὁ χορὸϲ ὅϲιοϲ.
ἄγε ϲὺ Φοῖβέ νιν· κατὰ ϲὸν ἐν δάφναιϲ
ἀνάκτορον θυηπολῶ.
Ὑμὴν ὦ Ὑμέναι' Ὑμήν.
χόρευε, μᾶτερ, χόρευμ' ἄναγε, πόδα ϲόν
ἕλιϲϲε τᾶιδ' ἐκεῖϲε, μετ' ἐμέθεν ποδῶν
φέρουϲα φιλτάταν βάϲιν.
βόαϲον ὑμέναιον ὦ

310 *ὦ* PQ: *ὦ ὑμὴν* VΣ^{1} 312 *βαϲιλικοῖϲ λέκτροιϲ* om. PQ 314 *ἄναξ*] *Ὑμήν* Hermann cl. 331 315 fort. *μᾶτερ* <*τορῶϲ*> [*ἐπὶ*] *δάκρυϲί* <*τε*> *καὶ* 316 *γόοιϲι τε* Q | *θανέντα* V | *πατρίδα τε*] fort. *πατρίδα τ' ε*<*ὖ*> 318 *φιλίαν* Q 319 *δ'* PQ: *τόδε* V 321 *ἐϲ* prius] *εἰϲ* PQ 322 *διδοῦϲ'* om. PQ | *ϲοι* PQΣ: *ϲύ* V | post h. u. *παρθένων* (-*ω*(*ι*) PQ) *ἐπὶ λέκτροιϲ* e 324 deriuata habent VPQ 323 *φάουϲ* PQ 324 *παρθένων ἐπὶ λέκτροιϲ* (quae habet post 322) om. V | *ἆ*(*ι*) PQΣ^{l}: *ἃ* V 325 *πάλαι* P | <*ἄναγ'*> Hermann | *ἄναγε* PQ: *ἄνεχε* V 326 *εὖ ἂν εὖ οἶ* (uel *οἶ*) VPQΣ 328 *ὅϲιοϲ* <*ὅϲιοϲ*> Hermann 328 *ϲὺ* PQ: *ϲοι* V 329 *νιν* Musgrave: *νῦν* VPQ 330 *θυηπόλωι* ut uid. Σ^{i}, sicut coni. Musgrave 331 *ὑμέναι'* P^{ac} ut uid.: *ὑμὴν* VP^{pc}Q 332 *χόρευμ' ἄναγε, πόδα ϲὸν* Diggle: *χόρευ'* (-*ευε* Q) *ἄναγε πόδα ϲὸν* PQ: *ἀναγέλαϲον* V 333 *τᾶδ'* Q: *τάδ'* VP | post *ποδῶν* habuit *πόδα ϲὸν* Q^{ac} 335 *βόαϲον* Diggle: *βοάϲατε τὸν* V: *βοάϲατ'* (*βάϲατ'* P) *εὖ τὸν* PQ

μακαρίαις ἀοιδαῖς
ἰαχαῖς τε νύμφαν.
ἴτ’, ὦ καλλίπεπλοι Φρυγῶν
κόραι, μέλπετ’ ἐμῶν γάμων
τὸν πεπρωμένον εὐνᾶι
πόςιν ἐμέθεν.

Χο. *βαςίλεια, βακχεύουςαν οὐ λήψηι κόρην,*
μὴ κοῦφον ἄρηι βῆμ’ ἐς Ἀργείων ςτρατόν;

Εκ. *Ἥφαιςτε, δαιδουχεῖς μὲν ἐν γάμοις βροτῶν,*
ἀτὰρ λυγράν γε τήνδ’ ἀναιθύςςεις φλόγα
ἔξω τε μεγάλων ἐλπίδων. οἴμοι, τέκνον,
ὡς οὐχ ὑπ’ αἰχμῆς <*ς’*> *οὐδ’ ὑπ’ Ἀργείου δορὸς*
γάμους γαμεῖςθαι τούςδ’ ἐδόξαζόν ποτε.
παράδος ἐμοὶ φῶς· οὐ γὰρ ὀρθὰ πυρφορεῖς
μαινὰς θοάζους’, οὐδέ ς’ αἱ τύχαι, τέκνον,
ςεςωφρονίκας’ ἀλλ’ ἔτ’ ἐν ταὐτῶι μένεις.
ἐςφέρετε πεύκας, δάκρυά τ’ ἀνταλλάξατε
τοῖς τῆςδε μέλεςι, Τρωιάδες, γαμηλίοις.

Κα. *μῆτερ, πύκαζε κρᾶτ’ ἐμὸν νικηφόρον*
καὶ χαῖρε τοῖς ἐμοῖςι βαςιλικοῖς γάμοις·
καὶ πέμπε, κἂν μὴ τἀμά ςοι πρόθυμά γ’ ἦι,
ὤθει βιαίως· εἰ γὰρ ἔςτι Λοξίας,
Ἑλένης γαμεῖ με δυςχερέςτερον γάμον
ὁ τῶν Ἀχαιῶν κλεινὸς Ἀγαμέμνων ἄναξ.
κτενῶ γὰρ αὐτὸν κἀντιπορθήςω δόμους
ποινὰς ἀδελφῶν καὶ πατρὸς λαβοῦς’ ἐμοῦ.
ἀλλ’ αὔτ’ ἐάςω· πέλεκυν οὐχ ὑμνήςομεν,
ὃς ἐς τράχηλον τὸν ἐμὸν εἶςι χἀτέρων,
μητροκτόνους τ’ ἀγῶνας, οὓς οὑμοὶ γάμοι
θήςουςιν, οἴκων τ’ Ἀτρέως ἀνάςταςιν.

338 *ὦ* PQ: *ἔξω* V 339 *ἐμῶν γάμων* VP: *-ὸν -ον* Q: *ἐμοῖς γάμοις* Diggle | *μέλπετέ μοι γάμων* Willink 341 *Χο.* VP: om. Q: *Τα.* P. Oxy. 4564, 'quidam' apud *Σ* 342 *ἄρηι* Wecklein: *αἴρη(ι)* PQ: *αἶρε* V 344 *λυγράν* V*Π*: *λυπράν* Q: *πικράν* P | *γε* PQ: *τε* V | *ἀναιθύςεις* P 345 *τέκνων* V 346 <*ς’*> Musgrave 347 *τοῦδ’* V 350 *ςεςωφρονίκας’* Σ^{i} (*ςώφρονα πεποιήκαςι*): *ἐςωφρονήκας’* VPQΣ^{l}: *ςεςωφρόνηκας* Nauck: *-ήκας* gE 351 *δάκρυά* PQ*Σ*: *δάκρυςί* VΣ^{l} | *ἀνταλάςςετε* VPQΣ^{l}: *-άξατε* *Σ* 352 *τῆςδε* VQ: *τοῖςδε* P 355 *πέμπετε* PQ | *κἂν* PQ: *καὶ* V | *ςοι* om. Q 356 *βιαίως* PQ: *αἰςίας* V | *εἰ* VQ: *οὐ* P 357 *δυςτυχέςτερον* PQ 359 *-ω δόμους* om. Q 361 *ἀλλ’ αὔτ’* Musgrave: *ἄλλα* (*ἄλλά* V) *τ’* VPQΣ^{l}: *ἀλλ’ αἴςχρ’* Parmentier | *ὑμνήςομαι* PQ 362 *τῶν ἐμῶν* Q 363 *μὴ προκτόνους* Q | *οὑμοὶ* P: *οἱ ’μοὶ* Q: *οὐμοὶ* V

πόλιν δὲ δείξω τήνδε μακαριωτέραν
ἢ τοὺϲ Ἀχαιούϲ, ἔνθεοϲ μέν, ἀλλ' ὅμωϲ
τοϲόνδε γ' ἔξω ϲτήϲομαι βακχευμάτων·
οἳ διὰ μίαν γυναῖκα καὶ μίαν Κύπριν
θηρῶντεϲ Ἑλένην μυρίουϲ ἀπώλεϲαν.
ὁ δὲ ϲτρατηγὸϲ ὁ ϲοφὸϲ ἐχθίϲτων ὕπερ
τὰ φίλτατ' ὤλεϲ', ἡδονὰϲ τὰϲ οἴκοθεν
τέκνων ἀδελφῶι δοὺϲ γυναικὸϲ οὕνεκα,
καὶ ταῦθ' ἑκούϲηϲ κοὐ βίαι λεληιϲμένηϲ.
ἐπεὶ δ' ἐπ' ἀκτὰϲ ἤλυθον Ϲκαμανδρίουϲ,
ἔθνηιϲκον, οὐ γῆϲ ὅρι' ἀποϲτερούμενοι
οὐδ' ὑψίπυργον πατρίδ'· οὓϲ δ' Ἄρηϲ ἕλοι,
οὐ παῖδαϲ εἶδον, οὐ δάμαρτοϲ ἐν χεροῖν
πέπλοιϲ ϲυνεϲτάληϲαν, ἐν ξένηι δὲ γῆι
κεῖνται. τὰ δ' οἴκοι τοῖϲδ' ὅμοι' ἐγίγνετο·
< >
χῆραί τ' ἔθνηιϲκον, οἱ δ' ἄπαιδεϲ ἐν δόμοιϲ
ἄλλωϲ τέκν' ἐκθρέψαντεϲ· οὐδὲ πρὸϲ τάφουϲ
ἔϲθ' ὅϲτιϲ αὐτοῖϲ αἷμα γῆι δωρήϲεται.
ἦ τοῦδ' ἐπαίνου τὸ ϲτράτευμ' ἐπάξιον.
[ϲιγᾶν ἄμεινον τἀιϲχρά, μηδὲ μοῦϲά μοι
γένοιτ' ἀοιδὸϲ ἥτιϲ ὑμνήϲει κακά.]
Τρῶεϲ δὲ πρῶτον μέν, τὸ κάλλιϲτον κλέοϲ,
ὑπὲρ πάτραϲ ἔθνηιϲκον· οὓϲ δ' ἕλοι δόρυ,
νεκροί γ' ἐϲ οἴκουϲ φερόμενοι φίλων ὕπο
ἐν γῆι πατρώιαι περιβολὰϲ εἶχον χθονόϲ,
χερϲὶν περιϲταλέντεϲ ὧν ἐχρῆν ὕπο·
ὅϲοι δὲ μὴ θάνοιεν ἐν μάχηι Φρυγῶν,
ἀεὶ κατ' ἦμαρ ϲὺν δάμαρτι καὶ τέκνοιϲ
ᾤκουν, Ἀχαιοῖϲ ὧν ἀπῆϲαν ἡδοναί.
τὰ δ' Ἕκτορόϲ ϲοι λύπρ' ἄκουϲον ὡϲ ἔχει·

365–83 del. Wilamowitz 365 τε Q 367 τοϲόνδε δ' ἐκτὸϲ Σ Or. 268 368 κύπριν V et gE: πόλιν PQ 376 ὑψίπυργον πατρίδ' Lenting: -γου -ίδοϲ VPQ | ἕλοι V^{sl}PQ: -η V 377 παῖδεϲ PQ 378 γῆ VQ: τῆ P 379 κεῖται Q | ἐγίνετο VQ: ἐγέν- P 380 ante h. u. aliquid excidisse putat Matthiae, <γυναῖκεϲ ἀνδρῶν ἐϲτεροῦντ' εὐκαρδίων> suppl. Kovacs 381 ἄλλωϲ Tyrwhitt: -οιϲ VPQ | ἐθρέψαντεϲ P| τάφουϲ VΣ^{1}: -οιϲ PQ 382 αὐτοῖϲ V: αὐτῶν PQ 383 ἦ Va: ἧι Q: ἢ VP | ἦ τοῦδ'] τοιοῦδ' Dobree | u. del. Wilamowitz 384–5 (quos habet gE) del. Reichenberger, post 364 trai. Weil 384 ϲιγᾶν <δ'> Bothe 386 πρῶτα Q 387 ἕλοι δόρυ PQ: ἄρηϲ ἕλοι V e 376 388 γ' V: δ' PQ | u. del. Dobree 394 λύτρ' Q

δόξας ἀνὴρ ἄριστος οἴχεται θανών,
καὶ τοῦτ' Ἀχαιῶν ἴξις ἐξεργάζεται·
εἰ δ' ἦσαν οἴκοι, χρηστὸς ἔλαθεν ἂν γεγώς.
Πάρις δ' ἔγημε τὴν Διός· γήμας δὲ μή,
σιγώμενον τὸ κῆδος εἶχ' ἂν ἐν δόμοις.
φεύγειν μὲν οὖν χρὴ πόλεμον ὅστις εὖ φρονεῖ·
εἰ δ' ἐς τόδ' ἔλθοι, στέφανος οὐκ αἰσχρὸς πόλει
καλῶς ὀλέσθαι, μὴ καλῶς δὲ δυσκλεές.
ὧν οὕνεκ' οὐ χρή, μῆτερ, οἰκτίρειν σε γῆν,
οὐ τἀμὰ λέκτρα· τοὺς γὰρ ἐχθίστους ἐμοὶ
καὶ σοὶ γάμοισι τοῖς ἐμοῖς διαφθερῶ.

Χο. *ὡς ἡδέως κακοῖσιν οἰκείοις γελᾶις*
μέλπεις θ' ἃ μέλπους' οὐ σαφῆ δείξεις ἴσως.

Τα. *εἰ μή σ' Ἀπόλλων ἐξεβάκχευσεν φρένας,*
οὔ τἂν ἀμισθὶ τοὺς ἐμοὺς στρατηλάτας
τοιαῖσδε φήμαις ἐξέπεμπες ἂν χθονός.
ἀτὰρ τὰ σεμνὰ καὶ δοκήμασιν σοφὰ
οὐδέν τι κρείσσω τῶν τὸ μηδὲν ἦν ἄρα.
ὁ γὰρ μέγιστος τῶν Πανελλήνων ἄναξ,
Ἀτρέως φίλος παῖς, τῆσδ' ἔρωτ' ἐξαίρετον
μαινάδος ὑπέστη· καὶ πένης μέν εἰμ' ἐγώ,
ἀτὰρ λέχος γε τῆσδ' ἂν οὐκ ἠιτησάμην.
καὶ σοῦ μέν (οὐ γὰρ ἀρτίας ἔχεις φρένας)
Ἀργεῖ' ὀνείδη καὶ Φρυγῶν ἐπαινέσεις
ἀνέμοις φέρεσθαι παραδίδωμ'· ἕπου δέ μοι
πρὸς ναῦς, καλὸν νύμφευμα τῶι στρατηλάτηι.
σὺ δ', ἡνίκ' ἄν σε Λαρτίου χρήιζηι τόκος
ἄγειν, ἕπεσθαι· σώφρονος δ' ἔσηι λάτρις
γυναικός, ὥς φασ' οἱ μολόντες Ἴλιον.

395 *δόξας*] *φανεὶς* Chr. Pat. 1656 396 *τοῦτ'* PQ: *ταῦτ'* V et Chr. Pat. 1652 | *ἴξις* Va^{pc}: *ἴξις* VPQΣ^{1}: *ἡ 'ρξις* uoluit Σ^{γρ} (*ἧρξις*) item *ἡ ἔρξις* Q^{γρ}: *ἶξις* Hesych. s.u. sine nom. auct.: *ἧξις* Bekker Anecd. 1.99.4 397 *ἔλαθεν ἂν γεγώς* VΣ^{1}: *ὢν ἐλάνθανεν* PQ et Chr. Pat. 1658, unde *ὢν ἐλάνθαν' ἄν* Burges, Schaefer 398 *δ'* PQ: *τ'* VΣ^{1} 399 *κῆδος* PQ: *κῦδος* VΣ^{1} et Chr. Pat. 1660 | *εἶχ' ἂν* Burges: *εἶχεν* PQ et Chr. Pat.: *εἶδεν* V: *ἔσχε* Σ 400 *οὖν* om. V | *πόλεμορ* Q^{ac} | *φρονεῖν* Q^{ac} 401 *ἔστ' ὅδ'* Q | *πόλει*] *πέλει* Nauck 402 *δυσκλεής* V et gE 404 *οὐ* V: *ἢ* PQ 407 *θ'* VPΣ^{1} et gE: *δ'* Q 408 *ἐξεβάκχευσε* VQ: *-χευε* PΣ^{1} 409 *οὔ τἂν* Lenting: *οὐκ ἂν* V: *οὔκουν* P: *οὐκοῦν* Q 412 *κρείσσων* P | *ἄρα* V^{pc} (*ἄγαν* V^{ac}) P: *ἆρα* Q 416 *ἠιτησάμην* Naber: *ἐκτησ-* VPQ 417 *σοῦ* Hermann: *σοὶ* VPQ (*σοι* Q) 421 *ἡνίκ' ἄν* PQ: *ἢν κάν* V | *λαερτίου* PQ | *χρήζηι* Q (*-η* Va): *-ει* V: *-οι* P 422 *ἕπεσθαι* V: *φέρεσθαι* PQ (*ἕπου* Q^{sl})

Κα. [ἦ δεινὸϲ ὁ λάτριϲ. τί ποτ᾽ ἔχουϲι τοὔνομα
κήρυκεϲ, ἓν ἀπέχθημα πάγκοινον βροτοῖϲ,
οἱ περὶ τυράννουϲ καὶ πόλειϲ ὑπηρέται;]
ϲὺ τὴν ἐμὴν φὴιϲ μητέρ᾽ εἰϲ Ὀδυϲϲέωϲ
ἥξειν μέλαθρα· ποῦ δ᾽ Ἀπόλλωνοϲ λόγοι,
οἵ φαϲιν αὐτὴν εἰϲ ἔμ᾽ ἡρμηνευμένοι
αὐτοῦ θανεῖϲθαι; τἄλλα δ᾽ οὐκ ὀνειδιῶ.
δύϲτηνοϲ, οὐκ οἶδ᾽ οἷά νιν μένει παθεῖν·
ὡϲ χρυϲὸϲ αὐτῶι τἀμὰ καὶ Φρυγῶν κακὰ
δόξει ποτ᾽ εἶναι. δέκα γὰρ ἀντλήϲαϲ ἔτη
πρὸϲ τοῖϲιν ἐνθάδ᾽ ἵξεται μόνοϲ πάτραν
οὗ δὴ <
> ϲτενὸν δίαυλον ὤικιϲται πέτραϲ,
δεινὴ Χάρυβδιϲ, ὠμοβρώϲ τ᾽ ὀρειβάτηϲ
Κύκλωψ, Λιγυϲτίϲ θ᾽—ἡ ϲυῶν μορφώτρια—
Κίρκη, θαλάϲϲηϲ θ᾽ ἁλμυρᾶϲ ναυάγια,
λωτοῦ τ᾽ ἔρωτεϲ, Ἡλίου θ᾽ ἁγναὶ βόεϲ,
αἳ †ϲάρκα φωνήεϲϲαν ἥϲουϲίν† ποτε
πικρὰν Ὀδυϲϲεῖ γῆρυν. ὡϲ δὲ ϲυντέμω,
ζῶν εἶϲ᾽ ἐϲ Ἅιδου κἀκφυγὼν λίμνηϲ ὕδωρ
κάκ᾽ ἐν δόμοιϲι μυρί᾽ εὑρήϲει μολών.
ἀλλὰ γὰρ τί τοὺϲ Ὀδυϲϲέωϲ ἐξακοντίζω πόνουϲ;
ϲτεῖχ᾽ ὅπωϲ τάχιϲτ᾽ ἐϲ Ἅιδου· νυμφίωι γημώμεθα.
ἦ κακὸϲ κακῶϲ ταφήϲηι νυκτόϲ, οὐκ ἐν ἡμέραι,
ὦ δοκῶν ϲεμνόν τι πράϲϲειν, Δαναϊδῶν ἀρχηγέτα.
κἀμέ τοι νεκρὸν φάραγγεϲ γυμνάδ᾽ ἐκβεβλημένην
ὕδατι χειμάρρωι ῥέουϲαι νυμφίου πέλαϲ τάφου

424–6 ut huic loco alienos suspectos habuit Friedrich, secl. Kovacs 424 ἦ Va: ἦι Q: ἢ VP | τοὔνομα] τἄμα Q 429 ηὑρμηνευμένοι P 433 ἀντλήϲαϲ PQ: ἐκπλήϲαϲ V 434 ἐνθάθ᾽ V | ἥξεται P^{ac} ut uid. | post h. u. lac. indic. Heath, post οὗ δὴ Kovacs 435 ὤκιϲτα V^{ac} ut uid. (ὤκ*ϲτα V^{pc}) | πέραϲ P 436 ὠμοβρώϲ τ᾽ ὀρειβάτηϲ Scaliger: ὠμοβροϲτορ- P: ὠμόβοροϲ τ᾽ ὀρ- Q: ὠμόφρων ἐπιϲτάτηϲ VQ^{γρ}: cf. Hesych. (iv.276 Schmidt) Χάρβυδιϲ ὠμόβροτοϲ 437 μορφάτρια PQ 438 δ᾽ PQ | ἁλμυρᾶϲ Va: -μηρᾶϲ V: -μυρὰ PQ 439 τ᾽ ἔρωτεϲ VQ^{sl} et Hesych. (ii.617 Latte): θ᾽ ἕρ- P: θ᾽ ἔρ- Q | ἰλίου P 440 ϲάρκα φωνήεϲϲαν V (-εϲαν) P (fort. φον- P^{ac}) Q: ϲαρξὶ φοινίαιϲιν Bothe | ἕξουϲίν Kirchhoff: sed fort. praestat ante ἥϲουϲίν lac. indicare 441 δὲ V: δὴ PQ | ϲυντεμῶ PQ 442 εἶϲ᾽ Q: εἶϲ᾽ P: om. V | ἅδην V^{pc} 444 ὀδυϲέωϲ ἐξαντίζω V 445 ἐϲ] ἐν Heiland | γημώμεθα PQ: γαμ- V: γαμούμεθα Porson 446 ἦ P: ἦι Q: ἢ V 447 πράττειν P | ἀρχηγέτα V: ϲτρατηλάτα PQ (-α cum ι subscr. Q) 448 τι Q | νεκρῶν VΣ^{1} | γυμνάδ᾽ V: -νάν θ᾽ P: -νάθ᾽ Q

θηρcὶ δώcουcιν δάcαcθαι, τὴν Ἀπόλλωνος λάτριν.
ὦ cτέφη τοῦ φιλτάτου μοι θεῶν, ἀγάλματ' εὔια,
χαίρετ'· ἐκλέλοιφ' ἑορτάς, αἷc πάροιθ' ἠγαλλόμην.
ἴτ' ἀπ' ἐμοῦ χρωτὸc cπαραγμοῖc, ὡc ἔτ' οὖc' ἁγνὴ χρόα
δῶ θοαῖc αὔραιc φέρεcθαί coι τάδ', ὦ μαντεῖ' ἄναξ.
ποῦ cκάφος τὸ τοῦ cτρατηγοῦ; ποῖ πόδ' ἐμβαίνειν με χρή;
οὐκέτ' ἂν φθάνοιc ἂν αὔραν ἱcτίοιc καραδοκῶν,
ὡc μίαν τριῶν Ἐρινύων τῆcδέ μ' ἐξάξων χθονόc.
χαῖρέ μοι, μῆτερ· δακρύcηιc μηδέν· ὦ φίλη πατρίc,
οἵ τε γῆc ἔνερθ' ἀδελφοὶ χὠ τεκὼν ἡμᾶc πατήρ,
οὐ μακρὰν δέξεcθέ μ'· ἥξω δ' ἐc νεκροὺc νικηφόροc
καὶ δόμουc πέρcαc' Ἀτρειδῶν, ὧν ἀπωλόμεcθ' ὕπο.
Χο. *Ἑκάβηc γεραιᾶc φύλακεc, οὐ δεδόρκατε*
δέcποιναν ὡc ἄναυδοc ἐκτάδην πίτνει;
οὐκ ἀντιλήψεcθ'; ἦ μεθήcετ', ὦ κακαί,
γραῖαν πεcοῦcαν; αἴρετ' εἰc ὀρθὸν δέμαc.
Εκ. *ἐᾶτέ μ' (οὔτοι φίλα τὰ μὴ φίλ', ὦ κόραι)*
κεῖcθαι πεcοῦcαν· πτωμάτων γὰρ ἄξια
πάcχω τε καὶ πέπονθα κἄτι πείcομαι.
ὦ θεοί· κακοὺc μὲν ἀνακαλῶ τοὺc cυμμάχουc,
ὅμωc δ' ἔχει τι cχῆμα κικλήcκειν θεούc,
ὅταν τιc ἡμῶν δυcτυχῆ λάβηι τύχην.
πρῶτον μὲν οὖν μοι τἀγάθ' ἐξᾶιcαι φίλον·
τοῖc γὰρ κακοῖcι πλείον' οἶκτον ἐμβαλῶ.
ἦ μὲν τύραννοc κἀc τύραννν' ἐγημάμην,
κἀνταῦθ' ἀριcτεύοντ' ἐγεινάμην τέκνα,

452 *ἐκλέλοιπα δ'* V 454 *αὔρεc* P^{ac} | *coὶ* Page (noluit Burges): *coῦ* Burges 455 *ποῦ* PQ: *ποῖ* V | *τὸ τῶν Ἀτρειδῶν* Cic. ad Att. 7.3.5 | *ποῖ* Q: *ποί* P: *ποῦ* V | *πόδ'* Elmsley: *ποτ'* VPQ | *με* om. P 456 *οὐκέτ'* spat. uac. relicto om. Q, suppl. q 457 *τρωιῶν* Q | *Ἐρινύων* Burges: cf. *IT* 931, 970, 1456: *Ἐρινὺν* VΣ^{l}: *-νῦν* P: *-ννῦν* Q | *ἐξάζων* Q 458 *δακρύcῃ* V 459 *χ' ὡ* Q: *χ' ὁ* V: *καὶ ὁ* P 460 *μακρα* V | *ἥξω* PQ^{pc} (*ἄξω* Q^{ac} ut uid.): *ἥκω* V 461 *ἀπολλόμεθα* P^{ac} 463 *ἐκτάδην* Verrall: *εἰc ἅδην* P: *εἰc ἅιδου* Q: *ἐc πέδον* V | *πιτνεῖ* VPQ 464 *ἀντιλήψεcθ'* PQ: *-ψετ'* V | *ἦ* Musgrave: *ἢ* VPQ | *μεθήcετ'* V: *-cεcθ'* PQ 465 *ἔρρετ'* P^{ac} ut uid. | *δέμαc* V: *πάλιν* PQ 466 *οὔτι* fere codd. Chr. Pat. 1034 (~gB) 468 *καὶ ἔτι* P 472 *φίλον*] *δέον* Chr. Pat. 535 (~Apsines p. 327 Hammer) 473 *τοῖ γὰρ* V | *κοῖcι* Q 474 *ἦ μὲν τύραννοc* Elmsley: *ἦμεν τύραννοι* VPQ: *ἤμην τύραννοc* Apsines p. 311: *ἤμην (ἄνανδροc)* Chr. Pat. 537: ad *μὲν* uide Denniston, GP 382–3 | *τύραννν'* VQ: *τύραννοc* P^{ac} ut uid. (*-ον* P^{pc}): *-ου* et *-ίαν* codd. Aps. 475 *ἐγεινάμην* V et Aps. et Chr. Pat. 558: *-νόμην* PQ

οὐκ ἀριθμὸν ἄλλωϲ ἀλλ' ὑπερτάτουϲ Φρυγῶν·
οὐ τοιάδ' οὔθ' Ἑλληνὶϲ οὐδὲ βάρβαροϲ
γυνὴ τεκοῦϲα κομπάϲειεν ἄν ποτε.
κἀκεῖνά τ' εἶδον δορὶ πεϲόνθ' Ἑλληνικῶι
τρίχαϲ τ' ἐτμήθην τάϲδε πρὸϲ τύμβοιϲ νεκρῶν,
καὶ τὸν φυτουργὸν Πρίαμον οὐκ ἄλλων πάρα
κλυοῦϲ' ἔκλαυϲα, τοῖϲδε δ' εἶδον ὄμμαϲιν
αὐτὴ καταϲφαγέντ' ἐφ' ἑρκείωι πυρᾶι,
πόλιν θ' ἁλοῦϲαν. ἃϲ δ' ἔθρεψα παρθένουϲ
ἐϲ ἀξίωμα νυμφίων ἐξαίρετον,
ἄλλοιϲι θρέψαϲ' ἐκ χερῶν ἀφῃρέθην.
κοὔτ' ἐξ ἐκείνων ἐλπὶϲ ὡϲ ὀφθήϲομαι
αὐτή τ' ἐκείναϲ οὐκέτ' ὄψομαί ποτε.
τὸ λοίϲθιον δέ, θριγκὸϲ ἀθλίων κακῶν,
δούλη γυνὴ γραῦϲ Ἑλλάδ' εἰϲαφίξομαι.
ἃ δ' ἐϲτὶ γήραι τῶιδ' ἀϲυμφορώτατα,
τούτοιϲ με προϲθήϲουϲιν, ἢ θυρῶν λάτριν
κλῇδαϲ φυλάϲϲειν, τὴν τεκοῦϲαν Ἕκτορα,
ἢ ϲιτοποιεῖν, κἀν πέδωι κοίταϲ ἔχειν
ῥυϲοῖϲι νώτοιϲ, βαϲιλικῶν ἐκ δεμνίων,
τρυχηρὰ περὶ τρυχηρὸν εἱμένην χρόα
πέπλων λακίϲματ', ἀδόκιμ' ὀλβίοιϲ ἔχειν.
οἳ 'γὼ τάλαινα, διὰ γάμον μιᾶϲ ἕνα
γυναικὸϲ οἵων ἔτυχον ὧν τε τεύξομαι.
  ὦ τέκνον, ὦ ϲύμβακχε Καϲϲάνδρα θεοῖϲ,
οἵαιϲ ἔλυϲαϲ ϲυμφοραῖϲ ἅγνευμα ϲόν.
ϲύ τ', ὦ τάλαινα, ποῦ ποτ' εἶ, Πολυξένη;
ὡϲ οὔτε μ' ἄρϲην οὔτε θήλεια ϲπορὰ
πολλῶν γενομένων τὴν τάλαιναν ὠφελεῖ.

476 *ἀλλ'* om. V   477 *τοιάδ' οὔθ'* Weil: *Τρωιὰϲ οὐδ'* VPQ   479 *καὶ ταῦτα ἐπεῖδον* (uel *ἴδον*) Aps.: fort. *κἀκεῖν' ἐϲεῖδον*   480 δ' V | *τύμβον* PQ | u. om. Aps. (qui 472–9 et 481–3 citat)   482 *κλυοῦϲα* West: *κλύουϲα* VPQ | *τοῖϲδε δ'* V: *τοῖϲδέ γ'* Q: *τοῖϲδ'* P | *ἤκουον ἀλλὰ τοῖϲδ' ἐπεῖδον* Aps. 483 *ἑρκείω* p: *-ίω(ι)* V (*ἐφερκίω*) Q et Aps. (*-ίου Διὸϲ* pars codd.): *-ίο* P ut uid. 484 *θ' ἁλοῦϲαν* V: *θανοῦϲαν* PQ   485 *νυμφίον* V   486 *χειρῶν* VQ 487 *ὀφθήϲομαι* VP: *ἀφιγμέναι* Q   489 *θριγγὸϲ* P | *ἔϲτι τόδε* in fine add. gB   490 *Ἑλλάδ'* om. PQ   491 *τῶνδε ϲυμφορ-* P   493 *κλῇδαϲ* P^pc: *κληίδαϲ* P^ac Q: *-είδαϲ* V | *φυλάττειν* V   494 *καὶ* P | *π*δω* P (*πέδω* p) 496 *τρυχηλὸν* PQ | *εἱμένη* PQ   498 *οἵ 'γὼ* Q: *οἳ ἐγὼ* P: *οἶ' ἐγὼ* V | *γάμων* V et gE | *μιᾶϲ* om. gE   499 *ὧν*] *ἔτι* Broadhead   500 *ϲὺ βάκχε* P | *καϲϲάνδρα* pQ: *καϲά-* VP   504 *γινομένων* Q

τί δῆτά μ᾽ ὀρθοῦτ᾽; ἐλπίδων ποίων ὕπο;
ἄγετε τὸν ἁβρὸν δή ποτ᾽ ἐν Τροίαι πόδα,
νῦν δ᾽ ὄντα δοῦλον, cτιβάδα πρὸc χαμαιπετῆ
πέτρινά τε δέμνι᾽, ὡc πεcοῦc᾽ ἀποφθαρῶ
δακρύοιc καταξανθεῖcα. τῶν δ᾽ εὐδαιμόνων
μηδένα νομίζετ᾽ εὐτυχεῖν, πρὶν ἂν θάνηι.

Χο. ἀμφί μοι Ἴλιον, ὦ str.
μοῦcα καινῶν ὕμνων,
ἆιcον cὺν δακρύοιc ὠιδὰν ἐπικήδειον·
νῦν γὰρ μέλοc ἐc Τροίαν ἰαχήcω,
τετραβάμονοc ὡc ὑπ᾽ ἀπήναc
Ἀργείων ὀλόμαν τάλαινα δοριάλωτοc,
ὅτ᾽ ἔλιπον ἵππον οὐράνια
βρέμοντα χρυcοφάλαρον ἔνο-
πλον ἐν πύλαιc Ἀχαιοί·
ἀνὰ δ᾽ ἐβόαcεν λεὼc
Τρωϊάδοc ἀπὸ πέτραc cταθείc·
Ἴτ᾽, ὦ πεπαυμένοι πόνων,
τόδ᾽ ἱερὸν ἀνάγετε ξόανον
Ἰλιάδι Διογενεῖ κόραι.
τίc οὐκ ἔβα νεανίδων,
τίc οὐ γεραιὸc ἐκ δόμων;
κεχαρμένοι δ᾽ ἀοιδαῖc
δόλιον ἔcχον ἄταν.

πᾶcα δὲ γέννα Φρυγῶν ant.
πρὸc πύλαc ὡρμάθη,
πεύκαν οὐρεΐαν, ξεcτὸν λόχον Ἀργείων
καὶ Δαρδανίαc ἄταν, θεᾶι δώcων,
χάριν ἄζυγοc ἀμβροτοπώλου·

506 ἁβρὸν Q: ἀ- VpΣ: αὖρον P 507 χαμερπτῆ V 508 δέμνι᾽ Dobree: κρήδεμν᾽ VPQ | ἀποφθαρῶ Vp: -φαρῶ P: -φθερῶ Q 510 θάνοι P[ac] 513 ἆιcον cὺν Burges (cὺν) et Bothe: ἄειcον ἐν VPQ | ἐπικήδειον Σ: ἐπιτήδ- VPQ 515 ἰcχήcω P[ac]Q 516 ἀπήνηc PQ 517 ὀλόμαν Musgrave: ὀλοίμ- VPQ 518 δωριάλωτοc V 519 ἔλιπον PQΣ: ἔλειπ- V 520 χρυcοφάλαρον Seidler: χρυcεο- VPQ 522 ἐβόαcεν Aldina: -cε VPQ: -c᾽ ὁ Hesych. (i.149 Latte) 523 Τρωϊάδοc Dobree: τρω(ι)άδοc VP (ὁ τ- P)Q 525 ἱρὸν P | ἄγετε VΣ | ξοάνων PQ 528 γεραιὸν V[ac] 534 πεύκαν οὐρεΐαν Dobree: πεύκα(ι) ἐν οὐρεία(ι) VPQΣ[i] | λόχων P 535 Δαρδανίδαc Σ[i] | θεᾶι Aldina: θέα VPQ: θέαι Σ[i] 536 χάριν Aldina: καὶ χάριν VPQΣ | ἀμβροτοπώλου post Barnes (ἀμβροτα-) Musgrave: ἀμβρότα πώλου VΣ: ἀμβρῶτα πώλου P (πόλ-) Q

κλωϲτοῦ δ' ἀμφιβόλοιϲ λίνοιο, ναὸϲ ὡϲεὶ
ϲκάφοϲ κελαινόν, εἰϲ ἕδρανα
λάινα δάπεδά τε, φονέα πατρίδι, Παλλάδοϲ θέϲαν θεᾶϲ.
ἐπὶ δὲ πόνωι καὶ χαρᾶι
νύχιον ἐπεὶ κνέφαϲ παρῆν,
Λίβυϲ τε λωτὸϲ ἐκτύπει
Φρύγιά τε μέλεα, παρθένοι δ'
ἄειρον ἅμα κρότον ποδῶν
βοάν τ' ἔμελπον εὔφρον', ἐν
δόμοιϲ δὲ παμφαὲϲ ϲέλαϲ
<μήνηϲ> μέλαιναν αἴγλαν
πυρὸϲ ἔδωκεν ὕπνωι.

ἐγὼ δὲ τὰν ὀρεϲτέραν ep.
τότ' ἀμφὶ μέλαθρα παρθένον,
Διὸϲ κόραν, ἐμελπόμαν
χοροῖϲι· φοινία δ' ἀνὰ
πτόλιν βοὰ κατεῖχε Περ-
γάμων ἕδραϲ· βρέφη δὲ φίλι-
α περὶ πέπλουϲ ἔβαλλε μα-
τρὶ χεῖραϲ ἐπτοημέναϲ.
λόχου δ' ἐξέβαιν' Ἄρηϲ,
κόραϲ ἔργα Παλλάδοϲ.
ϲφαγαὶ δ' ἀμφιβώμιοι
Φρυγῶν ἔν τε δεμνίοιϲ
καράτομοϲ ἐρημία
νεανίδων ϲτέφανον ἔφερεν
Ἑλλάδι κουροτρόφον,
Φρυγῶν δὲ πατρίδι πένθοϲ.

538 λίνοιο Bothe e Σ (λίνου): λίνοιϲι VPQ | ὡϲεὶ Matthiae e Σ (καθάπερ): ὡϲ εἰϲ V: ὧϲ PQ 540 φονέα Diggle: φοίνια PQ: φοίνιά τε V: φονία (φόνια uel φοίνια Σ^{i}) τε Σ^{1}: φόνια Aldina 542 ἐπὶ PQ: ἐν VΣ^{1} 543 ἐπεὶ Reiske: ἐπὶ VPQ 546 ἄειρον ἅμα Diggle: ἀέριον ἀνὰ VPQ et gE, quibus seruatis τ' 547 del. Burges: αἰθέριον ἀνὰ Wecklein cl. 325 547 ἐνὶ VΣ^{1} 549–50 <μήνηϲ> μέλαιναν αἴγλαν πυρὸϲ ἔδωκεν Robert: πυρὸϲ μ. αἴ. ἔδωκεν VPQ 554 κόραν Seidler: κόραν ἄρτεμιν VPQ 556 κατέϲχε Wilamowitz 558 ἔβαλλε V^{sl}: ἔβαλε VPQ | ματρὶ Q: μρὶ P: μητρὶ V | ἐπτοημένα West 560 ἐξέβαιν' Q: -νεν VP 561 ante h. u. fort. excidit aliquid, e.g. <ἐμέλποντο δ' ἀλαλαγάϲ> 562 ἀμφὶ βώμιοι VΣ^{1}: ἀμφὶ βωμοῖϲι(ν) PQ 564 καράτομοϲ V:-τόμοϲ PQ 566 κουροτρόφον V: -ω(ι) PQ: -ων Diggle 567 δὲ πατρίδι πένθοϲ VΣ^{1}: πατρίδι πένθη PQ

—Ἑκάβη, λεύccειc τήνδ᾽ Ἀνδρομάχην
ξενικοῖc ἐπ᾽ ὄχοιc πορθμευομένην;
παρὰ δ᾽ εἰρεcίαι μαcτῶν ἕπεται
φίλοc Ἀcτυάναξ, Ἕκτοροc ἶνιc.
ποῖ ποτ᾽ ἀπήνηc νώτοιcι φέρηι,
δύcτηνε γύναι,
πάρεδροc χαλκέοιc Ἕκτοροc ὅπλοιc
cκύλοιc τε Φρυγῶν δοριθηράτοιc,
οἷcιν Ἀχιλλέωc παῖc Φθιώταc
cτέψει ναοὺc ἀπὸ Τροίαc;

ΑΝΔΡΟΜΑΧΗ

Ἀχαιοὶ δεcπόται μ᾽ ἄγουcιν. str. 1
οἴμοι. *Εκ.* τί παιᾶν᾽ ἐμὸν cτενάζειc;
Αν. αἰαῖ. *Εκ.* τῶνδ᾽ ἀλγέων,
ὦ Ζεῦ, καὶ cυμφορᾶc.
τέκεα, πρίν ποτ᾽ ἦμεν.

Αν. βέβακ᾽ ὄλβοc, βέβακε Τροία ant. 1
τλάμων. *Εκ.* ἐμῶν τ᾽ εὐγένεια παίδων.
Αν. φεῦ φεῦ. *Εκ.* φεῦ δῆτ᾽ ἐμῶν
κακῶν· οἰκτρὰ τύχα
πόλεοc ἃ καπνοῦται.

Αν. μόλοιc, ὦ πόcιc μοι... str. 2
Εκ. βοᾶιc τὸν παρ᾽ Ἅιδαι
παῖδ᾽ ἐμόν. ὦ μέλεοc,
†cᾶc† δάμαρτοc ἄλκαρ;

568 *λεύcειc* V | *τὴν* V 569 *πορθμευομέναν* PQ 572–6 choro contin. | Kirchhoff: *Εκ.* VPQ 573 *δύcτηνε* Dindorf: *-ανε* VPQ 575 *ἀχιλέωc* V 578 *οἴμοι Σ*, sicut coni. Burges: *ἰώ μοί μοι* fere VPQ | *οἴμοι* Andromachae contin. Willink: Hecubae trib. VPQ | *Εκ.* Willink: *Αν.* VPQ | *παιὰν* V 579–81 *τῶνδ᾽…ἦμεν* Hecubae trib. Willink: *Ἀν. τῶνδ᾽ ἀλγέων Εκ. ὦ Ζεῦ Αν. καὶ cυμφορᾶc. Εκ. τέκεα Αν. πρίν* VPQ 579 *αἰαῖ* Bothe: *αἶ αἶ αἶ αἶ* VPQ 580 *ὦ* Seidler: *ἰὼ* VPQ 581 *τέκνα* P[ac] 582 *Αν.* Willink: *Εκ.* VPQ | *βέβακ᾽* Burges: *-κεν* VPQ et gB 583 *τλάμων* uersui priori contin. Willink: *Αν.* VPQ | *τλήμων* PQ 584 *φεῦ* tertium spat. uac. relicto om. Q, suppl. q 584–5 *φεῦ δῆτ᾽…καπνοῦται* Hecubae trib. Willink: *Αν. κακῶν. Εκ. οἰκτρὰ τύχα Αν. πόλεοc Εκ. ἃ καπνοῦται* P: *κακῶν* uersui priori contin. V et spat. uac. relicto Q, tum *Αν. οἰκτρὰ τύχα Εκ. πόλεοc Αν. ἃ καπνοῦται* VQ 585 *οἰκτρὰ* Burges: *οἰκτρά γε* VPQ 586 *πόλεοc* Burges: *-εωc* VPQ 587 *Αν.* P: om. VQ | *μόλιc* P | *πόcιc* Burges: *πόcι* V (*ποcί*) PQΣ 588–90 Hecubae trib. Willink: *Εκ. βοᾶιc…ὦ μελέα. Αν. cᾶc…ἄλκαρ* VPQ 589 *μέλεοc* Willink: *μελέα* VPQ

Αν. *ϲύ τ', ὦ λῦμ' Ἀχαιῶν...* ant. 2
Εκ. *λεχέων δέϲποθ' ἁμῶν*
πρεϲβυγενὲϲ Πρίαμ' ὦ
κόμιϲαί μ' ἐϲ Ἅιδαν.

Αν. *†οἷδε πόθοι μεγάλοι ϲχέτλια† τάδε πάϲχομεν ἄλγη* ep.
οἰχομένας πόλεωϲ, ἐπὶ δ' ἄλγεϲιν ἄλγεα κεῖται
δυϲφροϲύναιϲι θεῶν, ὅτε ϲὸϲ γόνοϲ ἔκφυγεν Ἅιδαν,
ὃϲ λεχέων ϲτυγερῶν χάριν ὤλεϲε πέργαμα Τροίαϲ·
αἱματόεντα δὲ θεᾶι παρὰ Παλλάδι ϲώματα νεκρῶν
γυψὶ φέρειν τέταται, ζυγὰ δ' ἤνυϲε δούλια Τροίαι.
Εκ. *ὦ πατρίϲ, ὦ μελέα... Αν. καταλειπομέναν ϲε δακρύω...*
Εκ. *νῦν τέλοϲ οἰκτρὸν ὁρᾶιϲ. Αν. καὶ ἐμὸν δόμον ἔνθ' ἐλοχεύθην.*
Εκ. *ὦ τέκν', ἐρημόπολιϲ μάτηρ ἀπολείπεται ὑμῶν.*
οἷοϲ ἰάλεμοϲ οἷά τε πένθεα
δάκρυά τ' ἐκ δακρύων καταλείβεται
ἁμετέροιϲι δόμοιϲ· ὁ θανὼν δ' ἐπιλάθεται ἀλγέων.
Χο. *ὡϲ ἡδὺ δάκρυα τοῖϲ κακῶϲ πεπραγόϲιν*
θρήνων τ' ὀδυρμοὶ μοῦϲά θ' ἣ λύπαϲ ἔχει.
Αν. *ὦ μῆτερ ἀνδρὸϲ ὅϲ ποτ' Ἀργείων δορὶ*
πλείϲτουϲ διώλεϲ' Ἕκτοροϲ, τάδ' εἰϲορᾶιϲ;

591 *Αν.* Hermann: *Εκ.* P: om. VQ | *ϲύ τ'* P: *ϲύ τε* VQΣ: *ϲὺ δ'* Page 592–4 Hecubae trib. Willink: totam antistropham trib. Hecubae P, Andromachae VQ 592 *λεχέων* Willink: *τέκνων* VPQ, quo seruato *δή ποθ'* pro *δέϲποθ'* Seidler 593 *Πρίαμ' ὦ* Willink: *Πρίαμε* VPQΣ: *Πριάμωι* Musgrave 594 *κόμιϲαί* VP (-*ϲέ* P) Q: *κοίμιϲϲαι* (non -*αί*) Haun.: *κοιμίϲαι* Burges: *κοίμιϲαί* Seidler | *Ἅιδαν* Kovacs: *ἄδου* VPQ 595 *Αν.* Murray: *Χο.* VPQ | *οἷδε* V | fort. *ὧδε ποθῶ·* | *μεγάλ' ὦ* Willink | *ϲχετλία* Burges: *ϲχέτλιαι* Scaliger | ante *ϲχέτλια* nulla nota Q: *Εκ.* P: *Αν.* V 596 ante *οἰχομένας* nulla nota VQ: *Χο.* P | ante *ἐπὶ* nulla nota VQ: *Εκ.* P | *κεῖνται* V 597 nulla nota VQ: *Χο.* P | *ὅτε* V: *ὁ δὲ* PQ | *ἔκφυγεν* Aldina: *ἔφυγ'* VPQ | *ἅ(ι)δαν* PQ: *ἅδην* V 600 *τέτακται* V | *ἤνυϲε* Willink: *ἦν-* VPQ | *δούλεια* VQ et (-*εία*) Σ | *τροίαι* QΣ: -*α* VP 601 *Αν.* Murray: nulla nota VPQ | *καταλειπομέναν* VQ (*κάτω λ-* Q) Σ^{i}: -*μένα* P: *κατερειπομέναν* Jacobs 602 *Εκ.* Murray: *Χο.* VPQ | *Αν.* Murray: *Εκ.* VPQ | *ἐμὸν δόμον* V: *ἐγὼ δόμων* PQ 603 *ἐρημόπολιϲ* Seidler: *ἔρημοϲ πόλιϲ* VPQ | *ἡμῶν* Q 604 *Εκ.* praescr. P | *πένθεα* Willink: -*θη* VPQ 605 *καταλείβετε* P^{ac} 606 *δόμοιϲ* Aldina: -*οιϲιν* VPQ | *ἀλγέων* post Seidler Dobree: *ἀλγέων ἀδάκρυτοϲ* VPQ 608 *ἁδὺ* Q | *πεπραγόϲι* V et gB: *πεπονθόϲι* PQ et gE et Stob. 4.54.4 609 *ἣ* PQΣ et gE: *ἃ* V et gB | *λύπαϲ ἔ* Q 610 *ὅπποτ'* V | *δορὶ* om. Q, qui post h.u. explicit

Εκ. ὁρῶ τὰ τῶν θεῶν, ὡς τὰ μὲν πυργοῦς' ἄνω
τὸ μηδὲν ὄντα, τὰ δὲ δοκοῦντ' ἀπώλεςαν.
Αν. ἀγόμεθα λεία cὺν τέκνωι· τὸ δ' εὐγενὲς
ἐς δοῦλον ἥκει, μεταβολὰς τοςάςδ' ἔχον.
Εκ. τὸ τῆς ἀνάγκης δεινόν· ἄρτι κἀπ' ἐμοῦ
βέβηκ' ἀποςπαςθεῖςα Καςςάνδρα βίαι.
Αν. φεῦ φεῦ·
ἄλλος τις Αἴας, ὡς ἔοικε, δεύτερος
παιδὸς πέφηνε cῆς. νοςεῖς δὲ χἄτερα.
Εκ. ὧν γ' οὔτε μέτρον οὔτ' ἀριθμός ἐςτί μοι·
κακῶι κακὸν γὰρ εἰς ἅμιλλαν ἔρχεται.
Αν. τέθνηκέ ςοι παῖς πρὸς τάφωι Πολυξένη
cφαγεῖς' Ἀχιλλέως, δῶρον ἀψύχωι νεκρῶι.
Εκ. οἲ 'γὼ τάλαινα. τοῦτ' ἐκεῖν' ὅ μοι πάλαι
Ταλθύβιος αἴνιγμ' οὐ cαφῶς εἶπεν cαφές.
Αν. εἶδόν νιν αὐτή, κἀποβᾶςα τῶνδ' ὄχων
ἔκρυψα πέπλοις κἀπεκοψάμην νεκρόν.
Εκ. αἰαῖ, τέκνον, cῶν ἀνοςίων προςφαγμάτων·
αἰαῖ μάλ' αὖθις, ὡς κακῶς διόλλυςαι.
Αν. ὄλωλεν ὡς ὄλωλεν· ἀλλ' ὅμως ἐμοῦ
ζώςης γ' ὄλωλεν εὐτυχεςτέρωι πότμωι.
Εκ. οὐ ταὐτόν, ὦ παῖ, τῶι βλέπειν τὸ κατθανεῖν·
τὸ μὲν γὰρ οὐδέν, τῶι δ' ἔνειςιν ἐλπίδες.
Αν. [ὦ μῆτερ, ὦ τεκοῦςα, κάλλιςτον λόγον
ἄκουςον, ὥς ςοι τέρψιν ἐμβάλω φρενί.]
τὸ μὴ γενέςθαι τῶι θανεῖν ἴςον λέγω.
[τοῦ ζῆν δὲ λυπρῶς κρεῖςςόν ἐςτι κατθανεῖν.]
ἀλγεῖ γὰρ οὐδὲν <

613 *τὸ* Elmsley: *τὰ* VP et gE | *ἀπώλεςαν* V et gE: *-ςα* P 615 *τοιάςδ'* V 616 *κατ'* gE 617 *καςςάνδρα* pq: *καςά-* VP 620 *μοι*] *τις* Chr. Pat. 41 (~gB) | *τῶν κακῶν* in fine add. gB 621 *κακὸν* V et gB et gE et Chr. Pat. 42: *-ῶν* P | *γὰρ* om. gE (~gB) | *ἅμιλαν* gB 623 *ἀχιλέως* V 624 *οἲ 'γὼ* Aldina: *οἲ* (*οἶ* V) *ἐγὼ* VP | *τοῦτ'* P: *τοῦ* V | *ἐκεῖν' ὅ* Fix: *ἐκεῖνό* VP (*-ο* P) 625 *οὐ cαφῶς*] *οὐςαθ'* P^{ac} 626 *αὐτὴν ἀποβᾶςα* V 628 *τέκνον* P et Chr. Pat. 716: *-ων* V | *προςςφαγμάτων* V 631 *γ'* om. gE 632 *τῶ* P: *τὸ* VΣ^{1} et gB et Stob. 4.53.25a | *τὸ* VP et Stob. cod. S: *τῶι* gB et Stob. cod. A 633 *τῶι μὲν* Stob. cod. S^{pc} sicut coni. Burges (~gB et Stob. codd. A et S^{ac}) 634 om. P neque habet Stob. (qui 632–3 et 635–6 separatim citat): habent VΣ 634–5 del. Dindorf 637 del. Cron 638 lacunam (*οὐδὲν <…οὐδὲν> τῶν*) indic. Seidler, *<τῶν ἀγεννήτων πλέον | ὁ νεκρός, οὐδὲν>* suppl. e.g. Kovacs

> τῶν κακῶν ᾐcθημένοc·
ὁ δ' εὐτυχήcαc ἐc τὸ δυcτυχὲc πεcὼν
ψυχὴν †ἀλᾶται† τῆc πάροιθ' εὐπραξίαc.
κείνη δ', ὁμοίωc ὥcπερ οὐκ ἰδοῦcα φῶc,
τέθνηκε κοὐδὲν οἶδε τῶν αὑτῆc κακῶν.
ἐγὼ δὲ τοξεύcαcα τῆc εὐδοξίαc
λαχοῦcα πλεῖcτον τῆc τύχηc ἡμάρτανον.
ἃ γὰρ γυναιξὶ cώφρον' ἔcθ' ηὑρημένα,
ταῦτ' ἐξεμόχθουν Ἕκτοροc κατὰ cτέγαc.
πρῶτον μέν, ἔνθα (κἂν προcῆι κἂν μὴ προcῆι
ψόγοc γυναιξίν) αὐτὸ τοῦτ' ἐφέλκεται
κακῶc ἀκούειν, ἥτιc οὐκ ἔνδον μένει,
τούτου παρεῖcα πόθον ἔμιμνον ἐν δόμοιc·
ἔcω τε μελάθρων κομψὰ θηλειῶν ἔπη
οὐκ εἰcεφρούμην, τὸν δὲ νοῦν διδάcκαλον
οἴκοθεν ἔχουcα χρηcτὸν ἐξήρκουν ἐμοί.
γλώccηc τε cιγὴν ὄμμα θ' ἥcυχον πόcει
παρεῖχον· ᾔδη δ' ἅμ' ἐχρῆν νικᾶν πόcιν,
κείνωι τε νίκην ὧν ἐχρῆν παριέναι.
καὶ τῶνδε κληδὼν ἐc cτράτευμ' Ἀχαιικὸν
ἐλθοῦc' ἀπώλεcέν μ'· ἐπεὶ γὰρ ἡιρέθην,
Ἀχιλλέωc με παῖc ἐβουλήθη λαβεῖν
δάμαρτα· δουλεύcω δ' ἐν αὐθεντῶν δόμοιc.
κεἰ μὲν παρώcαc' Ἕκτοροc φίλον κάρα
πρὸc τὸν παρόντα πόcιν ἀναπτύξω φρένα,
κακὴ φανοῦμαι τῶι θανόντι· τόνδε δ' αὖ
cτυγοῦc' ἐμαυτῆc δεcπόταιc μιcήcομαι.
καίτοι λέγουcιν ὡc μί' εὐφρόνη χαλᾶι
τὸ δυcμενὲc γυναικὸc εἰc ἀνδρὸc λέχοc·
ἀπέπτυc' αὐτὴν ἥτιc ἄνδρα τὸν πάροc
καινοῖcι λέκτροιc ἀποβαλοῦc' ἄλλον φιλεῖ.
ἀλλ' οὐδὲ πῶλοc ἥτιc ἂν διαζυγῆι
τῆc cυντραφείcηc ῥαιδίωc ἕλκει ζυγόν.
καίτοι τὸ θηριῶδεc ἄφθογγόν τ' ἔφυ

640 ἀλύει Schenkl 642 αὑτῆc Aldina αὐ- VP 644 πλεῖcτον Hartung et Σ[i]: πλεῖον VP 649 εἴ τιc Chr. Pat. 543 pars codd. 650 πόθον παρεῖc' Chr. Pat. 544 651 τε P et gE: om. V et Chr. Pat. 545 655 ᾔδη Heath: ἤ(ι)δειν VPΣ[1] et gE et Chr. Pat. 551 | ἅμ' ἐχρῆν P: ἅμε χρὴ VΣ[1] (ἐχρῆν Σ): ὥc μ' ἐχρῆν gE: οἷc μ' ἐχρῆν Chr. Pat. 657 Ἀχαιικὸν Aldina: -αικὸν VP 659 ἀχιλέωc V | ἐβολήθη P[ac] 664 cτέργουc' Lenting 668 κοινοῖcι gE (~gB) 670 ἕλκει gE et P[pc] (ἕλκει* P): ἕλξει V

ξυνέςει τ᾽ ἄχρηςτον τῆι φύςει τε λείπεται.
 cὲ δ᾽, ὦ φίλ᾽ Ἕκτορ, εἶχον ἄνδρ᾽ ἀρκοῦντά μοι,
†ξυνέςει† γένει πλούτωι τε κἀνδρείαι μέγαν,
ἀκήρατον δέ μ᾽ ἐκ πατρὸς λαβὼν δόμων
πρῶτος τὸ παρθένειον ἐζεύξω λέχος.
καὶ νῦν ὄλωλας μὲν cύ, ναυςθλοῦμαι δ᾽ ἐγὼ
πρὸς Ἑλλάδ᾽ αἰχμάλωτος ἐς δοῦλον ζυγόν.
 ἆρ᾽ οὐκ ἐλάςςω τῶν ἐμῶν ἔχει κακῶν
Πολυξένης ὄλεθρος, ἣν καταςτένεις;
ἐμοὶ γὰρ οὐδ᾽ ὃ πᾶςι λείπεται βροτοῖς
ξύνεςτιν ἐλπίς, οὐδὲ κλέπτομαι φρένας
πράξειν τι κεδνόν· ἡδὺ δ᾽ ἐςτὶ καὶ δοκεῖν.
Χο. ἐς ταὐτὸν ἥκεις ςυμφορᾶς· θρηνοῦςα δὲ
τὸ cὸν διδάςκεις μ᾽ ἔνθα πημάτων κυρῶ.
Εκ. αὐτὴ μὲν οὔπω ναὸς εἰςέβην ςκάφος,
γραφῆι δ᾽ ἰδοῦςα καὶ κλυοῦς᾽ ἐπίςταμαι.
ναῦται γάρ, ἢν μὲν μέτριος ἦι χειμὼν φέρειν,
προθυμίαν ἔχουςι ςωθῆναι πόνων,
ὁ μὲν παρ᾽ οἴαχ᾽, ὁ δ᾽ ἐπὶ λαίφεςιν βεβώς,
ὁ δ᾽ ἄντλον εἴργων ναός· ἢν δ᾽ ὑπερβάληι
πολὺς ταραχθεὶς πόντος, ἐνδόντες τύχηι
παρεῖςαν αὑτοὺς κυμάτων δραμήμαςιν.
οὕτω δὲ κἀγὼ πόλλ᾽ ἔχουςα πήματα
ἄφθογγός εἰμι καὶ παρεῖς᾽ ἔχω ςτόμα·
νικᾶι γὰρ οὐκ θεῶν με δύςτηνος κλύδων.
 ἀλλ᾽, ὦ φίλη παῖ, τὰς μὲν Ἕκτορος τύχας
ἔαςον· οὐ μὴ δάκρυά νιν ςώςηι τὰ cά.
τίμα δὲ τὸν παρόντα δεςπότην ςέθεν,
φίλον διδοῦςα δέλεαρ ἀνδρὶ ςῶν τρόπων.
κἂν δρᾶις τάδ᾽, ἐς τὸ κοινὸν εὐφρανεῖς φίλους,

672 *φύςη* V 674 fort. *πάντως*: u. del. Paley 675 *δόμον* V 676 *παρθένιον* V 678 *αἰχμάλωτον* V^ac 679 *ἔχειν* V 680 *ὄλεθρον* V 681 *φαίνεται* gB et gE (~Chr. Pat. 591) 683 *ἕξειν* Chr. Pat. 593 (~gB et gE) 686 *αὐτὴ* VΣ^1 et Chr. Pat. 622: *-ὴν* P 687 *γραφῆ(ι)* PΣ et Chr. Pat. 623: *-ήν* V | *κλυοῦςα* West: *κλύ-* VP 688 *ναῦται* Diggle: *ναύταις* VPQ | *μὲν* om. gB et Chr. Pat. 624 691 *ἄντλων* gB | *ναός* P et gB et Chr. Pat. 627: *νηός* V 692 *τύχηι*] *φορᾶι* Chr. Pat. 628 (~gB) 693 *παρῆκαν* gB et Chr. Pat. 629 | *αὑτοὺς* gB: *αὐ-* VP et Chr. Pat. | *δραμήμαςιν* Cobet: *δρομ-* VP et gB et Chr. Pat. 695 *ἔχω* Bothe: *ἐῶ* VP et gB et Chr. Pat. 631 696 *οὐκ* V 698 *οὐ μὴ … ςώςη* P: *οὐ γὰρ … ςώςει* V 700 *φίλων* gE 701 *φίλους* P et gE: *-ος* V

καὶ παῖδα τόνδε παιδὸϲ ἐκθρέψειαϲ ἂν
Τροίαι μέγιϲτον ὠφέλημ᾽, ἵν᾽ ἦι ποτε
ἐξ οὗ γενόμενοι παῖδεϲ ὕϲτερον πάλιν
κατοικίϲειαν καὶ πόλιϲ γένοιτ᾽ ἔτι.
ἀλλ᾽ ἐκ λόγου γὰρ ἄλλοϲ ἐκβαίνει λόγοϲ,
τίν᾽ αὖ δέδορκα τόνδ᾽ Ἀχαιικὸν λάτριν
ϲτείχοντα καινῶν ἄγγελον βουλευμάτων;

ΚΗΡΥΞ

Φρυγῶν ἀρίϲτου πρίν ποθ᾽ Ἕκτοροϲ δάμαρ,
μή με ϲτυγήϲηιϲ· οὐχ ἑκὼν γὰρ ἀγγελῶ
Δαναῶν τε κοινὰ Πελοπιδῶν τ᾽ ἀγγέλματα.
Αν. τί δ᾽ ἔϲτιν; ὥϲ μοι φροιμίων ἄρχηι κακῶν.
Κη. ἔδοξε τόνδε παῖδα... πῶϲ εἴπω λόγον;
Αν. μῶν οὐ τὸν αὐτὸν δεϲπότην ἡμῖν ἔχειν;
Κη. οὐδεὶϲ Ἀχαιῶν τοῦδε δεϲπόϲει ποτέ.
Αν. ἀλλ᾽ ἐνθάδ᾽ αὐτὸν λείψανον Φρυγῶν λιπεῖν;
Κη. οὐκ οἶδ᾽ ὅπωϲ ϲοι ῥαιδίωϲ εἴπω †κακά†.
Αν. ἐπήινεϲ᾽ αἰδῶ, πλὴν ἐὰν ϲτέγηι κακά.
Κη. κτενοῦϲι ϲὸν παῖδ᾽, ὡϲ πύθηι κακὸν μέγα.
Αν. οἴμοι, γάμων τόδ᾽ ὡϲ κλύω μεῖζον κακόν.
Κη. νικᾶι δ᾽ Ὀδυϲϲεὺϲ ἐν Πανέλληϲιν †λέγων†
Αν. αἰαῖ μάλ᾽· οὐ γὰρ μέτρια πάϲχομεν κακά.
Κη. λέξαϲ ἀρίϲτου παῖδα μὴ τρέφειν πατρόϲ
Αν. τοιαῦτα νικήϲειε τῶν αὑτοῦ πέρι.
Κη. ῥῖψαι δὲ πύργων δεῖν ϲφε Τρωϊκῶν ἄπο.
ἀλλ᾽ ὣϲ γενέϲθω, καὶ ϲοφωτέρα φανῆι·
μήτ᾽ ἀντέχου τοῦδ᾽, εὐγενῶϲ δ᾽ ἄλγει κακοῖϲ,
μήτε ϲθένουϲα μηδὲν ἰϲχύειν δόκει.
ἔχειϲ γὰρ ἀλκὴν οὐδαμῆι. ϲκοπεῖν δὲ χρή·
πόλιϲ τ᾽ ὄλωλε καὶ πόϲιϲ, κρατῆι δὲ ϲύ,
ἡμεῖϲ δὲ πρὸϲ γυναῖκα μάρναϲθαι μίαν
οἷοί τε. τούτων οὕνεκ᾽ οὐ μάχηϲ ἐρᾶν

703 *τροίαϲ* P | *ἵν᾽ ἦι* Kovacs: *ἵν᾽ εἴ* VP 704 *ἐξ οὗ* P: *ἐκ ϲοῦ* V | *ὕϲτερον* V: *ἴλιον* P 707 *ἀχαιικὸν* p: *-αικὸν* VP 708 *καινῶν* Vp: *-ὸν* P 709 *ΚΗΡΥΞ* post *Σ* et Elmsley (*ΑΓΓΕΛΟϹ*) Kovacs: *Τα.* VP 710 *οὐχ* V: *οὔθ᾽* P 711 *τὲ* V: *δὲ* P | *τ᾽* om. P 712 *ἄρχη(ι)* P: *-ὴ* V 716 *ἔνθά θ᾽* V | *αὐτὸν* P: *-οῦ* V 718 *ϲτέγηι* Lane: *λέγηιϲ* VP | *καλά* p 719 *κτείνουϲι* P | *τὸν* V 721 *λόγωι* West 724 *τῶν* P et gE: *τὸν* V | *αὑτοῦ* Barnes: *αὐ-* VP et gE 725 *δεῖν* Jacobs: *δεῖ* VP 728 *ἰϲχύειν* P: *-ύϲειν* V 731 *δὲ* V: *τε* P

οὐδ᾽ αἰcχρὸν οὐδὲν οὐδ᾽ ἐπίφθονόν cε δρᾶν
οὐδ᾽ αὖ c᾽ Ἀχαιοῖc βούλομαι ῥίπτειν ἀράc.
εἰ γάρ τι λέξειc ὧν χολώcεται cτρατόc,
οὔτ᾽ ἂν ταφείη παῖc ὅδ᾽ οὔτ᾽ οἴκτου τύχοι.
cιγῶcα δ᾽ εὖ τε ταῖc τύχαιc κεχρημένη
τὸν τοῦδε νεκρὸν οὐκ ἄθαπτον ἂν λίποιc
αὐτή τ᾽ Ἀχαιῶν πρευμενεcτέρων τύχοιc.
Αν. *ὦ φίλτατ᾽, ὦ περιccὰ τιμηθεὶc τέκνον,*
θανῆι πρὸc ἐχθρῶν μητέρ᾽ ἀθλίαν λιπών,
[ἡ τοῦ πατρὸc δέ c᾽ εὐγένει᾽ ἀποκτενεῖ,
ἣ τοῖcιν ἄλλοιc γίγνεται cωτηρία.]
τὸ δ᾽ ἐcθλὸν οὐκ ἐc καιρὸν ἦλθέ coι πατρόc.
ὦ λέκτρα τἀμὰ δυcτυχῆ τε καὶ γάμοι,
οἷc ἦλθον ἐc μέλαθρον Ἕκτορόc ποτε,
†οὐχ ὡc cφάγιον† Δαναΐδαιc τέξουc᾽ ἐμόν,
ἀλλ᾽ ὡc τύραννον Ἀcιάδοc πολυcπόρου.
ὦ παῖ, δακρύειc· αἰcθάνηι κακῶν cέθεν;
τί μου δέδραξαι χερcὶ κἀντέχηι πέπλων,
νεοccὸc ὡcεὶ πτέρυγαc ἐcπίτνων ἐμάc;
οὐκ εἶcιν Ἕκτωρ κλεινὸν ἁρπάcαc δόρυ
γῆc ἐξανελθὼν coὶ φέρων cωτηρίαν,
οὐ cυγγένεια πατρόc, οὐκ ἰcχὺc Φρυγῶν·
λυγρὸν δὲ πήδημ᾽ ἐc τράχηλον ὑψόθεν
πεcὼν ἀνοίκτωc πνεῦμ᾽ ἀπορρήξειc cέθεν.
ὦ νέον ὑπαγκάλιcμα μητρὶ φίλτατον,
ὦ χρωτὸc ἡδὺ πνεῦμα· διὰ κενῆc ἄρα
ἐν cπαργάνοιc cε μαcτὸc ἐξέθρεψ᾽ ὅδε,

733 *ἐπίχθονον* P^{ac} | *δρᾶν* V: *χρὴ* P 734 *οὐδ᾽* Hartung: *οὔτ᾽* VP | *ἀχαιῶν* V | *ῥιπτεῖν* P 736 *ταφοίη* P | *ὅδ᾽ οὔτ᾽* P: *οὐδ᾽* V | *οἴκτου τύχοι* p: *οἴκτου τύχη* V: *οἶκτοc ἔχοι* P 737 *ταῖc τύχαιc κεχρημένη* Hartung: *τὰc τύχαc κεκτημένη* VP 738 *λείποιc* uel *λοίποιc* P^{ac} 739 *πλευμενεcτέρων* P^{ac} 741 fort. *αἰχθρῶν* P^{ac} 742–3 (quos una cum 744 habent gB et gE et testatur Chr. Pat. 1515–16) del. Nauck: cf. fr. 62i 742 *δέ* om. gE (~gB) | *ἀποκτενεῖ* P et gE et (*-κτένει*) Chr. Pat. 1515: *ἀπώλεcεν* V et gB: cf. Hip. 1390 744 *τ᾽* gE et Chr. Pat. 1517 (~gB) | *coι* om. gE (~gB et Chr. Pat.) 745 *τἀμὰ*] *τάλανα* Schmidt | *κἄγαμα* Wecklein 745–8 del. West (747–8 iam Paley) 747 *οὐχὶ cφάγιον* Chr. Pat. 77: *οὐ cφάγιον <υἱὸν>* Nauck: fort. *οὐχ ὡc ὕβριcμα* uel *οὐχ ὥc τι θῦμα* 748 *ἀcιάτιδοc* V 751 *ὡc cεὶ* P: *ὡc* V 752 *κλεινὸν* P: *-ὸc* V et gE et Chr. Pat. 1534 756 *ἀπορρήξει* P^{ac} 757 *ὦ* P et gE: *ὧν* V 759 *cπαργάνοιc cε* P: *cπαργάνοιcι* V

μάτην δ' ἐμόχθουν καὶ κατεξάνθην πόνοιϲ.
νῦν, οὔποτ' αὖθιϲ, μητέρ' ἀϲπάζου ϲέθεν,
πρόϲπιτνε τὴν τεκοῦϲαν, ἀμφὶ δ' ὠλέναϲ
ἕλιϲϲ' ἐμοῖϲ νώτοιϲι καὶ ϲτόμ' ἅρμοϲον.
ὦ βάρβαρ' ἐξευρόντεϲ Ἕλληνεϲ κακά,
τί τόνδε παῖδα κτείνετ' οὐδὲν αἴτιον;
ὦ Τυνδάρειον ἔρνοϲ, οὔποτ' εἶ Διόϲ,
πολλῶν δὲ πατέρων φημί ϲ' ἐκπεφυκέναι,
Ἀλάϲτοροϲ μὲν πρῶτον, εἶτα δὲ Φθόνου,
Φόνου τε Θανάτου θ' ὅϲα τε γῆ τρέφει κακά.
οὐ γάρ ποτ' αὐχῶ Ζηνὸϲ ἐκφῦναί ϲ' ἐγώ,
πολλοῖϲι κῆρα βαρβάροιϲ Ἕλληϲί τε.
ὄλοιο· καλλίϲτων γὰρ ὀμμάτων ἄπο
αἰϲχρῶϲ τὰ κλεινὰ πεδί' ἀπώλεϲαϲ Φρυγῶν.
<ἀλλ'> ἄγετε φέρετε ῥίπτετ', εἰ ῥίπτειν δοκεῖ·
δαίνυϲθε τοῦδε ϲάρκαϲ. ἔκ τε γὰρ θεῶν
διολλύμεϲθα παιδί τ' οὐ δυναίμεθ' ἂν
θάνατον ἀρῆξαι. κρύπτετ' ἄθλιον δέμαϲ
καὶ ῥίπτετ' ἐϲ ναῦϲ· ἐπὶ καλὸν γὰρ ἔρχομαι
ὑμέναιον, ἀπολέϲαϲα τοὐμαυτῆϲ τέκνον.

Χο. τάλαινα Τροία, μυρίουϲ ἀπώλεϲαϲ
μιᾶϲ γυναικὸϲ καὶ λέχουϲ ϲτυγνοῦ χάριν.

Κη. ἄγε παῖ, φίλιον πρόϲπτυγμα μεθεὶϲ
μητρὸϲ μογερᾶϲ, βαῖνε πατρῴων
πύργων ἐπ' ἄκραϲ ϲτεφάναϲ, ὅθι ϲοι
πνεῦμα μεθεῖναι ψῆφοϲ ἐκράνθη.
λαμβάνετ' αὐτόν. τὰ δὲ τοιάδε χρὴ
κηρυκεύειν ὅϲτιϲ ἄνοικτοϲ
καὶ ἀναιδείαι τῆϲ ἡμετέραϲ
γνώμηϲ μᾶλλον φίλοϲ ἐϲτίν.

Εκ. ὦ τέκνον, ὦ παῖ παιδὸϲ μογεροῦ,

760 del. Valckenaer: cf. *Med.* 1030 | δ' ἐπόνουν gE et Chr. Pat. 1336 pars codd. (~gB et Chr. Pat. 910 et 1336 pars codd.) 761 οὔποτ' Stephanus: εἴ ποτ' VP 762 πρόϲπιπτε P | ὠλέναιϲ V 769 φόνου VP et gE: φθ- gB: utrumque codd. Chr. Pat. 336 | τε γῆ V et gB et Chr. Pat.: τε gE: γῆ P 770 Ζηνὸϲ Reiske: Ζῆνά γ' P et gE: Ζῆνά ϲ' V | ἐκφῦναί P^{pc} (-φῆναι P^{ac}) et gE: ἐκφῦϲαι V 774 <ἀλλ'> Hermann | ῥιπτεῖν P 775 δαίννυϲθε P 776 διολλύμεθα P | δυναίμεθ' ἂν V: -μεθα P 779 ἀπόλεϲα P^{ac} 782 Κη.] Τα. Tyrwhitt: Αν. VP 783 om. V 786 τοιάδε VΣ^{l}: τοιαῦτα PΣ 788 ἀναιδείαϲ P | ἡμετέραϲ Tyrwhitt: ὑμ- VP 790 μονογενοῦ V

ϲυλώμεθα ϲὴν ψυχὴν ἀδίκωϲ
μήτηρ κἀγώ. τί πάθω; τί ϲ᾽ ἐγώ,
δύϲμορε, δράϲω; τάδε ϲοι δίδομεν
πλήγματα κρατὸϲ ϲτέρνων τε κόπουϲ·
τῶνδε γὰρ ἄρχομεν. οἳ ᾽γὼ πόλεωϲ,
οἴμοι δὲ ϲέθεν· τί γὰρ οὐκ ἔχομεν,
τίνοϲ ἐνδέομεν μὴ οὐ πανϲυδίαι
χωρεῖν ὀλέθρου διὰ παντόϲ;

Χο. *μελιϲϲοτρόφου Ϲαλαμῖνοϲ ὦ βαϲιλεῦ Τελαμών,* str. 1
νάϲου περικύμονοϲ οἰκήϲαϲ ἕδραν
τᾶϲ ἐπικεκλιμέναϲ ὄχθοιϲ ἱεροῖϲ ἵν᾽ ἐλαίαϲ
πρῶτον ἔδειξε κλάδον γλαυκᾶϲ Ἀθάνα,
οὐράνιον ϲτέφανον λιπαραῖϲί <τε> κόϲμον Ἀθάναιϲ,
ἔβαϲ ἔβαϲ τῶι τοξοφόρωι ϲυναρι-
ϲτεύων ἅμ᾽ Ἀλκμήναϲ γόνωι
Ἴλιον Ἴλιον ἐκπέρϲων πόλιν ἁμετέραν
τὸ πάροιθεν < > [ὅτ᾽ ἔβαϲ ἀφ᾽ Ἑλλάδοϲ].

ὅθ᾽ Ἑλλάδοϲ ἄγαγε πρῶτον ἄνθοϲ ἀτιζόμενοϲ ant. 1
πώλων, Ϲιμόεντι δ᾽ ἐπ᾽ εὐρείται πλάταν
ἔϲχαϲε ποντοπόρον καὶ ναύδετ᾽ ἀνήψατο πρυμνᾶν
καὶ χερὸϲ εὐϲτοχίαν ἐξεῖλε ναῶν,
Λαομέδοντι φόνον· κανόνων δὲ τυκίϲματα Φοίβου
πυρὸϲ <πυρὸϲ> φοίνικι πνοᾶι καθελὼν
Τροίαϲ ἐπόρθηϲε χθόνα.
δὶϲ δὲ δυοῖν πιτύλοιν τείχη πυρὶ Δαρδανίαϲ
φονία κατέλυϲεν αἰχμά.

μάταν ἄρ᾽, ὦ χρυϲέαιϲ ἐν οἰνοχόαιϲ ἁβρὰ βαίνων, str. 2
Λαομεδόντιε παῖ,

794 *κόπουϲ* Seidler: *κτύπουϲ* VP 795 *οἳ ᾽γὼ* Seidler: *οἳ ἐγὼ* P: *οἵ ἐγὼ* V 800 *ἕδραϲ* V 801 *ἐπικεκλημέναϲ* P | *ἱεροῖϲ ἵν᾽* VΣ^{l}: *ἱεροῖϲιν* P 802 *κελάδον* P^{ac} ut uid. | *γλαυκὰϲ* P | *Ἀθάνα* Σ^{i} sicut coni. Aldina: *-ναϲ* VP | *Ἀθάνα*] fort. *Διὸϲ παῖϲ* 803 *λιπαραῖϲ* V | <*τε*> Seidler | *Ἀθάναιϲ* Burges: *ἀθήν-*VP 804 *τῶι* om. P | *ϲυναριϲτεύϲων* P 805 *ἅμ᾽* om. V 807 *πάροιθ᾽* P | uerbis *ὅτ᾽ ἔβαϲ ἀφ᾽ Ἑλλάδοϲ*, quae habent VP, seclusis lac. indic. Bothe; supplere possis e.g. *πάροιθ᾽* <*ἐπ᾽ ἀκύμον᾽ ἅλμαν*> 809 *ἀτιζόμενοϲ* Jackson: *ἀτυζ-*VPΣ^{i} 810 *δ**ευρείταο*V(*δ᾽ ἐπ᾽ εὐρ-*Va) 812 *πρύμναν* V 813 *χειρὸϲ* P 814 *τυκίϲματα* Aldina: *τεκ-* P: *τυκτ-* V: *τυχ-* Maas 815 <*πυρὸϲ*> Meineke | *πνοᾶ* P: *βοᾶ* V 817 *πυρὶ* Seidler: *περὶ* V: *παρὰ* P: *πέρι* (tum *Δαρδανίδαϲ* 818) Diggle 818 *Δαρδανίαϲ* V: *-δάναϲ* P | *φονία* Aldina: *φοιν-* 820 *μάτην* V | *ϲὺν* Wecklein 822 *λαομεδόντειε* P

Ζηνὸc ἔχειc κυλίκων πλήρωμα, καλλίcταν λατρείαν,
ἁ δέ cε γειναμένα πυρὶ δαίεται.
ἠϊόνεc δ' ἅλιαι
ἴακχον οἰωνὸc οἷ-
ον τέκνων ὕπερ βοῶc',
αἱ μὲν εὐνάc, αἱ δὲ παῖδαc,
αἱ δὲ ματέραc γεραιάc.
τὰ δὲ cὰ δροcόεντα λουτρὰ
γυμναcίων τε δρόμοι
βεβᾶcι, cὺ δὲ πρόcωπα νεα-
ρὰ χάριcι παρὰ Διὸc θρόνοιc
καλλιγάλανα τρέφειc· Πριάμοιο δὲ γαῖαν
Ἑλλὰc ὤλεc' αἰχμά.

Ἔρωc Ἔρωc, ὃc τὰ Δαρδάνεια μέλαθρά ποτ' ἦλθεc ant. 2
οὐρανίδαιcι μέλων,
ὡc τότε μὲν μεγάλωc Τροίαν ἐπύργωcαc, θεοῖcιν
κῆδοc ἀναψάμενοc. τὸ μὲν οὖν Διὸc
οὐκέτ' ὄνειδοc ἐρῶ·
τὸ τᾶc δὲ λευκοπτέρου
φίλιον Ἁμέραc βροτοῖc
φέγγοc ὀλοὸν εἶδε γαίαc,
εἶδε Περγάμων ὄλεθρον,
τεκνοποιὸν ἔχουcα τᾶcδε
γᾶc πόcιν ἐν θαλάμοιc,
ὃν ἀcτέρων τέθριπποc ἔλα-
βε χρύcεοc ὄχοc ἀναρπάcαc,
ἐλπίδα γᾶι πατρίαι μεγάλαν· τὰ θεῶν δὲ
φίλτρα φροῦδα Τροίαι.

825 *γειναμένα* Musgrave: *γ- τροία* VP 827 *κίονεc* P | *δ'* om. P 828 *ἴακχον* Hartung: *ἴαχον* V Σ[i] (*ἐβόηcαν*): *ἴcχον* P | *οἰωνὸc οἷον* Hermann: *οἷον οἰ-* VP 830 *τέκνων ὕπερ* post Bothe (*τεκέων* cum Stephano) Diggle: *ὑ- τέκνων* V: *ὑ- τοκέων* P | *βοῶc'* Wecklein: *βοᾶ(ι)* VP 830–1 *αἱ* ter V: *ἁ...ἃ...αἱ* P: *ἇι* ter Wilamowitz | *εὐνάc* Seidler: *εὐνάτοραc* VP 833 *προcόεντα* P 839 *ὤλεcεν* P 840 *τὰ* V: *παρὰ* P | *Δαρδάνεια* Dindorf: *-νια* VP 844 *θεοῖcι* V 847 *ὄνειδοc οὐκέτ'* P 848 *τᾶc δὲ* Victorius: *τᾶcδε* VP 849 *φίλιον Ἁμέραc* Murray: *ἁμ- φίλιον* V: *ἁμ-φίλαc* P 850 *εἰ δὲ* V | *γαίαc* Bothe et fort. Σ[i]: *γαῖαν* VP 853 *τᾶcδε* P: *τάδε* V 854 *θαλάμοιcιν* P 857 *πατρίδι* V

ΜΕΝΕΛΑΟϹ

ὦ καλλιφεγγὲϲ ἡλίου ϲέλαϲ τόδε,
ἐν ὧι δάμαρτα τὴν ἐμὴν χειρώϲομαι
Ἑλένην· ὁ γὰρ δὴ πολλὰ μοχθήϲαϲ ἐγὼ
Μενέλαοϲ <
> *εἶμι καὶ ϲτράτευμ' Ἀχαιικόν.*
ἦλθον δὲ Τροίαν οὐχ ὅϲον δοκοῦϲί με
γυναικὸϲ οὕνεκ', ἀλλ' ἐπ' ἄνδρ' ὃϲ ἐξ ἐμῶν
δόμων δάμαρτα ξεναπάτηϲ ἐλήιϲατο.
κεῖνοϲ μὲν οὖν δέδωκε ϲὺν θεοῖϲ δίκην
αὐτόϲ τε καὶ γῆ δορὶ πεϲοῦϲ' Ἑλληνικῶι.
ἥκω δὲ τὴν Λάκαιναν (οὐ γὰρ ἡδέωϲ
ὄνομα δάμαρτοϲ ἥ ποτ' ἦν ἐμὴ λέγω)
ἄξων· δόμοιϲ γὰρ τοῖϲδ' ἐν αἰχμαλωτικοῖϲ
κατηρίθμηται Τρωιάδων ἄλλων μέτα.
οἵπερ γὰρ αὐτὴν ἐξεμόχθηϲαν δορὶ
κτανεῖν ἐμοί νιν ἔδοϲαν, εἴτε μὴ κτανὼν
θέλοιμ' ἄγεϲθαι πάλιν ἐϲ Ἀργείαν χθόνα.
ἐμοὶ δ' ἔδοξε τὸν μὲν ἐν Τροίαι μόρον
Ἑλένηϲ ἐᾶϲαι, ναυπόρωι δ' ἄγειν πλάτηι
Ἑλληνίδ' ἐϲ γῆν κἆιτ' ἐκεῖ δοῦναι κτανεῖν,
ποινὰϲ ὅϲοιϲ τεθνᾶϲ' ἐν Ἰλίωι φίλοι.
ἀλλ' εἶα χωρεῖτ' ἐϲ δόμουϲ, ὀπάονεϲ,
κομίζετ' αὐτὴν τῆϲ μιαιφονωτάτηϲ
κόμηϲ ἐπιϲπάϲαντεϲ· οὔριοι δ' ὅταν
πνοαὶ μόλωϲι, πέμψομέν νιν Ἑλλάδα.
Εκ. *ὦ γῆϲ ὄχημα κἀπὶ γῆϲ ἔχων ἕδραν,*
ὅϲτιϲ ποτ' εἶ ϲύ, δυϲτόπαϲτοϲ εἰδέναι,
Ζεὺϲ εἴτ' ἀνάγκη φύϲεοϲ εἴτε νοῦϲ βροτῶν,

863 lac. post *Μενέλαοϲ* indic. west | *εἰμι* VP | lac. post 863 indic. Porson | *Ἀχαιικόν* Aldina: *-αικὸν* VP 866 *ἐλήιϲατο* Aldina: *ἐληίϲ-* VP 867 *ἔδωκε* V 868 *γῆι* V869 *λάκαιναν* P: *τάλαιναν* V 873 *ἐξεμόχθευϲαν* V 875 *ἀργείων* V876 *δ'* V et tab. Berolin. (Schubart et Wilamowitz 1907: 98): *γ'* P877 *ἄγειν*] *αλγει[ν* ut uid. tab. 879 *πο ὰϲ* V | *ὅϲοιϲ* Canter: *ὅϲοι* P: *ὅϲων* V: *ωϲων* pot. quam *εοϲων* tab. sec. edd. pr. | *τεθνᾶϲ'* Heath: *-ᾶϲιν* VP: *τεθν[* tab. 883 *πνοιαὶ* P 885 *εἰϲιδεῖν* Clem. Alex. protr. 2.25.3 et Sext. Emp. adu. math. 1.288 et 7.128 886 *[εἴ]τ' ἀνάγκ[η φύϲεω]ϲ εἴτ[ε* P. Oxy. 1176 (Satyrus), fr. 37 | *φύϲεοϲ* Aldina: *-εωϲ* VP et Plut. mor. 1026 B et Sext. Emp. utrobique et ps.-Iustin. de mon. 5

προϲηυξάμην ϲε· πάντα γὰρ δι᾽ ἀψόφου
βαίνων κελεύθου κατὰ δίκην τὰ θνήτ᾽ ἄγειϲ.
Με. *τί δ᾽ ἔϲτιν; εὐχὰϲ ὡϲ ἐκαίνιϲαϲ θεῶν.*
Εκ. *αἰνῶ ϲε, Μενέλα᾽, εἰ κτενεῖϲ δάμαρτα ϲήν.*
ὁρᾶν δὲ τήνδε φεῦγε, μή ϲ᾽ ἕληι πόθωι.
αἱρεῖ γὰρ ἀνδρῶν ὄμματ᾽, ἐξαιρεῖ πόλειϲ,
πίμπρηϲιν οἴκουϲ· ὧδ᾽ ἔχει κηλήματα.
ἐγώ νιν οἶδα καὶ ϲὺ χοἰ πεπονθότεϲ.

ΕΛΕΝΗ

Μενέλαε, φροίμιον μὲν ἄξιον φόβου
τόδ᾽ ἐϲτίν· ἐν γὰρ χερϲὶ προϲπόλων ϲέθεν
βίαι πρὸ τῶνδε δωμάτων ἐκπέμπομαι.
ἀτὰρ ϲχεδὸν μὲν οἶδά ϲοι ϲτυγουμένη,
ὅμωϲ δ᾽ ἐρέϲθαι βούλομαι· γνῶμαι τίνεϲ
Ἕλληϲι καὶ ϲοὶ τῆϲ ἐμῆϲ ψυχῆϲ πέρι;
Με. *οὐκ εἰϲ ἀκριβὲϲ ἦλθεν, ἀλλ᾽ ἅπαϲ ϲτρατὸϲ*
κτανεῖν ἐμοί ϲ᾽ ἔδωκεν, ὅνπερ ἠδίκειϲ.
Ελ. *ἔξεϲτιν οὖν πρὸϲ ταῦτ᾽ ἀμείψαϲθαι λόγωι,*
ὡϲ οὐ δικαίωϲ, ἢν θάνω, θανούμεθα;
Με. *οὐκ ἐϲ λόγουϲ ἐλήλυθ᾽ ἀλλά ϲε κτενῶν.*
Εκ. *ἄκουϲον αὐτῆϲ, μὴ θάνηι τοῦδ᾽ ἐνδεήϲ,*
Μενέλαε, καὶ δὸϲ τοὺϲ ἐναντίουϲ λόγουϲ
ἡμῖν κατ᾽ αὐτῆϲ· τῶν γὰρ ἐν Τροίαι κακῶν
οὐδὲν κάτοιϲθα. ϲυντεθεὶϲ δ᾽ ὁ πᾶϲ λόγοϲ
κτενεῖ νιν οὕτωϲ ὥϲτε μηδαμοῦ φυγεῖν.
Με. *ϲχολῆϲ τὸ δῶρον· εἰ δὲ βούλεται λέγειν,*
ἔξεϲτι. τῶν ϲῶν δ᾽ οὕνεχ᾽, ὡϲ μάθηι, λόγων
δώϲω τόδ᾽ αὐτῆι· τῆϲδε δ᾽ οὐ δώϲω χάριν.
Ελ. *ἴϲωϲ με, κἂν εὖ κἂν κακῶϲ δόξω λέγειν,*
οὐκ ἀνταμείψηι πολεμίαν ἡγούμενοϲ.
ἐγὼ δ᾽, ἅ ϲ᾽ οἶμαι διὰ λόγων ἰόντ᾽ ἐμοῦ

887 *ἐπευξάμην* Sext. Emp. adv. math. 7.128 (~1.288 et ps.-Iustin.) | *διὰ ψόφου* V[ac] 891 *ὁρᾶν* Stanley: *-ῶν* VP et gE | *πόθοϲ* P[ac] ut uid., sicut coni. Heiland 893 *πίμπρηϲιν* Dobree: *-ϲι δ᾽* V et gE: *-ϲι δι᾽* P | *ὡϲ δ᾽* gE 896 *τιδ᾽* (*τόδ᾽* p) *ἐϲτὶ πρὸϲ γὰρ* P 898 *ϲτυγουμένη* V: *μιϲουμένη* P 900 *ϲὺ* P 901 *ἦλθεν* *Σ*: *-εϲ* VP et gB | *ἀλλὰ πᾶϲ* V 905 *κτενῶν* Stephanus: *κτανών* P: *κτενῶ* V 909 *λόγουϲ* P 910 *μηδαμῶϲ* P 912 *μάθηιϲ* q (*-ηϲ* Va): *-η* VP 913 *τῆδε* P 914 *με* P: *μὲν* V 916 *λόγων* P*Σ*: *-ον* V

κατηγορήϲειν, ἀντιθεῖϲ᾽ ἀμείψομαι
τοῖϲ ϲοῖϲι τἄμ᾽ ἰϲαίτατ᾽ αἰτιάματα.
πρῶτον μὲν ἀρχὰϲ ἔτεκεν ἥδε τῶν κακῶν,
Πάριν τεκοῦϲα· δεύτερον δ᾽ ἀπώλεϲεν
Τροίαν τε κἄμ᾽ ὁ πρέϲβυϲ οὐ κτανὼν βρέφοϲ,
δαλοῦ πικρὸν μίμημ᾽ Ἀλέξανδρον τότε.
ἐνθένδε τἀπίλοιπ᾽ ἄκουϲον ὡϲ ἔχει.
ἔκρινε τριϲϲὸν ζεῦγοϲ ὅδε τριῶν θεῶν·
καὶ Παλλάδοϲ μὲν ἦν Ἀλεξάνδρωι δόϲιϲ
Φρυξὶ ϲτρατηγοῦνθ᾽ Ἑλλάδ᾽ ἐξανιϲτάναι·
Ἥρα δ᾽ ὑπέϲχετ᾽ Ἀϲιάδ᾽ Εὐρώπηϲ θ᾽ ὅρουϲ
τυραννίδ᾽ ἕξειν, εἴ ϲφε κρίνειεν Πάριϲ·
Κύπριϲ δὲ τοὐμὸν εἶδοϲ ἐκπαγλουμένη
δώϲειν ὑπέϲχετ᾽ εἰ θεὰϲ ὑπερδράμοι
κάλλει. τὸν ἔνθεν δ᾽ ὡϲ ἔχει ϲκέψαι λόγον·
νικᾶι Κύπριϲ θεάϲ, καὶ τοϲόνδ᾽ οὑμοὶ γάμοι
ὤνηϲαν Ἑλλάδ᾽· οὐ κρατεῖϲθ᾽ ἐκ βαρβάρων,
οὔτ᾽ ἐϲ δόρυ ϲταθέντεϲ, οὐ τυραννίδι.
ἃ δ᾽ ηὐτύχηϲεν Ἑλλάϲ, ὠλόμην ἐγὼ
εὐμορφίαι πραθεῖϲα, κὠνειδίζομαι
ἐξ ὧν ἐχρῆν με ϲτέφανον ἐπὶ κάραι λαβεῖν.
οὔπω με φήϲειϲ αὐτὰ τἀν ποϲὶν λέγειν,
ὅπωϲ ἀφώρμηϲ᾽ ἐκ δόμων τῶν ϲῶν λάθραι.
ἦλθ᾽ οὐχὶ μικρὰν θεὸν ἔχων αὑτοῦ μέτα
ὁ τῆϲδ᾽ ἀλάϲτωρ, εἴτ᾽ Ἀλέξανδρον θέλειϲ
ὀνόματι προϲφωνεῖν νιν εἴτε καὶ Πάριν·
ὅν, ὦ κάκιϲτε, ϲοῖϲιν ἐν δόμοιϲ λιπὼν
Cπάρτηϲ ἀπῆραϲ νηὶ Κρηϲίαν χθόνα.
εἶέν.

918 *τἄμ᾽ ἰϲαίτατ᾽* Pearson: *τἀμὰ καὶ τὰ ϲ᾽* VP | *τοῖϲοῖϲι* V[ac] ut uid. (fort. *τοῖϲ ϲοῖϲι* V[pc]) 921 *κἄμ᾽ ὁ* Bothe: *κἀμὲ* VP 922 *τότε* Lenting: *ποτε* VP | u. del. West 923 *ἐνθένδε* Va (et q): *ἔνθεν δὲ* P: *ἐνέδε* V 924 *τριϲϲὸν* Vp: *-ῶν* P | *τριῶν* Wunder: *τριϲϲῶν* VP 927 *δ᾽* P et Tzetzes exeg. in Il. p. 39 Hermann (Hermanni cod. Lipsiensi accedit cod. Cantab. S. Trin. Coll. 981): *θ᾽* V | *ἀϲίαϲ* V et Tzetzes 928 om. Tzetzes (qui 925–7 et 929–31a citat) 930 *δώϲειϲ* P[ac] | *θεᾶϲ* V | *ὑπερδράμοι* Tzetzae cod. Lips. (sec. Hermann) sicut coni. Canter: *ὑπεκδ-* VP et Tzetzae cod. Cantab. 931 *ἔνθεν δ᾽* q sicut coni. Tyrrell: *ἐνθένδ᾽* VP | *ἔχειϲ* P 932 *θεὰ* V | *οὑμοὶ* p: *οὔ μοι* P: *οἱμοὶ* VΣ[1] 935 *ἃ δ᾽* p: *ἄρ᾽* VP | *ὠλόμην δ᾽* V 936 *κὠνειδίζομαι* Va (et q): *κὀν-* P: *καὶ ὀν-* V 938 *τάμ* V 940 *θεῶν* V | *αὑτοῦ* Schaefer: *αὐ-* VP 941 *θέλειϲ*] *θέμιϲ* Nauck 942 del. Hartung

οὐ ϲ', ἀλλ' ἐμαυτὴν τοὐπὶ τῶιδ' ἐρήϲομαι·
τί δὴ φρονοῦϲά γ' ἐκ δόμων ἅμ' ἑϲπόμην
ξένωι, προδοῦϲα πατρίδα καὶ δόμουϲ ἐμούϲ;
τὴν θεὸν κόλαζε καὶ Διὸϲ κρείϲϲων γενοῦ,
ὃϲ τῶν μὲν ἄλλων δαιμόνων ἔχει κράτοϲ,
κείνηϲ δὲ δοῦλόϲ ἐϲτι· ϲυγγνώμη δ' ἐμοί.
  ἔνθεν δ' ἔχοιϲ ἂν εἰϲ ἔμ' εὐπρεπῆ λόγον·
ἐπεὶ θανὼν γῆϲ ἦλθ' Ἀλέξανδροϲ μυχούϲ,
χρῆν μ', ἡνίκ' οὐκ ἦν θεοπόνητά μου λέχη,
λιποῦϲαν οἴκουϲ ναῦϲ ἐπ' Ἀργείων μολεῖν.
ἔϲπευδον αὐτὸ τοῦτο· μάρτυρεϲ δέ μοι
πύργων πυλωροὶ κἀπὸ τειχέων ϲκοποί,
οἳ πολλάκιϲ μ' ἐφηῦρον ἐξ ἐπάλξεων
πλεκταῖϲιν ἐϲ γῆν ϲῶμα κλέπτουϲαν τόδε.
[βίαι δ' ὁ καινόϲ μ' οὗτοϲ ἁρπάϲαϲ πόϲιϲ
Δηίφοβοϲ ἄλοχον εἶχεν ἀκόντων Φρυγῶν.]
πῶϲ οὖν ἔτ' ἂν θνήιϲκοιμ' ἂν ἐνδίκωϲ, πόϲι,
<   >
πρὸϲ ϲοῦ δικαίωϲ, ἣν ὁ μὲν βίαι γαμεῖ,
τὰ δ' οἴκοθεν κεῖν' ἀντὶ νικητηρίων
πικρῶϲ ἐδούλωϲ'; εἰ δὲ τῶν θεῶν κρατεῖν
βούληι, τὸ χρῄζειν ἀμαθέϲ ἐϲτί ϲου τόδε.

Χο. βαϲίλει', ἄμυνον ϲοῖϲ τέκνοιϲι καὶ πάτραι,
πειθὼ διαφθείρουϲα τῆϲδ', ἐπεὶ λέγει
καλῶϲ κακοῦργοϲ οὖϲα· δεινὸν οὖν τόδε.

Εκ. ταῖϲ θεαῖϲι πρῶτα ϲύμμαχοϲ γενήϲομαι
καὶ τήνδε δείξω μὴ λέγουϲαν ἔνδικα.
ἐγὼ γὰρ Ἥραν παρθένον τε Παλλάδα
οὐκ ἐϲ τοϲοῦτον ἀμαθίαϲ ἐλθεῖν δοκῶ,
ὥϲθ' ἡ μὲν Ἄργοϲ βαρβάροιϲ ἀπημπόλα,
Παλλὰϲ δ' Ἀθήναϲ Φρυξὶ δουλεύειν ποτέ,
αἳ παιδιαῖϲι καὶ χλιδῆι μορφῆϲ πέρι
ἦλθον πρὸϲ Ἴδην. τοῦ γὰρ οὕνεκ' ἂν θεὰ
Ἥρα τοϲοῦτον ἔϲχ' ἔρωτα καλλονῆϲ;

946 φρονοῦϲ' ἐκ V 951 ἐνθένδ' VΣ^{1} 959–60 (quos citat Σ Lycoph. 168) del. Wilamowitz 961 πόϲει P | post h. u. lac. indic. Murray: supplere possis <πῶϲ δ' οὐχὶ πολλῶι μᾶλλον ἐλεηθεῖμεν ἂν> 964 ἐδούλωϲ' Dobree: -ευϲ' VP 965 ϲου Dobree: ϲοι V: om. P 966 ἄμεινον P^{ac} | πάτραν V 969 τοῖϲ θεοῖϲ Arist. rhet. 1418 B 970 ἐνδίκωϲ V 971 Παλλάδοϲ P^{ac} 974 εὐθύναϲ P 975 παιδιαῖϲ V | καὶ] κοὐ Lenting, fort. recte 976 πρὸϲ P: ἐπ' V

πότερον ἀμείνον' ὡϲ λάβηι Διὸϲ πόϲιν;
ἢ γάμον Ἀθηνᾶ θεῶν τινοϲ θηρωμένη,
ἢ παρθενείαν πατρὸϲ ἐξῃτήϲατο
φεύγουϲα λέκτρα; μὴ ἀμαθεῖϲ ποίει θεὰϲ
τὸ ϲὸν κακὸν κοϲμοῦϲα, μὴ <οὐ> πείϲηιϲ ϲοφούϲ.
Κύπριν δ' ἔλεξαϲ (ταῦτα γὰρ γέλωϲ πολύϲ)
ἐλθεῖν ἐμῶι ξὺν παιδὶ Μενέλεω δόμουϲ.
οὐκ ἂν μένουϲ' ἂν ἥϲυχόϲ ϲ' ἐν οὐρανῶι
αὐταῖϲ Ἀμύκλαιϲ ἤγαγεν πρὸϲ Ἴλιον;
ἦν οὑμὸϲ υἱὸϲ κάλλοϲ ἐκπρεπέϲτατοϲ,
ὁ ϲὸϲ δ' ἰδών νιν νοῦϲ ἐποιήθη Κύπριϲ·
τὰ μῶρα γὰρ πάντ' ἐϲτὶν Ἀφροδίτη βροτοῖϲ,
καὶ τοὔνομ' ὀρθῶϲ ἀφροϲύνηϲ ἄρχει θεᾶϲ.
ὃν εἰϲιδοῦϲα βαρβάροιϲ ἐϲθήμαϲιν
χρυϲῶι τε λαμπρὸν ἐξεμαργώθηϲ φρέναϲ.
ἐν μὲν γὰρ Ἄργει ϲμίκρ' ἔχουϲ' ἀνεϲτρέφου,
Cπάρτηϲ δ' ἀπαλλαχθεῖϲα τὴν Φρυγῶν πόλιν
χρυϲῶι ῥέουϲαν ἤλπιϲαϲ κατακλύϲειν
δαπάναιϲιν· οὐδ' ἦν ἱκανά ϲοι τὰ Μενέλεω
μέλαθρα ταῖϲ ϲαῖϲ ἐγκαθυβρίζειν τρυφαῖϲ.
εἶέν· βίαι γὰρ παῖδα φήιϲ ϲ' ἄγειν ἐμόν·
τίϲ Cπαρτιατῶν ἤιϲθετ'; ἢ ποίαν βοὴν
ἀνωτότυξαϲ, Κάϲτοροϲ νεανίου
τοῦ ϲυζύγου τ' ἔτ' ὄντοϲ, οὐ κατ' ἄϲτρα πω;
ἐπεὶ δὲ Τροίαν ἦλθεϲ Ἀργεῖοί τέ ϲου
κατ' ἴχνοϲ, ἦν δὲ δοριπετὴϲ ἀγωνία,
εἰ μὲν τὰ τοῦδε κρείϲϲον' ἀγγέλλοιτό ϲοι,
Μενέλαον ἤινειϲ, παῖϲ ὅπωϲ λυποῖτ' ἐμὸϲ
ἔχων ἔρωτοϲ ἀνταγωνιϲτὴν μέγαν·
εἰ δ' εὐτυχοῖεν Τρῶεϲ, οὐδὲν ἦν ὅδε.
ἐϲ τὴν τύχην δ' ὁρῶϲα τοῦτ' ἤϲκειϲ, ὅπωϲ
ἕποι' ἅμ' αὐτῆι, τἀρετῆι δ' οὐκ ἤθελεϲ.
κἄπειτα πλεκταῖϲ ϲῶμα ϲὸν κλέπτειν λέγειϲ
πύργων καθιεῖϲ', ὡϲ μένουϲ' ἀκουϲίωϲ.
ποῦ δῆτ' ἐλήφθηϲ ἢ βρόχοιϲ ἀρτωμένη

978 *ἄμεινον* V | *λάβοι* Hermann 979 *Ἀθάνα* Seidler: *-ηνὰ* V: *-ηνᾶ* P | *πειρωμένη* P 980 *παρθενίαν* V 982 <*οὐ*> Seidler 984 *ξυμ* V 985 *ϲ'* Hermann: *γ'* VP 991 *ὃν εἰϲιδοῦϲα* P et gE: *ὃν ἰδοῦϲα* V: *ἰδοῦϲα τοῦτον* gB 992 *λαμπρῶι* gE 993 *ϲμίκρ'* Burges: *μί-* VP (*μι-* P) 998 *ϲ'* Va: om. VP 1000 *ἀνωτότυξαϲ* Wecklein: *ἀνωλόλυξαϲ* VP 1001 *τ'* om. V 1012 *ποῖ* V | *ἐλείφθηϲ* P^{ac} | *βρόχοιϲ* Burgesii amicus: *-ουϲ* VP | *ἢ 'ν βρό-* Diggle cl. Hip. 779

ἢ φάϲγανον θήγουϲ', ἃ γενναία γυνὴ
δράϲειεν ἂν ποθοῦϲα τὸν πάροϲ πόϲιν;
καίτοι ϲ' ἐνουθέτουν γε πολλὰ πολλάκιϲ·
Ὦ θύγατερ, ἔξελθ'· οἱ δ' ἐμοὶ παῖδεϲ γάμουϲ
ἄλλουϲ γαμοῦϲι, ϲὲ δ' ἐπὶ ναῦϲ Ἀχαιικὰϲ
πέμψω ϲυνεκκλέψαϲα καὶ παύϲω μάχηϲ
Ἕλληναϲ ἡμᾶϲ τ'. ἀλλὰ ϲοὶ τόδ' ἦν πικρόν.
ἐν τοῖϲ Ἀλεξάνδρου γὰρ ὑβρίζειν δόμοιϲ
καὶ προϲκυνεῖϲθαι βαρβάρων ὕπ' ἤθελεϲ·
μεγάλα γὰρ ἦν ϲοι. κἀπὶ τοῖϲδε ϲὸν δέμαϲ
ἐξῆλθεϲ ἀϲκήϲαϲα κἄβλεψαϲ πόϲει
τὸν αὐτὸν αἰθέρ', ὦ κατάπτυϲτον κάρα;
ἣν χρῆν ταπεινὴν ἐν πέπλων ἐρειπίοιϲ,
φρίκηι τρέμουϲαν, κρᾶτ' ἀπεϲκυθιϲμένην
ἐλθεῖν, τὸ ϲῶφρον τῆϲ ἀναιδείαϲ πλέον
ἔχουϲαν ἐπὶ τοῖϲ πρόϲθεν ἡμαρτημένοιϲ.
Μενέλα', ἵν' εἰδῆιϲ οἷ τελευτήϲω λόγον,
ϲτεφάνωϲον Ἑλλάδ' ἀξίωϲ τήνδε κτανὼν
ϲαυτοῦ, νόμον δὲ τόνδε ταῖϲ ἄλλαιϲι θὲϲ
γυναιξί, θνήιϲκειν ἥτιϲ ἂν προδῶι πόϲιν.

Χο. Μενέλαε, προγόνων τ' ἀξίωϲ δόμων τε ϲῶν
τεῖϲαι δάμαρτα κἀφελοῦ πρὸϲ Ἑλλάδοϲ
ψόγον τὸ θῆλύ τ', εὐγενὴϲ ἐχθροῖϲ φανείϲ.

Με. ἐμοὶ ϲὺ ϲυμπέπτωκαϲ ἐϲ ταὐτὸν λόγου,
ἑκουϲίωϲ τήνδ' ἐκ δόμων ἐλθεῖν ἐμῶν
ξέναϲ ἐϲ εὐνάϲ· χἠ Κύπριϲ κόμπου χάριν
λόγοιϲ ἐνεῖται. βαῖνε λευϲτήρων πέλαϲ
πόνουϲ τ' Ἀχαιῶν ἀπόδοϲ ἐν ϲμικρῶι μακροὺϲ
θανοῦϲ', ἵν' εἰδῆιϲ μὴ καταιϲχύνειν ἐμέ.

Ελ. μή, πρόϲ ϲε γονάτων, τὴν νόϲον τὴν τῶν θεῶν
προϲθεὶϲ ἐμοὶ κτάνηιϲ με, ϲυγγίγνωϲκε δέ.

Εκ. μηδ' οὓϲ ἀπέκτειν' ἥδε ϲυμμάχουϲ προδῶιϲ·
ἐγὼ πρὸ κείνων καὶ τέκνων ϲε λίϲϲομαι.

Με. παῦϲαι, γεραιά· τῆϲδε δ' οὐκ ἐφρόντιϲα.

1013 *γεναία* P^{ac} 1014 *τὸν* P: *τὸ* V 1015 *ϲ' … γε* Burges: *γ' … ϲ'* VP 1017 *Ἀχαιικὰϲ* Aldina: *-αικὰϲ* VP 1018 *πέμψω* Va (et q): *πέμπω* VP | *παύϲω* Bothe: *παῦϲον* VP 1020 *ὑβρίζειν* Lehrs: *ὕβριζεϲ* VP 1025 *ἐριπίοιϲ* V 1027 *ἀναιδίαϲ* P^{ac} 1033 *τ' ἀξίωϲ* Seidler: *ἀξίωϲ τε* P: *ἀξίωϲ* V 1034 *τεῖϲαι* Herwerden: *τῖϲαι* P: *τί-* V 1035 *ψόγον* om. P 1040 *τ'* V: *δ'* P | *ϲμικρῶι* Diggle: *μι-* VP 1042 *νόϲων* P^{ac} 1044 ante h. u. aliquid desiderat Wecklein: <*μέμνηϲ' ἃ πᾶϲαν Ἑλλάδ' εἴργαϲται κακὰ*> supplere possis

λέγω δὲ προςπόλοιςι πρὸς πρύμνας νεῶν
τήνδ' ἐκκομίζειν, ἔνθα ναυςτολήςεται.
Εκ. μή νυν νεὼς ςοὶ ταὐτὸν ἐςβήτω ςκάφος.
Με. τί δ' ἔςτι; μεῖζον βρῖθος ἢ πάροιθ' ἔχει;
Εκ. οὐκ ἔςτ' ἐραςτὴς ὅςτις οὐκ ἀεὶ φιλεῖ.
Με. ὅπως ἂν ἐκβῆι τῶν ἐρωμένων ὁ νοῦς.
ἔςται δ' ἃ βούληι· ναῦν γὰρ οὐκ ἐςβήςεται
ἐς ἥνπερ ἡμεῖς· καὶ γὰρ οὐ κακῶς λέγεις·
ἐλθοῦςα δ' Ἄργος ὥςπερ ἀξία κακῶς
κακὴ θανεῖται καὶ γυναιξὶ ςωφρονεῖν
πάςαιςι θήςει. ῥάιδιον μὲν οὐ τόδε·
ὅμως δ' ὁ τῆςδ' ὄλεθρος ἐς φόβον βαλεῖ
τὸ μῶρον αὐτῶν, κἂν ἔτ' ὦς' ἐχθίονες.

Χο. οὕτω δὴ τὸν ἐν Ἰλίωι str. 1
ναὸν καὶ θυόεντα βω-
μὸν προύδωκας Ἀχαιοῖς,
ὦ Ζεῦ, καὶ πελανῶν φλόγα
ςμύρνας αἰθερίας τε κα-
πνὸν καὶ Πέργαμον ἱερὰν
Ἰδαῖά τ' Ἰδαῖα κιςςοφόρα νάπη
χιόνι κατάρυτα ποταμίαι
τέρμονα τε πρωτόβολον †ἁλίωι†,
τὰν καταλαμπομέναν ζάθεον θεράπναν;

φροῦδαί ςοι θυςίαι χορῶν τ' ant. 1
εὔφαμοι κέλαδοι κατ' ὄρφ-
ναν τε παννυχίδες θεῶν,
χρυςέων τε ξοάνων τύποι
Φρυγῶν τε ζάθεοι ςελᾶ-
ναι ςυνδώδεκα πλήθει.
μέλει μέλει μοι τάδ' εἰ φρονεῖς, ἄναξ,

1050 *πάροιθ'* V: *πάρος γ'* P 1051 *οὐκ ἔςτ'*] *οὐδεὶς* Arist. rhet. 1394 B et (*οὐθεὶς γὰρ*) eth. Eud. 1235 B (~gB) 1052 *Με.* Aldina (non q): om. VP 1053 *Με.* praescr. VP | *δ'* P: *τάδ'* V | *βόλει* P^{ac} 1058 *τῆς* V 1059 *αἰςχίονες* Hermann 1060 *ςὸν* Willink 1062 *προύδωκά ς'* P 1064 *ςμύρνας* Diggle: *-ης* VPΣ^1 1065 *ἱρὰν* Heath 1066 *κιςςηφόρα* P 1067 *κατάρυτα* Seidler: *κατάρρ-* VP 1069 *ἕω* Wilamowitz 1070 *ζάθεον* Wilamowitz: *-θέαν* VP | *θεράπναν* VΣ: *-άπναιναν* P | interrogationis notam add. Denniston, *GP* 209 1072 *εὔφαμοι* Dindorf: *εὔφημοι* VP 1073 *παννυχίδες θεῶν* om. P 1076 *ςυνδώδεκα* Va (et q) sicut coni. Barnes: *ςὺν δώδεκα* VP

οὐράνιον ἕδρανον ἐπιβεβὼϲ
αἰθέρα τε, πόλεοϲ ὀλομέναϲ
ἃν πυρὸϲ αἰθομένα κατέλυϲεν ὁρμά.

ὦ φίλοϲ ὦ πόϲι μοι, str. 2
ϲὺ μὲν φθίμενοϲ ἀλαίνειϲ
ἄθαπτοϲ ἄνυδροϲ, ἐμὲ δὲ πόντιον ϲκάφοϲ
ἀίϲϲον πτεροῖϲι πορεύϲει
ἱππόβοτον Ἄργοϲ, †ἵνα τείχεα†
λάϊνα Κυκλώπι' οὐράνια νέμονται.
τέκνων δὲ πλῆθοϲ ἐν πύλαιϲ
δάκρυϲι †κατάορα ϲτένει βοᾶι† βοᾶι·
Μᾶτερ, ὤμοι, μόναν δή μ' Ἀχαιοὶ κομί-
ζουϲι ϲέθεν ἀπ' ὀμμάτων
κυανέαν ἐπὶ ναῦν,
εἶθ' ἁλίοιϲι πλάταιϲ
ἢ Ϲαλαμῖν' ἱερὰν
ἢ δίπορον κορυφὰν
Ἴϲθμιον, ἔνθα πύλαϲ
Πέλοποϲ ἔχουϲιν ἕδραι.

εἴθ' ἀκάτου Μενέλα ant. 2
μέϲον πέλαγοϲ ἰούϲαϲ,
δίπαλτον ἱερὸν ἀνὰ μέϲον πλατᾶν πέϲοι
†αἰγαίου† κεραυνοφαὲϲ πῦρ,
Ἰλιόθεν ὅτε με πολυδάκρυον
Ἑλλάδι λάτρευμα γᾶθεν ἐξορίζει,
χρύϲεα δ' ἔνοπτρα, παρθένων
χάριταϲ, ἔχουϲα τυγχάνει Διὸϲ κόρα,
μηδὲ γαῖάν ποτ' ἔλθοι Λάκαιναν πατρῶι-
όν τε θάλαμον ἑϲτίαϲ,

1078 ἕδραν P | ἐπιβεβὼϲ Seidler: -βεβηκὼϲ VPΣ 1079 πόλεοϲ Seidler: -εωϲ VPΣ[1] 1081 cho. contin. Stephanus (et Neap. teste Wecklein): Εκ. praescr. VP 1083 φθίμενοϲ Aldina: -οιϲ VPΣ[i] 1086 ᾄϲϲον Hermann 1087 ἕδραν' ἵνα Willink 1088 Κυκλώπι' Bothe: -ια P: -εια V 1089 τέκνον P 1090 κατάροον Willink | ἀϲθενῆ βοὰν Paley 1091 ὤμοι V: ἔμοι P 1095 εἶθ' ἁλίοιϲι post Musgrave (εἶθ' ἁλίαιϲι) Willink cl. Hcld. 82: ἐναλίαιϲι V: ἐν ἁλ- P: εἰναλ- Aldina 1097 δίπορ*ον V[pc] (fort. -ιον V[ac]) 1100 εἴθ' Stephanus: ἔνθ' VPΣ | μενέλαε P 1102 δίπλατον P | πλατᾶν Burges: πλάταν VPΣ 1104 Ἰδαίου Musgrave: αἰθαλοῦν Diggle: Δῖον (cum ᾄϲϲον 1086) Schenkl 1105 πολυδάκρυον Bothe: -δακρυν VP 1106 ἐξορίζοι Wecklein

μηδὲ πόλιν Πιτάνας
χαλκόπυλόν τε θεάν,
δύcγαμον αἶcχοc ἑλὼν
Ἑλλάδι τᾶι μεγάλαι
καὶ Cιμοεντιάcιν
μέλεα πάθεα ῥοαῖcιν.

—ἰὼ ἰώ,
καίν' ἐκ καινῶν μεταβάλλουcι
χθονὶ cυντυχίαι· λεύccετε Τρώων
τόνδ' Ἀcτυάνακτ' ἄλοχοι μέλεαι
νεκρόν, ὃν πύργων δίcκημα πικρὸν
Δαναοὶ κτείναντεc ἔχουcιν.

Κη. Ἑκάβη, νεὼc μὲν πίτυλοc εἷc λελειμμένοc
λάφυρα τἀπίλοιπ' Ἀχιλλείου τόκου
μέλλει πρὸc ἀκτὰc ναυcτολεῖν Φθιώτιδαc·
αὐτὸc δ' ἀνῆκται Νεοπτόλεμοc, καινάc τιναc
Πηλέωc ἀκούcαc cυμφοράc, ὥc νιν χθονὸc
Ἄκαcτοc ἐκβέβληκεν, ὁ Πελίου γόνοc.
οὗ θᾶccον οὕνεκ', οὐ χάριν μονῆc ἔχων,
φροῦδοc, μετ' αὐτοῦ δ' Ἀνδρομάχη, πολλῶν ἐμοὶ
δακρύων ἀγωγόc, ἡνίκ' ἐξώρμα χθονόc,
πάτραν τ' ἀναcτένουcα καὶ τὸν Ἕκτοροc
τύμβον προcεννέπουcα. καί cφ' ᾐτήcατο
θάψαι νεκρὸν τόνδ', ὃc πεcὼν ἐκ τειχέων
ψυχὴν ἀφῆκεν Ἕκτοροc τοῦ coῦ γόνοc·
φόβον τ' Ἀχαιῶν, χαλκόνωτον ἀcπίδα
τήνδ', ἣν πατὴρ τοῦδ' ἀμφὶ πλεύρ' ἐβάλλετο,
μή νιν πορεῦcαι Πηλέωc ἐφ' ἑcτίαν
μηδ' ἐc τὸν αὐτὸν θάλαμον οὗ νυμφεύcεται
[μήτηρ νεκροῦ τοῦδ' Ἀνδρομάχη, λύπαc ὁρᾶν],
ἀλλ' ἀντὶ κέδρου περιβόλων τε λαΐνων

1113 θεάν Musgrave: θεᾶc θάλαμον VP 1114 ἔχων Wilamowitz 1115 τὰ P 1116 Cιμοεντιάcιν Hermann: -τίcιν VP 1117 ῥοαῖcιν post Musgrave (ῥοῆιcιν) Blomfield: προῆcιν P: τρωῆιcιν VΣ[i] 1118 καίν' ἐκ post Dobree (καιναὶ 'κ) Wilamowitz: καινὰ VPΣ[i] | καὶ νῶν P | μεταβάλλουcι Dobree: -ουcαι VPΣ[i] 1119 λέυcετε V 1122 κτείνοντεc P 1123 Κη. post Elmsley (Αγ.) Kovacs (uide ad 709): Τα. VP | λελειμένοc V 1124 ἀχιλείου V 1129 οὐ Bothe et Σ[i] ut uid.: ἢ VP 1130 δ' V: τ' P 1131 ἐξορμᾶ P 1132 τ' om. P 1134 νεκρῶν τῶνδ' P[ac] 1137 πλεῦρ' V: τήνδ' P 1138 μή νιν PΣ[i]: μῆνιν V 1140 del. Herwerden, Paley 1141 κε*δρου P | τ' ἐλαίνων V

ἐν τῆιδε θάψαι παῖδα· cὰc δ’ ἐc ὠλέναc
δοῦναι, πέπλοιcιν ὡc περιcτείληιc νεκρὸν
cτεφάνοιc θ’, ὅcη coι δύναμιc, ὡc ἔχει τὰ cά·
ἐπεὶ βέβηκε καὶ τὸ δεcπότου τάχοc
ἀφείλετ’ αὐτὴν παῖδα μὴ δοῦναι τάφωι.
ἡμεῖc μὲν οὖν, ὅταν cὺ κοcμήcηιc νέκυν,
γῆν τῶιδ’ ἐπαμπιcχόντεc ἀροῦμεν δόρυ·
cὺ δ’ ὡc τάχιcτα πρᾶccε τἀπεcταλμένα.
ἑνὸc μὲν οὖν μόχθου c’ ἀπαλλάξαc ἔχω·
Cκαμανδρίουc γὰρ τάcδε διαπερῶν ῥοὰc
ἔλουcα νεκρὸν κἀπένιψα τραύματα.
ἀλλ’ εἶμ’ ὀρυκτὸν τῶιδ’ ἀναρρήξων τάφον,
ὡc cύντομ’ ἡμῖν τἀπ’ ἐμοῦ τε κἀπὸ coῦ
ἐc ἓν ξυνελθόντ’ οἴκαδ’ ὁρμήcηι πλάτην.

Εκ. θέcθ’ ἀμφίτορνον ἀcπίδ’ Ἕκτοροc πέδωι,
λυπρὸν θέαμα κοὐ φίλον λεύccειν ἐμοί.
ὦ μείζον’ ὄγκον δορὸc ἔχοντεc ἢ φρενῶν,
τί τόνδ’, Ἀχαιοί, παῖδα δείcαντεc φόνον
καινὸν διηργάcαcθε; μὴ Τροίαν ποτὲ
πεcοῦcαν ὀρθώcειεν; οὐδὲν ἦτ’ ἄρα,
ὅθ’ Ἕκτοροc μὲν εὐτυχοῦντοc ἐc δόρυ
διωλλύμεcθα μυρίαc τ’ ἄλληc χερόc,
πόλεωc δ’ ἁλούcηc καὶ Φρυγῶν ἐφθαρμένων
βρέφοc τοcόνδ’ ἐδείcατ’· οὐκ αἰνῶ, φόβον
ὅcτιc φοβεῖται μὴ διεξελθὼν λόγωι.
ὦ φίλταθ’, ὥc coι θάνατοc ἦλθε δυcτυχήc.
εἰ μὲν γὰρ ἔθανεc πρὸ πόλεωc ἥβηc τυχὼν
γάμων τε καὶ τῆc ἰcοθέου τυραννίδοc,
μακάριοc ἦcθ’ ἄν, εἴ τι τῶνδε μακάριον·
νῦν <δ’> αὔτ’ ἰδὼν μὲν γνούc τε cῆι ψυχῆι, τέκνον,
†οὐκ οἶcθ’, ἐχρήcω† δ’ οὐδὲν ἐν δόμοιc ἔχων.

1142 δ’ ἐc pVa (et q): δέ c’ V: c’ ἐc P 1144 cτεφανοῖcθ’ P 1145 τὸ P: τὸ τοῦ V 1148 τόδ’ P^{ac} | ἐπαμπιcχόντεc praemonente Elmsley Matthiae: ἐπαπίcχ- P (-αμπ- p): ἀμπιcχόντεc V | ἀροῦμεν Burges: αἰρ- VP 1149 πράccετ’ ἀπεcταλμένα P^{ac} 1150 ἀπαλλάξαc $P\Sigma^{i}$: ἀνταλλ- V 1153 ἀναρήξων V 1155 ὁρμήcηι Reiske: -μήcει V: -μίcη P 1157 λεύcειν V et gE 1158 μείζον’ Va (et q): μεῖζον $VP\Sigma^{1}$ 1160 διηργάcαcθε P^{ac}: διειργ- VP^{pc} 1163 διωλλύμεcθα p: -μεθα P: διολλύμεcθα V^{sl}: διολύ- V | μυρίουc V: μυρίου Nauck 1167 cυcτυχήc P^{ac} 1171 <δ’> Reiske | αὔτ’ Aldina: αὖτ’ VP | cῆι] cὰ (sc. ὄντα) Munro 1172 fort. cύνοιcθα, χρῆcθαι (cύνοιcθ’ iam Hartung)

δύϲτηνε, κρατὸϲ ὥϲ ϲ’ ἔκειρεν ἀθλίωϲ
τείχη πατρῶια, Λοξίου πυργώματα,
ὃν πόλλ’ ἐκήπευϲ’ ἡ τεκοῦϲα βόϲτρυχον
φιλήμαϲίν τ’ ἔδωκεν, ἔνθεν ἐκγελᾶι
ὀϲτέων ῥαγέντων φόνοϲ, ἵν’ αἰϲχρὰ μὴ ϲτέγω.
ὦ χεῖρεϲ, ὡϲ εἰκοὺϲ μὲν ἡδείαϲ πατρὸϲ
κέκτηϲθ’, ἐν ἄρθροιϲ δ’ ἔκλυτοι πρόκειϲθέ μοι.
ὦ πολλὰ κόμπουϲ ἐκβαλών, φίλον ϲτόμα,
ὄλωλαϲ, ἐψεύϲω μ’, ὅτ’ ἐϲπίπτων πέπλουϲ,
Ὦ μῆτερ, ηὔδαϲ, ἦ πολύν ϲοι βοϲτρύχων
πλόκαμον κεροῦμαι πρὸϲ τάφον θ’ ὁμηλίκων
κώμουϲ ἐπάξω, φίλα διδοὺϲ προϲφθέγματα.
ϲὺ δ’ οὐκ ἔμ’, ἀλλ’ ἐγὼ ϲὲ τὸν νεώτερον,
γραῦϲ ἄπολιϲ ἄτεκνοϲ, ἄθλιον θάπτω νεκρόν.
οἴμοι, τὰ πόλλ’ ἀϲπάϲμαθ’ αἵ τ’ ἐμαὶ τροφαὶ
†ὕπνοι τ’ ἐκεῖνοι† φροῦδά μοι. τί καί ποτε
γράψειεν ἄν ϲοι μουϲοποιὸϲ ἐν τάφωι;
Τὸν παῖδα τόνδ’ ἔκτειναν Ἀργεῖοί ποτε
δείϲαντεϲ; αἰϲχρὸν τοὐπίγραμμά γ’ Ἑλλάδι.
ἀλλ’ οὖν πατρώιων οὐ λαχὼν ἕξειϲ ὅμωϲ
ἐν ἧι ταφήϲηι χαλκόνωτον ἰτέαν.
ὦ καλλίπηχυν Ἕκτοροϲ βραχίονα
ϲώιζουϲ’, ἄριϲτον φύλακ’ ἀπώλεϲαϲ ϲέθεν.
ὡϲ ἡδὺϲ ἐν πόρπακι ϲῶι κεῖται τύποϲ
ἴτυόϲ τ’ ἐν εὐτόρνοιϲι περιδρόμοιϲ ἱδρώϲ,
ὃν ἐκ μετώπου πολλάκιϲ πόνουϲ ἔχων
ἔϲταζεν Ἕκτωρ προϲτιθεὶϲ γενειάδι.
φέρετε, κομίζετ’ ἀθλίωι κόϲμον νεκρῶι
ἐκ τῶν παρόντων· οὐ γὰρ ἐϲ κάλλοϲ τύχαϲ

1173 ὥϲ ϲ’ P: ὃϲ V: ὥϲ ϲ’ et ὡϲ codd. Athen. 66A (hanc lect. commendat anonymus ap. Wecklein 1901) 1174 τείχη V et Athen.: τύχη P (et πατρῶα) 1177 ϲτέγω Diggle: λέγω VPΣ et Athen. et Eust. in Il. p. 757.47, quo seruato δὴ pro μὴ Denniston 1178 εἰκοῦϲ VP$Σ^{1}$ 1179 κέκληϲθ’ P^{ac} ut uid. | πρόϲκειϲθε (om. μοι) VΣ 1180 ἐκβαλὸν φίλιον V | post ἐκβαλών dist. Burges 1181 πέπλουϲ P: λέχοϲ V 1183 θ’ V: δ’ P 1184 ἐπάξω Nauck: ἀπ- VP 1187 ἀϲπάμαθ’ V 1188 πόνοι τ’ ἐκεῖνοι noluit Seidler: ἀυπνίαι τε Heimsoeth: ὕπνοι τε κοινοὶ Munro: ἄυπνοι τε κλῖναι Lane per litt. 1189 ϲοι Burges: ϲε VPΣ: ϲῶι Dobree 1191 τοὐπίγραμμα γ’ V (fort. -α γ’ V^{pc}, -α V^{ac}): -γραμμ’ P (-γραμμ’ ἐν p) 1194 ὧι V 1195 θέθεν P^{ac} 1196 ϲῶι Barnes: ϲὸϲ VP$Σ^{li}$ 1199 ἔϲταζεν P: -ξεν VΣ: -ζέ ϲ’ Bothe

δαίμων δίδωϲιν· ὧν δ' ἔχω, λήψηι τάδε.
θνητῶν δὲ μῶροϲ ὅϲτιϲ εὖ πράϲϲειν δοκῶν
βέβαια χαίρει· τοῖϲ τρόποιϲ γὰρ αἱ τύχαι,
ἔμπληκτοϲ ὡϲ ἄνθρωποϲ, ἄλλοτ' ἄλλοϲε
πηδῶϲι, †κοὐδεὶϲ αὐτὸϲ εὐτυχῇ ποτε†.
Χο. καὶ μὴν πρὸ χειρῶν αἵδε ϲοι ϲκυλευμάτων
Φρυγίων φέρουϲι κόϲμον ἐξάπτειν νεκρῶι.
Εκ. ὦ τέκνον, οὐχ ἵπποιϲι νικήϲαντά ϲε
οὐδ' ἥλικαϲ τόξοιϲιν, οὓϲ Φρύγεϲ νόμουϲ
τιμῶϲιν, †οὐκ ἐϲ πληϲμονὰϲ θηρώμενοι†,
< >
μήτηρ πατρόϲ ϲοι προϲτίθηϲ' ἀγάλματα
τῶν ϲῶν ποτ' ὄντων, νῦν δέ ϲ' ἡ θεοϲτυγὴϲ
ἀφείλεθ' Ἑλένη, πρὸϲ δὲ καὶ ψυχὴν ϲέθεν
ἔκτεινε καὶ πάντ' οἶκον ἐξαπώλεϲεν.
Χο. ἓ ἕ, φρενῶν ἔθιγεϲ ἔθιγεϲ. ὦ
μέγαϲ ἐμοί ποτ' ὢν ἀνάκτωρ πόλεωϲ.
Εκ. ἃ δ' ἐν γάμοιϲι χρῆν ϲε προϲθέϲθαι χροῒ
Ἀϲιατίδων γήμαντα τὴν ὑπερτάτην,
Φρύγια πέπλων ἀγάλματ' ἐξάπτω χροόϲ.
ϲύ τ', ὦ ποτ' οὖϲα καλλίνικε μυρίων
μῆτερ τροπαίων, Ἕκτοροϲ φίλον ϲάκοϲ,
ϲτεφανοῦ· κάτει γὰρ οὐ θανοῦϲα ϲὺν νεκρῶι·
ἐπεὶ ϲὲ πολλῶι μᾶλλον ἢ τὰ τοῦ ϲοφοῦ
κακοῦ τ' Ὀδυϲϲέωϲ ἄξιον τιμᾶν ὅπλα.
Χο. αἰαῖ αἰαῖ·
πικρὸν ὄδυρμα γαῖά ϲ', ὦ
τέκνον, δέξεται.
ϲτέναζε, μᾶτερ Εκ. αἰαῖ.
Χο. νεκρῶν ἴακχον. Εκ. οἴμοι.
Χο. οἴμοι δῆτα ϲῶν ἀλάϲτων κακῶν.
Εκ. τελαμῶϲιν ἕλκη τὰ μὲν ἐγώ ϲ' ἰάϲομαι,

1203–4 πράϲϲων δοκεῖ . . . χαίρειν Bothe 1206 αὐτῶν gE | εὐτυχῇ P: εὐτυχεῖ Vp et gE | κοὔποθ' αὐτὸϲ εὐτυχὴϲ ἀεί Barthold (αὐ- iam Scaliger): sed praestat tradita seruare lacuna post κοὐδεὶϲ indicata 1208 ἐξάπειν V 1211 τιμῶϲι, νείκουϲ Eden | post h. u. lac. indic. Scaliger 1212 προϲτίθημ' Herwerden 1213 δέ] τὰ Kovacs dubitanter 1216 ἓ ἓ VP 1218 γάμοιϲι χρῆν Prinz: -οιϲ ἐχρῆν VP 1220 om. V 1223 κάτει Wecklein: θανῆι VP 1229 ϲτέναξον V 1230 Χο. . . . Εκ. Aldina: om. VP | νεκρῶν Aldina: -ὸν VPΣ | οἴμοι Wecklein (ὤμοι iam Hermann): οἴμοι (οἴ μοί V) μοι VP 1232 Εκ. om. V | ἰήϲομαι V

τλήμων ἰατρός, ὄνομ' ἔχουςα, τἄργα δ' οὔ·
τὰ δ' ἐν νεκροῖςι φροντιεῖ πατὴρ ςέθεν.
Χο. ἄραςς' ἄραςςε κρᾶτα
πιτύλους διδοῦςα χειρός,
ἰώ μοί μοι.
Εκ. ὦ φίλταται γυναῖκες.
Χο. †Ἑκάβη, ςὰς† ἔνεπε· τίνα θροεῖς αὐδάν;
Εκ. †οὐκ ἦν ἄρ' ἐν θεοῖςι πλὴν οὑμοὶ πόνοι†
Τροία τε πόλεων ἔκκριτον μιςουμένη,
μάτην δ' ἐβουθυτοῦμεν. εἰ δὲ μὴ θεὸς
ἔςτρεψε τἄνω περιβαλὼν κάτω χθονός,
ἀφανεῖς ἂν ὄντες οὐκ ἂν ὑμνήθημεν ἂν
μούςαις ἀοιδὰς δόντες ὑςτέρων βροτῶν.
  χωρεῖτε, θάπτετ' ἀθλίωι τύμβωι νεκρόν·
ἔχει γὰρ οἷα δεῖ γε νερτέρων ςτέφη.
δοκῶ δὲ τοῖς θανοῦςι διαφέρειν βραχὺ
εἰ πλουςίων τις τεύξεται κτεριςμάτων·
κενὸν δὲ γαύρωμ' ἐςτὶ τῶν ζώντων τόδε.
Χο. ἰὼ ἰώ·
μελέα μήτηρ, ἣ τὰς μεγάλας
†ἐλπίδας ἐπὶ ςοὶ† κατέκναψε βίου.
μέγα δ' ὀλβιςθεὶς ὡς ἐκ πατέρων
ἀγαθῶν ἐγένου
δεινῶι θανάτωι διόλωλας.
ἔα ἔα·

1234 φροντιεῖ Chr. Pat. 1383 sicut coni. Matthiae: -ίςει VP 1235 κρᾶτα Bothe, Seidler: χειρὶ κρᾶτα V(κρά-) P 1238–9 Εκ.... Χο. om. V | uersus lacuna laborare suspicatus est Diggle 1239 θαρςήςας' Hermann: ςιγώςαις Willink | ἔνεπε Bothe: ἔνν- VP 1240 ἐν θεῶν γόναςι Wecklein 1240–1 πλὴν ἐμοὶ πόνοι (πόνος malit Wecklein) Τροίαι τε...μιςουμένηι Bothe 1241 ἔκριτον P^{ac} 1242 δὲ μὴ Stephanus: δ' ἡμᾶς $VP\Sigma^{i}$ 1243 ἔςτρεψέ τ' ἄνω P (et q): ἀφανεῖς ἂν ὄντες V 1244 ὑμνηθεῖμεν Hermann 1245 ὑςτέρων Wecklein: ὑςτέραν P: ἀοιδοῖς V: ὑςτέραις Wilamowitz 1246 ἄθλιον Pierson 1247 δεῖ P: δή V 1250 κενὸν $Vp\Sigma^{li}$ (κενὸς δὲ κόμπος Chr. Pat. 1452): καινὸν P et gE | γαύρωμ' $Vp\Sigma^{li}$ et gE: γαῦρον μ' P | τάδε Chr. Pat. (~gE) 1251 μήτηρ Dindorf: μάτηρ V: μᾶτερ P: μῆτηρ Σ^{l} 1252 post ἐλπίδας uerba excidisse suspicor | ἐπὶ] ἐν Porson | κατέκναψε Porson: -γναψε VP: -σκαψε gE 1253 ὀλβιςθεῖς' V 1253–4 ἐξ ἀγαθῶν (deletis πατέρων et ἐγένου) Hermann

τίνας Ἰλιάσιν τούϲδ᾽ ἐν κορυφαῖϲ
λεύϲϲω φλογέας δαλοῖϲι χέρας
διερέϲϲοντας; μέλλει Τροίαι
καινόν τι κακὸν προϲέϲεϲθαι.

Τα. αὐδῶ λοχαγοῖϲ, οἳ τέταχθ᾽ ἐμπιμπράναι
Πριάμου τόδ᾽ ἄϲτυ, μηκέτ᾽ ἀργοῦϲαν φλόγα
ἐν χερϲὶ ϲώιζειν ἀλλὰ πῦρ ἐνιέναι,
ὡϲ ἂν καταϲκάψαντεϲ Ἰλίου πόλιν
ϲτελλώμεθ᾽ οἴκαδ᾽ ἄϲμενοι Τροίας ἄπο.
ὑμεῖϲ δ᾽, ἵν᾽ αὑτὸϲ λόγοϲ ἔχηι μορφὰϲ δύο,
χωρεῖτε, Τρώων παῖδεϲ, ὀρθίαν ὅταν
ϲάλπιγγοϲ ἠχὼ δῶϲιν ἀρχηγοὶ ϲτρατοῦ,
πρὸϲ ναῦϲ Ἀχαιῶν, ὡϲ ἀποϲτέλληϲθε γῆϲ,
ϲύ τ᾽, ὦ γεραιά, δυϲτυχεϲτάτη γύναι,
ἕπου. μεθήκουϲίν ϲ᾽ Ὀδυϲϲέωϲ πάρα
οἷδ᾽, ὧι ϲε δούλην κλῆροϲ ἐκπέμπει πάτραϲ.
Εκ. οἲ ᾽γὼ τάλαινα· τοῦτο δὴ τὸ λοίϲθιον
καὶ τέρμα πάντων τῶν ἐμῶν ἤδη κακῶν·
ἔξειμι πατρίδοϲ, πόλιϲ ὑφάπτεται πυρί.
ἀλλ᾽, ὦ γεραιὲ πούϲ, ἐπίϲπευϲον μόλιϲ,
ὡϲ ἀϲπάϲωμαι τὴν ταλαίπωρον πόλιν.
ὦ μεγάλα δή ποτ᾽ ἀμπνέουϲ᾽ ἐν βαρβάροιϲ
Τροία, τὸ κλεινὸν ὄνομ᾽ ἀφαιρήϲηι τάχα·
πιμπρᾶϲί ϲ᾽, ἡμᾶϲ δ᾽ ἐξάγουϲ᾽ ἤδη χθονὸϲ
δούλαϲ· ἰὼ θεοί. καὶ τί τοὺϲ θεοὺϲ καλῶ;
καὶ πρὶν γὰρ οὐκ ἤκουϲαν ἀνακαλούμενοι.
φέρ᾽ ἐϲ πυρὰν δράμωμεν· ὡϲ κάλλιϲτά μοι
ϲὺν τῆιδε πατρίδι κατθανεῖν πυρουμένηι.
Τα. ἐνθουϲιᾶιϲ, δύϲτηνε, τοῖϲ ϲαυτῆϲ κακοῖϲ.
ἀλλ᾽ ἄγετε, μὴ φείδεϲθ᾽· Ὀδυϲϲέωϲ δὲ χρὴ
ἐϲ χεῖρα δοῦναι τήνδε καὶ πέμπειν γέραϲ.

1256 *Χο.* praescr. V: *Εκ.* P | τίναϲ semel Haun. (teste Wecklein): bis VP | τούϲδ᾽ Lenting: ταῖϲδ᾽ P: παῖϲδ᾽ V 1257 λεύϲω VΣ^1 1258 μέλει V 1260 τέταχθ᾽ ἐμπιμπράναι Dindorf: τέταχθεν πιμ- V: -χθε πιμ- PΣ^1 1262 χερϲὶ V: χειρὶ P 1265 αὑτὸϲ Aldina: αὐ- VP | ἔχη V: -ει P: -οι P[sl] 1267 ἠχὼ P: -ῶν V 1269 δ᾽ Blaydes, fort. recte 1271 οἶδ᾽ ὦ V | πάτραϲ P: χθονόϲ V 1272 οἲ ᾽γὼ Aldina: οἲ (οἶ V) ἐγὼ VP 1273 τῶν ἐμῶν ἤδη Musgrave: ἤδη τ- ἐ- VP 1276 ἀϲπάϲομαι V 1277 ἐμπνέουϲ᾽ q et Chr. Pat. 1704 sicut coni Wakefield 1279 πιμπρᾶ*ἡμᾶϲ* P (πιμπρᾶϲὶ δ᾽ ἡμᾶϲ p) 1283 πατρίδη P 1284 *Τα.* V: *Χο.* P | ϲαυτῆϲ P: αὑτοῖϲ V 1285 δ᾽ ἐχρὴ V

Εκ. ὀτοτοτοτοτοῖ. str. 1
Κρόνιε, πρύτανι Φρύγιε, γενέτα
[πάτερ, ἀνάξια τῆϲ Δαρδάνου]
γονᾶϲ, τάδ' οἷα πάϲχομεν δέδορκαϲ;
Χο. δέδορκεν, ἁ δὲ μεγαλόπολιϲ
ἄπολιϲ ὄλωλεν οὐδ' ἔτ' ἔϲτι Τροία.

Εκ. ὀτοτοτοτοτοῖ. ant. 1
λέλαμπεν Ἴλιόϲ <τε> περ-
γάμων τε πυρὶ τέραμν' ἄκρα τε τειχέων.
Χο. πτέρυγι δὲ καπνὸϲ ὥϲ τιϲ οὐρίαι πεϲοῦϲα δορὶ καταφθίνει γᾶ.
[μαλερὰ μέλαθρα πυρὶ κατάδρομα
δαΐωι τε λόγχαι.]

Εκ. ἰὼ γᾶ τρόφιμε τῶν ἐμῶν τέκνων. str. 2
Χο. ἒ ἔ.
Εκ. ὦ τέκεα, κλύετε, μάθετε ματρὸϲ αὐδάν.
Χο. ἰαλέμωι τοὺϲ θανόνταϲ ἀπύειϲ.
Εκ. γεραιά γ' ἐϲ πέδον μέλεα τιθεῖϲα καὶ
χερϲὶ γαῖαν κτυποῦϲα διϲϲαῖϲ.
Χο. διάδοχά ϲοι γόνυ τίθημι γαίαι
τοὺϲ ἐμοὺϲ καλοῦϲα νέρ-
θεν ἀθλίουϲ ἀκοίταϲ.
Εκ. ἀγόμεθα φερόμεθ' *Χο.* ἄλγοϲ ἄλγοϲ βοᾶιϲ.
Εκ. δούλειον ὑπὸ μέλαθρον. *Χο.* ἐκ πάτραϲ γ' ἐμᾶϲ.
Εκ. ἰὼ ἰώ, Πρίαμε Πρίαμε,
ϲὺ μὲν ὀλόμενοϲ ἄταφοϲ ἄφιλοϲ
ἄταϲ ἐμᾶϲ ἄιϲτοϲ εἶ.
Χο. μέλαϲ γὰρ ὄϲϲε κατεκάλυ-
ψε θάνατοϲ ὅϲιοϲ ἀνοϲίοιϲ ϲφαγαῖϲιν.

1287 *ὀτοτοτοτοτοῖ* post Schroeder (*ὀττ-*) Diggle: *ὀττοτοτοτοτοτοῖ* VP: item 1294 1289 *ἀνάξια τῆϲ δαρδανίου* P: *ἄξια τᾶϲδε δαρδάνου* V: u. secl. Willink 1293 *οὐδ' ἔτ'* q: *οὐδέ τ'* VP 1294 uide ad 1287 1295 *Ἴλιόϲ <τε>* Kovacs: *Ἴλιοϲ* VP: *-ον Σ* 1296 *τε* om. P | *πυρὶ* post Diggle Willink, scholiorum silentio fretus: *πυρὶ καταίθεται* VP | *τέραμν'* Hartung: *τέραμνα καὶ πόλιϲ* VP 1298 *οὐρίαι* Wilamowitz: *οὐρανίαι* VPΣ 1300–1 secl. Diggle, post 1297 trai. Hermann 1303 *ἒ ἔ* VP | post *ἒ ἔ* habet V *μέλαθρα τῶ πυρὶ καταδέδρακεν* (*τὸ πῦρ καταδεδρά<μη>κεν* Kirchhoff), quod est scholium ad 1300 pertinens | *τέκεα* West: *τέκνα* VP | *μητρὸϲ* V 1305 *Εκ.* om. P | *γ'* Seidler: *τ'* VP | *μέλεα τιθεῖϲα* West: *τ- μ-* VP 1307 *Χο.* om. P | *διάδοχά* Dindorf: *-όν* VPΣ^1 1312 *ἰώ* bis V: semel P | 1315 *Χο.* Seidler: om. VP | *κατεκάλυψε* Stephanus: *κατακαλύψει* VP

Εκ. ἰὼ θεῶν μέλαθρα καὶ πόλις φίλα, ant. 2
Χο. ἒ ἔ.
Εκ. τὰν φόνιον ἔχετε φλόγα δορός τε λόγχαν.
Χο. τάχ' ἐς φίλαν γᾶν πεςεῖςθ' ἀνώνυμοι.
Εκ. κόνις δ' ἴςα καπνῶι πτέρυγι πρὸς αἰθέρ' ἄις-
 cους' ἄοικον δόμων με θήςει.
Χο. ὄνομα δὲ γᾶς ἀφανὲς εἶςιν· ἄλλαι δ'
 ἄλλο φροῦδον, οὐδ' ἔτ' ἔ-
 ςτιν ἁ τάλαινα Τροία.
Εκ. ἐμάθετ', ἐκλύετε; Χο. περγάμων <γε> κτύπον.
Εκ. ἔνοςις ἅπαςαν ἔνοςις Χο. ἐπικλύζει πόλιν.
Εκ. ἰὼ <ἰώ>, τρομερὰ τρομερὰ
 μέλεα, φέρετ' ἐμὸν ἴχνος· ἴτ' ἐπὶ
 δούλειον ἁμέραν βίου.
Χο. ἰὼ τάλαινα πόλις· ὅμως
 δὲ πρόφερε πόδα ςὸν ἐπὶ πλάτας Ἀχαιῶν.

1316 *ὅςιος* PΣ[i]: *-ον* VΣ[l] | *ἀνοςίοις* L. Dindorf: *-αις* VP | *ςφαγαῖς* P 1317 *Εκ.* Seidler: om. VP 1318 *Χο.* P: om. V | *ἒ ἔ* VP | *Εκ.* Seidler: om. VP 1319 *Χο.* Seidler: om. VP | *γᾶν* V: *γὰρ* P 1320 *Εκ.* Seidler: om. VP | *καπνοῦ* Seidler 1320–1 *αἰθέρ' ἄιςςους' ἄοικον δόμων* West: *αἰθέρα ἄιςτον οἴκων ἐμῶν* VP 1321 *ἄιςτον οἶκον ἐμὸν* et *ἀίςτων οἴκων ἐμῶν* Σ[i] | *μεθήςει* V 1322 *Χο.* Seidler: om. VP | *ἄλλαι* Victorius et Σ[i]: *ἄλλα* VP 1323 *οὐδ' ἔτ'* q: *οὐδέ τ'* VP 1325 *Χο.* Seidler: om. VP | <*γε*> Seidler | *κτύπων* P 1326 *Εκ.* Seidler: om. VP | *ἔνωςις* utrobique V | *Χο.* Kirchhoff: om. VP | *ἐπικλύζει* Burges: *-κλύςει* VPΣ[i] 1327 *Εκ.* Bothe: om. VP | <*ἰώ*> Kirchhoff | *τρομερὰ* bis P: semel V 1329–30 (*ἴτ' κτλ.*) Hecubae continuat Seidler: Talth. trib. VP | *ἐπὶ* Burges: *ἐπὶ τάλαιναν* VP 1331 *Χο.* post Bothe Dindorf: om. VP

Commentary

METRICAL SYMBOLS

⏑	a short syllable or position
–	a long syllable or *princeps* position
×	an *anceps* position, where either a short or a long syllable may stand
○○	two positions of which at least one must be long
⏒	the strophe has a long syllable, the antistrophe a short
⏓	the strophe has a short syllable, the antistrophe a long
⏖	two short syllables making a *biceps* in double-short metres
⏕	two short syllables standing in place of a *princeps*
⏔	the strophe has a long syllable, the antistrophe two shorts
⏕	the strophe has two short syllables, the antistrophe a long
⌒	a short syllable standing in the last position where the pattern calls for a long (*breuis in longo*)
||	period end
|||	stanza end
∫	indicates word overlap between verses
an	anapaestic metron (⏖ – ⏖ –), with allowable substitution of – ⏖ or – – for ⏖ –
ba	bacchius (⏑ – –)
cho	choriamb (– ⏑⏑ –)
cr	cretic (– ⏑ –)
D	hemiepes (– ⏖ – ⏖ –)
D^2	– ⏖ – ⏖ – ⏖ –
D^3	– ⏖ – ⏖ – ⏖ – ⏖ –
^cD	– – – ⏖ – (hemiepes with its first double short contracted)
d	– ⏖ –
d^2	⏖ – ⏖ –
δ	dochmius (× – – ⏑ –)
da	dactyl (– ⏖)
dod	dodrans (– ⏖ – ⏑ –)

¨dod	reversed dodrans (◯◯ – ⏖ –)
e	– ⏑ – (in dactylo-epitrite)
E	– ⏑ – × – ⏑ –
gl	glyconic (◯◯ – ⏖ – ⏑ –)
gl¨	anaclastic glyconic (◯◯ – × – ⏖ –)
hag	hagesichorean (× – ⏖ – ⏑ – –)
hδ	hypodochmius (– ⏑ – ⏑ –)
hi	hipponactean (◯◯ – ⏖ – ⏑ – –)
hi¨	anaclastic hipponactean (◯◯ – × – ⏖ – –)
ia	iambic metron (× – ⏑ –)
ith	ithyphallic (– ⏑ – ⏑ – –)
kδ	kaibellian dochmius (× – ⏓ – ⏑ –)
lk	lekythion (– ⏑ – × – ⏑ –)
mol	molossus (– – –)
par	paroemiac, a catalectic anapaestic dimeter (⏖ – ⏖ – ⏖ – –)
ph	pherecratean (◯◯ – ⏖ – –)
prax	praxillean (– ⏖ – ⏖ – ⏖ – ⏑ – – = D^2 + ba)
reiz	reizianum (× – ⏖ – –)
sp	spondee (– –)
tr	trochaic metron (– ⏑ – ×)
tl	telesillean (× – ⏖ – ⏑ –)

THE *HYPOTHESIS*

The introductory notice prefixed to *Tro.* in our mss. is called in Greek a *ὑπόθεϲιϲ*, a word suggesting the information that one should have in place before reading the play. Of *hypotheseis* originating in antiquity there are two kinds (see *SFP* i: 2n1 with literature cited and add Zuntz 1955: 129–46, Parker's commentary on *IT*, pp. 51–2, and the exhaustive treatment of Meccariello 2014), one supplying didascalic and other material available in the library of Alexandria together with a brief plot summary in the present tense, the second giving a narrative summary, in the past tense, of what happens before the play and during its course. The second sort, of which the present *hypothesis* is an example, has its origin in a collection of plot summaries of the plays of Eur., arranged in alphabetical order. These were apparently intended as a substitute for the reading of the plays themselves. We have a partial plot summary on papyrus of *Alexandros* (see Introduction § 3.2.1). That for *Tro.* is transmitted in our medieval mss. An earlier form of this is found on an Oxyrhynchus papyrus cited in the app. crit. to the *hypothesis*. There is a reassessment of the readings of the papyrus in Luppe 1985. The most recent edition of the two *Tro.* summaries (the papyrus fragment and the medieval version) is Meccariello 2014: 402–12. Diggle 2005 notes that the collection exhibits the kind of metrical clausulae that were in fashion 'at any date between the 2nd century BC and the 1st century AD'. For further references see Parker on *IT*, p. 54.

8 Luppe commends τοῦ προειρημένου, the reading of Q, citing P. Oxy. 2455 fr. 14, ἡ δὲ τ[ο]ὺϲ π[ρ]οειρημέν[ουϲ] ξενοδοχήϲαϲα.

9–10 The placing of Agamemnon's removal of Cassandra (first episode) after Menelaus' taking away of Helen (third episode) shows that the author of the *hypothesis* considered pairing of like actions to be more important than accurate dramatic chronology.

12 The plural attributive participle is justified either by the laments of Hecuba and the Chorus at 1302–16 or as an allusive plural, on which see 1016–17n. Another possibility is to emend it to a singular with Diggle.

PROLOGOS (1–152)

In the Introduction, §§ 2.2 through 2.4, I describe the layout of the acting area and the three principal points of entry and exit available to tragic poets. In this play the *skēnē* (stage building) represents part of the Greek encampment before Troy, a military hut ('tent' would suggest something made of canvas cloth, but in the *Iliad* the quarters of the chieftains are semi-permanent structures) housing those of the Greek army's Trojan captives who have not yet been assigned to masters and also Helen. Of these the Chorus, Cassandra, and Helen will issue from its doors. On the roof of the *skēnē* is a space available for acting, the so-called *theologeion*. If it is used in this play, it represents a high spot on which Poseidon and Athena stand. In addition to the door of the *skēnē*, there are two other points of entry into the acting area, the *eisodoi* or entrance ramps leading offstage to left and right. In our play one of these (let us arbitrarily pick the one on the audience's right) is used by persons coming from the assembly place of the Greek army, and the other leads to the ships of Agamemnon, Menelaus, and Neoptolemus and also to the city of Troy, imagined as just offstage. (For the evidence on which these two assignments rest see the Introduction, §§ 2.3 and 2.4.) Until the very end of the play, when the Herald returns with Astyanax's body (from Troy) and with the shield of Hector (received from Neoptolemus, who is about to leave in his ship), characters enter either from the *skēnē* (Chorus, Cassandra, and Helen) or by the right *eisodos* (heralds, Andromache and Astyanax, Menelaus). All the exits are leftward, toward the ships or the city.

The *prologos* in the technical sense—the part of the play that precedes the entrance of the Chorus—consists of three parts: (1) the opening monologue of Poseidon, a non-dramatic exposition of the situation as it stands at the play's beginning; (2) the dialogue between Poseidon and Athena in which they plot the destruction of the Greek fleet; and (3) the lament of Hecuba.

Virtually all of Eur.'s plays begin with a monologue: an exception is *IA* in its present state, which begins with dialogue that has a monologue embedded in it.[1] In such a monologue a character comes out and describes the antecedent action, as Poseidon does here. There is no attempt at dramatic realism but neither are the audience ever explicitly addressed or alluded to. The monologue is usually followed by a dialogue (*Cyc.*, *Hec.*, *Supp.*, *Ion*, and *Ba.* are exceptions), sometimes involving the monologue speaker and a new arrival (as here and in *Alc.*, *Med.*, *Hcld.*, *Andr.*, *Herc.*, *Hel.*, and *Or.*) and sometimes between two other characters (*Hipp.*, *El.*, *IT*, and *Pho.*). Some plays have, in addition to or instead of the dialogue, a sung section, either by a new character (*Tro.*, *Med.*, *Hec.*, *Ion*, and *Pho.*, where Antigone's part of the dialogue is sung) or by one of the dialogue partners (*Andr.*, *El.*, *Hel.*, where Helen sings the strophe, the entering Chorus the antistrophe, *IA* in its present state). Here a lament by Hecuba (98–121 non-lyric and 122–52 lyric) is the last prologue element before the *parodos*.

Of Eur.'s other extant plays the following have a prologue involving one or more divine (or other-worldly) characters: *Alc.*, *Hipp.*, *Hec.* (a ghost), *Ion*, and *Ba.* Among the lost plays a divine prologue is highly likely for *Erechtheus* and is probable for *Alexandros* (see Introduction § 3.2.1) and an attractive possibility for *Palamedes* (see § 3.3, final paragraph). Only five of the extant plays have a divine (or spectral) speaker, and it would seem that a divine προλογίζων is the more 'marked' option. The use of both a monologue by Poseidon and a dialogue between him and Athena serves to establish the divine background of the action, a background already on display in *Alexandros*. If interpreters ignore this or producers edit it out (as modern productions frequently do), they distort the poet's meaning. On the losses attendant on this way of proceeding see Lefkowitz 2016: 8–20.

[1] We are told that the duet between Andromeda and Echo in Eur.'s lost *Andromeda* was the beginning of the play. If so, this would be an exception among his genuine works to the rule that he always began with an expository prologue. It is, however, quite possible that 'the beginning of the play' in our sources does not mean its very first lines but, e.g., the second half of the prologue. *Rhesus* begins with anapaestic dialogue, but it is almost certainly not a work of Eur.

1–47. Prologue monologue

Staging: Some Greek plays (*Hcld.*, *Andr.*, *Supp.*, *Herc.*, *Tro.*, *Hel.*, and *Or.*; *Ag.*; *OT*) begin with one or more characters imagined as being already in place for some time. In the absence of a curtain their entrance takes place in front of the audience, but this entrance is by convention 'cancelled', i.e. the play is deemed to begin only when they are in place. (See Burian 1977, Taplin 1977: 134–6.) Before the start of the play, the actor playing Hecuba comes out of the *skēnē* and lies down on a bed or pallet (see 507) situated in front of it, holding this position for a short time before Poseidon enters and begins the play. Hecuba has the mask and costume of an old woman of royal status. Poseidon is masked as a male in the prime of life, he wears splendid clothing that suggests divinity, and he carries a trident that identifies him as Poseidon before he utters a word. Mastronarde 1990: 277–8 argues that Poseidon takes his place on the roof of the *skēnē*; that he arrives not by means of the stage crane (*mēchanē*) but simply climbs the stairs or ladder within or behind the *skēnē*; that at 45 Athena arrives by *mēchanē* and departs at 94 or 97 by the same means; and that Poseidon descends into the *skēnē* at 97. In favour of this staging is Poseidon's command to Athena to make her way to Olympus, which suggests flight. But Hourmouziades 1965: 161, followed by Halleran 1985: 10, argues for staging at ground level, as does Spitzbarth 1945: 45. An argument in favour of this is that in the other plays with divine προλογίζοντες, Apollo and Thanatos in *Alc.*, Hermes in *Ion*, and Dionysus in *Ba.* are plainly at ground level. (The case of Aphrodite in *Hipp.* is unclear, though in my Loeb edition I put her on the *theologeion*.) I would argue, with Gregory on *Hec.* 30 and Mastronarde 1990: 276–7, that the ghost of Polydorus in *Hec.* is at height (*pace* Lane 2007a). In *Tro.* too there is something to be said for staging the gods at height. Their elevation would make it less unnatural that the conversation of the two gods is not heard by Hecuba. If, however, Poseidon delivers his lines at ground level, Athena might still have arrived by *mēchanē*, alighting next to him.

That Hecuba is there during the dialogue of the two divinities without being aware of their presence contributes to an ironic dissonance. The two gods discuss the divine dimension of what has happened to Troy and what will happen to the Greeks. Hecuba, by contrast, will show herself throughout the play to hold views (plural and mutually inconsistent) of the gods and their role in the world that are contradicted by this opening dialogue and by other things in this play and in *Alexandros*: see the introduction to the third episode, the introduction to the *exodos*, and the notes on 973–4 and 1280–1.

Poseidon's monologue takes the form of the god's sad farewell to the city he helped to build and whose champion he is. It conveys the facts of the situation, including the fall of Troy (Epeius' trick of the Wooden Horse is mentioned), the killing of Priam at the altar of Zeus Herkeios, the bereavement of the Trojan women and their coming servitude, and in particular the situation of Hecuba: her husband and sons have been killed, her daughter Polyxena has been sacrificed to Achilles, and her other daughter Cassandra is to become Agamemnon's concubine. But beyond this it conveys a mood of desolation, as Poseidon describes the wailing of the captive Trojan women and gives voice to his own sadness that this great city has fallen victim to the hatred of Athena and Hera. In the *Iliad*, Poseidon is a pro-Greek divinity, so making him pro-Trojan (see 6–7, 23–4) represents a mythical innovation on Eur.'s part, one which he adopts also at *IT* 1414–15. (The claim of Fontenrose 1967 that Poseidon is pro-Greek and that his affection is only for Troy's walls, not for its inhabitants, requires an implausibly restrictive interpretation of *πόλει* in 7 and ignores the implications of 23–4 and 50.) The innovation means that the god can be moved with grief at Troy's fall, which contributes powerfully to the play's mood. It also means that the following dialogue—in which Athena, now angered at the Greeks she had previously helped, conspires with Poseidon to wreck their fleet on their homeward journey—represents the coming together, in order to punish the Greeks, of two divinities previously on opposite sides.

As Gollwitzer 1937: 24 points out, Poseidon's prologue assumes that the audience know quite a bit about the antecedents of the play's action, e.g. the reason for the expedition against Troy, the cause of Athena's and Hera's hatred of the city, the reason for the sacrifice of Polyxena, and the identity of Priam, Hecuba, Agamemnon, and Helen. See also Meridor 1989: 18n11 and 19n14, who notes that where information is supplied, it is because Eur. is innovating. It is curious that of the three women besides Hecuba who figure in the three episodes Poseidon mentions Cassandra and Helen but says not a word to prefigure Andromache. Meridor (21–8) suggests that this is because Eur. is innovating with regard to the first two and not with regard to the third.

1–2 **ἥκω λιπών**: this formula of self-presentation is used by gods (Thetis at *Andr.* 1232, Dionysus at *Ba.* 1 and 13) and the ghost of Polydorus (*Hec.* 1). (For *ἥκω* with starting-point omitted see *Cho.* 3, *PV* 1 and 284–5, and *Ion* 5.) It seems to convey the impression of supernatural ease of movement, though *ἥκω* is used by an ordinary human prologue speaker at *Cho.* 3.

Αἰγαῖον: the etymology of the word was disputed in antiquity and is still unclear: see Fowler 1988. Eur. may have derived it from Aigai, the name of several localities, most with connections to Poseidon. At *Il.* 13.21 Poseidon comes to Troy by way of Aigai, where he harnesses his chariot, and the Townleian scholia *ad loc.* identify this with the Euboean Aigai. The Aegean is Poseidon's natural element, which he has left in order to say farewell to Troy.

ἁλμυρὸν βάθος | πόντου: 'briny' belongs properly to 'sea' but the epithet is transferred to 'depth' in a procedure called *enallage* (less correctly *hypallage*): for instances see Campbell 1879: 1.80, Griffith on *Ant.* 791, Smyth § 3027, *Andr.* 159–60 ἠπειρῶτις…ψυχὴ γυναικῶν, 1194–5 πατρὸς αἷμα τὸ διογενές, *Ion* 1486–7 δεκάτῳ…μηνὸς ἐν κύκλῳ, *IT* 1272–3 χθονίαν…μῆνιν θεᾶς; there is a thorough discussion of the phenomenon in Bers 1974. In most instances, the adjective can be thought to modify a compound idea, 'sea-depths' in the present case. The phrase 'briny sea-depths' is here modified by a further adjective, *Αἰγαῖον*. —Burges proposed ἁλμυροῦ. It is difficult to know whether the change is desirable. On the one hand Diggle, *Studies* 48–9 cites cases of 'the attachment of two epithets to the governing noun and the denial of an epithet to the noun which is governed' and the reverse. On the other hand Diggle 1993: 136–7 gives examples of interlacing like that produced by the conjecture.

2–3 ***ἔνθα Νηρῄδων χοροὶ | κάλλιστον ἴχνος ἐξελίσσουσιν ποδός***: the Nereids 'whirl their lovely feet'. The choruses of Nereids (catalogues of Nereus' daughters are given at Hom. *Il.* 18.37–51 and Hes. *Th.* 240–64) are a favourite Euripidean subject: see *Andr.* 1267, *El.* 432–51, *IT* 274, *Ion* 1080–6, *Hel.* 1585, *IA* 239–41, 1054–7. Here perhaps they serve to emphasize the divinity of the element in which Poseidon is at home.

χοροί: because 'the chorus of Nereids' is in itself a singular notion and is singular at *Andr.* 1267 and *IT* 274 (though plural at *IT* 428), it is just possible that χορός (PQ) may be right: for a collective singular governing a plural verb see *Ag.* 578 and KG 1.53.

3 ***κάλλιστον***: this could be predicative (cf. *Or.* 140), but attributive meaning, as above, seems easier here.

ἴχνος…ποδός is a periphrasis for 'foot' (or, distributively, 'feet'). On the distributive singular see 392n.

ἐξελίσσουσιν: ἑλίσσω (and compounds ἐξ- and ἀμφελίσσω: evidently a noticeably Euripidean word to judge from Ar. *Ran.* 1314) are used by Eur. to describe circular motion of various kinds (dance steps, unrolling a scroll, the circuit of the sun and moon).

4–6 The reason (γάρ) for Poseidon's arrival from the depths is his goodwill toward the city of Troy, which he built. His stay is brief: he has just arrived and by 23–5 he announces his intention to depart. The farewell that he actually says at 45–6 is the entire purpose of his visit.

4 **τήνδε Τρωϊκὴν χθόνα**: forms of ὅδε are used in all of Eur.'s prologues to indicate the location of the play's action: 'the Troad here'. (The use of such deictics in prologues is discussed by Kassel 1976.) Since the city itself is not visible to the audience, it is not strictly accurate to say that he enclosed 'the Troad here' with walls, but it is a pardonably abbreviated way of saying 'This is the Troad; Apollo and I put fortifications around (a part of) it.'

4–5 **ἀμφὶ... πέριξ**: on pleonastic adverbs reinforcing prepositions, see Jaeger 1957: 384–5 and Renehan 1963: 269–70.

5 **πύργους**: 'towers' is synecdoche for the whole encircling fortification.

6 **ὀρθοῖσιν ἔθεμεν κανόσιν**: Poseidon and Apollo used the tools of the stonemason's art. A κανών can be either a plumbline, for producing a straight vertical, or a rule. For Apollo as builder of Troy see *Andr.* 1009–18, *Hel.* 1511, *Or.* 1387–9, *IA* 756, and *Rhes.* 224–32.

6–7 **οὔποτ' ἐκ φρενῶν | εὔνοι' ἀπέστη τῶν ἐμῶν Φρυγῶν πόλει**: 'Never has goodwill for the city of the Phrygians left my heart.' I take τῶν ἐμῶν with φρενῶν rather than with Φρυγῶν. It stands, to be sure, next to Φρυγῶν, but 'my Phrygians' would claim an implausible level of identification between Poseidon and the Trojans, and φρενῶν is better with a possessive (see *Hcld.* 709, *Hipp.* 685, 983, 1262, 1454, *Andr.* 361, *Hec.* 85, etc.).

Φρυγῶν πόλει: 'Phrygian' is a synonym for 'Trojan' throughout Greek tragedy, which also uses 'Pergamos' or 'Pergama' and 'Ilios' or 'Ilion' for Troy and 'Idaean' for Trojan. —JD suggests that Eur. might have written πόλει Φρυγῶν, which would eliminate the ambiguity. The corruption would be an instance of *vitium Byzantinum*, the tendency of scribes to rearrange words so that the penultimate syllable bears an accent, on which see Barrett on *Hipp.* 1315. Eur. seems to prefer the order Φρυγῶν πόλει: his mss. give these words five times (*Andr.* 363 [with one ms. dissenting], *Hec.* 4, *Tro.* 994, *IA* [682, 773], 1290, the present passage) and only one instance of the reverse order (*Ba.* 58, where, however, a secondary witness has Φρυγῶν πόλει, adopted in Diggle's OCT). Eur. might have written πόλει Φρυγῶν here; alternatively, he could have relied on the actor to make his meaning clear. For another instance where delivery would eliminate ambiguity see 1184n.

8 **καπνοῦται**: the present tense means that the city is still smouldering (though the firing of the citadel itself still lies in the future: cf. 1260–4). For the verb, used of a city, see Pi. *P.* 5.84 καπνωθεῖσαν πάτραν.

πρὸς Ἀργείου δορὸς: πρός + genitive is used to express personal agent: see LSJ s.v. A.II.1 (of things only in Soph.: see LSJ s.v. A.II.2). But 'Argive spear' is put by metonymy for 'Argive army' (cf. *Hcld.* 674, 834, *Herc.* 61, *Pho.* 1082; *Rh.* 20), hence the personal agent construction.

9 **ὄλωλε πορθηθεῖϲ'**: 'has been sacked and is no more'. The aorist participle indicates antecedent action and the perfect indicative a present state. The line lacks the usual caesura after the fifth or seventh element and has only a *caesura media* (i.e. after the sixth element, dividing the line into two equal parts): in that case, as Diggle 1994: 82–3 has shown, there is always in Eur., as here, elision of the following vowel, which would have constituted the seventh element. Further examples in this play (not noted in the commentary below) are 475, 483, 658, 660, 879, 903, 922, 923, 1013, 1124, 1150, 1181, 1270, and 1285.

9–12 The building of the Wooden Horse is ascribed in the poetic tradition to Epeius, Athena having supplied the strategem (μηχαναῖϲι Παλλάδοϲ). At *Od.* 8.492–3 he makes the horse with her help. At the beginning of Stesichorus' *Iliupersis* (fr. 100 F.), Epeius is a lowly carrier of water for the Greeks, and Athena reveals to him the idea of the horse out of pity for him. (On the fragment see Finglass 2013 and for its inspiration of Simias see Finglass 2015b.) His name is a byword for cowardice (Ἐπειοῦ δειλότεροϲ) in Zenob. vulg. 3.81 (= Cratin. test. 15 KA). Eur. wrote an *Epeius*, probably a satyr play: see Pechstein 1998: 143–4. The mention of Athena prepares the way for the goddess's appearance in 48, and her aid to the Greeks makes their failure to punish Ajax's violation of her sanctuary all the more reprehensible (69–73).

A bronze statue of the Wooden Horse by the sculptor Strongylion was dedicated on the Athenian acropolis, perhaps shortly before our play was produced: see Paus. 1.23.8 and the scholiast on Ar. *Av.* 1128. Strongylion's pro-Athenian bias is evident in the choice of persons shown emerging from the horse: the sons of Theseus, Menestheus, and the Salaminian Teucer. Eur. devotes the first stasimon of our play to the Wooden Horse. Later in the prologue (31) he mentions the sons of Theseus. —Παρνάϲϲιοϲ appears to be the correct spelling: see Mastronarde on *Pho.* 207.

10 **μηχαναῖϲι Παλλάδοϲ**: the first of many references in the prologue and throughout the play to the role of Athena (or Athena and Hera or the gods generally) as destroyers of Troy or the Greeks: see 23–4, 46–7, 72, 356–8, 457, 597–600, 775–6, and 867. See also 799–819n.

11–12 **ἐγκύμον' ἵππον τευχέων**: the genitive with ἐγκύμων, 'pregnant', is analogous to that with adjectives meaning 'full' or 'empty': 'a horse pregnant with armour'. Vergil's *feta armis* (*Aen.* 2.238) renders the metaphor exactly. The phrase should be taken as object only of ϲυναρμόϲαϲ, the main verb governing βάροϲ.

12 **πύργων ἔπεμψεν ἐντόϲ**: for the meaning of πύργων see 5n.

ὀλέθριον βάρος: object of ἔπεμψεν. The 'deadly weight' is what the horse is pregnant with, its offspring of armed soldiers. At *Cho.* 992 *βάρος* is used of a child in the womb, and at *IT* 1228 τόκοις βαρύνεται means 'is pregnant'. See the LSJ Supplement s.v. —V's βρέτας is also possible. A βρέτας is normally a statue of a god, but 'statue (offered to a god)' seems a reasonable extension: cf. ξόανον below at 525 and Hor. *Carm.* 4.6.9–10, *equo Mineruae sacra mentito*. With this reading, ἵππον would be object both of συναρμόσας and ἔπεμψεν, and ὀλέθριον βρέτας would be an appositive or secondary object ('as an image meant for ruin'), and a comma after ἔντος would then be appropriate. I print βάρος without full conviction but note that anyone who found the abstract βάρος puzzling might have been moved to substitute the more concrete βρέτας. Hornblower on *Alexandra* 948 notes that Lycophron draws heavily on *Tro.* and that 948, which refers to the Wooden Horse as a βρέτας, may be evidence for βρέτας as the correct reading here. But (a) we do not know that Lycophron derived βρέτας from *Tro.*; (b) even if he did, the variant might still be secondary.

[13–14] The basic meaning of δόρυ is 'tree', then by extension 'plank of wood'. Hence a horse made of planks is called δουράτεος ἵππος (Hom. *Od.* 8.493 etc.) or δούρειος ἵππος (Plat. *Theat.* 184d). By a different extension δόρυ can mean 'spear-shaft'. Whoever wrote 13–14 is claiming that the adjective δουράτεος or δούρειος should be derived from the meaning 'spear'. This is a bizarre etymology (ψυχρῶς ἠτυμολόγησε τὸν ἵππον ἀπὸ τῶν δοράτων, says the scholiast *ad loc.*), and it is hard to see why Eur. should make it. But proving these lines spurious is difficult. Wilson 1968 attempts to do so on the grounds that Euripidean prologues do not contain etymologies that relate to the post-play future, but, quite apart from the counter-example of *Hipp.* 32–3 (where Jortin's ὀνομάσουσι is inevitable with τὸ λοιπόν), I can see no inherent reason why a divine prologue speaker should always avoid referring to later customs and nomenclature. Many scholars share with the scholiast the subjective feeling that this is a bad pun, but this is scarcely proof that the lines are spurious, and Parmentier 1923: 46–9, Erbse 1984: 63, and Stieber 2011: 185–9 argue for genuineness, the first and third principally as an allusion to Strongylion's statue, on which see 9–12n. But while these lines might be a reference to the fame given the horse by Strongylion's statue, no one would have concluded from its being in bronze that the etymology of δούρειος ἵππος had to be revised. Stieber says that the new etymology is clever, but others, including the scholiast, would demur. We cannot prove, of course, that Eur. never had temporary lapses of judgement. In bracketing the lines (with Burges) I am giving him the benefit of the doubt. Excision has one other slight benefit:

without 13–14 Poseidon moves from the destruction of the city (8–9), with a glance at its human and divine agents (9–12), to the particulars of the city's present state without a detour into what future men will call the horse. Fraenkel 1963: 10–11 cites as a parallel interference the interpolated etymology of Theoclymenus' name in *Hel.* 9b–10a.

15–17 The desertion of temples and groves and their defilement with blood are signs both of the religious dislocation of Troy (only the altar, outside the temple, would normally be reddened, and with the blood of animals) and also of the impious behaviour of the Greeks (cf. Clytaemestra's hope at *Ag.* 338–40 that the Greeks will act piously toward the gods' temples, and Heracles' similar warning at *Phil.* 1440–1). The killing of Priam at the altar of Zeus, ascribed in the *Iliupersis* (*GEF* arg. (2)) to Achilles' son Neoptolemus, is an act of impiety parallel to the forcible removal of Cassandra from the altar of Athena (70). Zeus Herkeios (Zeus of the Enclosure) protected the house, and his altar was situated in front of it. (For the possibility that in *Alexandros* Priam's son sought refuge at an altar see Introduction § 3.2.8, n. 108.) It is curious that there is no mention specifically of Neoptolemus in connection with Priam's death (here, 134–6, and 481–3) or with the sacrifice of Polyxena (39–40, 622–3). For a possible reason see the introduction to the second episode and Meridor 1989: 30–1.

15–16 **ἔρημα δ' ἄλϲη καὶ θεῶν ἀνάκτορα:** Biehl makes ἔρημα predicative, supplying ἐϲτίν, but the adjective could be attributive with both nouns, and both nouns could be subject of καταρρεῖ. Kiefner 142 takes θεῶν with both ἄλϲη and ἀνάκτορα (ἀπὸ κοινοῦ). With φόνωι καταρρεῖ cf. *Il.* 4.451 ῥέε δ' αἵματι γαῖα.

17 **ἑρκείου:** the form was conjecturally restored by Musgrave. Several converging arguments showing that ἑρκεῖοϲ is to be written everywhere in tragedy are given by Finglass 2009: 216–17. The correct form survives by a hair in 483.

28–44 —Several things about the sequence 18–47 suggest that these lines are not transmitted in the correct order. (1) Poseidon in 25–7 announces his departure, but that announcement is separated from his actual farewell by 28–44. (2) In their turn 28–44 contain further description of fallen Troy that looks like a continuation of 8–17. The shrines awash with blood in 15–16 and the death of Priam in 16–17 are more naturally followed by the miseries of the Trojan women (28–44) than by the removal of Trojan treasure (18–19). (3) Ludwig 1954: 39 notes that Poseidon begins and ends with his personal involvement, but that the otherwise objective and factual central section is interrupted by 23–7. Wecklein 1901: 6 notes a proposal by G. (Wilhelm) Wagner (possibly unpublished: Barthold 1864: 31 says 'communicavit nuper mecum amicus

Wagnerus') to put 23–7 after 44 and delete 45–7. But there is no obvious way to explain the transposition, and the proposal solves only the first problem. Instead, put 18–27 after 44. For this dislocation an obvious explanation lies to hand, homoearkton (πολύϲ 18, πολλοῖϲ 28). The words might have stood at the top of adjacent columns in a papyrus: the first column would have contained 1–17 (seventeen lines plus title if 13–14 were included) and the second 28–44 (seventeen lines if 38 was included), while the third would have begun with 18.[2] Rearrangement addresses the above problems. (1) It brings Poseidon's announcement and his leave-taking together. Lines indicating Poseidon's personal involvement thus begin (1–7) and end (23–7, 45–7) the speech, and we do not have the interruption of the factual by the personal noted by Ludwig. (2) The sequence ending at 17 with the death of Priam then continues with further Trojan misery, ending with Cassandra. (3) Furthermore, the reference to Agamemnon's bringing Cassandra home as his concubine (44) leads naturally to the thought of other booty (see below on 18–21) and of the Greek departure (18–22). This in turn leads to the announcement of Poseidon's own departure (25–7) and his leave-taking (45–7).

28–9 Now the catalogue of Trojan miseries, interrupted in our mss. by 18–27, continues. The Scamander, one of the two rivers in the plain of Troy, rings with the cries of captive women being assigned as slaves to their masters. —LSJ s.v. 3 take κληρουμένων as middle, 'have allotted one, obtain by lot', but the other passages they cite exemplify a different usage. Lane 2007b: 294 suggests that it is not the women, but their Greek masters, who ought to be doing the allotting and that the verb ought to be passive, as it is at 240 and *Hec.* 100, and that we should read δεϲπόταιϲ, which I have adopted. In 30 the three -αϲ endings in τὰϲ μὲν Ἀρκάϲ τὰϲ may have interfered with the copying of 29.

30–1 The three groups mentioned as having received women by allotment are clearly not meant to be an exhaustive list but are *exempli gratia*. Why these three? The Arcadians are mentioned in the *Iliad* only in the Catalogue of Ships (2.603–14). Parmentier 22 suggests that they are mentioned here because of their important role in international politics following the Peace of Nicias in 421. Stephanopoulos 1985: 116 gives evidence that Arcadian mercenaries were highly

[2] Many literary papyri have considerably more lines per column than this, but see P. graec. mon. 340 (published by F. Maltomini in Carlini 1986: 1–7), where we appear to have seventeen lines in one column and sixteen in the next. Turner 1980: 37 lists several Ptolemaic literary papyri of roughly the same small format. If the error is as old as the Ptolemaic period, it could well have spread far. For other short columns of about twenty lines see P. Oxy. 3215 and 4639.

thought of and that the Athenians made use of them in Sicily shortly after the date of our play. As for the Thessalians, Westlake 1953 sees a contemporary reference in their mention here and in the second antistrophe of the *parodos*. For further discussion see 214–17n. Whether or not we invoke contemporary history we can note that the progression from Arcadians (insignificant in the *Iliad*) to Thessalians (Achilles' contingent) to Athenians shows both increasing mythical interest to the audience and increasing phrase length (ascending tricolon).

31 The scholiast *ad loc.* says that the sons of Theseus (Demophon and Acamas) are mentioned to gratify the Athenians: the story, known from Proclus' summary of the *Iliupersis* and this scholium, was that they refused any share of the booty since they had come to Troy for the sole purpose of recovering their grandmother Aethra, who had been made a slave to Helen. In the *Ilias parva* (*GEF* fr. 17) Demophon and Acamas won Aethra back not by sortition but by requesting her from Agamemnon, who first asked Helen's permission. (We also have good reason to believe that Aethra and her grandsons figured in Stesichorus: see Davies–Finglass on fr. 105.) If that is the version alluded to by Poseidon here, we should take εἴληχ' in its more general sense of 'obtain', without any reference to sortition: cf. e.g. 644, *Hipp.* 80, *Supp.* 539, *IT* 1009; *Sept.* 690; *OT* 1366; *Il.* 4.49 and *Od.* 11.304. (In the *Iliupersis* (*GEF* fr. 6) it is Menestheus who leads the Athenian contingent, not the sons of Theseus, as, apparently, here.)

32–5 The women described here (the group includes Trojan noblewomen and Helen of Sparta) are chosen or picked out (ἐξῃρημέναι) as prizes for the army's leaders. Helen is, for other reasons, also a special prize and is properly (ἐνδίκωϲ) classed among these select women (cf. 871–2). In most accounts of Helen after the capture of Troy—in the *Iliupersis* (*GEF* arg. (2)), by implication in the *Ilias Parva* (fr. 17), in the scenes on vases where Helen is either grabbed or menaced with a sword or where Menelaus drops his sword (*LIMC*, s.v. 'Helene', IV.1.528–30 and 537–50)—Menelaus is quickly reconciled with his errant wife. (Only in Stesichorus' *Iliupersis* (fr. 106 F.) is the stoning of Helen by the Greeks threatened.) In our play, by contrast, Helen is held by the Greeks, and Menelaus has not yet seen her. When they meet in the third episode, it is for the first time since Helen's elopement, and Menelaus has already decided to have her executed.

32 **ὅϲαι δ' ἄκληροι Τρῳάδων**: 'all the Trojan women who are not (as yet) assigned by lot'. ἄκληροι might mean that these women were not subject to sortition, and indeed it appears from 249 and 274 that Cassandra and Andromache were not. But language at 185–6, 240, 263, 296, and

1271 suggests that the usual way these special women were to be distributed was by lot.

ὅcαι: what is meant is that the tent contains all those not yet assigned to masters, not that *all* the women set aside for the chiefs are in this tent: Andromache will enter by an *eisodos* at 568.

34–5 Poseidon's point in saying that Helen is justly regarded as a captive is that, despite the difference of nationality, she is a captive like them: contrary to other versions of the story Helen has not been quickly reconciled with Menelaus, which is why she is *properly* confined to the hut with the other captives. There is no moral disapprobation of Helen here, as claimed by Koniaris 1973: 97, who thinks that Poseidon's ἐνδίκωc shows that he thinks she is guilty and that her action of leaving Sparta was completely free and unconstrained. See also 373n.

36–7 The opening monologue of a Euripidean tragedy is addressed in non-dramatic fashion to the audience, telling them what they need to know. But Eur., unlike Menander, does not refer to the audience with, e.g., 2nd-person pronouns or verbs. These two lines are as close as a Euripidean προλογίζων comes to recognizing the existence of his hearers. As noted by Battezzato 1995: 33n27, they are an implicit appeal for audience sympathy. —There are two sets of variants. In one, Ἑκάβη κειμένη πυλῶν πάροc is the subject of πάρεcτιν, which means 'is present'; in the other, Ἑκάβην κειμένην πυλῶν πάροc is in apposition to τὴν ἀθλίαν τήνδ', and πάρεcτιν means 'it is possible (to see her)'. Each half of the tradition continues the same construction into the next line. Diggle, Lee, and Biehl all choose the former, Murray and Parmentier the latter. The choice between 'If anyone wants to see this poor woman, Hecuba is before you, lying in front of the gates' and 'If anyone wants to see here (τήνδ') the poor woman Hecuba lying in front of the gates, he may do so' (with interlacing of the protasis and apodosis) is not an easy one. I have hesitantly adopted the latter.

[38] Prinz deletes the line. Without it, 39–44 give further facts about Hecuba that substantiate ἀθλίαν. (You can be ἄθλιοc for things of which you are as yet unaware.) With it, 39–44 must be the things for which Hecuba is weeping many tears (the ᾗι in this setting giving the reason for her tears), yet she cannot weep for things she does not know about, and both Polyxena's sacrifice and Cassandra's enslavement to Agamemnon are unknown to her (see 107, 134–42, 247–8, and 260–5 for what Hecuba knows and does not know). It is also arguably undesirable for Poseidon's speech to be punctuated by cries and groans from Hecuba (throughout? or only just before or just after Poseidon mentions them? Neither is without its problems). A possible motive for interpolation is to increase pathos: for possible 'melodramatic' interpolations (the term is from Page 1934: 222 and throughout) see *Med.* 1233–5, *Andr.* 397–8, *Herc.* 452, *Ion* 844–58, *Hel.* 892–3, and *Or.* 957–9.

40 Most recent editors (Murray, Diggle, Biehl in both his commentary and his Teubner, and my own Loeb: Parmentier, Lee, and Schiassi are exceptions) print λάθραι, which is hard to defend, as Musgrave notes. λάθραι was probably intended by its author to convey the idea that Hecuba does not know about Polyxena's death, but as Nauck 1862: 126 points out, that would require e.g. λάθραι μητρός: by itself λάθραι would mean that her sacrifice was carried out in secret, but a secret sacrifice is without parallel in fifth-century tragedy. By contrast, οἰκτρά is unobjectionable style: the adjective and the adverb reinforce each other as at *Med.* 1386. see also *Tro.* 141–2 (where οἰκτρῶϲ reinforces πενθήρη), 446, and *Ion* 1226. The origin of λάθραι is easy to account for: with 38 interpolated, someone felt the need to explain that Hecuba did not yet know of her daughter's death.

41–4 Agamemnon, disregarding both the god's will and piety, means to make Cassandra, who by Apollo's gift was to be unwed and running wild (παρθένον δρομάδα), his concubine. Poseidon's emphasis falls on the violence (βιαίωϲ) of the act. In 618–19 Andromache regards it as the equivalent of Ajax's assault. The antecedent of ἣν is Καϲϲάνδραν (antecedent incorporated into the relative clause). The word order is unusually interlaced, δρομάδα and ἄναξ being separated from παρθένον and Ἀπόλλων. The mention of Cassandra serves to prepare for her scene of prophecy, 308–461.

41 **φροῦδοϲ:** a favourite of Eur. (forty-plus times in his works, six times in *Tro.*) and a noticeable predilection, to judge from the parody at Ar. *Ran.* 1343. —Priam was mentioned in 17, also in the nominative, and with a similar predicate, πέπτωκε. Lane 2007b: 294–5 shows that such multiple repetition of name and statement is unexpected in a Euripidean prologue and proposes φροῦδοϲ δὲ πρέϲβυϲ, comparing *Hec.* 160 and *Tro.* 921. Another possibility is φροῦδοϲ δ' ἀκοίτηϲ, giving a relationship word parallel to τέκν'.

44 **γαμεῖ:** a future, not a present.

ϲκότιον: 'secret' (literally 'dark') here means 'unsanctioned by marriage' (cf. 252 below). It is used of an illegitimate son at Hom. *Il.* 6.24, and of clandestine affairs at *Ion* 860.

18–21 We have been told that Cassandra, the last of the women specifically named, is about to be brought home. Now we hear of the homeward removal of Troy's treasures by the victorious Achaeans. (The two actions correspond to the common idiom ἄγειν καὶ φέρειν, in which the first verb applies to humans, cattle, and other sentient booty and the second to everything else: see LSJ s.v. ἄγω A.I.3.) They are waiting for a favourable wind (πρύμνηθεν οὖρον) so that they can go home after ten years of war to their wives and children.

18 **πόλυς δὲ χρυςὸς Φρύγιά τε ςκυλεύματα:** 'Phrygian' is to be understood with 'gold' as well as 'spoils' (ἀπὸ κοινοῦ).

19–20 In *Hec.* the Greeks are also waiting for a favourable wind (see 900).

20 **δεκαςπόρωι χρόνωι:** the dative indicates elapsed time, '*after* ten seed times'. Lee compares πολλῶι χρόνωι at *Ag.* 521. See also χρόνωι τοςούτωι at *Phil.* 598–9 with Jebb's note. At *IT* 306 Nauck's οὐ (for L's ἐν) μακρῶι χρόνωι is probably right. Eur. uses simple χρόνωι to mean 'after a while' at *Alc.* 1036, *Med.* 904, 1218, *Hcld.* 869, 941, 1029, *Hipp.* 1181, *El.* 578–9, *Herc.* 607, 740, *IT* 1336, *Ion* 659, *Pho.* 166, 295, 304, 872, 1043, *Or.* 1201, *Ba.* 294, but ἐν χρόνωι only at *Andr.* 782, as noted by Diggle 1994: 344. Jebb on *OC* 88, citing *Ant.* 422 and *Phil.* 235, notes that in Attic ἐν + quantitative adj. + χρόνωι is the standard way to say 'after a long, etc. time'. Eur. makes little use of this idiom.

[22] The line is unneeded after Ἀχαιῶν (19), and it feels like an afterthought. Hartung 1837: 47 plausibly deletes. Klinkenberg 1881: 47–8 notes that Eur. elsewhere in the play does not use forms of ὅδε to describe the *city* of Troy, which is offstage, visible to those on stage (see 45–7, 1256–8) but not to the audience.

23–7 Poseidon announces his intention to leave Troy behind. First, he has been defeated by Troy's great adversaries, Hera and Athena, who have destroyed the city. (The genitive is one of comparison since νικῶμαι is a comparative notion, 'I am bested': cf. *Med.* 315, *Hcld.* 233, etc.) Second, his worship there has been discontinued. For the idea that gods leave a defeated city see *Sept.* 76–7 and 217–18 and Verg. *Aen.* 2.351–2. The collocation κλεινὸν Ἴλιον occurs in the first line of *Alex.* (fr. 41a K.).

24 **Ἀθάνας:** on the 'Doric' vocalism of this name even in trimeters, see Björck 1950: 133 and Barrett on *Hipp.* 1120–5 *ad finem*.

45–7 Poseidon's farewell now follows its announcement in 25–7. In 46–7 it is further emphasized that the fall of Troy is the work of Athena. ἀλλά is used at the end of a speech when the speaker moves to depart: see *Hipp.* 51–3, *GP* 8. It is also used with prayers and wishes (*Med.* 759, *GP* 15), and with imperatives (*Hipp.* 887, *GP* 13). All three are relevant here.

ποτ' εὐτυχοῦςα: the present participle refers to a time before that of the main verb, the so-called 'imperfect' participle: see Diggle 1994: 233n13 and *MT* § 140. —Tragedy seems to prefer πόλις to πόλι when addressing a city: see Stevens on *Andr.* 1.

48–97. Dialogue between Poseidon and Athena

Staging: Poseidon turns to depart, but his departure is delayed by the following entry. (On departures delayed by the entrance of a new character see Taplin 1977: 162–3 and 299–300.) Enter Athena, costumed as a female divinity with helmet, aegis, and spear. Her entrance is probably airborne by means of the *mēchanē* (Poseidon in 92 specifies that she is to depart for Olympus, which suggests a different kind of departure from his own). It is unclear whether she and Poseidon converse on the *theologeion* or at ground level.

Athena, Troy's implacable enemy, now wishes to punish the Greeks for their impiety in condoning the crime of Ajax the Lesser, who had dragged Cassandra from the goddess's altar. She wants Poseidon's help in punishing them. (On the similarity of this scene to the description in the Herald's speech at *Ag.* 650–2 of two former enemies, fire and sea, conspiring to destroy the Greek fleet, see 78–84n.) Their dialogue, after a three-line first speech, continues in nine distichomythic exchanges, quickens into *stichomythia* for eight lines, and concludes with ten-line and eleven-line speeches by Athena and Poseidon.

48–50 Athena arrives pat upon the mention of her name. She addresses her uncle in flattering terms and expresses her intention to bring their previous hostility to an end.

49 In view of the plentiful examples of μὲν...τε collected at *GP* 374–6, Elmsley's μέγαν δὲ (adopted in my Loeb) should be considered possible rather than necessary.

50 **λύcαcαν**: agreeing with understood accusative subject of προcεννέπειν rather than dative with the understood complement of ἔξεcτι. On the use of either the accusative or the dative of a participle or other modifier after an impersonal verb, see Mastronarde on *Med.* 57–8 and, for an accusative participle where a dative is more logical, Diggle, *Studies* 44.

ἔχθραν τὴν πάροc: i.e. their being on opposite sides in the war. (The context, especially 46–7, 59–60, and 64–8, make it unlikely that the audience were meant to understand this as a reference to the contest for supremacy in Attica, as suggested by Biehl.) The delicacy of Athena's address to Poseidon does not mean (*pace* Fontenrose 1967) that Poseidon's sympathies are pro-Greek. Rather, since Poseidon had been Athena's adversary in the war, she anticipates that it may be difficult to get him to cooperate with her in anything.

51–2 Poseidon shows his willingness to be mollified. Though it is not universally true that 'the words of blood relatives have no small power to charm the heart', it makes here a plausible explanation for Poseidon's willingness to listen to his niece.

σμικρόν: Diggle 1975: 289–90 and *Studies* 50 shows that σμικρός is Eur.'s preferred form and μικρός is to be read only where σμικρός is metrically impossible.

53 **ἐπῄνεσ' ὀργὰς ἠπίους**: 'I commend (or 'I thank you for') your kindly attitude.' On αἰνεῖν and ἐπαινεῖν in expressions of thanks see Quincey 1966: 148–57. The aorist is of the so-called 'tragic' or 'instantaneous' kind, in which the speaker represents an emotion as having occurred a moment before. It is to be translated as a present. On these see Mastronarde on *Med.* 223 with his introduction, pp. 87–8, and Lloyd 1999.

53–4 'I bring a theme for you and me both (κοινούς) to discuss.' Both κοινούς and ἐς μέσον emphasize that Athena's topic is of interest to both parties.

55–6 'I hope you are not going to tell me of some new (i.e. unwelcome) pronouncement from one of the gods, either Zeus or one of the other deities?'

55 **μῶν**: Barrett on *Hipp.* 794 observes that this particle does not, as commonly alleged, expect a negative answer. Rather 'I ask "μῶν X" *when I am reluctant to accept X as true*'. This reluctance can stem from apprehension or surprise as well as from the belief that X is false. 'Reluctance sometimes weakens to hesitation, and the particle then may mark the question as a mere guess', he says, citing this passage, 'sometimes serving as little more than a sign of interrogation.' Its exact force here depends on the nature of the supposition Poseidon is putting forward, for this will determine his attitude toward it. I suggest that reluctance applies here as well, as in the above translation. —καινόν (only in V) is correct: 'new' commonly means 'new and unwelcome, untoward'. For this sense see 511, 1118, 1126, and 1259 below, Gregory on *Hec.* 83, Bond on *Herc.* 1118, Willink on *Or.* 239–40 and 1503–5 and also *Hipp.* 370, 1160, *Hec.* 177, 689, *Or.* 1327; *Trach.* 867, 873, *Phil.* 560. By contrast a κοινὸν ἔπος (PQ) would be a general edict, not the same as one from 'Zeus or one of the gods'. The forms of κοινός in 54 and 58 may have caused the corruption. V's future ἀγγελεῖς ('Do you mean to announce') seems to suit the deprecatory tone of μῶν (cf. the future in the common οἴμοι, τί λέξεις; on which see Barrett on *Hipp.* 353). But the present might also be right.

56 In my translation above I have taken the first ἤ to mean 'either' ('one of the gods, that is, either Zeus or even one of the [other] gods'), with, e.g., Wilamowitz, Parmentier, and Lattimore. Since a pronouncement of this kind is more likely to come from Zeus, the καί makes sense,

emphasizing that 'one of the other gods' is the more remote supposition. The omission of the word 'other' in 'Zeus and the gods' is illustrated by Page on *Med.* 1172 and Henry 1967: 50 (add Antiph. 6.40 to their examples). For synonymous δαίμων and θεός in the same sentence see 49. The other possibility is to take ἤ as 'or' ('one of the gods, or Zeus, or even one of the δαίμονες': thus, e.g., Murray² and Lee). But in tragedy δαίμων is rarely contrasted with θεός (Mikalson 1991: 242n26 claims that in tragedy identification of the two terms is normal and regards *Med.* 1391, *Hec.* 164, and *El.* 1234 as exceptional), and it is a somewhat implausible idea that one of the non-Olympians (a malevolent divinity, as at *Pers.* 345 or *Ag.* 1468–9, or a chthonic divinity, as at *Pers.* 628–9, *Eu.* 302, 929) has made some pronouncement. In the present passage it is likely to be a synonym for θεός, as it is at 49. Poseidon imagines that Zeus or another god has made some pronouncement that will upset things again.

57–8 'No: I have approached you (lit. 'your power') to win you as an ally (κοινήν) for the sake of Troy, where we now are walking.' This suggests to Poseidon that Athena has had a change of sympathies without making this absolutely clear. The combination of suggestion and unclarity perhaps explains 63, where he agrees without qualification to cooperate with Athena and then (implicitly retracting his assent) asks her to clarify her aims.

ἔνθα βαίνομεν: we cannot conclude from this phrase that Poseidon and Athena are at ground level, for gods tread the air above a territory: see *El.* 1233–7.

59–60 οὔ πού: this and οὔ τι που are used, especially by Eur., to ask incredulous or reluctant questions ('Surely it is not the case that…?'): see Denniston on *El.* 235 and *GP* 492. Poseidon can scarcely believe that Athena has exchanged her hatred of Troy for pity. —The mss. give ἦ που, which would be coolly ironical ('I suppose you have dropped your hatred of Troy and taken pity on her'), less in keeping with Poseidon's attitude elsewhere in the scene. οὔ που is corrupted to ἦ που in some witnesses at *El.* 235 and *Hel.* 135. (Note also the variants οὐ and ἤ at 404 and εἰ and οὐ at 356.) It has to be conjecturally restored, as here, at *Med.* 695, *Supp.* 153, *Herc.* 1101, 1173, and *Pho.* 1072. It is arguably the truth when it occurs in a papyrus at *Med.* 1308. It or οὔ τί που is the sole reading at *El.* 630, *Herc.* 966, *IT* 930, *Ion* 1113, *Hel.* 95, 475, 541, 575, 600, 791, and *IA* 670. See for discussion and further references Diggle, *Studies* 58 and Wecklein 1896: 533–5, who was the first to propose οὔ που here. For the contrary view, that ἦ που is correct here and elsewhere, see Caspers 2010.

νιν…ἐς οἶκτον ἦλθες πυρὶ κατηιθαλωμένην: ἐς οἶκτον ἦλθες is a periphrastic expression equivalent to a transitive verb, and like a transitive verb it can take an accusative object, *νιν . . . κατηιθαλωμένην*. For other examples see Diggle, *Studies* 58, who argues persuasively for Elmsley's conjecture here.

61 **ἐκεῖϲε πρῶτ' ἄνελθε**: i.e. return to the subject of your cooperation with me. Diggle 1994: 287–8 notes that when *ἀνέρχομαι* means 'return' it is generally accompanied by *πάλιν*. He agrees that the verb means 'return' here but claims it is a metaphorical 'going up' the page to what one has read earlier.

61–2 **κοινώϲηι λόγουϲ | καὶ ϲυμπονήϲειϲ ἂν ἐγὼ πρᾶξαι θέλω**: 'Will you share counsels with me and toil with me to bring about whatever I wish to accomplish?' —It is difficult to decide between *ϲυμπονήϲειϲ* (PQ) and *ϲυνθελήϲειϲ* (V). The former emphasizes active effort, the latter volition. Lee argues that *ϲυμπονήϲειϲ* 'looks like an attempt to do away with the repetition' of *θέλ-*, and Biehl points out the piling up of expressions for volition in 62, 63, 73, 74, and 75, which he thinks favours the reading of V. But the reading of PQ seems on balance the more likely. Athena's purposes do not require that Poseidon should *want* what she does, only that his *actions*, whatever their motivation, should complement her own. The combination of *λόγοι* (61) and *πόνοϲ* is a variation on the *λόγοϲ–ἔργον* distinction. As for the alteration, anticipation of words the scribe knows is coming is a well-known cause of corruption: see West 1973: 23–4, Jackson 105–7 and 223–7, and Diggle 1984: 60 and 1994: 469–70.

63–4 **μάλιϲτ'**: 'certainly'. Stevens 1937: 137–8 calls this a colloquial expression.

ἀτὰρ δὴ καὶ τὸ ϲὸν θέλω μαθεῖν: 'But in fact I want to know your interest in the matter.' Poseidon retracts his unqualified assent. His subsequent question whether Athena has come to aid the Achaeans or the Trojans indicates the source of his hesitation: 57–8 have suggested a change of sides, but Poseidon wishes to make sure.

65–6 Athena's formulation, which puts causing joy to the Trojans ahead of giving the Achaean army a grim homecoming, seems calculated to appeal to Poseidon's pro-Trojan sympathies.

67–8 'Why do you leap about in this way, now assuming one character, now another? Why hate and love so excessively whomever you chance to hate or love?' Poseidon implies that there is no rationale for Athena's loves and hatreds, but in fact, as Athena explains, the change of attitude has a clear motivation.

67 **τρόπουϲ**: the regular word for a person's 'character' (Lat. *mores*), seen as a set of habitual responses.

68 —Either the personal *τύχηιϲ* (sc. *μιϲοῦϲα καὶ φιλοῦϲα*) or the impersonal *τύχηι* (sc. *μιϲεῖν ϲε καὶ φιλεῖν*) gives possible sense. For impersonal

τυγχάνω, see *Hipp*. 428, 929, *El*. 1169, *IT* 722, *Pho*. 765, *Or*. 780, and LSJ s.v. A.I.3.a. I print the personal form without clear conviction.

69 **οὐκ οἶcθ' ὑβριcθεῖcάν με καὶ ναοὺc ἐμούc**: Athena has been treated with violence or contempt because her temple has been so treated.

70 Ajax the son of Oïleus (Ajax the Lesser) dragged Cassandra from her place of refuge in the temple of Athena. In the *Iliupersis* (*GEF* arg. (3)) she clings so tightly to Athena's statue that it is pulled from its base as she is dragged off. In Alc. fr. 296.4–5 Voigt the speaker attributes a similar significance to Ajax's act, saying that it would have been better if the Greeks had killed him.

71 'Yes (γ'), and what is more (καί), he received no punishment or criticism from the Achaeans.' For γε in replies see *GP* 130–8. In the *Iliupersis* (*GEF* arg. (3)) the Greeks reacted to the sacrilege by resolving to stone Ajax, who for his part took refuge at Athena's altar. Eur.'s version makes Athena's anger against the Greek army as a whole more clearly justified. —There is no reason to regard the reading of PQ and Cyril as in need of alteration, as Diggle does: cf. κοὐδέν γε θαῦμα ('Yes, and it is not surprising') in dialogue at *OT* 1132. Nauck's κοὐ δείν' gives worse sense since it appears to imply that there was *some* reaction from the Greeks, just not a dreadful one, as pointed out by Stephanopoulos 1988: 488–9.

72 'And yet they *sacked Troy* by your might.' καὶ μήν is adversative (see *GP* 357) and γ' stresses the reason (*GP* 119–20). It was Athena's ruse of the Wooden Horse that brought about the fall of Troy.

74 **τἀπ' ἐμοῦ**: 'as far as my part is concerned', qualifying ἕτοιμ' ἃ βούληι, 'What you wish is yours to command'.

δράcειc δὲ τί: for the interrogative postponed to last position (or to a position later than expected) see Diggle 1978b: 170, Willink on *Or*. 101, and Thomson 1939.

75 **δύcνοcτον . . . νόcτον**: 'a calamitous homecoming', lit. 'a homecoming of evil homecoming'. Tragedy is especially fond of a type of oxymoron in which a noun is modified by an adjective or adjectival expression that is privative (e.g. *OT* 1214 ἄγαμον γάμον or *OT* 1255 γυναῖκά τ' οὐ γυναῖκα: cf. *Hec*. 948, *Hel*. 1134, *Pho*. 1495) or dyslogistic (formed with δυc-, αἰνο-, κακο-, or ἀπο-) and whose second element is either identical with or a synonym of the modified noun. In his fundamental 1968 discussion Fehling notes the similarity in meaning between such privative adjectives and such German locutions as *Untier*, *Unwetter*, and *Unstern*, where the prefix conveys qualification ('horrid beast', 'nasty weather', 'baleful star') rather than negation. He also notes the construction's affinity with the pleonasm seen in λιμέναc εὐόρμουc, discussed below on 125. Fehling shows that, apart from a few examples listed under (4)

below, there is no essential difference between, e.g. *γάμος ἄγαμος* and *γάμος δύσγαμος*: both describe a wedding as calamitous or pitiable but neither denies that it is a wedding. (Further literature on this topic and further references in Finglass's note on *Aj.* 664–5.) I divide the tragic examples into four groups, adding in some cases semantically similar uses from epic.

1. The adjective conveys the idea that its substantive is an X *manqué*, that it lacks one or more of an X's usual characteristics: *Ag.* 1142 *νόμον ἄνομον* ('tune lacking music's joy'), *Ag.* 1545 *ἄχαριν χάριν* ('a favour that is unwelcome to the recipient'), *Cho.* 42 *χάριν ἀχάριτον* ('a favour that lacks kindly intent'; cf. also the spurious *Pho.* 1757), 600 *ἀπέρωτος ἔρως*, *PV* 69 *θέαμα δυσθέατον*; *Aj.* *ἄδωρα δῶρα* (here predicative: an enemy's gifts are not meant to do good), *El.* 1153 *μήτηρ ἀμήτωρ*, *Phil.* 534 *ἄοικον εἰσοίκησιν* (*ἐξοίκησιν* Frederking); perhaps the present passage belongs here ('homecoming that lacks a homecoming's joy'), though it could be classed under (2) as well.

2. The adjective conveys a generally negative qualification, often accompanied by rejection or revulsion ('horrid, calamitous X'): *Hipp.* 1143–4 *πότμον ἄποτμον* ('a fate, and a nasty specimen it is!'). See also *Od.* 5.493 *δυσπονέος καμάτοιο* ('toil, and an unpleasant kind at that'); *Eu.* 266 *πώματος δυσπότου*, 1034 *Νυκτὸς παῖδες ἄπαιδες* (according to Fehling 1968: 154, 'calamitous Erinyes'), *PV* 904 *ἀπόλεμος πόλεμος*; *OT* 1214 and 1256, cited above, *Ant.* 587 *δυσπνόοις πνοαῖς*, 1276 *πόνοι δύσπονοι*; *Hec.* 194 *δυσφήμους φήμας*, 661 *κακογλώσσου βοῆς* (and cf. *Med.* 420, *Andr.* 1144, *Ion* 1090–7), *Supp.* 960 *δυσαίων βίος*, *Herc.* 1133 *ἀπόλεμον πόλεμον*, *IT* 143 *δυσθρηνήτοις θρήνοις*, 146 *ἀλύροις ἐλέγοις* (and perhaps *οὐκ εὐμούσου μολπᾶς*: cf. *Pho.* 808, 1028), 203 *δυσδαίμων δαίμων* (also Soph. fr. 210.37), 566 *χάριν ἄχαριν* ('ob causam, quae causa esse non debebat' Seidler: see also the similar turn at *Hipp.* 678); *Ion* 783 *ἄφατον αὖ φάτιν* (Murray: *ἄφ. ἄφ.* L), *Hel.* 213 *αἰὼν δυσαίων*, *Pho.* 1047 *γάμους δυσγάμους*, 1306 *πότμος* (Dindorf: *ἄποτμος* codd.) *ἄποτμος*, *Or.* 163–5 *ἀπόφονον φόνον*, 192 *ἀπόφονον αἷμα*, 318 *ἀβάκχευτον θίασον*. Similar, though based on proper names, are *Il.* 3.39 and 13.769 *Δύσπαρι* (cf. *Hec.* 945, *Or.* 1387, *IA* 1316), *Od.* 19.260 *Κακοΐλιον*, and 18.73 *Ἶρος Ἄϊρος* (though this last may express ironical pity and belong in the next group).

3. The adjective conveys an attitude of pity or sympathy ('poor, luckless X'): *Od.* 23.97 *μῆτερ ἐμὴ δύσμητερ* ('my poor mother'); *Cho.* 315 *πάτερ αἰνόπατερ*; *IT* 216 *νύμφαν* (Scaliger: *-φαιον* L) *δύσνυμφον*. Here we may put *Herc.* 1061. a *ὕπνος ἄυπνος* (Dobree: *ὕπνον ὕπνον* L) is not 'a sleep that is no sleep', since Heracles is in fact asleep, but 'a pitiable sleep'. (But corruption may lie deeper: see Willink 1989.)

4. Only occasionally is a literally negatory interpretation (where the adjective denies that the person or thing is truly an X) certain or plausible. Certain examples are *Eu.* 457 †*Τροίαν*† *ἄπολιν Ἰλίου πόλιν*; *Phil.* 848 *ὕπνοϲ ἄυπνοϲ* ('sleepless sleep', i.e. light); *Supp.* 32 *δέϲμον ἄδεϲμον* ('bond that does not bind'), *Hel.* 363 *ἔργ' ἄνεργα* ('deeds that never happened'), 690 *γάμον ἄγαμον* ('a marriage that never took place'); there are formally dissimilar examples in Fehling 1968: 153–4 and prose examples in Wackernagel 2.291. Plausible are *Pers.* 680 *νᾶεϲ ἄναεϲ ἄναεϲ* (though 'calamitous ships' is thinkable), *Hec.* 612 *νύμφην τ' ἄνυμφον παρθένον τ' ἀπάρθενον* ('bride who is no bride—because her 'marriage' to Achilles is a sacrifice—and maiden who is no maiden—because she will be united to Achilles'; but one could take both adjectives pityingly: 'poor young woman, poor maiden'), *IT* 889 *ὁδοὺϲ ἀνόδουϲ* (but perhaps 'dreadful journeyings'), and *πόρον ἄπορον* in the justly obelized *IT* 897.

The adjective, while usually derived from the modified noun, is sometimes derived from its synonym, as in *Hec.* 661, *Supp.* 960, and *IT* 146. Other discussions in Bruhn § 222, Meyer 1923: 103–6, Wackernagel 2.291, Breitenbach 236–8, Moorhouse 1959: 66–8, Garvie on *Cho.* 43–6, Page and Mastronarde on *Med.* 199–200, Stevens on *Andr.* 278 and 1154–5, Collard on *Supp.* 32, Kyriakou on *IT* 143–7, Dodds on *Ba.* 112 and 1203–7, and Gibert 2004 on *Archelaus* F 242. In this play see 125 and 144.

76 **ἐν γῆι μενόντων**: sc. *αὐτῶν*. According to *MT* § 850. 'The gen. absol. is regularly used only when a new subject is introduced into the sentence and not when the participle can be joined with any substantive already belonging to the contruction. Yet this principle is sometimes violated in order to make the participial clause more prominent and to express its relation (time, cause, etc.) with greater emphasis.' Here Poseidon wants to know precisely where and when he is to intervene (with the Greeks on land or at sea?), and the genitive absolute, in contrast to the construction with the dative *αὐτοῖϲ*, helps to make the emphasis on the timing of his action clearer. For further examples of such unexpected absolutes (many without genitive noun) see Appendix 1 to Pearson's *Helen* (pp. 198–9) and KG 2.110–11. —The reading of PQ, *μένουϲιν*, is clearly secondary, being an obvious smoothing out of a difficult construction. If we supposed it genuine, we could not account for the reading of V.

ἁλμυρὰν ἅλα: when *ἅλϲ* means 'sea', it is feminine, when it means 'salt' masculine.

77 Athena answers the question: the attack will be at sea.

78–84 Zeus will send bad weather and has promised to give Athena the thunderbolt with which to strike the Greek ships and set them on fire. Poseidon for his part is to make the sea turbulent. This agreement of two former enemies to join forces and punish the Greeks by means of lightning-bolt and turbulent sea reads almost like a dramatization of the Herald's words at *Ag.* 650–2, *ξυνώμοϲαν γάρ, ὄντεϲ ἔχθιϲτοι τὸ πρίν, | πῦρ καὶ θάλαϲϲα, καὶ τὰ πίϲτ' ἐδειξάτην | φθείροντε τὸν δύϲτηνον Ἀργείων ϲτρατόν* (though curiously his subsequent narrative, which describes *θάλαϲϲα* fully, says nothing about *πῦρ*).

78 ***ὄμβρον καὶ χάλαζαν ἄϲπετον***: *ἄϲπετοϲ*, 'unutterably great', a word of epic flavour, modifies both *ὄμβρον* and *χάλαζαν*. (It derives from *ἀ-* privative plus the verbal root seen in *ἔϲπετε* [< **ἐν-ϲπετε*] and Lat. *insece*.)

79 ***δνοφώδη τ' αἰθέροϲ φυϲήματα***: logically 'murky' should modify *αἰθέροϲ* instead of *φυϲήματα*. On *enallage* see above on 1–2.

δνοφώδη: another word of epic register (*δνοφερόϲ* occurs in Homer). —The word is restored by Dindorf (all the mss. here give *γνοφώδη*, its later spelling).

80–1 To avoid the repetition *πῦρ ... πυρί* Cobet 1873: 593 proposed *φλογί*. But repetition, without obvious point, of the same word at short intervals is common in the tragic poets: see Jackson 220–2. Some evidence that the Greeks were more aware of this than is sometimes claimed is given in Pickering 2003, especially the criticism of Pausimachus *ap.* Philodemus cited on pp. 493–5. (An earlier article, Pickering 2000, makes no distinction between repetition belonging to established tropes such as anadiplosis and non-figural or 'careless' repetition, and so the statistics comparing the poets do not address the present question.) I owe the Pickering references to PJF.

82 ***τὸ ϲὸν* (sc. *μέροϲ*)**: for examples of this adverbial use, 'you (for your part)', see Bruhn § 247.

83 ***τρικυμίαιϲ***: for the sense 'huge wave' (developed from the original sense 'series of three waves' of which the last is the largest), see Barrett on *Hipp.* 1213–14. Sedley 2005, elucidating *τρικυμία* in Plato's *Republic* by citing its occurrence elsewhere in Greek literature, comes to the conclusion that the word alludes to a tsunami, which often involves three successive waves. But a tsunami does not belong in the present context.

84 ***κοῖλον Εὐβοίαϲ μυχόν***: possibly an etymological allusion to *τὰ Κοῖλα*, the part of the coast of Euboea between Chalcis (opposite Aulis) and Geraestus at its southeastern tip (see Strabo 10.1.2). The prominence of Euboea here and at 90 below perhaps reflects the plot of *Palamedes*, performed immediately before *Tro.*: see Introduction § 3.3.

85–6 'So that the Greeks may learn in future to act reverently toward my temples and to revere the other gods'.

85 ***εὐcεβεῖν***: the use of this verb with an external accusative seems guaranteed by *Ag.* 338, *Eu.* 1019, and *Pho.* 1321 (see Mastronarde on the last), as well as by fr. 752k.20–1 (*Hypsipyle*), and the personal passive use of the verb at Antiph. 3 γ 11.

86 ***εἰδῶc'***: for οἶδα + infinitive meaning 'learn to' see *Hipp.* 729, likewise minatory. —The occurrence of the same two syllables (cεβειν) at the ends of successive lines has excited suspicion. Norden 1909 1.28–9 and 2.832–3 gives examples of such rhymes in Eur. Most of them, such as *Med.* 408–9, involve some kind of antithesis, though Eur. shows himself capable of producing a gratuitous jingle at *Alc.* 782–5 and at *Andr.* 198–9. (But see Kovacs 1980: 20–8, where on other grounds a transposition is suggested.) A possible replacement for cέβειν is Herwerden's τίειν.

90 Scyros, where Achilles was hidden disguised as a girl to prevent his going to Troy and being killed, is the birthplace of Achilles' son Neoptolemus; Lemnos figures in the story of Philoctetes; Caphereus in Euboea is the home of Palamedes, whose father Nauplius, learning of his son's judicial murder by the Greeks, set false beacons to wreck the Greek fleet. According to a notice about *Palamedes* (fr. 588a), Palamedes' brother Oeax wrote about his fate on the blades of oars and set them adrift. The oars (miraculously?) reached Nauplius. Koniaris 1973: 92 points out that the reference to these cliffs does not imply that the judicial murder of Palamedes is the reason for the coming destruction of the Greeks. Nevertheless, given the certainty that Nauplius' activity was forecast at the end of *Palamedes* it seems fairly likely that a reference here to the earlier play is intended.

91 ***θανόντων cώμαθ'... νεκρῶν***: for the pleonasm see 623, *Alc.* 664, 995, *Supp.* 44–5, 107, *Hel.* 1252, *Pho.* 1476–7.

92 ***ἀλλ' ἕρπ' Ὄλυμπον***: the terminal accusative without a preposition is a common poeticism in tragedy: see Stevens on *Andr.* 3 and Bers 1984: 62–85.

93–4 ***καραδόκει... κάλωc***: i.e. 'Wait for the moment when the Greek fleet is proceeding full sail'.

94 ***ἐξιῆι κάλωc***: 'Let out the brailing ropes', i.e. expose the full sail to the wind, means to sail at full speed: see Mastronarde on *Med.* 278.

Staging: as argued above on 48–97, Athena departs by means of the *mēchanē*. Though her departure after 97 is conceivable, I would prefer her to exit after 94. This separates the two departures and allows Poseidon to utter the gnomic 95–7 to himself and the audience.

95–7 'Foolish is that mortal who sacks cities but who, having made desolate temples and tombs, holy precincts of the dead, perishes later himself.' As I argued in 1983 and again in 1996, Poseidon is not claiming that it is always foolish to sack cities. (Sacking cities does not, in itself, amount to or involve sacrilege: see Kovacs 1983: 335–6 and Scully 1990: 38.) Rather, foolish is that mortal who sacks cities *but*, when he has done so, perishes later himself (as the result of impieties like that of Ajax the Lesser and his fellow Greeks). In other words, both ἐκπορθεῖ and ὤλετ' belong to the relative clause. The idea of destroying cities is stated once in 95, then repeated for the sake of the contrast with perishing. For a similar pointed contrast see *Hel.* 105–6. *Ελ. ἦλθες γάρ, ὦ ξέν', Ἰλίου κλεινὴν πόλιν; Τε. καὶ ξύν γε πέρςας αὐτὸς ἀνταπωλόμην.* The text I print here makes use of the easy alteration of τε to δέ in 96, a conjecture by Blomfield published in Duncan 1821, p. 611. (It was proposed again by Headlam 1895: 287.) Sacking cities is only the first part (quasi-concessive: understand μέν) of a contrast that constitutes the folly in question: such a man, to be sure, sacks cities, *but* since he perishes later himself he shows himself to be a fool. Other treatments are less satisfactory. Biehl marks a colon at the end of 95, but this implies that sacking cities is always foolish and the victors always perish for doing so, which I have shown to be unlikely: see Kovacs 1983 and 1996. Diggle punctuates at the end of 96 (as suggested to him by Page) and writes Page's δούς <cφ'>, but this means that ἐκπορθεῖ takes an oddly assorted set of objects (cities, temples, and tombs: the latter two are parts of cities) and likewise implies that city-sackers always perish. The last objection applies also to Sansone 1982: 36, who punctuates after τύμβους θ'. I discuss the passage at greater length in Appendix 1.

96 **ναούς**: the tragic poets make liberal use of λεώς as well as λαός, but νεώς for ναός only at *Pers.* 810.

ἱερὰ τῶν κεκμηκότων: tombs are sacred to the dead in the way that the gods' precincts are sacred to them. The attributive perfect participle of κάμνω is used in tragedy for 'the dead, those whose toil is finished' once in Aesch., once in Soph., and twice in Eur. Epic prefers the aorist participle.

97 **ἐρημίαι δούς**: a periphrasis for ἐρημώσας. Similar periphrases at 1146, 1176, *Hec.* 850, *IA* 850, Biehl on 535, and Kannicht on *Hel.* 868–70. The point is that the people who worship at the shrines and bring offerings to the dead have been killed or removed.

Staging: Poseidon descends into the *skēnē* by a stairway or ladder. Alternatively, if his entrance was at ground level, he uses an *eisodos*.

98–152. Solo lament of Hecuba

Staging: Hecuba, prostrate on the ground in front of the *skēnē*, now stirs, raising her head up (but not yet rising to her feet, as I mistakenly said in the Loeb). She presumably rises from the ground at 143, when she calls the Chorus out of the *skēnē*.

The third part of the *prologos*, part of which is sung, has formal resemblances to solo monodies in two of Eur.'s plays, *Hec.* and *El.*, and in Soph.'s *El.*, as noted by Finglass on 86–120. Here, as in *Hec.* and the two Electra plays, the monodist took no part in the preceding portion of the *prologos*. Here, as in these plays, the monody precedes the entrance of a female chorus who have come to sympathize with the monodist. Here, as in the two Electra plays, the *parodos* consists of lyric dialogue.

Hecuba's lament consists of two distinct sections, one in non-lyric ('marching' or 'recitative') anapaests and one in lyric anapaests, with the possible admixture of other metres. Non-lyric anapaests were performed in a fashion perhaps mid-way between speaking and singing. They can be distinguished from the lyric variety by the following: (1) they exhibit Attic eta, not Doric alpha; (2) they occur in systems of full dimeters (or trimeters) rounded off by a clausular catalectic dimeter (paroemiac), which has seven elements instead of the full dimeter's eight; (3) paroemiacs are avoided except at the end of a system; (4) a sequence of four short syllables is usually avoided (i.e. an anapaest directly following a dactyl is rare); and (5) full dimeters and trimeters show caesura (diaeresis) at metron boundary. Lyric anapaests by contrast show Doric alpha; make frequent use of non-clausular paroemiacs, sometimes in successive lines (these are often in the fully 'contracted' form of seven long syllables); more frequently admit a sequence of four shorts; and sometimes bridge over the metron break.

98–121. Hecuba's non-lyric anapaests

As printed by me, 98–121 exhibit the following pattern: 12 full metra + paroemiac (98–104); 7 full metra + paroemiac (105–9); 7 full metra + paroemiac (110–14); 12 full metra + paroemiac (115–21), forming an ABBA pattern. Without the alteration of 114 the pattern would be 12 + paroemiac; 7 + paroemiac; 21 + paroemiac.

98–9 The frequency in Eur. of commands addressed by speakers to themselves is noted by Spitzbarth 1945: 87–8. See 101–4, 279–80, 308–10, 445, *Med.* 401, *Hec.* 1069, *El.* 112–13, 150, *Ba.* 594–5. We must make a complete sentence of ἄνα, δύϲδαιμον. (For the elliptical ἄνα, which = ἀνάϲτηθι or the like, in tragedy, see *Alc.* 276 and *Supp.* 45, where it is conjecturally restored. Since she does not rise until later, ἄνα is best taken non-literally, 'come now', as presumably at *Alc.* 277.) —The accusative κεφαλήν cannot be governed by this construction. We cannot adopt V's vocative κεφαλά and adjust the vocalism to κεφαλή, since this involves an impermissible hiatus with the next line. (In addition, 'Rise up from the ground, unlucky head! Lift up the neck!' asks the head, implausibly, to raise the neck.) Hecuba, after exhorting herself to action, bids herself raise her head and neck. Diggle 1973: 243n15 suggests achieving this by means of the ἀπὸ κοινοῦ construction, i.e. by supplying (ἐπάειρε) πεδόθεν κεφαλήν, ἐπάειρε δέρην on the analogy of Soph. *El.* 105–6 ἔϲτ' ἂν παμφεγγεῖϲ ἄϲτρων ῥιπάϲ, λεύϲϲω δὲ τόδ' ἦμαρ. Biehl cites other cases of ἀπὸ κοινοῦ in 322–3, 527–8, and Soph. *El.* 1434. An examination of Kiefner's appendix of examples (129–54) fails to discover any reassuring parallel for the absence of both connection ('and' or 'or') and anaphora. Later at *Studies* 64 Diggle rejects this interpretation in favour of Musgrave's δέρην <τ'>. This makes the sentence easier to read, but on the rarity of elision at metron boundary coinciding with strong punctuation see below on 114. We might consider Matthiae's γεραιάν (Matthiae actually proposed the incorrect γεραρήν) in place of κεφαλήν. Powell 1939 gives instances where τράχηλοϲ means 'neck and head' (see 755), and that could be the meaning of δέρη here. In that case κεφαλήν might be an explanatory gloss that has invaded the text. I print the unaltered text without conviction.

99–100 For the sense 'What you see here is no longer Troy', cf. *Andr.* 168–9, οὐ γάρ ἐϲθ' Ἕκτωρ τάδε, | οὐ Πρίαμοϲ οὐδὲ χρυϲόϲ. In tragedy if a woman uses the 1st-person plural to refer to herself, modifying nouns or adjectives are masculine (see Barrett on *Hipp.* 287), and so βαϲιλῆϲ ἐϲμεν = βαϲίλειά εἰμι.

101 **μεταβαλλομένου δαίμονοϲ**: the genitive could be either absolute or the one that is frequent with ἀνέχομαι: see LSJ s.v. ἀνέχω C.II.4 and add *Andr.* 340 (possibly spurious but written by someone competent in tragic Greek). —The reading δαίμονοϲ ἀνέχου (all mss.) contains a sequence of four shorts. Diggle, *Studies* 45–6 discusses the instances of tetrabrachs in the non-lyric anapaests of tragedy and concludes that where they are not spurious (*Septem* 827–8, 867–8, *Hec.* 145) or possibly lyric (*Ion* 226), most (*Eu.* 948, fr. 91 [Radt deletes καὶ τὸν ἐλάϲϲονα with

Bothe], Eur. *El.* 1319) are easily emendable and should be emended. But *El.* 1322–3 is not emendable, and *Ion* 226 is, as Diggle says, 'not prima facie lyric', so the present passage, as transmitted, has the company of two other non-lyric instances. To avoid the tetrabrach the OCT prints Nauck's conjecture ἄνcχου. The form is not without analogy (apocope of ἀνά is plausibly conjectured in Eur. at *Or.* 1501, and *Il.* 24.529 has ἄνcχεο; the aorist imperative ἀνάcχου is transmitted at *Alc.* 304, *Hcld.* 380, and *Ion* 947), but we would feel more confidence about admitting it here if it were actually transmitted elsewhere in Greek literature (it was conjectured by Meineke in Eur. fr. 1080, but Kannicht properly adopts Heath's ἀνέχου). The present imperative seems better here, to go with those at 99, 102, and 103 (and cf. ἀνέχου at *El.* 1320 and *Or.* 1599). The only reason for adopting it is the tetrabrach, but δαίμονοc could be challenged as an anticipation of δαίμονα in the next line, and we could write, e.g., μεταβαλλομένηc αἴcηc or Lenting's μεταβαλλομένων ἀνέμων, improved perhaps by the insertion of <δ'> between the two words. (Burges suggested <δ'> as part of a different proposal.)

102–4 The best commentary on this extended metaphor is 686–93 below. There Hecuba says that when there is a chance of avoiding shipwreck, sailors work hard to manage the tiller and the sails and to bail water, but when they despair of safety, they surrender the ship to the motion of the waves. Here Hecuba exhorts herself to adopt the second course of action, sailing in whatever direction the water is moving, and recommends against turning the prow of the ship into the wave. This is a counsel of despair, not an encouragement to prudence, as some interpreters imply. Turning the prow into the waves is the way to avoid capsizing. NL draws my attention to an American sailing publication: 'It should be obvious that one of the major goals of heavy weather tactics is to keep the bow or stern of the boat end-on into the waves.' Such advice is implied in phrases such as *Hipp.* 824 ἐκπερᾶcαι κῦμα τῆcδε cυμφορᾶc.

Eur.'s fondness for nautical metaphor, on which see Pot 1943, gave rise to the story in Eur.'s life (Kannicht T 1.69–71) that he wrote his plays in a cave on Salamis that looked out to sea. On the nautical metaphors here and at 118 see Barlow 1971: 50–2, 105, and 117–18.

102 **πλεῖ κατὰ πορθμόν, πλεῖ κατὰ δαίμονα:** in view of the second phrase, 'down the strait' must mean 'with the current'.

103–4 **μηδὲ προcίcτη πρῷραν βιότου | πρὸc κῦμα πλέουcα τύχαιcιν:** 'and do not turn your life's prow and sail into fortune's waves', i.e. there is no point in even trying to avoid shipwreck, as one can by turning the prow into the waves. Lee takes πλέουcα τύχαιcιν as 'sailing as you do by the winds of chance' but the participle should not express Hecuba's *general* circumstances but an action accompanying the main verb *προςίςτη*, as in the translation above. (Note also that if the main verb is negatived, we expect a participial phrase going with it to take the same negative colouring.) The dative is one of interest and has possessive force: see KG 1.429. This involves a slight personification of *τύχαι*. (A further possibility would be to suppose that the dative is governed by an adverb such as *κατέναντα*, that may once have stood where *πρὸς κῦμα* now stands.) —The choice between active and middle imperative (*pace* Lee, *προςίςτω* would be middle, not passive here) is not easy, and I print the active without conviction: either voice gives good sense.

105–7 The exclamation is followed by its cause (*γάρ*). The catalogue of Hecuba's miseries is surprisingly brief by Euripidean standards: she has lost country, children, and husband. For longer catalogues see 472–97, 745–56, and 1167–88 below and *Alc.* 939–61, *Andr.* 399–405, *Hec.* 349–66, *El.* 304–31, *Herc.* 1258–1302, *Ion* 862–9, *Hel.* 196–210, and *Ba.* 1352–62.

108–9 ***ὄγκος***: the noun and the corresponding verb are used by Eur. at *Andr.* 320, *Hec.* 623, *El.* 381, *Pho.* 717, and *IA* 450 to describe glory and high position. See also 1158n. The glory of Hecuba's ancestors has now been sharply abridged or reduced (*ςυςτελλόμενος*). Since this word is used as a nautical term for shortening sail, it continues the nautical metaphors of 102–4. The verb describes the action of a god 'reducing' mortal greatness at fr. 716.3–4 (*Telephus*): *τά τοι μέγιςτα πολλάκις θεός | ταπεὶν' ἔθηκε καὶ ςυνέςτειλεν πάλιν.*

109 ***ὡς οὐδὲν ἄρ' ἦςθα***: *ὡς* is exclamatory: with *οὐδέν* it can be translated 'how insignificant' ('how nothing' is unnatural English): see also *Med.* 62 and *Herc.* 62, where 'how little' is a good translation. The imperfect of 'to be' is used with *ἄρα* to mark the realization of something that is true and has been true all along: 'how insignificant you are (and were, had I known it), I now see.' See *GP* 37, KG 1.144, *MT* § 39, Mastronarde on *Med.* 703, and Barrett on *Hipp.* 359. (There may be an instance without *ἄρα*: see Liapis on *Rhes.* 324, though Fries *ad loc.* offers a different explanation.)

110–11 the three-fold division—(a) What shall I wrap in silence? (b) What shall I not wrap in silence? (c) What shall I bewail?—seems less natural than a binary opposition since (b) and (c) are arguably the same thing. Hence Tyrrell's deletion of 111. (One could consider deleting *τί δὲ μὴ ςιγᾶν* instead.) But the symmetry of four anapaestic systems—the first and last with 12 metra + paroemiac, and middle two with 7 metra + paroemiac—speaks in favour of the transmitted text.

112–14 ***τῆς βαρυδαίμονος ἄρθρων κλίςεως***: the genitive is one of cause ('How miserable I am because of the woeful disposition of my limbs').

113 **ὡc διάκειμαι:** such expressions with ὡc are partly causal, partly exclamatory: 'In such (a miserable) fashion am I disposed.' For examples see KG 2.370–1 and Barrett on *Hipp.* 877–80.

114 **νῶτ' ἐν cτερροῖcι ταθεῖcα:** 'with my back stretched out on the hard ground'. For the anarthrous neuter plural adjective used as a noun cf. *Med.* 122 ἐπὶ μὴ μεγάλοιc, *Med.* 1103 ἐπὶ φλαύροιc and ἐπὶ χρηcτοῖc, *Supp.* 884 cκληρά, *El.* 408 ἐν cμικροῖcιν, and *Ba.* 277 ἐν ξηροῖcιν. —I print the text as trimmed by Hartung 1837: 64 and Hermann 1847: 5 to make a paroemiac. We must either make 114 a full dimeter by marking an elision (first in the Aldine edition of 1503: unelided ταθεῖcα is the reading of the mss.); or trim in the middle to make a paroemiac. In favour of the second are two considerations. (1) In the extant plays there are approximately 1560 genuine anapaestic metra arranged in systems that conclude with a paroemiac (I include also sung metra arranged in systems). Elision at metron boundary coinciding with a strong mark of punctuation occurs only four times, *Alc.* 744, *Med.* 1109, 1398, and *Supp.* 1233 (plus *Tro.* 99 if Musgrave's δέρην <τ'> is correct). With an exclamation immediately following there is only *Med.* 1398. The phenomenon is arguably too rare to be introduced by conjecture. (2) Trimming produces the ABBA symmetry noted above. Hartung's deletion is preferable to that of Seidler 1812: 15 because the addition is more easily explained (cτερροῖcι seemed to need a noun), whereas the genuineness of νῶτα seems guaranteed by the physical discomforts mentioned in 115–18.

Staging: Hecuba rocks her body back and forth in time with the anapaestic rhythm.

115–18 κεφαλῆc, κροτάφων, and πλευρῶν are genitive of cause (the first two are hendiadys for 'temples of my head'). ὡc is exclamatory: 'How I long….'

εἱλίξαι: either this is intransitive or we must take νῶτον ἄκανθάν τ' (hendiadys for 'back') ἀπὸ κοινοῦ.

διαδοῦναι: the prefix indicates alternate distribution to one or the other side of her body (εἰc ἀμφοτέρουc τοίχουc μελέων). The plural μέλεα is a synonym for 'body'. The 'walls' are the sides of a ship and continue the nautical metaphor. For τοῖχοc in a nautical context see *Hel.* 1573.

119 —Musgrave's ἐπιοῦc' (ἐπέρχομαι is used with μοῦcαν as object at *Hel.* 165. cf. also Ar. *Ach.* 627) gives better sense than transmitted ἐπὶ τούc, since no parallel has been produced for ἐπί + accusative meaning 'to the accompaniment of'. For ἐπὶ τοὺc αἰεί Scheidweiler 1954: 250 suggests ἐπαειδούcῃι, the dative modifying μοι in 116. This would attractively prepare for the switch to sung anapaests at 122.

120–1 'This in fact (*καί*) is poetry for those in misfortune, to sing aloud their joyless ruinations.'

ἀχορεύτουϲ: lit. 'not fit to be celebrated in dance'. Euripidean characters elsewhere note the paradox that giving poetic voice to misery helps to alleviate it: see *Andr.* 91–5, *El.* 125–6, *Tro.* 608–9, and de Romilly 1980: 88.

Staging: Hecuba is on her feet, we may suppose, when she summons the Chorus out of the tent at 143–52. She may have risen to a sitting position at 122 (cf. 138–9).

122–52. Hecuba's monody

Hecuba evokes the Greek ships that came to Troy in quest of the hateful Helen and caused Troy's ruin (121–37), then laments her own enslavement (138–42) before calling the Trojan women of the Chorus out of the tent to sing of her woes antiphonally (143–52).

1. 122	– – – – – – – –	par
2. 123	– ⏖ ⏖ – – – –	par
3. 124	†⏑ ⏑ ⏑ – ⏖ – ⏖ –	?
4. 125	⏑ ⏑ ⏑ – ⏑ ⏑† – – –	?
5. 126	– – – – – – – – –	2an
6. 127	– – – – – – – – –	2an
7. 128	– – – – – – – – –	2an
8. 129	– – – – – – – – –	2an
9. 130	– – – – – – – –	par
10. 131	– ⏖ – – ⏖ – ⏖ –	2an
11. 132	– – ⏖ – – ⏖ – –	2an
12. 133	– – – – – – ⌒ ‖	par
13. 134	– – – –	an
14. 135	– – – – ⏖ – ⏖ –	2an
15. 136	† ⏑ ⏑ ⏑ ⏑ ⏑ ⏑ ⏑ ⏑ – ⏖ – †	?
16. 137	– – – – – – – –	par
17. 138	– – – – – – – – –	2an
18. 139	– – ⏖ – ⏖ – ⏖ –	2an
19. 140	– – ⏖ –	an
20. 141	– – – – – – – –	par
21. 142	– – – – – – – –	par
22. 143	– – – – – – – – –	2an
23. 144	⏖ – ⏖ –	an
24. 145	– – – – – – – – –	2an
25. 146	– ⏖ – ⏖ † – – ⏑ – †	2an
26. 147	– – – – – – – – –	2an
27. 148	– – – – – – – – –	2an

28. 149	– – – – – – ⏑⏑ –	2an
29. 150	– – ⏑⏑ – ⏑⏑ – ⏑⏑ –	2an
30. 151	⏑⏑ – ⏑⏑ – – – ⏑⏑ –	2an
31. 152	– – – – – – – – |||	par

Metrical analysis

Sung delivery is marked by Doric alpha (127, 132, 136, 137, etc.) and the frequent use of non-clausular paroemiac, often fully contracted (130, 141, etc.). Most lines as transmitted are anapaestic. Where they are not, metre is unconvincing.

122–5 The word-order shows the high degree of artificiality characteristic of Euripidean monody: the relative pronoun is postponed to the fourth place in its clause, and *ὠκείαιϲ* is separated from *κώπαιϲ* by four words. —Tyrrell's *ὠκείαιϲ* avoids hiatus and gives *κώπαιϲ* a modifier. I have obelized 124–5. (1) The metre is unconvincing. (2) The text gives *διά* in 124 two objects, the sea and the lovely harbours of Greece, an odd pairing since the harbours are a negligible part of the journey and are oddly mentioned second, though they belong at the beginning (unless, implausibly, we say that they are harbours called at on the way to Troy). (3) The relative pronoun in 123 has no verb except *ἐξηρτήϲαϲθ'*, and (4) there is no main verb. The so-called *vocativus pendens* (a vocative with modifiers but no main verb) is a feature of Euripidean lyric (e.g. *El.* 432–41), and so (4) is not in itself suspicious. But with *ἐξηρτήϲαϲθ'* being the clause's only finite verb, the terminal accusative *Ἴλιον ἱεράν* has to depend upon *βαίνουϲαι*, which is (a) already busy with 126–7 ('proceeding to the accompaniment of pipes and syrinxes') and (b) the wrong tense for an action antecedent to *ἐξηρτήϲαϲθ'*. A reconstruction that meets these objections is *πρῷραι ναῶν, ὠκείαιϲ* | *Ἴλιον ἱερὰν αἳ κώπαιϲ,* | *δι' ἅλ'* <*Αἰγαίαν*> (Willink unpub.) *πορφυροειδέα,* | *λιμέναϲ* <*τ'*> *ἔπτεϲθ' εὐόρμουϲ, κτλ.* (both Seidler 1812: 151 and Hermann 1847: 5–6 proposed [*καὶ*] *λιμέναϲ* <*τ'*>): 'Ship-prows, that flew on your way with swift oars against holy Troy through the dark-blue <Aegean> sea and against her fair-havened harbours, moving to the hateful peal of shawms and the tuneful voice of pan-pipes, etc.' For verbs of flying applied to the motion of a ship see *Med.* 1, Page *ad loc.*, and West on *WD* 628. Now the honorifically mentioned harbour is that of Troy and stands properly at journey's end, after the mention of the Aegean, and it has become a second terminal accusative parallel to *Ἴλιον ἱεράν*, not a second object for *διά*. (For *λιμένεϲ* used for a single harbour see Trag. Adesp. fr. 83, *Andr.* 749, and Arist. *Rhet.* 3.1407b32–5, who attributes it explicitly to poets.) Once the (mistaken) explanation Ἑλλάδοϲ had obliterated the verb together with preceding τ', someone would have felt the need for a connective and inserted καί.

124 **δι' ἅλα ... πορφυροειδέα**: cf. Aesch. *Supp*. 529 λίμναι ... πορφυροειδεῖ.

125 **λιμένας ... εὐόρμουϲ**: on the pleonasm, typical of lyric (though found in dialogue as well), where the second element of the compound adjective repeats the meaning of the modified noun, see 75n.

126–7 Wind instruments (aulos and syrinx) were used to mark the beat for rowers: see West 1992: 29 and n. 83 and Eur. *El*. 435–7. For the singing of *paianes* on shipboard see Rutherford 2001: 45n41 and 79n40 on the connection of *paian* with the aulos. There is a typically tragic oxymoron (a *paian* is normally lovely) in παιᾶνι ϲτυγνῶι. Curiously this figure is not continued in the next line, which is univocally eulogistic. —Page's <ϲύν> makes the dative of accompaniment ('moving to the tune of') easier and gives a pair of 2an lines.

127 —As Busche 1886. 14 points out, Eur. prefers the distributive singular (the reading of PQ) even when there is a plurality of singers, as at *Or*. 1897. For the distributive singular see 392n.

128–30 The ships hang ropes down from their prows in the bays of Troy to moor them to the shore. The moment when the Greek fleet ties up in the Troad (in the *Iliad* boats were pulled ashore) is a fatal one, and the exclamations are in order. '... and ropes, which Egypt taught you to make, you hung down—<ah me,> ah me—in the bays of Troy!'

128–9 **πλεκτάϲ, Αἰγύπτου παίδευμ'**: nouns in -μα denote the thing produced as the object of the corresponding verb. 'Thing taught by Egypt' means that the Egyptians taught others to make ropes. On papyrus as the material for ropes see Morrison, Coates, and Rankov 2000: 189–90, who cite Hdt. 7.25, 34, and 36.3, where in the bridging of the Hellespont the Phoenicians are instructed to produce cables of white flax (λευκόλινον) and the Egyptians ones of papyrus. For hawsers of flax see 537–8n. —The transmitted text gives difficult sense ('plaited education of Egypt') and unlikely metre (the end of a paroemiac is not elsewhere elided). For πλεκτή, 'plaited rope', in Eur. see 958 and 1010 below (not elsewhere used in this sense in tragedy).

ἐξηρτάϲαϲθ' <αἰαῖ>: —I have restored the lyric alpha to this alpha-contract verb: cf. βοάϲω, αὐδάϲω, etc. in lyric contexts. Page's supplement is *metri gratia*.

131–3 ϲτυγνάν repeats ϲτυγνῶι in 126 and conveys Hecuba's attitude toward both the expedition and its cause. Helen is called a disgrace to Castor and a (source of) ill fame to the river Eurotas (Sparta's principal river). —Nauck 1862: 136–7 proposed δυϲκλείαν to avoid *brevis in longo*. But see Diggle, *Studies* 96–7, who shows that *brevis in longo* is not rare in lyric anapaests.

134–6 Helen has slain Priam, father of fifty sons, and made Hecuba go aground in misfortune. —As transmitted, 136 gives impossible metre. Further, one expects after *σφάζει μέν* a *δέ* with the next clause. Lenting's [*Πρίαμον*] *ἐμὲ δ' αὖ μελέαν* [*Ἑκάβαν*] gives metre. A periphrasis for a person is commonly given a gloss, which is then frequently incorporated into the text, as at 554. Priam has been mentioned three times (17, 41, 107) and Hecuba twice (36–7 and 100), so Eur. might have dispensed with their names here. If we keep the names, Burges' insertion of <*τάν*> before *μελέαν* gives 2an with the first long element resolved.

137 ***ἐξώκειλ'***: the verb, 'has run me aground', continues the nautical metaphor of 102–4.

138–9 Hecuba may have risen to a sitting position, here or earlier. The identification of the *skēnē* as the hut of Agamemnon occurs only here and at 177, where see note.

140–2 The first explicit mention by Hecuba of her coming life as a slave. She additionally describes herself as having her grief-stricken head ravaged, i.e. her hair is cut short. —Before *πενθήρη* the mss. all have *κουρᾶι ξυρήκει*, 'by means of razor cutting', words that destroy the metre and are a quotation from *Alc.* 427. This was presumably written in the margin as a parallel and mistakenly copied into the text.

Staging: Hecuba rises to her feet to call the Trojan women out of the tent.

143–6 Hecuba asks the Trojan women to lament Troy as it smoulders.

144 ***καὶ κοῦραι, δύσ<νυμφοι> νύμφαι***: on compound adjectives whose second element is redundant with the noun they modify, as here *δύσνυμφοι* is with *νύμφαι*, see on 75 and 125. For the collocation see *IT* 216 *νύμφαν δύσνυμφον*. I take *νύμφη* in both noun and adjective to mean 'young woman', not 'bride'. The meaning of 144 is 'and (unmarried) girls, maidens most miserable'. —The postulated omission is a case of haplography. Diggle's *δυσνυμφ<όταт>αι* is another possibility, giving good sense as well as metre: for the superlative in expressions of this type see *Pho.* 808. By contrast, we can eliminate conjectures that involve deleting *καὶ κόραι* on the grounds that the interpolation seems unmotivated. In addition, it is reasonable that some of the Chorus should be matrons and others unmarried.

146 ***τύφεται Ἴλιον***: 'Ilion is smouldering.' Cf. *καπνοῦται* (10).

†αἰάζομεν†: —all the mss. give *αἰάζομεν* in 145. This is unmetrical, and the Aldine prints *αἰάζωμεν*. This simple substitution of one o-vowel for another looks inevitable, but in fact no 1st-person plural or any volitional subjunctive form of this verb is recorded in the TLG. I have accordingly daggered. We could mend the metre with *αἰάζω μέν*. In addition, marking a lacuna before the verb might be a way to address the problem discussed in 159–60n. We can restore consistency by writing, e.g., <*αἰαῖ· πρὸϲ ναῦϲ ἤδη χωρεῖ ϲτρατὸϲ Ἑλλάνων·*> *αἰάζω μέν, κτλ.* The contrast between 145 (*μέν*) and what follows (δ') would be that between matter and manner. An alternative would be to write <*ἔα ἔα*> or <*ἰοῦ ἰοῦ*> after 152. This would be consistent with her later statement (159–60) that the reason she raised a shout was that she saw Greek sailors descending to their ships.

147–52 'As a mother bird (utters, leads off) a cry to her winged brood, so I lead off the song, not at all like the one I led off, with the confident beat of a chorus leader's foot, in praise of Troy's gods as Priam leaned upon his sceptre.' Hecuba combines two comparisons in describing her role: (1) she is like a mother bird crying to her chicks (*κλαγγάν*, which belongs to the simile, is *vox propria* for the sound made by birds or other animals: understand either *κλάζει* or *ἐξάρχει* in the simile); (2) she is like an *ἔξαρχοϲ*, a singer who announces a theme for other singers to repeat or embellish. What she will sing, however, makes a sharp contrast with her former songs in honour of the gods of Troy when Priam stood by and the beat of her foot was confident. —Diggle pp. vii–viii notes that when P and Q are at variance, if P or Q disagrees with V, its reading is to be regarded as a peculiar error. Here P has *ὡϲεί τιϲ* where the others have *ὡϲεί*. Though P's reading is attractive (see Fraenkel on *Ag.* 288–9 and *Cyc.* 460, *Supp.* 961, 1046, *El.* 1163, etc.) and though Diggle's n. 7 lists some places where P alone has the truth, including 206, where P has a word omitted by V and Q, I have adopted the reading of VQ. Thereafter Dindorf's *ὄρνιϲ* [*ὅπωϲ*] gives good sense and metre: *ὅπωϲ* should not be regarded as akin to the imperatival-admonitory construction [sc. *ὅρα*] *ὅπωϲ*, as is done by Jackson 159, for there is nothing imperatival about *ἐξάρξω*; if *ὅπωϲ* were genuine it could only be a comparative particle, superfluous after *ὡϲεί*. (Since there is something to be said for 'As a mother to her winged brood' instead of 'As a mother bird to her birds' we might consider changing Dindorf's conjecture to *θρέμμαϲιν* or *ἔρνεϲιν* [*ὅπωϲ*]; it is plausible to regard transmitted *ὄρνιϲιν* as an incorporated gloss.) Since Hecuba should not be leaning on Priam's sceptre and since 'Phrygian' is not needed to modify *πλαγαῖϲ*, both Herwerden's *διερειδομένου* and Wilamowitz's *Φρυγίουϲ* deserve to be accepted.

Staging: at or before 153 seven or eight of the fifteen chorus members, alarmed by Hecuba's cry of distress, emerge from the *skēnē*. They are dressed and masked as either widowed matrons or unmarried girls (see 144n). The remainder will emerge at or before 176, summoned by the first group (164–7). Either there or before 176 perhaps enter two extras, costumed as Trojan women, who will carry out Hecuba's or the Chorus Leader's orders at 351–2, 462–5, 466–7, 506–9, and 1200–1.

PARODOS (153–229)

153–96 The first stanzaic pair of the Chorus's entrance song takes the form of an *amoibaion* or lyric interchange between the Chorus and Hecuba. The *amoibaion* is then followed by a pair of stanzas sung by the Chorus alone.

153–75 ~ 176–96

1. 153 ~ 176	*Ημ.*	⏕ – ⏖ – ⏕ – ⏔ –	2an
2. 154 ~ 177		– ⏖ – ⏔ ⏖ – ⏖ –	2an
3. 155 ~ 178		⏔ ⏕ ⏔ – – – – –	2an
4. 156 ~ 179		⏕ – – – – ⏕ ⏔ –	2an
5. 157 ~ 180		– ⏖ – – – – – –	2an
6. 158 ~ 181		– – – – – – ⏓ ||	par
7. 159 ~ 182	*Εκ.*	– ⏖ – – – – – –	2an
8. 160 ~ 183		– – – – – – –	par
9. 161 ~ 184	*Ημ.*	– – ⏖ – ⏔ – – –	2an
10. 162 ~ 185		– – – – ⏕ – – –	2an
11. 163 ~ 186	*Εκ.*	– – – – – – – ||	par
12. 164 ~ 186	*Ημ.*	– – – –	an
13. 165 ~ 187		⏕ – – – ⏕ – ⏕ –	2an
14. 166 ~ 188		– ⏕ – – ⏕ – – –	2an
15. 167 ~ 189		– – – – – – – ||	par
16. 168 ~ 190	*Εκ.*	⏓ ⏓	
17. 168 ~ 190		– – – –	an
18. 169 ~ 190		– – – – – – – –	2an
19. 171 ~ 191		– – – – – – –	par
20. 170 ~ 192		– – – –	an
21. 172 ~ 193		⏔ ⏕ ⏔ ⏕ ⏔ – ⏒ ||	par
22. 173 ~ 194		– – – –	an
23. 173 ~ 194		– ⏔ ⏔ – ⏔ – ⏔ –	2an
24. 174 ~ 195		– – – – – – – –	2an
25. 175 ~ 196		– – – – – – – |||	par

Metrical analysis

The predominance of Doric forms (155, 162, 163, 168, 171 (V), 173, 174, 175, 177, 182, 183, 184, 185, 187, 189, 190, 191, 192, 193, 194, 195, 196), the use of fully contracted paroemiac (158 ~ 181, 160 ~ 183, 163 ~ 186, 167 ~ 189, 171 ~ 192, 175 ~ 196), and several full dimeters without caesura at metron end (166, 169, 182, 195) mark these anapaests as sung.

153–96 The tone of the first stanzaic pair, the *amoibaion*, is anxiety for what is to come. The two hemichoruses emerge to learn the meaning of

Hecuba's loud lament. The first group fear imminent departure from Troy; the second, who begin with the unmotivated fear that they have been sentenced to death, turn their thoughts to their allotment as slaves.

153–8 'Hecuba, what is the cry, the shout, you are uttering? What is the purport of your words? Through the (walls of the) hut I heard the lament you are making, and there darted a pang of fear through the breast of the Trojan women who within this house are lamenting their servitude.' Choral entrances are similarly motivated by shouts or noises at *Med.* 131–8, *Hcld.* 73, *Hel.* 179–90, and *PV* 133–5. Elsewhere they are motivated by rumour (*Hipp.* 121–40), desire to help (*Andr.* 117–21, *Herc.* 107–18, *Or.* 132–3) or to bring news (*El.* 167–74), or because the Chorus were sent for (*Hec.* 59–64, *IT* 137–8, *Ba.* 55–61). For the anaphora of the interrogative pronoun see 110–11 and e.g. *Alc.* 29, *Hec.* 695, 1056, *Or.* 831, and Collard on *Supp.* 603–7 (p. 268); for the synonymy of θροεῖϲ and θωΰϲϲειϲ see, e.g. *Alc.* 77–8, *Hec.* 629, and *IT* 832. For ποῖ, 'to what end', see LSJ s.v. A.II. For the dative of advantage or disadvantage (Τρωιάϲιν), often used with parts of the body in place of a genitive, see 558–9n and KG 1.429.

153 —Since these are sung anapaests (see *Metrical analysis* above) I have restored Ἑκάβα here. Scribes sometimes write Doric forms where Attic ones are correct (see e.g. 1251 and *Ion* 827), but sometimes, as here, the reverse (see e.g. 171, 223, 228). Some further points in *Eur. Tert.* 173.

154 **μελάθρων**: on the tendency to treat military huts in tragedy as if they were more permanent structures see 871n.

156 KB 2.355 cites our passage as the single tragic exception to the rule that in tragedy ἀΐϲϲω has a short alpha. Diggle, *Studies* 71–2 suggests that at 1086 the alpha may be long, but the text is too uncertain in both strophe and antistrophe for this to count as a reassuring instance. I have adopted Wecklein's τάρβοϲ ἀΐϲϲει (1901: 11; it was thought of earlier by Seidler, who rejected it on the mistaken grounds that Homeric prosody defends long alpha here).

159–60 'My daughters, the crew with their oars are moving toward the Greek ships.' χείρ here means 'band', 'body of men', as at *Hcld.* 337, *El.* 629, and Aesch. *Supp.* 958. cf. Latin *manus.* —Schroeder's conjecture restores metre. As regards content, two things puzzle about Hecuba's response. First, her earlier lament (143–52), which the Chorus have asked her to explain, was not about movement toward the Greek ships but about her coming slavery as an old woman (140–2) and the smouldering of Troy (145), so that there is a contradiction between Hecuba's actual lament and what she tells the Chorus she had been lamenting. Second, as far as the text allows us to see, there has been in fact no such movement, and while we could imagine sailors with oars marching past at the end of Hecuba's monody, such 'dumb show' would violate the general rule, established with a high degree of probability by Taplin 1977: 28–31, that all significant stage action is marked in the text when it happens. At 145 the text implies that Hecuba looks down the left *eisodos* toward Troy (invisible to the audience but directly addressed by Poseidon at 45–7). That is also the direction in which the ships lie: see Introduction § 2.4. The last word in the line is corrupt. If words of Hecuba were lost before †αἰάζομεν†, she may have seen and lamented the movement of the Greek sailors toward the shore. For an *exempli gratia* supplement see 146n.

161–2 'Ah me, what is their purpose? I suppose (ἦ που) that soon (ἤδη) they will be transporting me from the land of my father(s).' —Burges's conjecture πατρίας restores metre. Forms of πάτριος are frequently altered, to the detriment of the metre, into πατρῷος, apparently a deliberate change based on the rule—not in fact observed by poets—that the first means 'ancestral' and the second 'belonging to one's father': see LSJ s.v. πατρῷος II, Parker on *Alc.* 248–9, Page on *Med.* 431, and Jebb on *Phil.* 724. (It is not clear why the alteration was made here since the meaning 'ancestral' is as appropriate as 'of my father', but clearly πατρίας was the original reading.)

163 οὐκ οἶδ', εἰκάζω δ' ἄταν: Hecuba's uncertainty, coupled with her description of the sea-voyage as 'ruin', increases the mood of helpless terror that is this ode's chief note.

164–7 The first hemichorus, accepting as fact Hecuba's guess (ἦ που) that departure is imminent, proceed to call out the other captive women from the *skēnē* to hear the bad news. The picture is one of women overwhelmed by misery and all too ready to believe the worst.

166 ἔξω κομίσασθ' οἴκων: the Aldine edition's substitution of aorist for present imperative restores metre. Diggle adopts Headlam's ἐξορμίζεσθ', noting 'frequens est Hecuba in figuris maritimis (102–4, 108, 118, 137)', but the speaker here is not Hecuba, and the idea of 'unmooring' from the hut seems a less attractive metaphor than those he cites. For κομίζομαι in similar contexts see *Pho.* 593, Aesch. *Supp.* 949, *Ag.* 1035, and *PV* 392.

168–72 'Ah, ah! Therefore please do not send out the god-crazed Cassandra, the maenad, to be shamed by the Greeks: may I not suffer griefs on top of griefs!' The 'therefore' (νυν) has in view either her determination to call the other women out of the tent or (as Biehl suggests) it refers to the sudden thought of Cassandra expressed in the interjection.

169 ἐκβακχεύουσαν Κασσάνδραν: here, as in *Hec.* 121, 676, and 827, Cassandra is likened to a maenad. See also 342, 349, 415, and *Alexandros*

F 62e. The verb is more frequently transitive (see e.g. 408 below) but note also Alexis fr. 145.13 KA.

171 ***αἰϲχύναν Ἀργείοιϲιν***: 'to cause (us) disgrace in the eyes of the Argives'. The accusative, though conceivably in apposition to Cassandra, is better taken as expressing the result of the verb. On the 'accusative in apposition to the sentence' see 536n. For the simple dative meaning 'in the eyes (judgement) of' see KG 1.421–2. —It cannot mean 'to be degraded by the Argives' (Barlow) or 'to be outraged by the Greeks' (Lee) since *αἰϲχύνω* is not a synonym of *ὑβρίζω*. The Greek in itself could mean 'as a disgrace to the Argives', perhaps calling to mind the crime of Ajax (thus Biehl). But Hecuba is more likely to worry about disgrace to the Trojans than to the Argives. Though the paradosis is not clearly wrong, clarity is improved by my suggestion (*Eur. Tert.* 173–4) *αἰϲχύναν <ἔν γ'> Ἀργείοιϲ*, 'to cause us disgrace in the eyes of the Greeks'. (For this sense of the preposition see LSJ s.v. A.I.6.) We could also consider *αἰϲχύναν Ἰδαίαιϲιν*, 'disgrace to the Trojan women': for the word as a synonym for 'Trojan' see 199, *Hec.* 325, 354, *Hel.* 658, and *Or.* 1380. Murray's transposition of 171 to precede 170 eliminates the hiatus between 170 and 171 and restores responsion with 192.

172 ***ἐπ' ἄλγεϲι δ' ἀλγυνθῶ***: the force of the negative continues from 168. For the 1st-person jussive or voluntative subjunctive see *MT* § 255–7. —Willink (unpub.) calls a paroemiac (here and 193) ending in ⏖ – – – a freak and also notes the irregularity of the responsion ⏔ ⏕ ⏔ ⏕ – – ⏒ and proposes to make both lines full dimeters: *μανίαιϲι δ' ἐπ' ἄλγεϲιν ἀλγυνθῶ* ~ *νεκύων ἀμένηνον ἄγαλμ', αἰαῖ.*

173–4 'Ah, ah, unhappy Troy, you are destroyed, and unhappy are those who are leaving you, both the living and the dead'. Strictly speaking the dead have left Troy already, and so when applied to them *ἐκλείποντεϲ* is best regarded as an instance of zeugma.

173 ***ἰὼ ἰώ***: —Seidler deleted these words since in the antistrophe V and the scholiast have *νεκύων ἀμενηνὸν ἄγαλμ'· ἤ* (the other manuscripts give a badly mutilated text). But at 194 Diggle, following Hermann, restores interjections, replacing the (clearly incorrect) *ἤ*.

175 ***δμαθέντεϲ***: for the word in this sense (= *θανόντεϲ*) see *Alc.* 127, *IT* 199 and 230.

Staging: the remaining chorus members emerge from the *skēnē*. It is possible that Hecuba here moves down into the *orchestra*: she appears to be at a distance from the *skēnē*, to judge from 306–7.

176–81 The second hemichorus was summoned by the first (164–7), but they have come out, they say, to hear a report from Hecuba, perhaps because they too have heard her laments. Like the first hemichorus (156–8) they are afraid. Their two fears are that a sentence of death has been passed on them and that their departure from Troy is imminent. The latter was explicitly affirmed by the first hemichorus (167). Auditory contact between those on stage and those in the *skēnē* can be perfect or imperfect depending on the playwright's wishes. (For imperfect contact see *Hipp.* 185.) Here, perhaps, the slippage adds to the atmosphere of uncertainty.

177 **Ἀγαμέμνονος**: only here and at 139 is it said that the *skēnē* represents the hut of Agamemnon. This is a fact of no consequence in the play, and it may be a reflexive reuse from *Hec.*, where the ownership of the hut was important. —Since these are lyric anapaests the sequence of four shorts is unremarkable; in non-lyric anapaests it is quite rare: see 101n.

178–9 **μή με κτείνειν | δόξ' Ἀργείων κεῖται μελέαν**: it is best to punctuate this as a direct question. On questions introduced by μή or μῶν see Barrett on *Hipp.* 794 and 55–6n above. 'Has an Argive decision been taken (as I hope it has not) to kill me, the unblest?'

179 **δόξα... κεῖται**: a periphrasis for δέδοκται, κεῖμαι being often used as the perfect passive of τίθημι.

180–1 **ἢ κατὰ πρύμνας ἤδη ναῦται | cτέλλονται κινεῖν κώπας**: 'Or are the sailors already setting forth in order to put their oars in motion aboard their ships?' I take κινεῖν as infinitive of purpose and πρύμνη, 'stern', as synecdoche for 'ship', on which see Breitenbach 174. For the spatial meaning of κατά + accus. see LSJ s.v. B.I.2.

182–3 'My daughter, in my soul, awake since dawn, I have become fear-struck.' Since Hecuba has been on stage since before the play began, ἦλθον is not likely to refer to movement on her part (as in the Loeb translation 'My daughter, I came in fear, panic-stricken in my soul, awake since dawn'), and we should probably see this as an instance of the verb being used in the sense 'become', as suggested by Wilamowitz 358, who compares Soph. *OT* 1358, οὐκ ἂν πατρὸc φονεὺc ἦλθον.

184–9 Hecuba has not answered either of the second hemichorus's questions (possible death sentence and imminent departure), and they turn from these to the question whether she has definite news and who their new masters are to be. Hecuba, who knows that no herald has yet come to announce this, again replies vaguely that no doubt (που) the hour of their assignment is not far off. The hemichorus reply with speculation on their new masters: Argive? Phthian? An islander? —The transmitted text, with νηcαίαν... χώραν, starts with two partitive genitives dependent on τίc naming inhabitants and then, as a third alternative, names a destination for ἄξει. Biehl suggests that we understand the destination ἀπὸ κοινοῦ for the first two and the inhabitants for the third, but this is unconvincing. (In theory we could make Ἀργείων and *Φθιωτᾶν* depend on *χώραν*, but a Greek hearing *τίϲ* followed by the genitive of an ethnic substantive would inevitably take the two together.) Wecklein's conjecture (1901: 12) gives us three inhabitants: 'what man of the Argives or the Phthiotes or of an island nation will take me, the unblest, far from Troy?' With *νηϲαίαϲ χώραϲ* Diggle compares *τᾶϲδε γᾶϲ* in 853–4. Now there is only one expression of destination, *πόρϲω Τροίαϲ*, 'far from Troy'.

186 ἐγγύϲ που κεῖϲαι κλήρου: 'The hour of your allotment is not far off, it seems.' Most of the women are assigned to masters by sortition: see 32n. —Tragic lyric uses *κλῆροϲ*, not *κλᾶροϲ*: see Björck 1950: 177, the single exception being a title of Zeus used by Aesch.

190–6 Hecuba applies to her own case the theme of the unknown master and destination (*τῶι... ποῦ πᾶι γαίαϲ*) and adds the question what duties she as an old woman, all but dead, will be asked to perform: will she keep the door? mind the children?

192 κηφήν: the Suda s.v. says this word is used to mean *ἄνθρωποϲ ὁ μηδὲν δρᾶν δυνάμενοϲ*. The drones in a beehive are sometimes represented (Hesiod *WD* 304; Ar. *Vesp.* 1114) not as unable but as unwilling to work, but 'drone' here seems to connote inability.

193 νεκύων ἀμενηνὸν ἄγαλμα: the phrase is modelled on *Od.* 10.521, *νεκύων ἀμενηνὰ κάρηνα*. Both *νεκύων ἄγαλμα* and *νεκροῦ μορφά* emphasize Hecuba's weakness: she is not merely a corpse but a mere image of one. With this double expression of nullity compare Pi. *P.* 8.95–6, *τί δέ τιϲ; τί δ' οὔ τιϲ; ϲκιᾶϲ ὄναρ | ἄνθρωποϲ*.

195–6 For this pity-evoking Euripidean trope, in which those who formerly enjoyed high status feel a fall into slavery more acutely, see 472–3, 489–97, 506–7, 639–40, *Hec.* 375–6 (with 350–8), *Herc.* 1291–3 (possibly genuine Eur. from another play), *IT* 1117–22, and *Hel.* 417–19, on which see Kannicht's note citing frr. 285.6–20, 821, and 964. In a later formulation (Caesar *BG* 1.14.5) it is said that when the gods wish to punish someone, they frequently increase his prosperity temporarily so that he will feel the change of his fortunes for the worse all the more acutely.

197–229 In this non-amoebaean pair of stanzas the Chorus imagine their future lot of toil and sexual slavery in Greece. The singers sharpen their previously unfocused question 'Of what city is the man who is to be my master?' by revealing that some destinations are worse than others: Sparta and Corinth are the worst (the former because of the presence of Helen), Athens is the best, and there is much to be said in favour of Thessaly, Sicily, and Thurii in southern Italy. As noted in the Introduction § 1.4, the places singled out for eulogistic mention are (or, in the case of Sicily, have in them) allies of Athens in the Peloponnesian

War, whereas the Chorus pray not to be sent to Athens' implacable adversaries, Corinth and Sparta.

197–213 = 214–29

1. 197 ~ 214	– – – – – – – –	2an
2. 198 ~ 215	– – – – – – – –	2an
3. 199 ~ 216	– – – – – – – ⏕	2an
4. 200 ~ 217	– – – – – – –	par
5. 201 ~ 218	⏖ – ⏖ – ⏔ ⏕ ⏔ –	2an
6. 202 ~ 219	⏕ – ⏔ – – – – –	2an
7. 203 ~ 220	– – – – – – – –	2an
8. 204 ~ 221	– – – – – – – –	2an
9. 205 ~ 222	⏔ – ⏔ – – ⏔ ⏕ –	2an
10. 206 ~ 223	– ⏕ – – ⏔ – ⏖ –	2an
11. 207/8 ~ 224	– – – – – – –	par
12. 209 ~ †225†	– – – – ⏖ – –	par
13. 210 ~ 226	– – – – – – – –	2an
14. 211 ~ 227	– – – – ⏕ – ⏕ –	2an
15. 212 ~ 228	– – ⏔ – ⏕ – ⏔ –	2an
16. 213 ~ 229	– – – – – – – |||	par

Metrical analysis

Sung anapaestic dimeters, many fully contracted, with interspersed paroemiacs, all but one fully contracted.

197–8 'Ah me, ah me! Yet (δ') with what lamentations could one (lit. 'you') bewail this outrage?' —I have repunctuated to make the interjection an independent utterance and *ποίοις δ' οἴκτοις κτλ.* a second utterance commenting on it. (Normally *αἰαῖ* is followed by asyndeton.) The other option is to delete δ' with Wecklein 1901: 12. (On the tendency of scribes to interpolate connectives see Barrett on *Hipp.* 40.) Wilamowitz's conjecture is clearly necessary, for without his two alterations the line means 'with what lamentations are you lamenting this outrage?', which makes no sense in this context.

199–202 'No more shall I shift (*ἐξαλλάξω*) my shuttle on a Trojan loom, circling it back and forth (I look my last now on the house of my parents, my last), and I shall have greater toils than these.' Weaving is the job of the wife or daughter of a free man, though the Chorus at *Hec.* 466–74 imagine themselves doing such work as slaves in Athens. At *Il.* 6.456 Hector fears that Andromache may weave at a loom in Argos. —Diggle's app. crit. suggests taking *λύμαν* as the understood object of *ἐξαλλάξω*, citing *Hel.* 380, where the verb means 'put from oneself' something unpleasant. But plying a shuttle on the loom is not an obvious way to put outrage from oneself.

201–2 **νέατον τοκέων δώματα λεύσσω | νέατον**: transmitted νέατοι... νέατοι is grammatically impossible, and Seidler's correction has been almost universally accepted. But, *pace* Lee and Biehl, we must also correct τεκέων σώματα. 'I look my last on the bodies of my children' refers either to their dead or their living bodies. If the first, elsewhere in the play children are being sent into slavery (1089–99), and if we were to imagine others being killed, this means that the death of Astyanax is deprived of its force as a unique occurrence (cf. the Herald's hesitation at 709–19 and Andromache's outburst at 764–5). If it is their live bodies, the assumption that the children will not accompany them into servitude is unmotivated. By contrast 'I look my last on the house (Parmentier's δώματα) of my fathers, my last, and I shall have greater woes than these as a slave' makes an intelligible sequence, loss of home trumped by the greater woe of involuntary servitude. It is hard to think of servitude trumping the death of one's children. Good sense is given also by Wilamowitz's τοκέων σήματα (1906. 358): the mention of tombs (implying their tendance) would resonate with their mention at 96 and 381–2.

202–6 'Either brought to the bed of Greek masters (a curse on that night and its fate!) or going as a wretched slave to fetch water from Peirene's holy spring'. The aorist may be 'coincident' (on which see Barrett on *Hipp*. 289–92), as suggested by Lee, but equally it could refer to what is preliminary to the distress of forced sexual relations. At *Il*. 6.457–8 Hector imagines Andromache fetching water from Greek springs.

203 **λέκτροις πλαθεῖσ' Ἑλλάνων**: as Lee notes, there is no implication that the speaker envisions more than one sexual liaison forced upon her. The plural is 'generalizing': see Bers 1984: 25–6 and n5.

206 **σεμνῶν ὑδάτων**: even a destination like Corinth, deprecated by the Chorus, has a spring that receives a eulogistic adjective. Cf. 1097–9 and the general tendency noted at 799–818n and 1087n. Rivers and springs generally receive the epithet 'holy', e.g. at 228 below and *Med*. 410.

207–9 The Chorus wish for Athens as the place of their servitude. On compliments to Athens in Eur. see Introduction § 1.3.3; on the analogous compliment at Soph. *El*. 731 see the scholiast *ad loc*. and the discussion by Fraenkel published in Appendix 2 of Finglass's *Electra*. The wish is introduced by asyndeton, possible when there is a change in the mode of expression (see Smyth § 2167e), as here from statement to wish or, as at 358, from statement to command, or, as at 214, from wish to statement. —Meridor 1978 points out that the Chorus elsewhere in the play use the 1st-person singular of themselves and that instead of the plural here the scholiast seems to have read ἔλθοιμι. To replace a collective destination here with an individual one is welcome (the idea that fifteen choreuts are bound toward the same location is implausible even if the audience have not yet heard 243). Paroemiacs with *brevis in longo* do occur: 133 and 193 may be examples, the latter, as restored by Diggle. Both, however, have more by way of pause than does the present passage. I have retained the reading of the mss. without firm conviction.

210–13 'No, let me not go to the whirling waters of the Eurotas and the hateful dwelling place of Helen, there as a slave to encounter Menelaus, the sacker of Troy.'

212 ἔνθ' ἀντάϲω Μενέλαι δούλα: Lee says plausibly that ἀντάϲω is future indicative in a relative clause of purpose, citing *Aj.* 658–9. The three-syllable form of Menelaus' name is not found in Aesch. or Soph.; Eur. uses it only in lyric.

214–17 The Thessalian plain, located south of Mt Olympus, is described as its 'most lovely plinth (κρηπῖδ')'. The prayer for Thessaly as a place of servitude is unmotivated from within the play (it was the home of Achilles, the Trojans' most powerful foe). This praise is most plausibly interpreted as a compliment to some of Athens' fifth-century allies. During the Peloponnesian War various Thessalian cities helped Athens against Perdiccas of Macedon, who was hostile to Athens: see Thuc. 4.78 and Hornblower *ad loc.*

218–19 'This is my second choice of destination after the sacred, divine country of Theseus.' The infinitive goes with δεύτερα (see Smyth §§ 2001–2) and is sometimes called 'epexegetic'. With 'sacred, divine' cf. 801 ὄχθοιϲ ἱεροῖϲ, describing Athens. —Diggle, *Studies* 6 proposes τὰ δὲ for τάδε, claiming that an adversative is needed. But 218–19 in no way stands in opposition to the admiration for Thessaly expressed in 214–17 ('These things are my second choice' is more plausible than 'But these things are my second choice'), and asyndeton is perfectly in order here. The neuter plural perhaps takes in the river Peneus, Thessaly's mountain setting, its wealth, and its fertility.

220–3 The references to Sicily and Italy are, of course, anachronistic in that Greek colonization of the west (which began in the eighth century) took place considerably after the fall of Troy (twelfth century). Likewise the pan-Hellenic games had not yet been founded (the earliest dates from 776). In similar fashion to Thessaly, Sicily is mentioned as a compliment to Athens since Athens had strong ties there: Egesta (Thuc. 6.6.2) and Leontini (3.86.2–3) were allies; Nicias regarded Naxos and Catane as friendly states (6.20.3), and Camarina and Acragas had also been persuaded to help Athens (5.4.6). The claim (first made by

Steiger 1900: 364–70 and 397n35) that this reference is designed to warn the Athenians against conquest of Sicily lacks plausibility: see Introduction § 1.4.

220 ***Αἰτναίαν*****:** for identification of Sicily by its most impressive mountain cf. 215, where proximity to Olympus defines Thessaly. See also *Cyc.* 20, 62, 95, 114, 366, 395.

221 ***Φοινίκας ἀντήρη χώραν*****:** the country to which Sicily is 'opposite' is not Phoenicia itself but its colony Carthage, whose position opposite the Italian peninsula is noted by Verg. *Aen.* 1.13–14, *Carthago, Italiam contra Tiberinaque longe ostia.* The Carthaginian presence in Sicily continued even after the defeat of Carthage by Gelon and Theron in the battle of Himera (480).

224–5 'The neighbouring place' is a reference to Thurii, a pan-Hellenic colony founded on the instep of Italy under the leadership of Athens in 444/3 on a spot once occupied by the city of Sybaris, destroyed *c.*510. The river Crathis (see 228) flows nearby into the Tarentine gulf and is mentioned with Sybaris at Ov. *Meta.* 15.315. —The transmitted text of 225 seems highly dubious for more than one reason. (1) Although a locative dative can stand near another noun, *Ἰονίωι ναύται πόντωι* gives a dative complementary to 'near' awkwardly sandwiched between two locative datives. (2) It is pointless to say 'near a sailor on the Ionian sea' when one means 'near the Ionian sea'. (3) Word-end after an initial choriamb in a paroemiac is also metrically anomalous, as pointed out by Parker 1958: 86. The general sense suggests that the Chorus name Thurii as a place nearby (*ἀγχιστεύουσαν sc.* 'to Sicily') and are saying something different about it from what they said about Sicily: the *τ'* in 224 should not merely tack on Thurii as another place 'proclaimed by heralds because of its garlands of excellence' but should introduce, along with the new accusative subject, a new predicate. A possible indication of this predicate is the relative clause 226–9, describing the effects on Thurii of the river Crathis, which colours the hair gold and makes the land rich (see below). Perhaps therefore *ἄιον αὖ θάλλειν πάντως*, 'I have heard, further, that its neighbour land prospers in all ways.' But equally some other feature of the city could have been mentioned. Perhaps someone else can repair the damage.

226–9 'A land that is watered by him, surpassing fair, who colours hair gold, Crathis, who nurtures it with his holy streams and makes rich this land of stalwart men'. Several authors (Ov. *Meta.* 15.315, Strabo 6.263, Pliny the Elder *N.H.* 31.2) note the effect its water have on the hair colour of those who bathe in it. —Of the variants *ὑγραίνει* and *ὑδραίνει*, the second means 'cleanse with water'. For the wider use of irrigating or moistening the first is to be preferred, as here: see Diggle 1976: 42.

FIRST EPISODE (230–510)

The episode centres around Cassandra, Hecuba's daughter, thought mad but actually possessed of prophetic gifts received from Apollo. Her appearance in the play was adumbrated when Hecuba asked the Chorus (168–72) not to bring the mad girl out and bring shame on the Trojan women in the eyes of the Greeks. We know that she appeared in *Alexandros* and prophesied that the young shepherd later revealed to be Hecuba's son would prove to be the destruction of Troy. Cassandra's prophecies in *Alexandros*—one fragment gives a clear indication of the gods' involvement in the fate of Troy—and the contribution of the Cassandra episode to the themes of *Tro.* are discussed in the Introduction §§ 3.2.3 (with n. 76) and 4.2.

The scene also provides the first interactions between the Trojan women and their Greek captors in the person of Talthybius, the first of two heralds in the play. (On the necessity of distinguishing Talthybius from the herald who enters in the second episode see the Introduction § 2.3 and 707n.) In the Introduction § 1.3.4 I point out that the Greeks in the play are portrayed not as cruel and abusive but as humane, surprisingly if Eur. intended them as an indictment of his countrmen's cruelty at Melos and elsewhere. Talthybius is by no means as tender-hearted as the herald of the second episode. At 240 he announces calmly that the women have been allotted. At 252 he announces coolly that Cassandra will not be Clytaemestra's slave but Agamemnon's concubine. He seems at 259 not to understand what this means to Hecuba or Cassandra. He takes no notice of the Chorus Leader's question at 292–3. In 304–5 he sees a direct clash between his interests and those of the Trojan women who are, he thinks, immolating themselves. Still, he is far from being cruel or abusive: he spares Hecuba the knowledge of Polyxena's sacrifice. A plausible explanation for the humanity of the heralds in this play and of Talthybius in *Hec.*, who weeps at Polyxena's sacrifice, is that in neither play does Eur. want his audience to see the Greeks as the main problem. In *Hec.* a greater source of Trojan misery is the treacherous barbarian Polymestor; in *Tro.* it is the gods who are primarily responsible for the destruction of Troy. On the gods in both play and trilogy see Kovacs 1997 and the Introduction §§ 4.6 and 4.7.

The episode is articulated as follows. After the anapaests announcing and accompanying Talthybius' entrance (230–4) and his lines of self-introduction (235–8), the episode consists of five parts: (1) an *amoibaion* (239–92) between Talthybius and Hecuba in which Hecuba learns who are to be the new masters of Cassandra, Andromache, and herself and is deliberately misled about the fate of Polyxena; (2) an interlude of dialogue 'covering' the business of fetching Cassandra from the *skēnē* and drawing attention to the flaming torches she will be carrying (293–307); (3) Cassandra's lyric 'mad song' celebrating her coming 'marriage' to Agamemnon (308–41) followed by reactions from the Chorus Leader and Hecuba (342–52); (4) *rheseis* by Cassandra in trimeters (353–405) and in trimeters succeeded by tetrameters (424–61) on the respective fates of the Greeks and the Trojans, these two speeches separated by interventions from the Chorus Leader and Talthybius (406–23) and followed by Cassandra's departure with Talthybius; and (5) a scene in which Hecuba responds to what has happened in a *rhesis* on her multiple miseries past, present, and future (462–510).

Eur. seems to be encouraging his audience to compare his treatment of Cassandra with that of Aesch. in *Ag.* 810–1330. (Although there is some reason to doubt that entire Aeschylean trilogies were revived at the Dionysia—see Biles 2006–7—the plays of the Oresteia could well have been revived individually: see 885n.) In both *Ag.* and *Tro.* Cassandra begins in lyric mode, which betokens an excited state of mind, and then explains herself in spoken verse. In both, those to whom she addresses her prophecies either fail to understand or disbelieve her. In both she strips off the badges of her office. But the differences are great. Aesch.'s Cassandra is portrayed as the victim of Apollo's enmity, which she incurred because she cheated the god who had given her prophetic powers. She says explicitly that the god has sent her to Argos so that she will be killed by Clytaemestra. She flings away the badges of her office with a curse (ἴτ' ἐϲ φθόρον πεϲόντ', *Ag.* 1267). In Eur., Cassandra is still on friendly terms with the god, and there is no hint that he is trying to punish her or that she hates him. She strips off her sacerdotal garments to protect them from desecration: she is about to become Agamemnon's concubine, and it is not fitting that she should wear the clothing of Apollo's virgin when she is deflowered. The two poets' dramaturgy, though equally striking, is entirely different. In *Ag.* Cassandra is silent for a long time, and the Chorus Leader cannot get her to speak. Then she bursts into a prophetic speech that hints at Apollo's enmity, the criminal past of the house of Atreus, and the murder of Agamemnon and herself at the hands of Clytaemestra. In Eur. she enters on the run, brandishing torches and singing a hymn in honour of her coming union with her master, which she treats as a marriage. She explains this attitude toward her coming sexual enslavement, bizarrely inappropriate as it seems at first, in lucid trimeters: Apollo has revealed to her that her concubinage to Agamemnon will cause his death and the ruin of his house and that she will thus repay him for the destruction of Troy. Both poets achieve ἔκπληξιϲ but their means are entirely different. See further Neblung 1997: 68–71.

Staging: enter Talthybius by the right *eisodos*. He carries the herald's staff or κηρύκειον (he is immediately identified as a herald by the Chorus Leader) and walks briskly. He is accompanied by servants.

230–4 Halleran 1984: 5–32 and 117–19, preceded by Hamilton 1978b: 72, argues that there is a tendency for the entrance immediately following what he calls 'an uninterrupted strophic song' not to be announced, perhaps because after a choral ode an entrance is the expected thing, not requiring announcement. But the present passage constitutes an exception, and there are enough exceptions (more than the 'moving tableaux' recognized by Halleran) that we may well wonder whether the rule has been correctly stated. Riemer 1991: 20–2, with notes 37 and 39, reformulates it: the Chorus may announce entrances at the beginning of an episode when there is an actor still on stage to whom the announcement can be made but not otherwise. Since Hecuba never leaves the stage, she is on hand to receive an announcement here, at 568–75, and 1118–22. (There is none before 860 since Menelaus' opening speech is meant to be a monologue with no intended audience.)

230 **καὶ μήν**: this is a frequent collocation (with or without a form of ὅδε) to mark the appearance of someone or something new, whether expected (e.g. *Alc.* 507) or unexpected (e.g. *Alc.* 611). See *GP* 356 and 586.

ὅδ': a form of ὅδε modifying the entrant is extremely common in entrance announcements. In the eighteen plays there are some fifty-nine instances (in *Tro.* see 568, 707, 1120, 1207, 1256), plus two in *Rhes.* It is, however, by no means universal. In Eur. the following entrance announcements are without one: *Cyc.* 36–7, 85–6, *Alc.* 611–13, *Med.* 269–70, *Andr.* 823–4, *Hec.* 216–17, *El.* 963–4, *Herc.* 815–17, *Tro.* 306–7, *Ion* 515–16, 1549–50, *Hel.* 1184–5, *Pho.* 696, *Or.* 456–8, 1366–8, *Ba.* 657–8, 1165–7, and *IA* 590–5.

231 **νεοχῶν μύθων ταμίας**: this should be taken not as a general description of a herald (thus Lee) but predicatively with στείχει ταχύπουν ἴχνος ἐξανύτων, 'comes as dispenser of (distressing) news with speed in his step'. It is an inference from his haste that he must have news: cf. *Med.* 1119–20, *Hipp.* 1151–2, *Andr.* 879–80, *Hec.* 216–17, *IT* 236–7, *Ion* 1109–10, *Or.* 1504–5, *Ba.* 212; also *Sept.* 369–74; Soph. *El.* 871–2; and *Rhes.* 85–6. The overtone of νέος and similar words when modifying 'report' or the like is that the news is troubling: see 55n, 708 below, and Page on *Med.* 37.

233–4 'For surely by now we have been made slaves of a Dorian land', i.e. slaves of someone living there. It appears that 'Dorian' here means 'Greek': the Chorus have concluded that they have by this time been assigned to their Greek masters. At the same time, in view of their distaste for a Spartan or Corinthian home and their pointed preference for Athens and its allies (see 207–9, 214–17, and 220–3 with notes), 'Dorian' suggests that the worse lot is already theirs.

235–8 Talthybius, in the course of explaining why Hecuba knows who he is, gives his name. The first two lines are introduced by anticipatory *γάρ* (see *GP* 68–9) and the last two give the fact to be explained. —With transmitted δέ in 237, the line would continue the explanatory clause, but 237 is part of the thing to be explained, namely that Hecuba knows who Talthybius is. Also, this reading would imply that Hecuba knows Talthybius not only from his service in the Trojan War but also on some previous occasion, which the audience are given no help at identifying. Mistchenko 1877: 268 proposed δή, which has much to recommend it. The particle shows that *ἐγνωϲμένοϲ* summarizes the preceding anticipatory *γάρ* clause: see *GP* 226 (ii). We might translate 'accordingly'.

239–91. *Amoibaion* between Hecuba and Talthybius

Hecuba in thirteen lyric utterances of varying length and metre (dochmiac, iambic, and dactylic or dactylo-epitrite) asks Talthybius who is to be the master of each member of the Trojan royal family and reacts to the news. She ends with a fifteen-line lyric outburst against Odysseus, her own new master. Lyric utterance by an actor (as opposed to the Chorus) often betokens an extreme state of mind, madness, possession by a god, awareness of approaching death, or (as here) great agitation. Talthybius' replies (all spoken, all single lines), are mostly factual and objective and make a stark contrast to Hecuba's sung utterances. Talthybius is not an utterly unsympathetic character, and one interpretation of the ambiguous phrasing of 264, 268, and 271 is that it is intended to spare Hecuba's feelings. But the formal structure of this dialogue does not suggest ready sympathy, and other replies seem decidedly cold: see the blunt 252 and the uncomprehending 259 and his failure to answer the Chorus's 292–3. We should not retroject into this scene the tender-heartedness of 709–19 and 786–9, especially since there is evidence that the herald in the Andromache episode is a different character: see the Introduction § 2.3 and 707n.

1. 239	*Εκ.*	†⏑ ⏑ ⏑ ⏑ ⏑ – ⏑ – ⏑† ⏑ ⏕ – ⏑ –	2δ?
2. 240	*Τα.*	trimeter	
3. 241	*Εκ.*	– – ⏕ ⏑ – | – ⏕ – ⏑ –	2δ
4. 242		– – – ⏑ –	δ
5. 243	*Τα.*	trimeter	
6. 244	*Εκ.*	⏑ ⏕ ⏕ ⏑ ⏕ | ⏑ ⏕ – ⏑ –	2δ

7. 245		– ⏖ – ⏑ –	δ
8. 246	*Τα.*	trimeter	
9. 247	*Εκ.*	– – – ⏑ –	δ
10. 248		⏑ ⏔ ⏔ ⏑ ⏔ | – ⏔ – – –	2δ
11. 249	*Τα.*	trimeter	
12. 250	*Εκ.*	– – ⏖ – ⏖ – – –	– D sp
13. 251		– – – – –	δ
14. 252	*Τα.*	trimeter	
15. 253	*Εκ.*	– – – – – | – ⏖ – ⏑ ⏔	2δ
16. 254		– ⏖ – ⏑ – | ⏑ – – – ⏑ –	2δ
17. 255	*Τα.*	trimeter	
18. 256	*Εκ.*	– ⏖ – ⏖ – ⏑	D ⏑
19. 257		– ⏖ – ⏖ – ⏑	D ⏑
20. 258		– ⏖ – ⏖ – – –	D sp
21. 259	*Τα.*	trimeter	
22. 260	*Εκ.*	⏑ ⏔ ⏔ ⏑ ⏔ | ⏑ ⏔ ⏔ ⏑ –	2δ
23. 261		– – <– ⏑ –>	δ
24. 262	*Τα.*	trimeter	
25. 263	*Εκ.*	– – – ⏖ – | – –	¨dod sp
26. 264	*Τα.*	trimeter	
27. 265	*Εκ.*	– ⏖ – ⏑ – | – ⏖ ⏔ ⏑ –	2δ
28. 266		⏑ | – ⏖ – ⏖ – | ⏑	⏑ D ⏑
29. 267		– ⏖ – ⏖ – | – –	D sp
30. 268	*Τα.*	trimeter	
31. 269	*Εκ.*	⏖ ⏑ ⏖	cr
32. 270		– ⏖ – ⏖ – | – –	D sp
33. 271	*Τα.*	trimeter	
34. 272	*Εκ.*	⏑ – – | – ⏖ – ⏖ – | ⏑ – ⏑ ⌒ ||	ba D ⏑ e
35. 273		– ⏖ – ⏑ – | ⏑ ⏔ – ⏑ –	2δ
36. 274	*Τα.*	trimeter	
37. 275		⏑ – ⏑ – | – ⏖ – ⏖ – | ⏑	ia D ⏑
38. 276		– ⏖ – ⏖ – | – –	D sp
39. 277		⏑ – – ⏑ –	δ
40. 278	*Τα.*	trimeter	
41. 279	*Εκ.*	⏑ ⌒	extra metrum
42. 279		⏑ – ⏑ – ⏑ | – ⏖ – ⏖ – | ⏑	⏑ e ⏑ D ⏑
43. 280		– ⏑ – ⏑ – –	ith
44. 281		– – – –	an
45. 282		⏖ – ⏖ – ⏑ –	tl
46. 283		⏑ – ⏑ – | – –	ia sp
47. 284		⏑ ⏔ – ⏑ – | ⏑ ⏔ – ⏑ – ||	2δ
48. 285		– – ⏑ – | – ⏑ – ⏑ – ⏑ –	ia lk
49. 286		⏑ | – ⏖ – ⏖ – | ⏑	⏑ D ⏑
50. 287		– ⏑ – | – –	cr sp

51. 288	⏑ ⏑͡⏑ ⏑͡⏑ ⏑ ⏑͡⏑ | ⏑ ⏑͡⏑ – ⏑ –	2δ
52. 289	⏑ – ⏑ – | – ⏑ –	ia cr
53. 290	⏑ – ⏑ – | ⏑ – <⏑ –>	2ia?
54. 291	– ⏑⏑ – ⏑ – | ⏑ – ⏑ – ⏑ –	δ kδ
55. 291	⏑ ⏑͡⏑ – – – |||	δ

Metrical analysis

Hecuba's lyrics move easily between dochmiac and iambic cola and dactylo-epitrite and aeolic ones. The lyric outbursts contrast with the terse and businesslike single trimeters of Talthybius.

239 'This is what I have long feared, dear women!' —That is the required sense, but the transmitted text in either V or PQ is unmetrical. If with Matthiae we delete the second *τόδε*, the resultant *τόδε, φίλαι γυναῖ-* gives us a dochmius. (PQ's *τρω(ι)άδεϲ* would then be a gloss.) Eur.'s scribes not only remove genuine cases of anadiplosis but also sometimes import false ones: see *Ion* 759 with Diggle 1994: 381 and 460n83. Diggle's restoration in his app. crit. continues with *-κεϲ, τόδε, Τρωϊάδεϲ*, relocating the deleted demonstrative and rescuing the variant reading. But it seems transcriptionally unlikely that the original had both *γυναῖκεϲ* and *Τρω(ι)άδεϲ* and that then each branch of the tradition deleted a different word and rearranged what was left. Simpler is *τόδε, φίλαι γυναῖκεϲ, φόβοϲ ἦν πάλαι*, conjectured by Nauck 1854: xxiv, though this involves deleting the relative pronoun. I have preferred to obelize.

241–2 'Ah, what city do you mean of Phthia or Boeotia?' —The mss. have, with minor varations, *αἰαῖ, τίνα* (*τίν'* V) *ἢ Θεϲϲαλίαϲ πόλιν ἢ Φθιάδοϲ εἶπαϲ ἢ* (*ἢ καὶ* V) *Καδμείαϲ χθονόϲ*; Hartung's deletion (1848. 25) of the second *ἤ*, adopted by Diggle, eliminates the absurdity of 'Thessaly *or* Phthia' (Phthia is a part of Thessaly) and also reduces hemiepes plus dochmiac to the much more natural 2δ. But the result is still not wholly satisfactory. 'Phthian Thessaly' is not plausible Greek (Phthia is a part of Thessaly, not the other way round), and 'Thessalian Phthia' would work only if (1) there were an adjective *Θεϲϲάλιοϲ* (which LSJ does not recognize and Hermann's conjecture eliminates from its single occurrence at *Andr.* 1176), and (2) if *Φθιάϲ* could be a noun (it is the separate feminine form of *Φθῖοϲ*: see LSJ s.v. *Φθία*). I take *Θεϲϲαλίαϲ* to be a gloss. The text I adopt, in which *Φθιάδοϲ* and *Καδμείαϲ* are both adjectives, is the result of further trimming in Willink unpub.

244–5 'Who of the Trojan women has blessedness awaiting her?' The irony is of an unusual kind: not 'What blessed fate awaits them?' but the assumption that some, and only some, have blessedness in their future. Are the blessed ones, implicitly, those who will be sent to Athens, Thessaly, Sicily, and Thurii, as suggested by 208–9 and 214–29?

247–8 —The transmitted text gives ia | 2δ, certainly possible. But Nauck produced 3δ by writing *τοὐμὸν* <*δή*>, on which *τοὐμὸν* <*μέν*> (Willink unpub.) is an improvement in sense and transmissional plausibility.

249 ***ἐξαίρετον***: after a victory the booty was divided up by sortition, but some items (princesses, for example) were exempted from this process and assigned by deliberate award to persons thought deserving. Such reserved chattels are mentioned in *Il.* 2.226–8 and *Ag.* 954–5, as well as Xen. *Cyr.* 8.4.29. See 32n above and 274n below.

250 ***τᾶι Λακεδαιμονίαι νύμφαι***: Clytaemestra. As Lee notes, *Λακεδαιμόνιοϲ* occurs nowhere else in tragedy.

252 'No, (not a slave to Clytaemestra) but the clandestine sharer of his bed.' For *ϲκότιοϲ*, 'unsanctioned by marriage', see 44n.

253–4 Cassandra is sacred to Apollo, who has granted her a life of virginity, says Hecuba. Some in the audience would remember another version, represented notably by Aesch., *Ag.* 1202–12, in which Cassandra cheats Apollo of her promised sexual favours after receiving his gift of prophecy, and he, unable to retract his gift, retaliates by ensuring that she will never be believed. (For suggestions on the text and interpretation of the Aesch. passage see Kovacs 1987b.) But neither in this scene nor in the fragments of *Alexandros* is there any hint of enmity between Cassandra and Apollo, and in our play the reverse is attested here and at 41–2, 329–30, and 451. The motif of Cassandra's prophecies being disbelieved is more easily accommodated to the Aeschylean model. But see Introduction § 3.2.4 for a way in which Eur. may have made Trojan disbelief compatible with his chosen version. (Making Cassandra guiltless toward Apollo may be intended to make her a paradigm of the proper relation of mortals to gods in contrast to Laomedon and other Trojans, possibly including Hecuba.)

Whatever may have been the case in earlier poetry, where Cassandra may have been deflowered by Ajax or Agamemnon before her departure for Greece, here Cassandra is presented as being still a virgin: see also 70 (where only abduction from the altar is mentioned), 324, and 453. Discussion of the mythical variants in Debnar 2010.

254 ***χρυϲοκόμαϲ***: for this epithet of Apollo see *Supp.* 975, *IT* 1236; and Pi. *O.* 6.41 and 7.32. —On the distribution of *ζόα* versus *ζωά* and the corruption of the first into the second see Barrett on *Hipp.* 811, p. 319.

255 Agamemnon, it is implied, would have respected the virginity of Apollo's prophetess if he had not been overcome by the arrows of love.

Later Talthybius will say (411–16) that, poor man though he is, he would not have taken this woman as his bedmate. The audience might guess that Agamemnon's aberrant and ultimately ruinous choice is the work of a divinity bent on destroying him: see 411–16n.

—Since 253–4 is a yes-or-no question ('Do you mean [he wants to take as his concubine] Phoebus' virgin, to whom the god of golden hair has given the boon of an unwedded life?'), we might expect a 'Yes' answer, and so perhaps *ἔρωϲ* <*γ'*>: for *γε* in answers as the equivalent of 'yes' or 'no' see *GP* 130–1.

256–8 'Cast away, my child, the sacred shoots (of laurel) and from your body (cast away) the holy accoutrement (*ἱεροὺϲ ϲτολμούϲ*) of the adornments you have on (*ἐνδυτῶν ϲτεφέων*).' Both *ἐνδυτῶν* and *ἀπὸ χροόϲ* (cf. LSJ s.v. *χρώϲ* I: 'generally, one's *body, frame*', citing *Ba.* 821, *Trach.* 605) suggest that *ϲτεφέων* refers to a garment, something to be 'got into', not e.g. something worn on the head, which is the normal meaning of *ϲτέφοϲ*. What kind of garment does Cassandra wear? As explained below, the evidence indicates a garment of net, referred to by Pollux as an *ἀγρηνόν* and worn by several divinities (including Apollo) and their human attendants. What about the first item, which she is to cast away? Stanley 1896 proposed *κλάδαϲ* (heteroclite accusative plural of *κλάδοϲ*: see LSJ s.v.), adopted here. It refers to garlands (presumably of laurel) for her head. (Both the 3rd-declension ending and the meaning occur in the Attic *skolion* *ἐν μύρτου κλαδὶ τὸ ξίφοϲ φορήϲω*, 'wearing a spray of myrtle'.) Hecuba's command to her daughter to cast away the emblems of her consecration is carried out later at 451–3. On the prosody of *ἀπὸ χροόϲ* see Barrett on *Hipp.* 760.

—Different views have been taken about the first object, which the mss. transmit as *κλῇδαϲ*. This would have to mean 'keys', presumably to the god's temple. Although we have no other evidence that Cassandra was represented as *κληιδοῦχοϲ*, like Iphigenia at *IT* 131 or Io at Aesch. *Supp.* 291, and although the command to throw away the key to a place to which she will not in any case return could be regarded as pointless, 'keys' are not impossible here. (Hopkinson on Callim. *H. Dem.* 44 defends 'keys' here, and Keyßner 1932: 81 talks about the symbolism of the key in poetry.) An item of personal adornment makes a more natural parallel with the second object, but that is not decisive. Metre, however, inclines me to accept *κλάδαϲ*: in the verses in this *amoibaion* that like 256 are composed of dactylic sequences separated by link elements, all but one of the latter are short: 257, 266, 272, 275, 279–80 (best analysed as ⏑ e ⏑ D ⏑ ith), and 286, with only the first syllable of 250 to set against these. (The absence of 3rd-declension forms of *κλάδοϲ* from tragedy need cause no concern: 3rd-declension *Ἄϊδοϲ* occurs only at *PV* 433 and *OC* 1221, and 3rd-declension πτύχα only at Eur. *Supp*. 979.) The corruption of the rare heteroclite word for 'sprays' to the much commoner word for 'keys' (familiar to Christian scribes from Matthew 16:19) is quite plausible whether or not there was an intermediate stage in which κλάδας was interpreted as Doric κλᾶιδας before being Atticized.

A different view of κλῆιδας was initiated by Meuli 1975: 1064–5 and continued by Bannert 1994–5: 197–200, who cites Pollux 4.116 on a garment called ἀγρηνόν, a πλέγμα δικτυῶδες περὶ πᾶν τὸ σῶμα worn by Teiresias and other prophets. (Picture in Kühnel 1992: 3.) This garment seems likely to be what Aesch.'s Cassandra wore: see Fraenkel's *Ag*., 584n3, Mau, *RE* 1 (1893) 891 s.v. ἀγρηνόν with literature cited. Hesych. κ2954 s.v. κληΐδες says that in the Ephesian dialect κληΐδες means τῆς θεοῦ τὰ στέμματα. On the basis of this Meuli tries to show that κλῆιδας has the meaning *'Schloss'-Gewand*, a garment originally denoting that a god was bound or chained, and that this is its meaning here and in a fragment of the epic poem *Phoronis* (*GEF* 4). Bannert says in effect that κλῆιδας here means ἀγρηνόν and that it designates the same object as ἐνδυτῶν... στολμούς.

On the one hand, it seems to me quite plausible that Cassandra wears an ἀγρηνόν and that this is what she strips off at 451–4. On the other, there are good reasons for thinking that κλῆιδας is not another name for it and that Hesychius' entry is irrelevant to this passage. (1) Synonymy would be pointlessly confusing here. (2) We would have to take ἀπὸ χροός as an instance of ἀπὸ κοινοῦ (or *Versparung*), even though in Kiefner's list of cases of *Versparung* in tragedy (1964: 129–44) there is no instance in Eur. where a whole prepositional phrase is set in a second clause but understood in the first. (3) Since Hesychius implies that the usage he cites is confined to speakers in Ephesus, it seems highly unlikely that a tragic poet, writing for an audience used to dialogue written in old Attic and to lyric in a superficially Doricized version of the same, would have risked misunderstanding by using a local dialect word. Only Hecuba's second direct object designates the ἀγρηνόν, and the first is either sprays of laurel or keys.

259 'What? Is it not a great thing for her to win the king's bed?' For γάρ introducing questions expressing surprise, see LSJ s.v. I.4.

260–71 Hecuba questions Talthybius about the fate of Polyxena, lately (νεοχμόν) taken from her. Talthybius replies euphemistically that she has been assigned to serve Achilles' tomb. In reality (the story is alluded to in 39–40) she was sacrificed to appease the shade of Achilles, who asked for her—or for a Trojan princess—as his γέρας according to *Hec*. 37–41 and 94–5 (on the discrepancy in the demand of Achilles see Kovacs 1987a: 113–14). Hecuba is surprised at this and asks for an explanation. Talthybius replies ambiguously and in a way that might suggest that she is dead. Hecuba questions him no further, apparently satisfied by his explanation that her daughter is a tomb-attendant.

Modern readers may be surprised that Hecuba probes no further after hearing 268 and 271. (So too was the scholiast at 268.) But tragedy has numerous examples where ambiguous language, like that of Talthybius, is perspicuous to the audience but opaque to the characters. Often it is dramatically necessary *both* that a character should be deceived by ambiguous language *and* that the audience should be made aware of the truth it masks, e.g. *Hipp.* 516–21, where it is essential that Phaedra be taken in by the Nurse's ambiguous language and that the audience not be so that they can immediately understand the shouting Phaedra hears at 565–90. Here it suits Eur.'s dramatic purpose that the audience should be reminded of what they know about the sacrifice of Polyxena and that Hecuba should for the time being be kept unaware of her daughter's death. (For a different view see Dyson and Lee 2000: 149–50.) For a discussion of ambiguous language in the whole genre see Nelson 1989.

260–1 ***τί δ'***: for verbless questions of the form 'But what about X?', often followed by a further question with X as subject, see *IT* 543 *τί δ' ὁ cτρατηγὸc ὃν λέγουc' εὐδαιμονεῖν*, 576–7 *τί δ' ἡμεῖc οἵ τ' ἐμοὶ γεννήτορεc; | ἆρ' εἰcίν; ἆρ' οὐκ εἰcί* and the other examples in Diggle 1994: 428–9. The parallels suggest that a main verb is missing in 261, as suggested by Diggle, and tell against Dindorf's deletion of *ποῦ μοι*.

ὃ νεοχμὸν ἀπ' ἐμέθεν ἐλάβετε τέκοc, ποῦ μοι <νῦν κυρεῖ>: 'The child that you recently took away from me, where is she now?' The antecedent of the relative is 'incorporated' into the relative clause: see Smyth §§ 2536–8. —Tyrwhitt's *δ' ὅ* gives two standard dochmii and avoids the epicism of *τό* as relative pronoun. Diggle's supplement restores sense and metre.

266–7 ***τίc ὅδ' ἢ νόμοc ἢ τί θέcμιον***: 'What law or what ordinance is this?' As at *Med.* 847, the first *ἤ* is postponed: if it were to stand in parallelism with the second, it would have to have preceded *τίc*, which would be awkward. Eur. always repeats the interrogative in a different form when two nouns of different gender or number are made parallel: see *Eur. Alt.* 32–3.

267 ***ὦ φίλοc***: according to West 1967: 139–44, the nominative *φίλοc*, used as a vocative, does not imply that the addressee is really a friend to the speaker. Instead it appears 'in earnest entreaties, exhortations, recommendations, or where the speaker is moved by fear, hope, impatience, or similar emotions' (140). Perhaps here 'I entreat you'. Apart from the single case of bare *φίλος*, *Med.* 1133, all instances are lyric: see Aesch. fr. 47a.807; [Aesch.] *PV* 546; *OT* 1321 (*ἰὼ φίλος*), *OC* 1700; *Cyc.* 73, *Andr.* 510, 530, 1204, *Supp.* 277 (with Collard's note), *Tro.* 1081, *IT* 830, and [Eur.] *Rhes.* 368 (with Fries's note). Its sole appearance in comedy, *Nub.* 1168, is also lyric. On nominative for vocative generally see KG 1.47–8, Wackernagel *VS* 1.306–7 (Engl. trans. 385–6), Stevens on *Andr.* 71 and 348, Diggle 1994: 155n3 (citing Schmidt 1968) and Diggle 1994: 476n162 (citing Fraenkel on *Ag.* 1072, Svennung 1958: 206–7, and Moorhouse 23–6).

268 **εὐδαιμόνιζε**: to declare someone *εὐδαίμων* is safe only when he or she is dead (see on 509–10 for the sentiment), hence Hecuba's question in the next line is a natural one. What is unnatural is that she does not conclude from Talthybius' 271 that her daughter is dead, which puzzled the scholiast *ad loc.* See 260–71n on the reason for Hecuba's lack of curiosity.

269 **τί τόδ' ἔλακες**: 'What is this you have uttered?' On the combination of interrogative and demonstrative see below 707n.

272–3 **τί δ' ... Ἀνδρομάχη τάλαινα**: on a question of the type 'But what about X?' followed by a further question about X see 260–1n above.

272 **χαλκεομήςτορος**: the word (credibly restored by Burges) is *ἅπαξ λεγόμενον*. It seems to be derived from *μήδομαι*, 'contrive or do skillfully' (LSJ) and to mean 'skilled with bronze weapons'. The restoration is confirmed by the analogous *δοριμήςτωρ* at *Andr.* 1016. For the etymology of *μήδομαι* see Beekes s.v.

274 Dyson and Lee 2000: 151 translate 'She too has been specially selected, by Achilles' son', where the comma seems designed to limit the similarity to her being *ἐξαίρετος* and deny that Neoptolemus took someone else as well as Andromache. (Similar interpretation in Lee.) Yet I cannot see how *καὶ τήνδ' Ἀχιλλέως ἔλαβε παῖς* could have any other meaning than that Neoptolemus took more than one prize. I therefore print Burges's *κοίτην* and my own *cφ'* (cf. 249 and 277 where *νιν* and *c'* are also part of a double accusative construction). Words for 'bed' (*λέχος*, *λέκτρον*, *εὐνή*) are used to mean 'bedfellow'. I know of no other transmitted instance of *κοίτη* in this sense, but see Rufinus 1.5 Page (= *A.P.* 5.9.5), where Page restores *κοίτην* for transmitted *καὶ τήν*. The extension of meaning is logical, and *εὐνή* in this sense (only at *Hipp.* 1011 and *Andr.* 907) is also rare.

275–7 'But whose slave am I, I, who need a third-foot staff for my hand, aged person that I am?'

275 **τῶι πρόςπολος**: omission of 1st-person *εἰμί* ('To whom *am* I a slave?'), though usual with *ἕτοιμος* (see Denniston on *El.* 796), is otherwise rare.

τριτοβάμονος: an adjective of this kind usually modifies a person ('going about on three feet'), but it is reasonable for it to modify the staff here. There is a similar extension at *Ag.* 80 τρίποδας ὁδούς, describing the road taken by the old and infirm.

276 **γεραιὸν κάρα**: like Soph. (see *Ant.* 1 with Griffith's note) Eur. is very fond of tragic periphrases of this type: see *Cyc.* 438, *Hcld.* 539, *Hipp.* 651, 1054, *Hec.* 676, *Supp.* 163, *El.* 1196, *Herc.* 1046, *Tro.* 661, 1024, *IT* 983, *Ion* 1476, *Pho.* 612, *Or.* 237, 476, 481, 682, 1380, and *Ba.* 1312. For further discussion see Barrett on *Hipp.* 651–2 and Finglass on *OT* 40–3.

—Wilamowitz, followed by Diggle, emends transmitted χερὶ δευομένα βάκτρου γεραιῶι κάραι to δευομένα βάκτρου γεραιᾶι χερί. This involves altering γεραιῶι to γεραιᾶι and transposing χερί to replace κάραι. But Wecklein's γεραιὸν κάρα (1901: 59) for γεραιῶι κάραι (with no transposition) is more economical. For the neuter expression in apposition to a person, see *Or.* 476 Ζηνὸς ὁμόλεκτρον κάρα, 480 στύγημ' ἐμόν, 481 ἀνόσιον κάρα, and 1380 Ἰδαῖον κάρα. The text I adopt, without Wilamowitz's transposition, gives plausible metre in all three verses (my 276 is scanned as D sp and preceded by ia D ⏑: cf. similar ⏑ D ⏑ | D sp in 266–7), whereas while Diggle's 276 is a respectable 2δ, his 275 is ia | D | ⏑ –, ending in an isolated iambic foot.

Staging: Hecuba strikes her head and draws her fingernails along her cheeks in a gesture of mourning.

279–91 Hecuba laments loudly that she has been given as a slave to her enemy Odysseus, who is crafty, unjust, and without loyalty to his friends. The strength of this outburst is a bit surprising since Odysseus does not appear in this play, nor is he named, as he is in *Hec.*, as the man who urged the necessity of sacrificing Polyxena. (His recommendation to kill Astyanax will be mentioned at 721–5.) But Odysseus had the villain's role in the immediately preceding *Palamedes*. Later Cassandra, in attempting to console Hecuba, will devote thirteen lines (431–43) to his future woes. On imperatives addressed to oneself see 98–9n above.

279 **κρᾶτα κούριμον**: Hecuba's hair is cut in mourning for the dead of her family.

280 **ὀνύχεσσι**: the Aldine edition's restoration of the epic dative is clearly correct. For the dative plural in -εσσι see *Ion* 883, *Ba.* 135, Parker on *Alc.* 756–7, Platnauer on *IT* 428, and Dodds on *Ba.* 76.

δίπτυχον παρειάν: for δίπτυχος modifying a singular noun (where we might expect a plural) see *Med.* 1136, *Hec.* 1156, and *Ion* 1010. Aesch. has no instance of the adjective, and the sole example in Soph. is fr. 152 (Radt cites scholars sceptical about the authorship).

282 **μυσαρῶι**: this word of religious denotation ('infected with μύσος, defilement') is a favourite of Eur. but is not found in Aesch. or Soph.

284 πολεμίωι δίκας, παρανόμωι δάκει: 'enemy of justice, beast that knows no law'. Biehl notes the isocola (2δ) and the repeated sequence of words beginning with *pi* and *delta*. For δάκος, 'biting beast', see Barrett on *Hipp*. 645–8.

285–6 For the idea that a clever speaker can make his hearers believe the opposite of what they know to be the case see Plat. *Apol.* 17a2–3. Translate 'who twists everything from that place to this and back again (from here) to there with his deceitful (lit. 'double') tongue'.

—The absence of a verb to govern τἀκεῖθεν suggests that the passage is lacunose. Diggle's supplement, adopted here, restores sense and explains the omission (the scribe's eye jumped from ἀνστρέφει to ἀντίπαλ').

288 φίλα τὰ πρότερ' ἄφιλα τιθέμενος πάλιν: 'reversing direction (πάλιν) and regarding as friendly what was previously not friendly'. The adverb does not imply in itself that there is more than one change of attitude: see LSJ s.v. I.2.

—Seidler's conjecture (1811–12: 140) restores metre (2δ). Wilamowitz's restores sense since transmitted πάντων has no plausible construction (τιθέμενος must mean 'considering, making in his own eyes': this leaves no room for 'everyone').

289–91 —Clearly προσέπεσον κλήρωι is a dochmius. Since ἁ is likely to be genuine (it is idiomatic in expressions of self-pity, as at *Med.* 277, 711, *Hipp.* 1066, 1374, 1387, 1446, *Andr.* 534, 751, *Hec.* 936, *Supp.* 924, *El.* 1183, *Ba.* 1282, 1284, etc.) and since it cannot stand at the end of a colon (as it does in Diggle's daggered text), we should take οἴχομαι ἁ τάλαιν- together as another dochmius. To be sure, Conomis 1964: 40–1 notes the rarity of correption in dochmiacs, but he cites twenty-one certain instances involving exclamations (the more numerous of his two divisions: these include *Tro.* 265) and seven certain instances where, as in the present instance, no exclamation is involved. He also cites numerous instances where a commonly accepted conjecture involves correption in dochmiacs. Here no conjecture is involved, so οἴχομαι ἁ τάλαιν- is a prima facie transmitted instance. This leaves -α δυστυχεστάτωι as kδ (or δ if we read, e.g., μελεωτάτωι). In 289 I print γοᾶσθέ μ', ὦ Τρωιάδες (ia cr) with Hartung 1848: 30, in preference to γοᾶσθ', ὦ Τρωιάδες (ba cr) with Stinton 1975: 96, on the grounds that sense seems to call for the pronoun. In 290 we do not know what rhythm is to be restored. Transmitted βέβακα δύσποτμος could be kδ except that the *brevis in longo* is unwelcome *within* a purely dochmiac sequence. If 2ia should happen to be what Eur. intended, both βέβακα δύσποτμος <λίαν> and βέβακα δύσποτμος, <φίλαι> are thinkable. (The hiatus created by the latter is quite normal at change of metre: see Conomis 1964: 42–3.)

Little change is needed in 289–90, and the two lines I number 291 make good sense and metre as transmitted. Much more complicated and less plausible are the two reconstructions Wilamowitz attempted. The first, *βέβακ᾽, οἴχομαι. δύϲποτμοϲ ἁ τάλαινα δυϲτυχεϲτάτωι προϲέπεϲον κλήρωι*, treats *τάλαινα* as an attributive adjective and its synonym *δύϲποτμοϲ* as a (somewhat awkward) predicate. The second, *βέβακ᾽, οἴχομαι. τάλαινα δυϲτυχεϲτάτωι προϲέπεϲον κλήρωι*, requires deletion at two separate places, one of them the idiomatic article (see above).

292–307. Interlude of dialogue

292–3 The Chorus Leader's question who are to be *their* masters is never answered.

293 ***τίϲ . . . Ἀχαιῶν ἢ . . . Ἑλλήνων***: normally these are synonyms. Perhaps the latter is used in its older sense to denote a region of Thessaly or even northern Greece as a whole in contrast to the Peloponnese.

294–7 Talthybius gives the order for servants to bring Cassandra forth so that he may take her to Agamemnon and later bring the other assigned women to their masters. This suggests that Talthybius is the herald who appears at 1260, where see note.

295 ***δμῶεϲ***: one might have expected Talthybius' retinue to consist of Greek soldiers at his command, not slaves. But perhaps a herald is not himself part of the army.

295–7 'So that once I have handed her over to our general I may next bring the assigned captive women to the other men'. —PQ's *δούϲ νιν* is superior to V's *δῶμεν* in that the pronoun seems indispensable. For *εἶτα* after a participial phrase see *Hcld.* 1023, *Hipp.* 703, *Supp.* 297, and *Ion* 833.

Staging: in response to Talthybius' order two members of his retinue move quickly toward the door of the *skēnē*. (On the use of extras to fetch things or people see Spitzbarth 1945: 60–1.) This double door opens inward, possibly only partway. (It is not clear whether one of the attendants opens it or someone from inside the hut.) Immediately the audience (or at least a portion of it) can see the gleam of fire produced by a pair of torches.

298–305 Talthybius, seeing the gleam, guesses that the Trojan captives are attempting to immolate themselves and orders one of his men to intervene so that he himself may not get into trouble if the Greek leaders do not receive their allotted property.

298 ***ἔα***: this and ἔα, ἔα are frequent exclamations in Eur. and are usually followed by a question expressing astonishment. Sometimes they are *intra metrum*, as here, more often *extra metrum*.

299 The parenthetic ἢ τί δρῶcι does not affect the structure of what surrounds it, which is a yes-or-no question with two clauses joined by τε. For a similar case see Diggle 1994: 428–9.

302 ***τοὐλεύθερον***: the substantivized neuter adjective could refer either to the women themselves or to the impulse in them that rejects enslavement.

303 ***ἐν τοῖc τοιούτοιc***: 'in circumstances like this', i.e. imminent slavery. The short scansion of the first syllable of τοιοῦτοc by internal correption is common in Eur., occurring some eighteen times (e.g. *Alc.* 551, *Med.* 626, 810, and *Hcld.* 266) in the plays and fragments.

304 ***ἄνοιγ' ἄνοιγε***: the command is addressed to one of the attendants. If he is the one who opened the door partway (see the preceding stage direction), the present imperative means 'Keep opening', if not, 'Open'. Anadiplosis, common in Euripidean lyric (see 804n), is rare in trimeters: see Stevens on *Andr.* 980, Willink on *Or.* 219–20, and add *Pho.* 1280. For duplication as underlining the urgency of the command, see Diggle 1998b: 45–6.

Staging: a servant obeys Talthybius' order to open the door. Cassandra, visible in the doorway with a lighted torch in either hand, begins to move on the double in the direction of Hecuba, who is downstage from her. Once she is in Hecuba's vicinity, she executes dance steps (332–4) in which she invites her to share. For the entrance of a character in a divinely caused ecstasy cf. *Ba.* 1165.

308–40. Cassandra's monody

1. 308 ~ 325	⏓ ⏑͡⏑ ⏕ ⏑ ⏔ | ⏑ ⏑͡⏑ ⏔ ⏑ –	2δ
2. 309 ~ 326	⏑ – ⏑ –	ia
3. 310 ~ 327	– ⏖ ⏑͡⏑ ⏑ ⏓? | ⏒ ⏖ – ⏑ –	2δ
4. 311 ~ 328	⏑ ⏕ ⏑ ⏑͡⏑ ⏑ ⏔	kδ
5. 312 ~ 329	⏑ ⏑͡⏑ – ⏑ – | ⏑ ⏑͡⏑ – ⏒ –	2δ
6. 313 ~ 330	⏑ – ⏑ – | ⏑ – ⏑ – ||	2ia
7. 314 ~ 331	⏑ – – ⏖ – ⏑ –	gl
8. †315† ~ 332	⏑ – ⏑ – | – ⏑ – | ⏑ ⏖ ⏑ ⏖	ia cr ia
9. 316/7 ~ 333	⏑ – ⏑ – | ⏑ – ⏑ ⏑͡⏑ | ⏑ – ⏑ ⏕ ?	3ia
10. 318 ~ 334	⏑ – ⏑ – | ⏑ – ⏑ –	2ia

11. 319 ~ 335	⏑ – ⏖ | ⏑ – ⏑ –	ba ia
12. 320 ~ 336	⏖ ⏑ – ⏑ – –	ith
13. 321 ~ 337	⏑ – – | ⏑ – –	2ba
14. 322 ~ 338	⏑ – – ⏑⏑ – ⏑ –	gl
15. 323 ~ 339	⏑ – – ⏑⏑ – ⏑ –	gl
16. 324 ~ 340	– ⏑ – ⏑⏑ – – ||	ph
17. 324 ~ 340	⏒ ⏖ ⏑ – |||	ia

Metrical analysis

Cassandra's verses, apart from 7, 14, 15, and 16, are dochmiacs and iambics. Long *anceps* predominates in the iambics (all except the last verse).

308–40 The manner of Cassandra's appearance and her 'mad aria' are a Euripidean *coup de théâtre*. Instead of being downcast at the loss of her sacred virginity and her coming sexual servitude to the general who destroyed her city, Cassandra sings an ecstatic marriage hymn in honour of this union. In all Greek marriages torches played a role, so there is an appropriateness about their appearance here, though in a wedding they were carried by the mother of the bride. Additionally, the appearance of a female figure with a torch in each hand would suggest a different reference, an Erinys. See Ar. *Plut.* 423–5 ἴϲωϲ Ἐρινύϲ ἐϲτιν ἐκ τραγῳδίαϲ... —ἀλλ' οὐκ ἔχει γὰρ δᾷδαϲ and the other passages cited by Diggle 1970: 143 and Arnott 1962: 120. Erinyes are portrayed in art as carrying snakes, whips, swords, or torches. (For the last see Sarian 1986: 841 and items 4, 8, 9, 10, 11, 19, 23, 26, 31, 32, 35, 45, 55, 57, 58, 61, 66, 71, 72, 73, 75, 80, 81, 82, 85, 87, 90, 92, 94, 95, 99, 100, 102, 103, 107, 109, and 111.) That Cassandra is figurally an Erinys becomes explicit at 457.

The audience must have thought Cassandra's wedding song an insane reaction to her new situation but have expected that it would ultimately be shown to make sense.

308 **ἄνεχε, πάρεχε**: Cassandra is conducting a one-woman procession and speaking to herself as if she had a torch-bearing follower. I take the two verbs as transitive, with 'torchlight' *vel sim.* as understood objects ('Raise it up! Bring it on!'). The alternative, taking the first as 'stand up!' and the second as 'make way!' (with ὁδόν understood: cf. Ar. *Vesp.* 949 for the 'make way' sense), results in a lack of parallelism between the two imperatives. (Likewise the active of ἀνέχω is not usually intransitive, though there may be an instance at *Trach.* 203.) A torchbearer is possible at *Cyc.* 203 and at Ar. *Vesp.* 1326, though equally these could be a loose application to a daylight setting of a formula for noctural processions. A similar phrase occurs in a wedding context at Ar. *Av.* 1720.

φῶς φέρε· σέβω φλέγω κτλ.: theoretically one could punctuate after *φῶς* and take *φέρε* with *σέβω φλέγω* regarded as subjunctives: cf. LSJ s.v. *φέρω* IX.2 and for this usage in our play see 1282. (On the voluntative 1st-person subjunctive, often preceded by *φέρε* or *ἄγε* see Barrett on *Hipp.* 567.) But *ἰδοὺ ἰδού* is more intelligible if *σέβω φλέγω* are indicative, not subjunctive. The object of the two verbs, with the transmitted text, is *τόδ' ἱερόν*, but for doubts about the text see 310n.

—VPQ give *φέρω*, but *φέρε*, which gives 2δ, is preserved in *Σ* Ar. *Vesp.* 1326. The corruption is a simple anticipation of the ending of the next word.

309 —The mss. put *ἰδοὺ ἰδού* after *ἄναξ* (310), but comparison with the antistrophe shows that they belong before *λαμπάσι*. (The other option, moving *εὐὰν εὐοῖ* to a place between *μακαριωτάταις* and *τύχαις*, would make an awkward break between noun and adjective.)

310 —(1) The sense of this line is wrong, and (2) the metre may be imperfect. (1) As transmitted, *τόδ' ἱερόν* would have to mean 'this holy place', and Cassandra would be imagining that she is in a temple or shrine. (Thus the scholiast *ad loc.*: *καθαίρω, φησί, τὸ ἱερόν, οὐχ ὅτι ἐν ἱερῶι ἦν, ἀλλ' ὅτι μαινομένη ἐν ἱερῶι ἐνόμιζεν εἶναι.*) But does she imagine she is in a temple? 329–30 are no evidence for this: see 330n. Her being a bride does not involve a temple since Greek weddings were not held in temples. (2) We can get the required 2δ only if we take the last syllable of *ἱερόν* as *brevis in longo*. But according to Conomis 1964: 45, *brevis in longo* or hiatus at metron end 'is always accompanied by change of speaker, change of metre, pause, or any combination of these'. The pause after *ἱερόν* is arguably too light to justify the *brevis*. If so, it is further evidence of corruption. I have therefore obelized. We could replace *τόδ'* with *φῶς*: 'with torches I make gleam a holy light.' For the collocation *ἱερὸν φῶς* see *Eu.* 1005 and *Herc.* 797. The repetition of *φῶς* at a brief interval need cause no alarm: see 80–1n. (The repetition could be eliminated by writing *πῦρ* instead of *φῶς*.)

311–12 ***μακάριος ὁ γαμέτας, μακαρία δ' ἐγώ***: felicitation of the bridal pair is a topos of the marriage hymn: see *Alc.* 918–21 with Parker on 915–17 and *Phaethon* 240 with Diggle's note. For *μακάριος* as particularly appropriate in a context of marriage see McDonald 1978: 302–3.

—311 could be scanned as kδ, as could the corresponding 328, *τύχαις ὁ χορὸς ὅσιος*. In view of this Diggle's suggestion of lacunae in both lines (<⏑–> *μακαρία* and Hermann's *ὅσιος* <*ὅσιος*>) seems unnecessary.

312–13 ***βασιλικοῖς λέκτροις | κατ' Ἄργος ἁ γαμουμένα***: best to take the dative and the prepositional phrase with *γαμουμένα*: 'Blessed am I, about to marry a royal bridgroom in Argos.' The participle is future, not present. For *λέκτρον vel sim.* as spouse or bedfellow see 274n.

314 Ὑμὴν ὦ Ὑμέναι' ἄναξ: the address to Hymenaios is an expected feature of a marriage hymn. —Hermann emended *ἄναξ* to *Ὑμήν* to match the antistrophe, but the variation (cf. 309 ~ 326) could well be original.

315–24 'For although you, mother, with tears and groans keep lamenting my dead father and our dear country, I nevertheless, in honour of my marriage, am lighting a flame of fire for shine, for gleam, giving light to you, Hymenaeus, and to you, Hecate, as custom holds when maidens marry.' Cassandra contrasts her mother's gloomy lamentation for Priam and Troy with her own joyous one of celebrating her marriage. 315–24 are nominally a subordinate clause dependent on what precedes (hence my colon at the end of 314) but have the effect of a new sentence. (The alternative would be to take the *ἐπεί*-clause as subordinate to *ἀναφλέγω*, but then the asyndeton at 315 is unwelcome, and this reading would mean apodotic *δέ* after a simple causal clause, which is apparently without example: see *GP* 180.) For *ἐπεί* = *γάρ*, see 1145, 1224, *Med.* 426, *Hipp.* 1331, *Hec.* 1208, and *Herc.* 270 and Diggle's discussion of our passage at *Studies* 61. Since Hecuba's behaviour is mentioned only as a foil to Cassandra's own, we might expect *cὺ μέν, μᾶτερ*, but for omission of *μέν* see 95–7 with note and also Theogn. 1369–70, and *Hipp.* 535–40, cited in Appendix A, point (1). I have translated the clause concessively.

315–17 Cassandra comments on her mother's loud lamentation. Like the Chorus at 153–5 she was in auditory contact before emerging from the *skēnē*.

315 —Even without the corresponding 332 we can tell on metrical grounds that the line is corrupt. As transmitted it scans ⏑ – ⏑ – ⏑ ⏖ ⏑ ⏖ –, that is, it ends with long *anceps*, and this is followed in the next line by *anceps*, which would mean period end, impossible after prepositive *καί*. Emendation must proceed on the basis of the metre of 332 as transmitted in PQ, ia cr ia. (See 332–4n for a defence of PQ against V.) Additionally, the occurrence of *μᾶτερ* in the identical place in strophe and antistrophe looks genuine and should be retained. We could therefore write *ἐπεὶ cύ, μᾶτερ, <τορῶc> [ἐπὶ] δάκρυcί <τε> καί* (*pace* Lee *ἐπί* is otiose here and was already deleted by Wilamowitz). The last iamb of 332, however, has both its *longa* resolved. To achieve this in the strophe we will have to remove the *καί*. Perhaps Eur. wrote *ἐπεὶ cύ, μᾶτερ, <τορῶc> δάκρυcι <δάκρυcι> | γόοιc τε κτλ.* (note Q's *γόοιcι τε*). For Euripidean anadiplosis see 804n.

316 —The line makes metre only if we scan the last iamb *-α πατ'ρίδα τε* as ⏑ – ⏑ ⏖. (The alternative, treating *τε* as *brevis in longo*, puts period end at an implausible place.) In lyric iambics it is rare for *τρ* to lengthen the previous syllable: I can find only *Andr.* 1028 (an iambelegus), *Supp.*

1151, *Herc.* 1053 (cho ia?), and *IA* 266 as opposed to some forty-eight instances of short value in iambic or trochaic metres. Furthermore none of the twenty instances of πατρίϲ elsewhere in Euripidean lyric has a long first syllable, and the same is true of the ten instances of πάτρα, πατριῶτιϲ, and πατροφόνοϲ and of the second syllable of εὐπατρίδαϲ and εὔπατριϲ. (These cases of single- and double-value τρ were found by an electronic search, which means that some transmitted instances may have been removed by conjecture or by adoption of different ms. readings and hence could not be caught. But the general picture is unlikely to have been affected.) I conclude that the transmitted text of 316 is unlikely to be correct.

The simplest way to alter the prosody is to add another word at the end, allowing πατρίδ- to be scanned as two shorts. Since we need connective τε, the word could be either a pyrrhic disyllable beginning and ending with a vowel (e.g. πατρίδα θ' ἅμα) or a long monosyllable beginning with a vowel. The latter gives exact correspondence with 333. I accordingly suggest πατρίδα τ' ε<ὖ>: 'For you, mother, piercingly, with tears and groans, are <thoroughly> lamenting my dead father and your dear country, whereas I, etc.' For εὖ, 'thoroughly', see LSJ and also *Cyc.* 237, *Alc.* 548, *Hipp.* 504, *El.* 694, *Hel.* 712, and *Pho.* 991. In some minuscule hands the ligature for ευ can be easily mistaken for simple *epsilon*. The reverse error is exhibited in our play at 335.

317 καταϲτένουϲ' ἔχειϲ: 'You keep on lamenting.' ἔχω with aorist participle is a familiar tragic periphrasis for the perfect: see KG 2.61–2, Smyth §§ 599b and 1963, and Moorhouse 206–7. KG cite only this passage for ἔχω with present participle, but there is another at *Trach.* 648, where see Davies's n. According to Bentein 2016: 236–8 this use of ἔχω with present participle indicates not completed action (like its use with the aorist participle) but continuous action. There may, he says, be a connection with the colloquial idiom ἔχων in e.g. ληρεῖϲ ἔχων, 'You keep on talking nonsense'.

319 ἐπὶ γάμοιϲ ἐμοῖϲ: according to Bers 1984: 28–34 we find the plural used to mean 'wedding' in non-tragic texts. Its use in tragedy to mean 'wedlock' or 'intercourse' he regards as an innovation peculiar to the genre. Since Cassandra is pretending to regard herself as a bride here, the ordinary Attic meaning 'wedding' is to the fore, though the others may be present as well. For ἐπί 'because of' see LSJ s.v. B.III.1.

322–3 The mention of Hecate along with Hymenaeus might have been unsurprising since this goddess is closely allied in function with Artemis, who is connected with weddings: the Σ says ὅτι γαμήλιοϲ ἡ Ἑκάτη, though this could be a guess. Her underworld associations, however, as the Σ also says, anticipate her death.

324 Theoretically we could translate 'on the occasion of the lawful (reading V's ἃ νόμος ἔχει) bedding of maidens'. But the plural relative pronoun suggests not a reference to the present situation (in which only one maiden is being bedded) but to marriages in general. V puts 324a after 322, and it seems unlikely that its ἅ is a bit of genuine tradition. Read ᾇι with P, Q, and the scholiast, take it as a postponed conjunction, and punctuate at the end of 323. For postponed ᾗι or ᾇι, see *Andr.* 863 and *Herc.* 295.

325 The singular imperatives are presumably, like those in 308, addressed by Cassandra to herself. On such imperatives see 98–9n. She tells herself to kick her feet skyward and to lead the dance. For the latter verb see LSJ s.v. I.5, corrected in the supplement.

—Hermann's <ἄναγ'> restores metre and is Euripidean in style (on Eur.'s fondness for anadiplosis see 804n). Its omission is easily explained.

326 εὐὰν εὐοῖ: comparison with Lat. *euhius*, etc. shows that this Bacchic cry has an internal *h* not represented in the Greek writing system.

327–30 'As (you did) at the time of my father's greatest blessedness. The dance is holy. Lead it, Phoebus: (for) it is in your shrine that I serve as priestess, crowned with laurel.' Asyndeton with imperative is common, so the absence of connective at 325 and 329 needs no further explanation. By contrast the asyndetic κατὰ cὸν κτλ. is clearly explicative, as is that in ὁ χορὸc ὅcιοc, which means, in effect, '[Dance joyfully:] for it is not ἀνόcιον to dance now since our ill fortune, which would have made dance shocking and irreligious, is only apparent.'

329 ἐν δάφναιc: 'wearing a wreath of laurel'. For the preposition in this sense see 1025 and *Ba.* 249 and the Attic skolion (*PMG* 893) ἐν μύρτου κλαδὶ τὸ ξίφοc φορήcω. Many translations, including my Loeb, take it with ἀνάκτορον ('laurel-girt shrine'), but see Diggle, *Studies* 60, who cites among other passages *IA* 759, where Cassandra is described as χλωροκόμωι cτεφάνωι δάφναc κοcμηθεῖcα. It is likely that Cassandra wears the wreath still: probably it is mentioned by Hecuba at 256–7 and is among the emblems she strips off at 451–4.

330 Not 'I am (now) serving in your temple (here)' but 'I am your priestess'. (Against the idea that Cassandra imagines herself to be in a temple see 310n.) The asyndeton is explicative: she can reasonably call on Apollo to lead the dance since she is the god's minister. In *Alexandros* (fr. 45.11–12) the Chorus almost certainly announce her arrival from the shrine of Apollo: see Introduction § 3.2.3.

332–4 'Dance, mother, strike up the dance, whirl your feet this way and that, joining with me in moving those feet I love!' —Since πόδα cόν is needed as the object of ἕλιccε, it is not available for ἄναγε, which is incomplete without an object. Hence Diggle's alteration of the second *χόρευ'*. My text, like his, is based on the reading of PQ. V omits the second *χόρευ'* and has *ἀναγέλαcον* for *ἄναγε πόδα cόν*. This gives less good sense since the rest of the sentence is about dance movement, not utterance, and in any case *ἀναγελάω* occurs nowhere else in tragedy. V's reading is the result of omitting *ΠΟ* from the sequence *ΑΝΑΓΕΠΟΔΑCΟΝ*, which, with one easy misreading (*Δ* is often mistaken for *Λ* in uncial hands), produced *ΑΝΑΓΕΛΑCΟΝ*.

335–7 **βόαcον ὑμέναιον... νύμφαν**: the compound expression 'cry hymenaios' takes a further object in the accusative. There is a similar use of *ἐc οἶκτον ἦλθεc* with further direct object at 59–60, where see n. The singular imperative is addressed to Hecuba. —Diggle's *βόαcον* for *βοάcατε τόν* restores both sense and metre.

338–40: With the exhortation to the maidens (*κόραι*) to sing the praises of her bridegroom we might compare Sappho frr. 105 (b), 112, and 115.

340 **πεπρωμένον**: Agamemnon may be 'destined' for her bed in a more than trivial sense. For an indication that Agamemnon's choice of her may have been influenced by the gods see 411–16n.

341–52. Spoken reactions of Chorus and Hecuba

341–2 The Chorus Leader fears that Cassandra will go dancing lightly off to the Argive army. She is not worried about an objective calamity (Cassandra will end up there whatever happens) but presumably fears that it would diminish Cassandra's dignity and that of her mother if she were to proceed there in her present mad state.

341 **οὐ λήψηι**: 'Won't you seize?' is frequently used in tragedy as the equivalent of the imperative 'Seize!', e.g. *Hipp*. 780. (A corollary of this is that, e.g. *οὐ μὴ λήψηι*, 'Won't you not seize?' means 'Stop seizing!': see Barrett on *Hipp*. 212–14.)

343–50 Hecuba contrasts the usual employment of torches in weddings (343) with their present employment, which, she says, is both painful and contrary to her great hopes for her daughter: she never expected Cassandra to marry constrained by the Argive spear. She asks her daughter to give her the torches since her carrying them is evidence of madness: her troubles have not brought her to a sensible frame of mind.

343–4 **μὲν... ἀτὰρ λυγράν γε**: for *μὲν... ἀτάρ* see *GP* 54 and for *ἀτὰρ... γε* *GP* 119.

345–7 'Ah me, daughter, how little did I imagine that you would ever make this marriage under constraint of Argive sword or spearpoint.' This is probably exclamatory *ὡc* going with the negative and meaning 'how little', as apparently at *Ba*. 358 and *IA* 644. (Cf. 109n on *ὡc οὐδέν*.) Alternatively, *ὡc* often means *ἴcθι ὡc*, on which see Collard on *Supp*.

294 and Diggle, *Studies* 88. The man γαμεῖ, the woman γαμεῖται, even when, as here, there is an internal accusative. For the poetic plural γάμοι see above on 319. We are not entitled to conclude, with Meridor 1989: 27, that 'before Troy fell Cassandra was expected to make a suitable match'. This would contradict statements (41–4, 253–4) about the virginity (ἄλεκτρον ζόαν in 254 implies life-long) granted to Cassandra by Apollo. Hecuba is expressing her dismay that her daughter is about to become Agamemnon's concubine, not contrasting her situation with some other possible marriage. —Hecuba had no reason to think that Cassandra would make *this* marriage (to Agamemnon) whether at spearpoint or otherwise. Apparently 'this marriage' means 'a marriage like this', i.e. concubinage. I know of no parallel for ὅδε meaning τοιοῦτος, and wonder whether Eur. might have written τῇιδ', 'in this fashion'. Expressions like γάμους γαμεῖσθαι with the noun unmodified seem protected by ὕβρεις ὑβρίζειν at *Ba*. 247 and the other examples cited in Dodds's note.

346 No worse than Musgrave's αἰχμῆς <c'> is Hermann's ὥς <c'>.

348 οὐ γὰρ ὀρθὰ πυρφορεῖς: i.e. your carrying of torches is out of place, crazy. Hecuba's reaction is likely at this point to have been shared by the audience.

349–50 οὐδέ c' αἱ τύχαι, τέκνον, cεcωφρονίκαc': i.e. 'your misfortunes have not brought you into your right mind, sobered you.' It is a constant feature of Cassandra's portrayal that she speaks the truth but is disbelieved, here because she is regarded as mad: see *Ag*. 1212 and *Tro*. 341–2, 406–7. (On the question why a Cassandra on friendly terms with Apollo is disbelieved see Introduction § 3.2.4.) —I have adopted the reading lying behind the scholiast's interpretation. cωφρονίζω is attested in tragedy but is much rarer there and elsewhere than cωφρονέω, so a scribe was more likely to write the perfect of the second than that of the first (they sounded identical in the medieval period). By contrast, if we adopt Nauck's conjecture (supported by gE's near miss of it), we must also adopt Heath's cαῖc τύχαιc in 349. It is uneconomical to make two alterations in order to achieve sense that is not demonstrably better than what is transmitted.

351–2 Hecuba tells two Trojan women to take the torches indoors (these are probably extras who entered with the second semi-chorus: see note on *Staging* before 153). She tells the Chorus to reply to Cassandra's wedding song with tears. This is a perfectly natural response to the scene the audience have just witnessed, but Cassandra will claim that it is mistaken.

Staging: in response to Hecuba's command two of the Trojan women remove the lighted torches from Cassandra's hands and take them inside.

353–461. Cassandra's *rheseis* with interventions

This whole spoken section allows Cassandra to set forth the reasoning that lies behind her joyful embrace of concubinage to Agamemnon. The two long speeches also express the surprising character of reality: often what seems like a great triumph has a sinister side to it, and what seems like unmitigated disaster contains elements of consolation. This, I argued in Kovacs 1997, is one of the unifying themes of the trilogy. It is also characteristically Euripidean: see Introduction § 4.2.

353–405 *Cassandra's first rhesis.* Up to this point everyone on stage (and perhaps most of the audience) have been puzzled by the discrepancy between Cassandra's future lot (concubine to Agamemnon, destroyer of her city) and her jubilant celebration of this fact as if it were a proper marriage. (Her monody has revealed nothing of the thought processes that would make this union a thing to celebrate.) Now in spoken trimeters she discloses the reasons for her jubilation. (For the sequence of lyric monody followed by spoken *rhesis*, see Dale on *Alc.* 280ff.) Cassandra makes two arguments. (1) In 353–64 (recapitulated at 404–5) she claims that Agamemnon's relation to herself will cause not only his death at the hands of his wife but also the ruin of his house when Orestes avenges his father's death. The Trojans will thus be avenged. Eur.'s first audience will not have felt this to be a trivial point, as is apparent from the commonly cited formulation of one's duty as helping friends and harming enemies (see Blundell 1989). And the sentiment 'they'll get me, but I'll take a few of them with me' is not utterly unintelligible to a modern audience. (2) In 365–402 she makes the two-part claim that the Greeks, though victorious, have paid heavily for their victory by doing things that are personally repugnant to themselves, while the Trojans, despite their defeat, suffered no such personal losses and can console themselves not only with the fame Hector won by fighting nobly in defence of their country but also with the fame Paris won as son-in-law to Zeus.

353 ***νικηφόρον***: Cassandra sees herself as victorious even though one of the defeated. Eur. has produced ring composition by repeating the same word at 460.

355–6 'Escort me, and if my attitude is not in your view (sufficiently) keen, thrust me on by force.' For *πέμπω* as 'escort', not 'send', see LSJ s.v. III and Platnauer on *IT* 171.

356–8 'For if Loxias exists (i.e. has really prophesied truly), the Achaeans' glorious general Agamemnon will get in me a bride more disastrous than Helen.' The if-clause does not express doubt but confidence. For *εἰ* meaning 'if (as is surely the case)' see LSJ s.v. VI.

357 γαμεῖ: the form could be either future or present but from context it must be future. It here takes both an internal (*γάμον*) and an external (*με*) object. It is an exaggeration to say that Cassandra will prove *more* ruinous to Agamemnon than Helen proved to Paris. Agamemnon, like Paris, will be killed, but his city will not be destroyed, only his house (364). Perhaps by 'more ruinous than' Cassandra means 'as ruinous as', which is true since Agamemnon will soon be as dead as Paris. Cassandra in *Alexandros* (see Introduction § 3.2.3, last paragraph) had called Helen 'one of the Furies (i.e. Erinyes)', and she later applies the same image to herself: see 457n.

δυςχερέςτερον: on the tendency of scribes to gloss forms of *δυςχερής* with those of *δυςτυχής* (as here has happened in the PQ branch) see Zuntz 1965: 152–3.

358 κλεινός: Mueller-Goldingen 1996: 37 compares *El.* 327 where Electra applies the adjective ironically to Aegisthus. Cf. also *Or.* 17, questioning its application to Agamemnon.

359 δόμους: tragedy has a decided preference for the plural of this word, even when it refers to a single dwelling: twenty-one plurals in this play and only one singular (602). Bers 1984: 43–4 notes that this preference does not extend to the nominative of the word, where the poetic plural is much rarer.

360 λαβοῦς': the aorist participle here describes an action coincident in time with the main verb. See Barrett on *Hipp.* 289–92.

361–4 The allusions to Clytaemestra's murder of her husband and his concubine and her death in turn by the hand of Orestes and his trial for murder will have been clear to the audience though opaque to the other characters.

361 ἀλλ' αὐτ' ἐάςω: this is a form of *praeteritio*, for Cassandra goes on to mention, albeit allusively, what she says she is leaving alone. —Anaphoric *αὐτός* may not stand first in its clause (see KG 1.654) or first in a line of verse and is thus quasi-enclitic. *ἀλλ' αὐτό* is rare (*Hec.* 973, *Ba.* 932; *Phil.* 64; *PV* 441) and so is anaphoric *αὐτός* in analogous positions (*Supp.* 330, *El.* 979, *Ba.* 306). (By contrast *ἀλλά με* and *ἀλλά ςε* are common.) But rare is not non-existent, and word position constitutes no reason to reject Musgrave's restoration of transmitted *ἄλλα τ'*. For the corruption of *αυ* to *α* see Bast 1811: 705–6. As at *Hec.* 973 and *El.* 979 the word here is closer to 'these things' than to 'them'.

πέλεκυν οὐχ ὑμνήςομεν: most sources make Clytaemestra's weapon the axe rather than the sword: see Davies 1987 and Marshall 2001. (Davies tries to prove that this is true also in Aesch., but Sommerstein 1989 demonstrates that she used a sword.) It is odd that *ὑμνεῖν*, 'chant in praise of', takes as object the axe that will kill Cassandra. The other objects are things hurtful to her Greek enemies where *ὑμνεῖν* is appropriate, so perhaps we might speak here of zeugma.

362 χἀτέρων: on the allusive plural see 1016–17n. Here the plural refers only to Agamemnon.

363 μητροκτόνουϲ τ' ἀγῶναϲ: the plural is again allusive and refers only to one *ἀγών*. The phrase could mean 'mother-killing struggles', i.e. struggles involving matricide or (with a less literal use of the adjective) 'trials *for* matricide'.

363–4 οὓϲ οὑμοὶ γάμοι | θήϲουϲιν, οἴκων τ' Ἀτρέωϲ ἀνάϲταϲιν: for the plural *γάμοι* see 319n. The active of *τίθημι* is used of setting up athletic contests: see LSJ s.v. A.VI. *ἀνάϲταϲιϲ* derives from *ἀνίϲταμαι*, 'be made to leave a place', usually one's own country. Roger Dawe *per litteras* suggests deleting *τ'*, which would make *ἀνάϲταϲιν* the so-called 'accusative in apposition to the sentence' (on which see 536n), 'the mother-killing struggles which my marriage will set up to make desolate the house of Atreus'.

365–405 Cassandra's demonstration that the Greeks are more to be pitied than the Trojans has separate sections on Greeks and Trojans, each subdivided. (1a) (368–73) The decision to sail against Troy cost more in terms of the lives of Iphigenia and of the Greek soldiers than the recovery of one woman could possibly justify. (1b) (374–82) The Greek army in the Troad sustained huge losses (death far from their families, burial in alien soil), and so did their loved ones at home (widowhood and childless old age). (2a) (386–7) The Trojans died defending their country (*ὑπὲρ πάτραϲ*), which gives the greatest glory. (2b) (387–93) The Trojans who were killed in battle received burial at the hands of their kin, while those who were spared enjoyed the company of their wives and children, pleasures denied to the Greeks. (2c) (394–7) Hector's fate is not as sad as appears: had it not been for the Greek expedition, his heroic valour would never been been seen. (2d) (398–9) Though Paris' decision to marry Helen may seem disastrous, she is the daughter of Zeus, and had he chosen otherwise, the marriage he made would have brought him no fame. There is a recapitulation of (2a) in 400–2. Death in battle is a crown of glory. Cassandra then repeats in 403–5 that she will now exact vengeance on Agamemnon, their common enemy.

—Wilamowitz 1875: 221–4 proposed to delete 365–83, but in a note to his 1906 translation he restores the verses to Eur.; Page 1934: 72–4 answers his original objections.

365 πόλιν δὲ δείξω . . . μακαριωτέραν: sc. *οὖϲαν*. For the ellipse of the participle of *εἰμί* in indirect statement see Smyth § 2119.

366–7 ἔνθεοϲ μέν, ἀλλ' ὅμωϲ | τοϲόνδε γ' ἔξω ϲτήϲομαι βακχευμάτων: Cassandra claims that, although she is Apollo's inspired priestess, what she has to say about why the Trojans are better off than the Greeks will not be uttered in a state of possession. (With this mention of her *βακχεύματα* cf. *Alexandros* fr. 62e.) In general Cassandra, unlike her namesake in *Agamemnon*, does not exhibit prophetic 'second sight'. The authority her words possess derives principally from what Apollo has told her: see 356 and 428–30.

—In a number of cases Eur. uses ἀλλ' ὅμωϲ elliptically, with no expressed adjective or predicate: see *Hipp*. 47, 358, *Hec*. 843, *El*. 753, *Hel*. 645, *IA* 904. In other cases a conceivably elliptical ἀλλ' ὅμωϲ is followed by an expression that makes clear the meaning of the two words. Sometimes the expression in question is clearly genuine: *Alc*. 353, *Hipp*. 795, 1325, *Andr*. 955, and *Hel*. 1232. In other cases scholars have deleted the line (or lines) that follow: *Hcld*. 319 (suspectum habuit Wecklein, del. Diggle), *Herc*. 1366 (del. Nauck), *Pho*. 1070–1 (del. Reeve, praeeuntibus Bruhn et Harburton), *Or*. 139 (del. Diggle, praeeunte Willink), 1024 (del. Kirchhoff cl. *Σ*), *Ba*. 1028 (del. Dobree cl. *Med*. 54). In a few of these cases deletion is manifestly justified (*Herc*. 1366 is quite weak, and the *Σ* to *Or*. 1023–4 clearly did not have 1024 in his text), but it would be a mistake to conclude that every time line-ending ἀλλ' ὅμωϲ could be read elliptically, anything completing it is clearly spurious. *Tro*. 367 is sufficiently protected against Wecklein's deletion (1901: 19) by *Alc*. 353–4, *Or*. 1168–9, and *Ba*. 324, all of which show an analogous lack of parallelism between the contrasted expressions.

368–9 'They, because of one woman and one object of desire, in their quest for Helen destroyed countless men.'

370 **ὁ ϲοφόϲ**: this is either ironic or it indicates that Agamemnon was (in other respects) skilled or wise but made a horrific blunder where it meant the most.

ἐχθίϲτων ὕπερ: it is clear that in sacrificing Iphigenia, Agamemnon has lost 'what is most dear', his beloved daughter. What does 'for the sake of what is most hateful' mean? Not his brother Menelaus, despite 372. The reference is to Helen. Women in general are ἐχθραί (cf. 1059n). But a woman who disgraces her husband by her infidelity is naturally more so.

372 **δούϲ**: the aorist participle is coincident, as often when the main verb is aorist or future: see Barrett on *Hipp*. 289–92.

373 **καὶ ταῦθ' ἑκούϲηϲ κοὐ βίαι λεληιϲμένηϲ**: for καὶ ταῦτα + participle of something that aggravates an existing circumstance see Smyth §§ 947 and 2083. Cassandra's rhetorical point is that Agamemnon is a fool for sacrificing both his daughter and the lives of so many Greeks to get back a woman, and, at that, one who was not forcibly abducted but left of her own free will. Her words should not be taken, *pace* Koniaris 1973: 97, as an authoritative refutation of Helen's claim (940–2, 953) that her responsibility was diminished by the role of Aphrodite. Helen admits that she was not abducted. The emphasis here, in any case, is not on Helen's choice but on that of the Greek kings.

374 **ἤλυθον**: this epic form, rare in tragic trimeters, is protected by *El.* 598.

375 **ἔθνῃϲκον**: an 'inchoative' imperfect (see Smyth § 1900): 'They proceeded to die.'

375–6 The Greeks had no *national* reason for war. Only their kings had been injured.

375 **γῆϲ ὅρι'**: like Latin *fines*, ὅρια, 'boundaries', appears here to mean 'territory'.

ἀποϲτερούμενοι: several Greek verbs of 'taking' or 'depriving' are construed with two accusatives, the thing taken and the person from whom it is taken. When such locutions are used in the passive, as here, the person becomes nominative but the thing remains accusative, the so-called 'retained accusative', on which see Smyth § 1747. There are further examples at 480, 486, 936–7, and 1278.

376 **ὑψίπυργον πατρίδ'**: the adjective is decorative. The scansion πατ'ρίδ' in trimeters is protected by *Med.* 328, *Supp.* 323, *Herc.* 1405, *Ion* 261, *Hel.* 16, *Pho.* 280, 406, *IA* 1407 (?), and numerous cases (e.g. *Alc.* 332, *Med.* 406) of πατ'ρόϲ and πατ'ρί.

377 —The reading παῖδεϲ (PQ) gives a defensible parallelism: the children of the Greek dead never see them again, their wives are not allowed to prepare them for burial. But the reading of V means that the dead Greek warriors are the subject of both verbs, arguably better style.

δάμαρτοϲ: for the 'distributive' singular see 392n.

379–82 There are analogous costs to the families at home, where some die in widowhood, others childless.

380 The sense of the passage is restored if we realize that a line has fallen out: 'Matters at home were no better than at Troy: <wives were bereft of their valiant husbands> and died in widowhood, while others [the fathers of the fallen] died childless, having raised children in vain.'

—Matthiae thought a line had been lost before 380. In Kovacs 2002: 274–5 I argued that he was right on the grounds that χῆραι and ἄπαιδεϲ make better sense taken predicatively ('died in widowhood, died childless') than as the subjects of ἔθνῃϲκον and that the verb had as subject a now missing word for 'wives' plus οἱ δ', taken pronominally. If we mark a lacuna, Diggle's γ' for τ' can be dispensed with.

381 **ἄλλωϲ**: those whose children do not survive to tend them in old age have raised them in vain since parents expect their children to tend them in old age and to give them burial: see *Alc.* 662–4, *Med.* 1029–34,

1098–1111, *Supp.* 918–24, 1134–7, *Pho.* 1432–5; *Cho.* 750–3; and Soph. *El.* 1143–5.

—Transmitted ἄλλοιϲ could be defended: those whose sons are killed in war have raised them 'for others'. But on balance Tyrwhitt's conjecture seems the better course: the fact that the children are not there to make tomb offerings (381–2) explains 'in vain'.

381–2 'There is no one who will offer blood to the ground at their tombs.' Attested as offerings at graves are both libations and animal sacrifice. The former, consisting of the pouring of liquids (milk, honey, oil, and wine), were made at the time of burial and repeated at intervals. Here we have the latter practice, much less often attested. At *Il.* 23.30–4 the blood of bulls, sheep, goats, and swine runs in such abundance at the tomb of Patroclus that it could be drawn up in cups. The use of blood sacrifice to honour heroes is mentioned in Pi. *O.* 1.90 (αἱμακουρίαιϲ) and by Arist. *Rhet.* 1.5.9. The pouring of blood at the graves of war dead is attested for the Plataeans at Plut. *Arist.* 21.5. Solon (Plut. *Solon* 215) forbade the sacrifice of an ox at the grave, though presumably he allowed a smaller animal. In tragedy both kinds of offerings are mentioned at *Hcld.* 1040–1, where Eurystheus seems to be demanding both libations and animal sacrifice at his tomb: see on this passage *Eur. Alt.* 21–3. It is possible that sacrifices at the grave began to wane by the fifth century. In literature the memory of them lingers on in Vergil (*Aen.* 3.63–8, 5.77–8) and beyond. On blood for the ghosts see von Fritze 1893: 70–87, Eitrem 1915: 417–21, Stengel 1910: 142–3, and Ekroth 2000.

—In 381 PQ's τάφοιϲ gives 'place where', easier sense but therefore an easy corruption for V's τάφουϲ, which implies motion toward. To defend the latter Lee cites Soph. *El.* 931, τὰ πολλὰ πατρὸϲ πρὸϲ τάφον κτερίϲματα. He points out that word order in 382 makes PQ's αὐτῶν awkward and recommends V's αὐτοῖϲ as dative of advantage. I have adopted V's readings as on balance more likely.

383 —There are two objections to the reading of the mss. 'The army is worthy of *this* praise' is difficult because no praise has been uttered (though 'praise' could be an ironic way to describe her criticism). More important, as Diggle notes, ἦ in Eur. is never followed by ὅδε. Dobree's τοιοῦδ' (1833. 89) meets the latter objection: 'That is the kind of encomium the army deserves' might stand (said ironically, of course) as a comment on 368–82. Wilamowitz 1875: 222 deleted the verse.

[384–5]: Cassandra is here made to recommend silence to herself: she will not mention what is shameful or have a muse that sings of κακά.

—Even with ϲιγᾶν <δ'>, proposed by Bothe 1801: 370, 384–5 are hard to square with context, for it is hard to see what Cassandra at this point is going to leave unmentioned since she has already told of Greek 'woes' that are 'shameful'. Weil put them after 364, where they arguably show to better advantage. (Wilamowitz achieved the same juxtaposition by deleting 365–83.) But 361–4 already show Cassandra passsing over unpleasant subjects, and 384–5 are unnecessarily repetitious. They are possibly borrowed (by an actor?) from another play. On the various senses of *μοῦϲα* in Eur. see 511–12n.

386 τὸ κάλλιϲτον κλέοϲ: the 'accusative in apposition with the sentence' expresses the result of their action, achieving 'the fairest renown': see 536n.

387 οὓϲ δ' ἕλοι δόρυ: —the wording of 376 has here infected V, which has *οὓϲ δ' Ἄρηϲ ἕλοι*.

388 γ': 'The opening of an apodosis is seldom stressed by *γε* (normally by *δή*)' according to *GP* 126, but Denniston nevertheless cites quite a few examples. —Dobree 1833: 89 considered deleting this line, as anticipating 390. Biehl accepts this deletion, pointing out that *νεκροί* duplicates the meaning of *οὓϲ δ' ἕλοι δόρυ* and *φίλων* that of *ὧν ἐχρῆν ὕπο*. Though the case is not proved, he could be right.

390 χερϲὶν περιϲταλέντεϲ ὧν ἐχρῆν ὕπο: 'wrapped for burial by those at whose hands they should have been buried'. *ὧν ἐχρῆν ὕπο* = *τούτων ὑφ' ὧν ἐχρῆν περιϲταλῆναι αὐτούϲ*. In many of its occurrences the imperfect of *χρή*, *δεῖ*, and the like indicates unfulfilled obligations but here it means that the obligation belonged to the past.

391 Φρυγῶν: partitive with *ὅϲοι ... θάνοιεν*.

392 δάμαρτι: for the distributive singular, illustrated in English by the biblical phrases 'by the mouth of his holy prophets', 'out of the hand of our enemies', and 'all the days of our life' (Luke 1:70 and 74–5) and in Latin by Suetonius' title *De vita Caesarum*, see Smyth § 998, KG 1.14–15, and, in our play, 3, 127, 377, and 558–9.

394–9 Cassandra argues that the Trojans are compensated for their loss by fame. The point is introduced at 386–7 and it finds an echo in Hecuba's words at 1242–5, where see note. Mills 2014: 171, while admitting that Cassandra is voicing the Iliadic view that participation in war brings eternal remembance, says that 'here it is too embedded in Euripides' trademark irony to be uncomplicatedly credible'. But although Cassandra's argument is paradoxical, nothing indicates irony in the sense that its ostensible and actual meaning are at variance or that 386–7 do not represent Cassandra's view of the matter. Gregory 1991: 164 is right to call it a 'serious benediction'. As noted in the Introduction § 1.2.2(2), Cassandra assigns intrinsic value to fame for martial bravery and says that Hector would have been the poorer if the Achaeans had stayed at home. (This is not a view compatible with any species of aversion to war as such, and the reading of this speech as quasi-pacifistic is, as argued there, mistaken.) Even more striking is the case of Paris' fame, based solely on his his elopement with Helen, which made him Zeus's son-in-law. Such fame, even when the elopement has proved ruinous to Paris and Troy, is a compensation for loss. See also 400–2n.

394 ***τὰ δ' Ἕκτορός cοι λύπρ'***: 'the aspects of Hector's fate that are painful to you'.

395 ***δόξας ἀνὴρ ἄριcτος οἴχεται θανών***: for Cassandra it is an important ingredient in Hector's success that he was not only brave but also *perceived* to be brave: 'He met his death after proving himself a hero.' On the persistence of shame-culture values in Euripidean tragedy see Kovacs 1987a: 25 with n8 and 134–5.

397 ***ἔλαθεν ἂν γεγώς***: —as I argued in 2002. 175–6, the reading of V and the scholiast's paraphrase gives good sense (the imperfect would mean 'we would not have been marking how brave he was being', the aorist, more synoptically, 'we would not have marked how brave he was') and style (*γεγώc* is good tragic Greek). The other reading is to be regarded as a banalization.

398–9 Cassandra claims that even Paris' disastrous abduction of Helen contributes to Trojan fame.

399 ***cιγώμενον τὸ κῆδος εἶχ' ἂν ἐν δόμοιc***: 'He would have had a marriage tie no one spoke of.' The imperfect *εἶχ'* can be used with reference to a past unreal circumstance. —Burges's *εἶχ' ἄν* is necessary. For a refutation of Elmsley's mistaken doctrine that Attic poets did not elide -*ε* before *ἄν* see Diggle 1974: 16n61.

400–2 Many interpreters treat these three lines as a profession by the poet of quasi-pacifist sentiments (war is justifiable only when one's country is attacked), but see Introduction, § 1.2.2(2). The point that sensible people avoid war is preliminary and subsidiary, as the *μέν* makes clear: 'To be sure, anyone with sense avoids war.' The main point Cassandra is making is that war, if it comes to that, is a source of glory. The Trojan War brought fame to the principal Trojan combatant, Hector, and even Paris, the seducer of Helen, won fame he would not otherwise have received. She does not say 'But if war is forced on you' for the good reason that, as the mention of Helen shows, the Trojan War was a war of choice for the Trojans, who could have given Helen back. This is no ringing denunciation of wars of choice.

400 ***μὲν οὖν***: the two particles function separately, *οὖν* drawing the general moral from what precedes and *μέν* marking 400 as concessive and a foil to 401–2. The moral is that while it is sensible to avoid war, if it comes to war, to perish nobly is a fine crown for a city, just as to perish ignobly is a disgrace. It is unclear whether *πόλει* goes with *οὐκ αἰςχρός* (meaning that the noble death of the individual is a crown of glory to the city) or with *ὀλέςθαι* (meaning that the noble death of the *city* is a glorious thing). The first interpretation is suggested by *Supp.* 315, the second by the fact that Troy has in fact perished and perished nobly. See also Hecuba's conclusion at 1242–5 that fame compensates Troy for the loss of its existence.

403–5 Cassandra deprecates lament for Troy for the reasons just given and then returns in ring fashion to her coming vengeance on the Greeks.

406–7 Despite the authoritative forcefulness of 353–64 and the rational discursiveness of 365–402, the Chorus Leader can make nothing of Cassandra's words. Ignoring the seer's words of consolation, she expresses scepticism about her prediction of revenge on the Greeks.

407 ***μέλπεις θ' ἃ μέλπους' οὐ caφῆ δείξεις ἴcως:*** 'You sing of things which you will perhaps show yourself to be singing unreliably.' The expression is rather contorted, but I know of no proposal to improve the style. For *caφής*, 'true', see LSJ s.v. 2, Diggle 1970: 94, Bond on *Herc.* 55, and Dawe on *OT* 534–5.

408–23 Talthybius too thinks Cassandra crazy: otherwise she would be punished for sending the Greeks off on their long sea journey with such ill-omened words. He ponders on Agamemnon's strange choice in a concubine before telling Cassandra to follow him. As for Hecuba, she must go with Odysseus and should take comfort in being the handmaid of the virtuous Penelope.

408 ***c' . . . ἐξεβάκχευcεν φρένας:*** the two accusatives are 'construction of the whole and part', on which see Smyth § 985, Finglass on Soph. *El.* 99, with literature cited by him, and 1173–4 below. Talthybius is more indulgent than Agamemnon at *Hec.* 1280–4, who punishes Polymestor for prophesying Agamemnon's murder. Cassandra's words, regardless of their motive, could be thought harmful to the Greek cause.

409 ***οὔ τἂν ἀμιcθί:*** —*οὔ τἂν* is Lenting's metrically necessary correction for *οὐκ ἄν*. On the repetition of *ἄν* (next line) see Page on *Med.* 250 and Barrett on *Hipp.* 270.

411–16 Talthybius, who finds Agamemnon's predilection for this mad woman unaccountable, remarks that high station (*cεμνά*) and a reputation for skill or wisdom (*δοκήμαcιν cοφά*) are often deceptive and that the great and good are often of less account (*οὐ κρείccω = χείρω*) than their social inferiors. Similar sentiments at *Andr.* 319–20 and also at *Andr.* 699–700, which, though not written for their present context, are probably genuine Eur. As Dyson and Lee 2000: 170–1 point out, Talthybius is deficient in his appreciation for the divine in human affairs, and that is why he dismisses the ill-omened words of Cassandra on the grounds that she is mad. Here too he seems to miss a possible explanation for Agamemnon's strange predilection: when a choice is unaccountable, that is often because a god has distorted it. (*Ant.* 620–5 is the *locus classicus* for this idea.) Likewise pointing in the direction of divine causation is Cassandra's πεπρωμένον (340).

412 τῶν τὸ μηδέν: sc. ὄντων. On the use of οὐδέν, μηδέν, and their corresponding masculines in an extended sense, see KG 2.197–8, Denniston on *El.* 370, Moorhouse 1965, and Finglass on *Aj.* 766–9, 1231, and 1273–6. The sense of these expressions ranges from 'a nobody, someone unimportant or ineffectual' to 'someone reduced to ruin or extremities, on the point of death' to 'someone no longer (or not yet: see *Anth. Pal.* 10.118) existing'. Soph. and Eur. frequently put a neuter singular article in front of μηδέν: see *Aj.* 1275, Soph. *El.* 1166, and *Trach.* 1107; *Cyc.* 355, *Hcld.* 167, *Hipp.* 638, *Hec.* 622, *El.* 370, and *IA* 945 (the article is restored at *Tro.* 613); *Rhes.* 819. It is possible that the use of μηδέν instead of οὐδέν in clauses where μή is not the expected negative is a metrical convenience to avoid hiatus, as suggested by Moorhouse 1965: 38. When τὸ μηδέν is used, its case seems invariable, as here, which suggests that it is to be understood adverbially, 'one who exists (for a particular purpose) not at all'.

ἦν ἄρα: on the imperfect of εἰμί used with ἄρα to indicate that which has been true all along but only recently realized see 109n.

414 ἐξαίρετον: i.e. out of all possible slave women he chose her: she was not forced on him by the lot.

415 καὶ πένης μέν εἰμ' ἐγώ: the μέν is concessive: 'I am, to be sure, a poor man, but I would not have taken *her* as my mistress.' This may imply that a poor man has less choice in sexual partners and is presumed to be less choosy. For μὲν . . . ἀτάρ . . . γε see 343–4n.

416 ἂν οὐκ ᾐτηςάμην: 'I would not have asked for her as my mistress.' — Naber's ᾐτηςάμην gives better sense than transmitted 'I would not have acquired her', emphasizing that Agamemnon specifically chose her.

417–20 Talthybius' words about giving Cassandra's reproaches of the Argives and encomia of the Trojans to the winds to carry away have an apotropaic intent. (Cf. *Hec.* 1276–84, where both Hecuba and Agamemnon try to counter Polymestor's prophecy.) Mad she may be, but he feels the necessity to counter her words. For the idiom see 454 below and the collection of examples cited by Finglass on *El.* 435–6.

417 καὶ coῦ μέν: Talthybius has instructions for both Cassandra and Hecuba. —coῦ, Hermann's conjecture for coί, seems to lay a lot of stress on the genitive and even to suggest a contrast with another person's words. Might Eur. have written κἀγὼ μέν, making a different contrast

(Talthybius' apotropaic words on the one hand, Hecuba's action on the other)?

418–19 **Ἀργεῖ᾽ ὀνείδη καὶ Φρυγῶν ἐπαινέcειc | ἀνέμοιc φέρεcθαι παραδίδωμ᾽:** the infinitive is common with verbs such as 'give', 'receive', 'choose', 'send', etc. to show purpose or result: see KG 2.16–17, Moorhouse 237–8, *MT* §§ 770–5. In contrast to English Greek idiom tends to prefer the active for this infinitive (see 450, 878, and Plat. *Apol.* 33b παρέχω ἐμαυτὸν ἐρωτῆcαι, 'I offer myself to be questioned'), but here φέρεcθαι is passive.

419 **ἀνέμοιc:** I take this opportunity here to set out the usage of the three tragic poets as regards first-foot anapaests in trimeters. Unlike anapaests later in the line (on which see 1126n), a first-foot anapaest—perhaps because the basic × – ⏑ – rhythm has yet to be established—is not felt to be much of a licence: in later feet only proper names are allowed to make an anapaest, whereas in the first foot all three tragedians admit anapaestically beginning common nouns (e.g. *Pers.* 184; *Aj.* 1302; *Alc.* 344), adjectives (e.g. *Ag.* 337; *OT* 256; *Hipp.* 37), and verbs (e.g. *Ag.* 30; Soph. *El.* 818, *Med.* 971), and Eur. allows prepositional phrases (e.g. *Alc.* 375). That an anapaest in the first foot requires no excuse is inferrable from the fact that Aesch., who never admits anapaests elsewhere, even to accommodate proper names, uses it initially between three and eleven times per play in the six extant plays. In *Tro.* there are thirty-two instances: seventeen proper names of anapaestic shape (36, 235, 277, 357, 462, 711, 862, 877, 1029, 1123, 1239, 1261) and five with the scansion ⏑⏑–⏑ (863, 895, 907, 1005, 1033); two adjectives derived from proper names (1208, 1219), six common nouns of anapaestic shape (419, 672, 1131, 1144, 1183, 1197, plus 674, where see note), one adjective (1244) and one verb (1223) of anapaestic shape, and one verb scanned ⏑⏑–⏑ (1030). For anapaests outside the first foot see 1126n.

420 **καλὸν νύμφευμα:** Cassandra, of course, is both beautiful and a princess, so she is a creditable match for a great leader. Talthybius' palpable irony has in view her madness.

421–3 Talthybius shows his kind nature in reassuring Hecuba that she will be the servant of a chaste and modest woman. (There may be an implicit contrast with Cassandra, who, for all her chastity, is not 'sound of mind', cώφρων in another sense.)

427–61 *Cassandra's second long rhesis.* In trimeters Cassandra, in response to Talthybius' remarks about Odysseus, describes the sufferings that await him both on his journey and when he reaches home. Then switching to the livelier trochaic tetrameter she turns again to Agamemnon's fate (446–7) and her own (448–50) and then divests herself of the badges of her Apolline office (451–4). In a final seven lines she exults in her coming revenge, calling herself an Erinys and forbidding her mother and her dead relatives to lament: she will shortly go down to the dead having wreaked full vengeance on Troy's enemies.

[424–6]: 'How clever (how dangerous?) is this servant! Why do heralds enjoy the honorific name they have, heralds, the single object of hatred for all mankind, underlings who attend upon tyrants and cities?' I argued for deletion (*Eur. Alt.* 149–50; but Friedrich 1953: 70–1 had already suspected the lines) and summarize my arguments here. (1) Characters elsewhere in Eur. (*Hcld.* 292–3, 426, *Supp.* 458–62) heap opprobrium on heralds, but those heralds are the callous emissaries of cruel tyrants. Talthybius by contrast is not threatening or abusive and has just said words of comfort (421–3) to Hecuba. The abuse is unrelated to anything in the context. (2) *δεινόϲ* lacks point. There is nothing 'clever' (or, by irony, 'stupid') about him, nor is he particularly 'dangerous'. Dyson and Lee 2000: 154 and n16 claim that Cassandra's scorn arises because herald and seer 'live on different levels' and Talthybius is 'out of touch with her supernatural perception of events', but nothing in 424–6 helps the audience interpret *δεινόϲ* as 'obtuse about the divine': the only characterization of heralds the lines suggest is 'hateful and abusive'. (3) If *λάτριϲ* in 424 picks up the same word 422, one might expect this to be made explicit, e.g. *λάτριν καλεῖϲ cὺ μητέρ', αὐτὸϲ ὢν λάτριϲ;* As things stand, *λάτριϲ* in 422 and in 424 refers to two different people, yet no connection is made. (4) The asyndeton in 427 is hard to explain even if we punctuate that sentence as a question. (5) Further evidence (not cited by me) that the lines do not belong here is the split resolution *ἓν ἀπ-* in 425. According to Cropp and Fick 1985: 27–68, split resolution of the second *longum* of the shape ⏑|⏑ × – ⏑ (type 4.2d) occurs, apart from this passage, once in *Pho.* and twice in *Or.* but nowhere else. A similar word shape ⏑|⏑ ⏑ – ⏑ (×) (type 2.3c), again with split resolution of the second *longum*, occurs only in *Or.*, *Ba.*, and *IA*. The metrical evidence thus suggests that these lines are Euripidean but from another and later play.

[424–5] ***τί ποτ' ἔχουϲι τοὔνομα κήρυκεϲ***: this probably means 'Why do heralds have their honorific name' (thus Paley 1872, Way 1912, Lattimore 1958, Davie 1998). The alternative, 'Why are they called "heralds"?' (thus Parmentier and Vellacott 1954, joined by my Loeb) lacks adequate parallel: we need an instance where (*τὸ*) *ὄνομα ἔχειν* = *ὠνομάϲθαι* and takes a nominative, but KG 2.45 and 99 list only *Tro.* 1233. There, however, the words *ἔργα δ' οὔ* make against taking *τλήμων ἰατρόϲ* as predicate nominative with *ὄνομα ἔχουϲα*.

427–8 Better as a statement, 'You claim that my mother will go to Odysseus' house', followed by the question, 'But what then becomes of

Apollo's prophecy?', than as two successive questions. The lines follow on well from 422–3.

429–30 —Klinkenberg 1881: 69 proposes deleting *εἰς ἐμ' ἡρμηνευμένοι αὐτοῦ θανεῖσθαι* and punctuates with a dash after *αὐτήν* to indicate aposiopesis. He points to odd collocation *ἑρμηνεύειν εἴς τινα*. Biehl accepts this text with its aposiopesis, which he explains by saying that Cassandra cannot tell her mother about her transformation into a bitch. But in the text as transmitted she does not actually mention the transformation. I do not find the argument compelling and do not find the preposition use alarming enough to merit athetesis.

430 τἄλλα δ' οὐκ ὀνειδιῶ: the allusion is to the the story (see *Hec.* 1249–73) that Hecuba before her death in the Troad was transformed into a bitch with flaming eyes, her place of burial being called Cynossema. Plutarch cites from an unnamed Euripidean play the line *Ἑκάτης ἄγαλμα φωσφόρου κύων ἔσῃ*. If this is from *Alexandros* (Kannicht lists it as fr. 62h), Cassandra must have there prophesied the transformation alluded to here. For *ὀνειδίζω*, 'mention (something unpleasant)', see *Or.* 85.

432–3 'How golden one day will my troubles and those of Troy seem to him!' For *χρυσός* used metaphorically of what is precious or desirable, see LSJ s.v. 3. For exclamatory *ὡς* with no adjective or adverb see 109n and 345–7n.

433–43 Cassandra describes Odysseus' future troubles, beginning with his return home after twenty years without any of his men and alluding to incidents on his wanderings described in the *Odyssey*: Charybdis (12.234–59), the Cyclops (9.105–542), Circe (10.150–574), the land of the Lotus Eaters (9.82–104), Thrinacia where the Sun has his cattle (12.260–396), and his descent into the Underworld (11.13–330, 385–635). As Paley notes, this is the earliest epitome we have of the *Odyssey*. The order is oddly jumbled. The descent to the Underworld comes last, perhaps, to highlight it as the crowning misery (see below on 441–2). But there is no obvious reason for the placing of Charybdis before Cyclops and Circe before Lotus Eaters. May it be intended to suggest oracular obscurity?

433 —Of the variants it could be argued that V's *ἐκπλήσας* is recommended by the identical *δέκ' ἐκπλήσας ἔτη* at *Or.* 657. But in favour of PQ's *ἀντλήσας* is not only the notion of 'enduring something unpleasant' inherent in the verb (see LSJ s.v. II.2) but also the nautical metaphor: see Mueller-Goldingen 1996: 46n34.

435–9 —The paradosis makes no sense. (1) Ithaca is not the place where Charybdis dwells, so 435 cannot follow 434. (2) But Heath's lacuna before 435 (adopted by Diggle) is also unsatisfactory since *οὗ δή* would then imply that Charybdis, the Cyclops, and Circe are to be found in the same place. (3) Even apart from geography, *ναυάγια* and *ἔρωτεϲ* lack a construction since they cannot be subjects of *ὤικιϲται*. Awareness of the last two difficulties prompted Diggle to suggest altering 435 to *οὗ δὴ ϲτενὸϲ δίαυλοϲ ὥριϲται πέτραιϲ*, since this would allow Charybdis to be the subject of a verb that once stood in the lacuna, and the same could be true of the Cyclops, Circe, and the common nouns that follow them. But a well-placed lacuna normally allows one to avoid altering the text on either side of it. On that showing Heath's lacuna is ill-placed. If instead we set it after the first two syllables of 435, *οὗ δή* can refer to Ithaca, and the whole line, its parts divided, may stand unchanged. Here is an *exempli gratia* restoration:

δέκα γὰρ ἀντλήϲαϲ ἔτη
πρὸϲ τοῖϲιν ἐνθάδ' ἵξεται μόνοϲ πάτραν
οὗ δὴ <ϲτεναγμῶν ἄξι' εὑρήϲει κακά·
νόϲτου δ' ἐπιϲχήϲει νιν ἡ νηλεῖ φρενὶ
παρὰ> ϲτενὸν δίαυλον ὤικιϲται πέτραϲ,
δεινὴ Χάρυβδιϲ, ὠμοβρὼϲ τ' ὀρειβάτηϲ, κτλ.

'For having endured ten years in addition to those here (in Troy) he will arrive alone at his homeland, where indeed <he will find troubles worthy of his groans. But he will be kept from his homeward journey by her who with pitiless mind> dwells on the cliffs <beside> the current's ebb and flow, dread Charybdis, by the mountaineer Cyclops, who eats raw flesh, etc.' My suggested supplement provides an explanation for the omission.

435 **ϲτενὸν δίαυλον**: the Straits of Messina, where post-Homeric authors placed Scylla and Charybdis: see Thuc. 4.24.5, with Hornblower's comment, and *Med.* 1342–3 with Mastronarde's note. Since *δίαυλοϲ*, 'double aulos', is used to mean the up-and-back of a racecourse, there is probably a reference to the ebb and flow of currents in the strait. The word, as suggested by Sansone 1984a, may be a reminder that Odysseus was destined to sail this strait once in each direction.

ὤικιϲται πέτραϲ: for an accusative object with *οἰκίζομαι* see *Hcld.* 46, *ζητῶν ὅπου γῆϲ πύργον οἰκιούμεθα.*

436 **ὠμοβρὼϲ τ' ὀρειβάτηϲ**: Scaliger's restoration, which is based on the unintelligible readings of P and Q, restores a rare but attested word: *ὠμοβρώϲ* is preserved in Timotheus *Persae* 138 and restored also at *Herc.* 887 and Soph. fr. 799.5. The reading of VQ$^{\gamma\rho}$ would need to be emended by the addition of *τ'*. A more important objection to it is that it does not explain the other variants.

437–8 ***Λιγυϲτίϲ θ'—ἡ ϲυῶν μορφώτρια—Κίρκη***: Circe, who in Homer lives on the island of Aiaie off in the mythical east, is given an Italian location in later accounts, including a home in Latium. Here she is Ligurian, further north on the Tyrrhenian Sea. The phrase 'shaper of swine' refers to her turning some of Odysseus' men into beasts. —The phrase ἡ ϲυῶν μορφώτρια must be taken διὰ μέϲου, since with no parenthesis we have an adjective standing outside the article-noun group, which would be very odd.

440–1 '(Cattle) which with their bloodied flesh will one day utter speech unwelcome to Odysseus'. —The above translates a text incorporating Bothe's conjecture (1826) ϲαρξὶ φοινίαιϲιν, recommended by Jackson 242 and printed by Diggle and also in my Loeb. The paradosis, ϲάρκα φωνήεϲϲαν, has been challenged since the only other instance in tragic iambics of an adjective in -ήειϲ is the much-contested τολμήϲτατε at *Phil.* 984. (φωνήειϲ occurs once each in Hesiod and Sappho and several times in Pindar.) Accepting it would mean replacing ἤϲουϲίν with, e.g., Kirchhoff's ἕξουϲίν (1868) since the verb 'to utter' cannot have flesh as its object. (I do not find plausible the defence of ϲάρκα φωνήεϲϲαν ἤϲουϲίν in Lee 1969. He cites *Ion* 168–9, not a good parallel, and in any case Nauck's αἰάξειϲ for αἱμάξειϲ is better sense at trifling cost.) But we must note against Bothe that the corruption is difficult to explain: though we could imagine the phonetic equivalents ι = η, αι = ε, and ϲϲ = ϲ contributing, still φοίνιοϲ is a common word and φωνήειϲ a rare one, and the change from dative plural to accusative singular is hard to account for. Furthermore, 'speaking flesh' is exactly what the cattle of the Sun have according to *Od.* 12.395–6, κρέα δ' ἀμφ' ὀβελοῖϲι μεμύκει, | ὀπταλέα τε καὶ ὠμά. On the other hand, as against Kirchhoff, we should perhaps be reluctant to replace ἤϲουϲιν, the *mot juste* for 'utter'. So choice is difficult. We could, however, keep both ϲάρκα φωνήεϲϲαν and ἤϲουϲίν by marking a lacuna between them. I offer the following supplement *exempli gratia*:

> αἳ ϲάρκα φωνήεϲϲαν <ἠρταμημέναι
> φανοῦϲι καὶ μυκηδὸν> ἤϲουϲίν ποτε
> πικρὰν Ὀδυϲϲεῖ γῆρυν.

'(cattle) that one day, <when cut in pieces, will reveal> speaking flesh and utter <in mooing fashion> a sound unwelcome to Odysseus'.

441–2 For the descent to Hades as crowning misery, allowing the speaker to abbreviate a long catalogue, cf. *Hcld.* 951–2 followed by 948–9 as in Diggle's OCT.

442 λίμνης ὕδωρ: even though *λίμνη* is not used elsewhere in tragic trimeters to mean 'sea', this usage is Homeric (e.g. *Il.* 13.21, *Od.* 5.337), and Lee is right to see this meaning here. Davidson 2001 argues that this makes better sense than the escape from the lake in the Underworld preferred by Schade 1998.

444–61 The last eighteen lines of Cassandra's speech are in the livelier trochaic tetrameter. The change from trimeters to tetrameters within a single speech is unexampled; for the switch within a stichomythic interchange see *IT* 1203. If *Herc.* is earlier than *Tro.*, it is the earliest of the extant plays of Eur. to make use of the tetrameter, which according to Arist. *Poetics* 1449a20 was the original spoken metre of tragedy. All Eur.'s plays from this point on make use of this metre. *Herc.*, *Tro.*, and *IT* have only one passage of tetrameter each. *Ion* has three (510–65, 1250–60, 1605–22), *Hel.* one (1621–41 containing a *stichomythia* with *antilabe*), *Pho.* as transmitted four (588–637, 1307–8, 1335–9, 1758–63, of which the last three are under heavy suspicion), *Or.* three (729–806, 1506–36, 1549–53, of which the first has *stichomythia* with *antilabe*), *Ba.* one (604–41), and *IA* as transmitted four (317–75, 378–401, 855–916, 1338–1401, of which only the last is clearly genuine). There is no clear pattern of increasing use.

444 ἀλλὰ γάρ: the two particles coalesce here ('but in fact'), unlike instances where the force of each is separately felt. See *GP* 102–3 for its use as a breaking off formula.

ἐξακοντίζω: the metaphor of javelin-throwing for forthright or defiant speech occurs at *Supp.* 456 and *Ant.* 1084–5.

445 στεῖχ' ὅπως τάχιστ' ἐς Ἅιδου· νυμφίωι γημώμεθα: 'Go with all speed to Hades: let me marry my bridegroom.' The imperative may be addressed to herself: for such imperatives see 98–9n. The hortatory subjunctive specifies the means by which her death is to be brought about. For *ὅπως* + superlative instead of *ὡς* or *ὅτι*, see LSJ s.v. A.I.5. On the common ellipsis with *Ἅιδου* of a word such as 'house' see *Eur. Alt.* 150–1 and 594n below. —Editors punctuate after *τάχιστ'*, and Diggle adopts Heiland's *ἐν* for *ἐς*. But this gives worse sense since it is not in Hades that she expects to be bedded by Agamemnon but while she is still alive (451–4). The marriage will precede their deaths and cause them: see 356–60.

446 ἦ κακὸς κακῶς ταφήσηι νυκτός, οὐκ ἐν ἡμέραι: as the next line shows, this 2nd-person future is addressed to Agamemnon. He will be buried without pomp in hugger-mugger fashion by his wife and her lover. In *El.* the indignity suffered by Agamemnon takes the form of burial far from the palace (289) in a grave that receives no libations or sprays of myrtle (323–5).

κακὸϲ κακῶϲ: on these words and their order see 1055–6n.

447 ***ὦ δοκῶν ϲεμνόν τι πράϲϲειν***: 'you that seem to enjoy (or 'think you enjoy') high prosperity'. For *πράϲϲειν* + neuter pronoun or adjective (instead of adverb) meaning 'to fare' a certain way see *El.* 1359, *Or.* 355, *OC* 1704, *Ran.* 302, and *Plut.* 341.

448 ***τοι***: *GP* 540 translates this as 'mark my words'. The *καί* of *κἀμέ* emphasizes that Cassandra will join Agamemnon in death.

γυμνάδ': for the separate feminine see *Hipp.* 1134. At fr. 105.1 K. it modifies a masculine noun. Note also *El.* 311, where, as I argued 1985: 306–10, the reading of uncorrected L, *δὲ γυμνὰϲ οὖϲα*, alone gives sense.

450 For the infinitive of purpose after a verb of giving see 418–19n.

Staging: Cassandra removes and casts away the garlands and other finery (probably including the garment called *ἀγρηνόν*: see 256–8n) that mark her as Apollo's prophetess. On the casting away of significant objects see Spitzbarth 1945: 69–70.

451–4 The scene calls to mind Aesch. *Ag.* 1264–72, where Cassandra, stripping off her badges of office, says that the god himself is divesting her. In Aesch. Cassandra, who has alienated Apollo, claims that he has sent her to Argos to secure her death (*Ag.* 1136–9). By contrast Cassandra here refers to Apollo as *φιλτάτου μοι θεῶν*. In Aesch. she curses her finery (*ἴτ' ἐϲ φθόρον*, *Ag.* 1267); in Eur. she respectfully strips them off to avoid their desecration. In the prologue (41–4) Poseidon describes Cassandra's virginity as sacred to Apollo and granted by his dispensation. Hecuba (253–4, 500–1) says the same thing. It is a fair question how these friendly relations between god and maiden can be reconciled with Cassandra's being constantly disbelieved, which is elsewhere her punishment for betraying the god. Meridor 1989: 26–8 suggests that since Cassandra in *Alexandros* is doomed to be 'a Cassandra', a prophet whose unhappiness it is to be disbelieved, yet in *Tro.* feels satisfaction at her prophecies, this constitutes an argument against the two plays' belonging to a connected trilogy. But, first, no Cassandra lines survive from *Alexandros* from which we could clearly prove this contrast (*Alexandros* T iii and Ennius fr. 17 J. establish that she makes unheeded prophecies but not that she has alienated Apollo: on the contrary Ennius fr. 17.36 may imply the opposite). Second, *Tro.* too shows her as always disbelieved: see 348–50, 406–7, and 417. So the contradiction, if it is one, is not only between the two plays but within *Tro.* itself. See the Introduction § 3.2.4.

452 ***χαίρετ'***: 'farewell' in Greek is not a hostile word. She has no need of her garlands since she has left the festivals for which they are appropriate.

ἠγαλλόμην: the imperfect need not imply that her attitude toward the festivals has changed: the festivals are no longer part of her life.

453–4 She means to take off her sacred apparel while she is still a virgin, allowing it to be borne on the winds to the god.

455 ***ποῦ cκάφοc τὸ τοῦ cτρατηγοῦ***: Cicero, probably quoting from memory, gives *τῶν Ἀτρειδῶν*, which is unlikely to be right: in no version of the return from Troy do the brothers travel in the same ship.

ποῖ πόδ' ἐμβαίνειν με χρή: Elmsley's *πόδ'* (1826: 291) restores the idiomatic use of the accusative for 'foot' with verbs of motion: see Diggle, *Studies* 36–7.

456–7 'Now is not too soon for you to be on the lookout for a breeze for your sails, for in me you are taking from this land an Erinys, one of the three' (Loeb translation). The lines are perhaps addressed to Agamemnon, mentioned in 455.

456 ***οὐκέτ' ἂν φθάνοιc***: 'It is not too soon for you to be [doing a thing].' For the idiom see Stevens 1976: 24–5 and KG 2.65–6. It is essentially a jussive expression.

457 ***μίαν τριῶν Ἐρινύων***: when Cassandra describes herself as 'one of the three Erinyes', this reflects the same conception as her calling Helen *Furiarum una* (*fr. incert.* 151.16–18 M., *Alexander* fr. 17.47–9 J.). A human being may be the proximate cause of a destruction planned by Zeus, and in those circumstances he or she becomes metaphorically an Erinys or an Alastor. At *Ag.* 55–67 there is the strong suggestion that the Greek expedition against Troy is Zeus's Erinys (66–7 suggest, additionally, that Greek suffering is also intended). In that play's second stasimon the coming of Helen to Troy is described as the arrival of an Erinys (see 744–9). Lastly, Clytaemestra tells the elders of Argos that she is less the wife of Agamemnon than she is an Alastor sent to punish the crime of Atreus against his brother Thyestes. Eur. echoes the second of these statements when he calls Helen *Furiarum una*. di Giuseppe 2012: 171–2 gives the parallels, Aeschylean and Euripidean, for Helen as an instrument of divine punishment and counters Jocelyn's claim (on *Alexander* fr. 17.47–9) that *Furia* has no notion of divine punishment about it and is different from *Erinys* (on this point see Introduction § 3.2.3, n. 76). Cassandra regards herself an Erinys in the same sense, a human being used by the gods to bring ruin to mortals. She had earlier drawn a parallel between Helen and herself (357–8, where see note). Diggle, *Studies* 62–3 shows that the Erinyes are regularly conceived of as three in number. I do not see why he feels that such a reference here is 'pointless'. He thinks that here the three Erinyes are Cassandra, Clytaemestra, and Aegisthus, but this seems far-fetched, and by the time the audience worked this out (Cassandra has one relation to the murder of

Agamemnon, Clytaemestra and Aegisthus an entirely different one) they would have missed ten lines of dialogue. Cassandra's point is that she is an agent of divine justice. The idea (Mueller-Goldingen 1996: 43–4 and 51) that Eur. has resolutely excluded the divine as an explanatory principle for what has happened cannot be maintained. Cassandra's general thesis does not require her to talk about the gods as destroyers of Troy, but for the coming destruction of the house of Atreus she clearly thinks them responsible. —Burges's *Ἐρινύων* seems right in view of the parallels, cited in the app. crit., for trisyllabic treatment of the genitive plural.

458–61 Cassandra's last words are a solace to her mother, her country, her brothers, and her father: she will rejoin them soon, and she will arrive as victor over their foes.

460 ***νικηφόρος***: on the repetition of this word from the beginning of her first *rhesis* see 353n.

Staging: exeunt Cassandra, Talthybius, and retinue by the left *eisodos*.

462–510. Hecuba's reaction

Staging: Hecuba collapses to the ground.

462–5 ***Ἑκάβης γεραιᾶς φύλακες***: these are extras (see 351–2n) and may have entered with the Chorus. For choral concern with a character about to collapse see *Andr*. 1076–7.

Staging: two Trojan women move to carry out the Chorus Leader's order, but Hecuba prevents its execution by authoritatively countermanding it. She delivers her speech until around 505 from a position on the ground.

463 ***ἐκτάδην***: Verrall's conjecture (possibly published only in Murray's app. crit.: see his preface) restores a rare tragic adverb. The corruption to P's *εἰς ἅδην* was caused by the misreading of *K* as *IC*. For the opposite corruption see below 916–18n.

464 ***οὐκ ἀντιλήψεσθ'***: for the imperatival force of such questions see 341n.

466–8 Hecuba thinks that her sufferings are sufficient to merit lying in a fallen state. This is a prelude to the catalogue in 474–510 of all that she has lost.

469–71 When tragic characters tax the gods with disloyalty, as Amphitryon taxes Zeus for not protecting the family of his son Heracles (*Herc*. 339–47) or Ion Apollo for not saving Creusa's baby (*Ion* 436–51), they are often saying no more than the truth as far as it is known to them at that moment. The forthright criticism of the gods is touching and human. Hecuba's response here is curious in that she seems to call on the gods half-heartedly and merely as a matter of form (σχῆμα). The effect is quite different from the generous anger of Amphitryon or Ion and seems rather cynical. Further, it is not clear how much justification the charge of divine disloyalty has. The Chorus in the second stasimon rebuke the gods for taking a *puer delicatus* and a husband from among the Trojans and then forgetting their affection for the city, and in the third stasimon they tally up the delightful worship the Trojans used to offer to Zeus and accuse him of folly in letting these delights go. But the gods respond to slights to their honour. As regards Zeus, *Alexandros* almost certainly adumbrated the young prince's seduction of his host's wife, an offence against Zeus Xenios. Paris' removal of Helen from Sparta is what dooms Troy: that is the reason he appeared in Hecuba's dream as a firebrand. An earlier generation witnessed another Trojan offence against Zeus, also referred to in our play (809–10), Laomedon's breaking of his oath to Heracles.

472–3 For the thought that people who have had great prosperity in the past suffer more acutely when disaster strikes than those who have never been prosperous see 195–6n. Hecuba means to dwell in song (ἐξᾶισαι) on her good fortune as a way of increasing the pity her sufferings evoke.

477–8 'No (other) woman, Greek or barbarian, could ever boast she gave birth to their like.' On 'polar expressions', where a totality is expressed by the disjunction of two opposites, see the examples and the literature cited in Kannicht on *Hel.* 229–31, Bond on *Herc.* 647f., and Finglass on *El.* 305–6.

—Diggle prints Stephanus' οὕς for transmitted οὐ and keeps Τρωιάς, but the sense is unsatisfactory. Hecuba would be saying that no (other) woman, Trojan, Greek, or barbarian, gave birth to her sons, which though true is trivial since she and only she is their mother. Furthermore, tragedy does not elsewhere divide the world into three by distinguishing Trojans from barbarians. (There is a tripartite division at *Pho.* 1509–13, but it does not involve distinguishing Trojans or any other non-Greek nation from the class of βάρβαροι.) Non-Greeks in tragedy commonly refer to themselves as βάρβαροι (note in our play 771, 973, 991, 1021, and 1277 and e.g. *IT* 1170, 1174, and 1422), so there is no reason for Hecuba to distinguish Trojan from barbarian. Weil's οὐ τοιάδ' οὔθ' eliminates both the tripartite world and the vacuous 'no one else is their mother'. For οὔτε… οὐδέ see *GP* 193, though οὔτε βάρβαρος (also suggested by Weil) would be an inexpensive further change.

480 τρίχας: on the 'retained' accusative see 375n.

481–2 For the motif of autopsy ('I did not hear of it but saw it') see the examples in Diggle 1973: 262n60, the additional cases cited in his *Studies* 17–18, and the additions in Diggle 1994: 81n60. —West 1984: 174

restores here and at 687 the aorist accentuation of a verb whose present and aorist stems are identical.

483 **ἑρκείωι πυρί**: i.e. the altar of Zeus Herkeios. —The correct form ἑρκείωι (see 17n above) is here preserved by p, the sixteenth-century corrector of P. This is one of three places (see Introduction § 5, n. 138) where p gives a reading that *might* be thought too good to be his conjecture, though it is hard to see where the scribe could have found genuine tradition to pass on.

486 **ἐκ χερῶν ἀφηιρέθην**: 'I was robbed of them (the virgin daughters I raised): they were taken out of my arms.' The understood accusative is 'retained', on which see 375n.

489–97 On this Euripidean trope, that previous high status makes a fall more painful, see 195–6n. Hecuba lists aspects of her coming life of slavery that make a sharp and distressing contrast with the life she has known: (1) slavery, exacerbated by old age, in a foreign land; (2) lowly tasks that ill befit a former queen, the mother of Hector, such as being a doorkeeper or making bread; (3) sleeping on the ground instead of in a luxurious bed; and (4) wearing ragged clothing. The woes of slavery were mentioned above at 194–5 and 202–6. Similar catalogues of slave duties at *Il.* 6.454–63, *Cyc.* 29–35, *Andr.* 164–7, and *Hec.* 359–66.

489 **θριγκὸς ἀθλίων κακῶν**: for the metaphor see *Herc.* 1280.

490 **δούλη γυνὴ γραῦς Ἑλλάδ' εἰσαφίξομαι**: Andromache makes a similar complaint at *Andr.* 12–13 αὐτὴ δὲ δούλη τῶν ἐλευθερωτών | οἴκων νομισθεῖσ' Ἑλλάδ' εἰσαφικόμην.

491 **γήραι τῶιδ' ἀσυμφορώτατα**: abstract for concrete, 'most unseemly for me, an old woman'.

492–3 **ἢ θυρῶν λάτριν | κλῆιδας φυλάσσειν, τὴν τεκοῦσαν Ἕκτορα**: for doorkeeping as a lowly occupation see Psalm 84:10. It was mentioned along with minding children at 194–5. Polyxena at *Hec.* 361 likewise finds slavery intolerable for her as sister of Hector.

494 **σιτοποιεῖν**: the making of bread is among the menial tasks Polyxena will avoid by dying: see *Hec.* 362.

494–5 Electra at *El.* 305–6 contrasts in similar fashion the palace in which she was raised with the hovel she now occupies.

495 **βασιλικῶν ἐκ δεμνίων**: 'after sleeping on a royal bed'. The preposition is temporal, as at *Hec.* 55. See LSJ s.v. II.2.

496–7 Electra at *El.* 304 comments on the raggedness of her clothing. Aristophanes at *Ach.* 407–70 makes fun of the ragged costumes worn by so many of Eur.'s characters. In this Eur. probably differed not in kind but in degree from other tragic poets (it is part of a tragic poet's business to evoke pity), and when 'Aeschylus' at *Ran.* 1061–4 complains that

'Euripides' dressed his royal characters in rags, he omits to mention that he himself did the same with Xerxes at the end of *Pers.*

498–9 διὰ γάμον μιᾶς ἕνα | γυναικός: the juxtaposition of two forms of εἷς makes emphatic Hecuba's view that Helen and Helen alone is to blame for her miseries. This is true in one sense: her elopement with Paris was the sole reason for the Greek expedition. Other aspects of this claim are discussed below at 780–1n and in the introduction to the Helen episode.

499 οἵων ἔτυχον ὧν τε τεύξομαι: οἷος is commonly used to introduce exclamatory clauses, and ὅς is rarely so used. This consideration may be responsible for the suggestion (made but not argued for) of ἔτι for ὧν by Broadhead 1968: 179. But see Meridor 1982, who cites Men. *Epitr.* 187, ὦ Ἡράκλεις, ἃ πέπονθα, to defend this rare usage.

501 ἔλυσας... ἅγνευμα σόν: Barlow compares the Homeric λῦσε δὲ παρθενίην ζώνην (*Od.* 11.245).

Staging: in response to Hecuba's request Trojan servants (on these extras see 351–2n) help her to her feet and settle her on the pallet near the *skēnē*. She apparently remains in this position throughout the ensuing stasimon. The text does not make clear when she rises to her feet.

506–9 Hecuba, contrasting the softness and luxury of her previous life with her present lot as a slave who sleeps on the ground, asks to be escorted to her lowly bed so that she may fall down there and die, worn away by her tears.

506 δή ποτ': for the sense 'once, formerly' see *GP* 213, citing 1277, *Hec.* 484, and *Herc.* 444.

508 πέτρινά τε δέμνι': δέμνιον is a Homeric word for bed or bedstead (*Od.* 6.20, 8.282). That it should be made of stone is an oxymoron. —The transmitted word κρήδεμνα always refers to a thing situated atop someone or something, a headdress for a woman or goddess (e.g. *Od.* 6.100) or the towering battlements of a city (*Il.* 16.100). Since Hecuba's resting place is specifically called χαμαιπετῆ, we should reject the transmitted word in favour of Dobree's conjecture (1833: 90).

509–10 τῶν δ' εὐδαιμόνων | μηδένα νομίζετ' εὐτυχεῖν πρὶν ἂν θάνηι: the *locus classicus* for this sentiment is Solon's admonition to Croesus at Hdt. 1.30–2. Unlike Solon Hecuba omits any mention of the gods in the destruction of human happiness. It is curious that Solon calls the man who is only provisionally happy εὐτυχής and the man who achieves perfect good fortune ὄλβιος or εὐδαίμων (see also the Messenger's formulation at *Med.* 1228–30), whereas in Hecuba's formulation one who is prosperous thus far is εὐδαίμων and the actually blessed one is εὐτυχής. The difference in terminology might be without significance, but it *could* suggest that Hecuba regards prosperity more as a matter of luck than of having a kindly *daimon*.

FIRST STASIMON (511–67)

This stasimon is a lyric retelling, in three stanzas, of the capture of Troy by the ruse of the Wooden Horse. The opening three words suggest the objective narrative of epic (see 511n), but this is going to be a narrative of a completely different kind, a sung lamentation of miseries personal to the singer. In tragedy the Chorus are normally bystanders, making sympathetic comment on the woes of others. Here (as also in *Hec.*, whose third stasimon likewise tells the taking of Troy from the Chorus's own perspective) they are among those directly affected by what has happened. The Chorus's own involvement is signalled in the first six lines by *cὺν δακρύοιc*, *ἐπικήδειον*, and *ὀλόμαν τάλαινα δοριάλωτοc* (plus *ἰαχήcω*, which suggests lamentation rather than objective narrative) and later resumed by *ἐγὼ δέ* (551). The break with the more usual kind of poetry is marked even earlier by *μοῦcα καινῶν ὕμνων*, 'muse of new (or unwelcome) songs': see 511–12n, where there is also a discussion of significance of the invocation of the Muse, which seems to violate generic boundaries.[3] A salient subtheme of the ode is the turning of apparent joy into misery. This is a theme that runs throughout the whole trilogy (see Introduction §§ 3.4.1 and 4.2). The pathos of loss of city may be conveyed by the number and variety of words for Troy and Trojans: *Ἰλιάδι* (526), *Τροίαν* (515), *Τρωϊάδοc* (523), *Φρυγῶν* (531, 563, 567), *Φρύγια* (545), and *Περγάμων* (556–7).

511–30 ~ 531–50

1. 511 ~ 531	– ⏖ – ⏖ –	D
2. 512 ~ 532	– ⏑ – – – –	cr mol
3. 513/4 ~ 533/4	– – – ⏖ – – – ⏖ – – –	ᶜD—d sp
4. 515 ~ 535	– – ⏖ – – – ⏑ – – –	—d—e sp
5. 516 ~ 536	⏖ – ⏖ – ⏖ – –	⏖ D—(par)
6. 517/8 ~ 537/8	– – – ⏖ – ⏑ – ⏑ ⏕ ⏑ – ⏓ ||	ᶜD ⏑ ith
7. 519 ~539	⏑ ⏕ ⏑ – ⏑ – ⏑ ⏑͡⏑	2ia
8. 520 ~ 540	⏓ ⏔ ⏑ ⏔ ⏑ ⏑͡⏑ ⏑ ⏑͡⏑	2ia ∫

[3] I mention as a curious aberration (though it has often been cited more respectfully) the view of Kranz 1933: 228–9 that the ode's opening is a forecast by Eur. of the novel character of his later lyric production. He also describes the ode as 'dithyrambic', ignoring its self-description as tearful and funereal, and 'a balladesque narrative standing completely on its own' (254), though the singers are themselves involved in the action it describes.

9. 521 ~ 541	⏑ – ⏑ – ⏑ – – ‖	ia ba
10. 522 ~ 542	⏑ ⏑͡⏑ ⏑ – – ⏑ –	ia cr
11. 523 ~ 543	⏒ ⏑͡⏑ ⏑ ⏖ ⏑ – ⏑ –	2ia
12. 524 ~ 544	⏑ – ⏑ – ⏑ – ⏑ –	2ia
13. 525 ~ 545	⏑ ⏑͡⏑ ⏑ ⏑͡⏑ ⏑ – ⏑ ⏖	2ia
14. 526 ~ 546	⏒ ⏖ ⏑ ⏑͡⏑ ⏑ – ⏑ –	2ia
15. 527 ~ 547	⏑ – ⏑ – ⏑ – ⏑ –	2ia
16. 528 ~ 548	⏑ – ⏑ – ⏑ – ⏑ –	2ia
17. 529 ~ 549	⏓ – ⏑ – ⏑ – –	ia ba
18. 530 ~ 550	⏑͡⏑ ⏑ – ⏑ – – ‖‖	ith

Metrical analysis

The strophe and antistrophe begin in what is basically dactylo-epitrite. The opening D followed by cr mol establishes a dactylo-epitrite context for the first six cola. This might have reminded the audience of Stesichorus, who wrote an *Iliupersis*. (The first element of 514 ~ 534 and of 517 ~ 537, which could be called ¨dod, I have described as D with its first *biceps* contracted, which occurs in the first colon of the strophes and antistrophes of Pi. *N.* 8 and in responsion with uncontracted D in Stesich. fr. 97.230.) Thereafter the dactylic element recedes in favour of lyric iambics, mostly with short *ancipitia*: long *anceps* in 523, 526, 540, 546 (if ms. reading is kept), and 549 if Robert's conjecture is accepted.

511 ***ἀμφί μοι Ἴλιον*:** *HHom* 19 begins *ἀμφί μοι Ἑρμείαο φίλον γόνον ἔννεπε Μοῦϲα* (*HHom* 7, 22, and 33 likewise begin with *ἀμφί* + accusative, and Lyr. Adesp. fr. 938(e) begins *Μοῖϲά μοι ἀμφὶ Cκάμανδρον*), so both the words and the double-short rhythm here suggest narrative by an epic poet or a lyric poet like Stesichorus, whose *Iliupersis* was in dactylo-epitrite. But this expectation of established poetic form is contradicted by the next phrase.

511–12 ***ὦ μοῦϲα καινῶν ὕμνων*:** the Chorus's muse is a 'muse of new songs' not only because the events they are recounting are recent (an attractive feature for audiences, according to Telemachus at *Od.* 1.351–2, as PJF reminds me) but also because the narrators are participants in the narrative, which is quite different from an epic recital. This fact is revealed starkly at 517 (*ὀλόμαν τάλαινα δοριάλωτοϲ*) and also at 551 (*ἐγὼ δέ*). The phrase may also mean 'O muse that singest of what is unwelcome': for *νέοϲ* and *καινόϲ* in tragedy as 'untoward, unwelcome' see 55n. (That of the two words for 'new' *καινόϲ* is by far the more marked is argued by D'Angour 2011: 64–84.)

In tragedy *μοῦϲα* denotes (1) 'the Muse' (or 'a Muse'), one of the daughters of Zeus and Mnemosyne (*Med.* 831, *Herc.* 791, *Ion* 884, *Hel.*

1345; *OC* 691, fr. 588.3; *Rhes.* 387 and *passim*); and (2) 'song' or '(emotive) utterance' (*El.* 703, *IT* 182, *Ion* 757, 1097, *Pho.* 50, 788, 1028, *Ba.* 563; its only meaning in Aesch.: see *Supp.* 695 and *Eu.* 308; possibly *Ant.* 965 and *Trach.* 643). Additionally in Eur. it denotes (3) poetry as an activity (*Alc.* 344, 962, *Med.* 196, *Hipp.* 452, 1135, *Supp.* 489, 883, *Herc.* 674, 686?, *IT* 1105?, *Ion* 1091); and, of greatest relevance here, (4) what could be called 'muse with a qualification', a source of inspiration whose difference from the nine Muses is marked by a qualifier: with μοῦϲα καινῶν ὕμνων cf. 609 'muse that has griefs for its theme' and 384–5 'muse who is a singer of disaster' (the lines are probably from another Euripidean play); a further case is *Med.* 1085, where there is a muse who inspires only women; for further muses with dependent genitives see *Med.* 421 and *Tro.* 1245. These examples, showing parallels to the transmitted vocative and genitive phrase, are a defence against the comma after μοῦϲα that appears in nearly all editions, beginning with the Aldine and including my own Loeb. To separate the genitive from a plausible *regens* by a comma is arbitrary in the absence of any compelling cause. Likewise, attaching the genitive to ᾠιδάν is anything but inevitable: although Breitenbach 194 shows that it is a common form of pleonasm in poetry (see 816n) to make one noun in the genitive depend on another of kindred meaning, in all his examples and in those of Bruhn § 205 (our passage apart) the 'synonymous genitive' phrase is separated from its *regens* by a single word at most, and never are both *regens* and genitive modified by adjectives. So 'of new songs' makes good sense joined with its neighbour μοῦϲα and dubious style if joined to ᾠιδάν, from which it is separated by a verb and a prepositional phrase. It is hard to account for the near unanimity of earlier editions except by the supposition that the punctuation was established when editors believed that Eur. wrote ἐπιτήδειον (which seemed to call for some kind of complement). It was retained by force of habit (or the herd instinct that human beings share with sheep) even after the reason for it had disappeared.

The 'muse with a qualifier' can be seen in many cases to be something internal to the singer. Since the Chorus tell their muse of new songs to sing 'with tears', they are arguably calling on a capacity within themselves. This means that their vocative is not an epicism and a violation of generic boundaries but part of a command addressed to themselves. On such commands in Eur. see 98–9n.

513–14. ἄιϲον ϲὺν δακρύοιϲ ᾠιδὰν ἐπικήδειον: both ϲὺν δακρύοιϲ and ἐπικήδειον mark the narrative as far from detached. ἐπικήδειοϲ here means 'mournful, funereal' (< κῆδοϲ, LSJ s.v. I.2.b, 'funeral rites, mourning'). It is used in one other place in Eur., fr. 46a.12 (*Alexandros*), where the phrase ἐπικηδείους πόνους could mean either 'toils connected with funerals' or 'troubles connected with a marriage relation' (< κῆδος, LSJ s.v. II, 'connection by marriage'). Alexiou 2002: 84–5 presents evidence, including Eur.'s poem on the Athenians who perished at Syracuse (see T 92 and Kovacs 1994a: 18), that ἐπικήδειον was an established genre.

—The best way of restoring both sense and responsion to transmitted ἄεισον ἐν δακρύοις and πεύκα(ι) ἐν οὐρεία(ι) is, first, to realize that ξεστὸν λόχον Ἀργείων must be in apposition to the second expression, which therefore must be accusative: πεύκαν οὐρεΐαν. (The diaeresis on the latter word makes it correspond to σὺν δακρύοις: cf. Ἀργεΐων at *Hec.* 479.) To this hemiepes with contracted first biceps the natural correspondent in the strophe is the Seidler–Burges restoration ᾆισον σὺν δακρύοις.

516–17 τετραβάμονος ὡς ὑπ' ἀπήνας | Ἀργείων: an ἀπήνη is literally a mule-drawn wagon: the word may be deliberately chosen as a homely description of this conveyor of ruin. That it has four feet creates a sense of paradox and also reflects the situation as described by Vergil at *Aen.* 2.235–7. *accingunt omnes operi pedibusque rotarum | subiciunt lapsus et stuppea uincula collo | intendunt*. 'Destroyed by the Argives' four-footed wain' and 'captured by the spear' also make a paradox, a sort of γρῖφος.

519–20 ὅτ' ἔλιπον ἵππον οὐράνια | βρέμοντα: ὅτε may be quasi-causal (see LSJ s.v.B), but the temporal sense is suitable here: the downfall of the singers (ὀλόμαν) was accomplished the moment the horse was put in place. οὐράνια is an internal accusative: the Horse's neighing reached high heaven. The sound exists, apparently, only in the Chorus's imagination. In Vergil there is an actual noise of armour rattling: *insonuere cauae gemitumque dedere cauernae* (*Aen.* 2.53). On the taking of the Horse into Troy in the epic tradition see West 2013: 205–8.

520–1 χρυσοφάλαρον ἔνο- | πλον: 'with cheek-pieces of gold, decked with armour'. The first adjective is unique in Greek poetry though used in later prose. The normal meaning of ἔνοπλος is 'having armour on', and though LSJ s.v. II give the meaning 'containing arms or armed men' for our passage, the parallelism between the two adjectives suggests that the Chorus are referring to things they could see at the time. This is a gift fit for the goddess of war, gold trimming, armour, and all. Barlow 1971: 29 suggests that the gorgeous description, including the newly coined adjective, implies 'the susceptibility of the Trojans to superficial attractions'. It could just as easily show how powerful were the forces that misled them. Vergil likewise tells the story of the Wooden Horse in a way that downplays Trojan credulity and emphasizes their being overpowered by a persuasion whose origin was ultimately divine: on this see Heinze 1908, ch. 1. —I have adopted Seidler's conjecture: Willink 2004: 49n17 [= 2010. 508n17] shows that χρυϲε- with short *upsilon* is firmly attested only in the simplex adjective χρυϲεόϲ, not in compounds.

522–3 **ἀνὰ δ' ἐβόαϲεν λεὼϲ | Τρωϊάδοϲ ἀπὸ πέτραϲ ϲταθεὶϲ**: on tmesis in tragedy see Kannicht on *Hel.* 106 and Collard on *Supp.* 56–8a, both citing earlier literature. See also 762–3n. The prepositional phrase 'from Troy's rocky citadel' goes with the verb but by a zeugma is understood as 'on Troy's rocky citadel' with the participle: for a parallel see *Pho.* 1223–4 Ἐτεοκλέηϲ δ' ὑπῆρξ' ἀπ' ὀρθίου ϲταθεὶϲ | πύργου, κελεύϲαϲ ϲῖγα κηρῦξαι ϲτρατῷι. Similarly, prepositions of direction are used for location and those of location for direction in the *constructio praegnans*, on which see Smyth § 1659.

524–5 The use, in choral and monodic lyric, of quotations in *oratio recta* is characteristic of Eur.: see Bers 1997: 102, who points out that there is no instance in surviving Soph. and many fewer in Aesch.

525 **ξόανον**: the word normally applies to a statue of a god (e.g. 1074, *IT* 1359, *Ion* 1403), but here it is an image presented to the god. For a possible instance of similar transfer of meaning see 12n.

526 The Trojans thought of their goddess as Trojan Athena (Ἰλιάδι), equivalent to Athena Polias for Athenians. They made their offering to her in ignorance of her implacable hostility to the city. A similar irony in *Il.* 6.297–311.

527–8 **τίϲ οὐκ ἔβα νεανίδων, | τίϲ οὐ γεραιὸϲ ἐκ δόμων**: the pairing 'young women and old men' may be intended to suggest the whole range of the population. Alternatively, as suggested by Wilamowitz *GV* 174 they may represent two groups who normally οἰκουροῦϲι. For τίϲ οὐ as the equivalent of πᾶϲ and combined with anaphora see *Andr.* 299–300. The predicate ἔβα ἐκ δόμων is divided between the two clauses. There is asymmetry (*inconcinnitas*) in that a partitive genitive of a noun in the first part is answered by a nominative adjective in the second. On such asymmetry in Euripidean lyric see Breitenbach 209–13, esp. 212–13. Examples of similar rhyming isometric cola are given by Diggle 1970: 115 (on *Phaethon* 99).

530 **δόλιον ἔϲχον ἄταν**: 'They got ruin in deceitful disguise.' Ending a stanza with a grim word like ἄταν is characteristic of an older style of stasimon, according to Kranz 1933: 230.

534 **πεύκαν οὐρεΐαν**: the horse is made of pine cut from a mountain in the Troad. Paris' ship had the same origin: see *Hel.* 232. The connection is strengthened when the horse is compared in 538–9 to the hull of a ship. —See 513–14n for textual discussion.

ξεcτὸν λόχον: the phrase may recall *Od.* 4.272, where the horse is called *κοῖλον λόχον*. The noun both here and there means 'place of ambush': see LSJ s.v. I.1.

535 **θεᾶι δώcων**: the masculine participle agrees in sense with *πᾶcα γέννα Φρυγῶν*, 'every Phrygian'. For the *constructio ad sensum* (ignoring grammatical gender) see KG 1.53–4 and below 740, 853–4, and 1180. —The decision as between transmitted *θέαι* and the Aldine's *θεᾶι* is not an easy one. The collocation *θέαι διδόναι* is found at *Andr.* 1086–7 (though the object of the verb is of a different kind), and similar expressions may be found at *Hec.* 944–6 and *IA* 850. (See Kannicht on *Hel.* 868–70 for further examples.) The transmitted phrase is thus of a Euripidean type. Nevertheless, the context speaks for 'in order to present to the goddess' and against 'in order to behold'. The quoted cry of 524–6 has already exhorted the Trojans to offer the horse to Athena, and 527–30 indicate that the Trojans' departure from their homes was to do just this. At this point to represent them as going out merely to look seems a regression. 536 likewise reads better as the expression of their fully formed intention to give the horse to the goddess. The immediate dragging of the horse into the city follows better as well.

536 **χάριν ἄζυγος ἀμβροτοπώλου**: 'an act to gratify the goddess of the immortal steeds'. This stands in apposition to the idea of giving in 535 and is the so-called 'accusative in apposition with the sentence', on which see Barrett on *Hipp.* 752–7, who shows that it is a special case of the internal accusative, that it is not always a non-integral afterthought to be marked off by a comma (as it is at *Or.* 1105), and that the name is somewhat misleading. Further discussion in Diggle 1978b: 171–2 and 1982: 59–60.

537–8 **κλωcτοῦ δ' ἀμφιβόλοιc λίνοιο ναὸc ὡcεὶ | cκάφοc κελαινόν**: 'with nooses of spun flax, as if it were the dark hull of a ship'. *ἀμφιβόλοιc* is a substantivized adjective. Ships in Homer are regularly *μέλαιναι*. There may be something sinister in the comparison to a ship: the last mythically relevant ship, also cut from mountain firs (cf. *Hec.* 629–34), was that of Paris. For ropes of flax see *IT* 1043 and Morrison, Coates, and Rankov 2000: 189–90. —Restoration of the 'Homeric' genitive in *-οιο* (cf. 838, *Πριάμοιο*) is certain here. Eur. is fond of the form (Dodds on *Ba.* 873–6 notes that Aesch. has it only three times, Soph. only once), but it is often corrupted. See Page on *Med.* 135. For other Homeric features of this stasimon see Barlow on 511ff.

538–40 **εἰc ἕδρανα | λάϊνα δάπεδά τε, φονέα πατρί- | δι, Παλλάδοc θέcαν θεᾶc**: 'They brought it, instrument of murder against their fatherland, into the goddess' stone temple and her precincts.' It is ironic that they bring this gift intended to ruin the city into the temple of the very goddess whom they regard as its protector. —Diggle, *Studies* 63–4 refutes the idea that φόνια, a reading recovered from the scholiast (the mss. have φοίνια) and printed by several editors, can agree with δάπεδα and mean e.g. 'destined to run with the blood of their countrymen'. The only murderous thing in sight is the horse, and Diggle's φονέα restores sense.

542 **ἐπὶ δὲ πόνωι καὶ χαρᾶι**: 'toil and joy' is hendiadys for 'joyful toil'. ἐπί is 'after, supervening upon'.

543 For the postponement of a subordinating conjunction (here to the seventh place) in Euripidean lyric see Breitenbach 262–3.

544–5 **τε . . . τε**: the main clause begins with Λίβυς τε λωτός, and the first τε must be 'both'.

546–7 **ἄειρον ἅμα κρότον ποδῶν | βοάν τ' ἔμελπον εὔφρον'**: either 'They raised a noise of feet as they sang loudly a cheerful song' or 'They lifted up their clattering feet, etc.', taking κρότον ποδῶν as the kind of periphrasis discussed on 1123. Diggle, *Studies* 63 gives examples where ἀείρω is used both of raising a foot and of raising a noise, so either is a possible rendering. —Diggle's persuasive discussion should be read *in toto*. Some points he makes: (1) the form with dissyllabic stem (ἀείρ-) is a borrowing from Homer (*Il.* 11.637); (2) the tragic poets use the monosyllabic stem in both imperfect and aorist, but they use ἀείρ- in both imperfect and aorist when they are not augmented; and (3) omission of the temporal augment is plentiful in Eur. (all his examples but *Med.* 1413 are lyric).

547–50 'And within doors the radiant gleam <of the moon> put to sleep in blackness the glow of the hearth-fire'. —In the transmitted text (with e.g. Murray's <ἄκος> before ἔδωκεν to mend the metre) an 'all-shining gleam' (παμφαὲς σέλας) casts as an antidote to sleep a 'black glow or glare' (μέλαιναν αἴγλαν), a contradiction no attested meaning of μέλας removes. Then too παμφαὲς σέλας seems a bit bright for a hearth-fire or torch (cf. *Med.* 1251, of the sun). With Robert's conjecture (1920: 310) σέλας refers to the moon and αἴγλα to the fire. We may take μέλαιναν proleptically, as in the translation above, or render it as 'indistinct' (see LSJ s.v. III.3). Bringing in the moon is pure gain. Wilamowitz 1895b: 32–3 points out that according to the *Ilias Parva* (*GEF* fr. 14) the taking of Troy occurred around midnight on a brightly moonlit night (νὺξ μὲν ἔην μέσση, λαμπρὴ δ' ἀνέτελλε σελήνη; cf. *Hec.* 914), and here it is, appropriately 'all-shining'. (Wilamowitz's own conjecture to bring in the moon is unsuccessful.) We may give a prosaic paraphrase: because of the bright moonlight the Trojans had no need for fires and allowed them to die down. For fires 'sleeping' see Fraenkel on *Ag.* 597 and add Verg. *Aen.* 5.743 and 8.410, *sopitos suscitat ignis*. The corruption is not as easily explained as some, but *πυρόϲ* in the line below could have been copied by a careless scribe instead of *μήνηϲ*.

551–67

1. 551	⏑ – ⏑ – ⏑ – ⏑ –	2ia
2. 552	⏑ – ⏑ ⏕ ⏑ – ⏑ –	2ia
3. 553/4	⏑ – ⏑ – ⏑ – ⏑ –	2ia
4. 555	⏑ – ⏑ – ⏑ – ⏑ –	2ia
5. 556	⏑ – ⏑ – ⏑ – ⏑ –	2ia ∫
6. 557	⏑ – ⏑ – ⏑ – ⏑ ⏕	2ia ∫
7. 558	⏑ ⏕ ⏑ – ⏑ – ⏑ –	2ia ∫
8. 559	⏑ – ⏑ – ⏑ – ⏑ –	2ia
9. 560	⏑ – – ⏑ – ⏑ –	ba ia
10. 561	⏑ – – ⏑ – ⏑ –	ba ia
11. 562	⏑ – – ⏑ – ⏑ –	ba ia
12. 563	⏑ – – ⏑ – ⏑ –	ba ia
13. 564	⏑ – ⏕ ⏑ – ⏑ –	ba ia
14. 565	⏑ – ⏑ – ⏑ ⏕ ⏑ ⏕	2ia
15. 566	– ⏑⏑ – ⏑⏑ –	D
16. 567	⏑ – ⏑ ⏕ ⏑ – – |||	ia ba

Metrical analysis

The epode is all lyric iambics apart from a hemiepes (D) near the end. There are resolutions in several places and syncopation in 560–4 and 567, but no instance of long *anceps*, which imparts swiftness perhaps suggestive of the swiftness of the events described. There is also between 555 and 558 no sense-break at line-end (in 555–6 *ἀνὰ* | *πτόλιν* must go together, and the ends of 556–8 are marked by spillovers), making a tragic *pnigos* indicative of breathless haste. (On the *pnigos*, usually found in comedy, see West 93 and 103.)

551–4 ***τὰν ὀρεϲτέραν…παρθένον, Διὸϲ κόραν***: 'the mountain-dwelling maiden, Zeus's daughter' is, of course, Artemis. She figures very little in the action of the *Iliad* but appears at 20.39 and 71 on the Trojan side. —*Ἄρτεμιν* in the mss. is a gloss that has invaded the text.

553 ***τότ' ἀμφὶ μέλαθρα***: the noun refers to the same interior space as *δόμοιϲ* (548), either the chorus members' houses or (Barlow 1971: 30) the royal palace.

555–7 ***φοινία δ' ἀνὰ | πτόλιν βοὰ κατεῖχε Περ- | γάμων ἕδραϲ***: 'But a murderous shout throughout the city was filling (see LSJ s.v. *κατέχω* II.2) Troy's dwelling-places.' —Wilamowitz, *GV* 175 says that his κατέcχε for κατεῖχε 'commendatione non indiget', and it is adopted by Diggle. The conjecture is certainly possible, but the next two verbs, ἔβαλλε and ἐξέβαινε, both imperfect, might be thought to defend the paradosis.

558–9 **περὶ πέπλουc ἔβαλλε μα- | τρὶ χεῖραc ἐπτοημέναc**: 'threw their frightened arms about the skirts of their mothers'. As frequently happens, the dative of advantage or disadvantage (ματρί) is translated as if it were a genitive. It is a distributive singular: see 392n. —πτοέω is used with a person as object (or as subject of the passive verb) or with parts of him or her (such as καρδία or φρένεc) that could be said to feel emotions, but apart from ἐπτοημένωι ποδί at *Or.* 1505, which seems a more plausible phrase (see West 1984: 189 for things that can be predicated of feet), 'frightened arms' lacks any parallel, and there is something to be said for West's ἐπτοημένα.

561 **κόραc ἔργα Παλλάδοc**: in the text as transmitted we must take these words as accusative in apposition with the sentence: '(and this emergence was) the work of the virgin Pallas'. The plural, says Biehl, 'relates to the plurality of contributors to the action that the invention of Athena…brought about [bezieht sich auf die Vielzahl der durch die Erfindung Athenes…bewirkten Handlungsmomente]'. But despite the accusative plural cοφίcμαθ' at *Ba.* 30, the plural here seems difficult. More fundamentally, the Chorus do not seem elsewhere to be aware that Athena is hostile to Troy. They have just represented the Trojans, themselves included, as in favour of offering the horse to the goddess in her capacity as Athena Ἰλιάc, the city's protector, presumably in thanks for that protection. In 539–41 their emphatic language points up the irony that this gift offered to the city's protector proved destructive to the people Athena Ilias was protecting. The shift to Athena as the destroyer of Troy is therefore surprising. It also contrasts with the view of the situation they take elsewhere: in the second and third stasima they complain of the gods' carelessness and indifference, not of their hostility. None of the three words in this line is otherwise suspicious, and I suggest that what they need is not alteration but a new context. What plural 'works of the virgin Pallas' might the Chorus have mentioned? Athena as martial goddess is associated with the war-cry that encourages one side and causes panic in the other: see *Il.* 18.217–18, where she augments the shout of Achilles with her own. We could therefore mark a lacuna of one verse before 561, e.g. λόχου δ' ἐξέβαιν' Ἄρηc <ἐμέλποντο τ' ἀλαλαγάc>, κόραc ἔργα Παλλάδοc, 'The soldiery were emerging from their hiding-place <and were making their war-cries>, the invention of the virgin Pallas.'

562–4 ***σφαγαὶ δ' ἀμφιβώμιοι | Φρυγῶν ἔν τε δεμνίοις | καράτομος ἐρημία:*** the Chorus speak in allusive terms of the slaughter of their menfolk and their own desolation, 'slaughtering of Trojans at the altars and in (our) beds a desolation wrought by the cutting off of heads'. For the killing of someone claiming the protection of an altar see above 16–17. The proparoxytone καράτομος (V) seems preferable to PQ's -τόμος, though either makes a bold expression. For ἐρημία see 15, 26, and 97.

565–7 ***νεανίδων στέφανον ἔφερεν | Ἑλλάδι κουροτρόφον, | Φρυγῶν δὲ πατρίδι πένθος:*** 'won for Greece a prize (lit. a crown) of young women to bear (or nurture) children but for the Trojans' homeland a grief'.

SECOND EPISODE (568–798)

The theme of this episode, expressed in the dialogue between Andromache and Hecuba and in the aftermath of the announcement that Astyanax is to be killed, is human vicissitude. Andromache is convinced that no amelioration of her circumstances is possible since her husband and city are destroyed and she is about to become the concubine of the son of Achilles, her husband's slayer. Hecuba holds out hopes for a future in which Troy might rise again under the leadership of the children of Astyanax, but these hopes are cruelly dashed when a herald comes with the announcement that the boy will be killed. Andromache's gloomy view is thus confirmed, and Hecuba comes to see that the utter ruin of her happiness is what is in store for her.

The episode centres on Andromache and Astyanax. There are three scenes, the first two subdivided. (1a) Andromache enters on a wagon with Astyanax and engages with Hecuba in an *amoibaion* of lament. There follow (1b) a distichomythic interchange, where each woman learns from the other of new misfortunes, and a pair of *rheseis* on hopes for the future, with Andromache denying (1c) that there is hope of amelioration and Hecuba (1d) claiming that Astyanax represents such a hope. A herald enters (on his identity see 707n). (2a) In *stichomythia* he delivers the news that the Greeks have decreed that Astyanax is to be thrown to his death from the battlements of Troy. This is followed by (2b) a short *rhesis* from the Herald and (2c) a longer one from Andromache. (3) After boy and mother have made their exits, Hecuba utters an anapaestic lament.

Variation of mood is deftly handled. Meridor 1989: 28–35 argues that Eur. has deliberately lulled the audience into forgetting what they know about the death of Astyanax from other sources so that the conversation between Hecuba and Andromache, which culminates in Hecuba's hopeful 'his descendants might refound Troy', may seem plausible to the audience even though they know the epic account of his death. That way the shock of the Herald's announcement will be all the greater. (Petersen 1915: 463–4 compares *Andr.* 409–20 followed by 425–34.) The principal means for achieving this forgetfulness, she argues, is the suppression of two stories in which Neoptolemus' crueler side appears, his slaughter of Priam at the altar of Zeus Herkeios and his sacrificing of Polyxena to the shade of his father. Both Priam's death and Polyxena's have been mentioned or alluded to in the play (16–17, 39–40, 262–72) and the second will be revealed to Hecuba in this scene (622–3), but Neoptolemus' name is deliberately withheld. Also deliberately deceptive is the treatment of the boy in this scene up to 702. After the entrance announcement, he is not mentioned either in hope or in fear. Andromache discourses on her future while holding him in her arms, but there is no hint of worry.

Staging: enter by the right *eisodos* Andromache and Astyanax on a wagon (568–71). (On ἀπήνη and chariot as alternatives in tragedy see Finglass on *OT* 752–3.) The wagon is laden with Trojan spoils belonging to Neoptolemus, Andromache's new master. Among the spoils is the armour of Hector, including his shield, visible even though mentioned only later (1136). Mother and son are bound for the ship of Neoptolemus. The entrance of characters by chariot or wagon is much commoner in Aesch. (*Pers.* 155, made plain only at 607–9), *Ag.* 783, and possibly *Supp.* 234) than in Soph. (no examples) or Eur. (only here and *El.* 988 plus *IA* 590, part of an interpolation). Possibly its use in Aesch. may be connected with the absence of a *skēnē* in early tragedy. (This mode of entry may have enjoyed a revival in the fourth century; see Taplin 1977: 75–9.) Taplin points out (75) that there is something ironically different about this entry from other entries on vehicles since she is not travelling in state but being taken to the ships as booty.

568–76 The Chorus Leader addresses Andromache in pitying style. The address includes more detail visible to the audience, Hector's weapons (573) and the spoils from Troy with which, the Chorus Leader says, Neoptolemus will adorn the temples of the gods at home (574). On entrance announcements immediately following choral odes see above 230–4n.

568 **τήνδε**: on ὅδε in entrance announcements see above 230n.

570 **παρὰ δ' εἰρεςίαι μαςτῶν ἕπεται**: Diggle notes the obscurity of the phrase: 'εἰρεςίαι μαςτῶν non intelleguntur.' The metaphor involved in εἰρεςίαι has three possible referents, and for any of them to be correct alteration of the text would seem to be necessary. (1) A common meaning of *ἐρέccειν* is ‘to put in swift motion’, and if we refer this to *πορθμευομένην* in the previous line, we shall have to alter *μαcτῶν* to e.g. *χηλῶν*. (2) Lee takes it as a metaphor of repeated motion (cf. the common *πίτυλοc*) and translates ‘beside the rhythmic breathing of her breast’. This is possible but would seem to require supplementation since the context does nothing to make this meaning clear. (3) Tyrrell points to the meaning ‘strike the breasts in mourning’ at *Sept.* 855 and *Pers.* 1046, and in spite of the strictures of Lee 1973, this seems the best bet. Yet in this case too the phrase seems allusive while the text provides nothing for it to allude to. We can preserve the paradosis by marking a lacuna before 570 and supplying e.g. <*θάνατόν τε φίλων ἀποκοπτομένην*>, ‘mourning (beating her breast for) the death of her kin’. (For ‘beat one’s breast’ with further object see 627n.)

572–6 The *ποῖ* is not really a request for information (cf. 575–6, which indicate that the Chorus Leader knows that captives and spoils alike are bound for Phthia) but more of an exclamatory question: ‘Ah, are you really being carried off?’ Andromache’s 577 does not answer the nominal question but is likewise in the exclamatory mode.

577–606. *Amoibaion*

Two pairs of lyric stanzas in syncopated iambics, sung by Andromache and Hecuba, bewail the generally woeful situation (first pair) and the death of Hector and Priam (second pair). A third section in dactylic rhythm (without contraction except for 603) bemoans the role of the gods in the survival of Alexandros, the Trojan who, above all others, brought about Troy’s destruction. It is noticeable in this *amoibaion* that when Andromache laments her woes, Hecuba constantly interposes her own: see 578n.

577–81 = 582–6

1. 577 ~ 582	*Αν.*	⏑ – – | – ⏑ – ⏑ – ⏓ ||	ba ith
2. 578 ~ 583		– – *Εκ.* ⏑ – |– ⏑ – ⏑ – –	ia ith
3. 579 ~ 584	*Αν.*	– – *Εκ.* – |– ⏑ –	mol cr
4. 580 ~ 585		⏓ – – | – ⏑ –	mol (ba) cr
5. 581 ~ 586		⏕ ⏑ – ⏑ – – |||	ith

Metrical analysis

The metre is iambo-trochaic with syncopation.

—The manuscripts in the strophe assign *οἴμοι*, *αἰαῖ*, *ὦ Ζεῦ*, and *τέκεα* to Hecuba and the rest to Andromache, and in the antistrophe the paradosis seems to assign *τλάμων*, *φεῦ φεῦ*, *κακῶν*, and *πόλεοc* to Andromache and the rest to Hecuba. (The discrepancy between P and VQ in the antistrophe will be discussed below.) This arrangement, though accepted by editors, violates a general rule of *amoibaia*, that the same singer (whether actor or Chorus) must sing the corresponding parts of both strophe and antistrophe. (It also gives weirdly pointillistic sequences, e.g. 584–6.) Apart from 587–94 (where the strophe seems to promise this kind of mirror antistrophe but where it is impossible to carry it out, as we will see), and the putative stanzaic pair 595–600 ~ 601–6 (which are probably not in correspondence: see below), the only exceptions are *OC* 510–33 and 1724–50, only the first of which represents a similar 'counterchange', whereas in 1724–50 the strophe divides the words between Antigone and Ismene and the antistrophe between the Chorus and Antigone. (The rule enunciated above does not apply to *undivided* stanzas such as *Hel.* 167–78 ~ 179–90 and 191–210 ~ 211–28, nor does it apply to *spoken* verses within a strophic system, as at *Med.* 1271–92.) See below on 587–90 ~ 591–4 for a further irregularity entailed in the counterchange. We must therefore make Andromache, who began the strophe, begin the antistrophe and reduce the number of utterances in each stanza (currently nine) to an even number. Other constraints are given by the wording. At 584 φεῦ δῆτ' requires a change of speaker there and after the first two syllables of 579. Hecuba must get ἐμῶν τ' εὐγένεια παίδων (583) and the corresponding part of the strophe. It seems inadvisable to break up φεῦ δῆτ' ἐμῶν κακῶν or οἰκτρὰ τύχα πόλεος ἃ καπνοῦται, and the same would apply to their counterparts in the strophe. Because of its vocative we must give τέκεα, πρίν ποτ' ἦμεν to Hecuba. These considerations lead to the arrangement proposed by Willink unpubl. and adopted both in the Loeb and here. Advantages and disadvantages are discussed below.

577 Andromache's statement is not a reply to the Chorus Leader's 572–6 but a cry of woe addressed to all.

578 **τί παιᾶν' ἐμὸν ϲτενάζειϲ:** a παιάν is a joyful song in honour of Apollo. For the oxymoron of a *paian* connected with woe see *Alc.* 423–4 with Parker's note. On the genre of the paean see Rutherford 2001: 1–136.

Throughout this *amoibaion* Hecuba, instead of cooperating in Andromache's lament, seems to claim that she has greater woes to lament than her daughter-in-law: see below on 582–3, 584–6, 588–90, 592, and 610–20.

—The transmitted speaker assignments give τί παιᾶν' ἐμὸν ϲτενάζειϲ as Andromache's response to Hecuba's οἴμοι, which seems at first sight more natural. But the counterchange cannot be kept, and the reassignment of these words enables us to see a pattern in Hecuba's reactions. Hecuba's utterance is arguably more natural as a statement. We could write ϲύ for τί.

579–80 Hecuba's ἀλγέων and cυμφορᾶc are genitives of exclamation dependent upon Andromache's αἰαῖ: see Smyth § 1407.

581 **τέκεα**: the plural could refer to Andromache and Astyanax, though the reference might be to the totality of her offspring, most of whom are dead. Of the tragic poets only Eur. uses τέκοc. It is often corrupted, as in one ms. here, to τέκνον.

πρίν ποτ' ἦμεν: 'We once existed (but are no more).' Cf. Verg. *Aen.* 2.325–6, *fuimus Troes, fuit Ilium et ingens gloria Teucrorum.* The use of 'we were' (without further explanation) to mean 'exist no more' is common in Latin (see Austin on *Aen.* 2.325–6), and that is its meaning here even though I have found no further instance in Greek. (At *Hec.* 284, κἀγὼ γὰρ ἦ ποτ' ἀλλὰ νῦν οὐκ εἴμ' ἔτι, 'exist no more' is spelt out.) By 'we' Hecuba means Troy: insisting that Troy is no more is a common utterance for her: see 99–100, 107, 173, 584–6, 1277–8.

582–3 Andromache picks up Hecuba's theme and makes it her own. Hecuba then trumps her complaint by referring to the loss of her noble children. This seems characteristic of her: see 578n.

583 **ἐμῶν τ' εὐγένεια παίδων**: i.e. 'my noble children'. For the abstract noun plus genitive in place of the concrete noun and adjective see 1123n and *Pho.* 291, ὦ cυγγένεια τῶν Ἀγήνοροc τέκνων, *El.* 601 τί μοι κατ' Ἄργοc εὐμενὲc φίλων, *IT* 793, γραμμάτων διαπτυχάc, *Ba.* 112, 370–2, 866–70, and Stevens on *Andr.* 713.

584–6 Once again the competitive spirit. This time among her own woes Hecuba lists the fate of her city.

585–6 —V and Q seem to descend from a tradition in which the speaker indication at the beginning of 585 was left out and the next three indications were accordingly reversed.

587–90 ~ 591–4

1. 587 ~ 591	*Αν.*	⏑ – – | ⏑ – –	2ba
2. 588 ~ 592	*Εκ.*	⏑ – – | ⏑ – –	2ba
3. 589 ~ 593		– ⏖ – ⏖ –	
4. 590 ~ 594		⏖ – ⏑ – – |||	D^2 ba (prax)

Metrical analysis

The metre of the first three cola is straightforward: 2ba, 2ba, D. In the fourth colon the mss. transmit a discrepancy between strophe and antistrophe, ithyphallic vs ⏖ – ⏑ – –. Either is a plausible clausular rhythm: D ith is found at *Alc.* 440–1 ~ 450–1 and *Supp.* 598 ~ 608, and D^2 ba (= praxillean) at 1070 ~ 1080, *Alc.* 120–1 ~ 130–1 and *Or.* 1300. In the strophe 590 must be assigned to Hecuba and be adjusted to make sense in its context. No adjustment to 594 seems necessary: see below. I have chosen to adopt the metre of the latter and emend 590 to agree with it.

—As restored, the two stanzas are begun by Andromache—who addresses Hector in 587 and either Hector or Priam in 591—and finished by Hecuba. The mss. divide the strophe into three utterances (giving 587 and 590 to Andromache and 588–9 to Hecuba) but give the antistrophe undivided to either Hecuba or Andromache. (VQ have no mark at 591, which means it continues Andromache's 590, whereas P marks a speaker change.) Such a lack of responsion cannot be original. Furthermore, in an *amoibaion* speaker change at stanza boundary is normal (the only *prima facie* counter-examples, *Supp.* 1145 and 1152, have been convincingly regularized: in my Loeb I print Willink's restoration), and its absence at 591 (and also at 595) is suspicious. I therefore follow Willink unpub. and divide both strophe and antistrophe into two utterances, giving 587 and 591 to Andromache and the rest to Hecuba.

587 Andromache begins the second strophe by asking Hector to appear. Megara similarly addresses her husband Heracles, presumed dead, at *Herc.* 494–5.

ὦ πόcις μοι: for the dative see e.g. 1081, *Alc.* 313, *Herc.* 626, and *Or.* 124.

588–90 Andromache's forlorn plea to her husband for rescue is interrupted in competitive fashion by Hecuba, who points out that he (whom she identifies as *her son*) is dead and cannot help.

589–90 —The transmitted text gives defective sense if read as the utterance of a single person (see *Metrical analysis* for the reasons why it cannot be divided): in 'poor woman, the defence of your wife' the vocative (addressed to a woman) does not fit with 'your wife' (addressed to a man). Best is to read ὦ μέλεος: for μέλεος as vocative (the only masculine singular vocative the word has in classical authors) see *Herc.* 877 (used as feminine), *Or.* 447, 839, 1029, and *Ant.* 1319. For the minuscule corruption οc > α see Jackson 15. If we keep κόμιcαί at 594, the scansion of 594 and 590 is ⏕ – ⏑ – –. We therefore need a short syllable to replace cᾶc. I suggest ὦ μέλεος, cὺ δάμαρτος ἄλκαρ;, 'Poor man, (are) you your wife's defence?' or τί δάμαρτος ἄλκαρ;, 'What defence ('are you' or 'is there') for your wife?' For the omission of εἶ, see e.g. *Hcld.* 360, 771–2, *Hipp.* 578, and *Andr.* 590. The corruption of cύ to cᾶc would be an example of unconscious adjustment of an ending to make it agree with a neighbouring word: see West 1973: 23–4 and Jackson 186–7; similar cases of corruption through the influence of neighbouring words are listed in Diggle 1994: 288, 428, and 469–70.

590 ἄλκαρ: the word is rare in tragedy: in addition to this passage it is conjecturally restored at *Ion* 481 and *Sept.* 762. It is at home in epic and is appropriately applied to Hector as valiant warrior. The genitive indicates the person defended, as at *Il.* 11.823, though in post-Homeric Greek it elsewhere indicates what is warded off.

591–3 Is Andromache addressing Hector or Priam? Neither option is without difficulties, but those who think she is addressing Hector face graver ones. To be sure, in favour of Hector is that πρεϲβυγενήϲ is logically 'eldest-born', and Hector was Priam's eldest child, which suggests Musgrave's πρεϲβυγενὲϲ Πριάμωι (1788: 493), a conjecture that eliminates an unattractive *brevis in longo*. Diggle adopts this and also Seidler's δή ποτ' for δέϲποτ', eliminating 'owner of my children'. But (1) Diggle is forced to dagger ϲύ τ', since neither ϲύ τ' nor Page's ϲὺ δ' are a way to continue addressing the same person, and the phrase is *prima facie* evidence for different addressee. (2) λῦμ' Ἀχαιῶν is difficult as applied to Hector (see 591n). (3) Seidler's δή ποθ' is not wholly satisfactory since Hector was Priam's eldest-born not 'in days gone by' but right up to his death and even (in status) beyond. This seems a dubious conjecture, and in fact δέϲποθ' can be retained by making a change elsewhere.

If we opt for Priam, ϲύ τ' or ϲὺ δ', implying a change of addressee, is perfectly in place. We can save δέϲποθ' if we adopt λεχέων δέϲποθ' ἁμῶν (Willink unpub.: he compares *Hel.* 592, ποίων δὲ λέκτρων δεϲπότηϲ ἄλλων ἔφυϲ;), a plausible periphrasis for 'husband'. πρεϲβυγενήϲ need mean no more than 'old', just as ἀειγενήϲ means 'eternal' and μονογενήϲ 'only'. The one disadvantage is that transmitted Πρίαμε gives implausible *brevis in longo*. But a long syllable can be achieved here at little cost: read πρεϲβυγενὲϲ Πρίαμ' ὦ κόμιϲαί μ' κτλ. For ὦ placed between a vocative and an imperative see *Herc.* 781 (and the restoration of the same placement by Verrall at *Herc.* 791). For ὦ preceding an imperative see *Hec.* 1093, *El.* 112, and *Ba.* 152–3 and Fraenkel on *Ag.* 22; it follows an imperative at *Supp.* 60 and *Tro.* 335. (Willink unpub. suggests both λεχέων and Πρίαμ' ὦ in passing on his way to a different solution that I find less plausible.)

591 ὦ λῦμ' Ἀχαιῶν: LSJ s.v. λῦμα (A) III, together with the *Revised Supplement*, say that the word, which usually means something cast away such as wash water, filth, or defilement, can mean λύμη, 'ruin', citing *PV* 692 and *Hymni Orphici* 14.14. But (1) *PV* 692, lacking both metre and sense, is weak evidence; (2) though the word in the (much later) Orphic hymns *might* mean 'evil, scourge', it could also mean 'defilement'; (3) even if we had the word λύμη, this doesn't sound like a term of praise ('outrage, maltreatment' is its basic sense); and (4) λῦμα sounds even less like one. If, by contrast, Priam is the addressee, the word could bear its ordinary sense, 'O thing cast forth by the Greeks', a reference to his unburied corpse: cf. 16–17, 481–3, and 1313.

592–4 Hecuba once more claims the honours in the exchange of laments. If 591, as argued above, means Priam, she insists that this is *her* husband. (If it means Hector, she answers 'Yes, *my* eldest son'.)

594 'Bring me to Hades.' —Transmitted κόμιcαί μ' ἐc Ἅιδου is perfectly paralleled by *IT* 774, κόμιcαί μ' ἐc Ἄργοc. For Burges's κοιμίcαι (active infinitive for imperative) or Seidler's κοίμιcαι (middle imperative) the parallels are less good: at *Hipp.* 1387–8 the subject of this verb is 'the dark, nocturnal necessity of Hades', and at *Aj.* 831–2 it is 'Hermes of the Underworld'. Furthermore, one does not fall asleep 'into Hades'. Burges's and Seidler's conjectures appear to be anticipated in part by the reading of the Hauniensis. But the reading of the other mss. is more vigorous than the conjectures, which are motivated only by the metre of 590 as transmitted.

ἐc Ἅιδαν: at *Eur. Alt.* 150–1, I showed that while in Euripidean dialogue the Attic genitive Ἅιδου is used, in lyric the Doric genitive Ἅιδα or Ἀΐδα is the only well-attested form. (The 1984 vol. i of Diggle's OCT prints Ἅιδα for transmitted Ἅιδου at *Hipp.* 1388 and *Hec.* 1076, but his 1981 vol. ii does not correct the present passage.) Furthermore, in lyric after εἰc, πρόc, or ἐν we do not find the genitive with understood δόμον or δόμωι but ε(ἰ)c Ἅιδαν at *Andr.* 1217, *Supp.* 1004, *Herc.* 427, *Ion* 1495 and πρὸc Ἀΐδαν at *Hec.* 1033, with only *El.* 122, ἐν Ἅιδα as possible genitive (but easily reinterpretable as Ἅιδαι). I have accordingly written the accusative here.

595–607

1. 595	*Αν.*	† – ⏑⏑ – ⏑⏑ – ⏑⏑ – † ⏑⏑ – ⏑⏑ – –	6da
2. 596		– ⏑⏑ – ⏑⏑ – ⏑⏑ – ⏑⏑ – ⏑⏑ – –	6da
3. 597		– ⏑⏑ – ⏑⏑ – ⏑⏑ – ⏑⏑ – ⏑⏑ – –	6da
4. 598		– ⏑⏑ – ⏑⏑ – ⏑⏑ – ⏑⏑ – ⏑⏑ – –	6da
5. 599		– ⏑⏑ – ⏑⏑ – ⏑⏑ – ⏑⏑ – ⏑⏑ – –	6da
6. 600		– ⏑⏑ – ⏑⏑ – ⏑⏑ – ⏑⏑ – ⏑⏑ – –	6da
7. 601	*Εκ.*	– ⏑⏑ – ⏑⏑ – *Αν.* ⏑⏑ – ⏑⏑ – ⏑⏑ – –	6da
8. 602	*Εκ.*	– ⏑⏑ – ⏑⏑ – *Αν.* ⏑⏑ – ⏑⏑ – ⏑⏑ – –	6da
9. 603	*Εκ.*	– ⏑⏑ – ⏑⏑ – – – ⏑⏑ – ⏑⏑ – –	6da
10. 604		– ⏑⏑ – ⏑⏑ – ⏑⏑ – ⏑⏑	4da
11. 605		– ⏑⏑ – ⏑⏑ – ⏑⏑ – ⏑⏑	4da
12. 606		– ⏑⏑ – ⏑⏑ – ⏑⏑ – ⏑⏑ – ⏑⏑ – –	6da

Metrical analysis

As printed here this is a single stanza of 12 dactylic cola, ten of them 6da and two 4da. The 4da colon, usually uncontracted, is common in Eur., sometimes in pairs or threes (e.g. *Alc.* 463–4 ~ 473–4, *Pho.* 1502–4), sometimes with hexameters on either side (e.g. *Supp.* 281, *Pho.* 822).

This dactylic lament has the destruction of the city as its subject (596, 597–8, 599–600, 601–2) and ends with general expressions concerning the extent of Trojan troubles and the *gnōmē* that the dead forget their woes.

—This lament could be treated as an epode or could be restored as two responsive stanzas (595–600 ~ 601–6) each consisting of six hexameters (thus Diggle). It is clear that 601 and 602 must be divided between two singers (*δόμον* in 602 makes sense only as the object of *δακρύω*, not of *ὁρᾶιϲ*) and 603–6 assigned to the first of them. If we are to make two stanzas of these dactylic lines, it must be plausible to divide 595 and 596 between the same two singers and to give 597–600 to the first of them. Then 604 and 605, four dactyls each, must be convincingly supplemented. It would be reassuring to those wishing to create responsion if we had elsewhere in tragedy whole responding stanzas in hexameters, but we do not (the dactyls at *Supp.* 271–85, for example, are a single stanza). At first glance 595 and 596 look like good candidates for division at the caesura (they are divided between two speakers by one or another of the mss.: see app. crit.) since 595a and 596a could be taken as a single utterance ('These are great longings for a city that has perished') and likewise 595b and 596b ('We are suffering, and woes are piled on woes'). But closer inspection reveals problems. In 595a the mention of *these* great longings for a perished city lacks a reference: the last two stanzas have been about Hector and Priam (or Hector if we restore differently), and Troy was last mentioned in passing at 586. In 595b 'Unhappy woman, we are suffering these woes' (reading Burges's *ϲχετλία*) is jejune. Furthermore, as Willink unpub. points out, it is normal for the vocative of *ϲχέτλιοϲ* (or the nominative used in direct address) to be preceded by *ὦ* (see *Alc.* 824, *El.* 1152, *Andr.* 1179, *Hec.* 783, *Ba.* 358, *Ant.* 47, *Phil.* 364, 930) or *ἰώ* (*Alc.* 741). Additionally, 597 does not look like the beginning of a new utterance since the dative of cause goes better with 596b than with 596a. In view of these difficulties, we should consider whether Q in omitting speaker changes at 595b, 596, and 596a (joined in the last two omissions by V) is correct in making 595–600 an undivided utterance. This on balance seems the more plausible option.

595–600 In order to make an informed choice of speaker we must determine what is being said. The main point of 597–600 is that 'your son', because of the malice of the gods, escaped death and brought about the destruction of the city, exposing corpses near Athena's temple and bringing the yoke of slavery on the Trojans who survived. Both Andromache and the Chorus are possible speakers, and the lines are assigned to the latter in the mss. Still, 608–9 are more the kind of sentiments (unobjectionable, non-confrontational) we expect from a chorus, and giving those lines to the Chorus Leader with the mss. suggests that she has not been a participant in the preceding *amoibaion*. I have accordingly assigned 595–600 to Andromache.

I know of only two ways to make a sensible single utterance out of 595–6, and each involves finding an adjective to go with τάδε ἄλγη (an adjective being necessary if 595b is not to be tautologous). (1) Willink unpub. wants the sense 'great, poor woman, are the woes we are suffering', and he proposes μεγάλ', ὦ cχετλία, τάδε πάcχομεν ἄλγη, making transmitted μεγάλοι neuter and adding the expected ὦ to the vocative of cχέτλιοc. (For cχέτλιοc in this sense see *Hec.* 783.) To precede this, all that is necessary is an expression of assent to Hecuba's preceding wish for death, perhaps ὧδε ποθῶ, 'that is my longing', i.e. death. The proper punctuation would be a raised period introducing causal asyndeton. (2) Alternatively cχέτλια ἄλγη makes a good collocation, 'cruel are the woes we are suffering'. The short alpha can be eliminated by writing οἵδε πόθοι μεγάλοι cχέτλι' <ὡc> τάδε πάcχομεν ἄλγη, 'these longings (i.e. for death) are great since cruel are the woes we are suffering'. (The supplement <ὡc> was proposed by Kirchhoff 1852: 68.) In both cases I would construe οἰχομέναc πόλεωc with ἄλγη, 'woes for a city that is no more'. For the various meanings of cχέτλιοc (it can mean 'cruel' or 'miserable') see Finglass on *El.* 887/8–890.

596 οἰχομέναc πόλεωc, ἐπὶ δ' ἄλγεcιν ἄλγεα κεῖται: the loss of city supervenes on the loss of Hector and Priam.

597–600 Andromache attributes the ruin of Troy to the malice of the gods, who caused Paris to escape death. He was rescued not only at his birth, when he was raised by the shepherd who was to expose him, but also when he was on trial (see Introduction § 3.2.5, n. 90 and text thereto for indications that the prosecution asked for the death penalty), and again when the murder plot of Deiphobus and Hecuba was thwarted by the revelation of his identity (see Introduction § 3.2.9).

600 γυψὶ φέρειν τέταται: possibly an allusion to *Il.* 1.5 and (for vultures) 4.237, 11.161–2, 16.836, 18.271, and 22.42–3.

ἥνυcε: Willink unpubl. restores the aspirate in the light of West's Aeschylus *praefatio* p. xxx.

601–6 Hecuba's 601a and 602a make a single utterance, and Andromache's 601b and 602b a separate one. Mastronarde's term for this (1979: 61n25) is 'interlacing of syntax'.

—In view of the above, we must conclude that both 601 and 602 are to be divided between singers at the caesura (the mss. erroneously omit the division of 601). Manuscript speaker assignments have no authority, and VPQ have *Χο.* at 602a, *Εκ.* at 602b, and *Αν.* at 603. Several things speak in favour of Murray's assignments. It is Andromache who is in the process of leaving Troy, so 601b belongs to her, and so therefore does 602b, whose reference to childbed fits better in her mouth as she is holding Astyanax. The vocative in 603 is characteristic of Hecuba (see 159, 182, 256, 345, 349, 500, 628, 790, 1171, 1209, 1303), who would thus also get 601a and 602a. Possible counter-evidence is 606, ὁ θανὼν δ' ἐπιλάθεται ἀλγέων. Andromache later argues the desirability of death as the ender of trouble (636–8, 679–80) and Hecuba the claims of hope (701–5), so the line might seem out of character for the latter. But this is not decisive evidence as Hecuba elsewhere is inconsistent with herself.

601 καταλειπομέναν cε δακρύω: 'I weep for you as I leave you behind' (lit. 'as you are being left behind'). —P's nominative middle is less awkward sense, but the middle is difficult to justify. Jacobs's κατερειπομέναν (1790: 96–7) is attractive at first sight, but in fact neither Troy nor the house where Andromache gave birth are at the moment being 'razed to the ground', and both are being left behind. What claims the Trojan women's attention now is their leaving Troy: see 603.

603 ἐρημόπολιc μάτηρ ἀπολείπεται ὑμῶν: both Lee and my Loeb take ἐρημόπολιc μάτηρ as Hecuba, but it seems more likely to be a periphrasis for Troy. For μήτηρ as land of one's birth see LSJ s.v. I.3, who cite among other passages *Sept.* 416 and Pi. *I.* 1.1. For an adjective in -πολιc modifying something that is a city, see 1291–2. This is a case of the compound adjective whose second element is superfluous because it means the same as the modified noun: see 122–5n.

604–5 Since all the other lines in this sequence are full hexameters, 604–5 might be thought lacunose, as suggested by Seidler. But there is nothing clearly wrong with the sense. For the 4da length among hexameters see *Metrical analysis* above. The uncontracted dactyls of 605 suggest that πένθεα (Willink unpub.) in 604 is likely to be right.

604 ἰάλεμοc: this word for 'wailing' or 'lament' is a favourite of Eur.: see 1304, *Supp.* 281, *Herc.* 110, *Pho.* 1033, and *Or.* 1390, plus *Rhes.* 895. It derives from the cry ἰή: see Liapis on *Rhes.* 895–8.

605–6 'Tears following upon tears (i.e. the woes associated with them) are being poured out for our house.'

608–9 The paradox that tears and poetry consisting in lament may be sweet to those in misfortune see 120–1n. On μοῦcα in Eur. see 511–12n.

610–33. Distichomythic interchange between Andromache and Hecuba

In this passage spoken lament (610–15) is followed by Hecuba's telling Andromache about Cassandra and by Andromache's telling Hecuba about the sacrifice of Polyxena.

610–20 Andromache's question (610–11) implies that Hecuba as mother of the man who killed the most Greeks must feel the enslavement of his widow with peculiar intensity. Hecuba's reply (612–13) generalizes Andromache's point into the commonplace that the gods often raise what is of no account and destroy what is of great repute. Andromache (614–15) again points to her own case, that she and her son have become booty: she accepts Hecuba's description of the gods' destruction of the mighty but describes the latter as 'the noble', which might refer to high birth but equally might imply moral desert. Hecuba (616–17) once more generalizes, then cites her own loss of Cassandra. Andromache (618–19) reacts with sympathy and says that Hecuba has yet a further grief. Hecuba (620–1) again generalizes by insisting on her own sorrow and its incomparable magnitude. It is hard to know to what extent these lines characterize Hecuba as self-absorbed and to what extent they are written as they are to wring the last drop of pathos from the situation. In light of Hecuba's insistence in the *amoibaion* on her own troubles we are perhaps entitled to suspect that characterization may play a role.

611 ***τάδ' εἰcορᾷιc***: similar indignant questions at *Med.* 404, *Hipp.* 1363, *El.* 239, *Herc.* 1127, *Ba.* 550, and *Aj.* 364.

612 ***πυργοῦc'***: this metaphorical sense, 'raise high', is not found in Homer, where the verb's one occurrence (*Od.* 11.264) is literal. Wilamowitz on *Herc.* 475 says that the metaphorical use belongs exclusively to the fifth century with its joy in building. But Stieber 2011: 105 notes that it is absent from Soph. It is a verb characteristic of Eur.

613 ***τὸ μηδὲν ὄντα***: for τὸ μηδέν as 'of no account' see above on 412.—Elmsley (on *Hcld.* 168) restores the singular article that is idiomatic in expressions for 'nullity'. Nauck 1862: 144–5 and Moorhouse 1965: 39n1 defend what is transmitted on the grounds that τὰ μηδὲν ὄντα should be a further attributive specifying what τὰ μέν refers to, but since the article in τὰ δὲ δοκοῦντ' is not pronominal but simply the marker of an attributive participle, it seems better to take τὰ μέν closely with ὄντα.

τὰ δὲ δοκοῦντ' ἀπώλεcαν: for absolute δοκέω, 'enjoy reputation', see LSJ s.v. II.5. For the (uncommon) ellipsis of εἶναί τι with δοκέω Lee cites

Hec. 294–5, and Gregory *ad loc.* cites Dodds on Plat. *Gor.* 472a2, as well as Smyth § 1269. For the gnomic aorist coupled with a present see 693 with 689.

614 **ἀγόμεθα λεία cὺν τέκνωι:** 'I am being taken away as plunder together with my son.' Like the contents of the wagon Andromache is λεία, 'plundered goods', but the verb used, ἄγειν, is one applied to sentient booty, such as livestock (another meaning of λεία): see above on 18–21. For singular λεία in apposition to the subject of a plural verb see *Ba.* 56 and Diggle 1971: 42, restoring κῶμοc in a similar function.

616–17 **τὸ τῆc ἀνάγκηc δεινόν:** 'Fate is a dreadful thing': the periphrastic τὸ τῆc ἀνάγκηc means no more than ἡ ἀνάγκη. On such periphrases see Smyth § 1299.

618–21 Andromache reacts (φεῦ φεῦ) to the announcement that Cassandra has been forcibly removed but sees a precedent in Ajax's removal of Cassandra from Athena's altar. She also (619) has a further set of woes to report. Hecuba (620–1) in effect discounts in advance any surprise on her part: her woes are numberless, and one woe competes with another.

618 **ἄλλοc... δεύτεροc:** for the pleonasm cf. χἀτέρουc ἄλλουc at *Supp.* 573, where Diggle prints a conjecture but Collard *ad loc.* defends the paradosis.

νοcεῖc δὲ χἄτερα: 'But you have other (a second set of) woes.'

620 'Yes (γ'), [woes] of which I have (ἔcτί μοι) neither the measure nor the [means of] counting.' For assentient γε see *GP* 130–1. Again Hecuba ignores the particular in favour of the general and trumps Andromache's 'second set' with 'a countless number'.

621 **κακῶι κακὸν γὰρ εἰc ἅμιλλαν ἔρχεται:** for γάρ in third place Lee cites *Ion* 690 ἄτοποc ἄτοπα γὰρ παραδίδωμί coι, where the conjunction, as here, comes after a polyptoton. For the metaphor of woes vying with woes see *Supp.* 71–2.

622–33 Andromache reveals that Polyxena is dead (622–3): she has seen and adorned her body and lamented it (626–7). Andromache's news of her death (622–3) elicits from Hecuba (624–5) no more than the recognition that Talthybius had spoken in riddles but truly. Hecuba's next couplet (628–9) recognizes the awfulness of her death, thereby setting up Andromache's couplet (630–1) on the preferability of death and Hecuba's reply (632–3). This last motivates Andromache's long speech (636–83).

622–3 'Polyxena is dead, having been slaughtered at the grave of Achilles as a gift to a lifeless corpse.' Such a compressed announcement would in real life evoke a request for elaboration, but Eur. does not wish to dwell on Polyxena's death. The last phrase underlines the pointlessness of her death. Contrast *Hec.*, where Achilles' spirit must be appeased, and Odysseus makes a strong case to the Greeks (*Hec.* 130–40, 303–31) that his accusations of ingratitude must be answered by giving him Polyxena, the prize he feels he deserves.

624–5 'That is [the meaning of] the riddling utterance Talthybius spoke, true but unclearly spoken.' This refers to 264–71. The paradox *οὐ ϲαφῶϲ . . . ϲαφέϲ* is Euripidean: cf. *Alc.* 521, *Hel.* 138, and the parody of the Euripidean oxymoron at Ar. *Ach.* 396. Note the inherent ambiguity in *ϲαφήϲ*, which can mean 'true' as well as 'clear'.

627 **ἔκρυψα πέπλοιϲ κἀπεκοψάμην νεκρόν:** dressing the corpse for burial and making a lament over it was part of the duty of female relatives. The middle *ἀποκόπτομαι* means 'beat one's own breast'. For such a verb with a further object see KG 1.299.

628–9 When an interjection is repeated, *μάλ' αὖθιϲ* is often used with the second occurrence: see *Med.* 1008–9, *Hec.* 628–9, 1035–7, *Pho.* 1067–9, *Or.* 1018–20, and the examples in other authors cited by Finglass on *El.* 1415–16.

προϲφαγμάτων: on the genitive of exclamation see on 579 above. The prefix in *πρόϲφαγμα* seems to be without special meaning both here, at *Hec.* 41 and 265, and at *IT* 243 and 458. Casabona 1966: 170–4 discusses these passages and the cases where the word indicates a preparatory or preliminary sacrifice.

ὡϲ κακῶϲ διόλλυϲαι: with verbs of perishing *κακῶϲ* seems to mean 'painfully'. Hecuba's present tense seems to mark the proceeding as having duration and being vividly present to her mind.

630 **ὄλωλεν ὡϲ ὄλωλεν:** the effect of this and similar tautological expressions (see Mastronarde on *Med.* 889, Denniston on *El.* 1141, Willink on *Or.* 79, and Johnstone 1980) is to discourage further discussion of a topic. Like the colloquial English 'it is what it is', such tautologies often express resignation. Slightly different are *Hec.* 1000, *El.* 1122, and *IA* 649, where such language serves the purpose of avoiding an outright lie.

630–1 **ἐμοῦ | ζώϲηϲ γ' ὄλωλεν εὐτυχεϲτέρωι πότμωι:** 'She is dead by a luckier fate than mine, who am alive.' This is a *comparatio compendiaria*: grammatically, Polyxena's fate is being compared to Andromache herself rather than to Andromache's fate. See Smyth § 1076 and KG 2.310–11.

632 **οὐ ταὐτόν:** i.e. 'quite different'. On the figure of litotes see KG 2.180 and Smyth §§ 3032 and 2694. By itself the neuter *αὐτό* never gets a final *nu*, which belongs only to the masculine singular accusative, but if it coalesces by crasis with the definite article, a *nu* is usually added: in the extant plays of Eur. there are some thirty-eight instances, guaranteed by metre, of ταὐτόν and only three guaranteed instances of ταὐτό. The usage of other poets on this point is treated by Barrett on *Hipp.* 1178–9.

βλέπειν: for this verb, without object, as a synonym for 'to be alive', see *Alc.* 142, *Hec.* 311, *IT* 718, *Hel.* 583 and 1011 (plus the non-Euripidean *IA* 1612); see also *Ag.* 677; *Aj.* 962, 1067, and *OC* 1438.

κατθανεῖν: strictly speaking it is the state of being dead (perfect), not the act of dying (aorist), that should stand in contrast to 'being alive'. For similar inaccuracy see 636 below. For the opposite inaccuracy, perfect instead of aorist, see *Aj.* 479–80, ἀλλ' ἢ καλῶc ζῆν ἢ καλῶc τεθνηκέναι | τὸν εὐγενῆ χρή.

633 'For the one is nothing[ness], while in the other there reside hopes.' For οὐδέν as either 'non-existence' or '[counting for] nothing' see *IA* 1250–2 τὸ φῶc τόδ' ἀνθρώποιcιν ἥδιcτον βλέπειν, | τὰ νέρθε δ' οὐδέν· μαίνεται δ' ὃc εὔχεται | θανεῖν. κακῶc ζῆν κρεῖccον ἢ καλῶc θανεῖν, fr. 532 τοὺc ζῶνταc εὖ δρᾶν· κατθανὼν δὲ πᾶc ἀνὴρ | γῆ καὶ cκιά· τὸ μηδὲν εἰc οὐδὲν ῥέπει, Adesp. Trag. 95 πᾶcιν δὲ θνητοῖc βούλομαι παραινέcαι | τοὐφήμερον ζῆν ἡδέωc· ὁ γὰρ θανὼν | τὸ μηδέν ἐcτι καὶ cκιὰ κατὰ χθονόc.

[634–5], 636–83. Andromache's *rhesis*

In reply to Hecuba's *dum spiramus, speramus*, Andromache argues that her situation is really hopeless and death is preferable. Her very virtues have been her undoing, for her reputation as a good woman reached the ears of the Greeks, and Neoptolemus, the son of her husband's slayer, has chosen her as his concubine. This leaves her with a choice of evils: either she opens her heart to her new bedmate and is disloyal to Hector, which would make her less loyal than a brute beast and forgetful of all Hector's virtues, or she hates her new master and so is hated by him in return. Pleasurable as it is to imagine happiness, she can imagine none for herself in these circumstances, and Polyxena, whose troubles have been ended by her death, has the happier lot.

[634–5] As Diggle's app. crit. points out succinctly, these lines do not fit their context. There is no reason for Andromache to refer to her own words as 'a most beautiful speech', nor is it the kind of speech to 'put delight into' Hecuba's heart, nor is ὦ τεκοῦcα at all plausible. The last was emended to οὐ τεκοῦcα by Musgrave, who compared *Ion* 1324. The other two are intractable: with Kirchhoff's conjecture (1852) κάλλιcτον γόνον Andromache absurdly calls Hecuba 'mother of a most beautiful son' (for the meaning of καλόc and αἰcχρόc as applied to persons see

1059n); the second problem is untouched. In addition, Hecuba has already been apostrophized at 610–11. The couplet may have come from another play, added here by an actor who felt that 636 was too abrupt a beginning. For this motive see Haslam 1979. (I cannot explain why only 634 and not 635 is missing in P and Stobaeus.)

636, [637], 638–40 These lines are the preliminary statement of Andromache's thesis, argued in detail in 641–83, that since her own life is hopeless, Polyxena's lot, death, is preferable. She begins in abstract fashion by asserting the equivalence of being dead and not having been born. She explains this by noting that neither the dead nor the unborn have knowledge of trouble. By contrast, a living person like herself who has fallen into misfortune feels distress because of his former happiness.

636 The equation of two articular infinitives is an abstract means of expression. The idea that death and never having been born are somehow equivalent states is hard to parallel in literature of the classical period. Slightly different is the idea, first seen at Theogn. 425–9, that never to be born and to die as quickly as possible are the best and second-best options for a human being: *πάντων μὲν μὴ φῦναι ἐπιχθονίοιϲιν ἄριϲτον, | μηδ' ἐϲιδεῖν αὐγὰϲ ὀξέοϲ ἠελίου, | φύντα δ' ὅπωϲ ὤκιϲτα πύλαϲ Ἀΐδαο περῆϲαι | καὶ κεῖϲθαι πολλὴν γῆν ἐπιεϲϲάμενον*. The same sentiment at *OC* 1225–9 *μὴ φῦναι τὸν ἅπαντα νι- | κᾶι λόγον· τὸ δ', ἐπεὶ φανῆι, | βῆναι †κεῖθεν ὅθεν† περ ἥ- | κει, πολὺ δεύτερον, ὡϲ τάχιϲτα*. Eur. fr. 449 expresses the related idea that the newly born are to be pitied and the newly dead congratulated: *ἐχρῆν γὰρ ἡμᾶϲ ϲύλλογον ποιουμένουϲ | τὸν φύντα θρηνεῖν εἰϲ ὅϲ' ἔρχεται κακά· | τὸν δ' αὖ θανόντα καὶ πόνων πεπαυμένον | χαίρονταϲ εὐφημοῦνταϲ ἐκπέμπειν δόμων*. For closer, if later, parallels see 638n.

[637] Though the line is not genuine here (see below), it could well be from Eur. or another tragic poet, perhaps a roughly parallel passage that managed to be copied into the text of our play. For the idea that death is superior to a life accompanied by pain or grief see Aesch. fr. 177 (*Hoplon Krisis*); *PV* 750–1; *Hec.* 375–8 and *Hel.* 296–8. For the related idea that death is the healer of (or freer from) human woes see Aesch. *Supp.* 802–3, *PV* 747–51, fr. 255.2–3 (*Philoctetes*), fr. 353; Soph. *El.* 1170, *Trach.* 1173, 1209, *OC* 955, fr. 698 *ἀλλ' ἔϲθ' ὁ θάνατοϲ λοῖϲθοϲ ἰατρὸϲ νόϲων*, *Hcld.* 595–6, *Hipp.* 1373, *Tro.* 607, *Or.* 1522, and fr. 449.5. These passages are distinct from those expressing the idea that death is preferable to disgrace, e.g. *Aj.* 479–80, but there can be overlap, especially since *ζῆν κακῶϲ* can describe both a dishonourable and a painful life: in this respect Soph. fr. 488, *τὸ μὴ γὰρ εἶναι κρεῖϲϲον ἢ τὸ ζῆν κακῶϲ* (*Peleus*), and Critias fr. 12 [= Eur., fr. 596 Nauck], *οὔκουν τὸ μὴ ζῆν* *κρεῖϲϲόν ἐϲτ᾽ ἢ ζῆν κακῶϲ;* (*Peirithous*), are ambiguous to us, who cannot read them in context.

—Because 636 is both abstract and not a commonplace, the line is in need of explication. The explication is supplied by 638, that what is common to the unborn and the dead is that they have no knowledge of troubles. (See 638n, which argues for a lacuna.) In between stands 637, which is a commonplace in need of no explanation and is not explained by what follows. I have deleted it after Cron 1874: 336.

638 This line must explain why not being born and being dead are equivalent states. My supplement, giving the required explanation, can be translated 'For <the dead man> feels no <more> pain <than the unborn>, having <no> perception of his troubles.' That the dead and the unborn are alike is the burden of 636 and that the dead do not experience trouble that of 641–2. This may well be the first occurrence of an idea to be found in Lucretius, who argues (3.832–42) that just as Romans of his own day felt no pain when the Carthaginian was ravaging Italy long before they were born, so they will feel none after their death. There is a similar comparison at 3.972–5. The idea receives its fullest expression in Housman's poem 'Be still, my soul, be still' (*A Shropshire Lad* XLVIII, Burnett 1997: 51–2). For the perfect of *αἰϲθάνομαι* as equivalent to a present see e.g. *Hipp.* 1403 *ᾔϲθημαι*; Plat. *Pol.* 272b3 ('you know'); Xen. *Mem.* 1.4.13.5, *Cyr.* 1.1.6.5 ('we think we know'); and Thuc. 7.66.1.4 (where *ᾔϲθηται* explicates *εἰδέναι*). That the participle in *οὐδὲν τῶν κακῶν ᾐϲθημένοϲ* refers, *pace* Bluck 1961: 125, to a present state, not a prior action, is indicated by 642, *κοὐδὲν οἶδε τῶν αὑτῆϲ κακῶν*. See further Diggle 1994: 462–3.

—Attempts to construe the line as transmitted are futile: the subject of *ἀλγεῖ* cannot be supplied out of *κατθανεῖν*, and *οὐδὲν* cannot do double duty ('feels *no* pain, having *no* perception of his woes'). Various defences of what is transmitted, various conjectures not involving a lacuna, and some alternative supplements are discussed in Appendix B. Seidler's lacuna is expertly placed: it restores a second negative that is badly needed and allows us to supply a subject for the verb as well as accounting neatly for the omission.

639–40 The sense of the couplet is clear: when someone falls from good fortune into bad, he is disturbed by the contrast with his former happiness. (For the idea see 195–6n.) Unlike some earlier scholars, who took *τῆϲ πάροιθ᾽ εὐπραξίαϲ* as a separative genitive ('wanders in his mind from his former happiness'), Bluck 1961: 125–6, citing KG 1.388–9, suggests treating it as a genitive of cause and translates 'is distressed in his mind because of his former prosperity'. He has, however, no good parallel for *ἀλάομαι* in this sense (at *Aj.* 23 the word means something different). To replace ἀλᾶται Musgrave proposed ἀcᾶται, which is not quite the right sense ('feels disgust'). Better sense is given by Schenkl's ἀλύει, 'is distraught', though explaining the corruption would be difficult. I have daggered.

641–83 Andromache descends to the particular, contrasting Polyxena's painless state (641–2) with her own pain (643–78). In the latter there is not only the sharp change of fortune mentioned in 639–40 and recapitulated at 677–8 but also two further elements. First, it was her virtuous behaviour toward Hector that has led to the intolerable situation of her sharing a bed with the son of his killer: her reputation reached the Greeks, and Neoptolemus wanted her for his own. Second, her loyalty to her dead husband, which is a virtue, means that she cannot open her heart in welcome to her new lord, and if she is true to her principles, she will be hated by him. The irony of being brought low by your very virtues occurs in *Alexandros*: see fr. 62i, οἴμοι, θανοῦμαι διὰ τὸ χρήcιμον φρενῶν, ἣ τοῖcιν ἄλλοιc γίγνεται cωτηρία, and almost certainly in *Palamedes*, where the hero is falsely convicted thanks to his own invention of writing. See also notes on 742–3 and 744.

641 **κείνη δ'**: since Andromache is illustrating the generality she made in the previous five lines, we might have expected γάρ. For δέ in place of γάρ see *GP* 169–70.

642 **τέθνηκε κοὐδὲν οἶδε**: parataxis for hypotaxis since logically we should expect τεθνηκυῖα οὐδὲν οἶδε.

643–4 'I, however, who aimed at fair renown, though I obtained it to a high degree, have failed to obtain good fortune.'

645–56 Andromache explains that she strove to excel in wifely virtue, describing it as it was understood by fifth-century Athenian males. Much of her description is paralleled in other Euripidean plays. She did not go out of doors: cf. Heracles' daughter at *Hcld.* 474–7 and the Paedagogus' warning to Antigone not to be seen in public at *Pho.* 193–201. She did not invite women into her house, for their communications lead to corruption: cf. Hermione's criticism of her female companions at *Andr.* 930–53 and Phaedra's virtuous repudiation of μακραὶ λέcχαι at *Hipp.* 384. She was quiet and calm toward her husband, not trying to get her way on every occasion but prepared to win at times and lose at others: cf. Andromache's description of her complaisance at her husband's amours at *Andr.* 213–31.

645 **ἃ γὰρ γυναιξὶ cώφρον' ἔcθ' ηὑρημένα**: modest and chaste behaviour is treated as something discovered or invented at some point by women.

647–50 'In the first place, in circumstances where—whether or not blame attaches to (particular) women—the very fact of not remaining inside brings with it bad repute, letting go of any desire for this I remained indoors.'

649 ***ἥτις οὐκ ἔνδον μένει***: for the concrete construction whereby an agent is named instead of an action, see Barrett on *Hipp.* 426–7.

652 ***εἰσεφρούμην***: on -*φρέω* or -*πίφρημι* (only in compounds) see Barrett on *Hipp.* 866–7. There is a full discussion of this accident-prone verb in Cobet 1862: 441–5.

653 ***οἴκοθεν***: 'from my own resources': see LSJ s.v. A.2. Andromache needed no one else to teach her how to live. The same point is made by *ἐξήρκουν ἐμοί*.

655–6 'I knew in what matters it was right to win a victory over my husband and in what I should concede victory to him.' The two things Andromache knew are variations on 'when to be ruled and when to rule'. We might be surprised to hear a woman who regards submissiveness as a duty talk of victories over a husband, but even in patriarchal ancient Athens our sources allow us to see that women, though in principle powerless in the political realm, could exert influence at home. In the first expression the neuter plural relative is accusative of respect. In the second *νίκην ὧν ἐχρῆν παριέναι* means *ταῦτα ὧν νίκην ἐχρῆν παριέναι*, 'those things whose victory I should concede'. In both cases *ἐχρῆν* denotes a past, and not an unfulfilled, obligation.

657–8 It is ironic that Andromache's very virtues, coming to the notice of the Greeks, have proved her undoing. A different kind of irony results if we take seriously Pericles' words at Thuc. 2.45.2 that a virtuous woman will not be the subject of comment for good or ill. Thucydides' views, however, could well be idiosyncratic.

660 ***αὐθεντῶν***: if someone has killed a member of your family, both he and his kin stand in the relation of *αὐθέντης* to you: see Zucker 1962.

663 ***κακὴ . . . τῶι θανόντι***: for *κακός*, 'disloyal' or 'ungrateful' (not explicitly recognized by LSJ), see *Med.* 84, *Herc.* 223, 569, *Hel.* 726, 1632, *Or.* 424, 740, and 1057.

664 ***δεσπόταις***: Neoptolemus is the only one the poet has in mind. To be sure, in *Andr.* Hector's widow is hated by the wife and father-in-law of Neoptolemus, but this is not because of her loyalty to Hector's memory. On the allusive plural see 1016–17n. —Nauck 1862: 146 says that in the transmitted text both *τόνδε* and *δεσπόταις* refer awkwardly to the same person. He proposes for *στυγοῦσ'* either *φιλοῦσ'* or, reviving a conjecture of Lenting 1821: 83, *στέργουσ'*. But of the two expressions for Neoptolemus the first simply designates him, whereas the second shows why incurring his hatred would be a bad thing.

μισήσομαι: for the future middle in place of the future passive see 1278, Smyth §§ 808–9 and 1738 and KG 1.114–17. The dative of agent is more normal with the perfect passive stem and verbal adjectives in -τόϲ and -τέοϲ, but examples in other tenses may be found at KG 1.422.

665–72 The essence of Andromache's case here is that *although* it is commonly said that a single night of love serves to lessen a woman's enmity to a man, she regards such a transfer of affections as contemptible and unworthy of a human being: even a beast of burden, *although* not endowed with speech and reason, does not bear the yoke easily when separated from its yokefellow. The concessive points are introduced paratactically with καίτοι. The reply to the first takes the form of asyndeton (667). The second concession follows the main idea.

665–6 For the generality that sharing a bed with someone leads to good will toward that person see Tecmessa's explanation at *Aj.* 485–91 why she wishes Ajax well. Scodel 1998: 137–43 explores the various ways in which the ongoing relationship of enforced concubinage can cause the woman to transfer her affections from the family she has lost to the man who has destroyed them. See also Gregory 1991: 106–7.

667 **ἀπέπτυϲ'**: 'I reject with contempt.' On the instantaneous or tragic aorist, see 53n.

668 **καινοῖϲι λέκτροιϲ**: dative of cause, 'because of a new sexual liaison'. These words have the same referent as ἄλλον.

669–70 Andromache draws a non-sexual analogy: a horse that is unyoked from its familiar yoke partner will be affected by the loss.

671–2 'And yet a beast is unendowed with speech and incapable of reason and inferior in nature.'

ξυνέϲει τ' ἄχρηϲτον: the adjective is active here, 'making no use of'.

673–8 The section before her final summary, taking the form of an apostrophe to Hector, emphasizes the misery of losing so good a man and being enslaved.

673 'In you, dear Hector, I had a husband to content me.' There is understatement in ἀρκοῦντά μοι. For this sense of the verb see LSJ s.v. III.2.

674 —At *GP* 501 Denniston lists instances where a series begins asyndetically and then has a further item attached by τε or καί (A, B, C τε or A, B, C τε καὶ D). Still, the series 'great in intelligence, birth, wealth, and bravery' has seemed suspicious to some. Kirchhoff 1855 punctuates so as to take ξυνέϲει with ἀρκοῦντά μοι and the other three datives with μέγαν, but this seems artificial. Paley is inclined to delete the line. The occurrence of ξυνέϲει at the beginning of 672 and 674 (neighbouring lines in mss. where two verses are written per line) is suspicious. Perhaps a scribe, his eye wandering temporarily to 672, copied ξυνέϲει in 674, obliterating the original word. That could have been an adverb, e.g. πάντωϲ. Kayser proposed πόϲιν, which also gives good sense.

675–6 'You received me as a virgin from my father's house and were the first to yoke my maidenhood in love.'

ἀκήρατον: lit. 'unharmed'; the word means 'untainted', whether by sexual contact of any kind (it is used of a virginal meadow at *Hipp*. 73 and 76) or by adultery (see *Or*. 575).

676 **ἐζεύξω:** for ζεύγνυμι in a sexual context see *Hipp*. 545–9 and Barrett on *Hipp*. 545–6.

677 **ναυcθλοῦμαι:** 'I shall be taken by ship.' Cf. 162 for the verb. This could be present used as future, as translated above (see *MT* § 32) or it could be a present used in a non-literal sense, 'I am being carried ('shipped') off'.

679–83 In her peroration to Hecuba she compares Polyxena's fate with her own and explicitly denies that she can have hope (cf. 633).

682–3 'Nor am I deceived in my mind [into believing] that I will have any good fortune, pleasant though it may be to dream.' For κλέπτω, 'deceive', see LSJ s.v. II. For a neuter expression instead of an adverb with πράττω, 'fare', see on 447. For parataxis (δ') in place of hypotaxis see above on 665–72.

684–5 The Chorus Leader's comment, as usual, is general and fairly colourless: 'You have come to the same point in misfortune [as I have], and by lamenting your own [case] you teach me where I stand in woe.' For the genitive with ἐc ταὐτόν (a sort of genitive of the whole) see 1036 below and *Pho*. 38. This is a variation on the idiom, found in oratorical prose and in Eur., but not in Aesch. or Soph., εἰc τοῦτο/τόδε + genitive + verb of going + ὥcτε, for which see Mastronarde on *Pho*. 963.

686–705. Hecuba's *rhesis*

In the first part (686–96) Hecuba contrasts two situations at sea, one where the sailors think they have a chance of surviving a storm and one where they do not, and says that the latter is like her own situation, so overcome is she with misfortune. In the second (697–705) she urges Andromache to forget about Hector and win Neoptolemus' affections: this, she says, will benefit her son, whose sons may one day refound Troy. (She does not explain why, if she herself is without hope, she is encouraging Andromache to entertain hopes for herself and Astyanax.)

686–96 The comparison between political trouble and a storm at sea goes back to Archil. frr. 105–6 *IEG*; Alcaeus frr. 6, 73, 208 Voigt; and Theogn. [667–82]. (See Brock 2013: 53–67 for a survey of the image in Greek literature and Finglass on *OT* 22–4, references I owe to PJF.) Tragic examples are *Sept.* 114–15, 208–10, 343–4, 758–60, and 795–6; *OT* 22–4, 922–3, *Ant.* 162–3; Eur. *Supp.* 473–5, and *Pho.* 859–60. Hecuba is not speaking of the city's troubles but her own. Here, as in previous parts of this scene, her response to Andromache's woes is to dilate upon her own: see above on 578, 582–3, 584–6, 588–90, 610–20.

686–7 For paintings as a source of knowledge cf. *Hipp.* 451, 1004–5 οὐκ οἶδα πρᾶξιν τήνδε πλὴν λόγωι κλύων | γραφῆι τε λεύccων, and *Eu.* 50–1.

687 **κλυοῦcα:** see 481–2n.

688 —In transmitted ναύταιc γὰρ ἢν μὲν μέτριοc ἧι χειμὼν φέρειν, the dative must be construed with μέτριοc φέρειν, but the latter needs no qualifier. In the next line ἔχουcι needs a subject. Hence Diggle's highly attractive nominative, which I have adopted.

690–1 Hecuba describes the organized teamwork of sailors at their respective jobs.

690 **ἐπὶ λαίφεcιν βεβῶc:** for ἐπί + dative as 'in charge of, looking after' see LSJ B.III.6. For the perfect participle of βαίνω, translatable as 'standing', see *Cyc.* 15 (where it is plausibly conjectured), *El.* 777, *Herc.* 178, 1112, *Pho.* 172, and *Ba.* 646.

691–2 **ἢν δ᾽ ὑπερβάληι | πολὺc ταραχθεὶc πόντοc:** the finite verb is probably intransitive (see LSJ s.v. A.II.3 and add *Hipp.* 924), though it might mean 'overwhelms [them]'; πολύc is predicative, as at *Hipp.* 443, and it reinforces the idea of excess in ὑπερβάληι.

692–3 'Giving way before whatever may chance they yield themselves over to the motion of the waves.' There is an implied contrast between the τέχνη showed by the sailors and the element over which they have no control (τύχη). For the contrast see *IT* 89 and Polus' formulation at Plat. *Gor.* 448c5–7. As I argued above 102–4n, the despairing sailors give up the attempt to keep the ship at right angles to the force of the waves. For gnomic aorist coupled with present (689) see above on 613. —The mss. have the form δρομήμαcιν. Cobet 1873: 693 restored δραμ- here and at *Med.* 1180. In the latter place his conjecture was confirmed by a papyrus fragment. On the attestation of δραμ- and δρομ- in classical authors and the reasons for thinking the former correct see Finglass on *OT* 190/1–193/4, last paragraph.

694–5 **οὕτω δὲ κἀγὼ πόλλ᾽ ἔχουcα πήματα | ἄφθογγόc εἰμι καὶ παρεῖc᾽ ἔχω cτόμα:** 'So also I, who have so many woes, am mute, and letting them go I hold my tongue.' —On the conjecture in 695 see Diggle, *Studies* 66–7. (Diggle 1994: 521 assigns proper credit to Bothe 1802: 378.)

696 **δύcτηνοc κλύδων:** 'wave of misery'. For κλύδων as a metaphor for trouble Lee cites *Med.* 362, *IT* 316, *Ion* 60, and *Pho.* 859. See also 686–96n and Finglass on *Aj.* 205–7.

698 ***οὐ μὴ . . . cώcηι***: on *οὐ μή* + subjunctive see Goodwin § 295.

700 ***δέλεαρ . . . cῶν τρόπων***: Hecuba says that Andromache's honouring of Neoptolemus will be a bait or enticement to him, winning him over to her side. This part of Hecuba's exhortation may have reminded the audience (if they knew the play, which was probably not performed in Athens) of *Andr.* 206–28.

701 'And if you do this, you will gladden those you love, one and all.'

702–5 'And you might raise to manhood this my grandson as a very great boon to Troy, so that he may be the source from whom sons may later be born and settle it again and it will one day be a city.' For a relative clause with verb in the optative without *ἄν*, see *Alc.* 52 *ἔcτ' οὖν ὅπως Ἄλκηcτις ἐς γῆρας μόλοι;*, 113 *ἔcθ' ὅποι τις cτείλας παραλύcαι ψυχάν;*, *Hel.* 435–6; *Ag.* 620, *Cho.* 172; and *PV* 292. The antecedent of the relative is often omitted, as in *Alc.* 113, 'is there [a place] to which?' See also KG 2.419, *MT* § 241, and Fraenkel on *Ag.* 620. Unless with Wilamowitz 361 we delete 704 and write *κατοικίcειεν* in 705, it is not Astyanax himself but his descendants that Hecuba expects might refound Troy.

—The main problem with transmitted *ἵν' εἴ ποτε* is that there are two subordinating conjunctions but only one subordinate clause (having two verbs, *κατοικίcειαν* and *γένοιτ'*) to introduce. There are also two sets of variants in 704 to take into account. Seven principal ways of dealing with the conjunction problem have been proposed. (1) Diggle adopts the Aldine edition's *ἵν' οἵ ποτε | ἐκ coῦ γενόμενοι παῖδες*, but though Soph. frequently puts the article unaccompanied by any attributive just before line end with the noun in the next line (e.g. *OT* 231 *τὸ γὰρ | κέρδος*, 995 *τό τε | πατρῶιον αἷμα*, *Ant.* 67, 78, 238, 409, *Trach.* 383, 434, 742, *Phil.* 263, 449, 674, *OC* 265, 290, 351, 577), Eur. does not. Note further that if we enclose *ποτε* between the article and the aorist participle *γενόμενοι*, we make it difficult for it to refer to the future. (2) Pearson 1890 proposes *Τροίαι μεγίcτην ὠφέληcιν, εἴ ποτε | ἐκ coῦ κτλ.* The sense 'in the hope that, if haply' for *εἰ* + opt. is attested after a primary tense at Ar. *Av.* 120, but what is normal, to judge from *MT* § 489, is *ἐάν* + subjunctive. Furthermore, *ἐκ coῦ* in 704, required by this suggestion, means that pre-eminent importance is given to the fact that the children are Andromache's descendants, when it is arguably more important that they descend from Hector and the Trojan royal family. This applies also to (1), (3), and (4). (3) Murray repunctuates, making a parenthesis: *ἵν'—εἴ ποτε—ἐκ coῦ γενόμενοι παῖδες κτλ.* His parallel for the ellipsis is *Ion* 354, where ellipsis is introduced by himself and accepted by no one since. Biehl, who adopts this punctuation, cites passages where *εἴπερ ποτέ* (not *εἴ ποτε*) means 'if at any time in the past', which are irrelevant here. (4) Kirchhoff 1868 prints *εἴ νίν ποτε | ἐκ coῦ γενόμενοι παῖδες ὕcτερον πάλιν* | *κατοικίcειαν κτλ.*, '[a great benefit to Troy] if at a later time children descended from you should found her again and she should one day become a city', and regards *Ἴλιον* in 704 as a gloss on *νιν*. This is attractive since corruption of *ὕcτερον* to *Ἴλιον* is easier to explain than the reverse, and *EININ* is virtually an anagram of *INEI*. There is no redundancy in *ὕcτερον πάλιν* since the one word means 'later' and the other 'a second time'. Still, *ἐκ coῦ* is unappealing for the reason given above, and the future-less-vivid conditional clause treats the refounding of Troy as a remote possibility. (5) Nauck 1862: 147 writes *εἶναί ποτε*, and Lee, who prints it, cites *MT* § 774 for the 'redundant' *εἶναι*. This means we can adopt *ἐξ οὗ*, which gives better sense. Lee takes the clause *ἐξ οὗ* . . . *ἔτι* as a wish (with *οὗ* as connecting relative), though something more confident would arguably provide a better contrast between Hecuba's cheerful outlook and the bad news that is coming. (6) Mesk 1926: 13–14 suggests writing *ἦι* for *εἴ* and making a complete clause, with postponed conjunction, of *Τροίαι μέγιcτον ὠφέλημ' ἵν' ἦι ποτε*, followed by a colon. This leaves an independent clause (*οὗ* being connecting relative) to be an optative of wish, which for the reason given above seems a bit weak. (7) If we omit Mesk's colon after *ποτε*, as in the text I print, the relative clause has the function described above. In 704 I have adopted V's *ὕcτερον*, the reading recommended by the *utrum in alterum* principle: since Troy was mentioned in 702, it can be understood as object of *κατοικίcειαν*.

702 παῖδα τόνδε παιδόc: 'this grandson (of mine)'. We might expect the object of *ἐκθρέψειαc* to be the grandson of the subject and not of the speaker (read *παῖδα τοὐμοῦ*?), but for a parallel see *El.* 916, *κἄγημας αἰcχρῶc μητέρ'* ('You married my mother').

Staging: enter a herald (with servants: cf. 786) by the right *eisodos*. (His identity is discussed below on 707.)

706–89 This heart-rending scene, in which the Herald takes Astyanax from Andromache so that he may be hurled from the walls of Troy, is one of the two moments of deepest pathos in the play (the other is the *exodos*), not only because the death of a child is inherently affecting but also because the killing of Hector's son marks the end of Troy's existence. (Both themes are developed further in the *exodos*, where the boy is adorned for burial by Hecuba and the firing of the city marks the fulfilment of Hecuba's prophetic dream of giving birth to a firebrand.)

The scene dramatizes a narrative found in the *Ilias Parva* (*GEF* fr. 29), where the boy is killed by Neoptolemus, and the *Iliupersis* (*GEF* arg. 4), where his killer is Odysseus, and found in vase painting (*LIMC* s.v. Astyanax (I) 26–7). A version of the story seems to have been told by Stesichorus, though details are unclear (fr. 107 F. with commentary).

The story is alluded to by Homer: at *Iliad* 24.734–9 Andromache expresses the fear that after Hector's death some Greek, whose kinsman Hector has killed, will hurl the boy from the walls, and Priam (22.63–4) expresses a similar fear.

The function of this Herald in the rhetorical strategy of the play deserves to be discussed. As noted in the Introduction § 1.3.4, when the Herald wishes that someone more hard-hearted than himself had the duty of bearing his message, he implicitly indicts his masters for cruelty. But elsewhere (see Talthybius in the first episode and the Herald of the *exodos*) the portrayal of Greek heralds as decent and humane entails no such contrast with the other Greeks. In the introductory note to the first episode I suggested that the reason Eur., in contrast to his practice in *Hcld.* and *Supp.*, did not make the heralds of *Tro.* abusive is that it would be pointless for the audience to get worked up about how evil the Greeks are since it is in the last analysis the gods, not the Greeks, who are the destroyers of Troy: Eur. wants pathos and elegiac sadness, not outrage, to be the audience's response.

706–8 The entrance announcement as continuation of a preceding *rhesis* is common in prologues, e.g. *Alc.* 24–7 and *Hipp.* 51–7. For examples elsewhere see *Supp.* 394–8 and *El.* 107–11.

706 ἀλλ' ἐκ λόγου γὰρ ἄλλοϲ ἐκβαίνει λόγοϲ: the γάρ is anticipatory: see *GP* 68–70. For anticipatory γάρ in entrance announcements see, e.g., *Hipp.* 51 and *Hec.* 724. —ἐκ by itself could be temporal: see 495n. But none of the examples of ἐκβαίνω in LSJ shows the meaning 'come after, succeed'. The Greek says that the new topic 'comes out of' the old one, when in fact it does not, being introduced solely by the arrival of the herald. Lee's translation is 'another subject takes us away from this one'. Though wishful as a translation, this gives the sense we look for. To achieve it we need a transitive verb, so perhaps ἐκβάλλει, sc. ἡμᾶϲ, 'dislodges us'. I know of no passage that uses ἐκβάλλω in this sense, but its functional passive ἐκπίπτω is so used at *Herc.* 460 in the OCT. (There it is conjectural, the reading of L being ἧ πολύ με δόξηϲ ἐξέπαιϲαν. The transmitted verb might be genuine and the basis for a different reconstruction, and this suggests ἐκπαίει as another possibility here.)

707 τίν' αὖ δέδορκα τόνδ' Ἀχαιικὸν λάτριν: 'What Greek servant do I see here (τόνδ') this time (αὖ)?' This idiomatic combination of τίϲ and ὅδε (the demonstrative cannot be translated as 'this' without changing the sentence structure) is highly characteristic of Eur.: see 1256, *Cyc.* 222, *Hec.* 733, *Supp.* 600, *El.* 341, *Herc.* 1132, *Ion* 223 (conjectural), *Pho.* 915, *Or.* 1347, *IA* 821; with αὖ *Hipp.* 232 and *Or.* 790. That the interrogative normally precedes the demonstrative is demonstrated in Diggle, *Studies* 42.

Unless we emend the text (Schneidewin replaced τίν' with τί δ', but the connective is unwanted after anticipatory γάρ; conceivable are νῦν, πῶς, or οὐκ) we must explain two facts: (1) the person referred to here appears to be a new arrival, unknown to Hecuba; and (2) he has just left the Greek assembly, whose decisions he reports, which means that he has arrived by the right or local *eisodos*. Both these facts make it unlikely that Talthybius is the arriving character. (1) Why would Hecuba be unable to make out his identity as he enters? At *Hcld.* 638–9 Alcmene does not recognize Hyllus' servant, and at *El.* 767 Electra does not recognize that of Orestes. Yet both of these are *personae mutae*, unlike Talthybius, who has had a long conversation with Hecuba. We have also heard from Talthybius himself (237–8) that he and Hecuba have had dealings in the past. It could be argued that she is exhibiting aristocratic disdain for her inferiors and feigned indifference to their precise identity. This cannot be disproved, but I find no other evidence for such an attitude in the play. (2) On the visual scheme described in the Introduction §§ 2.3 and 2.4, the ships of Agamemnon, Neoptolemus, and Menelaus lie down the left *eisodos*. Talthybius therefore departed to the left at 461. For him to reappear from the right is contrary to the logical schematism of tragic practice, but if he reappears by the left *eisodos*, the audience will be puzzled by his having fresh news of the Greek assembly, which lies in the other direction. In fact, the scholiast on 709 already concluded (though on the inadequate ground that Hecuba refers to him as a 'servant' rather than calling him by name) that the entering figure must be someone other than Talthybius. Elmsley calls him *ΑΓΓΕΛΟϹ*. The character describes himself in 787 as a herald, but the *Iliad* (1.320–36, 10.170) knows of three Greek heralds, Talthybius, Eurybates, and Hodios, the first two of whom sometimes serve independently of the others (2.184, 3.118, 4.192–8). Dyson and Lee 2000: 155–8, trying to establish, against the scholiast, that this is Talthybius, argue that for Hecuba's question in 707–8 not to be answered by either the entrant or someone else is unparalleled if the entrant is new. But in their first example of standard practice, *Supp.* 395–7, Theseus asks the question and answers it himself by saying that the new arrival would seem to be a Theban herald. Precisely this amount of information is already conveyed in τόνδ' Ἀχαικὸν ... βουλευμάτων. Their explanation (156–7) of Hecuba's failure to recognize a major character from the previous episode relies on psychological assumptions that seem foreign to Greek tragedy. On 'Occam's razor' principles we should not multiply characters without necessity, but this is a case of necessity. I have accordingly called him *ΚΗΡΥΞ*. —Speaker indications lack authority since the author's autograph and its ancient apographs marked only speaker change, employing the paragraphos and (for mid-line changes) the dicolon: see Lowe 1962 for the evidence.

708 The verse is identical with *Med.* 270 but is defensible in both places: the speaker reasonably infers that something new and authoritative is going to be announced from the arrival of authoritative persons. Defence in Wesener 1866: 30–1; Page 1934: 105 excludes the line from those he suspects. Deletion would make the sentence end rather abruptly. For entrance announcements where the Chorus has a foreboding that the entrant bears unwelcome news see above 231n.

709–11 The Herald quickly establishes that he has bad news, news that he is reluctant to tell. The reluctance continues in the *stichomythia* below. There has been a tendency in scholarship (Gilmartin 1970, Dyson and Lee 2000) to read this tender-heartedness back into the figure of Talthybius in the first episode. It is true that Talthybius deceives Hecuba about the fate of Polyxena, presumably to spare her feelings, but he is otherwise more businesslike than the anonymous Herald here: see the second paragraph of the introduction to the first episode. The herald of the second episode complains (786–9) that his job requires someone more pitiless and shameless than himself.

711 'The pronouncement both of the Danaans and of the sons of Pelops'. The army as a whole (*Δαναῶν*) and their leaders, the descendants of Pelops, are of one mind.

712 'What a dreadful start you make [in your speech] to me!' There is a duplication of meaning in *φροιμίων ἄρχηι*. Eur. makes frequent use of *φροίμιον* and *φροιμιάζομαι*, almost always in situations of foreboding: see *Hipp.* 568, *Hec.* 181, 1155, *Herc.* 538, 752, *Ion* 753, *IT* 1162, *Pho.* 1336. Aesch. has *φροίμιον* at *Sept.* 7, *Supp.* 830, *Ag.* 31, 829, 1216, 1354, *Eu.* 20, 142. There are no examples in Soph. or the *tragici minores*.

713 The Herald cannot bring himself to speak plainly about the decision to kill Astyanax. For a similar deliberative question see *Ion* 859–60 and *Hel.* 1196.

714 Andromache continues the Herald's syntax with the infinitive required by *ἔδοξε*: 'You don't mean that [it has been decreed that this child] shall have a different master from me?' She does the same in 716. The Herald never completes his own construction. For *ὁ αὐτόϲ* construed with a dative see 1023–4, 1036, 1049 and Smyth § 1500. For other constructions see Smyth § 1501a.

μῶν: see 55n.

715 The phrasing, designed to present bad news in a good light, recalls 264–71. —The similarity might be thought an argument that this is the same herald. It is, but it is a weak one, insufficient in my view to counterbalance the evidence presented at 707n.

716 'Well, [has it been decided] to leave him here as the last remnant of the Trojans?'

717 'I do not know how I can easily (painlessly?) tell you of †troubles†.' For ῥάιδιος in this sense see *Hipp.* 1047, ταχὺς γὰρ Ἅιδης ῥᾶιστος ἀνδρὶ δυστυχεῖ. —I have daggered the last word because it seems weak (not 'your troubles' or 'these woes' but a colourless 'troubles') and also because of the likelihood that the last word of 718 may have been copied here by mistake, obliterating a more vigorous reading. (The presumption of some editors is that κακά was the original reading in 717 and was miscopied in 718, but that is not an inevitable conclusion: see 718n.) Wecklein 1922: 98 proposed τάδε, 'this', which has a definiteness of reference that κακά lacks. (The conjecture was repeated by Jackson 202.) But since other expressions (e.g. τὰ σά) are also possible, I have simply daggered.

718 We may intuit that Andromache is asking for the truth and deprecating any feeling of pity or consideration that might prevent the Herald from telling it. The conjecture I print gives the required sense: 'I praise αἰδώς (I thank you for your pity) except when it (pity) conceals bad news.' On the 'instantaneous aorist' see 53n. On αἰδώς as 'pity' see 788n.

—Lee translates the transmitted text 'I commend your consideration, but not if you are to tell me bad news' and paraphrases 'If you have bad news then I wish you would tell me without further hesitation, because I know that you are forced to do so sooner or later.' Biehl paraphrases 'I praise your timid restraint, except that (this is) not (appropriate) if you have bad news to tell (as I cannot doubt after your announcement).' Both paraphrases are contorted. *Prima facie* Andromache is making a generalization: she praises αἰδώς (her thanks to the Herald for his hesitation is particular but implies a general attitude) unless some particular circumstance obtains. What is that circumstance? Not 'if you are to tell me bad news', for one might just as easily think that 'consideration', 'scruple', or 'hesitation' might be a good thing precisely when there is bad news to tell. This consideration led Wecklein 1922: 89, followed by Jackson 202–3, to adopt the reading of p, the corrector of P, and to write καλά. But since it has been clear since 710–11 that bad news is coming, to speak of good news here sounds silly and pedantic ('unless, of course, there's good news to tell!'). So we can reject what is after all probably an early conjecture (on the readings of p see Introduction § 5). To return to what is transmitted, one reason to retain *κακά* in 718 is that it explains the corruption of 717. In a conversation with NL I suggested that the verb in the if-clause should probably be 3rd-person and have *αἰδώϲ* as its understood subject (the generalization we expect, not a particular statement about the Herald; the 2nd-person verb here would not be easily interpreted as 'one'), and that it should have the meaning 'if it conceals trouble' (as Andromache has good reason to think it is doing). I suggested *πλὴν ἐὰν κρύπτηι κακά*. He suggested the paleographically more plausible *πλὴν ἐὰν ϲτέγηι κακά*. (Cf. Diggle's highly plausible conjecture at 1177 and my note *ad loc.*)

An alternative is 'I praise consideration except when it says what is unsound (i.e. false or deceptive).' That might be *πλὴν ἐὰν λέγηι ϲαθρά*: cf. *Supp.* 1064 *αἴνιγμα... ϲαθρόν* and *Ba.* 487 *δόλιον καὶ ϲαθρόν*. But in that case the *falsa lectio κακά* of 717 is difficult to account for.

719 The purpose clause depends on an understood 'I am telling you': similar ellipses at 1029, *Andr.* 1073, *IT* 779, *Ion* 35, 804, *Or.* 534, *Pho.* 997; *Cho.* 439, 1021; *Phil.* 989; and *Od.* 2.111.

720 ***γάμων***: for the poetic plural of this word see above on 319.

ὡϲ κλύω μεῖζον κακόν: the *ὡϲ* could be causal, explaining the interjection, or the equivalent of *ἴϲθι ὡϲ*.

721 *—λέγων* duplicates *λέξαϲ* (723), and West proposes *λόγωι*. For the collocation *νικᾶν λόγωι* see *Hcld.* 253 and *OC* 1296. The conjecture, reported in Diggle's apparatus, may be an otherwise unpublished private communication: see the OCT Praefatio, p. ix.

722 ***αἰαῖ μάλ'***: for *μάλα* emphasizing an interjection see *Cyc.* 665, *Med.* 1009, *Hec.* 1037, *Pho.* 1069, and *Or.* 1020. Andromache shares Hecuba's view of Odysseus (cf. 279–91): the fact that it is his proposal is additional grounds for lamentation.

723 'Urging us not to allow the child of a valiant father to reach manhood.'

724 'May he win such victories where his own children are concerned!' Spitzbarth 1945: 22 suggests that the curses here, at 772, and at 1110ff. may have been accompanied by a gesture toward the gods who were to fulfil them.

725 'But (saying) that they must throw him from the Trojan battlements.'

726 This is a paratactic way of saying 'But this is the way it must be if you are to show yourself wiser'. If Elmsley's conjecture at *Med.* 600 is correct (see Diggle's OCT, vol. 1), there is a parallel parataxis there involving imperative and future.

727 ***μήτ' ἀντέχου τοῦδ'***: the advice promised by 726 is introduced asyndetically: see Diggle 1994: 500 for examples.

728–9 The Herald recommends a realistic attitude in the face of irresistible force. For the sentiment cf. *Hec.* 225–8.

731–4 'We are capable of fighting against a single woman' is, of course, an ironic understatement. At the same time the Herald's *βούλομαι* (734) suggests that he has a preference for a non-violent solution.

735–9 Dyson and Lee 2000: 159–63 argue that in promising Andromache that Astyanax will be buried if she does not resist, the Herald is acting on his own initiative. They could be right. They also admit the possibility that to raise the question at all would be 'a distracting triviality for the audience' as they concentrate on Andromache's situation.

735 ***εἰ γάρ τι λέξεις ὧν χολώσεται στρατός***: on the 'minatory' or 'emotional' future condition, see Smyth § 2328.

736 A hendiadys, 'He will not obtain the mercy of a burial.'

737 'But by keeping quiet and by treating prudently what befalls, etc.' The idea here is that Andromache should wisely acquiesce in what has happened, not make things worse. As Dyson and Lee 2000: 160–1 point out, the normal fate of the slain Trojans in this play (Priam, Polyxena, the husbands of the Chorus at 1085, the people mentioned at 599–600) is to lie unburied. If she accepts the Herald's bargain, her son will at least avoid that fate.

—The wording and context suggest the idea that the course of wisdom is not to grow pointlessly angry at what fortune has thrown up to you: at *Herc.* 1228 Theseus recommends bearing, and not rejecting, what the gods send, and Bond *ad loc.* cites *Phil.* 1316–17 *τὰς μὲν ἐκ θεῶν | τύχας δοθείσας ἔστ' ἀναγκαῖον φέρειν*. The same idea of making the best of the situation is combined with a metaphor from dicing at *Hipp.* 718 *αὐτή τ' ὄνασθαι πρὸς τὰ νῦν πεπτωκότα*, fr. 572.2 *φέρειν τὰ συμπίτνοντα μὴ παλιγκότως*, and Soph. fr. 947 *στέργειν δὲ τἀκπεσόντα καὶ θέσθαι πρέπει | σοφὸν κυβευτήν*. I do not find convincing Lee's paraphrase of the reading of the mss., 'bearing your fortunes with equanimity' (fr. 417, cited by him as a parallel, is irrelevant). When Diggle 1991: 125 cites as parallels for our passage *Or.* 127, where *τοῖς καλῶς κεκτημένοις* appears to mean '(a source of help) to those who have a good one, i.e. a good nature', and fr. 187.1, where *εὖ βίον κεκτημένος* means 'possessing a good livelihood', he implies that *εὖ... κεκτημένη* means 'having a good fortune', which is impossible in this context. At *Pho.* 892 *τοῖσι τὴν τύχην κεκτημένοις* lacks any adverb and is simply a way of saying 'those affected by the fate I am about to announce'. I have adopted *ταῖς τύχαις κεχρημένη*, proposed by Hartung 1848: 66. (For the corruption see *Or.* 127, where the variants are *κεχρημένοις* and *κεκτημένοις*.) At *Hipp.* 1035 Hippolytus says that he had chastity but did not make prudent use of it. There appears to be a lacuna before *Andr.* 242, as I argued at *Eur. Alt.* 45–7, but still it shows a meaning compatible with our passage, 'managing (a thing) well'. That one may manage well even something bad or adverse is shown by *Or.* 705, puzzling though the passage is. (See *Eur. Tert.* 90–5 for a discussion of the difficulties.) For κεχρῆcθαι used instead of χρῆcθαι see *Med.* 347, *Hipp.* 349, and *IA* 89.

740–79 Andromache's farewell.

740 τιμηθεὶc τέκνον: for the *constructio ad sensum* see 535n.

741 'You will be killed by your enemies, leaving your mother in wretchedness.' It may seem odd that Andromache uses ἐχθρόc, 'personal enemy', instead of πολέμιοc, but at *Il.* 24.734–9 she prophesies that someone with a personal grudge against Hector will take it out on his son. This motive is not in evidence in our play or in the Cycle, but the Greeks had reason not only to hate Hector but also to fear his son once he grew to manhood, so that it is plausible to see them as motivated by inherited ἔχθρα.

[742–3] —These were deleted by Nauck 1862: 143, who describes them as a paraphrase of 744. He thinks 742 may be modelled on *Hipp.* 1390 and points out that 743 is a virtual repetition of the second line of fr. 62i (*Alexandros*) οἴμοι, θανοῦμαι διὰ τὸ χρήcιμον φρενῶν | ὃ τοῖcιν ἄλλοιc γίγνεται cωτηρία.

744 'Your father's valour proved no benefit to you.' The sentence exhibits litotes, for 'proved no benefit' means 'proved harmful'. On litotes or meiosis see Smyth § 3032. For καιρόc as 'benefit' or 'advantage' see LSJ s.v. IV and Race 1981: 205–8.

745–8 'O unlucky marriage-bed and marriage ceremony of mine, by which I once came to the house of Hector, not to bear him a son to be a sacrificial victim for the Greeks but to be the ruler of fertile Asia.' Formally this is a *vocativus pendens*, on which see 860–2n. —West 1980: 15 condemns these lines for the following reasons: (1) there seems to be no parallel for the pattern in 745 ὦ, noun, article, possessive; (2) with Nauck's *metri gratia* emendation 747 is not a very convincing Euripidean sentence; in particular, Astyanax is to be killed by being thrown off the wall, not by having his throat slit. In favour of retention is the *vocativus pendens*, which an interpolator is arguably unlikely to have produced. We might see whether 745 and 747 can be plausibly repaired.

There is further trouble in 745 unmentioned by West, the position of τε. According to *GP* 515–18 it is normal for τε to stand after the first word in its sense group. If the first word is an article or a preposition followed by a nominal word (substantive, adjective, or participle), τε in the third place is not unusual; if the first two words are preposition and article and the third is nominal, τε may be found in the fourth place. Denniston gives no examples like our passage where τε stands in fourth place after three nominal words. If we wish to meet this objection and West's (1) above, we could write ὦ λέκτρα τάλανα δυϲτυχῆ τε (Schmidt 1887: 392–3), where τε stands in second place. Though Eur. has no instance of the neuter of τάλαϲ, it occurs twice at *Sept.* 983 and once at *Phil.* 1088. For the rest perhaps κἄγαμα (Wecklein 1901: 33), where the last adjective would be illustrated by 75n above. As for West's (2) in 747 we need not accept Nauck's οὐ[χ ὡϲ] ϲφάγιον <υἱὸν> Δαναΐδαιϲ (1862: 149). The deleted ὡϲ is arguably needed as much in the negative half of the participial phrase as it is in its positive half (748). We should consider οὐχ ὡϲ ὕβριϲμα Δ. Transmitted ϲφάγιον will have been a maladroit gloss. Another possibility is Paley's deletion (1872) of 747–8.

749 'My son, you are weeping: are you aware of your troubles?' Both actors and non-speaking characters, such as Astyanax, wear masks, and when facial expressions, tears, or other evidences of emotion are to be conveyed to the audience, words must describe what the actors cannot produce and the audience cannot see.

750–1 'Why do you grasp me with your hands and clasp my clothing as if you were a small bird casting yourself into the embrace of my wings?' The image is a common one in Eur.: see *Alc.* 403 (on which see both Dale and Parker), *Hcld.* 10, 239, *Andr.* 441, 504–5 (see Stevens), *Herc.* 72, 224, 982, and *IA* 1248. Aesch. uses it in fr. 47a.795 (*Dictyulci*).

752–6 'Hector will not snatch up his glorious spear and come out of the earth to rescue you, nor will your father's kinsmen or the mighty Trojans. Instead, falling from a height onto your head (lit. 'neck') you will cut off your breath.' On ϲυγγένεια as abstract for concrete see 583n, 1123n, and Mastronarde on *Pho.* 291. On τράχηλοϲ as 'neck and head' see Powell 1939.

757–60 'How sweet is the smell of your skin. It was for nothing, I now see, that this breast of mine gave you nourishment in infancy, and in vain were the toils and pains my labours caused me.' Though the 'in vain I raised you' motif is used to express dismay when one's child dies and cannot be a γηροβοϲκόϲ (see 381n), here Andromache means that she expected to have the pleasure of seeing Astyanax grown to manhood. The dashed hopes of Hecuba for the boy are a large part of her moving speech to his corpse at 1167–1202.

761–3 'Now, for the last time, embrace your mother, fall into the arms of her that begot you, put your arms around my body [lit. 'back'] and your lips against mine.'

ἀμφὶ . . . ἕλιϲϲ': on tmesis see 522–3n.

Staging: Andromache and Astyanax embrace and kiss one another as their final farewell. For such farewell gestures see *Hec.* 409–12, *El.* 1321–2, *Herc.* 1408, *Or.* 1042–4; and Spitzbarth 1945: 29–30.

764–5 'You Greeks, inventors of barbarian woes, why do you kill this innocent child?'

βάρβαρ᾽... κακά: most translations (my Loeb among them) render the phrase as 'inventors of barbaric cruelties', but it is hard to see why Andromache, who is non-Greek, should describe cruelties as characteristic of her own race. If we translate as 'barbarian woes', i.e. woes *suffered by* non-Greeks, Andromache does not insult her own kind in the process of upbraiding the Greeks.

766–71 Having named the Greeks as the authors of her present woe (accurately since it is they who have decided to kill Astyanax), Andromache assails Helen, blaming her for the destruction of Troy. This too is true. Her denial that Zeus is her father seems intended to diminish her, but among the many fathers she assigns to Helen are divine beings (an Alastor is a punishing divinity) and deified abstractions. Even with this novel parentage Helen is seen as an agent of divine punishment (see 457n), and Andromache asserts (775–6 and 597) that it is the gods who are destroying the Trojans. The statement that Helen is a trouble to both barbarians and Greeks recalls a fragment of an unknown play of Eur., possibly *Alexandros* (fr. 1082, quoted in the Introduction at § 3.2.1) in which someone says that Zeus in causing the Trojan War intended to cause woe to both sides. So in spite of Andromache's novel paternity for Helen, she sees her as carrying out divine purposes. Only Hecuba attempts to assert that Helen is a cause independent of the gods. (On the success of her argument see the introduction to the third episode.)

769 —After the genitives *πολλῶν πατέρων*, *Ἀλάcτοροc*, *Φθόνου*, *Φόνου*, and *Θανάτου* one wonders why the construction is not continued with *ὧν τε γῆ τρέφει κακῶν*, with attraction of the relative and incorporation of the antecedent.

770 ***οὐ γάρ ποτ᾽ αὐχῶ Ζηνὸc ἐκφῦναί c᾽ ἐγώ:*** perhaps 'I assert confidently that you were never born from Zeus'. This would be a case of '*οὐ* adherescent', in which the negative stands next to the verb of saying or thinking: see Smyth §§ 2691–3. Otherwise it is the much less forceful 'I could not confidently assert that you were ever born from Zeus.'

775–7 As at 597–600, Andromache asserts, with the poetic tradition, that the destruction of Troy is the work of the gods. That is why the Trojans are powerless to save Astyanax's life.

780–1 The Chorus leader chimes in on the subject of Helen as the cause of Trojan misery. The form of the utterance suggests that Troy itself was the agent of ruin: the city destroyed or lost countless Trojans for the sake of a single hateful bedfellow for Paris. The audience knew *Il.* 7.344–78, where Antenor says the Trojans are foolishly going into battle having broken the oaths taken before Paris' duel with Menelaus and suggests returning Helen and the treasure. There Paris refuses to give up Helen, and Priam acquiesces in his son's decision. They would also have known the portion of the *Cypria* (*GEF* arg. 10) where Odysseus and Menelaus try to negotiate the return and are refused (an embassy alluded to in *Il.* 3.207). The choral distich is fleeting enough, but it might serve to remind the audience that the Trojans rejected an option that was choiceworthy on both moral and prudential grounds.

Staging: the Herald takes Astyanax from his mother and at 785 gives the boy to his attendants, who take him down the left *eisodos*. It is not clear from the text at what point the wagon carrying Andromache moves down this same *eisodos* (see Introduction §§ 2.3, and 2.4). The two exits by the same *eisodos* were probably not simultaneous (see Taplin 1977: 90–1, who shows that when two characters exit together, 'there is almost always some clear and positive reason why they are together'), and it is likely that her exit takes place during Hecuba's anapaests. Hecuba apostrophizes Astyanax, who is possibly just visible when she begins 790.

782–5 The Herald's words, spelling out the fate that awaits Astyanax, are arguably addressed less to Astyanax (which would be unnecessarily cruel if he understood them) than to himself, making plain why he wishes his task on someone else (786–9).

—Taplin 1977: 91n2 suggests assigning 782–9 to Andromache, retaining *ὑμετέραϲ* in 788. this would give her some final words. But it is difficult to give *λαμβάνετ' αὐτόν* to Andromache, and 786–9 are more plausible as the Herald's complaint about his task than as anything Andromache might say.

Staging: in response to his command the Herald's servants remove Astyanax from his mother's grasp. Herald and servants exit leftward with the boy. Since there is no other indication in the text, we must assume that Andromache, still on her wagon, exits leftwards behind him after an interval.

786–9 'Take him! But these are herald duties that should be performed by someone without pity, more a friend than my heart is to ruthlessness.'

788 ἀναιδείαι: *αἰδώϲ* is frequently closer to 'pity' than to 'shame', and *ἀναιδήϲ* frequently has overtones of ruthlessness: see, e.g., *Herc.* 556–7. Cairns 1993: 290n88 points out that *αἰδώϲ* is felt not only toward those one is under an obligation to protect (e.g. suppliants or *xenoi*) but also more generally as a reluctance to cause *anyone* pain. —For correption in the non-lyric anapaests of Eur. see Barrett's addendum (pp. 432–3) to his note on *Hipp.* 246.

790–8 'O child, O son of my ill-fated son, we are unjustly robbed of your life, your mother and I. What is to become of me? What can I do for you, luckless one? To you we give these blows to the head and beatings of the breast: for that is what lies in our control. Alas for my city, alas for you! What do we not have—what do we still lack—so as not to perish wholly, with utter destruction?'

792 τί πάθω: this colloquial expression (see Stevens 1976: 57–8) occurs four other times in Eur. (*Andr.* 513, *Hec.* 614, *Supp.* 257, *Pho.* 895); see also *Sept.* 1057 (non-Aeschylean); *Trach.* 973, *OC* 216; Men. *Samia* 604, *Phasma* 8; *Il.* 11.404 and *Od.* 5.465. The subjunctive is perhaps less the marker of a deliberative question than the survival of the Homeric volitional-future use. For the idiom see Gomme–Sandbach on the two Menander passages and SD 2.318. Here τί πάθω; expresses 'What will become of me?' and τί... δράcω; is a bewildered and despairing deliberative. There is a similar pairing at *Sept.* 1057 and *Trach.* 973.

Staging: Hecuba beats her head and breast in a gesture of grief. She may sink to the ground and lie there during the second stasimon, as she did during the first.

SECOND STASIMON (799–859)

I argued above that the first stasimon is neither self-contained nor dithyrambic. By contrast, the first stanzaic pair of the present ode, with its narrative of an attack on Troy in a previous generation led by Telamon, king of the romantically described island of Salamis, could be plausibly described as both. Even the second pair, though taking as its theme the present desolation of Troy, seems curiously distanced as it describes the contrast between the gods' close relations with Ganymede and Tithonus and the failure of Zeus and Eos to do anything about the destruction of Troy. As a response to the sending of Astyanax to his death, the ode—and particularly the first stanzaic pair—seems at first shockingly wide of the mark, but there is a similar response to unendurable pain in the 'escape ode' at *Hipp.* 732–75, where the Chorus pray to be transported to a place untouched by sorrow.

The language is highly decorative. Note the compound adjectives μελιccοτρόφου, τοξοφόρωι, ποντοπόρου, καλλιγάλανα, and λευκοπτέρου, the ornamental epithets περικύμονοc, ἱεροῖc, εὐρεῖται, φοίνικι, φονία, χρυcέαιc, ἅλιαι, δροcόεντα, and χρύcεοc, and the genitive of quality ἀcτέρων.

799–807 ~ 809–19

1. 799 ~ 809	⏑ – ⏑⏑ – ⏑⏑ – ⏑ – ⏑⏑ – ⏑⏑ –	⏑ D ⏑ D
2. 800 ~ 810	– – ⏑⏑ – ⏑⏑ – – – ⏑ –	– D – e

3. 801 ~ 811/12	– ⏑⏑ – ⏑⏑ – – – ⏑⏑ – ⏑⏑ – –	D – D –
4. 802 ~ 813	– ⏑⏑ – ⏑⏑ – – – ⏑ – – ‖	D – e –
5. 803 ~ 814	– ⏑⏑ – ⏑⏑ – ⏑⏑ – ⏑⏑ – ⏑⏑ – – ‖	D ⏑⏑ D –
6. 804 ~ 815	⏑ – ⏑ – – – ⏑⏑ – ⏑⏑ –	⏑ e – D ∫
7. 805 ~ 816	– – ⏑ – – – ⏑ ⏓ ‖	– E
8. 806 ~ 817/18	– ⏑⏑ – ⏑⏑ – – – ⏑⏑ – ⏑⏑ –	D – D
9. 807 ~ 819	⏑⏑ – ⏑⏑ – ⏑ – – ‖‖	d² ba

Metrical analysis

The first strophic pair is dactylo-epitrite, with 3, 5, and 8 coinciding in scheme with the dactylic hexameter. There is period end at 803 ~ 814, where final *anceps* is followed by *anceps*: see Stinton 1977: 39–40 [= 1989: 325–7]. The last verse could also be described as ⏑⏑ hag. Link *anceps* is mostly long.

799–819 The Chorus tell in verse of *Märchen*-like charm the story of the first sack of Troy at the hands of an army led by Heracles with the help of Telamon. Priam's father Laomedon had promised Heracles horses of divine breed, given him by Zeus, in exchange for help against a sea-monster that was threatening his daughter Hesione. He broke his promise, and in anger Heracles raised a force to sack Troy. The story is alluded to at *Il.* 5.638–51 and 20.145–8 and in the Hesiodic *Catalogue of Women* (fr. 165.9–13 M.-W.). Other treatments are cited by Finglass on *Aj.* 434–6. The monster, not incidentally, was sent by Poseidon when Laomedon cheated him and Apollo of their promised reward for building the walls of Troy (see *Il.* 21.441–57). So Laomedon's dealings both with the two gods who built his city and with the hero who saved his daughter show disregard for oath-keeping. The Chorus evince no awareness that at least the first sack of Troy was just punishment. The moral dimension of the story disappears amid the poetic ornament, what Kranz 1933: 242–3 calls 'der schöne Stil'. This begins with the description of Telamon's island kingdom of Salamis, particular attention being paid to its proximity to 'shining Athens' with its patron goddess, giver of the olive. After lovingly relating how the first flower of the Greek soldiery, crack archers and all, disembarked at the streams of the river Simois, the charming narrative finally arrives at the realities of war, the burning of Troy's walls and the sacking of the city, though the emphasis falls more on the ruin of the walls and the land they protected than on loss of life: see 818n. Then in the last two verses of the antistrophe the connection is made with Troy's most recent destruction.

799 **μελιccοτρόφου**: like Yeats's 'bee-loud isle' of Innisfree Salamis is (apparently) famed for apiculture, though other ancient evidence on this point is lacking. The adjective occurs here for the first and only time in verse. (Its only other occurrence in Greek literature is in Josephus, *BJ* 4.469. It is hard to know what to make of this odd distribution.)

Cαλαμῖνοc: Salamis, in the Saronic Gulf and visible from the Piraeus, was an Athenian possession since the time of Solon. Ancient biographers report that Eur. was born on the island in the year of (and, some said, on the day of) the famous naval battle (T 1.2–3, 16–17, T 12.3–4). The Marmor Parium (T 10a and 10b), however, has an earlier year for his birth, which perhaps casts doubt on Salamis as the birth-place as well. A report (T 2.9–11, T 1.69–71) that he owned land on the island and that he wrote his plays in the solitude of a cave looking out to sea, though attested as early as Philochorus (*c*.340–260 BC), deserves to be treated with caution, especially since it may have arisen as an explanation for the poet's frequent use of imagery derived from the sea. The island is mentioned again in eulogistic style at 1096. With the phrasing here cf. *Aj*. 134–5 Τελαμώνιε παῖ, τῆc ἀμφιρύτου Cαλαμῖνοc ἔχων βάθρον ἀγχίαλον.

800 **νάcου περικύμονοc οἰκήcαc ἕδραν**: 'you that made your home in a sea-girt isle'. In 'a home (seat) consisting in a sea-girt isle' the genitive is the so-called appositive genitive, on which see KG 1.264–5 and 816n below.

περικύμονοc: this is the first use of the word in extant Greek literature and its only use in tragedy. It is likely, though, to have been used in hexameter verse before Eur. since it turns up again in the parodist Archestratus frr. 135.5 and 190.4.

οἰκήcαc: the aorist is inceptive, 'take up habitation' in a place, as at *Hcld*. 311, *Hel*. 928, fr. 360.11 (conjectural), 228a.18, 558.4, 819.4; and [Eur.] *Rhes*. 973. Neither Aesch. nor Soph. (apart from the dubious *OC* 92) uses the aorist of this verb. Telamon, son of the Aeginetan Aeacus, was exiled by his father for killing his half-brother Phocus and settled in Salamis.

801–2 'That lies over against the holy hill where Athena first showed forth the shoot of the grey olive-tree.' ἐπικλίνομαι is used only here in tragedy. In the contest between Athena and Poseidon to be the tutelary deity of Athens, Athena won by her gift of the olive. The result was that the city was named after her (Apollodorus 3.14.1). δείκνυμι here means 'bring to light' (LSJ s.v. 1), i.e. produce for the first time. Another relevant meaning (not recognized by LSJ, but see *Andr*. 706 and 1001) is 'teach': Athena taught the cultivation of the olive tree. —Although Greek poets show greater tolerance for word-repetition than we do (see 80–1n), it is mildly suspicious that *Ἀθάνα* and *Ἀθάναις* occur at the ends of successive lines. Eur. may have written, e.g., *Διὸς παῖς* in 802, which could have been replaced by a gloss. If so, this would be in keeping with Eur.'s etymological practice: when he derives, e.g. Athens from Athena, he most commonly does it riddlingly by using a synonym for the *etymon*: see 892–3n.

803 **οὐράνιον στέφανον λιπαραῖσί <τε> κόσμον Ἀθάναις**: '(to be) a heavenly crown (or 'a glory rising heaven-high') and an adornment to gleaming Athens'. The two accusatives are in apposition to *κλάδον*. The olive is an adornment to Athens because it is the product on which its fame rests: Athenian olive oil was sent all over the Greek world in jars adorned with vase painting. A more literal sense of 'crown' is possible since olive leaves, like those of laurel, celery, or parsley, could be worn as a chaplet.

λιπαραῖσι: like *κραναός*, 'rocky', the adjective is a standing epithet for Athens: see Pi. fr. 76; *Alc.* 452, *IT* 1130–1; and Ar. *Eq.* 1329, *Nub.* 300, and *Ach.* 639–40, where Dicaeopolis accuses the Athenians of being too susceptible to this flattering epithet, which he considers more suitable for sardines. (For the application of the adjective both to Athens and to other cities, see Olson on *Ach.* 639–40.) Though the olive has just been mentioned, the word here need not imply glistening with oil: cf. LSJ s.v. III. Even before the Periclean building programme, but especially after it, the acropolis must have gleamed in the distance.

804 **ἔβας ἔβας**: on Eur.'s fondness for anadiplosis in lyric see Breitenbach 214–21 and the parody of Euripidean monody at Ar. *Ran.* 1331–63. Note further examples in this ode at 806, 815 (conjectural), and 841 and elsewhere in the play at 173, 325, 1066, 1077, 1090, 1217, 1235, 1310, 1312, 1326, and 1328. (It is to be emended away at 1090, where see n.) Numerous as these instances are, this stylistic mannerism was destined to be used even more liberally in some of Eur.'s later plays, especially *Or.* For anadiplosis in trimeters see 304n.

τοξοφόρωι: the word is epic (*Il.* 21.483) and lyric (e.g. Pi. *P.* 5.41).

804–5 Telamon's war is an *aristeia* (*συναριστεύων*), a feat of martial excellence, performed in company with Alcmene's bow-bearing son, more romantic ornament. That Telamon won the prize of valour is emphasized by his son Ajax at *Aj.* 434–6.

συναριστεύων ἅμ': the prepositionally used adverb seems otiose with *συν-*, but see Jaeger 1957 on the tendency of adverbs to reinforce prepositional prefixes. There are further examples in Diggle, *Studies* 39.

806–7 **τὸ πάροιθεν < >**: —in my Loeb I printed Hermann's conjecture (1847: 14) *τὸ πάροιθεν* [*ὅτ' ἔβας*] *ἀφ' Ἑλλάδος* <*γᾶς*>. This gives good metre and good sense. Its style, however, is faulty, for in spite of the thematic importance of Greece here, the occurrence of Ἑλλάδος in two successive lines is stylistically implausible. Diggle follows Bothe 1802: 380 in deleting ἀφ' Ἑλλάδος as well, the four words presumably being a gloss on τὸ πάροιθεν. (The gloss would originally have used the Attic vocalism.) To guide possible reconstructions we have the rhythm of the antistrophe, which (with the Aldine's φονία for transmitted φοινία) is plausible, and its beginning agrees with τὸ πάροιθεν. Just what was obliterated is unclear. Point of departure might have been mentioned (e.g. τὸ πάροιθεν <ἀπ' Ἀπίας γᾶς>), the sea journey itself (e.g. τὸ πάροιθ' <ἐπ' ἀκύμον' ἅλμαν>), or its destination (e.g. τὸ πάροιθ' <ἐπὶ τάνδε γαῖαν>). For the spanning of two stanzas by a single sentence see *Hcld.* 362, *Hipp.* 131, *Hec.* 455, 647, *Supp.* 48, *El.* 157, and *Ba.* 997; *Rhes.* 351.

809–10 ***ὅθ' Ἑλλάδος ἄγαγε πρῶτον ἄνθος ἀτιζόμενος | πώλων***: 'when he [Heracles] took with him Hellas' finest flower, being deprived of the horses'. With Ἑλλάδος ἄνθος cf. Aesch. *Pers.* 59, 252, 925, and *Ag.* 197–8. The Chorus allude without emphasis to the justice of Heracles' cause.

—Jackson's ἀτίζομενος (1955: 203), 'deprived of the due honour of the horses', seems inevitable: for the genitive with the kindred verb ἀτιμάζω see LSJ s.v. 2 and for ἀτίζω with genitive see A.R. 1.615 γεράων μιν ἄτισσαν. By constrast, transmitted ἀτυζόμενος gives poor sense since the verb means 'be distraught from fear, be bewildered': see LSJ. The word is sharply at variance with the rest of the description of Heracles.

810–13 'And by the Simois' full-flowing stream checked his sea-going vessel(s) and tied the hawsers to their prows and put forth from the ships the bowcraft of his archers' hands to work death for Laomedon'.

810 ***εὐρείται***: the adjective in its Homeric form ἐυρρείτην is found at *Il.* 6.34 and *Od.* 14.257. Other adjectives of similar 1st-declension masculine form modify names of rivers: βαθυρρείταο at *Il.* 21.195 and Hes. *Th.* 265, καλλιρόαν at Bacchyl. 11.26 and 96, καλλιδίνας at *Herc.* 368, ὠκυρόαν at *Ba.* 568, and ἀργυροδίναν at Callim. *H.* 6.13–14; see also Renehan 1963: 269–71 on *Herc.* 385 (defending transmitted ἀργυρορρύταν).

πλάταν: for the common synecdoche of 'oarblade' for 'ship' see 877, 1095, 1155, and 1332. For the related synecdoche of κώπη, 'oar-handle', for 'ship' see *Hec.* 456, *IT* 116, 140, *Hel.* 394, etc.

ναύδετ' ἀνήψατο πρυμνᾶν: for the construction (unnatural in English) of attaching a rope *from* something, see *Med.* 770 and *Hipp.* 767–70. ναύδετον only here in Greek literature. Diggle 1989: 198 notes that the suffix -δετος is sometimes active in meaning.

καὶ χερὸς εὐστοχίαν ἐξεῖλε ναῶν: the abstract, 'keen shooting of the hand', is put for the concrete, 'hands that are keen shooters'. On this feature of the high style, the 'inverse genitive', see 1123n.

Λαομέδοντι φόνον: the 'accusative in apposition to the sentence' (see 536n) gives the result achieved by the landing and disembarkation.

814–16 'And having demolished with the fire's, the fire's, ruddy blast the walls made with Phoebus' plumbline (rule), they plundered the land of Troy.' The Chorus ascribe the building exclusively to Apollo, perhaps because unlike Poseidon, whose pro-Trojan sympathies in this play are an innovation (see 1–47n), Apollo both in this play and in the tradition is Troy's defender.

814 *κανόνων δὲ τυκίϲματα Φοίβου*: on *κανών* see 4–6n: Phoebus' walls were painstakingly made. —Maas 1956 proposed *τυχίϲματα*, a change of spelling that more easily explains the frequent corruption to *τειχ-*.

815 *πυρὸϲ <πυρὸϲ> φοίνικι πνοᾶι*: since it is the fire, not the blast, that is red, this is a case of enallage or transferred epithet, on which see 1–2n.

816 *Τροίαϲ ἐπόρθηϲε χθόνα*: *Τροίαϲ* is an instance of 'appositive genitive' or *genetivus inhaerentiae*, in which the noun in the genitive is used to express something that might have been expressed by apposition. (Moorhouse 53 calls it genitive of definition.) Breitenbach 194 cites Geisau 1916: 255–8 on this construction in Indo-European. A particular case is the 'synonymous genitive', for which see *Herc.* 663 *ζωᾶϲ βιοτάν*, *IT* 1255 *μαντείαϲ . . . θεϲφάτων*, and other examples in Breitenbach *loc. cit.*

817–18 'Twice, in two onslaughts, deadly spearmen have razed with fire the walls of Dardania.' For *Δαρδανία* = *Τροία* see 535, *Hel.* 384, and *Or.* 1391. On variation in the naming of Troy see 511n.

817 *δὶϲ δὲ δυοῖν*: on the figure of *paregmenon* or *polyptoton* see Breitenbach 221–6.

πιτύλοιν: on *πίτυλοϲ*, 'repeated rhythmical movement' (such as blows, onslaughts, or attacks of madness), see Barrett on *Hipp.* 1464. For further discussion see Parker on *Alc.* 796–8 (who doubts that 'repeated and rhythmic' is always inherent in the word) and Garvie on *Pers.* 974–7. For *αἰχμά* as 'soldiery' see 839, *Hcld.* 276, and *Or.* 1485, and on the similar use of *δόρυ*, see above on 8. The separation of a noun from its dependent genitive (*τείχη . . . Δαρδανίαϲ*) is discussed by Breitenbach 250–3.

818 —Diggle, *Studies* 68 proposes *τείχη πέρι Δαρδανίδαϲ*, 'The deadly spear has destroyed the sons of Dardanus about the walls.' This involves the alteration of only one letter and the addition of a second, but there are objections to this conjecture. (1) *τείχη πέρι* gives poor sense. Whatever may have been true of the first sack of Troy, in the second the principal place where the Trojans were destroyed (once for all, as the aorist shows) was not 'around the walls' but within the city. (*Il.* 6.327–8, cited by Diggle, does not describe the final destruction.) (2) Neither

Aesch. nor Soph. nor Eur. uses *Δαρδανίδαι* to mean 'Trojans': only the singular is used, and only of a specific descendant of Dardanus (Ganymede at *IA* 1049). Its use in the plural as a synonym for 'Trojans' occurs at *Rhes.* 230, as Diggle notes, but nowhere else in tragedy. By contrast *Δαρδανίας* is protected by 535, *Hel.* 384, and *Or.* 1391. (3) *καταλύω* with a person as object means 'depose', whereas 'destroy' is normal with 'city' or similar object (see 1080 quoted below and *Il.* 2.117 and 9.24). Diggle admits that the verb 'is properly used of destroying things' but says its application to people is 'an easy extension'. But it is one of which no other poet has availed himself. By contrast two considerations speak in favour of Seidler's *πυρί*, which allows us to retain most of what is transmitted. (1) The first firing of Troy's walls was mentioned in 814–15 and the second was emphasized above at 8, 60, 145, and 586, so that the parallelism speaks in favour of 'fire'. (2) The first two stanzas, apart from *Λαομέδοντι φόνον* (814), have had in view the destruction of the walls and the territory within it (816), not the Trojans themselves, so 'destroyed the walls' is more plausible than 'destroyed the Trojans'. We find the same verb with the city as its object at 1079–80, (*πόλεος*) *ἃν πυρὸς αἰθομένα κατέλυσεν ὁρμά*. Diggle calls Seidler's conjecture 'inapposite', presumably because 'spearpoint' and 'fire' are different and incompatible means of destruction. But given the frequent use in poetry of 'spearpoint' to mean 'soldiery' (see previous note) there is no absurdity in having spear-men firing the city walls. The Greeks did not bring to Troy a special team of experts in setting fires, and so the men who were there as spear-fighters necessarily performed this task.

820–39 ~ 840–59

1. 820/1 ~ 840/1	⏑ – ⏑ – – ⏑ – ⏑ – ⏖ – ⏖ – ⏒	⏑ e e ⏑ D ⏒
2. 822 ~ 842	– ⏖ – ⏖ –	D
3. 823/4 ~ 843/4	– ⏖ – ⏖ – – – ⏑ – – – – ⏑ – –	D – E
4. 825/6 ~ 845/6	– ⏖ – ⏖ – ⏖ – ⏖	D^2 ⏖
5. 827 ~ 847	– ⏖ – ⏖ – ||	D
6. 828 ~ 848	⏑ – ⏑ – – ⏑ –	⏑ e e
7. 829 ~ 849	⏔ ⏑ – ⏑ – ⏑ –	lk
8. 830 ~ 850	– ⏑ ⏔ ⏒ – ⏑ – ⏓	E
9. 831 ~ 851	– ⏑ – ⏑ – ⏑ – – ||	E
10. 832/3 ~ 852/3	⏖ – ⏖ – ⏑ – ⏑	hag
11. 834 ~ 854	– ⏖ – ⏖ –	D
12. 835 ~ 855	⏑ – ⏑ ⏕ ⏑ – ⏑ ⏑͡⏑	2ia ∫
13. 836 ~ 856	⏑ ⏑͡⏑ ⏑ ⏑͡⏑ ⏑ – ⏑ –	2ia
14. 837/8 ~ 857/8	– ⏖ – ⏖ – ⏖ – ⏖ – ⏑	D^3 ⏑
15. 839 ~ 859	– ⏑ – ⏑ – – |||	ith

Metrical analysis

The second strophic pair is in dactylo-epitrite with a brief admixture of aeolic at 832/3 ~ 852/3 (also describable as d^2 ba).

820–59 In the second strophic pair the Chorus make two complaints, that Zeus, who honoured Troy by choosing Ganymede as cupbearer in his feasts, has now allowed the city to fall; and that Eos, the goddess of the dawn, has looked on with indifference as the Trojans' high hopes aroused by her marriage with their own Tithonus were dashed by the destruction of his city. The style, highly ornamented and generally eulogistic, leaves little room for serious moral reflection. The elegiac contrast between the former favour of the gods toward Troy and their present indifference to her sufferings is poignant (the strophe begins and the antistrophe ends with the theme of divine favour nullified, as Biehl points out), but the audience may well have felt a tension between that favour and the Trojans' lack of reciprocation. The Chorus have alluded to Laomedon's perjury but show no awareness that Zeus as protector of oaths could be expected to take umbrage. They lament Zeus's disfavour in the strophe, but the audience will have been aware from *Alexandros* and from *Tro.* 598 that one of the causes of Troy's destruction was Paris' removal of Helen from Sparta, an offence against Zeus Xenios. Immediately after this ode comes a reference to Paris as ξεναπάτηϲ (866) and to his punishment as divinely sanctioned (867). In short, however much moderns may deprecate 'blaming the victim', it is hard to avoid the conclusion that the Chorus's complaints show that, in broad terms, the Trojans' fate is in some measure congruent with their actions.

820–5 'It is therefore to no purpose that you, son of Laomedon, who walk so gracefully with your wine-flasks of gold, have the task of filling Zeus's cups, a form of servanthood most creditable, while the land that gave you birth is consumed with fire.' What is 'to no purpose' is the double proposition, that (1) Ganymede serves as cupbearer to the gods (a high honour); and (2) *nevertheless* his city is being burnt to the ground. On this Greek 'figure of thought' see 95–7n and Appendix A, section (1). Note that μέν, as frequently, has to be supplied here with the first member of the contrast.

821 χρυϲέαιϲ ἐν οἰνοχόαιϲ: Barlow translates 'among golden wine jugs', which suggests vessels littering the scene. But ἐν, which can mean 'wearing' (see 329n), sometimes indicates other kinds of accompaniment (see *Ba.* 1166), and sometimes means 'equipped with', as here, *El.* 321, and Xen. *Cyr.* 2.3.14. See also LSJ s.v. A.I.3. For the prosody of χρύϲεοϲ see 856n.

ἁβρὰ βαίνων: Ganymede might be represented here as walking in delicate fashion because he is being kept immature and sexually ambiguous as befits one who takes the female role in his sexual encounters with Zeus. But *Med.* 829–30, *αἰεὶ διὰ λαμπροτάτου | βαίνοντες ἁβρῶς αἰθέρος*, of the blessed life of the Athenians, suggests rather that the point is that his life is one of luxury, as befits a favourite of the gods. This creates a better contrast with the misery of Troy, his city. Biehl cites Denniston's note on *El.* 549 regarding the gait and bearing of aristocrats, and this may also contribute to the meaning.

824 ***καλλίσταν λατρείαν***: there is an oxymoron here since *λατρεία*, servitude, is normally debasing: being a servant to the gods is an exception to this generality. For the sentiment see *Ion* 128–35.

827–30 ***ἠϊόνες δ' ἅλιαι | ἴακχον οἰωνὸς οἷ- | ον τέκνων ὕπερ βοῶς'***: the beaches ring with the lamentations of the women. Cf. 28–9 where the Scamander likewise 'shouts' (i.e. resounds) with the voices of captives. (Banks resound in similar fashion at *Il.* 17.265.) —Hermann's transposition in 829 and Bothe's in 830 restore metre. At the end of 830 the mss. read *βοᾶι*, but that leaves *ἠϊόνες* with no verb. To remedy this Seidler replaced *ἴα(κ)χον* with *ἀχοῦσιν*, which is certainly possible, but Wecklein's *βοῶς'* for *βοᾶι* (1897: 464) presupposes the common error where a word is mistakenly adjusted to agree with a neighbouring word, on which see 589–90n. See further Appendix C.

827 ***ἠϊόνες***: at *Or.* 995 Willink plausibly restores *ἀϊόσιν*. JD points out that the Doric form could be restored here.

831–2 ***αἱ μὲν εὐνάς, αἱ δὲ παῖδας | αἱ δὲ ματέρας γεραιάς***: it is not literally the beaches (826) that are wailing but the women on them, and here the women with their cries are distributively specified: some bewail husbands (for the use of 'bed' to mean 'bedfellow' see 274n), others sons, others aged mothers (young women lamenting the enslavement of their old parents). Note that the periphrastic expression *ἴακχον βοῶς'*, understood from what precedes, takes further accusative objects: see above 59–60n.

—Wilamowitz (reported in Murray's apparatus) proposed *ἇι μὲν*... *ἇι δὲ*...| *ἇι δέ*, 'in one place...in another...and in another'. This is adopted by Diggle. It avoids the necessity of supplying 'some women, etc.' from the cries that the beaches bellow forth. For *ὃς μὲν*...*ὃς δέ* see LSJ s.v. *ὅς* A.II.4. Paleographically this is scarcely a change at all. But against it is the virtual absence of this collocation from tragedy: neither Italie nor Ellendt recognizes it, and a TLG search of Eur. reveals only one *prima facie* instance, *οἷς μὲν*...*τοῖς δ'* at *IT* 420–1, which has naturally not gone unchallenged. To keep what is transmitted and supply 'some women...others...others' may seem difficult.

But (1) even if we adopt Wilamowitz's alterations it is not the beaches that bewail husbands, sons, and mothers but women who thus must in any case be conjured out of the wailing on the beaches. (2) We have here distributive apposition κατὰ ϲύνεϲιν. There are good parallels, where a crying out or a controversy is described, for naming the parties to it in loose apposition: *Ba.* 1131–2 ἦν δὲ πᾶϲ' ὁμοῦ βοή, | ὁ μὲν ϲτενάζων ὅϲον ἐτύγχαν' ἐμπνέων, | αἱ δ' ὠλόλυζον; *Ant.* 259–60 λόγοι δ' ἐν ἀλλήλοιϲιν ἐρρόθουν κακοί, | φύλαξ ἐλέγχων φύλακα; *PV* 200–3 στάϲιϲ τ' ἐν ἀλλήλοιϲιν ὡροθύνετο, | οἱ μὲν θέλοντεϲ ἐκβαλεῖν ἕδραϲ Κρόνον, | ... οἱ δὲ τοὔμπαλιν, and the prose examples in Bruhn § 19 and KG 2.107.

833–4 ***τὰ δὲ ϲὰ δροϲόεντα λουτρὰ | γυμναϲίων τε δρόμοι:*** the 'dewy, fresh' baths (δροϲόειϲ only here in tragedy) and the running-tracks of the gymnasia are both indicative of the high civilization of Troy. Gymnasia are anachronistic: male nudity in athletics dates to a time much later than the Bronze Age. They are also Greek: even in the archaic period real-life non-Greeks (see Hdt. 1.10.3) found nudity abhorrent. But just as tragedy readily admits elements of later Greek culture into its Bronze Age stories (e.g. the gymnasia mentioned at *Hipp.* 229, *Hel.* 208, and *Pho.* 368), so the *barbaroi* in tragedy are seldom sharply distinguished from the Greeks. In our play there is only one possible allusion to ethnic difference: see below 1209–15n. Hall 1989 claims that tragedy schematizes the difference between Greek and non-Greek. The thesis requires some qualification.

835 ***βεβᾶϲι:*** 'have perished', a common meaning in Eur.: see 289, 582, and e.g. *Med.* 439, *Andr.* 1022, *Supp.* 1138–9, *Herc.* 769, *IT* 1289; but also Aesch. *Pers.* 1002–3; Soph. *OT* 959, and *Trach.* 134.

835–7 ***ϲὺ δὲ πρόϲωπα νεα- | ρὰ χάριϲι παρὰ Διὸϲ θρόνοιϲ | καλλιγάλανα τρέφειϲ:*** Ganymede's face is 'youthful in its graces', and he keeps it in its lovely serenity. Eur. is fond of compound adjectives in καλλι- (some thirty are listed in Allen and Italie), and this element is always adjectival. The second element is usually in origin a substantive, as here. The word therefore is a *bahuvrihi* compound (i.e. formed like the Sanskrit adjective meaning 'of much rice, possessing much rice') and means literally 'possessing a calm that is beautiful' (LSJ 'beautiful in its calm'). For τρέφω, 'keep (someone or something) in a certain state' see *Hel.* 1278.

838–9 ***Πριάμοιο δὲ γαῖαν | Ἑλλὰϲ ὤλεϲ' αἰχμά:*** the δέ-clause has the force of subordination, 'although the Greek soldiery have destroyed the land of Priam'. αἰχμά, as at 819, is metonymy for 'spear-men, soldiers'. For the separate feminine form of Ἕλλην joined with the same noun see *Or.* 1485 Ἑλλάδοϲ αἰχμῆϲ. For the Homeric genitive in -οιο see 537n.

840–4 Eros came to the walls of Troy as an object of care to the gods, i.e. causing one of them to fall in love with a Trojan. The love of Eos for Tithonus is presented as something that greatly exalted Troy by making a marriage tie between the city and the gods.

844 **ἐπύργωcαc**: the verb has its metaphorical sense, 'raise to a towering height, exalt, elate' (cf. 612), but its literal meaning suggests Troy's fortifications, now in ruins. This crossing over from literal to metaphorical meaning is noted by Barlow 1971: 117.

845 **κῆδοc ἀναψάμενοc**: for κῆδοc ἀνα- or cυνάπτειν (the active used of the contracting parties, whether father or groom, the middle being causative) see *Andr.* 620 and 648, *Herc.* 35 and 477.

845–51 **μὲν οὖν**: the particles are to be taken separately, the οὖν being transitional: see *GP* 471–2. 'Now I am, to be sure, no longer upbraiding Zeus. But the light of white-winged Day, dear to mortals, looked in fatal wise upon the destruction of the land, looked upon the destruction of Pergama.' The Chorus leave off their dispraise of Zeus to focus on the culpable indifference of Eos. The Chorus do not mean literally that Eos destroyed Troy. Rather, when in Greek one talks of someone's fatal day (αἴcιμον, μόρcιμον, or νηλεὲc ἦμαρ or ἦμαρ ὀλέθριον), the day is spoken of as if it caused the death in question: see *Alc.* 147 πεπρωμένη γὰρ ἡμέρα βιάζεται, *Hec.* 285, *Pho.* 3–6, [543, 1689], fr. 420.2–3; Aesch. *Ag.* 1577; Soph. *Aj.* 131, *El.* 201–2, *OT* 438 with Finglass's note; Sosiphanes Syracusanus 92 F 3.3 *TrGF*; Lycophron *Alex.* 1056–8; Verg. *Aen.* 4.169–70 *ille dies primus leti primusque malorum causa fuit*, 6.428–9 *quos . . . abstulit atra dies et funere mersit acerbo*; and Ov. *Meta.* 15.873–4 *cum uolet ille dies, qui nil nisi corporis huius | ius habet.* Since Eos, dawning on the day of Troy's destruction, was that fatal day personified, the Chorus can reproach her with taking a fatal role in Troy's demise. But the main charge, as against Zeus, is indifference. —I translate Diggle's text, which incorporates Murray's φίλιον Ἁμέραc and Bothe's γαίαc. The former restores sense and metre; the latter rids us of having to take εἶδε with two disparate objects, 'land' and 'destruction', and restores a second genitive dependent on 'destruction'. Since φέγγοc is already modified by φίλιον βροτοῖc we must take ὀλοόν predicatively, as above.

853–4 **τεκνοποιὸν ἔχουcα τᾶcδε | γᾶc πόcιν ἐν θαλάμοιc**: 'though she had a husband of this land in her bedroom to father her children'. The feminine participle is the *constructio ad sensum*, agreeing with the goddess who personifies the φέγγοc: see 535n and 740. The tradition mentions two sons of this union, Memnon and Emathion.

855–7 The Chorus return to an earlier point in the story to mention the carrying away of Tithonus, 'whom a starry four-horse chariot of gold snatched up and removed, (an act that was) a source of great hope to his ancestral land'.

855 ***ἀcτέρων***: for the genitive of quality see KG 1.264, Barrett on *Hipp.* 802, and Finglass on Soph. *El.* 19. The genitive here could indicate what the golden chariot was made of or to what realm it belonged.

856 ***χρύcεοc***: everything connected with the gods can plausibly be described as 'golden': see Davies–Finglass on Stesichorus fr. 8.1–2 F., Diggle 1970: 153 (on *Phaethon* 238), and Finglass on *El.* 510 and *Aj.* 92–3. The first syllable of this adjective is long in epic and in the spoken parts of tragedy. In tragic lyric it is sometimes long (e.g. 820) but often, as here, short. For a list of tragic instances (all lyric, including three in Soph.), see Page on *Med.* 633–4, and see Braswell on Pi. *P.* 4.4(c) for this scansion in Pindar and Bacchylides and an explanation for the variation in the quantity of the *upsilon*.

857 ***ἐλπίδα γᾶι πατρίαι μεγάλαν***: for the 'accusative in apposition to the sentence' see 536n.

857–8 ***τὰ θεῶν δὲ | φίλτρα φροῦδα Τροίαι***: 'But Troy has lost (lit. 'vanished for Troy is') the gods' love.' The Chorus end by summing up their complaint: the gods have for some reason discontinued their favour of Troy. As we have seen, the audience could easily have supplied reasons. For *φίλτρα*, 'love, affection', see *El.* 1309. Eur.'s partiality for *φροῦδοc* (thirty-nine times in the extant plays, once in the fragments) was marked enough to be parodied at Ar. *Ran.* 1343. See also 1071 below.

THIRD EPISODE (860–1059)

The episode is built around an *agōn*, a trial in which Helen is the defendant, Hecuba the prosecutor, and Menelaus the judge. Its contribution to the play has been variously described. Some (e.g. Pohlenz 1954: 1.369–70) see it as a further misery for the Trojans that Helen is not going to be punished for her role in causing the destruction of Troy. But as Lloyd 1984: 303–4 points out, Eur. does not make Menelaus reverse his earlier decision, and his last words (1055–9) reaffirm it. Neither Hecuba nor the Chorus react with sorrow to the outcome of the trial. The audience, to be sure, cannot be in any doubt that Menelaus and Helen will eventually reconcile (in no ancient source is she put to death, and in the *Odyssey* she and Menelaus are living together contentedly), a reconciliation prefigured by Hecuba's 891–4 and 1049–51. But that future reconciliation has no effect on the Trojan women since they do not know about it, and Lloyd 1984: 304 seems to be right in saying 'Helen's escape, right or wrong, is not an issue in the play.' Several scholars have regarded the debate as non-integral to the play: see Steiger 1900: 375 ('interesting but not tragic'), Wilamowitz 282 ('all this of course does not belong in a tragedy, least of all one that has brought two gods bodily on stage'), and Lee xxii ('not entirely relevant' to the play). Rather than being content with such verdicts it seems better to look further to find a connection between the episode and the rest of the trilogy.

The debate centres around the question whether Helen bears sole responsibility for eloping with Paris and therefore (a further point nowhere explicitly argued for) is the person solely responsible for the destruction of Troy (Hecuba's position) or whether her responsibility is diminished because of the influence of Aphrodite (Helen's position). The majority of scholars have regarded Hecuba as the winner: see e.g. Steiger 1900: 375–86, Nestle 1901: 90–1, Wilamowitz 276–84, Parmentier 18–20, Pohlenz 1954: 1.369–70, Grube 1961: 27, Kitto 1961: 211–12, Stinton 1965: 35–9, Lesky 1972: 288, Koniaris 1973: 98–100, Lee xxi–xxiii, Erbse 1984: 68–72, Biehl's introduction (325–7) to the episode, Burian 2009: 173–4, Mastronarde 2010: 78 (qualified at 222), and Blondell 2013: 182–201. A few have declared that there is no winner, e.g. Barlow 205–7, who says the truth lies 'somewhere in between', and Lloyd 1992: 110–12, who thinks it is impossible to decide who is right or to find any middle ground. (Croally 1994: 134–62 shows the many paradoxes inherent in the debate without saying whether there is a winner.) Only occasionally is Helen's case taken seriously: Scodel 96–7 says that Hecuba cannot be right about the Judgement, and Rabinowitz 2008: 135 that the audience is unlikely to have agreed with Hecuba's rationalistic view.

If Hecuba is the winner, the episode centres around her thesis 'We are all solely responsible for what we do, no matter what mythology says.' This is a point of view quite removed from the world of tragedy, in which the gods are regularly seen as influencing the behaviour of characters by sending *atē* or otherwise shaping their actions, as the scholars quoted above admit. It is also distant from this play and trilogy. *Alexandros* begins with Hecuba's dream, and it is clear that the survival of the Trojan prince and the ruinous consequences of this are presented as divinely ordained, a point reiterated by Andromache at *Tro.* 597–600. *Tro.* itself contains other references to the working of the divine in the world. If Hecuba's speech is intended to be regarded as the truth, it is a truth at variance with the rest of the play. The scholars quoted above do not explain why Eur. chose this moment to propound his untragic thesis about human responsibility. A 'Troy means Melos' allegorist might attempt to argue that his purpose is to show that the Athenians cannot excuse themselves for their aggression in the world by appealing to divine compulsion. But the Athenians are unlikely to have done so (the compulsion mentioned at Thuc. 5.105.2 is not a compulsion by the gods but one that acts on both gods and men); furthermore, to equate Helen's role in the Trojan War with that of the Athenians in the Peloponnesian War would be a decided stretch.

In contrast to the thematic unconnectedness of the episode that results from regarding Hecuba's argument as the truth, consider what happens when we take Helen's argument seriously. If we recognize that, in the trilogy's terms, the three goddesses came to the Judgement in deadly earnest (I discuss the text at 975–6n below), the result of Paris' choice of Aphrodite was that Hera and Athena both conceived an implacable hatred of Troy (see for this hatred 23–4, 46–7, 59, 68, and 72, for which no explanation is offered other than the traditional one). Hecuba's claim that Hera and Athena could not have made the offers Helen says they made flies in the face of the poetic tradition (see 973–4n below) and is mere assertion.

Aphrodite, by contrast, became his determined champion, and the poetic tradition unanimously makes her intervention the decisive reason for Helen's elopement: see below. The trilogy bears this out. From a passage in Ennius' translation of *Alexandros* (*fr. incert.* 151.16 M., *Alexander* fr. 17(d). 47–9 J.) we learn of Cassandra's prophecy that because Paris judged the goddesses, Helen was going to come to Troy: *eheu uidete: | iudicauit inclitum iudicium inter deas tris aliquis | quo iudicio Lacedaemonia mulier Furiarum una adueniet*, which clearly implies that Aphrodite brought about Helen's elopement. Rather than imagine that Eur. used the third episode to propound a mythologically novel theory of individual responsibility, it is more plausible to think that he introduces this debate precisely to emphasize—directly through Helen's words and indirectly by using Hecuba's arguments as a foil to them—the divine background to the destruction of Troy.

Why have scholars generally thought that Hecuba's view was meant to seem the truth? I give what appear to be their reasons and some evidence to discount them.

1. There is the formal argument that Eur. has inverted the order of the speeches (defendant before prosecutor) so that 'the stronger argument and the speech of the sympathetic character come second' (Lee on 912–13). It is not, however, the case that the second speaker is always the one the

audience are expected to approve of. Lloyd 1984: 304 cites Medea (*Med.* 465–519) and Polynices (*Pho.* 469–96) as sympathetic characters with the stronger arguments speaking first. He also points out that in *Tro.* the defendant speaks first because her plea is an appeal against a judgement already made by Menelaus.

2. It is alleged that Helen's arguments of self-exculpation are poor, roughly the equivalent of 'the devil made me do it', and that Eur. would not have put such arguments in the mouth of someone he meant to win a debate. But though 'the devil made me do it' is a poor excuse, the same is arguably not true, for the audience of a fifth-century tragedy, of Helen's claim that Aphrodite, making good on her bribe to Paris, caused her to leave Sparta. There is, first, the Homeric background, which would have been familiar to Eur.'s audience: see 940–4n below. It is often maintained that Eur. and (many of) his contemporaries have moved on from Homer's world view, but *prima facie* the gods are active in his tragedies in a similar way. It would take skilful advocacy to prove, e.g., that Phaedra's responsibility is in no way diminished by Aphrodite's interference with her emotions or that Heracles is solely to blame for the death of his children. Second, as noted above, in *Alexandros* Cassandra prophesied that the Judgement of Paris would have disastrous results by bringing Helen to Troy as a spirit of destruction. The implication of this—that Helen's elopement had a divine causation—will not be countered in the audience's mind by Hecuba's assertion, unsupported by any new facts, that it simply could not have happened that way.

3. There is the feeling that Eur., in whose works untraditional ways of thinking are clearly in evidence, must of course be putting this correction of Homeric mythology in Hecuba's mouth in order to recommend it to his audience. (Steiger 1900: 378–82 and Wilamowitz 281–4 can tell us—because they simply know—that Eur. found the Homeric conception of divine intervention in human life utterly unsatisfactory.) But there is much less consensus than there once was either that Eur. held advanced views or that he used his plays to recommend them to his countrymen. Whatever his personal view of the gods may have been, his plays presuppose the archaic Greek universe in which human beings interact with and are influenced by anthropomorphic divinities. The flash of 'Greek enlightenment' found at *Herc.* 1341–6 does not alter the fundamental realities of the play's action.

4. Lastly, there is Hecuba's role as a focus of sympathy in the play: how could Eur. have put her on the wrong side of this debate? Yet sympathetic characters sometimes argue brilliantly but on mistaken presuppositions. Theseus in *Hipp.*, for example, argues with crushing logic that his son is guilty. His arguments ἐκ τῶν εἰκότων would be valid ordinarily, but in a

world where the gods intervene they miss the mark. Hippolytus, for his part, though in the right, is forced by circumstances to sound much less sympathetic than he might, much as Helen does in the present passage. Hecuba's being a focus of sympathy does not mean she is right. In brief, though Hecuba is 'the queen of sorrows', she is also wrong about the role of the gods in the world, and Helen, though having no argument except 'a god made me do it', is right.

The example of Theseus shows that a prosecutor can be mistaken without forfeiting the good will of the audience. We can also compare one of the 'optimistic rationalist' figures to which Mastronarde 1986 draws attention, Theseus at *Supp.* 195–249. The optimistic rationalist thinks the world is governed in such a way that tragedy can be avoided because the gods are perfectly good, and Theseus in *Supp.* blames Adrastus in a way that leaves no room for the possibility that he may have been set up to fail by the gods, but he still remains Theseus, the heroic recoverer of the Argive dead. On this showing Hecuba too can be wrong and also sympathetic.

We must also consider the possibility that Hecuba, though the focus of sympathy in one sense, is not intended to be seen as a fully sympathetic character. I have already drawn attention (610–20n) to her self-absorption, her inability to recognize that others may have griefs as great as her own. Here she attacks a woman who is a captive like herself, one who has already been sentenced to death. Having received permission to contribute to her condemnation she produces a zealous speech of prosecution, one concentrating in laser-like fashion on her role in the fall of Troy and refusing to acknowledge any contribution to it by the Trojans. Helen says (reasonably) that Priam and Hecuba share responsibility for the survival of Paris and hence for the fall of Troy, but the queen does not acknowledge the point at all. Likewise the Trojans, who were asked both before the war and during its course to return her and the treasure Paris stole (see 780–1n above) might have overridden Paris' objections and returned Menelaus' wife and property. Hecuba says that Helen's elopement was the sole cause of Troy's fall when it would not have had that effect if the Trojans had acted differently. Furthermore, it is quite possible that in *Alexandros* she learned about the Judgement from Paris and knew that it happened as Helen describes it. If so, her attack on her daughter-in-law is not only mistaken but also knowingly false. As it is, we can see in the play we have that her arguments are captious and unfair (see 998–1001n, 1010–14n, and 1015–22n). Likewise when she engages in Ionian cosmological speculation (see 884–8n) or in reductionist etymologizing *à la* Prodicus (see 987–90n) these may be intended to suggest a worldview that is radically rationalistic and has little room for piety as traditionally conceived.

The episode is articulated as follows: (1) Menelaus' entrance monologue and his orders to his men to bring Helen out (860–83); (2) the intervention of Hecuba, who thanks Zeus for bringing about Helen's just punishment and warns Menelaus not to look at her (884–94); (3) the entrance of Helen from the *skēnē* and a three-cornered dialogue setting up the *agōn* (895–913); (4) the *agōn* proper, consisting of defence and prosecution speeches by Helen and Hecuba (914–1035); (5) Menelaus' sentence of death and Helen's plea for understanding (1036–48); and (6) a dialogue in which Hecuba warns Menelaus not to travel in the same ship with Helen (1049–59).

860–83. Menelaus' entrance monologue and orders to his men

Hecuba is on stage when the episode begins, but Menelaus at his entrance makes no 'contact' with her (or the Chorus) until she speaks at 884–8. (On 'contact' see Mastronarde 1979: 2–3.) Further instances where a character, entering the acting area with others already present, speaks a non-dramatic monologue are *Herc.* 523–8 (Heracles), *Or.* 356–74 (Menelaus), and *Ba.* 215–51 (Pentheus). (The monologuists at *Alc.* 747–72 and *Hel.* 386–434 enter to an empty stage.) The monologue allows for a more complete self-presentation, permitting the audience to see how Menelaus views the coming confrontation with Helen.

Staging: enter Menelaus with retinue by the right *eisodos*.

860–2 'O fair-gleaming light of the sun I behold here (τόδε), in which I shall become master of my wife Helen.' The reference to the day that brought the fall of Troy and the recapture of Helen is perhaps an echo of 848–51. The phrase is a *vocativus pendens*, i.e. it is not integrated into any larger syntactical unit: on this originally hieratic device see Fraenkel on *Ag.* 1470–1 (p. 698), Stevens on *Andr.* 7, Bond on *Herc.* 798–9, and Dodds on *Ba.* 521–2. In Eur. see further examples at *Alc.* 1–2, *Hipp.* 752–6, *El.* 1–3, 54–8, 432–41, *Tro.* 122–37, *IT* 157–66, *Ion* 492–506, *Hel.* 1451–65, and *Ba.* 120–5. Eur.'s fondness for this construction may be parodied in Ar. *Ran.* 1309–16.

—Herwerden 1855: 377 deleted 862–3, and he is followed by Diggle. Certainly as they stand they give impossible sense, for 862 says 'I am the much toiling Menelaus and the Greek army', which is nonsense. (Biehl's suggestion that we supply ἐμόχθηcε with cτράτευμ' seems impossible.) Furthermore, the scholiast says περιccὸν τὸ Μενέλαόc εἰμι· αὐταρκὲc γὰρ τὸ δάμαρτα τὴν ἐμὴν χειρώcομαι, implying that the identification of Menelaus is unnecessary here. Third, some have thought Ἑλένην in 862 inconsistent with the preference announced at 869–70 (thus Page 1934: 74). But two considerations make against deletion. First, the lines cannot be dispensed with: the new arrival, *pace* the scholiast, needs either to be identified at once by another (like Heracles at *Herc.* 516–19 and Pentheus at *Ba.* 212) or identify himself (like Menelaus at *Hel.* 392 and *Or.* 366). Second, interpolators write in order to solve problems, not create them, and so if a passage makes no sense, as 863 does not, our first duty is not to delete but to emend. As for the supposed inconsistency between 862 and 869–70, the latter lines say that Menelaus takes no pleasure in mentioning his wife's name, not that he never does so, and Page's principle would require altering or deleting 877 as well. West 1980: 16 marks a lacuna after Μενέλαος in 863, supplying e.g. <αἰχμῆι καὶ καταςκάψας πόλιν | νῦν Ἑλλάδ'> εἶμι καὶ cτράτευμ' Ἀχαιικόν, 'For I, Menelaus, who have toiled so long <in war and razed the city,> am going <now to Greece>, and the Greek army with me.' (For the joining of the unexpressed subject of a 1st- or 2nd-person verb by 'and' to a further subject requiring a 3rd-person verb, see 1002–3, ἐπεὶ δὲ Τροίαν ἦλθες Ἀργεῖοί τέ cου | κατ' ἴχνος.) The change of εἰμι to εἶμι is welcome since nowhere does the speaker of a monologue (whether initial or mid-play) ever introduce himself with a bare 'X εἰμι' but always with an action verb such as ἥκω.

864–79 Menelaus explains that his purpose in coming to Troy was not, as generally thought, to get his wife back but to punish Paris, the deceitful guest friend who stole her from his home. Now, with the gods' help (cὺν θεοῖc), both Paris and his city have been punished. He means to fetch Helen from the hut where she is being held, take her to Greece, and there exact the death penalty that will satisfy all those affected by her elopement. The Greek army has explicitly given him permission to kill or to spare his errant wife.

Normally a monologue of the prologue type admits of no suggestion that the speaker is insincere. (*Or.* 356–79 *may* be an exception, as argued at Kovacs 2002: 284–5.) We should not therefore interpret 864–6 as a case of 'protesting too much'. Menelaus is not addressing anyone he hopes will think better of him, and he betrays no weakness toward Helen in the course of the episode. Obviously, unless Helen is going to be killed and the entire poetic tradition set aside, he must change his mind about her subsequently. But at this point he is firmly committed to killing her. That he feels distaste at using her name, calling her instead 'the Spartan woman' and 'her who was once my wife' (869–70), suggests the same thing. I see no evidence that Menelaus would dearly love to embrace his wife but suppresses his own feelings because he is 'strictly bound to his appointed task', as suggested by Biehl (p. 320).

866 ***ξεναπάτης***: the word occurs at *Med.* 1392 of Jason but nowhere else in tragedy (it is used of Paris at Ibycus fr. S151.10 [= fr. 282.10 *PMG*], a reference I owe to PJF). That Paris seduced Helen and persuaded her to leave Sparta was a crime against his *ξένος* Menelaus and hence a sin against Zeus Xenios. At *Ag.* 61–2 the Chorus claim that Zeus Xenios sent the Greeks to Troy to punish him and his city for this.

ἐλῄσατο: in saying that Paris took Helen away as plunder (see 614n) Menelaus regards his action as a crime against property. He does not mean that Helen did not leave of her own free will, and he clearly regards her as deserving of punishment: see 879 and 881–2.

867 ***σὺν θεοῖς***: a pious acknowledgement of higher powers not unlike that of Agamemnon at *Ag.* 810–13.

868 That not only Paris but also his city had to pay for his offence against Zeus Xenios is not at all surprising. The Trojans, as is plain from the *Iliad*, were complicit in Paris' theft. There is a parallel in the prologue to our play, where the whole Greek fleet is to be wrecked by Athena and Poseidon because the Greeks did not punish Ajax's removal of Cassandra from Athena's temple.

871 ***δόμοις***: here and at 880 the temporary structure of a military hut is described as if it were a permanent dwelling. See also 154. On this habit in plays set on battlefields see Arnott 1962: 100.

872 ***Τρωιάδων ἄλλων μέτα***: possibly not 'with the other women of Troy' (thus my Loeb) since Helen is not a Trojan by birth, but 'with the others, the Trojan women'. For this idiom (the 'Penelope and the other handmaids' construction), see LSJ s.v. *ἄλλος* A.II.8. For a similar usage see Finglass on Soph. *El.* 708 and Jebb on *OT* 290. For the sentiment that Helen is justly classed with the captives, see above 35n.

873–5 'Those whose labour won her have given her to me to kill, or, if I prefer, to spare and take back to Greece.' See Kiefner 142, who notes that *εἴτε* and *θέλοιμ'* are to be taken *ἀπὸ κοινοῦ*, expressed only in the second of the two clauses to which they apply. See also *GP* 507n1. Biehl (pp. 320–1) claims that the army have ordered Menelaus to kill his wife, either in Troy or in Greece, but here *μὴ κτανὼν ... ἄγεσθαι* clearly leaves him the option of not killing her at all. (Furthermore, if Menelaus has no choice but to kill Helen, the *agōn* loses its point.)

875 ***ἄγεσθαι***: the same verb is used, likewise in the middle voice, of a man marrying a woman. It is hard to know whether this nuance—that Menelaus' taking Helen back to Sparta is a second marriage—would have been felt.

ἐς Ἀργείαν χθόνα: in view of Elmsley's demonstration (on *Ba.* 1) that with *χθών* Eur. always uses adjectives like *Ἀργεία* in preference to the possessive genitive, we can reject the reading of V. With *πόλις* or *ἄστυ*, by contrast, he prefers the genitive: see Diggle 1994: 442–4.

877 ***ναυπόρωι...πλάτηι***: LSJ s.v. say that paroxytone *ναυπόρος* = *ναυσιπόρος*. At *Rhes.* 48 the latter modifies *στρατιά*, 'passing in a ship'. Here the former modifies a noun that is used by metonymy to mean 'ship', which is more difficult. But see above 122–5n for the phenomenon of the compound adjective one of whose elements repeats the idea of the modified noun. Both the present instance and the similar collocation at *IA* 172 (*pace* LSJ, not 'oars' but 'ships') mean 'sea-going vessel(s)'.

878 ***δοῦναι κτανεῖν***: 'give her over to be killed'. For the construction see 418–19n. As noted there, English idiom usually calls for the passive and Greek for the active infinitive.

879 'To satisfy all those whose kinfolk have been killed at Troy' (lit. 'as satisfaction to (all those) for whom near-and-dear have been killed'). On this construction, the so-called 'accusative in apposition to the sentence', see 536n. 'To all those for whom' is neatly expressed by Canter's *ὅσοις* (in his edition of 1571), which provides a dative of disadvantage with *τεθνᾶσ'*, while its understood antecedent, *τοσούτοις*, is dative of advantage with *ποινάς*.

—Canter's conjecture should be regarded as virtually certain, for without it we cannot explain what is transmitted. V's *ὅσων* is straightforward: supply *τοσούτοις* and the sense is 'for all those of whom near-and-dear perished in Troy'. But the corruption to *ὅσοι* would be unexplained since the result is more difficult, not less: 'for all those (being) near-and-dear who perished in Troy': the dative antecedent is not easily supplied out of the nominative pronoun, and the absence of *ὄντες* with *φίλοι* is awkward. By contrast we can explain *ὅσοι* as a careless truncation of an original dative plural. Once that happened, alteration to the genitive plural (no less good sense than the dative) would have been natural. Note that satisfaction made to the living, not the dead, explains why Helen's execution is to be held in Greece, another reason to reject *ὅσοι*.

880 ***ἀλλ' εἶα***: these words are used to mark a strong break in thought, here from reflection to action. According to *GP* 14, this collocation with the imperative is 'common in Eur., and perhaps confined to him'. (For its use by others see Ion fr. 22; Ar. *Thesmo.* 985, *Eccl.* 496, and *Plut.* 292 and 316.) Other collocations are discussed in Diggle 1970: 145 (on *Phaethon* 221). For the rough breathing on *εἶα* see Mastronarde on *Pho.* 970.

882 For the genitive with *ἐπισπάω* see LSJ s.v. 1.

883 ***πέμψομεν***: see above on 355–6 for the common meaning 'escort', not 'send'.

Staging: in response to Menelaus' command two of his retinue enter the *skēnē*.

884–8. Hecuba's prayer

Hecuba, on stage during Menelaus' entrance monologue and his instructions to his retinue, now breaks her silence, addressing not Menelaus but the divine or quasi-divine power that directs the universe. In Menelaus' announcement that he intends to execute Helen she sees the working of this power: 'For you, proceeding on a silent path, direct all mortal affairs in accordance with justice.'

Hecuba's prayer adds an abstract and philosophical conception of divinity to elements from the traditional language of prayer. Her emphasis on the divinity's hidden guidance of events makes a point of contact with traditional religious views (see below on 887–8). By contrast the prayer's first three lines are quite untraditional and show strong connections with Ionian cosmological speculation. Many scholars (e.g. Schadewaldt 1926: 113 and Scodel 94) have reasonably concluded that the source of the ideas here is Diogenes of Apollonia, the last representative of material monism, the belief that all things are derived, by e.g. condensation and rarefaction, from a single element. Like Anaximenes, Diogenes identified this element as air (ἀήρ): see frr. 1–2, 7–8 Graham. As far as we know, the Milesian monists Thales, Anaximander, and Anaximenes did not assign intelligence to this substrate, but for Diogenes air was breath, soul, and intelligence (νόηϲιϲ) and governed the universe so as to make it as good as possible: see frr. 6, 9, 11, 12, and 14 Graham. (By contrast, the scholiast here considers Anaxagoras to be the source of Hecuba's thought. For his belief in the governance of the universe by νοῦϲ, see frr. 4 and 31 Graham.)

Since Diogenes has been identified as the source of the view of the universe expressed in the prayer, some scholars (e.g. Lee) have said that the element surrounding the world is Diogenes' ἀήρ. Others (Schadewaldt 1926: 113, Matthiessen 1968: 699–701, Diggle 1978a: 30) suggest that, in view of several passages in Eur. where the divine is set equal to αἰθήρ, he must have had that element in mind. Egli 2003: 79 suggests that Eur. used αἰθήρ to mean 'air'. Discussions of the prayer in Parmentier 1893: 70–3, Decharme 1893: 85–7, Schadewaldt 1926: 113–18, Langholf 1971: 134–7, Scodel 93–5, Egli 2003: 81–94, Schorn 2004: 214–15 with further literature, and Lefkowitz 2016: 34–8.

884 ***ὦ γῆς ὄχημα κἀπὶ γῆς ἔχων ἕδραν***: 'you that support the earth and have your seat upon it'. Both halves of this are untraditional, for the gods' seat is in heaven or on Olympus, not upon earth or supporting the earth from beneath. It is characteristic of Ionic cosmological speculation (see Anaximenes, frr. 11 and 12 Graham, both using *ἐποχέομαι* and Thales frr. 18 and 20 Graham) to imagine the primal substance that replaces the anthropomorphic deities as surrounding the earth, not merely above it. The same idea of a surrounding element is found in frr. 919 and 941, while fr. 944 has the earth resting upon *αἰθήρ*. To say that divinity has its seat upon the earth seems to stress the idea that it is not an agent operating from without but is immanent within the cosmos it controls.

885 ***ὅcτιc ποτ' εἶ cύ, δυcτόπαcτοc εἰδέναι***: 'whoever you are, for you are hard to know by conjecture'. For the traditional prayer formula, indicating a willingness to call the god by any name he wishes, see Fraenkel on *Ag*. 160. Both *Ag*. 160–2 and this passage emphasize that Zeus's person and activity are mysterious.

886 'Either Zeus or the necessity of nature or the mind of mortals'. There are three possibilities for the force that governs the universe: (a) the anthropomorphic king of the gods, (b) the material necessity that makes things behave as they do, and (c) an intelligence (distinct from Zeus) that is visible in mortals (but presumably exists outside of mortals as well). These may represent an ascending order of probability for Hecuba, who criticizes myths about the gods she considers unworthy of them. Does she have a preference for (c) over (b)? The text does not make this clear, but the last item could be viewed as a sensible compromise between anthropomorphism and an impersonal necessity.

Ζεύc: it is preferable to put no comma after this word (as in the translation of Wilamowitz 336 and in Langholf 1971: 134), in which case the phrase *Ζεὺc εἴτ' ἀνάγκη φύcεοc εἴτε νοῦc βροτῶν* consists of three parallel expressions in apposition to *cύ*, Zeus being one of three possible designations for the force that surrounds the earth. (For the omission of the first *εἴτε* of a series of two or three see 874, *IT* 272, and fr. 912.2–3.) Less good is to punctuate after *Ζεύc* (Diggle and my Loeb), taking *Ζεύc* as nominative for vocative (on this see literature cited above 267n; *Ζεύc* for *Ζεῦ* is rare, but see Aesch. *Supp*. 26). This would mean that the name Zeus is a given but that there are two abstract and impersonal choices for what the name might designate. It seems more likely that Hecuba is not sure whether the name 'Zeus' is appropriate.

ἀνάγκη φύcεοc: though *φύcιc* is commonly employed with respect to *human* nature (and is so taken here by Scodel 94), sense here seems to call for the meaning 'the necessity that governs the natural world': if it referred to irresistible urges in the human being, it would not be distinct from *νοῦϲ βροτῶν*. In the title *περὶ φύϲεωϲ* given to cosmological works by Anaximander, Heraclitus, Empedocles, Diogenes of Apollonia, and Gorgias, *φύϲιϲ* appears to mean 'all that is, the universe'. The phrase *ἀνάγκη φύϲεοϲ* seems to mean the law or compulsion that governs the physical universe: Democritus, for example, is credited in Diog. Laert. 9.45 (= DK 68 A1(45); not in Graham) with the doctrine that everything happens necessarily since the motion of the vortex brings forth all things that are.

νοῦϲ βροτῶν: Anaxagoras called the principle governing the universe *νοῦϲ*, but there is no indication that he located it in human beings. Diogenes (fr. 9 Graham) says that the human spirit or mind is or partakes in the *ἀήρ* that is both the world's substrate and its governor. The phrase should perhaps be read as a brachylogy for 'the mind that governs the universe for the best, a mind in which the human mind participates'.

887 **προϲηυξάμην ϲε**: 'I offer my prayer of thanks to you.' On the instantaneous or tragic aorist see 53n. Lloyd 1999: 39 cites *Pers.* 498 and *El.* 415 for the meaning 'offer a prayer of thanks', which the context here requires. The prayer may be accompanied by the gesture of lifting the hands to heaven: see Spitzbarth 1945: 18–19 and Finglass on *El.* 636.

887–8 **δι' ἀψόφου | βαίνων κελεύθου**: 'proceeding on a noiseless track (or 'with noiseless step')'. The idea that the gods accomplish their purposes unobtrusively is found in tragedy at Adesp. Trag. fr. 486 and 493 (text uncertain) and at *TrGF* 76 (Dionysius) fr. 4. There may be a connection with Solon fr. 4.14–16 W., where Justice silently notes and in time punishes transgressions. At Eur. fr. 979.3 the tread of Justice is silent and slow.

889–94. Hecuba's dialogue with Menelaus

Menelaus, in reply, asks what Hecuba means and draws attention to the novelty of her prayer. Hecuba praises Menelaus' intention to kill Helen but warns him of the danger that he will fall once more under her spell: to underline this danger she hints that Helen's name is derived from *ἑλεῖν*, 'capture, destroy'.

889 **τί δ' ἔϲτιν**: the expression indicates surprise: 'What's this you say?'

εὐχὰϲ ὡϲ ἐκαίνιϲαϲ θεῶν: 'How novel your prayer to the gods is!' The 'novelty' of Hecuba's prayer is mostly in 884, which seems to describe Zeus in terms used by the physical philosophers, and 886, which conceives of him less as a person than as a personification of either the ineluctable force of nature or something inherent in the mind of mortals. As noted above, neither 885 nor 887–8 is particularly novel.

889 Hecuba's 'I approve your intention to kill your wife' does not answer Menelaus' comment about the novelty of her prayer but only his 'What's this you say?'

εἰ κτενεῖϲ δάμαρτα ϲήν: here εἰ means 'that': see Smyth § 2247. The construction is common with verbs such as ἀγανακτέω but found also with verbs, such as ἄγαμαι, expressing a favourable emotion.

891 'But avoid looking at her lest she take you captive with desire.'

—Stanley's and Reiske's ὁρᾶν is a necessary correction. For the construction see LSJ s.v. φεύγω, I.4.

892–3 These lines, which refer to ἕλῃι in 891, bring out the implicit etymology Ἑλένη < ἑλεῖν: cf. *Ag.* 681–92, where the chorus claim that Helen's name is eerily prophetic since she is ἑλέναυϲ, ἕλανδροϲ, and ἑλέπτολιϲ. Eur. makes the same pun at *Hec.* 443 and possibly at *Andr.* 106, *El.* 1279, and *Tro.* 1214. It is noteworthy that neither αἱρεῖ nor ἐξαιρεῖ uses the aorist stem on which the etymology depends. Euripidean etymologies sometimes explain a word by means of a synomym of the actual *etymon*: see *Ion* 9, 802, *IT* 32, and *Hel.* 13, and also Soph. *OC* 107–8 and Chaeremon *TrGF* 71 F 4, Πενθεὺϲ ἐϲομένηϲ ϲυμφορᾶϲ ἐπώνυμοϲ. On the prominence of etymology in tragedy see Collard on *Supp.* 496–7a and Finglass on *Aj.* 430–1.

893 **πίμπρηϲιν οἴκουϲ**: Housman 1888: 282 sees here a further etymology of Helen's name at work, from ἑλάνη, 'firebrand'. On this as a possible etymology in Aesch. see Kovacs 2000. The image of Helen as firebrand recalls Hecuba's dream of Alexandros as δαλόϲ. —Dobree's conjecture (1833: 92) restores the asyndetic connection of the three parallel phrases.

Staging: Menelaus' servants bring Helen out forcibly from the *skēnē*. If Menelaus' orders are obeyed literally, one of her captors pulls her along by her hair. We later learn that her clothing is not ragged nor is her hair shorn in mourning, but we cannot say for certain that she is spectacularly turned out (though this, of course, has in no way limited modern producers' instructions to their costume designers). Hecuba notes in 1022–3 that she has taken some trouble with her appearance.

895–913. Menelaus' conversation with both Helen and Hecuba

Brought forcibly out of the *skēnē* Helen expresses worry that this rough treatment may presage worse to come and wants to know what has been decided about her. When Menelaus explains that the army has given him the right to kill her if he likes, she asks whether she may speak in her own defence. Menelaus refuses the request, but Hecuba intervenes and asks that she be allowed to speak provided that Hecuba herself may speak for the prosecution: she will make it unmistakable that putting Helen to death is the just course. Menelaus gives his permission, emphasizing that he is granting this as a favour to Hecuba and not out of regard for Helen.

895–900 *φροίμιον* indicates that Helen regards the rough handling by Menelaus' men as an indication of her future fate. She recognizes, to be sure (*μέν*), that Menelaus hates her, yet she wants to ask what decision has been made regarding her fate.

898 Of the two transmitted participles *μιcουμένη* is the more ordinary and should be regarded as a banalization.

901 ***οὐκ εἰc ἀκριβὲc ἦλθεν***: the subject of *ἦλθεν* is impersonal: 'It did not come to an exactitude', i.e. a precise decision, with perhaps a hint of 'severe, in accordance with strict justice'. For the use of *ἀκριβ-* in detailed instructions see Plat. *Pol.* 295b2, *δι' ἀκριβείαc προcτάττειν τὸ προcῆκον*; for the sense 'severe, exacting', see Thuc. 1.99.1. (Much less plausible is the scholiast's paraphrase, 'the vote was not close and no exact counting was necessary': *ἅπαc cτρατόc* shows that the vote was unanimous, not merely lopsided.) *ἀκριβήc* and congeners occur nine times in Eur. and once in *Rhesus* but elsewhere in tragedy only at *PV* 328 and adesp. 348c.

—We owe the reading *ἦλθεν* to the scholiast alone: the mss. have *ἦλθεc*, less good sense, though 'You (i.e. your case) did not come to an exactitude' is not impossible. The adjacent *-εc* of *ἀκριβέc* may have caused the corruption. (Biehl retains the ms. reading, but his translation 'du hast den entscheidenden Punkt nicht getroffen' does not suit the context. LSJ s.v. *ἀκριβήc* II.1 give '[You did not come] at the right moment', but a comment on the timing of Helen's arrival makes no sense here.) Denniston 1936: 116 says that anarthrous *ἀκριβέc* lacks sufficient parallel and proposes *οὐκ ἦλθεc εἰc τἀκριβέc*. (It may be defensible in view of such expressions as *εἰc καλόν*.) In any case Menelaus has a free hand. Both Hecuba (1029–32) and the Chorus Leader (1033–5) likewise treat Menelaus as the deciding party.

901–2 ***ἅπαc cτρατὸc | κτανεῖν ἐμοί c' ἔδωκεν***: 'The entire army has handed you over to me to kill.' This is an abbreviated version of 873–9, where the army gives Menelaus the right to kill her if he wants. Menelaus' formulation here means the same thing, but the briefer version, omitting the possibility of mercy, may be intended to suggest to Helen that her doom is sealed.

902 *ὅνπερ ἠδίκειϲ*: adultery by a wife is conceived as damage to the husband's honour. Since Menelaus was the chief victim of Helen's elopement, the army has left it to him to determine her punishment.

903–4 Helen wants to know whether she may say anything by way of exculpation to show that her execution would be unjust.

905 Menelaus rejects any such plea in advance: he has already made up his mind.

906–10 Hecuba asks Menelaus to hear Helen out provided that she herself is allowed to speak for the prosecution.

906 *μὴ θάνηι τοῦδ' ἐνδεήϲ*: execution without trial is viewed in Greek sources as highly irregular: cf. Hdt. 3.80; Thuc. 2.67 and 8.48; Lys. 19.7; and Xen. *Hell.* 1.7.5.

908–10 909–10 mean 'When the entire account has been put together, it will bring about her death, and she will have nowhere to escape to.' (For the judicial sense of *ἀποκτείνω*, used of a prosecutor securing a defendant's death or a judge imposing it, see LSJ s.v. 2.) Menelaus knows about Helen's elopement and the woes it caused. What he does not yet know (908–9) is *τὰ ἐν Τροίαι κακά*. If this is to be fully relevant to Menelaus' verdict the phrase must mean not 'the troubles we endured in Troy' but 'her misdeeds in Troy', a meaning assisted by *κατ' αὐτῆϲ* immediately before it. (The neuter forms of *κακόϲ* normally refer to what is painful or troublesome, not to what is morally reprehensible, but for *κακά*, 'misdeeds', see *Hipp.* 425, 695, 707, 949, 998, 1383, *Andr.* 946, *Hec.* 1254, *Supp.* 253, *IT* 1193, *Hel.* 272, 1629, and *Ba.* 512.)

911–13 Menelaus' *ϲχολῆϲ τὸ δῶρον* implies that it would take leisure he does not have to grant this request. But his next statement, introduced by adversative *δέ*, allows Helen to speak. Menelaus is at pains, however, to point out that he does so as a favour to Hecuba, not to Helen. It is Hecuba's intervention that causes the trial scene to take place, and there may be a suggestion that the queen, by being so determined to have a hand in securing Helen's death, may be unintentionally protecting her from execution by giving her estranged husband a longer look at her.

914–65. Helen's *apologia*

Although she knows that Hecuba will be the prosecutor, Helen addresses her entire speech to Menelaus. In a brief *prooemium* she wonders whether he will regard her as an enemy and refuse to reply to her. She announces her intention to answer the accusations she thinks he will make by setting against them just accusations of her own. Her targets are five in number.

(1) Hecuba, not herself, is to blame for the troubles that have afflicted so many by giving birth to Paris. (2) Also to blame is 'the old man' (Priam: see 921n) for failing to kill the baby once he was born. (3) Paris judged the goddesses, rejected Athena's offer of success in war against the Greeks and Hera's of dominion over both Asia and Greece, and succumbed to Aphrodite's offer of the lovely Helen. Because he accepted Helen as a bribe, Greece was spared, but far from getting credit for Greece's good fortune, she is reviled. (4) As for her being persuaded by Paris to leave Sparta with him, that is to be attributed to the power of Aphrodite, for it is inexplicable in ordinary terms that she should leave both her country and her home to follow a foreigner. (5) Menelaus himself contributed to this result by departing for Crete, leaving her alone with Paris. She tries to counter an objection that once Paris had died and the liaison the goddess had inspired was a thing of the past, she should have left Troy for the Greek ships: that, she claims, is what she actually tried to do, though her escape was prevented by the city's watchmen. In sum, she does not deserve to be punished for her actions (which were not free), especially since these actions resulted in the preservation of Greece. To attempt to become master of a goddess such as Aphrodite convicts one of folly.

This defence is sometimes thought to be outrageous or sophistical, but as the above summary shows, it is sober and factual, quite different in spirit from Gorgias' *Encomium of Helen*. It is often claimed (see Guthrie 1971: 192n2, Scodel 144, and Goldhill 1986: 236–8) that Gorgias' treatment preceded Eur.'s and influenced it. But we have no evidence for the date of Gorgias' work, and his love of sophistical paradox (he claims that no matter what motivated Helen to leave Sparta, she was innocent) is not to be found in Helen's speech, which clearly envisages circumstances in which she might be culpable. For the case against the influence of Gorgias on Eur. see Lloyd 1992: 100–1.

914 ***κἂν εὖ κἂν κακῶς δόξω λέγειν***: *εὖ λέγειν* can mean either 'speak persuasively' (whether truly or not) or 'speak truthfully or usefully, make sound proposals'. Here Helen imagines that even if Menelaus thinks (understand *coι* with *δόξω*) that what she is saying is true or useful, he still may not deign to reply.

916–18 'As for me, the accusations which I think you in your attack will make against me I shall answer, setting against your complaints most just complaints of my own.' For idiomatic phrases of the type *διὰ λόγων ἰέναι τινί* see Barrett on *Hipp*. 542–4. The idiom often indicates hostility.

—The scholiast does not comment on 918, and Diggle, following Paley 1872, deletes it. But as transmitted the line is nonsense ('my and your accusations set against yours') and therefore not likely to be written as it stands. Furthermore, *ἀντιθεῖϲ'* must mean 'assert (something) in reply to something else', as at *Or.* 551, so that the dative and accusative objects in 918 are exactly what is needed. Pearson's palmary *τἄμ' ἰϲαίτατ'* gives the sense we need, 'my most just complaints'. On the uncial error of *K* for *IC* see Jackson 54 and West 1973: 25. *ἰϲαίτατοϲ* is not found in the remains of tragedy, but that it is a good tragic word is strongly suggested by *ἰϲαίτερον* at *Supp.* 441. Furthermore, *ἰϲαίτεροϲ* and *ἰϲαίτατοϲ* are the only comparative and superlative forms used by fifth- and fourth-century authors: see Thuc. 8.89.2; Xen. *Hell.* 7.1.14; Plat. *Leg.* 744c3; and [Arist.] *Ath.* 30.3. For *ἴϲοϲ*, 'just', see *Hec.* 805, *Supp.* 432, 441, and 908.

921 **ὁ πρέϲβυϲ**: this is Priam, not the servant Priam ordered to kill the baby. In favour of the latter Scodel 78n30 argues that *οὐ κτανὼν βρέφοϲ* describes the servant who disobeyed his master, not Priam, whose order was disobeyed. But Priam, who could have had the baby killed under his supervision, could reasonably be blamed for not doing so. The chorus at *Andr.* 292–300 blame Hecuba for failing to heed Cassandra's urgent plea to kill the child. (It is special pleading to suggest, as Scodel does, that in this version no measures, not even exposure, were taken: wherever Paris' infancy is mentioned at all, he is exposed.) Furthermore, the offhand reference by Helen to such a minor character seems unlikely, especially in a speech to Menelaus, who could not be expected to know the details of Paris' exposure. The frequent assertion that Paris' foster-father in the first play was called simply *πρέϲβυϲ* rests on the highly uncertain fr. 62d.54, on which see Kannicht. By contrast the use of 'the old man' to refer to Priam occurs at *Hec.* 160–1, *φροῦδοϲ πρέϲβυϲ, φροῦδοι παῖδεϲ*. Diggle 1981: 106 says 'After blaming Hecuba for giving birth to Alexander, the next step is for her to blame Priam for not killing him. To blame the herdsman would be a gross irrelevancy.' For bibliography see Huys 1985: 241n5.

922 —West 1980: 17 suggests deleting 922 as an addition 'designed to reinforce the connection' with *Alexandros*: 'The dream of the firebrand is not necessary to Helen's argument, and to call Paris *δαλοῦ πικρὸν μίμημα* is a clumsy way of dragging it in; *Ἀλέξανδρον* is intolerable, as the child has already been named; *ποτε* is equally intolerable, and Lenting's *τότε* (1821: 86) not much more welcome.' The case is not negligible even if the motive assumed—the tying together of plays in a trilogy—has not been shown to have motivated an interpolator elsewhere.

923–37 Helen has already mentioned Paris as the ἀρχὴ κακῶν, and this aspect of him is emphasized in 922 (if it is genuine). Her narration of the Judgement, however, lays less stress on his culpability and more on the fact that had he chosen otherwise (and therefore had Helen not been taken to Troy), Greece would have fallen under Trojan rule. Erbse 1984: 69–70 tries to argue that Helen's description of the bribes offered cannot be correct because it is different from those in P. Oxy. 663 (the *hypothesis* to Cratinus' *Dionysalexandros*) and Isoc. 10.41–2 (which he says represent the ordinary version (*Vulgatform*) of the Judgement). This is special pleading. In both Cratinus and Isocrates some kind of rule and success in war were promised to Paris, and in Isocrates Aphrodite promises the hand of Helen. In the supposed vulgate, therefore, the goddesses offered bribes. There is no good reason to deny that Helen's description of them is correct for the trilogy.

927–8 'Hera promised that he would have Asia and the territory of Europe as his kingdom if he named her the winner.' For Ἀϲιάϲ (sc. γῆ) see *Ion* 1356. For κρίνω, 'adjudge the winner', see LSJ s.v. II.7.

929 **ἐκπαγλουμένη**: we would expect 'greatly praising' instead of 'greatly admiring', but I know of no conjecture to achieve this sense.

930 **δώϲειν ὑπέϲχετ'**: Aphrodite admires Helen's beauty and so promises *it* to Paris. We might have expected her to promise Helen herself, hence NL's proposal δώϲειν <μ'> ὑπέϲχετ'. The corruption is easy to explain.

931 **τὸν ἔνθεν δ'**: the reading of VP involves asyndeton, which is unwelcome here. I print the reading of p: it looks sound and *might* be genuine tradition, though it could be a happy error: see Introduction § 5, n. 138.

932 **γάμοι**: on this poetic plural see 319n.

934 For οὔτε... οὐ see *GP* 510.

935–6 'And the favourable fortunes Hellas enjoyed I experienced as my destruction since I was sold because of my beauty.' Both ηὐτύχηϲεν and ὠλόμην govern internal accusatives, the first a relative pronoun and the second its understood antecedent.

935 **ηὐτύχηϲεν**: Lautensach 1899:146–9 maintained that compound verbs whose first element was εὖ were not augmented. His view was long accepted, but see now Mastronarde 1989 and Rijksbaron 1991: 133–5.

936–7 'And I am reproached for the (very) deeds on the basis of which I ought to receive a garland on my head.' There is a retained accusative (the antecent of ὧν) understood with ὀνειδίζομαι. For this construction see 375n.

937 **ϲτέφανον**: on crowning for public services in war or peace see LSJ s.v. ϲτέφανοϲ II.2.b and, in tragedy, see *Or.* 923–4 with Willink *ad loc.* For fifth-century examples of crowns awarded by the Athenian *demos* to those responsible for victory in war or other services to Athens see Blech 1982: 153–7.

938 ***αὐτὰ τὰν ποςίν***: 'the most obvious point', lit. 'the very things (that lie) at our feet'. This is explicated by the indirect question 'how I set off secretly from your house'.

940–4 The exculpatory circumstance for Helen is that Paris was accompanied by a powerful goddess, and Menelaus made matters worse by departing for Crete while he was in the house. Helen's account agrees with Homer. At *Il.* 6.355–7 Helen blames the gods for her elopement (Hector does not dispute this statement), and she blames Aphrodite in particular at *Od.* 4.261–6, where Menelaus explicitly says she is right. At *Il.* 3.399–402 she makes this claim to Aphrodite herself, and the goddess, though angered by her disrespectful tone, in no way disputes the truth of what she says. This is not Helen's judgement alone but is also shared by Priam at *Il.* 3.164–5.

940 ***οὐχὶ μικρὰν θεόν***: by litotes or meiosis (on which see 744n) this means 'a quite powerful goddess'.

941 ***ὁ τῆςδ' ἀλάςτωρ***: 'the spirit sent to ruin this woman'. τῆςδ' is probably Hecuba (thus Lloyd 1989: 78): Biehl suggests a reference to herself, but I cannot find an instance of bare ὅδε or ἥδε in this sense without any modified noun.

941–2 ***εἴτ' Ἀλέξανδρον θέλεις | ὀνόματι προςφωνεῖν νιν εἴτε καὶ Πάριν***: the double name Paris/Alexandros may have been explained in the prologue of *Alexandros*: see Introduction § 3.2.1, n. 72. Why is it relevant here that he has two names? Paley defends the lines by paraphrasing: 'You may call him by what name you please, but he was no man, but the devil.' The last phrase, however, is not an obvious thing to supply.

—Paley could be right, but to some the lines have seemed maladroit: the double nomenclature has been visible throughout the play, with Hecuba's son being called Paris at 398 (if genuine), 920, and 928 and Alexandros at 922, 952, and 1020, so it is not clear why attention should be called to it here. Hartung 1837: 47 proposed deleting 942, which would give us the ἀπὸ κοινοῦ use of εἴτε to be seen at 874: 'or Alexandros, if you so prefer' could be thought to make the point that he deserves a more sinister name. Another approach, however, might be 'the spirit sent to destroy this woman, whether you prefer to name him Alexandros or Spirit of Ruin', for which the Greek might be εἴτε καὶ Φθοράν or εἴτε δαίμονα (the latter suggestion was made by Wesener 1874: 8–9). Nauck 1854: 16–17 and 1862: 150–9 proposes εἴτ' ἀλάςτορα for the end of 942 and alters the beginning of 941 to ὁ τῆςδε ληιςτής or ληιςτήρ. He also proposes θέμις for θέλεις.

944 Menelaus' mother Aërope came from Crete, and Menelaus' continuing connection with the island is suggested by *Il.* 3.232–3. Apollodorus *Epit.* 3.3 says that he went to Crete on this occasion to bury his maternal grandfather Catreus.

945–7 'I let the point pass. Next I shall ask not you but myself: What was my purpose when I left my home in the company of a foreigner, abandoning my fatherland and my house?' The oblique phraseology conceals a forceful argument, that there is no natural explanation for her leaving house and country to follow a stranger. (Compare Pasiphaë's argument in Eur.'s *Cretans* fr. 472e, that her attraction to a bull is so unnatural that it must have a supernatural cause, though there the case is more easily made.) The divine causation is made explicit at 948–50, where it is pointed out that Zeus too fell under the compulsion of Aphrodite.

945 **εἶἑν**: on the internal aspiration of this word see SD 2.557 and 558n1 and Finglass on *Aj.* 101. For the word as 'introducing a transition to a fresh point by a backward glance at what has been established' see Stevens 1976: 34. It stands in front of a question, as here, at *Med.* 386, *Hipp.* 297, *Hec.* 313, *Supp.* 1094, *El.* 907, *Herc.* 451, *Tro.* 998, *Ion* 275, *Pho.* 849, 1615, and *IA* 454 and 1185.

948 'Go ahead and punish the goddess and become mightier than Zeus', as your accusation expects me to have done. The 2nd-person imperatives do not directly fit Menelaus' situation but rather those of humankind generally.

951–8 Helen answers a plausible (εὐπρεπῆ) objection Menelaus may raise: even on the supposition that your love for Paris was caused by Aphrodite and therefore irresistible, once Paris was dead should you not have left Troy for the Greek ships? Helen's response is that she tried to do just that but was stopped by guards on the walls. The point is implicitly conceded by Hecuba: see 1010–14 with note.

957–8 'Who often discovered me trying to abscond myself by ropes let down from the battlements.' Like δέμας (e.g. 465 above, *Alc.* 468, and *Hipp.* 131) cῶμα is used as, in effect, a reflexive pronoun: see 1010 below, *Herc.* 703, *IT* 757, 765, *Ion* 1228, *Or.* 1075, and *Ba.* 607. At the same time cῶμα τόδε directs attention to Helen's notorious physical charms. For the deictic applied by speakers to themselves see Spitzbarth 1945: 13.

[959–60] There are four reasons to delete with Wilamowitz 362. (1) The statement that the Trojans were unwilling (ἀκόντων Φρυγῶν) for Deiphobus to marry Helen but that he married her anyway is baffling. Is their reluctance to be explained by their desire for Helen to leave? If so, the guards who prevented her escape were (inexplicably) acting contrary to the wishes of the Trojans. Was there some other reason for their opposition to the marriage? We are entirely in the dark about it and also why their opposition was ineffective. (2) *οὗτος*, as Biehl points out, is a demonstrative without any discernible purpose. (In Soph. *El.* 301, cited by Lee, *οὗτος* does more work, adding a note of contempt that would be out of place here.) (3) If we retain the lines, we are forced to interpret 962 as a reference to Deiphobus' marriage to Helen, whereas it ought logically to refer to the marriage with Paris, described in 932, 939–42, and 946–7 (Grube 1961: 293n2). (4) When Hecuba in 998–9 refers to a forcible appropriation of Helen by a son of hers, it is clear that this is Paris, not Deiphobus. (Further discussion in Meridor 1996.) Wilamowitz describes 959–60 as a 'mythographische Interpolation'. As Page 1934: 74 says, there is nothing clearly histrionic about the passage, but that is true of some other 'explanatory interpolations', as he notes on p. 117. A similar tying up of a mythological loose end is *IT* 59–60.

961–5 Helen's peroration consists of two points: (1) it is unjust to put someone to death for actions that were not freely chosen, and (2) the attempt to win mastery over the gods is foolish.

961–2 —Murray marked a lacuna after 961. That something is missing here is certain since *πρὸς σοῦ δικαίως* cannot stand in the same clause with *ἐνδίκως*. (Biehl's attempt to avoid a lacuna by means of repunctuation does not succeed.) The line that fell out, like my *exempli gratia* supplement, could reasonably have begun with *πῶς*, which would both make an effective anaphora and account for the line's disappearance.

962–4 The relative clause, in two parts, gives the reason why Helen does not deserve to be put to death but rather deserves, e.g., pity. The first half makes the point that marriage with Alexandros was forced on her. The second is harder to interpret. With Dobree's *ἐδούλωσ'*, which I have adopted (see below), various things might be said to have 'gallingly enslaved' Helen 'instead of (conferring on her) a victory prize'. Since *οἴκοθεν* means 'from one's own resources, from oneself' (see above 653), *τὰ οἴκοθεν κεῖν'* might mean 'those well-known natural endowments of mine', though Eur. does not use the word elsewhere in this sense as an attributive. The phrase might also mean 'my domestic affairs', as suggested by Lee. Another possibility is 'my well-known departure from home': as she has already demonstrated, Greece's conquest of Troy (rather than vice versa) is intimately connected to her being used as a bribe and made to leave her husband, and the point here is similar to the one made at 935–7.

—In view of the large scope Greek gives to the internal accusative it is hard to be absolutely certain that the transmitted reading *ἐδούλευσ'* is wrong: at need we could translate 'I experienced my departure from home as a bitter enslavement instead of a victory prize (the one I clearly deserved)'. The omission of a second relative pronoun in a different case (nominative with ἐδούλευcα) is normal Greek: see Smyth §§ 2517–18. Nevertheless Dobree's conjecture (1833: 92) produces a marked gain in clarity and should probably be accepted.

964–5 The 2nd-person here is generalizing and has no particular reference to Menelaus. Cf. above on 948.

966–7 Three choral lines urge Hecuba to refute the specious rhetoric of Helen. Usually the sympathies of the Chorus align pretty well with the attitude the audience is being invited to take. That, however, is not a universal rule: at *Ion* 648–9 the Chorus are distinctly cool to Ion and express the wish that he will not move to Athens, a position excused by their ignorance of the facts and their desire to have autochthonous Athenians as their rulers. Here too the Chorus do not know the facts. There is also an element of Trojan *parti pris*, parallel to that of the *Ion* chorus, marked by both the vocative and πάτραι.

969–1032. Hecuba's prosecution speech

Hecuba makes eight main points. (1) The goddesses could not have offered the bribes that Helen says they offered since Hera would never have sold Argos into slavery or Athena Athens. Furthermore, Hera, already married to Zeus, and Athena, who received the gift of perpetual virginity from the same god, would have no reason to wish to have their beauty recognized. (2) Aphrodite would not have come with Paris to Sparta, as claimed by Helen, since she could have remained in heaven and accomplished the same result. (3) The real reason for the elopement was Helen's lust (Paris was very handsome) and greed (Troy had more luxuries than Sparta). (4) The charge that she was forcibly abducted (not actually what Helen says) is disproved from the fact that she did not cry out, which would have caused her brothers to come to her rescue. (5) Her behaviour in Troy showed her to be a frivolous person, now favouring Paris, now Menelaus, depending on how the war was going. (6) In reply to Helen's claim that she attempted to escape from Troy, Hecuba points out that she was never caught trying to commit suicide, as a good woman would have done for love of her former husband. (7) She also says that she urged Helen to leave Troy and free both Greeks and Trojans from war, but Helen refused: she preferred living insolently in Alexandros' house and enjoying προcκύνηcιc from the barbarians. (8) Now, instead of humbling herself by dressing shabbily and shaving her head, she has shamelessly adorned herself to go to meet her husband.

969–86 Arist. *Rhet.* 3.15, 1418b16–21 quotes the beginning of this speech as an example of the way a speaker may 'make room in the audience's mind for the speech to come' (χώραν ποιεῖν ἐν τῶι ἀκροατῆι τῶι μέλλοντι λόγωι) by attacking the arguments of his adversary. Here, he says, Hecuba has attacked Helen's 'least intelligent' (εὐηθεςτάτου) point, the one about the Judgement of Paris and its results. But Aristotle is not a typical member of Eur.'s audience, since to judge from the *Poetics*, where he mentions the gods only twice in passing, he had no appreciation for the divine in tragedy. His belief that the story of the Judgement of Paris was conspicuously foolish does not prove that Eur.'s contemporaries felt the same way.

969–70 μή replaces οὐ in indirect statement when the statement is a 'strong, emotional asseveration' (Mastronarde on *Med.* 593): see Smyth §§ 2723–7 and, for the verbs that commonly take this construction, § 2730.

—Aristotle quotes 969 and the beginning of 971, omitting 970, but it seems unlikely that he did not have 970 in his text: he was probably quoting from memory. (His mss. read τοῖς θεοῖςι, which is probably a misquotation on Aristotle's part.)

973–4 At *Il.* 4.51–4 Hera says that to secure the punishment of the Trojans she would give up Argos, Sparta, and Mycenae to destruction. So vis-à-vis the poetic tradition Hecuba is mistaken. Likewise, the present play lends no support to Hecuba's thesis since it gives no other reason for the two goddesses' hostility to Troy than the Judgement. Athena and Hera, as their subsequent actions attest, set great store by Paris' verdict, and the bribes Helen says they offered are consistent with this. Further evidence is Cassandra's prophecy in *Alexandros* (Ennius *Alexander* fr. 17.47–9 J.), quoted in the introduction to this episode.

973 Paley suggests that the indicative after ὥςτε here indicates that Hecuba is treating Helen's statement as if it were true.

974 **δουλεύειν**: for the infinitive (purpose or result) see 418–19n and Smyth §§ 2008–11.

975–6 The goddesses came to Ida 'in (a spirit of) playfulness and luxuriant pride in their beauty', i.e. they were not in such deadly earnest that either would have offered the bribes Helen mentioned.

—The scholiast *ad loc.* says that the sense is wrong and that Hecuba should have denied that the contest took place at all. He suggests punctuating interrogatively after Ἴδην, but this is an unattractive remedy. Diggle accepts οὐ for αἳ (Hartung 1848: 82 and 148; Bothe 1802: 382 had proposed κοὐ here), thereby achieving the denial directly. This is unlikely to be right. (1) In the transmitted text the two modal datives are doing work, explaining that, yes, the goddesses went to the contest on Ida but were not serious about winning. If the claim is that they never went, it is hard to see why the datives are added to the denial at all. (2) Their position directly after *οὐ* means that Hecuba could be interpreted as denying they came in a playful spirit rather than that they came at all. To be sure, Moorhouse 1959: 69–120 does not give hard and fast rules, and when *οὐ* is first in its clause (the usual position for the negative of fact in Indo-European), the verb often comes later even when the negative is 'nexal', i.e. negatives the whole utterance, as happens frequently in Homer. But he notes (96–120) a tendency in the later authors he discusses (Hdt., Thuc., and Ar.) for it to immediately precede the *Rhema* (the central point of the sentence), whether the verb or some other word or phrase. This suggests that the point of 975–6 is not whether the goddesses *went* to Ida but the spirit in which they went, that for them the verdict was of no great importance and their participation in the contest a matter of playfulness and pride in their beauty. That is the force of the question in 976–7: why would Hera have set *such store* by a beauty verdict, i.e. so as to act in such deadly earnest? (Hecuba does not deny that Hera or Athena had *any* desire to be recognized for their beauty, merely that in order to satisfy it they would have offered the bribes Helen claims they did.) Transmitted *καὶ χλιδῆι μορφῆϲ πέρι* is probably right too. Eur. might have written *κοὐ χλιδῆι* (as suggested by Lenting 1821: 86): Hecuba would be saying that no pride or insolence was involved (see LSJ s.v. *χλιδή* 2). On balance, however, it seems best to keep the transmitted text: in admitting that the goddess could have acted out of pride in their beauty Hecuba does not undermine her argument.

976–81 The arguments Hecuba offers against the idea that Hera and Athena each really wanted to win the beauty contest are inconclusive, the kind of arguments *ἐκ τῶν εἰκότων* that were a staple (and known to be a staple) of a kind of rhetoric concerned entirely with victory and not at all with truth. Their unspoken premise is that no woman or goddess desires to have her beauty recognized unless she is in quest of a husband. But it is likely that the audience would have been more impressed with how clever Hecuba's arguments are rather than how convincing, for the desire to be proclaimed the best or the wisest or the most beautiful does not always mean that the contestant is seeking something other than the recognition. In this case there was also the prize of a golden apple.

983–6 For the dative of accompaniment *αὐταῖϲ Ἀμύκλαιϲ* see Smyth § 1525. Hecuba's argument that Aphrodite could have remained in heaven and still brought Helen to Troy leaves open the possibility that she did just that. The addition 'Amyclae and all' to the supposition doesn't alter the main issue, the claim that it was Aphrodite who brought Helen to Troy. For the 'advanced' notion that the gods work at a distance, see Xenophanes frr. 37–8 Graham.

987–90 Hecuba argues that the 'Aphrodite' at work in the elopement was Helen's folly and lust. She suggests that the goddess's name derives from *ἄφρων*, 'foolish'. This is a novel etymology: ever since Hes. *Theog.* 190–8, her name had been derived from *ἀφρός*, 'sea foam', alluding to the foam that gathered about the severed genitals of Uranus when they were cast into the sea. The use of etymology to disprove the existence of the gods by claiming that they are names for beneficial (or harmful) phenomena or the inventors of them (as here, that Aphrodite is *nothing more than* human folly) was characteristic of some of the sophists, especially Prodicus: see Philodemus *De pietate* 1 (*PHerc* 1077, fr. 19.519–41 Obbink), Obbink's commentary on line 535, and Mayhew 2011: 175–80.

—*ἄρχειν* in the sense 'to begin with (from)' is usually middle (see LSJ s.v. I.2) and usually employs *ἐκ* or *ἀπό* (ibid. plus I.7). To make it do so here would require major surgery, e.g. *καὶ τοὔνομ' ὀρθῶϲ ἀφροϲύνηϲ ἄπ' ἄρχεται* (we would need to allow ourselves the licence described in 1021n). Wecklein 1897 479–80 regards 988–90 as spurious (Bothe 1802: 383 had already proposed deleting 989–90). 990 is quoted in Arist. *Rhet.* 1400 b 24. Musgrave proposed *θεᾶι*, presumably to avoid the awkward clash of genitives with *ἀφροϲύνηϲ*.

991–2 ***βαρβάροιϲ ἐϲθήμαϲιν | χρυϲῶι τε λαμπρόν***: hendiadys for 'splendid with barbarian gold-adorned garments'. Cf. Hor. *Carm.* 4.9.13–16, *non sola comptos arsit adulteri | crinis et aurum uestibus illitum | mirata regalisque cultus | et comites Helene Lacaena.* (The passage should be added to the list in Sansone 1984c.)

993 ***ϲμίκρ'***: see 51–2n.

996 ***Μενέλεω***: for the resolution of the fifth *longum* see 1170n.

998–1001 Hecuba seems to be referring to 940–50, in which Helen claims that Aphrodite compelled her to follow Alexandros. But she pretends to understand this as a claim of forcible abduction by Paris, answering not the defendant's argument but a straw man.

—Scodel 144 proposes deletion on several grounds. (1) The lines 'make sense only if we assume that Hecuba is deliberately distorting Helen's argument beyond recognition, but she shows no signs of this elsewhere'. This is debatable in view of 1010–19, which answer Helen's claim that once Paris was dead, she did attempt to flee by citing an instance during Paris' lifetime when Helen refused to go. (2) The passage 'disturbs the flow of the speech, since 997 marks the end of a psychological analysis of Helen's flight from Sparta, and 1002 takes up the next expected theme, Helen's behaviour in Troy'. But there is no clear objection to the sequence 'You found my son handsome and his wealth attractive'; 'You claim forcible removal, but no one heard you shout';

'Your behaviour in Troy showed double disloyalty.' (3) The lines, she claims, ruin what Eur. was clearly trying to do in his adaptation of the argumentation of Gorgias. I do not understand Scodel here but feel that since we cannot know for sure that Gorgias' *Helen* preceded *Tro.*, her remarks are made doubly speculative. (4) Of 1000 she says 'there is no parallel to my knowledge for the ὀλολυγμόϲ as a cry for help'. But Wecklein's ἀνωτότυξαϲ (1901: 42), recommended by Diggle 1994: 480, is a simple and inexpensive remedy, which I have adopted. (Herwerden's identical correction at Soph. *El.* 750 is printed in Lloyd-Jones and Wilson's OCT. The correct ἀνωτότυξαϲ is transmitted at *Ag.* 1074 but corrupted to ἀνωλόλυξαϲ in the indirect tradition.) Schulze 1918: 506–7 shows the legal reasoning behind Hecuba's words: if a woman does not shout when she could be heard, her later complaint of violence against her person will not deserve credence.

998 on εἶέν see above 945n.

1004 **τοῦδε**: this refers to Alexandros, mentioned in 998.

1008–9 'Keeping your eye on fortune it was your practice to follow her: you refused to follow virtue.'

1008 For ὅπωϲ at line end (an enjambment more characteristic of Soph.) see *Med.* 322, *Hcld.* 1051, *Hipp.* 392, *IT* 951, *Pho.* 1318, and *IA* 56.

1009 **τῆι ἀρετῆι**: for further examples of this kind of mixing of a final long with an initial short or long, usually called synaloephe, see Descroix 1931: 32.

1010–14 In replying to Helen's claim (951–8) that she did attempt to leave Troy after Paris' death Hecuba does not try to refute her. Instead she shifts the ground to the question why Helen did not try to commit suicide. This suggests that the facts are as Helen described them. Suicide also seems a rather unfair expectation under any circumstances.

1015–22 Hecuba urged Helen to leave, but Helen would not do so. *Prima facie* this is evidence of Helen's persistence in error even when *ex hypothesi* she was no longer under the influence of Aphrodite. But 1016–20 (see below on 1016–17) show that Hecuba is speaking of the time when Paris was still alive.

1015 —In contrast to καίτοι...γε (of which there are some fourteen examples in tragedy), καίτοι γε is very rare: apart from [Eur.] fr. 953 (= fr. com. adesp. 1000 KA) the only other tragic example is *IT* 720 (Diggle, however, prints Erfurdt's καίτοι κἀγγύϲ). Furthermore, enclitic personal pronouns normally take the second place in a clause ('Wackernagel's Law'): see Wackernagel 1892. I have adopted Burges's conjecture, which restores normal usage.

πολλὰ πολλάκιϲ: in some cases of polyptoton the two words have distinct functions, e.g. 38 above and *Supp.* 577 τοίγαρ πονοῦϲα πολλὰ πόλλ' εὐδαιμονεῖ. Here and at *Med.* 1165 we have emphatic redundancy as both words refer to number or frequency.

1016–19 Hecuba quotes herself in direct speech. Bers 1997: 99 notes that the number of cases where *oratio recta* occurs outside of messenger speeches in tragedy is quite small. He cites seven, two from *Tro.* (the present passage and 1182–4).

1016–17 ***οἱ δ' ἐμοὶ παῖδες γάμους | ἄλλους γαμοῦσι:*** παῖδες is an 'allusive' plural, in which a single person is meant 'with a glance at any and all persons in that relationship' (Bers 1984: 23–4; further discussion at 25n5 and 42–3). The sentence means 'There is no need for Paris (or any other son of mine) to be married to you.' If we took it as a genuine plural, e.g. Paris and Deiphobus (as we might be tempted to do if 959–60 were genuine), that would imply that if Helen leaves Troy, *two* of her sons will require other wives; or, at the very least, that she has been married to two, which is hard to reconcile with 1020. *Pace* Scodel 143 (who wants to defend 959–60 and so argues that παῖδες here means Paris and Deiphobus), the allusive plural is not 'impossibly confusing' but, given its wide employment in tragedy with relationship nouns, perfectly clear: for Soph. see Bruhn *Anhang* 3–5 and for Eur. e.g. *Med.* 823 (δεσπόταις = Medea), 897 (φίλους = Jason), *Andr.* 172, 359, 391, 632, 739, 1068 (αὐθεντῶν, γαμβροῖς, δεσπόταισι, τέκνων, γαμβρούς, and φίλοις all = Neoptolemus), *El.* 45 (ὀλβίων ἀνδρῶν τέκνα = Electra), *Hel.* 595 (οἱ φίλτατοι = Menelaus), *Ba.* 1033 (δεσπόταις = Pentheus), and Barrett on *Hipp.* 49. Latin examples in Löfstedt 1956: 1.38–40. Note the implication of Hecuba's words here and in 1020, that at the time she urged Helen to depart, Paris was still alive and married to her.

1018 ***καὶ παύσω μάχης:*** i.e. if you depart, as I am proposing, I will bring this war to an end. —The mss. have παῦσον, but we would expect asyndeton between an indicative (πέμψω) and an imperative, hence Bothe's alteration of the latter (1826). We could preserve an imperative by writing κατάπαυσον. Diggle's punctuation of 1016–18 is apparently intended to make a parenthesis of οἱ δ' ἐμοὶ... συνεκκλέψασα, which would make καὶ παῦσον a continuation of ἔξελθ'. But a parenthetical remark does not usually contain a connective particle, and so we would need to emend to οἵ τ' ἐμοὶ... σέ τ'. Bothe's alteration, my alteration, and Diggle's parenthesis, as emended, all give equally good sense as either Helen or Hecuba under the circumstances could be said to stop the Greeks and barbarians from fighting. I have adopted Bothe without clear conviction.

1021 ***καὶ προσκυνεῖσθαι βαρβάρων ὕπ':*** it is characteristic of barbarian (especially Persian) royalty to demand that their subjects bow down in abasement before them. For another possible indication in the play that the Trojans are culturally different from the Greeks see 1209–15n. It is rare for prepositions to be used anastrophically in the middle of a line. But cf. *Ba.* 732.

1022 **κἀπὶ τοῖcδε**: 'and on top of this'.

1023–4 **πόcει | τὸν αὐτὸν αἰθέρ'**: 'the same (upper) air as your husband'. For the various constructions with ὁ αὐτόc see above on 714.

1025 **ἐρειπίοιc**: on the correct spelling of this word see Finglass 2009: 224n77.

1026 **ἀπεcκυθιcμένην**: 'with your head cropped in Scythian fashion', i.e. with your hair cut down to the skin, shaved.

1027–8 'Showing modesty rather than shamelessness over your former misdeeds'.

1029 For purpose clauses of this kind, where the purpose depends on an understood 'I tell you' or 'listen', see 719n.

οἷ τελευτήcω λόγον: the usual Greek idiom is τελευτᾶν εἴc τι, as at *Hec.* 419; Aesch. *Pers.* 737, *Cho.* 526; Soph. *OC* 476. There is a counter-example at *Ba.* 909.

1032 'That any woman who betrays her husband must be put to death', the infinitive depending upon νόμον ... θέc, 'establish a law'.

1033–5 The Chorus Leader seconds Hecuba's condemnation on the grounds that killing Helen will be worthy of his ancestors and his house and will prove him a real man.

1034–5 'And remove from yourself (middle) the accusation of unmanliness Greece makes against you, proving yourself noble in the eyes of your detractors'. We must take πρὸc Ἑλλάδοc closely with ψόγον. The ἐχθροί in question are not the Trojans (who would be πολέμιοι) but Menelaus' personal enemies, perhaps those Greeks who regard him as uxorious. His nobility consists in his concern for his honour and his being superior to the temptation of Helen's beauty. —Diggle, *Studies* 68–70 argues for Dobree's suggestion (but Bothe had made it earlier) ψόγον τὸ θῆλυ, κεὐγενὴc ἐχθροῖc φανῆι, 'Remove from the female sex the blame Greece heaps on them, and you will appear noble in the eyes of your detractors.' He cites 726, *Med.* 600, *IA* 1208, fr. 188.3 for the pairing of imperative and future indicative. As regards sense, he claims that a taunt of effeminacy against Menelaus does not suit the context (i.e. is not a good move rhetorically?) and that the behaviour of women is the subject in 1031–2. But the implication of the conjecture is that women have a bad reputation because of Helen, whereas in 1031–2 the assumption is that the whole sex needs to be frightened into behaving better. It is perhaps tactless of Hecuba to imply that Menelaus is open to the charge of unmanliness, but this comment, tactless though it may be, could be an effective means to motivate Menelaus to kill

Helen. By contrast, I cannot see why Menelaus should care whether women are ill-spoken-of or why concern for *their* reputation would show his enemies that he is noble. I prefer the reading of the mss. here.

1035 **ψόγον τὸ θῆλύ τ'**: 'blame and womanliness' means by hendiadys 'the charge of unmanliness'. Cf. *Med.* 218, δύcκλειαν ἐκτήcαντο καὶ ῥαιθυμίαν, 'They have won for themselves a reputation for slackness', and *Ion* 600, γέλωτ' ἐν αὐτοῖc μωρίαν τε λήψομαι. On hendiadys in Greek see Sansone 1984c.

1036–59. Menelaus' verdict and Hecuba's second warning

1036 'You have arrived at the same consideration as I have.' For ἐc ταὐτὸν λόγου see 684–5n.

1038 **κόμπου χάριν**: Menelaus means that Helen exaggerates her beauty by claiming (falsely) that Aphrodite chose her as a bribe.

1039 **λόγοιc ἐνεῖται**: the verb is the perfect passive of ἐνίημι, 'has been added to' her speech.

βαῖνε λευcτήρων πέλαc: for the sense 'Go to face (not simply 'near') the stoners' see *OT* 782.

1040 **ἐν cμικρῶι μακρούc**: the juxtaposition emphasizes that Helen's punishment, even though it is capital, does not equal her offence. Her pain will be brief in contrast to the ten years of war she caused. On cμικρῶι see 51–2n.

1041 'So that she may learn not to disgrace me'. The offence of adultery is conceived of as principally the harm it does to the wronged husband's reputation: see above 902n. For οἶδα plus infinitive meaning 'learn (to one's cost) not to do a thing' see *Hipp.* 729. The active 'teach a person (to his cost)' is expressed by δείκνυμι at *Andr.* 706 and 1001.

Staging: Helen kneels before Menelaus and grasps his knees in supplication.

1042 **μή πρόc cε γονάτων**: on this elliptical expression, '[I beg] you by your knees', see Barrett on *Hipp.* 503–4.

1044 **μηδ'**: οὐδέ and μηδέ, when they are connective, are usually continuative (see *GP* 193, first line), not adversative. When a new speaker starts with either of these connectives, they continue the argument either of the previous speaker (*El.* 1332, *IT* 248, 570, *Rh.* 82) or of the same speaker's earlier utterance (*Hipp.* 1055, 1399, *IA* 308, *Rhes.* 82, 168). There are a few cases in Eur. where 'but (...) not' seems to be the sense: see *Ion* 305, 328, 956, *Hel.* 802, *Pho.* 398, 404, *Or.* 429 and 1056. But even that does not work here since 'But do not betray' would suggest that Hecuba is not challenging Helen's 'Do not kill me but spare me.' So Wecklein's suggestion (1901: 44) that a line has fallen out before 1044 is attractive. In the transmitted text Helen and Hecuba each have a pair of lines (1042–3 and 1044–5), but if Wecklein is right, a single couplet is followed by three lines each for Hecuba and Menelaus.

1046 **τῆcδε δ' οὐκ ἐφρόντιcα**: for δέ where we expect γάρ see *GP* 169.

Staging: at Menelaus' command two members of his retinue raise Helen to her feet and prepare to lead her away to his ship. This order may be carried out at once or, more likely, is delayed by Hecuba's intervention until 1059.

1049–50 Hecuba's command to Menelaus not to travel on the same ship with his wife is perfectly intelligible: she is afraid that he will fall under Helen's spell, a fear she expressed at 891–3. (The scholiast calls 1049 γελοῖον, but Gregory 1999–2000: 70 suggests that this may have in view the peremptory character of the line, absurdly inappropriate for a captive.) Menelaus' reply, by contrast, has provoked puzzlement and has seemed to many to be making a joke about weight gain, one in bad taste that detracts from the scene. But Gregory 1999–2000: 71 points out that such a joke would be anachronistic since in the economic conditions of ancient Greece emaciation was a greater danger to a person's attractiveness than obesity, and sleekness, as in many third-world countries today, was an indication of prosperity and held to be becoming. Gregory plausibly maintains that Menelaus' question expresses surprise and is a request for information, a reasonable one for someone about to set out in a flimsy ancient ship, more prone to sink from overloading than ones we are used to. (See especially her n. 55.) There is no need for my suggestion (1998a) that this is a reference (unconscious on Menelaus' part) to the weightiness Helen's body will take on after her eventual apotheosis.

1052 'That depends on how (lit. 'in whatsoever way') the mind of the beloved one turns out.' For the ellipsis 'that depends' see *Med.* 331 and Mastronarde's and Page's notes *ad loc.*

1055–6 **κακῶc | κακή**: Elmsley on *Med.* 787–8 notes that the order with adverb before the adjective occurs at *Phil.* 1369, *Tro.* 1055, *Cyc.* 267, and Ar. *Eq.* 2, but, with no words coming between, the order adjective–adverb is far more common: *Med.* 1353, *Tro.* 446; *Aj.* 839, 1177, 1391; Ar. *Eq.* 189–90, *Nu.* 554, *Lys.* 162, *Plut.* 65, 418, and 880. Cf. also Soph. *El.* 198 and *Phil.* 166. He suggests that the order adjective–adverb ought to be read at *Med.* 787–8.

1056–7 **καὶ γυναιξὶ cωφρονεῖν | πάcαιcι θήcει**: 'And she will lay down the law to all women that they should be chaste.' There seems to be a subaudition of νόμον, though I know of no parallel.

1059 **ἐχθίονεc**: as I pointed out at *Eur. Tert.* 185–6, the adjective has in view the hatred that immoral women incur: cf. μίcητοc, 'lecherous, promiscuous', and μιcητία, 'lewdness'. In the Loeb I translated 'though they be still more reprobate than she is'. (One may wonder whether Archil. fr. 206 West περὶ cφύρον παχεῖα μιcητὴ γυνή, contains the substantive claim that thick-ankled women are lecherous or the less interesting claim that they are hated.) —Hermann's paleographically plausible conjecture αἰcχίονεc (for the corruption see *Alc.* 1037, *Hec.* 200, *El.* 138, *Herc.* 293, *Pho.* 585; Aesch. *Sept.* 695; Soph. *Aj.* 1059; and the partial corruption at *Tro.* 741) is far from certain. Although καλόν and αἰcχρόν describing actions mean 'creditable' and 'discreditable', when they describe persons they usually mean 'beautiful' and 'ugly'. There seems to be a big difference between, on the one hand, αἰcχρὸc φανοῦμαι (*Phil.* 906) and ἐρωτηθεὶc γὰρ αἰcχίων φανῆι (Med. 501), both using φαίνομαι, which helps the meaning 'shown up in an ugly light', and, on the other, an expression such as αἰcχίονέc εἰcιν with the verb 'to be', which can scarcely mean 'They are more shameful'. To be sure, καλόc (as in ὁ ποιμὴν ὁ καλόc, John 10:11), becomes a later substitute for ἀγαθόc, but that lay centuries in the future. Hermann's conjecture receives no support from fr. 248.1 οὐκ ἔcτι Πενίαc ἱερὸν αἰcχίcτηc θεοῦ (*Archelaus*) because the quality the goddess represents is ugly and unattractive.

Staging: Menelaus exits down the left *eisodos*. Helen, escorted by members of his retinue, precedes or follows him. Hecuba remains during the third stasimon.

THIRD STASIMON (1060–1117)

Like its two predecessors, this stasimon expresses an emotive reaction, not to the preceding episode, which it mostly ignores (see 1100–17n), but to the fall of Troy. Its structure may be said to mirror that of its immediate predecessor. The second stasimon began with description (the first sack of Troy) and ended with complaint (that the Trojans have provided Zeus with a cupbearer and Eos with a husband and received no benefit). The present stasimon begins with complaint and puzzlement that Zeus has abandoned or betrayed so much in Troy that is dear to him and ends with description: the Chorus's own misery in the aftermath of Troy's fall and the fate they pray will overtake Menelaus and Helen on their homeward journey.

1060–70 ~ 1071–80

1. 1060 ~ 1071	– – – ⏑⏑ – ⏑ –	gl
2. 1061 ~ 1072	– – – ⏑⏑ – ⏑ –	gl ∫
3. 1062 ~ 1073	– ⏓ – ⏑⏑ – –	ph

4. 1063 ~ 1074	– – – ⏖ – ⏑ –	gl
5. 1064 ~ 1075	⏒ – – ⏖ – ⏑ –	gl ʃ
6. 1065 ~ 1076	– – – ⏖ – – ||	ph
7. 1066 ~ 1077	⏒ – ⏑ – – ⏑ – ⏑ ⏗ ⏑ –	ia lek
8. 1067 ~ 1078	⏓ ⏑͡⏑ ⏑ ⏑͡⏑ ⏑ ⏑͡⏑ ⏑ –	2ia
9. 1068 ~ 1079	– ⏑͡⏑ ⏑ ⏔ ⏑ ⏑͡⏑ ⏑ –	ia
10. 1069/70 ~ 1080/1	– ⏖ – ⏖ – ⏖ – ⏑ – – |||	D^2 ba

Metrical analysis

The first stanzaic pair begins with two instances of glyconics in pairs (1–2, 4–5), each followed by a pherecratean (3, 6). Iambics, with mostly short *ancipitia*, ensue followed by a final run of double shorts (D^2) with clausular bacchius, the whole sometimes called a praxillean. The metre is about as simple as Euripidean choral lyric ever gets.

1060–80 The first stanzaic pair lists all the things that Zeus, in allowing Troy to fall, has abandoned or betrayed. The items mentioned (his temple and altar with their offerings of batter and myrrh and the holy mountain of Ida) are things Zeus is presumed to delight in, and his abandoning of them seems pointless. The clear implication of *φροῦδαί coι* (1071) is that Zeus is the loser. (In similar fashion the psalmist, e.g. at *Ps.* 6:5, 30:9–10, and 88:10–12, reminds the Almighty of what He forfeits if the psalmist dies: if the latter goes down to Sheol, where the dead do not praise, God suffers loss.) This is a different complaint from the one made in the second stasimon, that the gods have forgotten their ties to Troy embodied in Ganymede and Tithonus. There the Chorus complained of ingratitude and disloyalty, here of unfathomable stupidity. The Chorus's sentiments make a contrast with 884–8, where Hecuba had seen Zeus operating with perfect justice. Note that although the views of the world that Hecuba and the Chorus hold are opposite, they are both, in mythical terms, mistaken. Contrary to Hecuba's view Zeus does not intend to punish Helen but rather Troy, and contrary to that of the Chorus his betrayal of Troy is not thoughtless but purposeful.

1060 ***οὔτω δή:*** *οὔτωc* often implies 'without further (expected) preliminaries, simply' (see LSJ s.v. IV). Here what the Chorus seem to complain of it is that Zeus has *summarily* or *without consideration* abandoned Troy. Denniston notes (*GP* 207) that with pronouns and pronominal adverbs the emphasis imparted by δή 'is often ironical, contemptuous, or indignant in tone'. At 209 he cites its use in surprised or indignant questions, as here.

1061 **ναόν**: the temple Zeus has betrayed to the Greeks must be his own, *τόν* being an unemphatic possessive: see LSJ s.v. B.1.a.

1061–2 **θυόεντα βωμόν**: the identical phrase at Pi. *Pae.* 3.8–9 (where it also follows a reference to a *ναός*); similar is the Homeric formula *βωμός τε θυήεις* at Hom. *Il.* 7.48, 23.148, *Od.* 8.363, *HH Ap.* 87–8, and *HH Ven.* 59; in Pi. fr. 75.3 we find *ὀμφαλὸν θυόεντ'*.

1063 **πελανῶν φλόγα**: an offering of meal, honey, and oil, which could be poured on the graves of the dead (where it would seep down to its recipients), was also burned on the altars of the gods (to whom it would ascend in smoke). —For the correct accentuation, *πελανός*, see LSJ s.v.

1064–5 **cμύρνας αἰθερίας τε καπνόν**: 'the smoke of myrrh that rises to high heaven'. For *τε* in third place see *GP* 517 and Diggle 1989: 198.

1066 **Ἰδαῖά τ' Ἰδαῖα κιccοφόρα νάπη**: 'ivy-covered vales of Ida, Ida'. The typically Euripidean anadiplosis (on which see 804n) perhaps here conveys some of the emotive importance for the Trojans of the shrine of Zeus on Ida's summit.

1067 **χιόνι κατάρυτα ποταμίαι**: 'flowing with rivery snow' means 'having snow-fed streams'. —Seidler's reduction of double *rho* to single achieves responsion with 1078. This scansion is strongly commended by the iambic character of 1066–8 ~ 1077–9.

1069–70 **τέρμονά τε πρωτόβολον †ἁλίω†, | τὰν καταλαμπομέναν ζάθεον θεράπναν**: 'and the boundary first struck by the †sun†, the holy dwelling-place illumined'. The 'boundary' is Mt Ida, on the Troad's eastern border. As Parmentier points out, there may be an allusion here to the phenomenon mentioned in Diod. Sic. 17.7.5–7, who says that from the summit of Ida, about the time of the rising of the Dog Star, one sees the sun before dawn, not in its customary round shape but dispersed along the horizon, only later to be gathered into its customary disk. Similar descriptions at Lucr. 5.663–5 and Pomponius Mela 1.18.94. Zeus's altar on this mountain is mentioned at *Il.* 6.47 and 12.352, and hence Ida is 'a holy place illumined'.

—Transmitted *ἁλίω(ι)* seems unsound: Biehl keeps 1069 as transmitted and scans as 3 cr, but 2ia is more plausible here and in the antistrophe. (Biehl is obliged to insert a syllable before *πόλεωc* in 1079: he chooses the unwelcome <*τᾶc*>.) Diggle originally adopted Wilamowitz's *ἕωι* for *ἁλίωι* (1895: 24), which gives metre, but in his note on *Phaethon* 64 he had already observed that tragic lyric uses *ἀώc* or *ἠώc* but not *ἕωc*, and at Diggle 1996: 193 he declares the conjecture unlikely. Lane 2006–7: 269–71 proposed *ἅλωι*, 'disk'. As he shows, this word, which can mean 'threshing floor', can also denote the circumference of the sun or moon or a halo around them. Yet without any genitive to identify it, 'by the disk' seems a long shot. But perhaps the corruption lies earlier in the line and Eur. wrote, e.g., *πρωτόβολά τ' ἐρύμαθ' ἁλίωι*, 'the rampart first struck by the sun's rays'.

1070 ***ζάθεον***: since there is no reason why this adjective should be three-termination here and two-termination five lines later, Wilamowitz's conjecture (1895: 24) commends itself. On the corruption of the 2nd-declension feminine into 1st-declension see Mastronarde on *Pho.* 1575.

1071–4 ***φροῦδαί cοι***: the Chorus remind Zeus what he has lost, among them sacrifices, choruses offered to him, and gilded statues. See above on 1060–80.

κατ' ὄρφναν τε παννυχίδες θεῶν: the expression is pleonastic, perhaps eulogistic in force. For *θεοί*, 'the (other) gods' in contrast to Zeus, see 56n. Allan on *Hel.* 1364–5 discusses the all-night festival as characteristic of female worship.

χρυcέων τε ξοάνων τύποι: another pleonastic expression, perhaps similar to the foregoing. The force of *ξοάνων τύποι* is that the statues have a shape pleasing to the eye. That the statues are gold, of course, increases the effect of their loss.

1075–6 Some commentators (e.g. Tyrrell) have taken *cελᾶναι* here to mean 'monthly festivals'. But a passage in Eur.'s *Erechtheus* (fr. 350) mentions 'moons made from young wheat', i.e. cake-offerings called *cελῆναι* from their shape, an offering mentioned in Athenaeus 489d; Suda *α* 2082 and *β* 458 Adler; Hesych. *σ* 379 Hansen, the scholia to this passage, and elsewhere. The same is suggested by 1063 *πελανῶν*. Stephanopoulos 1988: 489–90 cites a fragment of Plato Comicus (188.10 KA, from his *Phaon*), *λαγῷια δώδεκ' ἐπιcέληνα*, which may mean hare meat served on moon-cakes. The Trojan offering seems to be of twelve cakes at once (this is perhaps suggested by the prefix in *cυνδώδεκα*), not twelve spread over the year.

1077–80 'It matters, it matters to me whether you mark these things, my lord, having stationed yourself in your heavenly abode and the upper air, when the city has perished, destroyed by the blast of blazing fire.' (The anadiplosis matches that in 1066.) The Chorus ask whether Zeus, from his lofty position at the top of the heavens, notices the losses they have just described (*τάδε*). The genitive absolute *πόλεοc ὀλομέναc* could be concessive in relation to *ἐπιβεβώc* ('you sit enthroned above though the city has perished') or temporal/causal in relation to *φρονεῖc* ('you notice [the loss of] these things since the city has perished'). —The scholiast, after making *αἰθέρα* a second object of *ἐπιβεβώc*, as above, notes that Didymus explains it as 'conflagration', *ἐμπυριcμόν*. This would supply a noun on which the genitive *πόλεοc* could depend. But even if this were a sense attested in the classical period (which it is not), it means that 'the burning of Troy' is connected by *τε* to *τάδε*, which is awkward. Didymus is unlikely to be right.

ἂν πυρὸς αἰθομένα κατέλυςεν ὁρμά: 'blazing' more naturally modifies 'fire' (cf. *πυρὸς αἰθομένοιο* at *Il.* 16.81). It here modifies the compound idea *πυρὸς ὁρμά*, and is thus an instance of enallage, on which see 1–2n. The verb *καταλύω* was used in a similar context at 819.

1082–99 ~ 1100–17

1. 1082 ~ 1100	– ⏖ – ⏖ –	D
2. 1083 ~ 1101	⏑ – ⏑ ⏑͡⏑ ⏑ – – ‖	ia ba
3. 1084/5 ~ 1102/3	⏑ – ⏑ ⏑͡⏑ ⏑ ⏑͡⏑ ⏑ – ⏑ – ⏑ ⏓ ‖	2ia
4. 1086 ~ 1104	⏓ – – ⏑ – ⏖ – – ‖	hip¨
5. 1087 ~ 1105	– ⏑͡⏑ ⏑ ⏔ ⏑ ⏑͡⏑ ⏑ ⏑͡⏑	2ia
6. 1088 ~ 1106	– ⏑͡⏑ ⏑ – ⏑ – ⏑ ⏕ ⏑ – – ‖	2ia ba
7. 1089 ~ 1107	⏓ ⏔ ⏑ – ⏑ – ⏑ –	2ia
8. 1090 ~ 1108	⏑ ⏑͡⏑ ⏑ ⏕ ⏑ – ⏑ – ⏑ – ⏑ –	3ia
9. 1091/2 ~ 1109/10	– ⏑ – – ⏑ – – ⏑ – – ⏑ –	3cr ʃ
10. 1093 ~ 1111	– ⏑ ⏑͡⏑ ⏑ – ⏑ –	lk
11. 1094 ~ 1112	– ⏖ – ⏖ –	D
12. 1095 ~ 1113	– ⏖ – ⏖ –	D
13. 1096 ~ 1114	– ⏖ – ⏖ –	D
14. 1097 ~ 1115	– ⏖ – ⏖ –	D
15. 1098 ~ 1116	– ⏖ – ⏖ –	D
16. 1099 ~ 1117	⏑ ⏑͡⏑ ⏑ ⏔ ⏑ – – ‖‖	ia ba

Metrical analysis

An initial hemiepes (1) is succeeded by a run of nine verses (2 through 10) all in iambic metre except for one Aeolic verse (4). This is followed by five further cases of hemiepes (11–15), a repetition carrying an emotional affect hard to specify, and these are rounded off by clausular ia ba.

1081–1117 In the second strophe a more personal note is heard as the Chorus lament the loss of their husbands, their departure for Greece, and the weeping of their children, now to be separated from their parents and taken by ship to Salamis, perhaps, or Corinth. The second antistrophe utters a curse against Menelaus and Helen: may they perish en route to Sparta!

1081 ὦ φίλος, ὦ πόσι μοι: the singular 'O dear husband' corresponds to the 1st-person singular often used by the tragic chorus. On *ὦ φίλος*, nominative for vocative, see 267n. For the use of *ὦ* twice in the same vocative phrase, once each with an adjective and a noun, see 601, *Cyc.* 266, *Alc.* 460, *Med.* 990, *Hec.* 414, *IT* 983, *Ion* 112, and *Phil.* 799.

1082–3 cὺ μὲν φθίμενος ἀλαίνεις | ἄθαπτος ἄνυδρος: Finglass on *OT* 252–4 (see also Finglass on *Aj.* 323–5 and *El.* 164–5) notes that 'Alpha-privatives tend to occur in pairs, sometimes in asyndeton, for rhetorical emphasis'. The dead husband 'wanders' because unburied: see *Il.* 23.71–4. One would think that the soul wanders, but at *Hec.* 28–30 the wanderer is the sea-washed corpse, and *Supp.* 62 applies the verb to dead men's bodies. As Biehl notes, ἄθαπτος ἄνυδρος is *hysteron proteron*, 'unburied and without being washed' (as was customary before burial).

1086 ἀίccον πτεροῖcι: 'moving swiftly with the speed of its wings (oars)'. The metaphor is already implicit in *Od.* 11.125, ἐρετμά, τά τε πτερὰ νηυcὶ πέλονται. For tragic examples, including cases where it is a metaphor for a sail, see Kannicht on *Hel.* 147. —At 1104, the corresponding place in the antistrophe, the text is corrupt. Here there is doubt only whether we should read transmitted trisyllabic ἀίccον, giving anaclastic hipponacteum, or dissyllabic ᾆccον, giving anaclastic hagesichorean. In tragedy the present of ἀίccω normally has a short first syllable (for an apparent exception see 156n), but inexact responsion in syllables before the aeolic choriamb is not uncommon: see 1064 ~ 1075. How we mark accents and breathings here, therefore, depends on the highly uncertain 1104, where see n.

1087–8 'To horse-pasturing Argos where men dwell in heaven-high stone walls, built by the Cyclopes'.

1087 ἱππόβοτον Ἄργοc: 'horse-pasturing Argos' (cf. *Il.* 2.287 Ἄργεος ἱπποβότοιο, imitated by Eur. also at *Supp.* 365 and *Or.* 1621) is terminal accusative without a preposition. Despite the obvious reluctance of the Chorus to journey to Argos, it still receives an honorific epithet, and its Cyclopean walls are mentioned with admiration.

†ἵνα τείχεα†: —if, taking our cue from the antistrophe, we scan 1087 as iambs, the penultimate element in the line as transmitted (τειχ-) is long, impermissible except in choliambics. Diggle, *Studies* 20 prefers cr cr ba, found at *Andr.* 1205 ~ 1219, and he adopts Seidler's ἵνα <τε> τείχη (with 'epic' τε) and the same scholar's πολυδάκρυτον in 1105. But in view of 1088–90 ~ 1106–8, plausibly all iambic dimeters, an iambic analysis seems preferable. If we accordingly treat 1105 as 2ia, either with period end (transmitted πολύδακρυν would give *brevis in longo*) or without (reading Bothe's πολυδάκρυον), the possibilities for 1087 include ἵνα θ' ἕδρανα (Willink unpub.), again with epic τε, my earlier suggestion ἵν' ἐρύματα (Loeb apparatus: but the plural is not elsewhere found in poetry apart from the dubious Eur. fr. 1132.1 (*Danae*)), and, e.g., ἔνθ' ἕδρανα. Wilamowitz proposed τείχε' ἵνα, but the preponderance of short *anceps* in the iambics of this stanzaic pair is a reason to reject

(-γος) τείχε'. Furthermore, according to Parker 1966 word-break after any long *anceps* in most metres is suspicious.

1088 λάϊνα Κυκλώπι' οὐράνια νέμονται: in Hes. *Theog.* 139–45 the Cyclopes are the skilled workers who forge Zeus's thunderbolts. They are mentioned as builders of cities in the Argolid in Adesp. Trag. fr. 269b (Tiryns) and Bacchyl. 11.77 (Argos) and perhaps at Pi. fr. 70a.6 Snell-Maehler. The theme is frequent in Eur.: *El.* 1158 (and note similarity to the present passage), *Herc.* 15, 944, *Or.* 965, *IA* 152, 265, 534, and 845. The verb is best taken not as passive (the plural verb with a neuter plural subject would then be anomalous) but as middle, which is plentifully attested in the sense 'dwell in': see LSJ s.v. II.2.

1089–90 τέκνων δὲ πλῆθος ἐν πύλαις | δάκρυσι †κατάορα στένει βοᾶι† βοᾶι: 'the throng of children in the gates, . . . with tears, is . . . crying, crying'. —There are several problems here. (1) LSJ translate κατάορα 'hanging on their mother's neck', but the other occurrences of the word, all much later (A.R. 2.104, Nonnus *Dion.* 21.207, Paulus Silentarius, *A.P.* 5.259, *Descr. Sanctae Soph.* 544), mean simply 'hanging down' and refer not to people but to things (a sword-strap, a garment of skin, a cluster of grapes, etc.). This and the absence from the text of any noun that would turn 'hanging down' to 'hanging upon' means that we must view the word with deep suspicion. (The agreement of neuter plural with neuter singular πλῆθος is also surprising since agreement in sense would more naturally give masculine gender.) (2) As Diggle says in his app. crit., 'στένει βοᾶι βοᾶι a stilo Euripidis abhorret'. (3) The iambic trimeter lacks a caesura. We can begin our reconstruction at the end of the line, where the anadiplosis seems out of place. There are hundreds of examples of anadiplosis in Breitenbach 214–21, but at the end of a sentence or clause it is rare (JD cites, at sentence end, *Or.* 1469, and, at clause end, *IT* 138, *Hel.* 214 and 640, and *Or.* 162). Furthermore, the verb does not seem to be the element calling for Eur.'s trademark repetition. This means that Paley's alteration of the first βοᾶι to βοάν (changing the second is also possible) is attractive. His conjuring of an adjective to go with the cognate accusative (he suggests ἀσθενῆ) supplies the wanted caesura by redrawing the boundary with its daggered western neighbour. Though I cannot find a parallel for 'weak cry' in tragedy, ease of corruption to what is transmitted speaks in its favour.

As for a word to replace κατάορα, the scholia *ad loc.* translate 'covered in tears', which might point to a lost reading. Meridor proposed καταρροα. Willink unpub. adjusts this to κατάροον, allowing it to stand before ἀσθενῆ. This gives 'running with tears'. The adjustment also restores agreement with πλῆθος. κατάροος with a single *rho* is plausible in view of other single-rho compounds ending in -ροος such as ὠκύροος as well as transmitted variations such as αἱμό(ρ)ροος and καλλί(ρ)ροος.

1091–2. This is one of two instances of *oratio recta* in the lyrics of *Tro.* (see 524–6n). Bers 1997: 107 notes that in spite of πλῆθος (1089), this is the lament of one girl (note μόναν 1092). As NL points out, μόναν may mean 'bereft of' and be construed closely with ϲέθεν ἀπ' ὀμμάτων: see LSJ s.v. μόνος A.2.

1094 κυανέαν ἐπὶ ναῦν: the adjective is epicizing: see *Il.* 15.693 νεὸς κυανοπρῴροιο. Cf. also Aesch. *Pers.* 559 κυανώπιδες νᾶες. On the word see Irwin 1974: 79–110 (92–4 on its application to ships, 108 noting Homeric overtones here and at *El.* 436). The *upsilon* of κυάνεος is long in Homer. In Eur. the epic scansion is found here, at *Andr.* 1011, and at *IT* 392 and 889. It occurs once in Soph. (*Ant.* 966).

1095 εἶθ' ἁλίοιϲι πλάταιϲ: first down to the dark-hued ship and *then* aboard the sea-going vessel to various possible ports. —Musgrave suggested εἶθ' ἁλίαιϲι, the result of which is that ἐπί may mean 'to' and refer to the brief land part of the journey (ἐπὶ ναῦν could not mean 'onboard ship'). Eur. shows a propensity for making adjectives two-termination (see 1070n and, for this adjective, *Hcld.* 82). Since such forms are subject to frequent corruption (see Mastronarde on *Pho.* 1575), Willink's ἁλίοιϲι (unpub.) is attractive.

1096 Ϲαλαμῖν' ἱεράν: the eulogistic adjective (cf. *Od.* 1.2 Τροίηϲ ἱερὸν πτολίεθρον as well as 123 Ἴλιον ἱεράν and 1065 Πέργαμον ἱεράν) is surprising but lends, perhaps, a sense of distance from the painful reality of slavery. The reference in 1097–8 to Corinth and its peak Acrocorinth perhaps shows the same eulogistic tendency.

1100–17 This is the only part of the choral ode that might be regarded as a reaction to the previous *epeisodion*. But the connection is not very precise. Both Hecuba and the Chorus there showed their detestation of Helen, but they looked forward with approval to Menelaus' execution of his wife. Here both are execrated without differentiation. Despite Menelaus' assurance in 1053–4 the Chorus imagine them on the same ship.

1100–4 'How I wish that while Menelaus' bark is in mid-voyage over the sea the twin sacred †of the Aegean† fire of lightning might descend in the midst of the vessels.' In fact, we know from the prologue (80–1) that the thunderbolt will descend on the Greek fleet (though Menelaus' ship, in the tradition, is spared), hurled not by Zeus but by his daughter.

1100 ἀκάτου: 'light vessel, boat' (LSJ) may suggest how vulnerable Menelaus is on the sea. But it does not necessarily mean a small vessel: see Pfeijffer 1999: 103 on Pi. *N.* 5.2–3 (p. 103) on the meaning of ἄκατος.

Μενέλα: on the three-syllable form of Menelaus' name see 212n.

1101–2 μέϲον πέλαγοϲ... ἀνὰ μέϲον πλατᾶν: on the indifference of tragic poets to casual repetition of a word see 80–1n. Here we have both the partitive adjective μέϲοϲ, modifying a noun, and the substantive μέϲον with partitive genitive, seen e.g. at *Hec.* 1150, Hdt. 2.25.1, and places cited in LSJ s.v. III. —Burges's πλατᾶν is a necessary change, and Biehl's attempt to make transmitted πλάταν the object of 'the idea of igniting to be supplied from πέϲοι... πῦρ' lacks analogy among the instances of a periphrasis taking a further accusative given by Diggle, *Studies* 58.

1102 δίπαλτον: the adjective suggests that the god has a thunderbolt in each hand, like the image of Zeus Horkios described at Paus. 5.24.9. see Finglass on *Aj.* 405a–408/9, p. 259.

1104 †αἰγαίου† κεραυνοφαὲϲ πῦρ: —transmitted 'Aegean' is clearly wrong since it comes too late to go with μέϲον πέλαγοϲ. Wilamowitz wanted to save it by emending δίπαλτον to Αἰγαῖον and Αἰγαίου to δίπαλτον. But why this transposition should have involved corruption into the genitive is unexplained. Depending on whether we read ἀίϲϲον or ᾆιϲϲον in 1086 we need either ⏑ – – (for which – – – would be an acceptable substitute) or – –. Sense calls either for a further adjective modifying 'fire' or an expression specifying Zeus as its sender. Of dissyllabic proposals, Bannert's αἰγλᾶν, 'dazzling', a word used at *Andr.* 285, might have been corrupted to Αἰγαῖον, but the genitive is still unexplained. The same is true of Schenkl's Δῖον. Of trisyllables, αἰθαλοῦν (Diggle, *Studies* 71–2) gives good sense, is fairly close to the paradosis, and accounts for the corruption to the genitive (he cites this adjective in Hes. *Theog.* 72, 504, 707, and 854; *Pho.* 183; and *PV* 992), and he gives parallels for the responsion of – ⏑ with ⏑ –. An alternative that produces a more usual responsion, – – with ⏑ –, is Musgrave's Ἰδαίου, giving the lightning-bolt to 'Idaean Zeus', who is mentioned with this epithet at *Il.* 16.605 and 24.291 and also in Eur. fr. 472.10. For the use of an epithet of Zeus instead of his name cf. Φίλιοϲ at *Andr.* 603; Ar. *Ach.* 730; Pherecr. fr. 96 KA; and Ὀλύμπιοϲ at *Il.* 18.79, 22.130; Hes. *Op.* 474, etc. Ἑρκεῖοϲ is used by itself at Paus. 4.17.4.

1105–9 'When from the land of Ilios he is banishing me, tearful one, to be a slave in Greece and when Zeus's daughter, as it chances, is holding her golden mirror, the delight of maidens'. The Chorus here pray for the destruction of Menelaus and Helen even at the cost of their own death, perhaps considering death preferable to a life of slavery.

1105 πολυδάκρυνον: Bothe's conjecture avoids *brevis in longo*, unwelcome both here and in the strophe since the sense continues on without a break.

1106 λάτρευμα: Eur. employs a large number of deverbative nouns in -μα to describe persons. These are usually passive in sense, e.g. 425 ἀπέχθημα,

757 *ὑπαγκάλιϲμα*, 1121 *δίϲκημα*, and *μίϲημα*, *θρέμμα*, *πρόϲφαγμα*, *ὕβριϲμα*, etc. But some, being from verbs that have no passive, are active in sense: 420 *νύμφευμα*, 'object that will be a bride', and *λάτρευμα* here, 'object that will perform service' (cf. the similarly formed *δούλευμα* at *Ion* 748). See Barrett 2007 and Long 1968: 35–46.

γᾶθεν: —one occasionally finds two words with the archaic ablatival suffix -*θεν* (*Ἰλιόθεν*, *γᾶθεν*) in the same sentence, as *Od.* 5.490 and 7.52 *ποθεν ἄλλοθεν*. But I have found no other cases where two nouns referring to the same thing stand in the same sentence. None of the pleonasms cited by Lee, Biehl, Breitenbach 193, or KG 2.586 seems a close parallel. NL suggests *λάτρευμ' ἀγαθέϲ*, 'a downcast menial'. The adjective is a conjecture at *Trach.* 869. He notes the pleasing contrast this makes with Helen's life of pleasure.

ἐξορίζει: —It would certainly be reasonable for the indicative here to be attracted into the optative, as Wecklein 1901: 46 proposed. The same principle would give us *τυγχάνοι* in 1109, lending greater clarity to the structure.

1108–9 ***χρύϲεα δ' ἔνοπτρα, παρθένων | χάριταϲ, ἔχουϲα τυγχάνει Διὸϲ κόρα***: these words are a continuation of the *ὅτε*-clause begun at 1105. The Chorus, unlike Andromache at 766–71, call Helen the daughter of Zeus. (They fail to notice that this makes the chances of her death by lightning-stroke rather slim.)

1110–11 The subject of *ἔλθοι* is Menelaus (and not the more recently mentioned Helen), not only because of the masculine participle *ἑλών* (1114) but also because Menelaus is the one whose paternal home (*πατρῷιον θάλαμον ἑϲτίαϲ*) is in Sparta.

1112–13 Pitane was one of the districts (the Spartans called them *κῶμαι*) of Sparta: see Hdt. 3.55 and Paus. 3.16.9. Hdt. 9.53.2 mentions a Pitanate *λόχοϲ* or battalion, but Thuc. 1.20.3 insists that no such entity exists. *Πιτάναϲ* is the so-called appositive genitive on which see 816n.

1113 ***χαλκόπυλόν τε θεάν***: in Sparta Athena was worshipped as *Χαλκίοικοϲ*, the epithet derived from her temple, which had doors of bronze. Her temple and Menelaus' ancestral home are mentioned at *Hel.* 227–8 (where Bothe's *ὀλβιεῖ* restores the correct ownership of the halls). —Transmitted *θάλαμον* is clearly a gloss that has invaded the text. Wilamowitz, followed by Biehl, suggests that transmitted *θεᾶϲ*, not Musgrave's *θεάν*, is correct and that *χαλκόπυλον* is a noun, as *Δίπυλον* sometimes is. But all its other occurrences are adjectival, and so too is the epithet to which it alludes. 'The goddess of bronze gates' is a plausible way of referring to her temple, and it could easily have attracted the ministrations of a scribe or scholiast wanting to make it clear that the temple is meant.

1114–17 'Having won for mighty Hellas a disgrace consisting in an evil marriage and [having caused] woeful sufferings to [those who dwell by] the streams of the Simois.' There is a slight zeugma, indicated in the translation above. *δύcγαμον αἶcχοc* might be a periphrasis for Helen, but it is more likely that it means the disgrace itself: see *Hel.* 687 *δι' ἐμὰν . . . δύcγαμον αἰcχύναν*. —Wilamowitz 1895b: 26 proposed *ἔχων* for *ἑλών*, which makes the possession, not the acquisition, of Helen the reason for the Chorus's execration. But both the phrases here ought to refer to what Menelaus *accomplished* by the Trojan expedition.

1117 ***πάθεα ῥοαῖcιν***: —Diggle 1994: 456–8 shows that an open syllable ending in a short vowel is in spoken iambics usually treated as long before initial *rho* but in lyric usually as short, as here. The transmitted ending *-ηιcι(ν)*, the two-syllable ending of the 1st-declension dative plural, may have been used by Aesch., as it was used in contemporary inscriptions: see West's Aeschylus *praefatio*, p. xxxvi. But Barrett on *Hipp.* 101 discusses the evidence for Eur. and opts for *-αιcι(ν)*.

EXODOS (1118–1332)

The *exodos* has two principal sections, (1) 1118–1255 and (2) 1256–1332, each beginning with the entrance of a herald. (1) The first section consists of three scenes marked by entrances or exits. (a) 1118–55: after the body of Astyanax, laid out on his father's shield, is brought in, the herald who escorts it brings news and instructions for Hecuba. (b) 1156–1206: after his departure, Hecuba makes a speech over the body of her grandson. (c) 1207–55: after some Trojan women bring adornments for his body come four brief trimeter speeches by Hecuba, the first followed by a brief sung utterance by the Chorus, the second and third by brief *amoibaia*, and the last by a lamentation in spoken anapaests as the body of Astyanax is carried off. (2) In the second principal section there is, after the entrance with which it begins, no entrance or exit before the play's end. It falls into two parts, the first spoken, the second sung. (a) 1256–86: after the Chorus announces that soldiers in the distance are about to set fire to Troy, a herald enters. He orders the soldiers on the walls to proceed with the firing of the city and tells the Trojan women that they must depart for the ships when a trumpet sounds. Odysseus' underlings, who enter with him, are to escort Hecuba to his ship. When Hecuba urges the Chorus to commit suicide by running into the flames of Troy, he orders his men to take her away, the order to wait for the trumpet signal being cancelled. (b) 1287–1332: in spite of the Herald's order to depart at once, Hecuba and the

Chorus sing a strophic *amoibaion* in which they lament the fall of the city and their future lot as slaves. The play ends, as do virtually all Greek tragedies, with a general exit: Hecuba, Chorus, Herald, and Odysseus' underlings all depart by the left *eisodos*.

The two parts of the *exodos* have two separate but complementary focuses, the death of Astyanax and the burning of Troy. The former marks the end of the Trojan royal line. The latter rounds out the trilogy as a whole since it completes the prophecy made in *Alexandros* that Hecuba's son would prove a destructive firebrand for Troy: the ruin forecast in the prologue of the first play has finally come to pass. Though the *exodos* lacks most of Eur.'s customary closural gestures (see below), both halves of it convey the sense of an ending.

This portion of the play was clearly intended by Eur. to be a moving conclusion. We may guess that it was at this point in the play (our source does not tell us precisely when), that at a performance in Thessalian Pherae the tyrant Alexander of Pherae (who ruled 369–358) was reduced to weeping and had to leave the theatre: see Plut. *Pelopidas* 29.4–6, 293F and *Bellone an pace* 334A. The scholiast's comment on 1129, however, is suggestive of a wider range of reaction: 'In regard to the tragic plot, he [Eur.] has arranged that this episode should bring on stage both the shield and Astyanax. To motivate Neoptolemus' rapid departure he invented (εὗρεν: delete ὅτι) Peleus' expulsion by Acastus, and as regards the shield, he invented Andromache's request that Hector's shield should not be in the same bedroom with her. This is cleverly done. But he has removed some of the tragic apparatus. For if Andromache had been present, pity would have been more in evidence as she lamented her own child. He [Eur.] has given up such emotional effect in exchange for the introduction of the shield.' In other words, the scholiast thinks that Eur. may have had other effects than tragic pathos in mind.

In fact, the *exodos* contains, along with pathos, quite a bit of what Aristotle calls διάνοια, intellectual content, as Hecuba interprets what has befallen her. The pathos is unmistakable: the dead Astyanax; the adorning of his body with the tokens of vanished royal splendour; the shield of Hector and its mute witness to Trojan martial valour, a valour destined from the start to prove unavailing; and the final firing of the city and the collapse of its buildings. All this, however, must not stand in the way of our describing accurately what Hecuba says. Two things must be recognized, though interpreters have seemed reluctant to recognize them. First, Hecuba's argument is incoherent in what she says about the Greeks, not only captiously misrepresenting them but also contradicting herself. Second, she has learned little or nothing about the workings of the gods in the world and shows no understanding of the divine dimension of what has happened. Here too she contradicts herself as well as the facts.

1. Hecuba claims that the Greeks set more store by their spears than their intelligence (1158) and are nullities (1161) since they are irrationally afraid of a small boy, a charge she makes twice (1158–66 and 1188–91). But the Greeks are not afraid of the child Astyanax but of the man he will become if he lives. Every word Hecuba says about the bravery of Hector (see 1161–6n, 1194–5n, and 1221–3n) or his son's resemblance to him (see 1178–9n) proves that this fear has a rational basis. Furthermore, when she dismisses the idea that Astyanax might refound Troy (1160–1), the audience will have remembered that she had earlier commended a similar hope to Andromache (701–5).

2. What Hecuba says about the gods is similarly lacking in coherence. At one place (1204–6) she implies that the fall of Troy is the work of τύχαι whose operations are as causeless as the leaping about of a madman. At another (1213–15) she blames Helen for the death of Astyanax and the fall of Troy, as if the daughter of Zeus had done this on her own. At yet another the cause of what has happened is the gods' hatred of Troy (1240–2). Lastly, she asks incredulously whether Zeus sees the Trojans' sufferings (1290) and accuses the gods of deafness to prayer (1280–1), though these reproaches make no sense if the gods hate Troy.

Unwillingness to describe this intellectual content accurately may have its source in a feeling that mental clarity of some kind is to be expected at the end of a tragedy. Many extant tragedies bear out this expectation, yet others do not. In some tragedies, e.g. *Hipp*., clarity is achieved by the intervention of a *deus ex machina*, but it can also be achieved without authoritative informants. At the end of *OT*, for example, Oedipus sees for the first time that what he has suffered—his parricide, incest, and self-blinding—is the work of Apollo (see 1329–32). Creon at the end of *Ant*. likewise sees that his disregard of the ἄγραπτα κἀcφαλῆ θεῶν νόμιμα has brought ruin (see 1317–25). Some tragedies, however, achieve only suffering, the sufferer being still unable to understand what has happened or holding a view of it that events have decisively disproved. At the end of *Pers*. Xerxes laments the damage his invasion of Greece has done to Persia, but though the spectators know something of the divine background thanks to the ghost of Darius, all Xerxes has by way of explanation are his comments about a cruel δαίμων. After his final entrance in *Trach*. Heracles understands Zeus's prophecy to him that one of the dead would prove his undoing and that the Selli, in naming the present hour as the time of his release from labours, meant his death. But he does not achieve any larger insight into the workings of the world. His namesake in *Herc*. likewise suffers without any corresponding illumination. His particular contribution to the play's διάνοια—that gods who commit adultery or bind one another, or indeed have any needs at all, are not gods (1341–6)—contradicts not only the premise of the play but what he himself said earlier (1263–80, 1303–10). At the end of his life Ajax calls upon the Erinyes to punish his enemies (*Aj.* 835–44) but utters no word that recognizes his contribution to his own downfall. Cadmus (*Ba.* 1345–9) seems reluctant to accept the justice of Pentheus' punishment (though in 1377–8, if Kannicht's conjecture is correct, he includes himself among the blameworthy). Clearly the audience are not being asked to regard such διάνοια as deep insight. It may be that the very faults in its reasoning are designed to highlight the pathos. As Ismene says at *Ant.* 563–4, those in misfortune lose even the sense that they once had.

The ending of *Tro.* lacks most of the means Eur. usually employs to convey the sense of an ending: see Dunn 1996: 101–14. General reflection, which subsumes the events the audience have just experienced under generalities about the human condition, is a frequent closural device in tragedy and one much used by Eur., who normally assigns such thoughts to the Chorus's closing anapaests. Here there are neither anapaests nor general reflection. In place of anapaests, which end all but one of Eur.'s other extant plays (*Ion* ends in trochaic tetrameters) and all but one of Sophocles' (but the tetrameters that end *OT* are likely to be spurious, as argued by Kovacs 2009 and 2014, and the original ending may have had anapaests), *Tro.* ends with antistrophic lyric, which harks back to the practice of Aesch.'s *Pers.*, *Supp.*, and *Eu.* There is no *aition*, no reference to a feature of the audience's own day that is the memorial of the events just seen. (Aetiology as a closural gesture is seen at *Med.* 1381–3, *Hipp.* 1423–30, *Hec.* 1271–3, *El.* 1258–66, *Herc.* 1331–5, *IT* 1449–61, *Ion* 1575–88, *Hel.* 1670–5, and perhaps in *Hcld.* 1032–6.) Only the exhortation to depart (cf. the references to departure at the ends of *Hcld.*, *Hec.*, *Supp.*, *El.*, *Herc.*, *IT*, *Ion*, *Or.*, and *Ba.* plus those of *Pers.*, *Eu.*; *Aj.*, *Trach.*, and *Phil.*) serves to mark that the action is over. The most obvious closural element is the repeated insistence (1240–5, 1277–81, 1291–2, 1298–9, 1317–19, 1322–4) that Troy has perished for good.

Staging: accompanied by choral anapaests that call attention to the body of Astyanax, enter Herald by the left *eisodos* with two servants, who carry the boy on Hector's shield. This is the only time the left *eisodos* is used in this play for an entrance. On the significance of this see Introduction § 2.4, last paragraph. On entrance announcements immediately after a choral ode see 230–4n.

1118–22 'Ah, ah! From woeful change to woeful change go the fortunes of our land! See, unblest wives of the Trojans, Astyanax before us, dead! Sight unwelcome is he, hurled from the tower, killed by the Greeks!'

1118 ***καίν᾽ ἐκ καινῶν μεταβάλλουϲι***: *καιν(ά)* is internal accusative, 'undergo untoward changes'. For 'new' as 'unwelcome, untoward' see 55n. For temporal *ἐκ*, 'after', see 495n. The polyptoton is perhaps intensifying. —The transmitted participle gives an awkward sentence with no main verb. Dobree's deletion (1833: 92) of a single letter gives us the required indicative. The corruption may have been due to the influence of the diphthongs in *καινῶν*, *ϲυντυχίαι*, and *μέλεαι*. A further conjecture of Wilamowitz, *καίν᾽ ἐκ*, restores sense.

1119 ***χθονί***: the dative is one of interest, which often has the force of a possessive and is so translated above: see KG 1.429. Astyanax's death is viewed here as momentous for the city of Troy: he was the last of Troy's royal line and is now dead.

λεύϲϲετε: imperative or indicative? Neither 'See!' (*Herc.* 1029; *IA* 592 is part of a spurious addition) nor 'You see' (568, *Hec.* 1053) is common in entrance announcements, so it is difficult to decide.

1120 For *ὅδε* in entrance announcements and for entrance announcements immediately following a strophic choral song, see 230n.

1121 ***πύργων δίϲκημα πικρόν***: though this could in theory be accusative in apposition to the sentence ('an unwelcome hurling from the towers': Barrett 2007: 363), it seems better to take *δίϲκημα* as 'thing hurled', in apposition to Astyanax. For the loose ablatival genitive *πύργων* see *IT* 1384 *τό τ᾽ οὐρανοῦ πέϲημα*, and *Herc.* 1148 *πέτραϲ λιϲϲάδοϲ πρὸϲ ἅλματα*. As frequently in Eur. *πικρόϲ* is used of a thing that causes pain or is unwelcome: see 66, 922, 1019 and, of an unwelcome sight, 1227, *Med.* 1388, *Hipp.* 809, *Supp.* 783, 945, *Ion* 1257, *Or.* 952, *Ba.* 815, and P. Oxy. 5131.9 (*Ino*), where *πικρόν*, not *μικρόν*, may be the reading of the papyrus. (Differing views in Kovacs 2016: 5 and Finglass 2017: 64–5).

1122 ***κτείναντεϲ ἔχουϲιν***: 'have killed': on the aorist active participle with *ἔχω* as a periphrasis for the perfect, see 317n.

1123–55 *The Herald's rhesis.* The Herald begins by explaining why Andromache is not available to bury Astyanax: her master Neoptolemus had to leave Troy suddenly. (On the dramatic reason for this see 1126–8n.) He describes Andromache's requests to Neoptolemus (to arrange burial for the boy in his father's shield by bringing both to Hecuba) and to Hecuba herself (to adorn the body for burial). Departure is imminent: Hecuba must perform her role with all speed, and he himself will dig the grave, having already washed the body in the Scamander.

Biehl notes the help rendered by the Herald on his own initiative, the fullness of his explanation, unexpected where he could simply command, and his evident sympathy (*Solidarität*) with the queen-turned-slave, owing, he thinks, to their both being unfree. Heralds, however, are not slaves (see West on *Od.* 1.109–12; Van der Weiden on Pi. fr. 70b.24 Snell-Maehler notes their high status), so this explanation misses the mark. Eur. has simply made him more humane than he might have been in the circumstances. The same is true of Neoptolemus, who in the Herald's report accedes to all of Andromache's requests in spite of his need for a hasty departure.

1123 I have replaced the speaker indication *Τα.* with *Κη.* since this herald is the same one who took Astyanax away. For evidence that the herald of the second episode is not Talthybius, see 707n.

νεὼϲ μὲν πίτυλοϲ εἷϲ: 'one ship with its beating oars' (lit. 'one oar-beat of a ship'). The use of *regens* plus genitive *regimen* as a periphrasis for the dependent noun belongs to the high poetic style and is seen in Homeric expressions such as ἲϲ Τηλεμάχοιο and its congeners in tragedy such as *Sept.* 448 *Πολυφόντου βία*. Here the *regens* is a verbal idea ('rhythmic movement'): for parallels see Aesch. *Supp.* 487 ὕβριν ... ἄρϲενοϲ ϲτόλου, *Ag.* 947 ὀμμάτων ... φθόνοϲ; Soph. *Trach.* 656 πολύκωπον ὄχημα ναόϲ, 964 ξένων βάϲιϲ, *El.* 718 τρόχων βάϲειϲ, *Phil.* 868 οἰκούρημα τῶνδε τῶν ξένων; Eur. *El.* 601 τί ... εὐμενὲϲ φίλων, and *Hel.* 1322 θυγατρὸϲ ἁρπαγὰϲ δολίουϲ. To use 'oar-beat of a ship' to express 'ship with its beating oars' is a particular case of abstract for concrete, on which see Mastronarde on *Pho.* 291 and Kannicht on *Hel.* 50 and 1675. The same construction (*genetivus inversus*) is used in Latin: see LHS 2.152 and Pöschl 1967: 264–5 (= 1991: 252–3), explicating Horace's *regalique situ pyramidum*, 'and the pyramids in their royal decay'. For the meaning of πίτυλοϲ see 817n.

1126–8 According to the scholiast *ad loc.* the expulsion of Peleus by Acastus—which motivates the hasty departure of Neoptolemus and Andromache—was the invention of Eur. The result of this is that the preparation of Astyanax's body for burial falls to Hecuba, who thus continues to the end of the play as the focus of all Troy's woes.

1126 **Νεοπτόλεμοϲ**: scanned as four syllables, the first two vowels making a single syllable by synizesis and the last three syllables forming an anapaestic foot. The substitution in trimeters of double short for the *anceps* or short before a *princeps* position is governed by stricter rules than commentators have acknowledged, so I set them out here. There is a pronounced difference between a first-foot anapaest, which is scarcely felt to be a license (see 419n), and one in the second, third, fourth, or fifth foot. Anapaestic feet after the first are clearly felt to be an irregularity, one for which necessity is the only justification. Greek myth abounds in names of choriambic or adonean shape (e.g. Ἱππομέδων and Παρθενοπαῖοϲ) belonging to persons whose earliest home was hexameter verse. If these are to be accommodated in trimeters, there are precisely two ways to do so. Aesch. does so exclusively by anaclasis of the first metron, – ⏖ – replacing × – ⏑ –. Soph. and Eur. allow the double short in these names to stand before the second or fourth *princeps*, replacing single short (here the double short replaces the short before the fourth *princeps*), or before the third or fifth *princeps*, replacing *anceps*. Three rules are inferable from the evidence: (1) only proper nouns are accorded this metrical treatment, adjectives derived from proper nouns being excluded: see *Eur. Alt.* 97–8 and 102–3; (2) the proper noun must have the shape of a choriamb or an adoneus, and proper names beginning ⏖ – are accommodated at the beginning of the line. (The present passage, where the double short replaces the line's seventh (short) element, is paralleled at 1130, [1140], *Andr.* 14, *Or.* 65, 1654, 1655, and 1671.) (3) 2nd-declension choriambic names, when they are nominative or accusative, e.g., Ἱππόλυτον, can be scanned as – ⏖ ⏑, as at *Hipp.* 11, 22, etc., and are not normally treated anapaestically. But the present line is an exception to this generality, as are *IT* 825, 1457, and *Or.* 1655.

1129–30 **οὗ θᾶccον οὕνεκ᾽, οὐ χάριν μόνηc ἔχων, | φροῦδοc**: 'Accordingly, he has gone off more quickly, not having the pleasure of tarrying.' For the genitive with χάριc, 'pleasure', cf. *Med.* 226–7 βίου χάριν μεθεῖcα. For θᾶccον with no expressed point of comparison see *Med.* 100 and *Andr.* 551. —The paradosis could be translated 'Accordingly, more quickly than if he had the pleasure of tarrying, he has gone off.' But the emended text gives more natural sense, and the corruption of Bothe's οὐ (1802: 385) to ἢ is easy to explain after the comparative.

1130–3 The Greek herald describes how Andromache's farewell to her country and to the tomb of Hector brought tears to his eyes. (On the sociocultural aspect of tears see Fögen 2006.) He had earlier shown his tender-hearted side at 709–18. It would presumably have been easy for Eur. to make the Greek heralds cruel like Eurystheus' herald in *Hcld.* For a possible motive for the portrayal he actually adopts, see Introduction § 1.3.4.

1131 **δακρύων ἀγωγόc**: a similarly striking phrase at *Hec.* 535–6 χοάc ... | νεκρῶν ἀγωγούc.

1133–46 Andromache makes four requests of Neoptolemus, all in the infinitive: that he bury (i.e. cause the burial of) Astyanax; that he not bring Hector's shield back to Greece to be installed in the bedroom where she will become Neoptolemus' bed-fellow; that it be used instead as a coffin or sarcophagus for Astyanax; and that his body be sent to Hecuba for her to adorn as best she can.

1133 **προcεννέπουcα**: for the meaning 'bid farewell to' Lee cites *Ion* 1613.

1134–5 **νεκρὸν τόνδ᾽, ὃc πεcὼν ἐκ τειχέων | ψυχὴν ἀφῆκεν**: the Herald's deictic finally acknowledges what the audience have seen since 1118, the dead body of Astyanax. Here, as frequently, πίπτω serves as a passive, 'be thrown'. The Herald does not mention that it was he who in the second *epeisodion* led the boy away to his death. The actual hurling is ascribed to Neoptolemus in the *Ilias Parva* (*GEF* fr. 29) and to Odysseus in the *Iliupersis* (*GEF* arg. 4). In the present play we know only that it was Odysseus (721–5) who argued for this killing.

1135 **Ἕκτορος τοῦ σοῦ γόνος**: this nominative expression might have been accusative in apposition to νεκρὸν τόνδ' but is instead incorporated into the relative clause.

1136–9 'And this bronze-backed shield, terror of the Achaeans, which this boy's father used to put about his flanks, she begged him not to bring to the hearth of Peleus and to the same chamber where she will be made his bride.' In 1138 take νιν as 'him', resumptive of σφ' in 1133 rather than of ἀσπίδα in 1136 (*pace* Lee and Biehl). For resumptive or pleonastic pronouns see KG 1.660.

[1140] —The line is not only unneeded but also unwanted since 1138–42 are part of an *oratio obliqua*: the naming of the subject of νυμφεύσεται as 'the mother of this dead boy' would be out of place since that subject in *oratio recta* is simply 'I'. The interpolation may have had its origin as a glossing proper name, later filled out to a trimeter: see Mastronarde on *Pho.* 428.

1141–2 The shield will take the place of a cedar coffin or a stone sarcophagus. The compression of ἀντί here, 'instead of (burying him in)', is analogous to a *comparatio compendiaria*, on which see 631–1n.

1142–4 Neoptolemus is to give the dead boy into Hecuba's hands to adorn with grave-clothes and garlands as best she can. For the garlanding of the dead for burial see *Herc.* 562, where Heracles strips his children of the garlands Amphitryon and Megara had put on them when they were condemned to death, and *Ion* 1433, where Creusa mentions the garland she put on the child she expected would die (cf. 26–7). See also Hermann and Blümner 1882: 362–3 and Blech 1982: 81–9. For *peploi* covering a corpse see the new Ino fragment (P. Oxy. 5131), line 11 with Finglass 2014: 68n18, and, for other literature on this fragment, Kovacs 2016 and Finglass 2017.

1144 **ὅσῃ σοι δύναμις, ὡς ἔχει τὰ σά**: the second of these expressions of possibility qualifies or explains the first, 'to the extent that you are able *in view of* your circumstances'. For limitative ὡς see LSJ s.v. A.Ab.2. The first expression is a relative clause with incorporated antecedent, i.e. it is equivalent to 'with that ability, whatever size it is, that you have'. That Hecuba has so little scope to do anything for her grandson clearly marks how far she has fallen and contributes to the pathos of the situation. For πόσος, ὁπόσος, ὅσος, and the like in the sense 'how small' or 'so small' see 1165n. —Herwerden's ὥϲ <τ'> is not demonstrably necessary but might still be right.

1146 ἀφείλετ' αὐτὴν παῖδα μὴ δοῦναι τάφωι: 'robbed her of burying the boy'. An accusative of person and an accusative of thing are both found with ἀφαιρέω, combining the constructions of the English verbs 'rob' (of persons) and 'take' (of things). Here the second accusative is an action. For the 'redundant' or 'sympathetic' negative after verbs of hindering see Smyth §§ 2739–49. For the periphrasis with δίδωμι see 97n.

1148 ἐπαμπιϲχόντεϲ: aorist active participle of ἐπαμπέχω. In both ἀμπίϲχω and ἀμπέχω the prefix is deaspirated because a syllable with initial aspirate succeeds it, as happens, e.g., in the initial syllable of πέφευγα. —Diggle gives the conjecture to Matthiae 'praemonente Elmsley'. I have not found where Matthiae made it, but Elmsley in his 1822 edition of *Medea* proposed it at 282 (his 277).

ἀροῦμεν δόρυ: 'We will set sail.' For αἴρω with a ship or a fleet as object, see Thuc. 1.52 and *Ag*. 46. *IT* 117 shows the same construction with a more abstract object.

1151–2 The Scamander lies down the left *eisodos* and thus in the same direction as Troy: see Introduction § 2.3 and 2.4. The deictic perhaps underlines a gesture by the Herald in that direction: for ὅδε indicating what is vividly present to the mind see Taplin 1977: 150–1, Diggle 1971: 43n3, and Spitzbarth 1945: 9. The Greek herald has of his own accord performed the duty of washing the corpse that normally fell to the decedent's female relatives. This is of a piece with his general humanity, though since he was accessory to his killing, his taking a hand in his burial could be regarded as somewhat irregular.

1150 ἀπαλλάξαϲ ἔχω: on ἔχω plus aorist active participle as the equivalent of a perfect see 317n.

1153–5 'So I will go now and dig a grave for this boy so that actions on my part and yours, coming together, may quickly (ϲύντομ') speed the ship on its homeward journey.' For ἀλλά as transition from talk to action, where 'so' is sometimes a better translation than 'but', see *GP* 13–14. The adjective ὀρυκτόν is proleptic and describes the state of affairs after the action of the verb has been performed. For ῥήγνυμι with internal object see Pi. *N*. 8.29 ἕλκεα ῥῆξαν. For transitive ὁρμάω, less common than the intransitive, see LSJ s.v. A.I.

Staging: exit Herald. His ἀλλ' εἶμι strongly suggests an immediate exit. He uses the left *eisodos*: (1) it is plain from 1251–9 that the body is borne in the direction of Troy since the Chorus watch its departure and then see the men on the walls of Troy; (2) at 1256–9 we cannot have an exit to the right happening simultaneously with an entrance from the right; (3) burial near Troy makes more sense than near the Greek assembly place. Two of his retinue remain behind to bring Hector's shield with Astyanax's body down the same *eisodos* at 1250.

1156–1206 *Hecuba's rhesis.* After ordering the soldiers to lay the shield down, Hecuba upbraids the Greeks (1158–66) for murdering a boy who was no danger to them, his valiant father having perished. There follows a lament (1167–88) for the happiness the boy has lost (1167–72: he could, after inheriting the kingship, have died a glorious death in battle for his country), the sad state of his body with its gaping wounds and slack hands (1173–9), the tender moments Hecuba shared with him (1180–4), and the efforts, now lost, expended on his nurture (1185–8). She then imagines for the boy a fitting poetic epitaph (1188–91): the Greeks killed him because they were afraid of him. The only part of his paternal inheritance that he has received, she says, is his father's shield, which she then apostrophizes (1192–9). She gives orders for servants to fetch adornment from the hut of Agamemnon, then moralizes on the instability of human happiness (1203–6): fortune's changes are as unpredictable as the leaping about of a madman.

1156–7 In Hecuba's failure to say any word to the Herald Biehl finds evidence of contempt for an unfree person. But his immediate departure is a better explanation for her silence, and heralds are not slaves.

1156 ***θέcθ'***: for the meaning 'set down', as here, see line 8 of P. Oxy. 5131, a fragment of Eur.'s *Ino*. The object there is likewise a dead body, though Athamas seems to envisage the possibility that his son may still be alive.

ἀμφίτορνον: 'well rounded'. The word is *hapax eiremenon*. Eur. has in mind the kind of round shield used by hoplites in his day. On the *τόρνος*, 'compasses', in Eur. see Diggle 1998b: 47.

1157 ***λυπρὸν θέαμα κοὐ φίλον λεύccειν ἐμοί***: on the fullness of expression, common in tragedy, where the same idea is presented both positively and negatively ('painful and not pleasing'), see Stevens on *Andr.* 96, Denniston on *El.* 987, and Stockert on *IA* 1035. For the infinitive limiting an adjective, often called 'epexegetic infinitive', see Smyth § 2001–2 and *MT* § 763. The wringing of emotional effects from props consisting of weapons, here and at 1194–9 and 1221–5, has its parallel in *Herc.* 1377–85.

Staging: the two *personae mutae* put the shield on the ground.

1158 ***ὦ μεῖζον ὄγκον δορὸc ἔχοντεc ἢ φρενῶν***: 'You (Greeks), who pride yourselves more on (or 'are more highly esteemed for') your spears than your intelligence.' See LSJ s.v. *ὄγκοc* (B) II.2 for the sense 'pride, self-importance', and *Pho.* 717 for *ὄγκον ἔχειν*, 'enjoy esteem'. See also *Andr.* 320, where reputation 'makes impressive' the life of worthless persons.

1159–60 ***τί τόνδ', Ἀχαιοί, παῖδα δείσαντες φόνον | καινὸν διηργάσασθε:*** 'Why, Greeks, did you fear this child so that you committed an unprecedented slaughter?' (lit. 'Fearing this child for what reason, did you commit, etc.'). The interrogative belongs with the participial phrase, a state of affairs as natural in Greek as it is unnatural in English, where one does not ask 'Doing what were you arrested?' but 'What were you doing that you were arrested?'

In a Greek context it is neither unprecedented nor irrational to deal pre-emptively with the children of an enemy one has killed, children who will inherit the duty of avenging their father's death. A fragment of the *Cypria* (*GEF* fr. 31), *νήπιος ὃς πατέρα κτείνας παῖδας καταλείπει*, a line quoted in Arist. *Rhet.* 1395a16 and Plb. 23.10.10, is the first of a number of such expressions: see Stevens on *Andr.* 519–22, Bond on *Herc.* 166–9, and West 2013: 128.

1160–1 Hecuba implies that it is manifest nonsense that Astyanax might one day refound Troy. But just before the entry of the Herald at 706 with the news that the Greeks had condemned the boy to death, she expressed the hope to Andromache that if the boy grew to manhood Troy might be refounded by his descendants. Hecuba views the killing of Astyanax as an act of unfathomable cruelty, but she herself has provided evidence that it is (from the Greek perspective) a rational means of insuring that Troy will not rise again. The Greeks feared not the child Astyanax but the man he would become. Hector's heroism, embodied in the shield and frequently brought to the audience's attention (1136, 1162, 1194–9, 1221–2, 1253–4), contradicts her words.

1160 ***διηργάσασθε:*** this, rather than *διειργ-*, is the spelling of the aorist and imperfect of this verb that we find in fourth-century Attic inscriptions (it does not occur in fifth-century ones, where in any case there is until the end of the century no distinction between *ει* and *η*). On this question see Mastronarde's Teubner edition of *Pho.*, p. xxiii.

1161–6 Hecuba says that the Greeks are now shown to be—and have been all along—of no account. (On the idiom of the imperfect plus *ἄρα* see 109n.) This is because (*ὅτε* is causal here) it is true *both* that when Hector and other Trojan soldiers were enjoying success in battle, the Trojans were nevertheless on their way to their doom (and hence in the end not a threat); *and* that with that doom accomplished—Troy now fallen and its warriors dead—the Greeks are *still* afraid of a Trojan, a mere child. Thus the fear that leads to the killing of Astyanax is not rational but evidence of cowardice. (Here again, the mention of Hector's success in battle reminds the audience what was to be expected of his son.)

1165 **τοcόνδ'**: this could be adverbial with ἐδείcατ' ('were so afraid') but it seems better as adjectival with βρέφος, in which case it means 'so little': LSJ s.vv. τόcoc, τοcόcδε, and τοcοῦτοc allow for the meaning 'no bigger (or more numerous) than that' at e.g. Xen. *Ana.* 2.4.4 and *Cyr.* 6.3.22.

1165–6 'I disapprove (οὐκ αἰνῶ is litotes for ψέγω) of anyone who has (lit. 'fears') a fear that he has not examined rationally.' The ὅcτιc is postponed to the second place in its clause, and φόβον is the object of both φοβεῖται and διεξελθών. —The punctuation before φόβον was suggested by Dobree 1833: 93. This avoids 'a fear that fears without examining rationally'. The comma involves a break in sense before the final iamb, rare in Eur., as pointed out by Wilamowitz on *Herc.* 280 and Denniston 1936: 74. But rare is not the same as non-existent, and a pause here gives better sense than the alternative.

1167–72 Hecuba gives a summary of Astyanax's life that must, in view of his circumstances, be the opposite of a μακαριcμόc. A fortunate death is the appropriate end to a fortunate life, and the boy, who might have come to manhood, married, become king, and died gloriously in battle, has been robbed of both living happily and dying gloriously.

1169 **γάμων**: for this poetic plural see 319n.

τῆc ἰcοθέου τυραννίδοc: perhaps the article implies that 'godlike' is a standing epithet for royal power. —Normally putting a prepositive such as the definite article as fifth or seventh element would negate the caesura, but see West 83, who notes that 'a combination of two prepositives may stand before the caesura'. Cf. οὐκ ἐc before the caesura at 1211.

1170 **εἴ τι τῶνδε μακάριον**: when applied to things μακάριοc and μάκαρ can mean, as here, 'productive of blessedness': see 327, 336, *IT* 647, *Hel.* 1434, and *Or.* 1208. It is not clear whether Hecuba means to cast doubt on the blessedness produced by royal power and the like or whether she means 'if any of these things brings blessedness (as surely they do)'. (For εἰ in the sense 'if (as is surely the case)', see Smyth § 2246 and LSJ s.v. VI.) If the words express doubt, as seems likely, it is still a mistake to say that they express Eur.'s 'cynicism' (Lee *ad loc.*). The idea that kingship does not necessarily confer blessedness is expressed at Hdt. 1.32.5 by Solon, who is thought a wise man, not a cynic. The resolution of the fifth *longum* in the trimeter is rare in the earlier plays of Eur. but becomes more frequent in later plays. Cropp and Fick 1985: 50–1 give four instances before *Herc.*, three in *Herc.*, two in *Tro.* (here and 996), and some twenty-eight in the extant plays after *Tro.*

1171–2 I have daggered the first five syllables of 1172. In the app. crit. is a suggestion I have not ventured to put into the text, principally because it alters all three of the words in question. I translate this as follows: 'In your soul you are conscious that while (μέν) you have seen and known them, yet (δ') you were unable in your house to have any use of them.' The participles are those of *oratio obliqua*.

—The proposal addresses three problems. (1) Transmitted οὐκ οἶcθ' does not give good sense with ἰδὼν μὲν γνούc τε: it would have to mean 'You do not know that you have seen and known'. (2) The dative cῆι ψυχῆι lacks employment (it does not add anything to γνούc). (Munro 1882: 273–4 proposed cὰ for cῆι, taking it as 'seeing and knowing that they were yours', but this still leaves ψυχῆι weak in sense.) (3) In the text as transmitted, ἐν δόμοις ἔχων has to be taken (concessively: a καίπερ would be welcome) as 'though you had them in your house', and yet it seems inaccurate to say that Astyanax 'had' the things just mentioned (especially his young manhood and marriage) in his house. In the conjecture cύνοιcθα solves the first two problems (cύνοιcθα cῆι ψυχῆι means cύνοιcθα cεαυτῶι), and χρῆcθαι turns 'possessing' (ἔχων) into 'being able'. The μέν and δέ now mark the contrast between the first two participles and the third. The contrast is between what Astyanax saw and knew about his prospects and his inability to realize them. 'Hopes raised and dashed' is a variant on the idea that the experience of happiness makes subsequent unhappiness harder to endure: see 195–6n. The reference in cύνοιcθα to present time is not a problem: elsewhere Hecuba leaves open the possibility that Astyanax and the other dead are sentient: see 1248–50n.

1173–6 'Poor boy, how woefully your father's walls, Loxias' fortifications, have shorn you (c'), the locks (βόcτρυχον) of your head (κρατόc) that your mother often tended with care and kissed.' ἔκειρεν takes two objects, c' and βόcτρυχον, the latter being an antecedent incorporated into the relative clause. For the double accusative, 'construction of the whole and part', see 408n. —Word order would be less contorted if we omitted c' with some of the mss. of Athenaeus and allowed κρατόc to be an ablatival genitive. But the omission of the pronoun is poorly attested and is anyway the *lectio facilior*, whereas the bringing forward of κρατόc, though difficult, looks justifiable by its emotional effect.

1175 ὃν πόλλ' ἐκήπευc' ἡ τεκοῦcα βόcτρυχον: 'the hair your mother so often looked after'. The verb suggests careful tendence, as of a garden.

1176 φιλήμαcίν τ' ἔδωκεν: 'and (often) kissed'. For the periphrasis using δίδωμι see 96n.

1176–7 ἔνθεν ἐκγελᾶι | ὀcτέων ῥαγέντων φόνοc, ἵν' αἰcχρὰ μὴ cτέγω: 'where, with your bones shattered, the blood now forms a smiling gash—not to conceal what is shameful'. —Diggle, *Studies* 73–4, arguing that transmitted αἰcχρὰ μὴ λέγω is impossible since Hecuba *does* describe things that are shameful, replaces λέγω with cτέγω. This corruption has been diagnosed at *IA* 872, and I have adopted a similar conjecture at 718.

1178–9 'O hands, what a sweet resemblance you have to (the hands of) your father, and yet how slack in all your joints you lie!' On the *comparatio compendiaria*, where 'the hands of' needs to be supplied, see 630–1n. Exclamatory ὡς is to be supplied in the second clause of the sentence. On εἰκούς contracted from εἰκόνας see LSJ s.v. εἰκών. On the accent see Dover on *Nub.* 559. Biehl cites *Od.* 4.189, where similarity of hands and feet are mentioned as indicators of parentage. The genetic inheritance of Astyanax, visible in his hands, is the reason the Greeks thought it necessary to kill him.

1180 **ὦ πολλὰ κόμπους ἐκβαλών, φίλον στόμα, | ὄλωλας:** φίλον στόμα is a vocative, as recognized by Burges. (A similar vocative, ἀνόσιον στόμα, was detected at *OC* 981 first by Mähly 1862: 72–3 and then independently by Housman 1892: 156–7.) The neuter address does not affect the gender of the participle: on the *constructio ad sensum* see 535n. Finglass on *El.* 1508 notes that scribes do not usually alter the sense-construction to the gender called for by strict grammar, but V's ἐκβαλόν is a case where one scribe has.

1181–4 Hecuba remembers when the boy promised that after her death he would cut a large lock of his hair in mourning and bring his age-mates to her funeral.

1181 **ὄλωλας, ἐψεύσω μ'**: 'You are dead, your words to me proved false.' ψεύδομαι can mean to be factually incorrect without the intent to deceive: see LSJ s.v. A.4. (In modern Greek ψέμματα means 'Nonsense!' rather than 'Lies!') The asyndeton suggests that dying and proving false are closely connected actions since two verbs in asyndeton at the beginning of a trimeter are often synonyms: see Mastronarde on *Pho.* 1193, Collard on *Supp.* 699–700a, and the literature cited by both.

ἐσπίπτων πέπλους: the image of a child hurling himself into the clothing of an adult recalls 557–9, 750–1, *Alc.* 189, and *Herc.* 972, though these are children in distress. —V's λέχος is possible, and Parmentier suggests that as the aged are frequently represented as keeping to their beds (he cites *Herc.* 107 and 555), it is natural that Astyanax should hurl himself into the bed of Hecuba. If λέχος is right, however, it does not mean that the boy has gone there to sleep and should not be invoked to support 1188 ὕπνοι τ' ἐκεῖνοι; see 1187–8n.

1183–4 **πρὸς τάφον θ' ὁμηλίκων | κώμους ἐπάξω:** revellers and mourning do not belong together (cf. *Alc.* 831). Astyanax's words, though grotesquely inappropriate in an adult, are arguably charming in a child. The original audience, fighting tears at this point or past fighting them, may have smiled.

1184 φίλα διδοὺϲ προϲφθέγματα: do these words belong with the rest of the *oratio recta*? If so, they mean 'giving my loving farewell' (see 1133n for 'address' as 'last address'). But then the present participle is being used where we expect a future participle of purpose. They could just as easily be a comment by Hecuba on Astyanax's naive outburst, 'And your words to me brought me joy'. Since I have chosen (following the practice of the OCT) to dispense with quotation marks, using a capital letter to mark the beginning of a quotation but nothing to mark the end, my text bears either interpretation. I therefore declare my preference here for ending Astyanax's speech after ἐπάξω. The actor will have marked the *oratio recta* vocally, perhaps by raising his voice into a higher register to imitate the speech of a child.

1185–6 It is a shock when the old find themselves obliged to bury the young. That, according to Croesus at Hdt. 1.87.4, is the most important reason why no sensible person chooses war when peace is a possibility. θάπτω is not *praesens pro futuro*, 'I shall bury', but a present, 'I am engaged in burying'. —1186 contains ideas that either duplicate the point of 1185 (γραῦϲ) or are irrelevant to it (ἄπολιϲ, ἄφιλοϲ). It may be an interpolation designed to spell out what Hecuba has expressed elliptically: 'But you are not (performing acts of mourning for) me but I for you, the younger person.' (I admit that this ellipsis is difficult.) If so, an explanatory note, θάπτω, was padded out into a trimeter: see 1140n. To be sure, repetition of alpha-privative adjectives is common in genuine tragedy (see above on 1082–3), but for its use by an interpolator see *Hipp.* 1029 (del. Valckenaer).

1187–8 Hecuba mentions their many embraces, her nurturing of him, and one other item, which has apparently suffered corruption. —In spite of Jackson 87, cited in Diggle's apparatus, I doubt that ὕπνοι τ' ἐκεῖνοι is sound. Jackson, who proposed at *IT* 861 the palmary φεῦ φεῦ χερνίβων ἐκεί⟨νων· οἴμοι⟩, notes the emotive force of the demonstrative there. He then calls 'lamentable' any alteration of ὕπνοι τ' ἐκεῖνοι. But there is a big difference between, on the one hand, 'next to the altar there were tears and sighs. Oh, those lustral bowls: ah me!' where it is plain what lustral bowls are meant and why they deserve the demonstrative; or 'the <loosing> of my mother's girdle and that (clearly indicated and highly consequential) night' (*IT* 204–5); and, on the other, 'Ah me, the many embraces, my nurturings of you, and *those sleeps*', which provokes the question 'What sleeps, and why are they emotively charged?' As indicated at 1181n, ἐϲπίπτων λέχοϲ might be correct, as Parmentier 1923: 59–61 argues, pointing out how common it is for the aged to keep to their beds, but it does not prove that Astyanax hurled himself into his grandmother's bed in order to sleep there: Parmentier writes 'After her games and caresses, after their meal and the other attentions his grandmother bestowed on him, the child ended by falling asleep next to her' (p. 61), but this is pure eisegesis. Munro 1882: 274 proposed ὕπνοι τε κοινοί, which is at least less obscure. Wilamowitz 1879: 182 (= *Kleine Schriften* 19) proposed ὕπνοι τ' ἄυπνοι. But instead consider πόνοι τ' ἐκεῖνοι, thought of by Seidler and rejected by him without much conviction. (Dobree 1833: 93 repeated the suggestion, citing *Supp.* 1134 as parallel.) With this text 'toils' picks up on the nurturing mentioned in the previous line. This makes better sense of φροῦδά μοι. To complain that embraces and acts of feeding *qua* individual acts 'are gone' makes little sense since such acts are in themselves transitory. If, however, the subject is labour that has an expected return in the future, the complaint makes sense. A common lament when young persons die is that the efforts expended on raising them have proved vain: see 381n and 757–60n. For a plausible corruption of πόνοϲ to ὕπνοϲ see Willink 1988: 89–92 [= Willink 2010: 104–7].

1187 τὰ πόλλ' ἀϲπάϲμαθ' αἵ τ' ἐμαὶ τροφαί: probably '(my) many embracings and my (many) nurturings [of you]', each adjective being ἀπὸ κοινοῦ in the other half of the line.

1188–91 'What, pray, could a poet write for your tomb? "This boy the Argives once dispatched—in fear"? Such an epitaph brings disgrace on Hellas.' Lougovaya 2013: 265 notes the ways in which the conventions of inscriptions for war-dead are here inverted, with the dead boy no longer subject but object. A similar inversion is to be seen in the near-epitaph at *Il.* 7.89–91, where Hector imagines that the death of his as-yet-unspecified opponent will bring him glory: ἀνδρὸϲ μὲν τόδε ϲῆμα πάλαι κατατεθνηῶτοϲ, ὅν ποτ' ἀριϲτεύοντα κατέκτανε φαίδιμοϲ Ἕκτωρ. ὥϲ ποτέ τιϲ ἐρέει, τὸ δ' ἐμὸν κλέοϲ οὔ ποτ' ὀλεῖται. For the intensification of a question by καί see *GP* 312, 314. There is a similar quotation of a hypothetical inscription at *Pho.* 574–6. The implication of Hecuba's words is that this inscription will be widely known. There is a similar promise of widespread fame in the *Iliad* passage quoted above. —We must write either Burges's ϲοι or Dobree's ϲῶι (1833: 93) since γράφω is not construed with two accusatives like λέγω or ποιέω.

1190 ποτε: for this word in epitaphs (with perhaps a suggestion of boastfulness), see Fraenkel on *Ag.* 577, Bond on *Herc.* 1 and 1289, and Young 1983: 35–40. To boast of a triumph over a child would, of course, be no boast at all and would shame the boaster. But just as Hecuba's claim that the Greeks were afraid of a child is captious (see the introduction to the *exodos*), so is her suggestion that they will boast of killing him.

1192–9 Hecuba dwells on the irony that the only item Astyanax has inherited from his father is the makeshift coffin provided by his shield, an item that recalls his valour.

1192 **ἀλλ' οὖν πατρῴιων οὐ λαχὼν ἕξεις ὅμως**: 'But though you did not inherit your father's property, you will at any rate have....' In the collocation ἀλλ' οὖν the latter particle, according to *GP* 441, expresses 'essentiality or importance'. Here, as noted at *GP* 442, Hecuba is countering her own words ἄθλιον θάπτω νεκρόν with 'Still, you *shall* have your father's shield to be buried in', more emphatic, says Denniston, than the commoner καίτοι.

1194 **καλλίπηχυν**: for the compound adjective with redundant second element, repeating the idea of the modified noun, see 122–5n.

1194–5 **βραχίονα | cῴιζουc', ἄριcτον φύλακ' ἀπώλεcαc cέθεν**: the shield saves the warrior and the warrior the shield. That Hector saved his shield means that he was not a ῥίψαcπιc, abandoning it and his fellow hoplites in order to save his life.

1196–9 Hecuba draws attention to the imprint of Hector's chin and the marks of his sweat on the shield. The τύποc (made by the chin) is not fully explained until 1199. —Barnes's cῶι is necessary since 'you' in this sentence is the shield, not Hector. The apostrophe to the shield should not be broken off by adopting Bothe's ἔcταζεc, Ἕκτορ (1802: 386) in 1199.

1200 Hecuba ends by ordering the two servants attending on her (see 462–5n) to fetch adornment for Astyanax and then commenting bitterly on the instability of fortune.

Staging: two servants go into the *skēnē*, returning before 1207. If they leave immediately on hearing 1200, six lines are available to cover their going and coming. This is considerably less than the twelve lines that cover the fetching of Cassandra (294–305) or the fifteen lines during which someone goes into the *skēnē* to bring Helen out (880–94) and so may represent a minimum. But lines may have perished hereabouts: see 1206n.

1201–2 **οὐ γὰρ ἐc κάλλοc τύχαc | δαίμων δίδωcιν**: 'Our fate does not provide us circumstances that allow fine display.'

1202 **ὧν**: genitive of the whole or ablatival genitive, '(Out) of such store as I possess you shall receive these things'.

1203–4 Hecuba's sentence shows a formal resemblance to Poseidon's μῶροc δὲ θνητῶν ὅcτιc in 95. In content, though, the two are quite different. Poseidon draws the moral that it is foolish to offend the gods (see 95–7n and Appendix 1), Hecuba that it is foolish to imagine that your prosperity will last, all human happiness being subject to reverse, not only that of the impious: 'That mortal is a fool who rejoices in the belief that he enjoys stable prosperity.' The idea that prosperity cannot be counted on to last is, of course, one of the staples of Greek moralizing, but Hecuba's words take a decidedly untraditional turn at 1204–6: see note. —Biehl interprets the transmitted text thus, taking *βέβαια* with *εὖ πράccειν δοκῶν*. Bothe 1826 conjectured *εὖ πράccων δοκεῖ βέβαια χαίρειν*, 'imagines in his prosperity that his joy is reliably fixed'. This eliminates the awkwardness of taking *βέβαια* with the expression in the previous line and leaving *χαίρει* isolated. For cases where the corruption of one word by false concord or other misunderstanding causes corruption elsewhere in the sentence see *El.* 1263, *IT* 1004–5, *Hel.* 1033, *OT* 376, *OC* 266–7; and, e.g., Hor., *Carm.* 3.8.19–20. The conjecture could be right, but I have left it in the apparatus since arguably *βέβαια* goes better with an expression like *εὖ πράccω* than with *χαίρω*: see fr. 1074 *βέβαια δ' οὐδεὶc εὐτυχεῖ θνητὸc γεγώc*.

1204–6 Hecuba's words might be regarded as an encapsulation of the venerable theme that mortal life is always subject to unexpected change. Eur. is especially fond of this (see 509–10, *Alc.* 1159–63, *Med.* 1415–19 (found also at the ends of *Andr.*, *Hel.*, and *Ba.*), *Hcld.* 865–6, *Hipp.* 981–2, *Andr.* 100–2, *Hec.* 282–3, *Herc.* 509–12, *Ion* 381–3, 1510–15, *Or.* 340, frr. 62, 100, 101, 153, 157–8, 196, 262, 304, 330, 409, 420, 536, 549, 554, 617a, 618, 684, 765c, 901, 1041, 1073, 1074). Aesch. too sounds this note occasionally (*Ag.* 928–9, 1327–30), as does Soph. (*OT* 1186–96, [1529–30] with Jebb's note, *Trach.* 1–3, fr. 646). The 'call no man happy until he is dead' motif is often ascribed to Solon as reported in Hdt. 1.32.4 (e.g. by Arist. *EN* 1100a11–12), but the more general theme of the unreliability of human expectation is to found at *Il.* 16.684–91 and in other non-Attic sources such as Simonides *PMG* 521 and Pi. *O.* 12. (This sentiment, though Greek, is ascribed to Cyrus at Hdt. 1.86.6.) But it is one thing to sound the common tragic note that life is changeable and quite another to describe its changes as utterly random and uncaused: to Hecuba's denial of any rhyme or reason to human vicissitude there is only a partial parallel in fr. 901, where the Chorus ponder whether it is a god or chance that determines human life, and in fr. 1073, where someone wonders whether 'god' is the right term for the sender of vicissitude). Poseidon at 67–8 had also used the image of mad leaping about to express his puzzlement at Athena's change from loving to hating the Greeks. In fact, as she explained, her change of attitude was not random or unmotivated but provoked by the impiety of Ajax and of the Greeks' failure to punish it. Eur.'s first audience might well have thought that Hecuba's complaint deserved a similar reply.

1204 ***τοῖc τρόποιc***: 'in their character', as changeable. Contrast 67 *ἄλλοτ' εἰc ἄλλουc τρόπουc*, where the word indicates a succession of *different* characters.

1205 **ἔμπληκτος ὡς ἄνθρωπος**: derived from ἐμπλήσσω the adjective means 'stunned' and then 'stupid or senseless' (LSJ s.v. 1) then 'impulsive, unstable, capricious' (LSJ s.v. 2). Finglass on *Aj.* 1358 translates it as 'inconsistent'.

1206 In view of what precedes ('human fortunes leap about in unaccountable fashion like a madman'), we expect the line to say 'and no one is happy forever'. None of the ways of explaining or altering what is transmitted is without objection, and I have daggered most of the line. —As transmitted, 1206 is impossible, in spite of attempts to defend. Following the lead of Murray's app. crit. Wilamowitz 362–3 paraphrases 'οὐ παρ' ἑαυτοῦ οὐδὲ παρ' ἑαυτῶι ἔχει τὴν εὐτυχίαν, das Glück ist keine ἕξις wie die ἀρετή, sondern eine περίστασις, in späterer Terminologie zu reden' and translates 'der Mensch ist niemals seines Glückes eigner Herr'. But there is a considerable distance between the text and both the Greek and the German paraphrases. Lee translates 'and no one is ever happy of himself', meaning 'without any assistance from others', as Zeus begat Athena. But nothing in the context suggests that Hecuba is emphasizing the need for help in human life. Biehl takes εὐτυχεῖ as *praesens pro futuro* and translates 'and accordingly no one (of those now happy) will himself (i.e. in his own person) be happy at a future time'. But (1) one cannot be happy in someone else's person so αὐτός is meaningless; and (2) his translation denies that those who are fortunate now will be fortunate *at any time in the future*, implying that their luck must run out immediately. The defences fail. By contrast Barthold 1875: 10 emends to αὑτὸς εὐτυχῆς ἀεί (αὑτός was already proposed by Scaliger). In the report of this conjecture in Wecklein and Diggle one more word is altered, οὐδείς to οὔποθ'. I do not know whether this is a correct report (I cannot find a second discussion by Barthold), but the further alteration is arguably necessary since 'no man the same' is doubtful sense. The reported conjecture gives the kind of *sententia* the context leads us to expect: human fortunes are ever changing, and the same man is never fortunate forever. It achieves sense, however, only at the cost of altering three of the four daggered words, the reason why it has remained in the apparatus. Making the slightest of changes Jackson 145–6 proposed κοὐ δὶς αὑτὸς εὐτυχεῖ ποτε, but we expecct Hecuba not to deny that the same man is ever fortunate *twice* but that he is fortunate *forever*. Yet κοὐδείς, αὐτός, and ποτε all seem relevant words in a statement about changing human fortunes. The same is true of transmitted εὐτυχεῖ or εὐτυχῇ either of which could be plausibly interpreted as an adjective. This suggests not a corrupt but a lacunose text and that Eur. wrote, e.g. (the underlined words would explain the omission):

κοὐδείc, <αὐτίκ' εἰ πράccει καλῶc,
πράξει τὸ λοιπόν, οὐδὲ διὰ μακροῦ χρόνου
ἕν' ἔcχε βίοτον> αὐτὸc εὐτυχῆ ποτε.

'And no one, if he prospers at the moment, will do so for the rest of his life, nor throughout length of days has the same man ever enjoyed an unvaryingly happy life.' With the phrasing of the last line compare *Ion* 382–3, ἕνα δ' ἂν εὐτυχῆ | μόλιc ποτ' ἐξεύροι τιc ἀνθρώπων βίον. It is a further benefit that two more lines are available to cover the servants' journey into and out of the *skēnē*: see *Staging* note before 1201–2.

1207 πρὸ χειρῶν: on this phrase, which means 'visible in the hands', see Jebb on *Ant.* 1279.

1207–8 cκυλευμάτων | Φρυγίων: the genitive is ablatival as at 1202.

Staging while speaking 1209–15 Hecuba puts finery on Astyanax. The text nowhere mentions garlanding his head (contrast the garlanding of the shield in 1223). It may have been implied in a line lost before 1212, where see note.

1209–15 The burden of this speech is that the occasion of his being adorned ought by right to be a victory with the horse or the bow but that he has been robbed of this decoration by the god-hated Helen. Riding a horse and shooting the bow are two of the three accomplishments (the third is speaking the truth) that the Persians teach their sons according to Hdt 1.136. If we have an allusion to Persian practice, this is one of two places in the play (see 1021n) where it is suggested that the Trojans are culturally different from the Greeks.

1209–10 We have *Versparung* (ἀπὸ κοινοῦ) since ἥλικαc in the second member is to be understood in the first: see Kiefner 35.

1211 οὐκ ἐc πληcμονὰc θηρώμενοι: 'not pursuing (them) to satiety' was taken by Wilamowitz 363 as an attack by Eur. on his countrymen's excessive devotion to athletics. Though archery does not seem to have featured in any of the pan-Hellenic games, there is a bow contest in *Il.* 23, and at Soph. F 859 the Trojans use horse and bow in a context that suggests athletic endeavour. But 'not pursuing to satiety' could equally mean that the Trojans never get enough of such competitions. Another possibility: instead of athletic contests θηρώμενοι might suggest hunting, a pursuit in which horse and bow are used. Perhaps the Trojans 'do not hunt to the point of satiety', i.e. they never get enough of hunting.

—Eden 1990: 28–9 was puzzled by 'not pursuing them to the point of satiety' and proposed νείκουc πληcμονάc: 'pursuing satiety of feuding', i.e. 'pursuing their feuds until they have had enough'. νείκουc is an anagram of *-ν οὐκ εἰϲ*. (On anagrammatic corruptions see Jackson 208n1.) If this is right, the first audience, who in *Alexandros* had watched the attempt by Deiphobus to kill the upstart athlete who had bested him and his brothers in the games, would understand just how far a feud can be taken.

1212 —Lee explains the lack of concord between *νικήϲαντά ϲε* and *ϲοι προϲτίθηϲ'* as an anacolouthon. The change of case from accusative (1209) to dative (1212) can be paralleled (see Smyth § 2148d) but not the duplication of *ϲε* in 1209 by *ϲοι* in 1212. Scaliger marked a lacuna after 1211, and this, if accepted, would allow for different constructions for the two pronouns. A clue to the lacuna's contents is the phrase *μήτηρ πατρόϲ*: Hecuba is, to be sure, the boy's grandmother, but the particular reason for mentioning this here and writing 3rd-person *προϲτίθηϲ'* and not Herwerden's *προϲτίθημ'* is that the meaning is not 'I, his father's mother, am decorating him'; instead, Hecuba contrasts being decorated in private by one's (naturally prejudiced) grandmother, which confers no glory, with a state honour awarded in a public place, e.g.

ὦ τέκνον, οὐχ ἵπποιϲι νικήϲαντά ϲε
οὐδ' ἥλικαϲ τόξοιϲιν, οὓϲ Φρύγεϲ νόμουϲ
τιμῶϲιν, οὐκ ἐϲ πληϲμονὰϲ θηρώμενοι,
<ϲτεφάνοιϲι κῆρυξ δημίοιϲ πυργοῖ μέγαν,
ἀλλ' ἐν ταπεινοῖϲ κειμένωι μόνη μόνωι>
μήτηρ πατρόϲ ϲοι προϲτίθηϲ' ἀγάλματα κτλ.

'My child, not for a victory with horse or bow over your agemates (which customs the Trojans honour, who never get enough of hunting) <is a herald exalting you to greatness with a crown bestowed by your people; rather as you lie alone in humble state> your grandmother, <herself alone,> fastens these adornments on you.' If Hecuba did mention a publicly awarded crown, as *νικήϲαντα* suggests, the *ἀγάλματα* of 1212 may have been the garland for Astyanax, not otherwise mentioned in the text.

1212–13 **προϲτίθηϲ' ἀγάλματα | τῶν ϲῶν ποτ' ὄντων**: the genitive seems to be ablatival, 'finery from (the store of) those things that were once yours'.

1213–15 Hecuba (134–7), Andromache (766–73), and the Chorus (781–2) earlier blamed Helen for the fall of Troy. But Helen is not an independent agent. It is not surprising that the Trojan women are unwilling to acknowledge that it was Zeus who destroyed Troy.

1213–14 **νῦν δέ ϲ' ἡ θεοϲτυγὴϲ | ἀφείλεθ' Ἑλένη**: 'But now god-detested Helen has robbed you [of them].' I have punctuated with a comma after *ὄντων* since the contrast between then and now belongs in the same sentence: 'possessions once yours but now taken away by Helen'. For the shift in construction, where the expected participle of the second half of the contrast is replaced by an independent clause, see Smyth § 2147c, KG 2.100, and Dodds on *Ba.* 1131–3. —The transmitted text is ambiguous and could mean that Helen has taken Astyanax himself away, but this anticipates the point of *πρὸϲ δὲ καὶ ψυχὴν ϲέθεν ἔκτεινε*. We might consider *νῦν τὰ ϲ'.* This produces an unambiguous first element (robbing of possessions) to contrast with what follows (taking of his life and destruction of his whole house). The asyndeton would be explanatory, and the comma after *ὄντων* would be replaced by a raised period, eliminating the shift in construction mentioned above.

1214–15 There may be here the most elaborate of the etymological puns on Helen's name: *ἀφαιρεῖν*, *κτείνειν*, and *ἐξαπολλύναι* could all be regarded as synonyms of *ἑλεῖν*. On Eur.'s habit of giving not the *etymon* itself but a synonym see 892–3n.

1216–17

1. 1216	⏑ – ⏑ – | ⏑ ⏕ ⏕ ⏑ –	ia δ
2. 1217	⏑ ⏕ – ⏑ – | ⏑ – – ⏑ – |||	2δ

1216 *φρενῶν ἔθιγεϲ ἔθιγεϲ*: this could be addressed to Astyanax, who is addressed in 1217 (see 1217n). But in the absence of a good parallel for 'You (by your death) have touched my heart', we should take Hecuba as the addressee: cf. *Alc.* 108.

1217 *ἀνάκτωρ πόλεωϲ*: the vocative is addressed to Astyanax, not, *pace* Lee, Hector. The Chorus's point is that, as the etymology of his name implies, Astyanax was, in the Chorus's eyes (*ἐμοί*), the king of the city. In *Il.* 6.402–3 and 22.506–7 the boy was called Astyanax because his father rescued the city (for the *ἄναξ* part of his name in Homer see Schulze 1892: 505 and von Kamptz 1982: 85), but here the Chorus derive the name from Astyanax's own status. For a speculative argument that Homer's etymology is secondary and Astyanax himself was originally seen as the city's rescuer, see Roussel 1919. For a different view of the passage see Edinger 1992.

1218–25 Hecuba once more dwells on what would have been in store for Astyanax if he and his city had not been destroyed: marriage with a high-born Asian princess. She garlands and praises the shield of Hector, so much more worthy of praise than that of Odysseus.

Staging: Hecuba covers Astyanax's body with a rich garment. She then decorates the shield (1221–3) with a garland like that used to adorn the dead.

1218 *γάμοιϲι*: for this poetic plural see 319n.

1219 *Ἀϲιατίδων γήμαντα τὴν ὑπερτάτην*: either the aorist participle is coincident (on which see 372n) or the infinitive refers to getting dressed the morning after a marriage, which always takes place in the evening.

1220 ***Φρυγίων πέπλων ἀγάλματ'***: this could mean 'adornment consisting in Phyrgian garments' but also 'adornment for Phrygian garments', e.g. a jewelled pendant or the like. The former seems more likely in the context. Hecuba need not laboriously dress the boy in the robe but can simply lay it over him.

1221–3 Hector's shield is apostrophized as 'mother, glorious in victory, of countless routs', a further reminder of Hector's valour. The shield is addressed as female because several words for shield (*ἀcπίc, ἰτέα, πέλτη*) are feminine, even though the word used later in the line is neuter. The participles in 1221 and 1223 agree with *μῆτερ*, not with *cάκοc*. The present participle *οὖcα* refers to the past: on the 'imperfect' participle see 45n. For the predicate adjective *καλλίνικε* attracted into the vocative see *Pers.* 674 and *Phil.* 760.

1223 ***cτεφανοῦ· κάτει γὰρ οὐ θανοῦcα cὺν νεκρῶι***: 'Receive this garland: for you will be descending, though alive, with one who has died.' The shield is going down to the Underworld, and it is therefore appropriate that it be garlanded.

—Transmitted *θανῆι* (which could only mean 'you will die', not 'you will be dead') is wrong since the shield is not going to die; furthermore, it cannot die *in company with* Astyanax, since he is not going to die either, being already dead. Biehl sees this point, but his repunctuation as *θανῆι γὰρ οὔ, θανοῦcα cὺν νεκρῶι* gives feeble sense ('You will not die, having already died with the dead boy'), sense, moreover, that in no way justifies the *γάρ*. Lee, by contrast, takes *θανῆι γὰρ οὐ θανοῦcα* as a characteristically Euripidean oxymoron, citing *Alc.* 521 and *Hel.* 138 and the parody at Ar. *Ach.* 396. An oxymoron, however, is a contradictory expression that is nevertheless in some sense true in both of its halves (see the three examples cited by Lee and, e.g., *Andr.* 420 and *IT* 512 with Platnauer's note), yet there is no sense in which the shield *θανεῖται*. Instead of (failed) oxymoron we should notice the pointed juxtaposition of opposites in *οὐ θανοῦcα cὺν νεκρῶι*, which is Euripidean (cf. *Andr.* 1144 *ἐν εὐφήμοιcι δύcφημοc δόμοιc*, *Herc.* 199 *τυφλοῖc ὁρῶνταc*, *Pho.* 1506 *δυcξύνετον ξυνετόc*, *IA* 466 *οὐ ξυνετὰ ξυνετῶc*, and the juxtaposition of contrasting numbers in *Herc.* 328, *IT* 1065, *Ion* 530, *Hel.* 731–2, *Pho.* 894, and *Or.* 1244) but also Aeschylean: see Fraenkel on *Ag.* 320. The corruption presupposed by Wecklein's palmary conjecture (1901: 51) is caused by the scribe's anticipation of a word that is coming: see West 1973: 24 and many of the examples in Jackson 223–7 (who also demonstrates the reverse error of perseveration in a word or syllable already copied). See also above 62n.

1224–5 Odysseus is singled out as the cowardly (*κακοῦ*) counterpart to the brave Hector, perhaps because it was he who proposed killing Astyanax.

1226–31

1. 1226	*Χο.*	– – – –	2sp
2. 1227		⏑͡⏑ ⏑ – ⏑ – ⏑ –	cr ia
3. 1228		⏑ – – ⏑ –	δ
4. 1229		⏑ – ⏑ – ⏑ *Εκ.* – –	ia ba
5. 1230	*Χο.*	⏑ – ⏑ – ⏑ *Εκ.* – –	ia ba
6. 1231	*Χο.*	– – – ⏑ – ⏑ – – ⏑ – |||	2δ

1227–8 'It is as a painful object of lamentation that the earth will receive you.'

1231 ***οἴμοι δῆτα cῶν ἀλάcτων κακῶν***: 'Alas indeed for your unforgettable woes'. For *δῆτα* seconding the previous speaker's words see *GP* 276.

Staging: Hecuba puts straps (belonging to the shield?) or bandages of some kind around parts of Astyanax's body to close his wounds.

1232–4 Hecuba says that she is binding up her grandson's wounds in some respects whereas Hector in the Underworld will see to the other respects. It is unclear what this refers to.

1232 ***ἕλκη . . . c'***: on the 'construction of whole and part' see 408n.

1233 Kiefner 42 notes the *Versparung* of the definite article in *ὄνομ' ἔχουcα*.

1235–39

1. 1235	*Χο.*	⏑ – ⏑ – ⏑ – ∩ ||	ia ba
2. 1236		⏖ – ⏑ – ⏑ – ∩ ||	ia ba
3. 1237		– – – –	2sp
4. 1238	*Εκ.*	– – ⏑ – ⏑ – ∩ ||	ia ba
5. 1239	*Χο.*	†⏖ – –† ⏑ ⏑͡⏑ ⏑͡⏑ ⏑ – – –	2δ?

1235 On commands addressed by speakers to themselves see 98–9n.

1235–6 ***πιτύλουc διδοῦcα χειρόc***: the periphrasis means 'moving your hands in rhythm'. For 'regularly repeated rhythmic movement' as a meaning of *πίτυλοc* see Barrett on *Hipp.* 1464 and 817n above.

1238–9 Hecuba, who has said nothing to the Chorus since 289 (351–2, 466–7, and 505–6 are spoken to servants), now addresses them. Her words together with the Chorus's response suggest that this will be an important statement by Hecuba.

1239 ***Ἑκάβη cάc***: the vocative is unnecessary and unmetrical, and the second word is nonsense. Hermann 1847: 16 proposes *θαρcήcαc'* and Willink unpub. suggests *cιγώcαιc*. These conjectures presuppose that an intrusive vocative obliterated the beginning of a participle. Both give possible sense, but neither carries full conviction.

1240–50 This seems to be Hecuba's summary of what she has learned. (1) The gods have had no purpose in mind except to cause woe to her and to Troy, a city they hate beyond all others. (2) There is consolation for misery in the fame that Troy and she will win as the subject of later poetry. (3) As she sends the body off to be interred, she remarks that lavish funerals make little difference to the deceased and serve only as ostentation for the living.

1240–2 'There was not, it now appears, anything for the gods (meaning 'anything on their mind'?) except my woes and Troy hated beyond all other cities (a way of saying 'their superlative hatred for Troy'?), and it was in vain that we offered sacrifice.' For the imperfect + ἄρα see 109n. The parentheses above show areas of difficulty. To address the first problem Wecklein 1901: 51 proposed θεῶν γόναcι for θεοῖcι, which seems possible even if this epic phrase (*Il.* 17.514, *Od.* 1.267, etc.) happens not to be found anywhere in tragedy. To address the second—this cannot be solved by invoking the *ab urbe condita* construction, which would work out to 'Troy's being hated', not 'the gods' hatred of Troy'—Bothe 1826 suggested πλὴν ἐμοὶ πόνοι (Wecklein suggested altering this to πόνοc) | Τροίαι τε πόλεων ἔκκριτον μιcουμένηι: 'The only thing on the knees of the gods was, it now appears, woe for me and for Troy hated beyond all other cities.' But that means altering the fourth, sixth, and seventh words in 1240 (1241, from a palaeographic standpoint, is virtually unchanged). I have accordingly moved the second dagger to the end of 1240.

1242 **μάτην δ' ἐβουθυτοῦμεν:** for the gods' refusal of sacrifice to themselves see *Il.* 6.311.

1242–5 'But if a god had not overturned what is above, passing it over (what lay below it, i.e. transporting it) to a place below the earth, we, being unknown, would not be sung of, providing a theme for song to the Muses of men yet to be.' At *Il.* 6.357–8, in a speech to Hector expressing regret for her elopement with Alexandros, Helen says that Zeus brought an evil doom on them so that they might be a theme of song for men to come. Helen says this in (partial) exculpation of herself, and any thought of future fame as consolation for their misfortunes is implicit at best. There is also no explicit consolation in Alcinous' similar statement at *Od.* 8.579–80. Hecuba too ascribes the fall of Troy to the gods, but her contrary-to-fact statement is the explicit consolation 'We may have had pain, but at least we have fame in the future.' —A difficult passage, in which there are two areas of textual uncertainty. (1) The translation and summary given above presuppose that in 1242 Stephanus' δὲ μή for δ' ἡμᾶc is correct. This gives more natural sense: if Troy had not been destroyed, the Trojans would be obscure and not have fame. By contrast, with the reading of the mss. Hecuba says that if Troy had been completely buried, the Trojans would have been rendered invisible and would have no fame, somewhat bizarre sense.

The only thing in its favour is that a separate object for ἔϲτρεψε is welcome. But we can either supply 'us' as the object of the indicative or take τἄνω with both indicative and participle, as in the above translation. (2) In 1244 the reading of the mss., ὑμνήθημεν, has been thought to imply that the Trojans *have already* been sung of, and this has led to the adoption of Hermann's ὑμνηθεῖμεν. But Meridor 1985–8, citing the aorist indicatives at *Alc.* 360–2, *OT* 1372, and Plat. *Apol.* 38c5–6, argues that aorist indicative + ἄν can refer to a future event unrealizable under the condition stipulated. There is a further example at Pi. *P.* 4.43–8.

1246 **χωρεῖτε, θάπτετ' ἀθλίωι τύμβωι νεκρόν**: 'Go, bury the dead boy in his wretched tomb.' For two imperatives in asyndeton, a common feature in tragedy, see Finglass 2014: 67n10 and literature cited there.

—There are two reasons, however, to consider Pierson's ἄθλιον here. (The conjecture is cited in Wecklein 1901: 71, but I could not find where it was originally published; it was also made by Lenting 1821: 113.) First, νεκρόϲ, referring to Astyanax, is modified by ἄθλιοϲ in 1186 and 1200, in the latter case with interlaced word order as here. By contrast, nothing dyslogistic has been said or implied about his tomb, humble though it may be. Second, the adjective, plentiful in tragedy, means 'unhappy' and is properly applied to persons, then, by extension, to states of life (γάμοι, βίοϲ, τύχη) and to things that cause unhappiness. There is only one other case in all of tragedy where 'wretched' means 'a poor excuse for' (e.g. 'wretched dwelling' or the like), *El.* 519, where likewise the word does not seem immune to challenge (and was challenged by Lenting). The reading of the mss. is presupposed by *Christ. pat.* 1447 ὀλβίωι τύμβωι, but that does not prove it to be right.

1247 **ἔχει γὰρ οἷα δεῖ γε νερτέρων ϲτέφη**: 'For he has such funereal adornment as is necessary.' The γε may mark an implicit contrast between absolute needs and what may be in other circumstances desirable.

1248–50 Hecuba's reflection that receiving a rich burial may not matter much to the dead and that it is mere ostentation by their survivors presumably consoles her for not being able to provide it. It should be noted that in an *epitaphios* it is perfectly in order for the speaker to be agnostic on the question whether the dead have any knowledge of what the living do for them or whether they are sentient at all: see Mikalson 1983: 74–82, who cites, among other passages, Hyperides 6.43. Hecuba's βραχύ (rather than 'not at all') suggests, as does 1234, that she regards sentience in the dead as likely, though 1314 suggests otherwise. The dimness, in the Greek view, of the faculties of the dead is described by Vermeule 1979, ch. 1 and *passim*. See also Garland 1985: 1–12.

Staging: the shield with the body of Astyanax is carried by the two extras down the left *eisodos*. The allocutory anapaests in 1251–5 escort the body on its way to its final resting place, as at *Alc.* 741–6.

1251–2 Translators, including my Loeb, blur the grammar of these lines, and with good reason. In the Greek the feminine relative pronoun, referring to Andromache (or conceivably to Hecuba), is the subject of κατέκναψε. Yet the verb means 'tear to pieces, mangle', as with a tool for carding wool (see Finglass on *Aj.* 1029–31), and it describes far too destructive an action for either woman to be its subject: they did not tear to pieces his hopes or their hopes for him. Here are some translations, whose inaccuracies I have italicized: 'Mit Trauer gedenk' ich der Mutter, die die höchste Hoffnung des Lebens in dir *gescheitert sah*' (Wilamowitz); 'Hélas! ta malheureuse mère *a vu s'effondrer* avec toi le magnifique espoir de sa vie' (Parmentier); 'Unhappy mother, whose high hopes for your life *have been wrecked*!' (Loeb). Lee translates 'Wretched is the mother who brought to nought the hopes resting in you', accurate grammatically but not factually. A further point is that μελέα μήτηρ sounds like direct address (nominative for vocative), with the result that in 1253–5 ϲοί, ὀλβιϲθεὶϲ . . . ἐγένου, and διώλωλαϲ come as an awkward surprise.

All the elements of the transmitted text (including the securely restored *hapax* κατέκναψε and transmitted ἐπὶ ϲοί) look genuine and suggest that the passage is lacunose and requires supplementation. The first part, up through ἐλπίδαϲ, makes sense if we add to the Greek the verb 'saw', smuggled into their translations by Wilamowitz and Parmentier, and also a main clause. In the second, we may interpret ἐπί in a hostile sense, 'upon' in the sense 'against' (see LSJ s.v. II.*B*.1.d) and therefore find a participle (e.g. 'rushing') that can govern the prepositional phrase. If βίου has not been corrupted subsequent to the omission, it will have to depend upon a noun meaning 'destruction'. The object of κατέκναψε is likely to be 'you', so two 2nd-person pronouns are probably unavoidable. These considerations suggest the following *exempli gratia* supplement:

μελέα μήτηρ, ἣ τὰϲ μεγάλαϲ
ἐλπίδαϲ <εἶδεϲ πάϲαϲ φρούδαϲ,
ἐλεῶ ϲ᾽. ὦ παῖ, ϲὲ δ᾽ ὄλεθροϲ ἅπαϲ
ἄιξαϲ> ἐπὶ ϲοὶ κατέκναψε βίου, κτλ.

'Poor mother, who <saw> your great hopes <all disappear, I pity you; and you, boy, the total destruction> of your life, <rushing> upon you, has ground you to nought!' If the distance between βίου and its *regens* distresses, we could consider the possibility that the word was corrupted in transmission and that perhaps an original *βίον*, once serving as object for *κατέκναψε*, was altered after the omission to make it depend on *ἐλπίδας*. The second supplementary line would then not need *cέ*, though it could be retained as an instance of the 'construction of the whole and part', on which see 408n.

1256–9 The Chorus, following with their eyes the progress of the body of Astyanax down the left *eisodos* and catching sight of the walls of Troy with torch-bearing men on them, do not see, and therefore do not announce, the entrance of the Herald from the right, which occurs during their description of the torch-bearers. On simultaneous or closely successive exits see Taplin 1977: 90–1 and the *Staging* note above before 782–5.

1256 The deictic refers to persons visible to the Chorus but not to the audience. For similar scenes where Chorus or actors comment on offstage actions visible to themselves alone see *Supp.* 980–3 and *Pho.* 109–92. Both passages have instances, as does our passage, of *ὅδε* applied to things offstage, on which see Taplin 1977: 150–1. —Idiom here requires Lenting's *τούcδ'* (1821: 88). For questions employing an interrogative and a demonstrative in the same case (to be rendered into English only by paraphrase) see 707n.

1258 **διερέccοντας**: on the metaphor of rowing see 570n. The soldiers' hands are in swift motion.

Staging: while the Chorus are wondering about the men on the walls of Troy, enter a herald by the right *eisodos*. He is accompanied by two soldiers or servants of Odysseus. The latter will escort Hecuba during the final *exeunt omnes*.

1260 The mss. call the entrant here Talthybius, the name they give any herald in the play, including the entrant at 706, on whom see 707n. The present herald enters from the right, since the orders he passes on must come from the army or its leaders, which throughout the play have been located at the end of the right *eisodos*; furthermore it would make no sense to come *from* Troy in order to shout orders *toward* the city. He cannot be the same man who brought the dead Astyanax to Hecuba and left to dig his grave since that man almost certainly exited leftward: see the *Staging* note before 1156–1206. Most likely is a re-entry by Talthybius. As noted in the introduction to the first episode, he was less sympathetic to the Trojan women than the herald who enters at 706. The present entrant has some points of contact with Talthybius in that both worry about the possible suicide of their Trojan charges (298–305, 1284–6) and both are more businesslike than the herald who comes to fetch Astyanax. At 296–7 Talthybius promises to return for the other women, which suggests that he is the present entrant. His last exit, also leftwards, was eight hundred lines ago, and so even if the audience noticed the inconsistency between his earlier exit and his entrance here, they need not have felt surprise that over this long stretch of lines he has found his way back to the assembly of Greek soldiers. I have accordingly retained the person indication of our mss. An alternative would be to print *ΚΗΡΥΞ Β*: for three characters having the same function in a single play see the three announcing characters in *Ba.* (*Θεράπων*, *Ἄγγελος*, *Ἄγγελος Β*) as well as two each in *Hcld.* (*Θεράπων*, *Ἄγγελος*), *IT* (*Βουκόλος*, *Ἄγγελος*), *Hel.* (*Θεράπων*, *Ἄγγελος*), and *Pho.* (*Ἄγγελος*, *Ἄγγελος Β*).

1260–4 Talthybius gives the order to the soldiers, who have just been spotted on the top of Troy's battlements, to carry out the final destruction of Troy. Once they have done their work, all may depart for Greece. The deliberate firing of the city was recounted in the *Iliupersis* (*GEF* arg. 4).

1260 αὐδῶ λοχαγοῖς, οἳ τέταχθ' ἐμπιπράναι: for αὐδάω used of giving orders or admonitions see *Andr.* 619, *Herc.* 499, 1215; Aesch. *Sept.* 1042. The accusative is commoner than the dative (NL suggests λοχαγούς), but for the latter see *IT* 1226 and Ar. *Ran.* 369. On the Doricism λοχαγός in contrast to ἀρχηγός in 1267 see the various explanations cited by Björck 1950: 66 and 291–4.

1261–2 'Not to keep the flame idle in your hands but to set your fire in the midst (of the city's buildings)'.

1263 κατασκάψαντες Ἰλίου πόλιν: the verb means literally to bring a house or city down by digging up its foundations: the metaphor is still alive at *Ag.* 525–6. For the appositive genitive or genitive of definition see 816n.

In the Introduction § 2.4 I show that the city is to be imagined as lying down the same *eisodos* as the Greek ships. The firing of Troy is imagined as visible to the actors and chorus but not to the audience: see 1256n. We can dispense with Wilamowitz's idea (1921: 165) that stagehands (*operae*) set the stage or part of the *proscenium* on fire, Hourmouziades's (1965: 122) that torch-carriers marched from one *eisodos* to the other, or Lesky's (1972: 391–2 (Engl. trans. 290–1)) that smoke may have arisen from behind the *skēnē*. The audience will not have seen any stage action here.

1264 The mention of the Greeks' eagerness for their departure (ἄσμενοι) looks like a reminder, by way of irony, that the journey will not end well for them.

1265–8 The herald announces that the Chorus must go to the ships when they hear the sound of the trumpet. The sounding of the trumpet is not marked in the text. For an explanation see 1284–6n.

1269–70 'And you, greyhead, woman most unfortunate, accompany them.' Talthybius, having given instructions to the Chorus to depart for the ships at a signal to be given later, clearly means to leave before they do. This is likewise the implication of his order to Hecuba: servants of Odysseus, not the herald himself, are to escort the queen to her new master's ship. After Hecuba proposes to immolate herself, he changes the timing of her departure and thus, by implication, that of the Chorus. —*GP* 497 says that τ' here comes 'after a particularly strong pause' and tentatively recommends δ' (proposed by Blaydes 1901: 171). But if we interpret as above, the pause is not particularly strong, and we may punctuate with a comma at the end of 1268, as I have done. If, by contrast, we use a period and adopt Blaydes's δ', as does Diggle, this suggests two divergent commands ('Chorus, go to the ships when you hear the trumpet; Hecuba, follow me now'). But since the Chorus and Hecuba are in fact going to exit together, the suggestion of two separate commands gives less intelligible dramaturgy. It is better to keep transmitted τ'.

1270–1 'Accompany them (the Chorus). (For) these men have come for you from Odysseus: it is as his slave that the assigning lot is sending you from your homeland.' This is a compressed way of saying that Hecuba is leaving her home, has been assigned to Odysseus as a slave, and must follow the men he has sent.

Staging: the two servants of Odysseus who entered with Talthybius detach themselves from him and stand near her.

1272–3 Hecuba reacts to Talthybius' news by calling it the final blow to her fortunes. Though she is not always correct in her evaluations of circumstances, the closural intent of this statement suggests the dramatist's hand: no further blows remain. Whether the audience were meant to think that 'last of my woes' means that something other than woes will follow (see Cassandra's allusion at 427–30 to the transformation on Hecuba into the dog whose grave is commemorated as Cynossema) is unclear. On this legend see Roscher 1884–90: 1882–3, the Loeb Apollodorus 2.241n4, and Tarrant on Sen. *Ag.* 707f. The version at *Hec.* 1259–73 is our earliest, and Collard on *Hec.* 1265 may be right to suggest that the story is Eur.'s invention.

1273 —Musgrave's transposition restores to the line's seventh element the short syllable it must have.

1274 The line sums up the pathos of this second part of the *exodos*, forcible abandonment of country and the burning of Troy.

Staging: Hecuba, ignoring the Herald's order that Chorus and Hecuba should depart at the same time, begins to move slowly in a leftward direction. Her motive is to say farewell to the city of Troy before her departure.

1275 **ἐπίϲπευϲον μόλιϲ**: 'hasten with difficulty' is an oxymoron, though only a slight one given that haste for a woman of Hecuba's age is not easy.

1277 **ὦ μεγάλα δή ποτ' ἀμπνέουϲ' ἐν βαρβάροιϲ**: for the idiom 'draw great breaths' as a metaphor for pride see *Andr.* 189 and *Ba.* 640. On δή ποτ' see 506n, and on the present participle referring to previous action (the 'imperfect participle') see 45–7n.

1278 **τὸ κλεινὸν ὄνομ' ἀφαιρήϲηι τάχα**: that is, 'soon you will not be called "famous Troy"', as at 25 and in the first line of *Alexandros*. ὄνομα is 'retained accusative' with ἀφαιρήϲηι, on which see 375n. For the future middle used with passive sense see on 664.

1280–1 Here Hecuba reproaches the gods for failing to heed her ealier prayers to them. Given the references in this play and in *Alexandros* to the guilt of the Trojans (Paris' violation of *xenia* in seducing and removing the wife of his host Menelaus and Laomedon's perjury in relation to Heracles: see notes on 799–818 and 866), the audience may have felt that Hecuba's complaint lacked full justification.

1280 **ἰὼ θεοί. καὶ τί τοὺϲ θεοὺϲ καλῶ**: 'Hear me, you gods! Yet why am I calling on them?' For καί before a question word expressing surprise or contempt, see *GP* 309–11.

1281 'They also failed to hear me when I called on them earlier.'

1282–3 'Come let us run into the flames: it is for me the most honourable thing to perish being burnt up with my country!' This could be a genuine exhortation to the Chorus to immolate themselves, but μοι suggests that δράμωμεν refers to herself alone. πυρουμένηι could be taken with either μοι or πατρίδι. The former seems slightly better.

1284–6 Talthybius concludes that Hecuba has been driven mad by her misfortunes: cf. 408–10. There is pity in his δύϲτηνε, but his job is to make sure that Odysseus' γέραϲ reaches him—and the women of the Chorus their masters—unharmed, and he says to his men 'Show her no mercy' or 'Do not hold back' (μὴ φείδεϲθ'), bidding them lead her away at once. Apparently his order to take Hecuba away implies that his earlier plan that all should wait for the sound of the trumpet is now a dead letter (no sound of the trumpet is indicated in the text), and the movement toward the end of the play quickens. At the same time, although the departure is moved suddenly forward, it is artificially prolonged, allowing a final lyric interchange to end the play: see next note on *Staging*. In 1286 there is *Versparung* (ἀπὸ κοινοῦ), γέραϲ being supplied with the first infinitive and τήνδε with the second.

Staging: Odysseus' servants have been ordered to take hold of Hecuba and remove her at once. But before the departure of the Trojan women, the stage action freezes while Hecuba and the Chorus sing an *amoibaion*. See Bain 1981: 24–9 for other examples of this procedure, where an order (*Ant.* 885–90, *Herc.* 520–2) is ignored for a considerable space so that reactions to the situation may be expressed. (Against the idea, theoretically possible, that the last portion of the *exodos* is chanted while on a slow march Bain cites 1305–6.)

1287–1332 The final lyric interchange is in two stanzaic pairs. The first pair, with five cola each, laments the burning of the city and its walls, which Zeus does nothing to prevent. The second pair is considerably longer, with fifteen cola each. In the strophe Hecuba calls on her dead children and the Chorus their dead husbands and complains to them of their coming servitude. Last among the dead to be mentioned is Priam, described as 'unaware of my calamity' (1314). In the antistrophe the women turn to the physical remains of the city, including its temples. They are soon to be wiped from Hecuba's consciousness (1320–1), and Troy will be robbed of its name (1322–4). In the text there is a reference to the sound of falling masonry and the earthquake it produces, on which see 1325n. Hecuba and the Chorus lament their coming lot as slaves and then proceed down the *eisodos* to the ships of the Achaeans.

1287–93 ~ 1294–99 [–1301]

1. 1287 ~ 1294	*Ἑκ.*	⏑ ⏖ ⏑ –	ia
2. 1288 ~ 1295		⏑ ⏕ ⏑ ⏕ ⏑ ⏕ ⏑ ⏕	2ia ∫
3. 1290 ~ 1296/7		⏑ – ⏑ ⏔ ⏑ – ⏑ – ⏑ – – ‖	2ia ba
4. 1291 ~ 1298	*Χο.*	⏑ ⏔ ⏑ – ⏑ ⏕ ⏑ ⏕	2ia ∫
5. 1292 ~ 1299		⏑ ⏕ ⏑ – ⏑ ⏔ ⏑ – ⏑ – –	2ia ba

1287–93 Hecuba's exclamation to Zeus expresses astonishment that he as divine progenitor of the Trojan royal line could look on while the city is destroyed. The Chorus answer that Zeus does look on and yet the destruction of Troy has occurred.

[1289]: —The line gives neither metre nor sense and also has nothing to correspond to it in the antistrophe. It looks as if a gloss on γενέτα (πάτερ) and one on οἷα (ἀνάξια) have been thoughtlessly expanded: see 1140n.

1291–2 ἁ δὲ μεγαλόπολιϲ | ἄπολιϲ ὄλωλεν οὐδ᾽ ἔτ᾽ ἔϲτι Τροία: we may take Τροία as ἀπὸ κοινοῦ with ὄλωλεν and translate 'The great city Troy is now no city at all and no longer exists'.

1295–6 'Ilium glows in flame, and the chambers of its citadel, and the high peak of its walls!' —To mend the metre I have added <τε>. At 1296 Willink unpub. deleted καταίθεται, not paraphrased by the scholiast, and also adopted τέραμν᾽ [καὶ πόλιϲ] from Hartung 1837: 68.

1298–9 To Hecuba, who laments the burning of the city, the Chorus respond 'Like smoke on a following breeze our land, fallen to the spear, perishes.' —Wilamowitz 1879: 183 reduced *οὐρανίαι* to *οὐρίαι*. The trimming results in good metre and responsion with the strophe.

[1300–1]: —The origin of these two lines, which do not belong here, is mysterious.

1302–16 ~ 1317–32

1. 1302 ~ 1317	*Εκ.*	⏑ – – ⏖ ⏑ – ⏑ – ⏑ –	ba lk
	Χο.	⏑ ⏑	exclam.
2. 1303 ~ 1318	*Εκ.*	– ⏖ ⏑ ⏖ ⏑ ⏖ ⏑ – ⏑ – – ‖	2ia ba
3. 1304 ~ 1319	*Χο.*	⏑ – ⏑ – | – ⏑ – ⏑ – ⏑ –	ia lk
4. 1305 ~ 1320	*Εκ.*	⏑ – ⏑ – ⏑ – ⏑ ⏖ ⏑ – ⏑ –	3ia ∫
5. 1306 ~ 1321		– ⏑ – – ⏑ – ⏑ – – ‖	cr cr ba
6. 1307 ~ 1322	*Χο.*	⏑ ⏖ ⏑ – ⏖ ⏑ – ⏑ – –	ia cr ba ∫
7. 1308 ~ 1323		– ⏑ – ⏑ – ⏑ –	lk ∫
8. 1309 ~ 1324		⏑ – ⏑ – ⏑ – – ‖	ia ba
9. 1310 ~ 1325	*Εκ.*	⏑ ⏖ ⏑ ⏖ ⏑ *Χο.* – ⏑ – – ⏑ –	2ia cr
10. 1311 ~ 1326	*Εκ.*	⏒ ⏔ ⏑ ⏕ ⏑ ⏔ ⏑ *Χο.* ⏔ ⏓ – ⏑ –	3ia
11. 1312 ~ 1327	*Εκ.*	⏑ – ⏑ – ⏑ ⏖ ⏑ ⏖	2ia
12. 1313 ~ 1328/9		⏑ ⏖ ⏑ ⏖ ⏑ ⏖ ⏑ ⏖	2ia
13. 1314 ~ 1330		– – ⏑ – ⏑ – ⏑ –	2ia
14. 1315 ~ 1331	*Χο.*	⏑ – ⏑ – ⏑ ⏖ ⏑ –	2ia ∫
15. 1316 ~ 1332		⏑ ⏖ ⏑ ⏖ ⏑ ⏖ ⏑ – ⏑ – – ⦀	2ia ba

1302–4 Hecuba addresses the land as nurturer of her sons and then exhorts the sons themselves to hearken to a mother's words. That they are dead and cannot hear is apparently the burden of the Chorus 1304: 'It is on the dead that you call with your lament.' *ἠπύω* (*ἀπύω*) is a verb confined in tragedy to lyric, the sole exception being *Rhes.* 776. On *ἰάλεμος* see 604n. On the accusative object of *βοάω* and similar verbs expressing 'the content of the *βοή*' see Diggle 1994: 437–8.

1303 ***τέκεα***: West 1984: 189 proposes this in place of *τέκνα*: this not only gives exact responsion but also restores a word used by Eur. alone of the tragic poets and one frequently corrupted, e.g. at 248 and 581 above.

Staging: Hecuba at 1305 and the Chorus at 1307 kneel on the ground and strike it repeatedly with their hands.

1305–6 According to Spitzbarth 1945: 23–4 the act of kneeling here and of the sitting upon the grave at *Cho.* 501, as well as the striking of the earth here and at *El.* 678, are a means of making closer contact with the realm of the dead.

1307 ***διάδοχα***: adverbially, 'in succession to you, in my turn.'

1310 ***ἀγόμεθα φερόμεθ'***: this means that the Chorus and Hecuba are the booty of war. On the idiom *ἄγειν καὶ φέρειν* see 18–21n.

1312–14 These lines seem to imply that if Priam had been properly buried he would be aware of Hecuba's fate. I know of no ancient text attesting to this view. On the general question of whether the dead were believed to be aware of the doings of the living see 1248–50n.

1315–16 The Chorus agree that Priam has no knowledge of what is going on: his eyes have been closed by *θάνατος ὅσιος ἀνοσίοις σφαγαῖσιν*. The juxtaposition of two antonyms is common in tragedy (see 1223n). Why Priam's slaughter is called 'unholy' is clear but not why death is holy. Perhaps because Death is a divine figure?

1318 'You have (i.e. 'are affected by, your fate is') the murderous fire and the spearpoint.'

1319 'Soon you will collapse into the beloved earth and have no name.'

1320–1 ***κόνις δ' ἴσα καπνῶι πτέρυγι πρὸς αἰθέρ' ἄισσουσ' ἄοικον δόμων με θήσει***: 'Dust, keeping pace with smoke, winging its way aloft, will make me homeless' (trans. West 1984: 190). That is to say, the destructive processes that produce smoke and dust (the firing of the city, the collapse of its masonry) will destroy my home. For alpha-privative adjectives governing an ablatival genitive of kindred meaning see *Andr.* 714 *ἄπαιδας τέκνων*, *El.* 310 *ἀνέορτος ἱερῶν*, *Herc.* 114 *πατρὸς ἀπάτορα*, *Pho.* 324 *ἄπεπλος φαρέων λευκῶν*, and the other examples, mostly from tragedy, in KG 1.401–2 and Bruhn 28. —I have printed West's conjectural restoration, which addresses the difficulties that in the transmitted text *πτέρυγι πρὸς αἰθέρα* lacks a construction and that *ἄιστον οἴκων ἐμῶν με θήσει* yields the strained meaning 'will make me without knowledge of my house'. (By contrast *ἄιστος* makes good sense at 1314.) The participle solves the first, the elegant tragic locution *ἄοικον δόμων* the second. For an explanation of the corruption see West's discussion. At the corresponding place in the strophe West transposes *τιθεῖσα* and *μέλεα* to produce better responsion. It is only fair to warn readers that the absence of caesura in the trimeters 1305 and 1320 means that we still await a complete solution.

1322–4 'The name of the land will go off into oblivion: one thing in one way, another in another are disappearing, and unblest Troy is no more.'

1325–6 Though Hecuba's 'Did you mark, did you hear?' might have been a textual reference to the trumpet sound anticipated at 1266–7, the Chorus's reply indicates that it refers to the sound of falling masonry. The Athenian theatre may have had the resources to produce a loud noise (the scholiast to Ar. *Nub.* 294 mentions a *βροντεῖον* or thunder machine, an amphora filled with stones). Equally, the audience may have been expected simply to imagine it. *Ba.* 605 implies that the collapse of

Pentheus' palace is audible, if not visible, and *Herc.* 904–5 suggest the same. But in the premodern theatre the audience are asked to imagine a great deal, e.g. night-time conditions at *Ant.* 1–99 and *Rhes. passim.* The shaking or earthquake of 1326 presumably is what is felt when a heavy object nearby falls to the ground.

1327–30 Hecuba exhorts her trembling limbs to carry her (lit. her footsteps, which means 'feet') to her coming life of slavery.

1330 δούλειον ἁμέραν βίου: Eur. twice in trimeters (*Andr.* 99, *Hec.* 56) alters and adopts the epic phrase δούλιον ἦμαρ (*Il.* 6.463, *Od.* 14.340, 17.323). A further change here makes it suitable for lyric.

1331 ὅμως: the strong adversative marks the breaking off of the Chorus's lamentation and the acceptance of a lot they cannot avoid.

Staging: Hecuba, Odysseus' men, the Chorus, and Talthybius all exit by the left *eisodos*.

APPENDIX A: 95–7

I have explained the meaning of Blomfield's conjecture in English (1983) and German (1996) and above for a third time, but I believe the explanation can be made clearer and the case stronger. I therefore take this opportunity to set forth at greater length than a commentary usually permits what advantages it enjoys over its competitors.

I repeat from my commentary the translation I favour of the text I print: 'Foolish is that mortal who sacks cities but who, having made desolate temples and tombs, holy precincts of the dead, perishes later himself.' To show what I think this means I paraphrase: 'A mortal may be successful in war and destroy the enemy's city, but if having done so—having emptied its temples of worshippers and its tombs of those who make grave offerings—he subsequently perishes himself (before his time and needlessly, because of acts like those we have been discussing), he is a fool, and his earlier success only serves to highlight his folly.' Here are some clarificatory comments, which I amplify below. (1) Poseidon mentions sacking cities not as an act foolish or impious in itself or as itself causing the fool's death. Rather the fool's earlier success in war is a foil for his actual folly, *death caused by committing impiety*. (2) Poseidon's language, though elliptical on one point, refers to the case at hand and does not imply—the claim would be highly dubious under the dramatic circumstances—that a city-sacker always perishes as a result of sacking cities (or, with different punctuation, cities, temples, and tombs), and that the Greeks are about to perish *because they sacked Troy*. (3) The emptying of temples and tombs is likewise mentioned neither as foolish nor as impious nor as the cause of the Greeks' coming downfall (what offence have the Greeks committed against tombs? what offences against tombs are the gods thought to punish? is the emptying of either an offence against the gods?), but as an explication of what it means to sack cities. The phrase means the removal of the population that worships at the temples and makes offerings at the graves. It serves to draw a telling contrast between what some successful persons do to others and what they suffer themselves if they offend the gods. Since what is done to the temples and tombs is not to destroy them but only to depopulate them, there is no implication that offences against temples or tombs are the reason for the disaster that awaits the Greeks. Poseidon refers to tombs as 'sacred precincts of the dead' not to imply that any impiety has been committed against them but merely to show that they, like temples, are deserving of pious regard under ordinary circumstances. But the fall of a city changes all that. (4) Poseidon does not mention in 95–7 the reason for what is about to happen to the Greeks, that they perish because they connived at Ajax's impiety, but the thought must be present if his gnomic utterance is to have any relevance to the case at hand. It can easily be supplied because it is so prominent in the preceding dialogue (69–86). (5) The grammatical form in which Poseidon's reflection is cast is unusually complicated, but the three complicating elements can all be exemplified singly or in pairs from Eur., and syntactical complexity provides no good reason to reject a construal that gives the sense the context requires at the trifling cost of changing τε to δέ. I take these five points in order.

1. The relative clause that follows 'Foolish is that mortal who' is in two parts, built upon two verbs, ἐκπορθεῖ and ὤλετο. The first part is not in itself evidence of folly but serves as a foil for the second part: 'That man is a fool who though successful at sacking cities perishes later himself.' The unstated implication of the second is 'perishes as the Greeks are now about to perish, because of impiety like theirs'. The folly of the Greeks, he says, is that though successful in war (they sacked Troy and emptied it of its population), they are now about to perish in their turn. It need not have happened thus, which is why they can be reproached with folly. The lines employ a 'figure of thought' that we might call the 'He saved others' figure, a name derived from the mocking words spoken about Jesus on the cross: 'He saved others; himself he cannot save' (Mark 15:31). The first clause is not in itself a reproach but is there to add sting to the second, throwing Jesus' powerlessness to save himself into sharper relief. The orators make extensive use of paired verbal forms of which the first is a foil, e.g. Socrates' argument that he had to carry out the quest Apollo's oracle laid

on him (Plat. *Apol.* 28d–29a): I would have done something terrible, he says, if, on the one hand, I obeyed my human commanders and risked death in battle, but, on the other, disobeyed the god from fear of death. Obeying his human commanders, far from being something terrible, is the right thing to do. What is terrible is the second, and the first is mentioned as an aggravating circumstance. (Further exx. at Lys. 4.13, 6.15, 10.13, 11.6, 12.36, 14.17, 29.11, 34.11; Aeschin. 3.244; Lycurg. 57; Isocr. 2.36, 18.24; D. 21.61, 23.143, 24.31, 32.23, 39.21.) The poets likewise use this figure. The reproach of folly backed up by a bipartite relative clause appears in Theogn. 1369–70, which like our passage uses coordination but without *μέν*: *ἄφρονεϲ ἄνθρωποι καὶ νήπιοι, οἵ τε θανόνταϲ | κλαίουϲ', οὐδ' ἥβηϲ ἄνθοϲ ἀπολλύμενον*. Another case is *Hipp*. 535–40, *ἄλλωϲ ἄλλωϲ παρά τ' Ἀλφεῷι | Φοίβου τ' ἐν Πυθίοιϲ τεράμνοιϲ | βούταν φόνον Ἑλλὰϲ <αἶ> ἀέξει, | Ἔρωτα δὲ τὸν τύραννον ἀνδρῶν…οὐ ϲεβίζομεν*, where sacrificing to Zeus and Apollo is not what is pointless but the failure to sacrifice to Eros. Euripidean passages with *μέν* include *Hec*. 311–12, 592–7, and 814–19. These show how the present lines are to be understood. Sacking cities is not in itself foolish but the act of a successful man. The success in the first part of the relative clause serves to set off the failure in the second, a death like that of the Greeks on their homeward journey.

2. Several of the other ways of construing 95–7—versions (i) through (iv) discussed below—make Poseidon say that it is *ipso facto* foolish to sack cities (or, with different punctuation, to sack 'cities, temples, and tombs') because anyone who does so invariably perishes himself as a result. Poseidon is the speaker here, and he may reasonably be supposed to be talking about something the gods bring about. Yet the idea that the gods always destroy sackers of cities (or of cities, temples, and tombs) is (a) unGreek and (b) contrary to the dramatic situation in *Tro.* (a) The Greeks in literature and in life show little evidence of believing in such a principle. According to non-philosophical, popular religious views (see Mikalson 1983: 27–30, 103–4 and 1991: 155), the gods' concern is almost exclusively with offences against their own *τιμή*, and only those who diminish that *τιμή* by, e.g., false oaths taken in a god's name or the forcible removal of a suppliant from his altars, are subject to punishment. In literature and in life cities may be sacked without commission of sacrilege. In the *Iliad* we learn that the Greeks have sacked other cities in the Troad. They were not punished for this. Apollo sends a plague against the host *because Agamemnon mistreated his priest.* What is more, that priest, addressing the Greeks, prefaces his request for the return of his daughter with the words *ὑμῖν μὲν θεοὶ δοῖεν Ὀλύμπια δώματ' ἔχοντεϲ | ἐκπέρϲαι Πριάμοιο πόλιν εὖ δ' οἴκαδ' ἱκέϲθαι*. The clear implication of Chryses' words is that sacking Troy and getting home safely is a thing that can be done. The same tale is told at *Ag.*

338–44 where Clytaemestra prays that the Greeks will act piously in the captured city so that they can get home. Alexander in Plb. 5.10.6–8 believes the same thing and takes pains while destroying Thebes not to commit impiety. Some possible counter-examples are discussed in Kovacs 1983: 335. (b) Poseidon—who should be expected to punish the sackers of Troy if the gods generally punished people for sacking cities (or 'cities, temples, and tombs')—does nothing to the Greeks *for sacking Troy*. He is persuaded to punish them because they acquiesced in Ajax's impiety. Athena for her part makes no mention of the sack of Troy as a motive for punishing the Greeks, unsurprisingly since the Greeks sacked the city *with her help* (72: note also 10, 23–4 and 46–7). Her motive in punishing them (85–6) is to teach them to act piously toward her temples (as they have failed to do in Ajax's case) and show reverence for the other gods. The idea that sacking cities (or 'cities, temples, and tombs') always results in death of the sackers is thus contradicted by the events of the play so far, and there is very little *prima facie* evidence for such an idea in Greek literature as a whole. The Greeks offended Athena and Poseidon by failing to punish Ajax's impiety, not by sacking Troy.

3. It might be thought that the mention of temples in 96 is there to suggest that sacking cities always means an offence against them: when a city is burnt to the ground, they are destroyed. If we punctuate at the middle or the end of 96, 'temples' will be one of the objects of ἐκπορθεῖ. We have already noted that this produces an odd trio of objects for the verb. But if we take 96–7 together as a single clause, 96 has nothing to do with destroying or violating temples. As Biehl *ad loc.* shows, the periphrasis ἐρημίαι δούϲ means the same thing as ἐρημώϲαϲ: he compares 1146 δοῦναι τάφωι (= θάψαι), *Hec.* 945 κατάραι διδοῦϲα (= καταρωμένη), and *IA* 850 ἀμελίαι δόϲ (= ἀμέληϲον). What is mentioned here is the *emptying* of temples and tombs, the removal of the population who worship at the temples and tend the tombs, a removal which is not thought to anger the gods and in our play angers neither Poseidon nor Athena. That this participial phrase has nothing to do with punishable impiety is made even clearer by the mention of tombs: there is no evidence that the gods were thought to punish those who *destroyed* tombs, much less those who merely empty them (in the two other places in tragedy where temples and tombs are mentioned together, *Pers.* 404–5 and *Ba.* 1359, nothing is said or implied about divine punishment), and in any case the Greeks committed no offences against Trojan tombs either in this play or anywhere else in Greek literature. (Tombs being emptied of those who tend them are mentioned in the play at 381–2.) Both sacking cities and emptying temples and tombs are distinct from impieties like looting temples or setting them on fire (*Pers.* 809–12; Hdt. 8.109.3). If further proof is needed

that the gods are not angered by the 'making desolate' of temples and tombs, consider Poseidon's attitude to Troy's desolation (*ἐρημία*, 26). In 23–7 he announces his intention to leave: when a city is desolated, he says, the gods are not worshipped, and there is no reason for them to remain. There is nothing here to make us think that Poseidon is angry at this state of affairs: he accepts it as normal, and it is so regarded elsewhere in Greek literature (see the passages cited in 23–7n). So the words *ναοὺϲ δὲ τύμβουϲ θ', ἱερὰ τῶν κεκμηκότων ἐρημίαι δούϲ* do not indicate an offence against the gods. Rather, they are a restatement, in the second part of the relative clause, of the meaning of *ἐκπορθεῖ πόλειϲ*. The restatement lays stress on the removal of the population and helps to make an ironic parallel between what victorious fools do and what they suffer: 'They sent others to destruction but did not have the wit to avoid their own.' This is the precise contrast Clytaemestra makes in her hopes for the Greek army at *Ag.* 340: *οὔ τἂν ἑλόντεϲ αὖθιϲ ἀνθαλοῖεν ἄν*. In the event it can be said of the Greeks, in that play and in this, that 'Having destroyed they were destroyed in their turn', but it did not have to happen this way. Sacking Troy did not have perishing at sea as its inevitable consequence.

4. The omission from Poseidon's *gnōmē* of the reason why the fool perishes is no obstacle to the acceptance of Blomfield's conjecture. The preceding twenty-six lines have had only two themes, Greek impiety and Athena's and Poseidon's plan to punish it. It is this that brings about the Greeks' downfall, not sacking cities or emptying temples or tombs (destroying temples is not even mentioned). To be sure, the firing of the entire city at the end of the play will quite possibly entail a religious offence (cf. *Pers.* 810 and Hdt. 8.109.3), and part of the city has already been burnt (8), though burning of temples has not been mentioned. But it is not this (unmentioned) burning of temples that motivates Poseidon and Athena. Poseidon implies that the Greeks are fools. The most plausible grounds for this lies in their failure to punish Ajax. The Greeks had been successful at annihilating their enemies but failed thereafter to show gratitude, in the form of basic piety, toward their divine patroness. All this has been made abundantly clear in the preceding dialogue, and the audience can easily understand in Poseidon's 'Foolish the man who destroys others but perishes in his turn' the words 'by committing impiety'.

5. Poseidon's *gnōmē*, if construed as above, is grammatically complicated. There are three complicating factors: (a) the relative clause has two verbs; (b) *μέν* is omitted from the first part of the clause; and (c) the idea of sacking cities in the first part is repeated in the second in the form of a participial phrase, as happens in Greek at e.g. Hdt. 1.8.1 *Κανδαύληϲ ἠράϲθη τῆϲ ἑωυτοῦ γυναικόϲ, ἐραϲθεὶϲ δὲ ἐνόμιζέ οἱ κτλ.*, though here the repetition is of an idea, not of a word. All three of these complicating factors can

be paralleled. (a) Bipartite relative clauses are not rare in Eur.: see e.g. *Alc.* 751–5, *Hec.* 252–3, *Supp.* 220–31 (cf. *Eur. Alt.* 73–6 for Lueders's deletion of 222–8 and Wilamowitz's of 230), *Tro.* 949–50, *Ion* 1557–9, *Or.* 1095–6, *Ba.* 902, most of them clauses justifying criticism or praise. And (b) there are cases where *μέν* might have been expected but does not appear: *Andr.* 616–18, *Supp.* 523–7, and *Hipp.* 535–40 and Theogn. 1369–70 both cited above. (c) The repetition in participial form of an idea from the first of two coordinated clauses to the second is to be seen at *OT* 1189–92 *τίς γάρ, τίς ἀνὴρ πλέον | τᾶς εὐδαιμονίας φέρει | ἢ τοσοῦτον ὅσον δοκεῖν | καὶ δόξαντ' ἀποκλῖναι*; and *OT* 1404. Other Sophoclean and Euripidean examples in Bruhn § 230, to which add *El.* 1035–8, where *ὑπόντος τοῦδ'* carries over the idea of woman's folly into the second clause.

I here set out all the different proposals for taking these lines (different wording, different punctuation) together with the objections to which they are liable. I divide these proposals into two groups, depending on whether they give dramatically and culturally acceptable sense. Those in Group One are open to the objection that Poseidon is made to imply that the Greeks are about to be destroyed for sacking Troy or for doing something to its temples and tombs (the dramatic context objection) and that it was a plausible thing to say in fifth-century Athens that sackers of cities (or of cities, temples, and tombs) are always destroyed (the cultural context objection). Those in Group Two escape these objections.

Group One: (i) *μῶρος δὲ θνητῶν ὅστις ἐκπορθεῖ πόλεις | ναούς τε τύμβους θ'· ἱερὰ τῶν κεκμηκότων | ἐρημίαι δοὺς αὐτὸς ὤλεθ' ὕστερον* (the scholiast *ad loc.*, Sansone 1982: 35–6). In addition to the dramatic and cultural context objections, note that *ἐκπορθεῖ* takes three objects, of which the first includes the other two since temples and tombs are parts of cities (the disparate objects objection well described by Manuwald 1989: 240n23). Furthermore, one feels that *ἱερὰ τῶν κεκμηκότων* should stand in apposition to *τύμβους*, not in a separate sentence. This reading also implies that what is decisive in the downfall of the fool is his treatment of tombs. (ii) *μῶρος δὲ θνητῶν ὅστις ἐκπορθεῖ πόλεις· | ναούς τε τύμβους θ', ἱερὰ τῶν κεκμηκότων | ἐρημίαι δοὺς αὐτὸς ὤλεθ' ὕστερον* (Kirchhoff 1852, 1855, Biehl, Meridor 1984: 210n23, Manuwald 1989). This escapes the disparate objects objection but not the dramatic and cultural context objections. Furthermore, as Holzhausen 1999: 26n4 points out, it is odd and confusing for the asyndetically attached second sentence to have *τε* (so easily taken for a connective) as its second word. (iii) *μῶρος δὲ θνητῶν ὅστις ἐκπορθεῖ πόλεις | ναούς τε τύμβους θ', ἱερὰ τῶν κεκμηκότων· | ἐρημίαι δούς <σφ'> αὐτὸς ὤλεθ' ὕστερον* (Page *ap.* Diggle, *Studies* 59). This is subject to the dramatic and cultural context objections and the disparate objects objection. (iv) *μῶρος δὲ θνητῶν ὅςτις ἐκπορθεῖ πόλεις, | ναούς τε τύμβους θ', ἱερὰ τῶν κεκμηκότων | ἐρημίαι δούς· αὐτὸς ὤλεθ' ὕςτερον* (West 1980: 15). This escapes the disparate objects objection but not the dramatic and cultural context objections. It is also hard to see why *δούς*, now dependent upon *ἐκπορθεῖ*, should be aorist when it is not an antecedent action. Furthermore, as Manuwald 1989: 241 points out, it makes odd style for the trailing participle to be carrying the most crucial point, as in West's view it does.

Group Two: (v) *μῶρος δὲ θνητῶν ὅςτις ἐκπορθῶν πόλεις | ναούς τε τύμβους θ', ἱερὰ τῶν κεκμηκότων | ἐρημίαι δοὺς αὐτὸς ὤλεθ' ὕςτερον* (Hartung 1848). This escapes the dramatic and cultural context objections and the disparate objects objection: both the sacking of cities and the emptying of temples and tombs are now subordinate to the idea of perishing. The only objection is that the pairing of present with aorist participle is awkward. (vi) Reiske 1754: 93 gives the same wording and punctation as Hartung except that he reads *ἐκπέρςας*. This avoids the pairing of present and aorist participle, and the only drawback is a corruption that is more difficult to account for. Reiske's wording gives good sense: 'Foolish is the man who, having sacked cities and desolated temples and tombs, perishes later himself', sc. as the Greeks are about to do. I award this the third prize. (vii) *μῶρος δὲ θνητῶν ὅςτις ἐκπορθεῖ πόλεις, | ναούς τε τύμβους θ', ἱερὰ τῶν κεκμηκότων | ἐρημίαι δούς, <κ>αὐτὸς ὤλεθ' ὕςτερον* (Holzhausen 1999). (West 1980: 15 had suggested the possibility of *<κ>αὐτὸς* but preceded by a raised period.) This escapes the dramatic and cultural context objections and the disparate objects objection. It gives good sense: 'Foolish is the man who sacks cities and desolates temples and tombs <and then> perishes later himself.' Arguably, though, the aorist participial phrase *ναούς τε... δούς* goes less well with *ἐκπορθεῖ*, where it is hard to see why the aorist is used of contemporaneous action, than with *ὤλετο*, where the aorist helps to make the kind of contrast between having destroyed others and perishing oneself that we see at *Hel.* 106, *καὶ ξύν γε πέρςας αὐτὸς ἀνταπωλόμην* and *Ag.* 340, quoted above. Furthermore, to underline the contrast between the fool's success and his failure, additive *καί* is less effective than adversative *δέ*. Still, the sense is good, and the postulated corruption is slight. In my view Holzhausen deserves the second prize. (viii) Blomfield's conjecture escapes all the objections mentioned and involves a trivial alteration of the transmitted text. For the sake of completeness I mention its drawbacks. First, like (v), (vi), and (vii) it requires us to understand 'by actions like those of the Greeks' with *ὤλετο*. But without this the sentence lacks relevance to its context. Second, as Blomfield himself says, *μέν* must be understood after *ἐκπορθεῖ*. On this see (5) above. An additional point in favour of the conjecture is that, like (v), (vi), and (vii), it gives intelligible sense to *ναοὺϲ . . . δούϲ* in that depopulating temple and tomb precincts, which is not a religious offence, is not treated as one. For confusion of δέ and τε see Diggle, *Studies* 59 and n1, Diggle 1994: 91n4, and Kovacs 1996: 101n7.

These lines, as emended by Blomfield, can thus be understood as arising out of their dramatic context. The same is true of versions (v), (vi), and (vii) above. Those who reject all of these emendations in favour of any of versions (i), (ii), (iii), or (iv) must accept the consequences candidly described by Manuwald 1989: 242–6. Poseidon's lines, he says, are 'dramatically set off from what precedes' and 'cannot be derived without remainder' from it. Sacking cities, desolating temples and graves—in fact, being the aggressor in war—are all in themselves foolish. He concedes that these sentiments are 'unusual', but says that novelty is more to be expected from Eur. than from anyone else. But there is a further consequence: since there is no sign that either Poseidon or Athena is offended by the sack of Troy per se or by the emptying of its temple or grave precincts, Manuwald concludes that it is not the gods who bring about the destruction mentioned in 97: Poseidon, he says, is talking about 'a somewhat secularized justice of Solonian stamp, reduced to the empirical observation that whoever destroys cities runs the risk of suffering a similar fate himself'. These comments raise obvious questions. First, in the absence of divine intervention, what gives city-sackers such bad actuarial odds? If Poseidon is not talking about divine punishment, his words suggest nothing in particular. Manuwald earlier criticized the Blomfield interpretation (mistakenly) as equivalent to 'A fool is he who falls victim to a change of fortune', and it is difficult to see why this does not apply to the apparently causeless demise of city-sackers.

Second, if Eur. were trying to put forward a religious novelty, the idea that sacking cities per se is fatal ('a thoroughgoing warning against wars of aggression'), why would he write a prologue in which one of the two divinities is the principal divine patroness of the Greek conquest of Troy, and both react solely to offences against them that are recognized by conventional religion? Why not give his prologue to a pair of divinities who could express, instead of affronted honour, a sense of general and disinterested justice and a revulsion against wars of aggression? I can see no plausible answers to these questions, and I invite my unprejudiced reader to 'look here upon this picture and on this' and choose between Eur. the dramatist, whose characters speak words that arise out of their dramatic situation, and Eur. the propounder of newfangled ideas, ideas that are both confusingly expressed and contradicted by their dramatic context.

APPENDIX B: 638

The phrase 'construing [a passage] through a brick wall' suggests—what is true—that defending the text can be as wilful and violent as any conjecture. Several editors of *Tro.* construe 638 through a brick wall. I argue against their defences here at greater length than the commentary allows both because they are likely to come to the notice of beginners (Barlow's is in a standard series, and Bluck is cited prominently, for other reasons, in Diggle's app. crit.) and because the temperament that thinks it more virtuous to defend at all costs what is transmitted than to point out unintelligibility seems to be a permanent feature of the classical scene.

Paley 1872 says 'the meaning is, ὁ γὰρ κατθανὼν οὐκ ἀλγεῖ διὰ τὸ αἰϲθάνεϲθαι τῶν κακῶν, or perhaps, "after having known what misfortune is"'. The Greek paraphrase could only mean that the dead do not feel pain because they *experience* their misfortunes, inadequate sense. In the English paraphrase the participial phrase names a circumstance that does not explain the main clause but makes it less intelligible.

Parmentier 1948 translates 'On ne souffre pas quand on n'a nul sentiment de ses maux'. His note claims that οὐδέν negatives both the indicative and the participle, and he offers as examples of such 'illogisme d'expression' *Andr.* 706–7, *El.* 383, and *Or.* 393, none of which is parallel. None of these is relevant.

Bluck 1961 translates 638 as 'A man who has had experience of the ills of life has no grief', taking ἠιϲθημένοϲ as a substantive. He claims that 636–40 make a tripartite division, 'those who are dead and know nothing, those who experience misfortune but are used to it, and those who have once prospered but have lost their prosperity'. But this is inadequate in both grammar and sense. Grammatically, the use of the anarthrous participle as a noun is confined in tragedy to the neuter singular: see KG 1.36 and 608–9, SD 2.408–9. Furthermore, τῶν κακῶν with the article would naturally be 'his woes': Euripidean Greek for 'the ills of life' is normally the anarthrous κακά, as at *Cyc.* 172, 687, *Alc.* 211, etc. The sense labours in several ways. First, we might expect the man who has had experience of misfortune to be described as unmoved *by subsequent misfortune*, yet this is left unsaid. Second, it is not true that someone who has known misfortune feels *no* pain at subsequent woes: less pain, perhaps, than the hitherto fortunate, but not none. Third, the connection between having experienced misfortune and being inured to it is not obvious enough to be omitted. Fourth, in view of γάρ the line ought to give a reason for 636–7 (or 636 alone, if 637 is interpolated), but on Bluck's view it merely explicates what is meant by ζῆν λυπρῶϲ and advances no argument. Lastly, Bluck's threefold division is unnecessarily complicated and less effective than the twofold division essential to Andromache's argument—those with no existence, whether unborn or dead, and those who live in misery like herself.

Lee says 'I take the line to mean "for the dead man after having experienced the woes of life feels no pain". This is T[yrrell]'s second suggestion'. Note that here, as in Barlow's interpretation below, 'the dead man' has to be conjured up out of nowhere: the previous line refers to two states, life and death, and in this version only one of the two, or rather the dead man, becomes the unmentioned subject of ἀλγεῖ. Furthermore one feels that a participial phrase in that position ought to explain why the man feels no pain, not merely cite a fact that is neither here nor there to his present state. But Lee has construed the line to his satisfaction and sets out to answer Bluck's objection that this interpretation 'contributes nothing to the contrast with the next two lines'.

Barlow translates similarly ('For the dead man after experiencing the ills of life does not suffer') and comments 'i.e. the dead man feels no pain after having experienced (life's) troubles'. She continues 'The points being made here and in the next lines are therefore 1. being dead is better than having experienced the miseries of life [I do not understand this: both are frequently true of the same individual] but 2. in life it is better never to have known prosperity if one subsequently loses it, for then one always regrets it.' So Andromache is telling Hecuba that it would have been much better if she or they had been wretched all their lives? Is this a contribution to her argument? Lee's and Barlow's further elaborations of the argument put one in mind of the trenchant parody of conservative textual criticism made by Eicken-Iselin 1942: 280, 'Was sich interpretieren lässt, das ist auch in Ordnung'.

Biehl reverts to assigning double duty to οὐδέν. His answer to Bluck is not to produce examples of this phenomenon but to cite the unsupported assertion of Stiblinus, 'hic οὐδὲν una negatio duarum locum tenet', as if that settled the matter.

Alterations not involving a lacuna either entail rewriting to give ἀλγεῖ a subject, as do Blaydes's οὐδεὶϲ τῶν κακῶν ἀπαλλαγείϲ or οὐδὲν τῶν κακῶν ἀνὴρ λυθείϲ (1901: 163) or F. W. Schmidt's οὐδὲν τῶν κακῶν ὁ τεθνεώϲ (1887: 390); or they fail to supply this needed subject, as is the case with Pearson's τῶν κακῶν δ' ἔϲβη μένοϲ (1890) or Hermann's τῶν κακῶν ἡϲϲημένοϲ (1847: 13). By contrast Seidler's lacuna allows the needed sense to be expressed and (unlike the rewriting) can be given a plausible cause.

A supplement is necessary, then. Supplementation is, of course, *exempli gratia* only, but the supplementer should take advantage of all the clues provided by the context. Andromache, who has said that being unborn and being dead are equivalent, uses the phrase <οὐδὲν> τῶν κακῶν ᾐϲθημένοϲ. Of whom is she speaking, one unborn or one who has died? Surely it is the latter, for only one who has lived can be 'unaware of his (*τῶν*) troubles', since one who is not yet born does not yet have them. Furthermore, when she instances Polyxena (641–2) as the proof of her generality, she says that her sister-in-law, being dead, has no knowledge of her troubles. I have accordingly made 'one who is dead' the subject of *ἀλγεῖ*, adding that this person has no more trouble than does the unborn. Diggle supplements thus: *ἀλγεῖ γὰρ οὐδὲν <ὅϲτιϲ οὐκ ἔβλεψε πω | τὸ φέγγοϲ, οὐδὲν> τῶν κακῶν ἠιϲθημένοϲ*, but this makes the unborn person the subject. Wilamowitz's supplement, printed in Murray's apparatus, reads: *ἀλγεῖ γὰρ οὐδὲν <ὅντιν' ἡ φύϲαϲα γῆ | ἐδέξατ', οὐδὲν> τῶν κακῶν ἠιϲθημένοϲ*. This makes the dead person the subject but does not explain why such a person's situation is like that of the unborn. I do not claim that Eur. must have used my words, only that my supplement is more consistent than others with what is transmitted.

APPENDIX C: 827–30

With transmitted *βοᾶι*, the main clause of the sentence consists of subject (*ἠϊόνεϲ*) and direct object (*ἴακχον*) but no verb, which some editors have urged is to be mentally supplied from the comparative clause *οἷον οἰωνὸϲ βοᾶι*. By contrast Diggle adopts Wecklein's *βοῶϲ'* (1901: 36), which gives us a main verb in the plural, one which, being situated after the singular subject of the comparative clause, might easily have been corrupted into the singular. A singular verb for the comparative clause can then be mentally supplied. Diggle in adopting the conjecture presumably felt instinctively, as I do, that a sentence beginning with the subject and the object of the main clause cannot ask its readers to supply the missing main verb out of an ensuing subordinate clause. Consider the following English example, which employs the freedom of poetic word order. Most, I suspect, would feel instinctively that a sentence such as 'Husbands their wives, as a father his children cherishes' is unlikely or impossible and that *Sprachgefühl* can be satisfied only by emending and repunctuating to 'Husbands their wives, as a father his children, cherish'. (A sentence beginning with a comparative clause, 'As a father his children cherishes, so husbands their wives' is clearly on a different footing. Likewise, 'As a father his children, so husbands cherish their wives'.) In a case such as this, emendation seems a reasonable course of action. Such errors might occur with some frequency over the course of Greek literature, and one might hope that to make trifling emendations of even a score or more of them would not necessarily incur the charge of wading through blood to impose a theory on the facts of transmission.

Evidence that this instinctual belief is wrong, however, is collected by Vahlen 1895/6: 7–13 (= Vahlen 1907/8: 2.185–92), who cites a number of passages in Greek and Latin in which comparative and other subordinate clauses supply the verb for the superordinate clause (not always a main clause) that precedes them. (Some of these were in the pre-Gerth editions of Kühner and are repeated at KG 2.574–5, § 600.) Vahlen's evidence is taken at face value and cited with approval by Wilamowitz 361–2. But the evidence is less clear than Wilamowitz believes. Vahlen begins with passages remarkable only for their word order, not for their agreement: a verb that belongs to the superordinate clause and has the proper tense, person, and number for that clause is placed in the middle of the subordinate clause, as at Hor. *Car.* 4.4.44 *equitauit* stands wholly within the comparative clause *ceu flamma per taedas uel eurus per Siculas…undas.* This, I submit, does not outrage the *Sprachgefühl* but rather supplies a mild and agreeable surprise. Such cases are numerous: Vahlen cites, in addition to the Horace passage, Theocr. 12.8–9 (ἔδραμον), 7.76 (κατετάκετο), 17.107 (κέχυται); Catull. 64.238 (*liquere*); *Od.* 17.397 (κήδεαι), *Il.* 3.21 (ἐχάρη), 12.154 (πῖπτον), 8.306 (βάλεν); and Hor. *Serm.* 1.3.9 (*currebat*). It is obvious that a superordinate verb so placed is in danger of assimilation to the tense, person, or number of the subordinate clause that surrounds it. So when he cites A.R. 3.1293–5 in Merkel's edition:

αὐτὰρ ὅ τούϲ γε
εὖ διαβὰϲ ἐπιόνταϲ, ἅτε ϲπιλὰϲ εἰν ἁλὶ πέτρη,
μίμνεν, ἀπειρεϲίηιϲι δονεύμενα κύματ' ἀέλλαιϲ

he admits that Merkel's μίμνεν for transmitted μίμνει may be what Apollonius wrote, especially in view of the similar cases at 3.1317–20 and 3.1391–2. But his own view is that μίμνει is the correct reading, and to show that this is good Greek he cites *Tro.* 826, claiming that βοῶϲιν is to be understood with the main clause. (His Latin, which seems to have typographical errors, appears to concede, though this is unclearly stated, that when the simile precedes, such 'subaudition' is easier.) To bolster his claim further he cites Theogn. 1.541–2

δειμαίνω, μὴ τήνδε πόλιν, Πολυπαΐδη, ὕβριϲ
ἥ περ Κενταύρουϲ ὠμοφάγουϲ ὄλεϲεν,

but (1) as transmitted it could mean 'I am afraid that the same violence that destroyed the barbarous Centaurs has (already) destroyed this city' (see KG 2.394–5 for the indicative in clauses of fear); and (2) if fear for the future is meant, writing the aorist subjunctive ὀλέϲηι for the transmitted aorist indicative is an easy correction. Easily fixed likewise is Xen. *Cyr.* 4.1.3 τὰ μὲν γὰρ ἄλλα ὅϲαπερ, οἶμαι, καὶ πάντεϲ ὑμεῖϲ ἐποιεῖτε (ἐποίει pars codd.).

Bibliography

Alexiou, M. 2002. *The ritual lament in Greek tradition*. 2nd edn (Lanham, Boulder, New York, Oxford).

Arnott, P. 1962. *Greek scenic conventions in the fifth century B.C.* (Oxford).

Bain, D. 1981. *Masters, servants, and orders in Greek tragedy: a study of some aspects of dramatic technique and convention* (Manchester).

Bannert, H. 1994–5. 'Beobachtungen zu den Troerinnen des Euripides', *WS* 107–8: 197–220.

Barlow, S. A. 1971. *The imagery of Euripides* (London).

Barrett, W. S. 2007. 'A detail of tragic usage: the application to persons of verbal nouns in -μα', in *Greek lyric, tragedy, and textual criticism: collected papers* (Oxford), pp. 351–67.

Barthold, T. 1864. 'De nonnullis Euripidis locis e scholiis corrigendis', in *Liber miscellaneus editus a societate philologica bonnensi* (Bonn), pp. 19–33.

Barthold, T. 1875. *Kritische Besprechung einiger Stellen aus Euripides und seinen Scholiasten*, Gymn.-Progr. 4 (Altona).

Bast, F. J. 1811. *Commentatio paleographica*, in Schaefer's edition of Gregory of Corinth, pp. 701–861.

Battezzato, L. 1995. *Il monologo nel teatro di Euripide* (Pisa).

Bentein, K. 2016. *Verbal periphrasis in ancient Greek: have- and be-constructions* (Oxford).

Bers, V. 1974. *Enallage and Greek style*, Mnemosyne Supplements 29 (Leiden).

Bers, V. 1984. *Greek poetic syntax in the classical age* (New Haven).

Bers, V. 1997. *Speech in speech: studies in incorporated* oratio recta *in Attic drama and oratory* (Lanham).

Bethe, E. 1927. 'Sisyphos', *RE* 3A: 371–6.

Biehl, W. 1973. 'Beobachtungen zur Zeitkritik in Euripides' Troerinnen: mit Ausblicken auf die Wirkung des Stückes in der Gegenwart', in Hofmann and Kuch 1973, pp. 125–37.

Biles, Z. P. 2006–7. 'Aeschylus' afterlife: reperformance by decree in 5th c. Athens?', *ICS* 31–2: 206–42.

Björck, G. 1950. *Das alpha impurum und die tragische Kunstsprache* (Uppsala).

Blaydes, F. H. M. 1901. *Adversaria critica in Euripidem* (Halle).

Blech, M. 1982. *Studien zum Kranz bei den Griechen* (Berlin).

Blondell, R. 2013. *Helen of Troy: beauty, myth, devastation* (Oxford).

Bluck, R. S. 1961. 'Euripides, *Troades* 636–40', *CQ* 11: 125–6.

Blundell, M. W. 1989. *Helping friends and harming enemies: a study in Sophocles and Greek ethics* (Cambridge).

Bothe, F. H. 1802. *Euripides' Werk verdeutscht*, vol. 4 (Berlin).
Bothe, F. H. 1826. *Euripidis Dramata*, vol. 2 (Leipzig).
Bremer, J. M. and Calder III, W. M. 1994. 'Prussia and Holland: Wilamowitz on the two Kuipers', *Mnemosyne* 47: 177–216.
Broadhead, H. D. 1968. *Tragica* (Christchurch).
Brock, R. 2013. *Greek political imagery from Homer to Aristotle* (London and New York).
Burian, P. 1977. 'The play before the prologue: initial tableaux on the Greek stage', in J. H. D'Arms and J. W. Eadie (eds), *Ancient and modern: essays in honor of Gerald F. Else* (Ann Arbor), pp. 79–94.
Burian, P. 2009. 'Introduction', in A. Shapiro (tr.), *Euripides: Trojan Women* (New York), pp. 3–25.
Burnett, A. 1997. *The poems of A. E. Housman* (Oxford).
Cairns, D. L. 1993. *Aidōs: the psychology and ethics of honour and shame in ancient Greek literature* (Oxford).
Campbell, L. 1879. *Sophocles: the plays and fragments*, 2nd edn (Oxford).
Canter, W. 1571. *Euripidis tragoediae XIX* (Antwerp).
Carey, C. 2012. 'The victory ode in the theatre', in P. Agócs, C. Carey, and R. Rawles (eds), *Receiving the Komos: ancient and modern receptions of the victory ode*, *BICS* Supplement 112 (London), pp. 17–36.
Carlini, A. 1986. *Papiri letterari geci della Bayerischen Staatsbibliothek di Monaco da Baviera* (Stuttgart).
Carrara, P. 2009. *Il testo di Euripide nell' antichità* (Florence).
Carter, D. M. 2007. *The politics of Greek tragedy* (Exeter).
Casabona, A. 1966. *Recherches sur le vocabulaire des sacrifices en grec, des origines à la fin de l'époque classique* (Aix-en-Provence).
Caspers, C. L. 2010. 'The pragmatic function and textual status of Euripidean *οὔ που* and *ἦ που*', *CQ* 60: 327–44.
Clay, D. 2005. *Euripides: The Trojan Women* (Newburyport, Mass.).
Cobet, C. G. 1862. 'Euripidea', *Mnemosyne* 5: 435–48.
Cobet, C. G. 1873. *Variae lectiones: quibus continentur observationes criticae in scriptores Graecos*, editio secunda auctior (Leiden).
Coles, R. A. 1974. *A new Oxyrhynchus papyrus: the hypothesis of Euripides' Alexandros*. *BICS* Suppl. 32 (London).
Collard, C. 1995. 'The *Pirithous* fragments', in J. A. López Férez (ed.), *De Homero a Libanio: Estudios actuales sobre textos griegos II* (Madrid), pp. 183–93; rpt in Collard 2007, pp. 55–68.
Collard, C. 2004. 'Appendix 2: *Palamedes*' and 'Appendix 3: *Sisyphus*', in C. Collard, M. J. Cropp, and J. Gibert, *Euripides: select fragmentary plays*, vol. 2 (Oxford), pp. 92–104.
Conacher, D. J. 1967. *Euripidean drama: myth, theme and structure* (Toronto).
Conomis, N. C. 1964. 'The dochmiacs of Greek drama', *Hermes* 92: 23–50.
Croally, N. T. 1994. *Euripidean polemic: the* Trojan Women *and the function of tragedy* (Cambridge).

Cron, H. 1874. 'Kritische und exegetische Bemerkungen zu den Troades des Euripides', *ZöG* 26: 331–40.

Cropp, M. J. 2004. 'Alexandros', in C. Collard, M. J. Cropp, and J. Gibert, *Euripides: select fragmentary plays*, vol. 2 (Oxford), pp. 35–91.

Cropp, M. J. and Fick, G. 1985. *Resolutions and chronology in Euripides: the fragmentary tragedies*, Bulletin of the Institute of Classical Studies Supplement 43 (London).

D'Angour, A. J. 2011. *The Greeks and the new: novelty in Greek imagination and experience* (Cambridge, New York).

Davidson, J. 2001. 'Euripides, Troades 442 revisited', *RhM* 144: 107–8.

Davie, J. 1998. *Euripides: Electra and other plays* (Harmondsworth, Middlesex).

Davies, M. 1987. 'Aeschylus' Clytemnestra: sword or axe?', *CQ* 37: 65–75.

Debnar, P. 2010. 'The sexual status of Aeschylus' Cassandra', *CP* 2: 129–45.

Decharme, P. 1893. *Euripide et l'esprit de son théâtre* (Paris) [Engl. trans. by J. Loeb (Port Washington, 1968)].

Delebecque, E. 1951. *Euripide et la guerre du Péloponnèse* (Paris).

Denniston, J. D. 1936. 'Pauses in the tragic senarius', *CQ* 30: 73–9.

Descroix, J. 1931. *Le trimètre iambique des iambographes à la comédie nouvelle* (Macon).

Diggle, J. 1970. *Euripides: Phaethon* (Cambridge).

Diggle, J. 1971. 'Notes on the *Cyclops* of Euripides', *CQ* 21: 42–50; rpt in Diggle 1994, pp. 34–43.

Diggle, J. 1973. 'Supplices', *GRBS* 14: 241–69; rpt in Diggle 1994, pp. 59–89.

Diggle, J. 1974. 'On the *Heracles* and *Ion* of Euripides', *PCPS* 20: 3–36; rpt Diggle 1994, pp. 90–136.

Diggle, J. 1975. Rev. of Kambitsis, *L'Antiope d'Euripide*, *Gnomon* 47: 288–91; rpt in Diggle 1994, pp. 143–7.

Diggle, J. 1976. 'Notes on the *Iphigenia in Tauris* of Euripides', *PCPS* 22: 42–5; rpt in Diggle 1994, pp. 148–51.

Diggle, J. 1978a. Rev. of K. H. Lee, *Euripides: Troades*', *Proceedings of the African Classical Association* 14: 27–32.

Diggle, J. 1978b. 'On the *Helen* of Euripides', in R. D. Dawe, J. Diggle, and P. E. Easterling (eds), *Dionysiaca: nine studies in Greek poetry by former pupils presented to Sir Denys Page on his seventieth birthday* (Cambridge), pp. 159–77; rpt Diggle 1994, pp. 176–95.

Diggle, J. 1981. Rev. of Scodel 1980, *CR* 31: 106–7.

Diggle, J. 1982. 'Further notes on *Heraclidae*', *PCPS* 28: 57–63; rpt Diggle 1994, pp. 220–8.

Diggle, J. 1983. 'The manuscripts and text of *Medea*: I. the manuscripts', *CQ* 33: 339–57; rpt Diggle 1994, pp. 250–72.

Diggle, J. 1984. 'The manuscripts and text of *Medea*: II. the text', *CQ* 34: 50–65; rpt Diggle 1994, pp. 273–97.

Diggle, J. 1989. 'Notes on the *Phoenissae* of Euripides', *SIFC* 7: 196–206; rpt in Diggle 1994, pp. 341–52.

Diggle, J. 1991. *The textual tradition of Euripides' Orestes* (Oxford).
Diggle, J. 1993. '*Orestes* 225', in H. D. Jocelyn (ed.), *Tria Lustra: essays and notes presented to John Pinsent*, Liverpool Classical Papers 3 (Liverpool), pp. 135–7; rpt Diggle 1994, pp. 416–20.
Diggle, J. 1994. *Euripidea: collected essays* (Oxford).
Diggle, J. 1996. 'Epilegomena Phaethontea', *AC* 65: 189–99.
Diggle, J. 1998a. *Tragicorum Graecorum fragmenta selecta* (Oxford).
Diggle, J. 1998b. 'Euripides, *Bacchae* 1063–1069', *Eikasmos* 9: 41–52.
Diggle, J. 2005. 'Rhythmical prose in the Euripidean hypotheses', in G. Bastianini and A. Casanova (eds), *Euripide e i papiri* (Florence), pp. 29–67.
Diggle, J. and Goodyear, F. R. D. (eds). 1972. *The classical papers of A. E. Housman*, 3 vols (Cambridge).
di Giuseppe, L. 2012. *Euripide: Alessandro* (Lecce).
Dihle, A. 1977. 'Das Satyrspiel "Sisyphus"', *Hermes* 105: 28–41.
Dobree, P. P. 1833. *Adversaria*, vol. 2 (Cambridge).
Dover, K. J. 1974. *Greek popular morality in the time of Plato and Aristotle* (Oxford).
Duncan, A. and J. M. 1821. *Euripidis opera omnia* (Glasgow), vol. 5.
Dunn, F. 1996. *Tragedy's end: closure and innovation in Euripidean drama* (New York).
Dyson. M. and Lee, K. H. 2000. 'Talthybius in Euripides' *Troades*', *GRBS* 41: 141–73.
Eden P. T. 1990. 'Some skewered gobbets in Euripides', in E. M. Craik (ed.), *Owls to Athens: essays on classical subjects presented to Sir Kenneth Dover* (Oxford), pp. 25–9.
Edinger, H. G. 1992. 'Euripides, "Troades" 1217', *Hermes* 120: 381–2.
Egli, F. 2003. *Euripides im Kontext zeitgenössischer intellektueller Strömungen: Analyse der Funktion philosophischer Themen in den Tragödien und Fragmenten* (Munich).
Eicken-Iselin, E. 1942. *Interpretationen und Untersuchungen zum Aufbau der Sophokleischen Rheseis*, diss. Basel (Dortmund).
Ekroth, G. 2000. 'Offerings of blood in Greek hero-cults', in V. Pirenne-Delforge and E. Suárez de la Torre (eds), *Héros et héroïnes dans les mythes et les cultes grecs: actes du colloque organisé à l'Université de Valladolid du 26 au 29 mai 1999* (Liège), pp. 263–80.
Elmsley, P. 1826. 'Annotatio in Euripidis Iphigeniam Tauricam', *Museum Criticum* 6: 273–307.
Erbse, H. 1984. *Studien zum Prolog der euripidesichen Tragödie* (Berlin, New York).
Erp Taalman Kip, A. M. van. 1987. 'Euripides and Melos', *Mnemosyne* 40: 414–19.
Fehling, D. 1968. '*Νυκτὸϲ ἄπαιδεϲ παῖδεϲ*: A. *Eum*. 1034 und das sogenannte Oxymoron in der Tragödie', *Hermes* 96: 142–55.
Finglass, P. J. 2009. 'Orthographica Sophoclea', *Philologus* 153: 206–28.

Finglass, P. J. 2013. 'How Stesichorus began his *Sack of Troy*', *ZPE* 185: 1–17.
Finglass, P. J. 2014. 'A new fragment of Euripides' *Ino*', *ZPE* 189: 65–82.
Finglass, P. J. 2015a. 'Ancient reperformances of Sophocles', *TiC* 7: 207–23.
Finglass, P. J. 2015b. 'Simias and Stesichorus', *Eikasmos* 26: 197–202.
Finglass, P. J. 2017. 'Further notes on the Euripides *Ino* papyrus (*P. Oxy.* 5131)', *Eikasmos* 28: 61–5.
Finglass, P. J. forthcoming. 'The textual transmission of Euripides' dramas', in *Brill's Companion to Euripides* (Leiden).
Fögen, T. 2006. 'Tränen und Weinen in der griechisch-römischen Antike', *Zeitschrift für Semiotik* 28: 157–77.
Fontenrose, J. 1967. 'Poseidon in the *Troades*', *Agon* 1: 135–41.
Fowler, R. L. 1988. '*AIΓ*- early Greek language and myth', *Phoenix* 62: 95–113
Fraenkel, E. 1963. 'Zu den Phoenissen des Euripides', SB Bayerische Akademie der Wissenschaften, Phil.-hist. Kl. 1963.1.
Friedrich, W. H. 1953. *Euripides und Diphilos*, Zetemata 5 (Munich).
Fritze, J. von. 1893. *De libatione veterum Graecorum* (Berlin).
Funke, H. 1965/6. 'Euripides', *Jahrbuch für Antike und Christentum* 8/9: 233–79.
Gamel, M.-K. 2016. 'The post-classical reception of Greek tragedy', in M. Lefkowitz and J. Romm (eds), *The Greek plays* (New York), 815–24.
Gantz, T. N. 1979. 'The Aischylean tetralogy: prolegomena', *CJ* 74: 289–304.
Gantz, T. N. 1980. 'The Aischylean tetralogy: attested and conjectured groups', *AJP* 101: 133–64.
Garland, R. 1985. *The Greek way of death* (London).
Gebhard E. R. 1974. 'The form of the orchestra in the early Greek theater', *Hesperia* 43: 428–40.
Geisau, J. von. 1916. 'Syntaktische Gräzismen bei Apuleius', *Indogermanische Forschungen* 36: 70–98 and 242–87.
Gibert, J. 2004. 'Archelaus', in C. Collard, M. J. Cropp, and J. Gibert, *Euripides: Select Fragmentary Plays*, vol. 2 (Oxford), pp. 330–62.
Gildenhard, I. and Revermann, M. (eds). 2010. *Beyond the fifth century: interactions with Greek tragedy from the fourth century BCE to the Middle Ages* (Berlin, New York).
Gilmartin, K. 1970. 'Talthybius in the *Trojan Women*', *AJP* 91: 213–22.
Goff, B. 2009. *Euripides: Trojan women* (London).
Goldhill, S. 1986. *Reading Greek tragedy* (Cambridge).
Gollwitzer, I. 1937. *Die Prolog- und Expositionstechnik der griechischen Tragödie*, diss. Munich.
Goossens, R. 1962. *Euripide et Athènes* (Brussels).
Green, P. 1970. *Armada from Athens* (Garden City, N.Y.).
Green, P. 1999. 'War and morality in fifth-century Athens: the case of Euripides' *Trojan women*', *The Ancient History Bulletin* 13: 97–110.
Grégoire, H. 1933. 'Euripide, Ulysse et Alcibiade', *Bulletin de la Classe des lettres et des sciences morales et politiques de l'Academie royale de Belge*, ser. 5, vol. 19: 83–106.

Gregory, J. 1991. *Euripides and the instruction of the Athenians* (Ann Arbor).
Griffith, M. and Most, G. 2012. 'Introduction', in R. Lattimore (tr.), *Euripides III* (Chicago), pp. 77–80.
Groeppel, A. 1890. *De Euripidis versibus logaoedicis* (Leipzig).
Grube, G. M. A. 1961. *The drama of Euripides* (London).
Guthrie, W. K. C. 1971. *The sophists* (Cambridge), first published as Part 1 of *A history of Greek philosophy*, iii (Cambridge 1969).
Hall, E. 1989. *Inventing the barbarian: Greek self-definition through tragedy* (Oxford).
Hall, E. 2004. 'Introduction', in E. Hall, F. Macintosh, and A. Wrigley (eds), *Dionysus since 69: Greek tragedy at the dawn of the third millenium* (Oxford), pp. 1–46.
Halleran, M. 1984. *Stagecraft in Euripides* (Beckenham, Kent).
Hamilton, R. 1976. Rev. of Coles 1974, *AJP* 97: 65–70.
Hamilton, R. 1978b. 'Announced entrances in Greek tragedy', *HSCP* 82: 63–82.
Hartung, J. A. 1837. *Euripides: Iphigenia in Aulide* (Erlangen).
Hartung, J. A. 1848. *Euripides'* Trojerinnen, *Griechisch mit metrischer Übersetzung* (Leipzig).
Haslam, M. W. 1979. 'O suitably-attired-in-leather-boots: interpolations in Greek tragedy', in G. W. Bowersock, W. Burkert, and M. C. J. Putnam (eds), *Arktouros: Hellenic studies presented to Bernard M. W. Knox on the occasion of his 65th birthday* (Berlin, New York), pp. 91–100.
Headlam, W. 1895. 'Various conjectures III', *JPh* 23: 260–323.
Heath, B. 1762. *Notae sive Lectiones ad Euripidis quae supersunt dramata deperditorumque relliquias*. Oxford.
Heath, M. 1987a. *The poetics of Greek tragedy* (Stanford).
Heath, M. 1987b. 'Jure principem locum tenet: Euripides' *Hecuba*', *BICS* 34: 40–68.
Heinze, R. ²1908. *Vergils epische Technik* (Leipzig). [Engl. trans. Berkeley 1993.]
Henry, A. S. 1967. 'Sophocles, *Oedipus Tyrannus*: the interpretation of the opening scene and the text of l. 18', CQ 17: 48–51.
Henry, W. B. 2014. '5183: tragedy (Euripides, *Alexandros*?)', *The Oxyrhynchus Papyri* 89: 1–5.
Hermann, G. 1847. *De quibusdam locis Euripidis Troadum* (Leipzig).
Hermann, K. F. and Blümner, H. 1882. *Lehrbuch der griechischen Privatalterthümer* (Freiburg, Tübingen).
Herwerden, H. van. 1855. 'Euripidea', *Mnemosyne* 4: 358–82.
Holzhausen, J. 1999. 'Nochmal zu Euripides, Troerinnen 95–7', *Philologus* 143: 26–31.
Hornblower, S. 2008. *A commentary on Thucydides*, vol. 3 (Oxford).
Hourmouziades, N. C. 1965. *Production and imagination in Euripides: form and function of the scenic space* (Athens).
Housman, A. E. 1888. 'The *Agamemnon* of Aeschylus', *JPh* 16: 244–90, rpt in Diggle and Goodyear 1972, pp. 1.55–90.

Housman, A. E. 1892. 'The *Oedipus Coloneus* of Sophocles', *AJP* 13: 139–70; rpt in Diggle and Goodyear 1972, pp. 1.175–208.

Huys, M. 1985. 'Some reflections on the controversial identity of the πρέϲβυϲ in Euripides' *Trojan Women* (v. 921) and in his *Alexander* (fr. 43, col. III, 12)', *AC* 54: 240–53.

Irwin, E. 1974. *Colour terms in Greek poetry* (Toronto).

Isler, H.-P. 2002. 'Theater: II. Architektur', *DNP* 12: 259–66.

Jaeger, W. 1957. 'Adverbiale Verstärkung des praepositionalen Elements von Verbalkomposita in griechischen Dichtern', *RhM* 100: 378–85; rpt in *Scripta minora*, pp. 2.517–24.

Johnstone, Jr., H. W. 1980. 'Pankoinon as a rhetorical figure in Greek tragedy', *Glotta* 58: 49–62.

Kamptz, H. von. 1982. *Homerische Personennamen: Sprachwissenschaftliche und historische Klassifikation* (Göttingen).

Kannicht, R. 1996. 'Zum corpus Euripideum', in C. Mueller-Goldingen et al. (eds), *ΛΗΝΑΙΚΑ: Festschrift für Carl Werner Müller* (Stuttgart, Leipzig), pp. 21–31.

Karamanou, I. 2011. 'The Hecktor-Deiphobus agon in Euripides' *Alexandros* (frr. 62a–b K.: P. Stras. 2342, 2 and 2343)', *ZPE* 178: 35–47.

Karamanou, I. 2013. 'The attack-scene in Euripides' *Alexandros* and its reception in Etruscan art', in A. Bakogianni (ed.), *Dialogues with the past 2: classical reception theory & praceice* (London), pp. 415–31.

Karamanou, I. 2017. *Euripides,* Alexandros: *introduction, text and commentary* (Berlin, Boston).

Kassel, R. 1976. 'Euripides Bakchen 23', *ZPE* 21: 35–6; rpt in Kassel 1991, pp. 187–8.

Kassel, R. 1991. *Kleine Schriften*, ed. H.-G. Nesselrath (Berlin).

Keyßner, K. 1932. *Gottesvorstellung und Lebensauffassung im griechischen Hymnus* (Stuttgart).

Kiechle, F. K. 1958. 'Zur Humanität in der Kriegführung der griechischen Staaten', *Historia* 7: 129–56.

Kirchhoff, A. 1852. *Euripidis Troades* (Berlin).

Kirchhoff, A. 1855. *Euripidis fabulae*, vol. 1 (Berlin).

Kirchhoff, A. 1868. *Euripidis fabulae*, vol. 3 (Berlin).

Kitto, H. D. F. 1961. *Greek tragedy: a literary study*, 3rd edn (London).

Klinkenberg, J. 1881. *De euripideorum prologorum arte et interpolatione* (Bonn).

Knox, B. M. W. 1985. 'Euripides', in P. E. Easterling and B. M. W. Knox (eds), *The Cambridge history of classical literature I* (Cambridge), pp. 316–39.

Koniaris, G. L. 1973. '*Alexander, Palamedes, Troades, Sisyphus*—a connected tetralogy? a connected trilogy?', *HSCP* 77: 85–124.

Kovacs, D. 1980. *The* Andromache *of Euripides: an interpretation* (Chico).

Kovacs, D. 1983. 'Euripides, *Troades* 95–7: is sacking cities really foolish?', *CQ* 33: 334–8.

Kovacs, D. 1984. 'On the *Alexandros* of Euripides', *HSCP* 88: 47–70.

Kovacs, D. 1985. 'Castor in Euripides' *Electra*', *CQ* 35: 306–14.

Kovacs, D. 1987a. *The heroic muse: studies in the* Hippolytus *and* Hecuba *of Euripides* (Baltimore).
Kovacs, D. 1987b. 'The way of a god with a maid in Aeschylus' *Agamemnon*', *CP* 82: 326–34.
Kovacs, D. 1987c. 'Treading the circle warily: literary criticism and the text of Euripides', *TAPA* 117: 257–70.
Kovacs, D. 1993. 'Zeus in Euripides' *Medea*', *AJP* 114: 45–70.
Kovacs, D. 1994a. *Euripides: Cyclops, Alcestis, Medea* (Cambridge, Mass.; second printing with corrections 2001).
Kovacs, D. 1994b. *Euripidea* (Leiden).
Kovacs, D. 1996. '*ΜΩΡΟΣ ΔΕ ΘΝΗΤΩΝ ΟΣΤΙΣ ΕΚΠΟΡΘΕΙ ΠΟΛΕΙΣ*: Nochmal zu Euripides, Troerinnen 95–97', *RhM* 139: 97–101.
Kovacs, D. 1997. 'Gods and men in Euripides' Trojan trilogy', *Colby Quarterly* 33: 162–76.
Kovacs, D. 1998. *Euripides: Suppliant Women, Electra, Heracles* (Cambridge, Mass.).
Kovacs, D. 1998a. 'Euripides, *Troades* 1050: was Helen overweight?', *CQ* 48: 553–6.
Kovacs, D. 2000. 'Why is Helen fitly named (Aeschylus, Agamemnon 681–92)?', *Eikasmos* 11: 71–2.
Kovacs, D. 2002. *Euripides: Helen, Phoenician Women, Orestes* (Cambridge, Mass.).
Kovacs, D. 2005. 'Text and transmission', in J. Gregory (ed.), *The Blackwell companion to Greek tragedy* (Oxford), pp. 379–93.
Kovacs, D. 2009. 'Do we have the end of Sophocles' *Oedipus Tyrannos*?', *JHS* 129: 53–70.
Kovacs, D. 2015. 'The first line of Euripides' *Alexandros* (fr. 41a K.)', *Eikasmos* 26: 111–15.
Kovacs, D. 2016. 'Notes on a new fragment of Euripides' *Ino* (P. Oxy. 5131)', *ZPE* 199: 3–6.
Kovacs, G. 2014. 'Reception of Euripides', in Roisman 2014: 2.1044–50.
Kranz, W. 1933. *Stasimon: Untersuchungen zu Form und Gehalt der griechischen Tragödie* (Berlin, rpt Hildesheim 1988).
Kuch, H. 1973. 'Die troische Dramengruppe des Euripides und ihre historischen Grundlagen', in Hofmann and Kuch 1973, pp. 105–23.
Kuch, H. 1978. 'Zur Euripides-Rezeption im Hellenismus', *Klio* 60: 191–202.
Kuch, H. 1998. 'Euripides und Melos', *Mnemosyne* 51: 147–57.
Kühnel, H. (ed.). 1992. *Bildwörterbuch der Kleidung und Rüstung* (Stuttgart).
Lamari, A. A. 2015. 'Aeschylus and the beginning of tragic reperformances', *Trends in Classics* 7: 189–206.
Lane, N. 2006–7. 'Further notes on Euripides' *Troades*', *ICS* 31–2: 268–71.
Lane, N. 2007a. 'Staging Polydorus' ghost in the prologue of Euripides' *Hecuba*', *CQ* 57: 290–4.
Lane, N. 2007b. 'Notes on Euripides' *Troades*', *CQ* 57: 294–5.

Langholf, V. 1971. *Die Gebete bei Euripides und die zeitliche Folge der Tragödien* (Göttingen).

Lattimore, R. 1958. '*The Trojan Women*', in *Euripides III* (Chicago), pp. 122–75.

Lauriola, R. 2015. 'Trojan Women', in Lauriola and Demetriou 2015, pp. 44–99.

Lauriola, R. and Demetriou, K. (eds). 2015. *Brill's companion to the reception of Euripides* (Leiden, Boston).

Lautensach, O. 1899. *Grammatische Studien zu den griechischen Tragikern und Komikern* (Hannover).

Lee, K. H. 1969. 'Two illogical expressions in Euripides', *CR* 19: 13–14.

Lee, K. H. 1973. 'Observations on *EPECCEIN*, *MACTOC*, and Eur. Tro. 570–571', *Philologus* 117: 264–6.

Lefkowitz, M. R. 1986. *Women in Greek myth* (London).

Lefkowitz, M. R. 2016. *Euripides and the gods* (Oxford).

Lenting, J. 1821. *Animadversiones criticae in Euripidem*, Nova acta literaria societatis Rhenotraiectanae, n.s. 1: 1–120 (Utrecht).

Lesky, A. 1972. *Greek tragic poetry*, trans. by M. Dillon (New Haven, London).

Lloyd, M. 1984. 'The Helen scene in Euripides' *Trojan Women*', *CQ* 34: 303–13.

Lloyd, M. 1989. 'Paris/Alexandros in Homer and Euripides', *Mnemosyne* 42: 76–9.

Lloyd, M. 1992. *The* agon *in Euripides*. Oxford.

Lloyd, M. 1994. Rev. of Euripides' *The Trojan Women*: a new version by Brendan Kennelly, *Classics Ireland* 1: 54–60.

Lloyd, M. 1999. 'The tragic aorist', *CQ* 49: 24–45.

Lloyd-Jones, H. ²1983. *The justice of Zeus* (Berkeley, Los Angeles).

Löfstedt, E. 1956. *Syntactica: Studien und Beiträge zur historischen Syntax des Lateins* (Lund).

Long, A. A. 1968. *Language and thought in Sophocles: a study of abstract nouns and poetic technique* (London).

Lougovaya, J. 2013. 'Inscriptions on the Attic stage', in P. Liddel and P. Low (eds), *Inscriptions and their uses in Greek and Latin literature* (Oxford), pp. 255–70.

Lowe, J. C. B. 1962. 'The manuscript evidence for changes of speaker in Aristophanes', *BICS* 9: 27–42.

Ludwig, W. 1954. *Sapheneia: ein Beitrag zur Formkunst im Spätwerk des Euripides*, diss. Tübingen.

Luppe, W. 1985. 'Dikaiarchos' *ὑποθέϲειϲ τῶν Εὐριπίδου μύθων (mit einem Beitrag zur 'Troades'-Hypothesis)*', in Jürgen Wiesner (ed.), *Aristoteles Werk und Wirkung: Paul Moraux gewidmet* (Berlin, New York), pp. 1.610–15.

Luppe, W. 2011. 'Die "Palamedes"- und die "Polyidos"-Hypothesis: P. Mich. Inv. 3020(A)', *ZPE* 176: 52–5.

Luppe, W. and Henry, W. B. 2012. '5131: tragedy (Euripides, Ino?)', *The Oxyrhynchus Papyri* 78: 19–25.

Maas, P. 1956. '*τύχισμα*', *Glotta* 35: 300; rpt in *Kleine Schriften* (Munich 1973), pp. 219–20.

Macurdy, G. H. 1905. *The chronology of the extant plays of Euripides*, diss. Columbia University (Lancaster, Penn.).

Mähly, J. 1862. *Der* Oedipus Coloneus *des Sophocles: Beiträge zur inneren und äusseren Kritik des Stückes* (Basel).

Manuwald, B. 1989. '*Μῶρος δὲ θνητῶν ὅςτις ἐκπορθεῖ πόλεις*: zu Euripides, *Troerinnen* 95–97', RhM 132: 236–47.

Marshall, C. W. 2001. 'The next time Agamemnon died', *CW* 95: 59–63.

Mastronarde, D. J. 1979. *Contact and discontinuity: some conventions of speech and action on the Greek tragic stage* (Berkeley).

Mastronarde, D. J. 1986. 'The optimistic rationalist in Euripides: Theseus, Jocasta, Teiresias', in M. Cropp, E. Fantham, and S. E. Scully (eds), *Greek tragedy and its legacy: essays presented to D. J. Conacher* (Calgary), pp. 201–11.

Mastronarde, D. J. 1989. 'Lautensach's law and the augment of compound-verbs in *ευ-*', *Glotta* 67: 101–5.

Mastronarde, D. J. 1990. 'Actors on high: the skene-roof, the crane, and the gods in Attic drama', *ClAnt* 9: 247–94.

Mastronarde, D. J. 2010. *The art of Euripides: dramatic technique and social context* (Cambridge).

Mastronarde, D. J. 2017. 'Text and transmission', in L. K. McClure (ed.), *A companion to Euripides* (Chichester, West Sussex, and Malden, Mass.), pp. 9–26.

Matthiessen K. 1968. 'Zur Theonoeszene der euripideischen Helena', *Hermes* 96: 685–704.

Mayerhoefer, F. 1908. *Ueber die Schlüsse der erhaltenen griechischen Tragödien* (Erlangen).

Mayhew, R. 2011. *Prodicus the sophist: texts, translations, and commentary* (Oxford).

McDonald, M. 1978. *Terms for happiness in Euripides*, Hypomnemata 14 (Göttingen).

Meccariello, C. 2014. *Le 'hypotheseis' narrative dei drammi euripidei: testo, contesto, fortuna* (Roma).

Meiggs, R. and Lewis, D. 1969. *A selection of Greek historical inscriptions to the end of the fifth century B.C.* (Oxford).

Meridor, R. 1978. 'Eur. *Troades* 207: an unobserved variant reading', *AJP* 99: 426.

Meridor, R. 1982. 'Exclamations again', *Mnemosyne* 35: 141.

Meridor, R. 1984. 'Plot and myth in Euripides' *Heracles* and *Troades*', *Phoenix* 38: 205–15.

Meridor, R. 1985–8. 'Euripides' *Troades* 1244: *ὑμνήθημεν* PV, *ὑμνηθεῖμεν* Hermann', *SCI* 8–9: 25–9.

Meridor, R. 1989. 'Euripides' *Troades* 28–44 and the Andromache scene', *AJP* 110: 17–35.

Meridor, R. 1996. 'How many husbands has Helen in the *Troades*? A note on E. *Tro.* 959–60', *SCI* 15: 46–54.

Meuli, K. 1975. 'Die gefesselten Götter', in K. Meuli (ed.), *Gesammelte Schriften* (Basel), 2.1035–81.

Meyer, G. 1925. *Die stilistische Verwendung der Nominalkomposition im Griechischen*, Philologus Suppl. 16.3 (Leipzig).

Michelini, A. M. 1988. 'The unclassical as classical: the modern reception of Euripides', *Poetics Today* 9: 699–710.

Mikalson, J. D. 1983. *Athenian popular religion* (Chapel Hill).

Mikalson, J. D. 1991. *Honor thy gods: popular religion in Greek tragedy* (Chapel Hill).

Mills, S. 2014. 'Attitudes to war', in Roisman 2014: 1.171–3.

Mistchenko, T. 1877. 'Euripide, *Troyennes*, 237; Eschyle, *Prométhée*, 242'. *Revue de philologie* 3: 268

Moorhouse, A. C. 1959. *Studies in the Greek negatives* (Cardiff).

Moorhouse, A. C. 1965. 'A use of *οὐδείς* and *μηδείς*', *CQ* 15: 31–40.

Morrison, J. S., Coates, J. F., and Rankov, N. B. ²2000. *The Athenian trireme* (Cambridge).

Mueller-Goldingen, C. 1996. 'Die Kassandraszene in Euripides' *Troades* (308–461)', in C. Mueller-Goldingen, K. Sier, and H. Becker (eds), *AHNAIKA: Festschrift für Carl Werner Müller zum 65. Geburtstag am 28. Januar 1996*. Beiträge zur Altertumskunde 89 (Stuttgart), pp. 33–51.

Munro, H. A. J. 1882. 'Euripidea', *Journal of Philology* 11: 267–86.

Murray, G. 1932. 'The Trojan trilogy of Euripides (415 B.C.)', in *Mélanges Gustave Glotz* (Paris), pp. 2.645–56.

Murray, G. 1946. 'Euripides' tragedies of 415 B.C.: the deceitfulness of life', in *Greek Studies* (Oxford), pp. 127–48.

Murray, G. 1965 (1946). *Euripides and his age* (Oxford), repr. of the 2nd edn (London and New York).

Musgrave, S. 1788. In C. D. Beck (ed.), *Euripidis tragoediae fragmenta epistolae*, vol. 3 (Leipzig).

Musgrave, A. 1797. *Euripidis tragoediae* (Glasgow).

Nauck, A. 1854. Rev. of Kirchhoff's *Troades*, *Neue Jahrbücher für Philologie und Paedagogik* 70: 3–19.

Nauck, A. 1862. *Euripideische Studien: zweiter Teil*, Mémoires de l'académie impériale des sciences de St. Pétersbourg, vii série, tome v, no. 6 (St. Petersburg).

Neblung, D. 1997. *Die Gestalt der Kassandra in der antiken Literatur* (Stuttgart, Leipzig).

Nelson, J. A. 1989. *Ambiguity and deception in Greek tragedy*, diss. University of Virginia.

Nestle, W. 1901. *Euripides, der Dichter der griechischen Aufklärung* (Stuttgart; rpt Aalen 1969).

Norden, E. 1909. *Die antike Kunstprosa vom VI. Jahrhundert v. Chr. bis in die Zeit der Renaissance* (Leipzig).
Norwood, G. 1920. *Greek tragedy* (London).
O'Sullivan, P. 2012. 'Sophistic ethics, old atheism, and "Critias" on religion', *CW* 105: 167–85.
Paley, F. A. 1872. *Euripides with an English commentary*, vol. 1 (London).
Parker, L. P. E. 1958. 'Some observations on the incidence of word-end in anapaestic paroemiacs and its application to textual questions', *CQ* 8: 82–9.
Parker, L. P. E. 1966. 'Porson's law extended', *CQ* 16: 1–26.
Parmentier L. 1893. *Euripide et Anaxagore* (Paris).
Parmentier L. 1923. 'Notes sur les *Troyennes* de 'Euripide', *REG* 36: 46–61.
Pearson, A. C. 1890. 'Euripides, *Troades*', *CR* 4: 425.
Pechstein, N. 1998. *Euripides Satyrographos: ein Kommentar zu den euripideischen Satyrspielfragmenten*, Beiträge zur Altertumskunde 115 (Stuttgart).
Perrotta, G. 1925. 'L'Ecuba e le Troadi di Euripide', *A&R* n.s. 6: 264–93.
Pertusi, A. 1952. 'Il significato della trilogia troiana di Euripide', *Dioniso* 15: 251–73.
Petersen, E. 1915. *Die attische Tragödie als Bild- und Bühenkunst* (Bonn).
Pfeijffer, I. L. 1999. *Three Aeginetan odes of Pindar: a commentary on Nemean V, Nemean III & Pythian VIII* (Leiden).
Pickering, P. E. 2000. 'Verbal repetition in *Prometheus* and Greek tragedy generally', *BICS* 44: 81–101.
Pickering, P. E. 2003. 'Did the Greek ear detect "careless" verbal repetitions?', *CQ* 53: 490–9.
Planck, H. 1840. *De Euripidis Troica Didascalia* (Göttingen).
Pohlenz, M. 1954. *Die griechische Tragödie*, 2nd edn (Göttingen).
Pöschl, V. 1967. 'Die Horazode *Exegi Monumentum*', *GIF* 20: 261–72.
Pot, E. E. 1943. *De maritieme beeldspraak bij Euripides*, diss. Utrecht.
Powell, J. E. 1939. '*ΤΡΑΧΗΛΟΣ* "head"', *CR* 53: 58.
Quincey, J. H. 1966. 'Greek expressions of thanks', *JHS* 86: 133–58.
Rabinowitz, N. S. 2008. *Greek tragedy* (Malden, Mass., Oxford, Victoria).
Race, W. H. 1981. 'The word *καιρός* in Greek drama', *TAPA* 111: 197–213.
Rehm, R. 1992. *Greek tragic theatre* (London).
Rehm, R. 2002. *The play of space: spatial transformation in Greek tragedy* (Princeton, Oxford).
Reiske, J. J. 1754. *Ad Euripidam et Aristophanem animadversiones* (Leizpig).
Renehan, R. 1963. 'Some Greek textual problems', *HSCP* 67: 269–83.
Riemer, P. 1991. *Sophokes, Antigone: Götterwille und menschliche Freiheit*, Abhandlungen der Akademie der Wissenschaften und Literatur zu Mainz, Jahrgang 1991, Nr. 12.
Rijksbaron, A. 1991. *Grammatical observations on Euripides' Bacchae* (Amsterdam).
Roisman, H. M. 2014. *The encyclopedia of Greek tragedy*, 3 vols (Malden, Mass., Oxford).

Roisman, J. 1997. 'Contemporary allusions in Euripides' *Trojan Women*', *SIFC* 15: 38–47.

Romilly, J. de. 1980. *L'évolution du pathétique d'Eschyle à Euripide* (Paris).

Roscher, W. H. 1884–90. *Ausführliches Lexikon der griechischen und römischen Mythologie*, vol. 1.2 (Leipzig).

Roussel, P. 1919. 'Astyanax', *RÉG* 32: 482–9.

Rutherford, I. 2001. *Pindar's* Paeans: *a reading of the fragments with a survey of the genre* (Oxford).

Rutherford, R. 1998. 'Preface to *Trojan Women*', in J. Davie (tr.), *Euripides:* Electra *and other plays* (London), pp. 177–81.

Sansone, D. 1982. Rev. of Diggle, *Studies on the text of Euripides*, *GGA* 234: 31–41.

Sansone, D. 1984a. 'Euripides, *Troades* 435', *RhM* 127: 361.

Sansone, D. 2015. 'The place of the satyr-play in the tragic tetralogy', *Prometheus* 41: 3–36.

Sarian, H. 1986. 'Erinys', *LIMC* 3.1: 827–43 and 3.2: 595–606.

Schade, G. 1998. 'Euripides, *Troades* 442: κἀκφυγὼν λίμνης ὕδωρ', *RhM* 141: 206–8.

Schadewaldt, W. 1926. *Monolog und Selbstgespräch: Untersuchungen zur Formgeschichte der griechischen Tragödie* (Hildesheim).

Scheidweiler, F. 1954. 'Zu den Troerinnen des Euripides', *Hermes* 82: 250–1.

Schmidt, V. 1968. *Sprachliche Untersuchungen zu Herondas* (Berlin).

Schmidt, F. W. 1887. *Kritische Studien zu den griechischen Dramatikern*, vol. 2 (Berlin).

Schöll, A. 1839. *Beiträge zur Geschichte der griechischen Poesie* (Berlin).

Schorn, S. 2004. *Satyros aus Kallatis: Sammlung der Fragmente mit Kommentar* (Basel).

Schubart, W. and Wilamowitz-Moellendorff, U. von. 1907. 'Lyrische und dramatische Fragmente', *Berliner Klassikertexte*, vol. 2 (Berlin).

Schulze, W. 1892. *Quaestiones epicae* (Gütersloh; rpt Hildesheim 1967).

Schulze, W. 1918. 'Beiträge zur Wort- und Sittengeschichte II', *Sitzungsberichte der preußischen Akademie der Wissenschaften* pp. 481–511 (rpt in his *Kleine Schriften* (1966), pp. 160–89).

Scodel, R. 1980. *The Trojan trilogy of Euripides*, Hypomnemata 60 (Göttingen).

Scodel, R. 1998. 'The captive's dilemma: sexual acquiescence in Euripides *Hecuba* and *Troades*', *HSCP* 98: 137–54.

Scodel, R. 2012. 'Introduction', in D. A. Svarlien (tr.), *Euripides: Hecuba, Andromache, Trojan Women* (Indianapolis), pp. vii–xxv.

Scullion, S. 1994. *Three studies in Athenian dramaturgy* (Stuttgart, Leipzig).

Scully, S. 1990. *Homer and the sacred city* (Ithaca, London).

Seale, D. 1982. *Vision and stagecraft in Sophocles* (Chicago).

Sedley, D. N. 2005. 'Plato's tsunami', *Hyperboreus* 11: 205–14; rpt in P. G. McC. Brown, T. Harrison, and S. Instone (eds), *Θεῶι δῶρον: essays by past pupils in honour of Theo Zinn for his 84th birthday* (Gracewing), pp. 41–8.

Seidler, A. 1811–12. *De versibus dochmiacis tragicorum Graecorum* (Leipzig).
Sidwell, K. 2001. 'Melos and the *Trojan Women*', in Stuttard and Shasha, pp. 30–44.
Snell, B. 1937. *Euripides* Alexandros *und andere Strassburger Papyri mit Fragmenten griechischer Dichter*, Hermes Einzelschriften 5 (Berlin).
Sommerstein, A. H. 1989. 'Again Klytaimestra's weapon', *CQ* 39: 296–301.
Spitzbarth, A. 1945. *Untersuchungen zur Spieltechnik der griechischen Tragödie*, diss. Zürich (Wintertür).
Stanley, J. 1896. 'Euripides, *Troades* 256', *CR* 10: 34.
Steidle, W. 1968. *Studien zum antiken Drama: unter besonderer Berücksichtigung des Bühnenspiels*, Studia et testimonia antiqua 4 (Munich).
Steiger, H. 1900. 'Warum schrieb Euripides seine *Troerinnen*?', *Philologus* 59: 362–99.
Stengel, P. 1910. *Opferbräuche der Griechen* (Berlin).
Stephanopoulos, T. K. 1985. 'Euripides und die Arkader (*Troades* 30–31)', *Hermes* 113: 115–19.
Stephanopoulos, T. K. 1988. 'Kleinigkeiten zu den "Troerinnen"', *Hermes* 116: 488–90.
Stephanus (Estienne), H. 1568. *Annotationes in Sophoclem et Euripidem* (Basel).
Stevens, P. T. 1937. 'Colloquial expressions in Euripides', *CQ* 31: 182–91.
Stevens, P. T. 1956. 'Euripides and the Athenians', *JHS* 76: 87–94.
Stevens, P. T. 1976. *Colloquial expressions in Euripides*, Hermes Einzelschriften 38 (Wiesbaden).
Stieber, M. 2011. *Euripides and the language of craft*, Mnemosyne Supplements 327 (Leiden, Boston).
Stinton T. C. W. 1965. *Euripides and the judgement of Paris*, Journal of Hellenic Studies Supplements 11 (London); rpt in Stinton 1990, pp. 17–75.
Stinton, T. C. W. 1975. 'More rare verse-forms', *BICS* 22: 84–108; rpt in Stinton 1990, pp. 113–42.
Stinton T. C. W. 1977. 'Pause and period in the lyrics of Greek tragedy', *CQ* 27: 27–66; rpt in Stinton 1990, pp. 310–61.
Stinton T. C. W. 1990. *Collected papers on Greek tragedy*, ed. H. Lloyd-Jones (Oxford).
Strauss Clay, J. 2011. *Homer's Trojan theater: space, vision, and memory in the Iliad* (Cambridge).
Stuttard, D. and Shasha, T. (eds). 2001. *Trojan Women: a collection of essays* (Brighton).
Sullivan, J. J. 2007. 'The agency of the herald Talthybius in Euripides' *Trojan Women*', *Mnemosyne* 60: 472–7.
Svennung, V. 1958. *Anredeformen* (Uppsala).
Taplin, O. 1977. *The stagecraft of Aeschylus: the dramatic use of exits and entrances in Greek tragedy* (Oxford).
Taplin, O. 1978. *Greek tragedy in action* (London).

Thomson, G. 1939. 'The postponement of interrogatives in Attic drama', *CQ* 33: 147–52.

Timpanaro, S. 1996. 'Dall'*Alexandros* di Euripide all'*Alexander* di Ennio', *RFIC* 124: 5–70.

Turner E. G. 1980. 'Ptolemaic bookhands and Lille Stesichorus', *Scrittura e civiltà* 4: 19–40.

Turyn, A. 1957. *The Byzantine manuscript tradition of the tragedies of Euripides* (Urbana).

Tyrwhitt. T. 1762. In Musgrave 1762, pp. 133–76.

Vahlen, J. 1895/6. 'Index Lectionum Hibernarum 1895/96' (Berlin).

Vahlen, J. 1907/8. *Opuscula Academica*, 2 vols (Berlin).

van Zyl Smit, B. (ed.). 2016. *A handbook to the reception of Greek drama* (Chichester, West Sussex).

Vellacott, P. 1954. *Three plays: The* Bacchae *and other plays* (London, New York).

Vellacott, P. 1975. *Ironic drama: a study of Euripides' method and meaning* (Cambridge).

Vermeule, E. 1979. *Aspects of death in early Greek art and poetry* (Berkeley, Los Angeles).

Vitelli, G. 1890. 'Spicilegio florentino', *Museo italiano di antichità classica* 3: 287–318.

Wackernagel, J. 1892. 'Über ein Gesetz der indogermanischen Wortstellung', *IF* 1: 333–436.

Way, A. S. 1912. *Euripides with an English translation* (Cambridge, Mass. and London), vol. i.

Webster, T. B. L. 1966. 'Euripides' Trojan trilogy', in M. Kelly (ed.), *For service to classical studies: essays in honour of Francis Letters* (Melbourne), pp. 207–13.

Webster, T. B. L. 1967. *The tragedies of Euripides* (London).

Wecklein, N. 1896. 'Beiträge zur Kritik des Euripides [I]', *Sitzungsberichte der philosophisch-philologischen und der historischen Classe der k. b. Akademie der Wissenschaften zu München*, Jahrgang 1895, pp. 479–543.

Wecklein, N. 1897. 'Beiträge zur Kritik des Euripides [II]', *Sitzungsberichte der philosophisch-philologischen und der historischen Classe der k. b. Akademie der Wissenschaften zu München*, Jahrgang 1896, pp. 449–538.

Wecklein, N. 1901. *Euripidis Troades* (Leipzig).

Wecklein, N. 1922. 'Textkritische Studien zu den griechischen Tragikern', *Sitzungsberichte der Bayerischen Akademie der Wissenschaften*, Philosophisch-philologische und historische Klasse, Jahrgang 1921, 5 (pub. 1922).

Wesener, P. 1866. *De repetitione versuum in fabulis Euripideis* (Bonn).

Wesener, P. 1874. 'Zu Euripides', *Programm des kaiserlichen Lyceums zu Colmar* (Colmar).

West, M. L. 1967. 'Epica', *Glotta* 44: 135–48.

West, M. L. 1973. *Textual criticism and editorial technique applicable to Greek and Latin texts* (Stuttgart).
West, M. L. 1980. 'Tragica IV', *BICS* 27: 9–22.
West, M. L. 1984. 'Tragica VII', *BICS* 31: 171–92.
West, M. L. 1990. *Studies in Aeschylus* (Stuttgart).
West, M. L. 1992. *Ancient Greek music* (Oxford).
West, M. L. 2013. *The epic cycle* (Oxford).
Westlake, H. D. 1953. '*Troades* 205–229', *Mnemosyne* 6: 181–91.
Whitmarsh, T. 2014. 'Atheistic aesthetics: the Sisyphus fragment, poetics, and the creativity of drama', *Cambridge Classical Journal* 60: 109–26.
Wilamowitz-Moellendorff, U. von. 1875. *Analecta Euripidea* (Berlin).
Wilamowitz-Moellendorff, U. von. 1879. 'Parerga', *Hermes* 14: 161–86; rpt in Wilamowitz-Moellendorff, *Kleine Schriften* 4 (Berlin 1962), pp. 1–23.
Wilamowitz-Moellendorff, U. von. 1895. 'Commentariola metrica', *Index lectionum aestivarum Gottingae* (Göttingen; rpt in Wilamowitz-Moellendorff 1921: 154–209).
Wilamowitz-Moellendorff, U. von. 1921. *Griechische Verskunst* (Berlin).
Wiles, D. 1997. *Tragedy in Athens: performance space and theatrical meaning* (Cambridge).
Wiles, D. 2000. *Greek theatre performance: an introduction* (Cambridge).
Willink, C. W. 1988. 'Sleep after labour in Euripides' *Heracles*', *CQ* 38: 86–97; rpt in Willink 2010, pp. 99–115.
Willink, C. W. 2004. 'Euripides, *Hecuba* 905–22', *Mnemosyne* 57: 45–53; rpt in Willink 2010, pp. 504–11.
Willink, C. W. 2010. *Collected papers on Greek tragedy*, ed. W. B. Henry (Leiden, Boston).
Wilson, J. R. 1968. 'The etymology in Euripides, *Troades*, 13–14', *AJPh* 89: 66–71.
Wilson, N. G. 1966. Rev. of Zuntz 1966, *Gnomon* 38: 334–42.
Yoon, F. 2012. *The use of anonymous characters in Greek tragedy* (Leiden, Boston).
Yoon, F. 2016. 'Against a *Prometheia*: rethinking the connected trilogy', *TAPA* 146: 257–80.
Young, D. C. 1983. 'Pindar Pythians 2 and 3: inscriptional ποτέ and the "poetic epistle"', *HSCP* 87: 30–48.
Zucker, F. 1962. '*Αὐθέντης* und Ableitungen', *Sitzungsberichte der Sächsichen Akademie der Wissenschaften zu Leipzig, Philologisch-historische Klasse* 107.4.
Zuntz, G. 1955. *The political plays of Euripides* (Manchester).
Zuntz, G. 1965. *An inquiry into the transmission of the plays of Euripides* (Cambridge).

Indices

Numbers in italics refer to pages of the Introduction. Numbers in roman type refer to discussions of particular lines in the Commentary. The introductions to the constituent parts of the play are referred to as Prol., Par., Ep. 1, Stas. 1 (and similarly with the other episodes and stasima), and Exod. I have occasionally given pages references in italics if an introduction is long.

GREEK

SUBJECTS

Aeschylus, Sophocles, and Euripides are indexed selectively, as are Hecuba and other characters in the play. References to *Metrical analysis* are marked Metr. preceded by relevant line numbers. Sections on *Staging* are marked St. followed by a reference to the immediately succeeding lines of commentary.